# Auto Repair

## 2nd Edition

### by Deanna Sclar
#### John O'Dell, Technical Advisor

for dummies®
A Wiley Brand

## Auto Repair For Dummies®, 2nd Edition

Published by: **John Wiley & Sons, Inc.**, 111 River Street, Hoboken, NJ 07030-5774, www.wiley.com

Copyright © 2019 by John Wiley & Sons, Inc., Hoboken, New Jersey

Published simultaneously in Canada

For general information on our other products and services, please contact our Customer Care Department within the U.S. at 877-762-2974, outside the U.S. at 317-572-3993, or fax 317-572-4002. For technical support, please visit https://hub.wiley.com/community/support/dummies.

Wiley publishes in a variety of print and electronic formats and by print-on-demand. Some material included with standard print versions of this book may not be included in e-books or in print-on-demand. If this book refers to media such as a CD or DVD that is not included in the version you purchased, you may download this material at http://booksupport.wiley.com. For more information about Wiley products, visit www.wiley.com.

Library of Congress Control Number: 2018955357

ISBN: 978-1-119-54361-9; ISBN: 978-1-119-54369-5 (ebk); ISBN: 978-1-119-54370-1 (ebk)

Manufactured in the United States of America

V10006322_112118

# What's So Special about Auto Repair For Dummies, 2nd Edition

This book is designed for people who think that anything technical will make their brains shut like garage doors, who sincerely care about how their vehicles affect the environment, and although they believe they can't work on their cars themselves — and wouldn't like it if they could — are willing to give it a try. How do I know that it will work for these reluctant readers? Because it's written by a genuine, certified ex-Dummy who has found that, despite total ignorance and a complete lack of manual dexterity, getting personally involved with a vehicle is enjoyable, rewarding, and easy. Believe me: If I can do it, so can you!

### It Is *Not* Written for Confirmed "Do-It-Yourselfers." It *Is* for You If:

>> You have never held a wrench.

>> You are positive that, in your case, manual labor can lead only to disaster.

>> You haven't the vaguest idea of how a car works.

>> You have failed shop or arts and crafts.

>> You believe that if you do something wrong, your car can blow up.

### To Enjoy This Book, It Would Help If:

>> You don't believe that working on your vehicle can possibly be fun, but you're willing to give it a try for any reason whatsoever.

>> You are sincerely tired of being ripped off because of your own ignorance.

### Why Is That Enjoyable? Because You Will Be Delighted to Find:

>> Cars run on principles that are as easy to understand as common sense.

>> You can save a tremendous amount of money, extend the life of your vehicle, save on fuel, and do your bit for the environment if you know more about your car!

>> Most of the devices on your vehicle will not hurt you unless you really go out of your way to hurt yourself.

### Here's How *Auto Repair For Dummies* Accomplishes These Miracles:

>> It starts from scratch. It even shows you what a screwdriver looks like!

>> It explains each system in simple terms *before* you get to work on it.

>> It provides step-by-step instructions for even the simplest tasks.

>> It tells you exactly what you need and how to know if you've been given the wrong part, the wrong diagnosis, or an outrageous estimate.

### It Tells You the Truth About:

>> What makes your vehicle go (and how and why as well)

>> How the car you drive, how you drive it and maintain it, and how you recycle or dispose of used parts and toxic fluids affect fuel economy and global warming

>> The easy work involved in keeping your vehicle well maintained and running efficiently, and how to tell what's wrong if trouble strikes

>> How 15 minutes of "preventive medicine" avoids breakdowns

>> Whether you can handle a problem yourself, and how to get it fixed at a fair price if you can't

>> How to extend the life of your vehicle; keep it clean and healthy; and repair the minor dents and dings it acquires on the road

### These Features Will Make Life Even Easier:

>> A *Practical Glossary of Automotive Terms* that are in *special type* throughout the book so that you can refresh your memory if you've forgotten what something means

>> A detailed *Index* where you can look up a part, a problem, a symptom, or a specific job and find the page you need

>> A *Maintenance Record* so you can keep track of what you've done and when you did it

>> A *Specifications Record* for the data you need to buy the right parts

>> Tons of illustrations that show you how things look and where they are

**This Revised Edition Also Tells You:**

» About alternatively fueled vehicles and other innovations so you can choose a safe and efficient vehicle when Old Faithful finally heads for the Used Car Lot in the Sky

**You Have a Few Things to Supply, Too!**

» You have to buy the book . . . and read it!

» You have to try to do one small, easy job yourself (you can pick the job).

**There Are Fringe Benefits, Too!**

» Your vehicle will run better and live longer.

» Automotive technicians will respect you.

» You'll have more money to spend on other things.

» You'll no longer be a Dummy!

# Contents at a Glance

# Table of Contents

# Introduction

For many people, getting a driver's license is an event that runs second only to getting a diploma or a marriage license. Most of us succeed in passing the test and hop happily into our vehicles, headed for the freedom of the open road. Unfortunately, most of us don't know the first thing about the machines we're licensed to drive — and this can turn a ticket to freedom into a ticket to trouble.

I'm not necessarily talking about physical danger. State motor vehicle bureaus have made fairly sure that, before we can get a driver's license, we know how to drive defensively and can handle a vehicle under poor driving conditions. What I'm referring to is the kind of trouble that comes from depending on other people to care for and repair our vehicles. If you're like most people, you probably tend to drive around until something goes wrong and then incur the expense of replacing worn and burned-out parts — or the entire vehicle! — when low-cost, regular maintenance could have kept your wheels turning for a long time.

Whether you're trying to cut expenses, are tired of being patronized, or have just fallen in love with your first car, this book tells you how your vehicle works, what it needs in the way of tender loving care, how to reduce its impact on the environment, and how to keep from getting ripped off if you have to entrust repairs to someone else. By handling the simple maintenance and being able to diagnose trouble and perform the less complex repairs yourself, you'll earn the respect of your family, your mechanic, and your car — and you'll feel pretty good about it!

## About This Book

This new edition is about much more than auto repair. In this book, I introduce you to the wonders of the internal combustion engine and to the even more wondrous alternative fuels and alternatively fueled vehicles that reduce dependence on the rapidly dwindling supply of fossil fuel and will play a huge role in the battle against global warming that threatens the future of the planet. I'm proud to say that this edition of *Auto Repair For Dummies* is the first "green" automotive guide that focuses on how the vehicles you choose; the way you maintain them; and how you recycle used oil, parts you've replaced, and other waste products directly affects the environment.

The book starts off with the basics every driver should know, from how to get the hood open and fill up with fuel, to using a jack and changing a tire safely. You learn the basic safety rules to follow when dealing with your vehicle, and how to take *anything* apart and reassemble it without losing anything, including your mind! After identifying the basic tools you may need, I gently lead you into an easy preventive maintenance check-up that you can do to extend the life of your vehicle and keep it from breaking down on the road.

Next, there's a quick overview of how your vehicle's principal systems work together to start it, operate it efficiently on the road, and bring it safely to a stop. After you have a general idea of how things work, we explore each system, part by part, and what needs to be done to maintain it, troubleshoot it, and do minor repairs yourself. Don't worry about getting in over your head. If a repair can get you into trouble if you attempt to do it yourself, I tell you how to be sure the work is done properly by a professional at a fair price. So don't chicken out on me! Start with the easy stuff and then take on the more challenging tasks.

# How I Became Intimately Involved with My Car, and Why You Should Too

Before I moved to California, I was an ordinary urban cliff dweller: I had only a nodding acquaintance with cars. Ours was locked up in a garage, and I used subways, buses, and taxis. All the maintenance on our car was done by the garage that housed it. When we moved to California, my enthusiasm for a life in the sun was considerably dampened by the knowledge that this would also include a life on the freeways, but the first time I took the family car to the supermarket myself I had an epiphany in the parking lot: I could drive anywhere I wanted to, instead of just being driven home. It wasn't long before I was looking for a car of my own.

The best I could do was a secondhand Mustang with more than 70,000 miles on it. A friend of mine checked out the car and pronounced it drivable. He said that it might need "a little work." We took it to a reliable mechanic, who checked it over, tuned it up, and told me that it was "a classic."

Thus reassured, I drove the car to the Department of Motor Vehicles to register it. I parked the car, turned off the ignition, locked it, and found that the car was singing! A bit puzzled, I rechecked the ignition and the radio, but everything was truly shut off. And still the car sang. By the time I returned, all was quiet. But that night, when I took the family out to dinner, old Tweety Bird began to sing again. After several weeks of expensive and unsuccessful repairs, I found out that all she had needed was an inexpensive radiator cap. To my amazement, the shop was unwilling to refund the money I'd spent on all the other stuff they'd tried! I realized that it would be impossible to communicate with Tweety properly if I didn't know anything about her, and the repair bills were going to send both of us down the drain.

So I conned a friend of mine into taking an auto shop class with me at a local adult-ed center. Instead of a bewildering array of weird objects and miles of hoses that threatened to blow up if I turned a screw in the wrong direction, I soon found that a car was just a series of simple mechanisms linked together and that vehicles are very good about sending out signals telling you clearly what's wrong — if you know how to hear, see, smell, or feel them.

Before long, it was no longer enough to be able to communicate with a mechanic; I wanted to be the mechanic *myself* whenever possible. Not only did I save money, but Tweety began running better, and I found that not only was I saving money and fuel, I was having *fun!*

Today, vehicles are more complex because computers control many systems and even professional mechanics need specialized equipment to deal with them. The upside is that these vehicles usually need fewer repairs, and there are much greater intervals between basic maintenance tasks, most of which are still easily done yourself. The same goes for making a variety of minor repairs and adjustments.

Unlike professional mechanics, when *you* do the troubleshooting (that's CarSpeak for diagnosing a problem by analyzing the symptoms), you can try the cheaper solutions first. For example, if your engine has been overheating constantly, you check the radiator cap and the coolant level, look for leaks in the hoses, and check the thermostat *before* paying for a new water pump. If it's the cap, a hose, or the thermostat, you may be able to easily replace it yourself, and the money you'll save is well worth the effort. If it finally comes down to changing the water pump, you can ask the mechanic about installing a good rebuilt pump instead of an expensive new one.

With this book as your guide to how cars work, you may discover that your vehicle stops being a mystery and begins to be fun to hang around with. When you realize that a vehicle exhibits most of the symptoms of life — it's self-propelled, reacts to outside stimuli, consumes fuel and discharges wastes, and even manages to sing a little tune now and then — it's really hard not to respond to it as though it were another living thing.

# Conventions Used in This Book

The following conventions are used throughout the text to make things consistent and easy to understand:

>> All Web addresses appear in monofont.

>> Whenever you encounter a term set in *this font,* you'll find it defined in the glossary in Appendix A.

- » *Italic* is used to note technical terms that aren't defined in the glossary.

- » **Bold** is used to highlight the action parts of numbered steps as well as key information in lists.

- » Sidebars are the shaded boxes that appear here and there. They contain information that's interesting and insightful and that may help you out in your auto repair adventures. However, you won't be at a serious disadvantage if you stick to the regular text and save the sidebars to read later on.

# How I Picture You

In order to make this book as relevant, readable, and enjoyable as possible, I envision it as a friendly conversation with the kind of person I feel would want to read it. Here's my mental portrait of my readers:

- » You're intelligent and may know a great deal about a lot of things (law, business, literature, medicine, and other nonautomotive subjects), but you need some help when it comes to cars.

- » You're tired of living as a "closet dummy" who nods and smiles at the incomprehensible mutterings of your mechanic, only to end up shelling out money for repairs that you neither fully understand nor always need.

- » You've decided that it simply isn't worth the extra money to have other people do things for you that you can do yourself.

- » You're tired of other people assuming (especially if you're a teenager, a senior, or a woman) that you aren't capable of handling repairs yourself.

- » You want to keep a good vehicle in good condition without paying dearly to have someone else do the simple maintenance, or you want to keep your old heap running just a little longer without spending a lot of money on it.

- » You want to maintain your vehicle *without* devoting every weekend, weeknight, and spare lunch hour to poring over the intricacies, details, and mysteries of the internal combustion engine.

- » You've realized (I hope!) that a vehicle that runs inefficiently because it's poorly maintained or is running on fossil fuel pollutes the environment, and you want to do something to turn that around.

# How This Book Is Organized

Basically, this book covers everything you need to know to understand, care for, maintain, and troubleshoot your vehicle, or choose a new, more efficient, and safer one. You'll be relieved to know that I explain everything in everyday terms, with no jargon, no unnecessary technical details, and lots of simple illustrations.

To help you find information easily, this book is divided into seven parts, each containing chapters that deal with a particular topic. Because the key to doing *any* job is to understand what you're working on and how it functions, I strongly recommend that you read the chapter that deals with the system you want to work on *before* you head for the chapter that tells you how to do a specific job. The following sections describe the information that you can find in each part.

## Part 1: Getting to Know Your Vehicle

If you want the basics, this is the part for you. I cover things that everyone who drives should know, like how to decide whether you want to do a job yourself, how to get the hood open, how to use a jack and change a tire, and how to take *anything* apart and put it back together again. A monthly under-the-hood check that can prevent 70 percent of highway breakdowns will transform you from an "I-*can't*-do-it-myselfer" into a hands-on mechanic. I also describe the tools that you'll need to borrow or buy if you plan to do regular maintenance and simple repairs. Finally, a quick and simple run-through of how basic automotive systems work together gives you the confidence to explore further because what was once a mystery is now familiar territory.

## Part 2: Powering Up with Air, Fuel, and Fire

This part provides a closer look at the electrical and fuel systems in vehicles with internal combustion engines and tells you how to do simple jobs related to each one. If you own or would like to own an alternatively fueled vehicle, you'll find information on how diesel, hybrid, multifuel, natural gas, and hydrogen vehicles work; descriptions of a variety of alternative fuels; and the advantages and disadvantages of each.

## Part 3: Staying Cool and In Control

This part deals with the cooling system, how oil benefits your vehicle, and how the brake system works. You find out how to prevent and deal with chronic overheating, add and change coolant, find and repair leaks, change your oil, check and maintain your brakes, pack wheel bearings, and do a variety of other vital tasks.

## Part 4: Smoothing the Ride: Steering and Suspension, Tires and Transmissions

How comfortably and efficiently a vehicle operates is hugely influenced by the systems covered in this part of the book. This part tells you how all these systems operate and shows you how to choose the right tires, read the wealth of information on the sidewalls and the treads to prevent tires from wearing out prematurely, about balancing and alignment, and how to fill tires with the proper amount of air. The chapters on transmissions explain how they work, how to troubleshoot symptoms, and how to obtain the best deal on repairs, along with driving techniques that will extend the life of your transmission.

## Part 5: Staying Safe and Dealing with Emergencies

This part helps you deal with problems that may occur while you're away from home. It describes a variety of new safety systems that help children ride comfortably and securely, prevent accidents and injuries, increase traction and stability, avoid rollovers, and even call for help without your assistance when your car is disabled or stolen. It shows you how to decipher such symptoms as weird noises, smoke, smells, and leaks to determine what's wrong; I also share what to do to get off the road safely, jump a start, and cool things down if your car overheats in traffic.

If a job is just too hairy to deal with yourself, I tell you how to find a reliable service facility and establish a good relationship with it, describe a problem so a mechanic can diagnose it swiftly and accurately, decipher a mechanic's invoice, and get satisfaction on complaints if, despite your best efforts, you run into problems with *anything* you buy.

## Part 6: Helping Your Vehicle Look Its Best

Because keeping a vehicle clean — inside and out — can extend its life and value, in this part I cover washing and waxing the body, tidying up under the hood, cleaning the interior, and removing stains from fabric, carpeting, windows, and other surfaces. If your vehicle has suffered minor damage, I show you how to repair small dings, dents, and rust spots; touch up paint; and patch or install weatherstripping instead of paying big bucks for body shops to do it. If major work needs to be done I tell you how to choose the right type of parts, and how to evaluate body shops and get the best deal and highest quality work from them.

## Part 7: The Part of Tens

This part can save you money, time, and sanity. It lists the most important preventive maintenance you can do to keep your vehicle in good condition and offers "eco-logical" tips for saving fuel.

## Appendixes

I include two handy appendixes at the back of this book:

- ›› The *Dictionary of Acronyms* and the *Practical Glossary* not only tell you what automotive terms mean but give you advice about them as well. Throughout the book, glossary terms are set in a **special font** to remind you to go to the glossary when you see a word that you don't recognize or a term that you don't understand.

- ›› The handy *Specifications Record* makes sure that you have the numbers of the parts you need when you go to the auto supply store, and the *Maintenance Record* reminds you to get busy if you've let things go too long. The *Maintenance Record* also provides a history of maintenance and repair that will be an asset when it's time to sell your vehicle or trade it in. Each record can be photocopied (before you enter any information on it) so you have one for every vehicle you own.

# Icons Used in This Book

To make this book easier to read and simpler to use, I include some icons that can help you find and fathom key ideas and information.

**TIP**

This icon points to suggestions or hints that can make a task easier, save you money, help you avoid hassles, and otherwise make your life easier.

**WARNING**

This icon appears next to information you want to watch out for because it is attempting to keep you from something dangerous or that could cost you a lot of money. It is designed to help you achieve success in a particular situation.

**ECO-LOGIC**

This icon was specially created for this book to alert you to the relationship between a piece of information and its impact on the environment. The information will help you save fuel, cut air pollution, recycle parts, and dispose of toxic substances safely.

REMEMBER

This icon indicates information that you may have encountered elsewhere in the book and need to take into consideration and keep in mind.

TECHNICAL
STUFF

This icon appears beside technical information that, although interesting (at least to me), you can skip without risking anything important.

TRUE
STORY

This icon appears beside real-life stories that provide a relaxing respite from serious subjects and demonstrate what you should — or should not — do to avoid major trouble or to triumph in difficult situations.

## Where to Go from Here

You can use this book any way you want to. You can read it from cover to cover or jump from section to section as the mood strikes you. To find a general topic, head to the Table of Contents. If you're looking for more specific information, go to the Index.

No matter how you use the book, I recommend that you tuck it into your trunk compartment to keep it handy when it's time for maintenance or if you need to figure out what's gone wrong on the road.

If this book turns you on to automotive systems and repair, then by all means extend your knowledge by reading more and more sophisticated literature on your favorite automotive topics. But there's no substitute for hands-on experience. You won't be able to realize any of your goals unless you stop procrastinating and start *working.* If you're feeling timid about actually *touching* your vehicle's inner parts, try doing something simple, like checking the oil dipstick or changing the air filter. I hope that you find it as exhilarating as I did, and I know that your car will love you for it. May you and your vehicle have a long and happy life together!

## Beyond the Book

In addition to what you're reading right now, this book comes with a free access-anywhere Cheat Sheet. To get this Cheat Sheet, go to www.dummies.com and search for "Auto Repair For Dummies, 2nd Edition For Dummies Cheat Sheet" by using the Search box.

# 1

# Getting to Know Your Vehicle

Ever seen someone try to figure out how to open a can of sardines? They have the key in one hand, the can in the other, and they poke, prod, and pry until they finally decide that saltines alone are fine. If you've ever tried to open the hood of your vehicle or jack it up without the benefit of prior experience (or paying attention when someone else did it), you may feel as confused as the sardine-lovers seem. That's why this part covers the things every driver should be able to do, safety tips that everyone who works on cars should know, and the tools you can use to get your vehicle running smoothly again. You find out how to buy the right auto part on your first trip to the store and how to do a monthly under-the-hood check that can prevent breakdowns on the road by *70 percent!*

Finally, I take a quick trip through all the automotive systems involved in operating your vehicle to show you what each one does, how it does it, and how they relate to one another.

Chapter **1**

# Things Every Driver Should Know

I f you're not particularly mechanically inclined, you may watch those who *are* with admiration, amazement, and exasperation because they have something you don't: an understanding of how things work and how things fit together. When they take something apart, they can reassemble it the way it was. When they say that they want to take a look under the hood, they can actually get the darn thing open. And when they need to change a flat, they don't spend ten minutes trying to figure out which end of the jack is up.

The good news is that you don't have to be born with a wrench in your hand to know how to fix things — even things as seemingly complicated as a car. I know; I've been there. The Introduction tells you all about my automotive epiphany.

Of course, the simplest tasks can sometimes be the biggest hurdles to overcome. After all, if you can't even figure out how to open the hood, how can you check the *oil* or the *coolant* level? That's why I begin this book with the basics: simple jobs that you'll need to do again and again — like opening the hood, jacking up a car, and changing a tire. I also include instructions for filling the fuel tank yourself (it's cheaper than full-service), a surefire method for taking *anything* apart and putting it back together again, and safety pointers that *every* mechanic — experienced and beginner — should heed.

**REMEMBER**

Whenever you encounter a term set in *this font,* you'll find it defined in the glossary in Appendix A.

# Before You Tackle Any Job

It's wonderful to do things yourself. You spend less money, you get a sense of power knowing that you did it on your own, and you know that the job's been done right. Nevertheless, to avoid getting in over my head, I always ask myself the following questions before undertaking *any* job:

>> Do I really want to do this? Will it be fun — or horrendous? (I try never to do anything that doesn't *feel* good unless it's absolutely necessary.)

>> Do I know how to do it? If not, where do I go to learn?

>> Does it require such expensive tools that it would cost less to have someone do it for me than to buy those tools? Can I borrow or rent the tools I need?

>> If I goof, can something be seriously damaged? Can I be hurt?

>> How long will it take, and what is my time worth? From that perspective, how much money will I save by doing it myself?

You'll be happy to know that almost every job in this book should pass the test of these questions. If you find a task that doesn't, don't hesitate to turn it over to a professional — *after* you read enough to know that the job is definitely necessary, what it entails, whether the work has been done properly, and how to get satisfaction if it isn't. With that in mind, let's get on to the very first thing you need to know in order to work on your vehicle.

## Buying the right parts for your vehicle

Before you go shopping for parts to replace those on your vehicle, read the tips in this section carefully. They can help you avoid what's probably the most annoying part of any automotive job: disabling your vehicle to work on it only to find that you need it to drive back to the store to exchange the stuff they sold you in error! Before I learned how to do it right, this happened at least two out of every three times on every job I did.

## WHAT THE BIG GUYS TAUGHT ME ABOUT BUSTING THINGS LOOSE

If you try to remove a bolt or a spark plug and you can't budge it, don't feel like a weakling. At first I thought that I had trouble because I was female, so I asked the biggest guys in my auto class for help because it would have been embarrassing if some little guy could do it. To my amazement, I found that often the big guys struggled, too! The difference was that they always prevailed. What I learned from them is that strength depends less on size or sex and more on the way in which we've been taught to focus our strength. People who are handy with tools usually have learned to pour their strength down their arms and into their hands, and focus it on the tool they're using. The guys also showed me that the longer the handle, the more leverage you have. And from watching them struggle, I learned that the patience to persevere comes from having the confidence that eventually you will succeed. So now I approach hard-to-move objects with the proper tools, focus, and patience. It works!

**REMEMBER**

This section tells you what you need to know when buying *any* part. Sections in other chapters that deal with jobs that require buying replacement parts provide tips on buying them as well as what tools and other stuff you need for that task. Chapter 3 tells you how to buy specific tools and what they're used for.

To buy the proper parts for your vehicle, you must know its *specifications* (or "specs," as they're often called). Most of this information should be in your *owner's manual,* and a lot of it is also printed on metal tags or decals located inside your hood. You can usually find these in front of the radiator, inside the fenders, on the inside of the hood — anywhere the auto manufacturer thinks you'll find them. I know of one car that has its decal inside the lid of the glove compartment. These ID tags also provide a lot of other information about where the vehicle was made, what kind of paint it has, and so on.

The *service manual* for your vehicle should have the specs for the parts you need, and the parts department at your dealership or a reputable auto supply store can also look them up for you.

**WARNING**

It's a good idea to stick with parts from the same manufacturer as those that your vehicle originally came with. That brand may be listed in a service manual for your vehicle. If you don't have a service manual, tell the sales clerk at the auto parts store that you want *OEM (original equipment manufacturer)* parts. Quality *aftermarket* parts are available as well, but unless you trust your parts seller's recommendations, or you've already used a particular aftermarket brand and had good luck with it, stick with OEM parts.

# HOW TO DISPOSE OF EMPTY GASOLINE CANS SAFELY

Although gasoline simply burns, gasoline plus air forms an explosive vapor that can literally take out your entire neighborhood. For this reason, it's wise not to store or carry gasoline unless you're heading far away from any source of fuel (and in that unlikely event, use only a specialized, vented gas can). If you have an old gasoline can around, get rid of it, and do it in a way that won't pollute the environment: Fill the can with water, and, as soon as you can, take the can to a recycling center that handles toxic waste. If there's no center nearby, ask your local service station if they'll dispose of it for you.

Some people keep gasoline around to clean parts with, but this is extremely dangerous. Mechanic's solvent, available at gas stations and auto supply stores, works better and has been treated with a flame retardant to keep it from burning too freely.

TIP

If you can't find specs for buying and gapping spark plugs in your owner's or service manual or on your vehicle, you'll find them in a "Tune-Up Specification Guide" (called a "spec sheet" for short) at an auto supply store. "Buying the right plugs" in Chapter 6 provides a sample spec sheet and shows you how to use it.

REMEMBER

I provide a *Specifications Record* in Appendix B. Make a copy for each vehicle you own and record the specifications for that vehicle on it. I keep a duplicate in my glove compartment so that I always have it when I shop for parts.

TIP

When you go to buy parts, keep in mind that most professional mechanics get discounts at auto parts stores. Ask if you can get a discount given that you're installing the parts yourself. It can't hurt to try. Even if you don't get a price break on parts, you'll still be ahead of the game because you won't have to pay labor charges.

## Following safety rules

WARNING

The first time I tuned my car, I was sure that if I made the smallest mistake, the car would explode when I started it. This seems to be a common delusion, but it just isn't so. If you make a mistake, in most cases all you'll get is silence (which can be just as disconcerting, but not lethal after all). This isn't to say that working on a vehicle is free from danger. Before you do *any* work, be sure to observe the following safety rules:

>> **Don't smoke while you're working on your car — for obvious reasons!**

>> **Never work on your vehicle unless the *parking brake* is on, the *gearshift* is in Park or Neutral, and the engine is shut off.** If you have to run the

engine to adjust something, turn it on and off yourself to avoid the risk that a friendly helper may misunderstand and turn the engine on while your hands are in the way.

>> **Be sure that the parts of the engine you're working on are nice and cool so that you don't get burned.** If you're doing a job that calls for a warm engine, be very careful.

>> **Never jack a vehicle up unless the wheels are properly blocked.** I go into more detail about this later in this chapter in "How to Use a Jack Safely" and "How to Change a Tire."

>> **Use insulated tools for electrical work.**

>> **Before using a wrench or *ratchet* on a part that's "stuck," make sure that if the part suddenly comes loose, your hand won't hit anything.** To avoid the possibility of being injured because your hand slams into something, *pull on wrenches rather than push them whenever possible.*

>> **Take off your tie, scarf, rings, long necklaces, and other jewelry.** If they get caught on parts, they — and you — can be damaged.

>> **Tie back long hair.** If your hair accidentally gets caught in a moving fan or belt, you can literally be scalped.

**ECO-LOGIC**

>> **If you're working with toxic chemicals, such as *coolant,* cleaners, and the like, keep them away from your mouth and eyes.** Wash your hands thoroughly after using them, and either store them safely away from pets and children or dispose of them in a way that's safe for the environment.

>> **Know that gasoline is extremely dangerous to have around.** Not only is It toxic and flammable, but the vapor in an *empty* can is explosive enough to take out a city block. If you must keep a small amount of gasoline on hand for a lawn mower or chain saw, always store it in a ventilated gasoline can designed specifically for that purpose. Unless you're going far into the wilds, *never* carry a can of gasoline in or on your vehicle. (See the sidebar "How to dispose of empty gasoline cans safely.")

>> **Work in a well-ventilated area to avoid breathing in carbon monoxide if you have to run the engine, or breathing in toxic fumes from chemicals and gasoline.** If possible, work outdoors in your driveway, your backyard, or a parking lot. If you must work in your garage, be sure to keep the garage door open and move the vehicle as close to the door as possible.

>> **Use a work light in dark areas.** If you don't already have one, Chapter 3 tells you what you need to know about buying one.

>> **Keep a fire extinguisher handy.** Chapter 3 contains reasons for this precaution that may surprise you.

So much for the scary stuff. Auto repair safety is all a matter of common sense, really.

# How to Fill 'Er Up Yourself

More and more gas stations are shifting toward self-service. If you've been reluctant to abandon the luxury of the full-service lane, chances are that it's going to get more and more difficult to find one. Knowing how to fill 'er up yourself not only prevents you from being stranded with an empty tank when there's no one available to fill it for you, but it also saves you money on every gallon, every time.

**TIP**

Fill up in the morning, before the temperature rises or fuel is delivered to the gas station. Gasoline expands with heat, which also reduces its energy content per gallon. Since the sales meters at service stations are set for fuel at 60°F, you get less energy and pay more for fuel that's hotter than that. Fuel is often delivered to stations while still hot from the refineries and studies show that fuel in underground tanks can top 100°F even when the weather is cooler.

**WARNING**

Always extinguish your cigarette before you start to pump gasoline. If the flame comes in contact with gasoline fumes, it can cause an explosion.

Here are the steps for pumping your own gas:

1. **Look at the price window on the pump.**

   If a previous sale is registered there, reset it by following the next steps to activate the pump and select the grade of gasoline. If the price doesn't disappear, try inserting your credit card or have the attendant clear the machine so that the price window reads "$0.00."

2. **If you're using a credit card, insert it into the slot and follow the instructions in the credit card window.**

3. **Select the grade of fuel you want, and move the lever on the pump to ON.**

4. **Unscrew the cap from your *fuel tank*.**

5. **Unhook the pump nozzle and hose from the pump, and place the nozzle into the fuel tank opening.**

   Some nozzles have rubber vapor-recovery sleeves that must be depressed to allow the fuel to flow, so push the nozzle as deeply into the filler tube of your vehicle as it will go.

6. **Squeeze the trigger on the pump nozzle to allow fuel to flow out of the hose and into your fuel tank.**

   There's usually a little latch near the trigger that keeps the trigger open so that you don't have to stand there holding onto it and inhaling gasoline fumes. Don't worry about overflows; gas pumps shut off automatically when your tank is almost full.

**TIP**

Engaging the trigger latch gives you time to take advantage of the other services available. You can wash the windows or check the air pressure in your tires and add air if they need it (Chapter 17 has instructions). The trigger latch also enables you to get farther away from the pump instead of standing there breathing in the toxic fumes while the tank is filling.

7. **When the fuel stops flowing, the trigger clicks closed and the numbers in the pump window stop moving. Remove the nozzle from the fuel tank and hang it back on the pump.**

**ECO-LOGIC**

Never "top off" a tank by adding fuel after the pump shuts off automatically. If you overfill your tank, the fuel may overflow the fill hole or leak out onto the road through an overflow outlet. This is not just a waste of your money; spilled fuel ruins asphalt, pollutes the air, and is a fire hazard. This kind of leakage is especially prone to happen if it's a hot day because heat makes the fuel in your tank expand.

8. **If you used a credit card, press Yes for a receipt and replace the cap on your fuel tank while the receipt prints.**

# How to Open the Hood

How can you do even simple under-the-hood jobs — such as checking the oil, *coolant*, and *transmission fluid*; refilling windshield wiper fluid; and checking *accessory belts* — if you don't know how to get the hood of your vehicle open?

The good news is that opening the hood is easy and uncomplicated — *if* you know how to do it. Although the location of the hood release may differ from one vehicle to the next, all releases work in pretty much the same way.

**TIP**

If after reading the following instructions and consulting your *owner's manual* you still can't figure out how to get your hood open, head for the full-service bay the next time you stop for gas and ask the attendant to show you how to do it. You may pay a little more for fuel and a tip, but the lesson will be worth it — and you can get your windows washed and your tire pressure checked for nothing! (If you're really short of cash, just ask for $5 worth of gasoline; the difference in cost will be negligible.) (A sidebar in Chapter 2 tells you why you should check the oil yourself instead of having the attendant do it.)

Here's how to open the hood yourself:

1. **Find your hood release and pop open the hood.**

Either consult your owner's manual, or try to remember the last time a service station attendant opened the hood of your car. Did he or she ask you to pull a lever inside the vehicle? Or did he or she go directly to the front grill?

In newer models, the hood release is often inside the vehicle, somewhere near the steering column or on the floor next to the driver's seat. (It generally displays the word "Hood" or a picture of a car with its hood up.) In older models, the hood release is behind the grill or the bumper.

If the hood release is inside the vehicle, press, push, or pull it until you hear the hood pop open. If the hood release is at the front, look around and through the grill and feel under the grill and behind the bumper to find a handle, lever, arm, or button. Then press, push, or pull it from front to back and side to side until it releases the hood.

The hood will open a little, but it will probably be stopped by the safety catch — a metal lever that, when pressed one way or the other, releases the hood so that it can open all the way. This gizmo prevents the hood from opening accidentally and obscuring your vision while you're driving.

2. **With one hand, raise the hood as far as it will go. With the other hand, feel along the area between the hood and the grill for the safety catch. Release it and raise the hood the rest of the way.**

3. **Secure the hood if necessary.**

   If the hood stays up all by itself, fine. If it doesn't, look for a hood prop — a long, thin metal rod attached either to the underside of the hood or to the bottom edge of the hood opening. Either lower or lift the rod (depending on where it's located) and fit the end of it into the slot that's provided to hold it in place.

WARNING

On some vehicles, the hood is held up by two gas-pressurized cylinders known as *hood shocks*. If the hood doesn't feel secure, gas may have leaked out of these units and the hood could come down at any moment. If you're not sure, secure the hood with a broom handle or similar object and have these units checked — or replaced, if needed — as soon as you can.

# How to Take Anything Apart — and Get It Back Together Again

I'd never been able to follow the "easy" instructions to put my kids' toys together until I learned the technique that follows. Then I was able to get at my brakes to check them and even lubricate the *wheel bearings* and put everything back together again! The bonus is that this procedure works for *anything* that you need to take apart and put back together again — flat tires, toasters, bicycles, you name it.

> Never, ever do a job in a hurry.

Allow yourself plenty of time. If things get rough, have some water or a cup of coffee. You may get a whole new perspective when you go back to work. Limit distractions: Turn on your answering machine or take the phone off the hook, keep the kids and the dog away, and relax. If you hit a snag, sit quietly and think about it — don't panic. If the parts fit together before, they'll fit together again.

Follow these instructions, breathing slowly and deeply:

1. **Lay a *clean*, lint-free rag down on a flat surface, near enough to reach without having to get up or walk to it.**

   You'll lay each part on this rag as you remove it. Consequently, the rag shouldn't be in an area where oil or dust or anything else can fall on it and foul up the parts. If you plan to use something that blasts air for cleaning purposes, leave enough of the rag uncluttered to fold it over the parts resting on it.

2. **Before you remove each part, stop and ask yourself the following questions, and if you're worried about forgetting your answers, make notes:**

   - What is this thing?
   - What does it do?
   - How does it do it?
   - Why is it made the way it is?
   - How tightly is it screwed on (or fastened down)?

   Most amateurs put things back very tightly, in hopes that the part won't fly off. But some things, like bolts that hold **gaskets** in place, shouldn't be tightened too securely because, for example, the bolt threads could be stripped or the gasket could be squeezed out of shape, allowing whatever it's holding in to get out. It's helpful to make notes about how hard each thing was to remove. "Don't over-tighten" or "Be sure it's secure." Some parts require exact **torque** specifications, but we don't deal with them in this book.

3. **As you remove each part, lay it down on the rag *in clockwise order, with each part pointing in the direction it was in before you removed it.***

   This is the key to the whole system. When you're ready to reassemble things, the placement and direction of each part tells you when to put it back and how it was oriented.

4. **If you're making notes, assign each part a number indicating the order in which you removed it — Part #1, Part #2, and so on.**

You can even put numbers on the parts with masking tape if you're afraid that the rag may be moved accidentally. Also, note what each part was attached to; for example, "Part #6: Hook at end of arm on left hooks onto knob to right of Part #7." Add a sketch if it helps.

If you work systematically and understand the function of each part, you won't be left with what seem to be extra nuts and bolts at the end of the job.

5. **When you're ready to reassemble everything, begin with the last part you removed, and proceed counterclockwise through the parts on the rag. If you've numbered the parts, they should go on in reverse order.**

Now you're ready to tackle the first job that will give you a chance to apply this technique: Using a jack and changing a tire. You may never need to do it, but if you're stuck with the need to change a flat, you'd better know how.

# How to Use a Jack Safely

The most obvious reason to jack up a car is to change a tire, but other jobs such as inspecting brakes may also require you to get under the vehicle. (Even if you're skinny enough to squeeze yourself between the pavement and the underside of your car, you still need room to move around and manipulate tools.) Chapter 3 has detailed information about the different types of jacks as well as items such as *jack stands* (essential) and *creepers* (nonessential, but nice). This section explains how to use a jack safely and efficiently. The next section tells you how to change a tire after the vehicle is in the air.

WARNING

*Before* you attempt to jack up your vehicle, observe the following safety precautions:

>> **Jacks are used only to get a vehicle off the ground. They should *never* be used to hold a vehicle in place.**

>> **You must use jack stands when you work underneath your vehicle.** If you don't, you run the risk of serious injury or even death. People have been crushed to death when vehicles that were improperly secured fell on them.

>> **Never jack up a vehicle without blocking the wheels to keep it from rolling.** Use bricks, wooden wedges, or metal wheel chocks to block the wheels at the opposite end of the car from the end that is to be raised. (Chocks are available at a low cost at auto supply stores.) Keep whatever

you use for blocks in the trunk so that you don't have to go hunting around if you have to change a flat tire.

**TIP**

If you find yourself faced with the job of changing a tire and you have nothing with which to block the wheels, park near the curb with the wheels turned in. This may not keep you from getting hurt if the car rolls off the jack, but at least innocent motorists and pedestrians won't have to deal with a runaway driverless vehicle!

>> **Never change a tire on a freeway or highway.** Not only can you be seriously injured, but you can also fall prey to carjackers. *Don't exit the vehicle;* instead use a cellphone to call road service or an automobile association such as the AAA. If you don't have a cellphone, hang a white rag or a white piece of paper out of the driver's side window and wait for the highway patrol to rescue you.

**TECHNICAL STUFF**

Even if you hate cellphones, I recommend that you buy one and keep it in the vehicle for emergencies. You can find a very affordable model that just lets you call 911, road service, and those you'd want to notify in an emergency. It could save your life.

>> **Always park a vehicle on level ground before you jack it up.** If you get a flat tire on a hill and can't coast to the bottom without killing the tire completely, park close to the curb, turn the wheels toward the curb, and block the downside wheels securely to prevent the car from rolling.

**REMEMBER**

These precautions won't eliminate the risk of changing a tire on an incline. If you can't get to level ground or wait for assistance, you change the tire at your own risk.

>> **Be sure that your gearshift is in Park (or in First if you have a *manual transmission*) and that the *parking brake* is on *before* you jack up the vehicle.** The only time you don't want the parking brake on is when you have to be able to rotate a *rear* wheel or remove rear *brake drums* to inspect the brakes. In such a case, make sure that the front wheels are blocked *securely*.

**WARNING**

If you remove a wheel and begin to work without making sure that you jacked up the car and blocked it securely, the vehicle can do a lot of damage to itself — and to you — if it falls. (This is not meant to frighten you away from jacking up your car and working on or under it. It's just to emphasize the fact that taking a few simple precautions can keep you safe.)

After you've observed *all* the safety precautions, follow these steps to jack up a vehicle:

**1.** If you're going to remove a wheel to change a tire or check your brakes, remove the *wheel cover* or hubcap (if there is one) and loosen the *lug nuts.*

After the vehicle is jacked up, the wheel will turn freely, which makes it harder to get a wheel cover off and almost impossible to start turning the nuts. Instructions for removing a wheel cover and loosening lug nuts are in the next section, "How to Change a Tire."

2. **Place the jack under the part of the vehicle that it should contact when raised. If you're using jack stands, place them near the jack.**

   Where you place your jack depends on whether you're planning to do a one-wheel job, such as tire changing or brake checking, or a two-wheel, whole-end repair job. Many vehicles now have special flat spots on the underside specifically for jack placement.

TIP

   If you place your jack incorrectly, you can injure your car. To find the proper place to position the jack for your particular vehicle, check your **owner's manual.** If you don't have a manual, ask the service department at your dealership to show you the proper placement. In any event, follow these guidelines:

   - Never place the jack so that the weight of the vehicle rests on something that can bend, break, or give.

   - If your manual is incomprehensible or lacks jack placement information, try to place the jack so that it touches either the vehicle's frame or the big bar that supports the front wheel **suspension.**

   - You can also place jacks near the rear-wheel **axle,** but until you become more proficient at this, I'd stick to jacking up one wheel at a time.

3. **Lift the vehicle by using the jack. How you accomplish this depends on the type of jack you're using (see Figure 1-1):**

   - If you have a *scissor* jack, insert the rod or wrench over the knob, and then crank.

   - If you have a *hydraulic* jack, place the handle into the appropriate location and pump up and down. Use nice, even strokes, taking the jack handle from its lowest point to its highest point on each stroke to cut down on the labor involved.

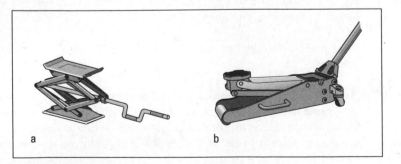

**FIGURE 1-1:**
A scissor jack (a) and a hydraulic jack (b).

a                    b

4. **Place the jack stands under the vehicle, near where the jack is touching it (see Figure 1-2). Raise the stands until they're high enough to just fit under, and lock them in place. Lower the jack until the vehicle is resting on the jack stands.**

Substituting boxes, stones, or bricks for jack stands is very dangerous. They can slip out or break while you're under the car. A jack can do the same thing, so be sure to buy a pair of jack stands and stow them in the trunk if you're traveling out of reach of help if you get a flat tire. You can find information about buying jack stands in Chapter 3.

5. **Before you begin to work, wiggle the vehicle a little to make sure that it's resting securely on the jack stands. Then remove the jack.**

Wiggling the vehicle also tells you whether you have the wheels blocked properly. It's better if the vehicle falls while all four wheels are in place. (It will bounce just a little.)

6. **When you're finished working, replace the jack, remove the stands, and lower the vehicle to the ground.**

If you're using a scissor jack, simply turn the crank in the opposite direction. If you're using a hydraulic jack, use the rod to turn the pressure release valve. The jack will do the rest of the work for you.

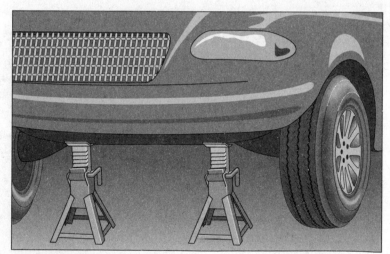

**FIGURE 1-2:** Jack stands hold your vehicle up safely.

# How to Change a Tire

These days, working on your vehicle at roadside can be risky, so the best thing is to use your cellphone to call an automobile association or another source of help. But if you have a flat tire in an area where you can't get a cellphone signal, you can be helpless unless you know how to change a tire yourself. For this reason, *everyone* should have a general idea of what's involved. The task seems easy enough to do:

1. **Secure the vehicle so that it won't roll.**

2. **Jack up the vehicle, following the instructions in the preceding section, "How to Use a Jack Safely."**

3. **Remove the old tire.**

4. **Put on the new tire.**

5. **Put away the jack stuff and the old tire.**

6. **Drive happily into the sunset.**

These may be the basic steps of changing a tire, but the job can get sticky in a couple of places if you're not properly equipped. The following sections explain the steps involved in changing a tire in detail and in order. Check out Chapter 3 for a list of the tools you need.

**TIP**

Because the location and type of spare tire differs from one vehicle to the next, if you aren't familiar with your vehicle it's a good idea to check out the spare (and the jack and *lug wrench*) *before* trouble occurs. While you're at it, make sure the spare has enough air in it and continue to check that periodically.

## Removing a wheel cover or hubcap

The first task in changing a flat is to remove the *wheel cover* or hubcap on the injured tire. The following steps tell you how:

1. **If your car has a standard wheel cover or hubcap, use a screwdriver or the flat end of a lug wrench (see Figure 3-16 in Chapter 3) to pry it off.**

   Just insert the point of the tool where the edge of the cover meets the wheel, and apply a little leverage (see Figure 1-3). The cap should pop off. You may have to do this in a couple of places, as if you were prying the lid off a can of paint.

**WARNING**

   If the cover has a delicate finish, consult your owner's manual for instructions on how to remove it without damage. It may pry off or unscrew.

**FIGURE 1-3:**
You can use a screwdriver to pry a wheel cover loose.

2. **Lay the cover down on its back so that you can put the *lug nuts* into it to keep them from rolling away and heading for the nearest sewer.**

   If you're afraid of marring the finish, lay the cover on a rag.

After you remove the wheel cover or hubcap, the next task is to loosen the lug nuts.

# Loosening the lug nuts

Lug nuts are those big nuts that hold the wheel in place. How you remove the lug nuts on your vehicle depends on whether you have *alloy wheels* that are held on by lug nuts with delicate finishes, or hubcaps or wheel covers with standard lug nuts behind them.

## Lug nuts with special finishes

**WARNING**

The delicate aluminum or chrome-plated lug nuts on alloy wheels need careful handling. *They should never be loosened or replaced with power tools that can scratch the delicate finish.* (Some power tools have rubberized or plastic-coated fittings to avoid damaging the nuts, but those will be of no use to you on the road with no power supply to run them.) Many mechanics prefer to do it all by hand using a special lug fitting to avoid scarring the finish or rounding off the corners of the nuts. You can find this fitting at many parts and tire shops.

**TIP**

Some alloy wheels come with one or more locking nuts on each wheel to help discourage wheel thieves, and you must use the special "key" that came with the car to unlock them before loosening. Be sure you know where your wheel locks are, if your vehicle has them.

## Lug nuts with standard finishes

Most garages retighten ordinary lug nuts with a power tool, and unless you've done the job yourself by hand, they're pretty hard to loosen yourself. (Take my advice in Chapter 3 and buy a *cross-shaft* lug wrench. Figure 3-16 shows what one looks like.)

**TIP**

To make the job easier if an emergency arises, you may want to go out and try to remove the lug nuts on your vehicle now, following these instructions. If you have problems, resolve them now so that you won't have to struggle at the side of the road.

1. **Find the end of the wrench that fits the lug nuts on your vehicle, and fit it onto the first nut.**

   Always work on lug nuts in consecutive order so that you don't forget to tighten any later.

2. **Apply all your weight to the bar on the *left*.**

This starts turning the nut *counterclockwise*, which loosens it.

TIP

I don't suggest using this kind of strong-arm tactic on lug nuts with special finishes, but if an ordinary nut has been put on with a power tool and you can't get it started, a piece of hollow pipe, fitted over that left-hand arm of the cross-shaft wrench, magically adds enough leverage to start the nut easily (see Figure 1-4). After you replace the nut yourself, this aid is no longer necessary. But remember, the longer the arms on your lug wrench, the more leverage you have.

**FIGURE 1-4:**
A hollow pipe and a cross-shaft wrench can loosen the tightest lug nuts.

REMEMBER

Don't remove the lug nuts completely; just get them loose enough to remove by hand *after* jacking up the vehicle.

## Changing the tire

Before you jack up your vehicle, remove the spare from the trunk. After the vehicle is safely jacked up and the lug nuts are off, follow these instructions to change the tire:

1. **Roll the spare tire to the scene of the action if you haven't already done so.**

2. **Grasp the flat tire with both hands and pull it toward you.**

The flat tire sits on the exposed bolts that the lug nuts screw onto. As you pull the flat off, it should slide along the bolts until, suddenly, it clears the end of the bolts and you find yourself supporting its full weight. Tires are heavy, and you'll be quite happy to lower it to the ground (if you haven't already dropped it).

3. **Roll the flat along the ground to the rear of the vehicle to get it out of the way.**

4. **Lift the spare onto the lug bolts.**

Because tires are heavy, you may have a little trouble lifting the spare into place — especially if you're not accustomed to lifting heavy things.

5. **After you have the spare tire in place, replace the lug nuts and tighten them by hand.**

Give each lug nut a jolt with the wrench to get it firmly into place, but wait until the car is on the ground before you really try to tighten the lug nuts.

6. **Replace the jack, use it to lift the vehicle off the jack stands and lower the car to the ground.**

7. **After the vehicle is resting on the ground, use the lug wrench to tighten the lug nuts as much as you can.**

WARNING

If your vehicle has alloy wheels, tighten the lug nuts until the lug wrench won't move any more, then press down on the wrench's cross arm with all your weight, but don't jerk it or kick it or jump on it as you could cause the wrench to damage the finish on the nut.

Standard lug nuts are sturdier than those on alloy wheels, but you don't want to twist them off the bolts or ruin the threads. However, you don't want the wheel to fall off, either. If you're worried about tightening them sufficiently, use your hollow pipe, or step on the right-hand arm of the lug wrench after the nut is tight.

8. **Replace the wheel cover or hubcap.**

If your car has wheel covers with a delicate finish, the owner's manual should provide instructions for replacing it. If not, reverse the order of things you did when removing it (if you had to pry it off, then it probably pops back in with a sharp tap of your hand; if it unscrewed like a big jar top, then it screws back in).

If your car has hubcaps, place the hubcap against the wheel and whack it into place with the heel of your hand. Cushion your hand with a soft rag first so that you won't hurt it. And don't hit the hubcap with a wrench or hammer — you'll dent it. Whack it a couple of times, in a couple of places, to be sure that it's on evenly and securely. (Even secondhand hubcaps can be expensive to replace, and that's *if* you can find the one you need.) If it's too much of a hassle, or if you don't have the time to replace the hubcap, you can take it home and install it later; it's mostly ornamental, and you can drive for a while without it. But do replace it soon because it helps keep dust and dirt out of your brakes and bearings.

9. **Put the flat in the trunk where the spare was located, and put your tools (including wheel blocks) away.**

WARNING

*Get that flat fixed immediately; you don't know when you may need it again!* And make sure that it's repaired properly. Instead of dismounting the tire from the wheel rim, inspecting it, fixing it, and remounting it, some service stations simply plug the flat from the outside. Several states now outlaw this procedure, known as "outside-in" repair, and patches should never be used if the hole is in the sidewall rather than the tread. In either case, be sure to tell the service facility that you *don't* want the tire plugged from the outside; you want the flat corrected the proper way.

TIP

If you get caught in the middle of nowhere with a flat tire and are unable to call or wait for service, and if you don't feel safe — or capable of — changing it yourself, a can of nonflammable inflator/sealant can get you rolling again in minutes. Simply screw the nozzle of the can onto the valve stem of the flat tire. It will fill the tire with air and some sort of goop that temporarily seals the puncture. Because there's still some question about how permanent this fix is and its ultimate effects on your tire, look for a major brand that's environmentally friendly and can be rinsed out of the tire with soap and water by a tire repair professional. Use this product *only* in emergencies, get to a service station as soon as possible, and be sure to tell them that you used canned inflator/sealant and that they should remove the stuff before fixing the tire.

TIP

If reading these instructions makes you think that you'd rather languish by the side of the road for hours than undertake changing a tire yourself, consider outfitting your vehicle with *run-flat* tires. Although these tires are more expensive and some require special wheels, they make it possible to drive with a flat to the nearest service station without ruining the tire. Chapter 17 has more information about run-flat tires.

# How to Get In When You're Locked Out

WARNING

If you tend to leave the keys in your car fairly often, consider hiding an extra key somewhere on the vehicle. A little magnetic key box that sticks to the metal surface of a steel body or frame is best, but *be sure to place it in an obscure and hard-to-reach area where it can't jiggle loose and fall off.* I leave the location up to you — be imaginative. Struggling a little to reach that extra key is better than having car thieves find it. And *don't* hide your house key with it.

Fortunately, many new vehicles come with electronic door openers or "digital keys" that don't allow you to lock the doors with the keys in the vehicle. The downside is that if you lose the gadget, it can take days and hundreds of dollars to replace it, and you'll probably need to have the vehicle towed to a dealer who will order a new key.

TIP

If your vehicle has an electronic door opener, you may be able to get the door open, but if you've lost the opener outside your vehicle, the ignition may fail to start without it. Some vehicles have override switches for this eventuality, so find out whether you'd be able to start your vehicle without your opener, and locate the override switch now, if there is one.

Assuming that you've decided not to risk hiding an extra set of keys on your car, here are a few things you can try to get in without a key:

>> **If your vehicle has door locks that are recessed inside the interior door handle,** get professional help.

>> **If you have the old-style door locks with little buttons on the window ledge,** straighten a wire coat hanger and bend the end into a little hook. Insert it between the rubber molding and the side window and then carefully hook it around the door button and pull it up.

>> **If you have smooth buttons,** you can try to hook one using the hanger technique, but most will refuse to budge.

>> **If you happen to lock yourself out of the vehicle while you have the trunk open,** you may be able to move the rear seat out of the way and gain access to the rear of the car (or you can hide an extra ignition key in the trunk).

TIP

If you need professional help, call emergency road assistance and ask if they will be able to open the door. If not, ask them to send a local locksmith. The good news is that each car key is coded by the auto manufacturer, and if you have the key code number and personal identification, a locksmith can make you a new key. Write down the key code number and leave it where someone at home can read it to you in an emergency. Also record it — without identifying what it is — in your pocket address book or in your wallet *before you lose your keys.* If you bought the vehicle, new or used, from a dealer, the dealer may still have the number on file or the automaker may have a record of it. Failing that, a good locksmith may be able to analyze a key in fairly new condition and come up with the proper code for it.

Chapter **2**

# Preventive Maintenance: A Monthly Under-the-Hood Check

Everyone knows a few chronic tire kickers. Before they get in and drive off, these people habitually walk around their cars and kick the tires to make sure that they aren't flat. The same people habitually open and close all the cabinet doors in the kitchen and check the gas jets every time they go past the stove. You may laugh at them, but they're probably rarely caught with flat tires, open cabinets, or leaking gas. Why not learn from these folks and make a habit of checking the little things under the hood of your vehicle — maybe not every time you drive somewhere, but definitely once a month and before starting out on long road trips.

**TIP**

If the idea of committing yourself to a regular under-the-hood checkup seems less than alluring, look at it this way: Spending 15 minutes a month checking under the hood can prevent 70 percent of the problems that lead to highway breakdowns!

What you need to check regularly is anything that can run out of fluid, lose air, jiggle loose, or fray after use — in other words, things like *coolant*, tire pressure, hoses, and *accessory belts.* This chapter explains what to look for, how to look for it, and what to do if you discover that something needs to be replaced or refilled. You'll be happy to know it doesn't require any special tools.

TIP

I provide a *Maintenance Record* in Appendix B. Make a copy for each of your vehicles to keep track of what you check and what you replace each time you do an under-the-hood checkup. Appendix B also contains a *Specifications Record*; to avoid having to return parts that don't fit your vehicle, make a copy of this "spec sheet" for each of your vehicles, fill in the appropriate part numbers, and keep it in the glove box so that you have it whenever you buy parts.

REMEMBER

Whenever you encounter a term set in *this font,* you'll find it defined in the glossary in Appendix A.

# Getting Your Bearings under the Hood

Once a month, in the morning before you've driven your vehicle, arm yourself with a clean, lint-free rag and the household tools mentioned in this chapter, and open the hood of your vehicle. (If you've never done that, flip back to Chapter 1.) Then check the items in the sections that follow. The checkup may take a bit longer the first time you do it, but after that you should be able to whip through this check in about 15 minutes. As a matter of fact, you may want to grab this book and your *owner's manual* (if you have one), go out to your vehicle, and locate each part while you read. Figure 2-1 helps you find each part. Make a game of it. Enjoy!

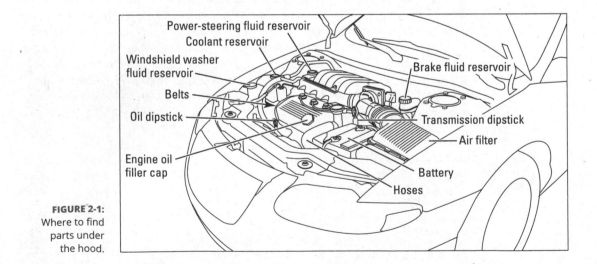

FIGURE 2-1: Where to find parts under the hood.

Power-steering fluid reservoir
Coolant reservoir
Windshield washer fluid reservoir
Belts
Oil dipstick
Engine oil filler cap
Brake fluid reservoir
Transmission dipstick
Air filter
Battery
Hoses

**TIP**

When you do the check for real, if you find that the *coolant,* oil, *transmission,* brake, or *power-steering* fluid levels are low, fill them to the proper levels and check again in a couple of days. If any of them are low again, visit a mechanic to find out why you're losing fluid and correct the problem.

**ECO-LOGIC**

To find out how to dispose of hazardous materials like batteries and the fluids in automotive systems, visit www.1800cleanup.org/default.asp. Just insert your zip code in the search box to find recycling centers in your area for many kinds of toxic materials. If you don't have access to the Internet, ask your local auto shop if they will accept your hazardous materials for recycling.

# Check the Air Filter

In most newer, fuel-injected vehicles, the air filter is found inside a rectangular box called a *cold air collector box* (see Figure 2-2). It's usually close to the front of the vehicle near the inside of one of the fenders. Air that's scooped up by the front of the vehicle moves through an air intake tube into the air filter inside the box (see Figure 2-2). On older fuel-injected engines and carbureted engines, the filter is found in the *air cleaner,* which sits atop the engine. As you can see in Figure 2-3, it's large and round with a snorkel sticking out of the side to facilitate the intake of fresh air. Your owner's manual should have instructions on how to locate and get at your air filter. If you have no manual, see Chapter 8 for general instructions.

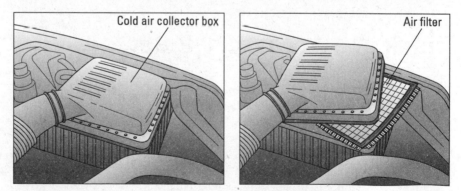

**FIGURE 2-2:**
The cold air collector box houses the air filter.

To find out if your air filter needs to be replaced, just lift it out (it isn't fastened down) and hold it up to the sun or to a strong light. Can you see the light streaming through it? If not, try dropping it *lightly,* bottom-side down, on a hard surface to jar some dirt loose. (Don't blow through the filter — you can foul it up that way.) If you drop the filter a few times and it's still too dirty to see through, you need a new one. Chapter 7 tells you more about air filters, and Chapter 8 has instructions for buying and replacing them.

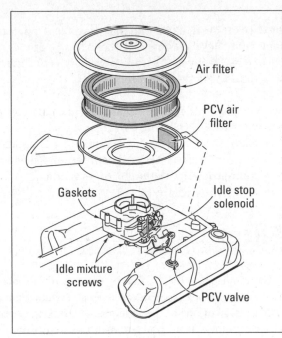

FIGURE 2-3:
On carbureted
vehicles, the air
filter is inside the
air cleaner.

Labels in figure: Air filter, PCV air filter, Idle stop solenoid, Gaskets, Idle mixture screws, PCV valve

REMEMBER

Because the air filter extracts dirt and dust particles from the air, you should change it at least once a year or every 20,000 miles, whichever comes first — unless yours gets very dirty before then. If you do most of your driving in a dusty or sandy area, you may need to replace your air filter more often.

# Check the Accessory Belts

If you're under the hood of your vehicle and can see without having to remove shields or cowlings, take a look at the serpentine *accessory belt* that drives the **alternator,** the *power-steering pump,* the air conditioning compressor, the water pump in many cases, and other parts of a modern vehicle. (If you drive an older car, look at the separate belts.) Figures 2-4 and 2-5 show you what both types of belts look like.

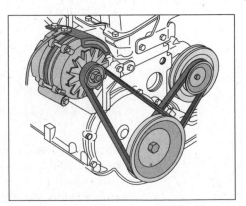

FIGURE 2-4:
Accessory belts.

**TIP**

If you can't access an accessory belt easily to check it yourself, have it checked when you have the vehicle serviced or if the belt gets noisy or any of the equipment it drives begins to malfunction.

If you can see an accessory belt easily, here's what to look for:

» **If the belt "gives" more than ½ inch when you press on it but otherwise is in good condition,** it may just need to be adjusted.

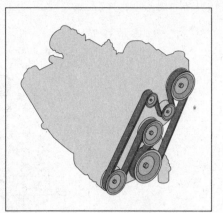

**FIGURE 2-5:**
Serpentine multi-accessory drive belt.

» **If the belt is glazed or has oil on it,** the slick surface will slip where it winds around the pulleys and it won't be able to efficiently drive the components connected to it. Your engine may overheat because the water pump isn't operating properly, or the air conditioner may fail to cool the interior of your vehicle. Have the belt replaced.

» **If you see chunks missing from the belt or many cracks across its surface, or if it's frayed or tearing,** debris may be embedded in it, or one of the pulleys may be out of alignment. The safest move is to replace the belt.

Chapter 12 provides more detailed information about how to inspect an accessory belt and whether you can deal with it yourself or have a professional work on it.

# Check the Battery

The *battery* stores the electrical current that your vehicle uses to start and passes electricity along to the parts of your vehicle that need it to function, such as the *ignition system*, lights, radio, and so on. (For more information about the ignition system in general and the battery in particular, see Chapters 5 and 6.)

A battery, like other parts of your vehicle, is subject to wear and tear and should be checked regularly. In particular, pay attention to the battery's trouble spots shown in Figure 2-6. Also, a battery that's kept clean should last longer than a cruddy one.

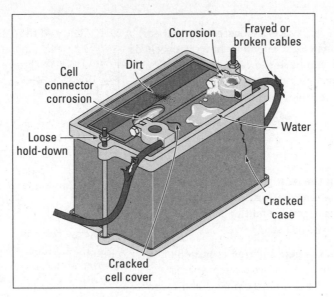

**FIGURE 2-6:**
The parts of the
battery to check.

WARNING

Before you work on your battery, be sure to read *all* the safety measures involved. Here's a rundown:

>> **Never work on a battery with a lit cigarette in your mouth.** (For that matter, you should not only never smoke while working around your vehicle, you should never smoke at all!) Batteries are filled with sulfuric acid that generates hydrogen gas, so you need to be careful when working around them. If you get acid deposits on your skin or clothes, wash them off with water immediately.

>> **Disconnect the battery whenever you work on it, but *be sure to shut the engine off first!*** On most modern vehicles, computers control functions of the engine, *fuel* and *ignition systems, automatic transmissions,* and other stuff. Therefore, when messing about with batteries and their cables, you need to be extremely careful not to inadvertently send a shot of unwanted voltage into one of the computers and destroy it. For this reason, it's important to disconnect the battery before you work on it.

>> **Always remove the negative cable from the battery if you plan to work on wiring under the hood.** This will prevent you from possibly damaging electrical components or receiving a shock.

>> **When removing and replacing both battery cables, always remove the *negative* cable first and replace it last.** If you attempt to remove the positive clamp first and your wrench slips and touches something metal, your wrench can fuse to the part like an arc welder.

>> **Tie the cables back while you work on the battery so that they don't flop back over onto the terminals.** Don't allow anything made of metal to connect the terminal posts; this can damage the battery. If the cables are connected to the posts when something else interferes, you can destroy the *onboard computers.*

The radio may be affected by disconnecting the battery. As a precaution, you can maintain power while the battery is disconnected by making a cheap tool with a cigarette lighter socket and a 9-volt battery. (Most electronics stores can set this up for you.) Plug the 9-volt battery into your cigarette lighter socket before disconnecting the vehicle's battery, and remove it after the battery is back on.

Don't let all the cautions that I list here turn you off the idea of checking your vehicle's battery. It's easy to check your battery if you follow these steps:

**1. Locate your battery.**

Figure 2-6 shows you what it looks like and what may be wrong with it.

**2. If you see powdery deposits on the *positive* and *negative terminals,* clean them off.**

The cruddy deposits that form in lovely colors on the top of your terminals are made by battery acid. Before you clean this stuff off, remove the cables from both terminals by undoing the nut on each cable clamp and wiggling the cable until the clamp comes off the terminal post.

This bears repeating: *Always remove the cable clamp from the negative terminal first.* (It's the one that's marked with a "–" sign.) When you're through with the job, *replace the positive cable first and the negative cable last.*

To brush the deposits off the terminal posts and cable clamps, sprinkle some baking soda straight from the little yellow box that keeps your refrigerator smelling nice onto each terminal, dip an old toothbrush or disposable brush in water, and scrub the deposits away.

If your cables and clamps won't clean up completely with baking soda and water, rotate an inexpensive battery terminal brush (see Figure 2-7) on each terminal to shine it up and ensure a

**FIGURE 2-7:**
A battery terminal brush (inside the cap) and clamp cleaner.

good, solid electrical connection. You can also shine up the insides of the cable clamps with the clamp cleaner that's usually sold as one unit with the brush. A *soapless* steel wool pad may also do the job.

**3.** **Dry everything off with a clean, disposable, lint-free rag.**

Try to avoid getting the powdery stuff on your hands or clothes. If you do, wash it off with water *right away*, and neither you nor your clothes will be damaged.

REMEMBER

**4.** **Reconnect the terminals to the battery, replacing the positive cable first and the negative cable last.**

After the battery terminals are reconnected, coat the terminals with thick automotive grease or petroleum jelly to prevent corrosive deposits from forming again.

**5.** **Examine the battery cables and clamps to see whether they're badly frayed or corroded.**

If the damage looks extensive, the cables and clamps may need to be replaced; otherwise, the battery may short-circuit, which could damage onboard computers. Have a professional check it out.

TIP

**6.** **If you've been having trouble starting your engine, if your headlights seem dim, or if the battery is old, check to see whether the electrolyte in the battery is strong enough. If it's weak, the battery may need to be recharged or replaced before it dies and leaves you stranded.**

Ask your local service station to test the battery (assuming you trust them not to sell you a new one you may not need).

**7.** **Check the battery case and the terminals.**

If you see major cracks in the battery case or obvious terminal damage, replace the battery regardless of its electrical performance. Chapter 6 tells you how to replace a battery and recycle the old one.

# Check the Coolant

The *radiator* in your vehicle cools your engine and needs water and *coolant* (sometimes called *antifreeze*) to function. This section focuses on checking the coolant and adding more, if necessary. (Chapter 11 familiarizes you with the parts of the *cooling system* and how they work; Chapter 12 tells you how to flush the cooling system and replace the coolant, and how to do minor repairs on it; and Chapter 21 tells you what to do if your vehicle overheats on the road.)

Keep the following points in mind as you check the level of the liquid in your cooling system and add more, if necessary:

>> **Rather than open the cap on the radiator, just check to see whether the liquid reaches the "Full" line on the side of the coolant reservoir.** (That's the plastic bottle connected to the radiator that holds an extra supply of liquid, as shown in Figure 2-1. It's part of the *coolant recovery system.*) If the liquid doesn't reach the "Full" line, open the bottle and add a 50/50 mix of water and coolant until it does.

TIP

Always use a 50/50 mixture of coolant and water to fill or top off the cooling system. Use just water only in an emergency. Most modern engines have aluminum cylinder heads, which require the protective anticorrosive properties of antifreeze. For the purposes of brevity, I refer to that 50/50 mix simply as "liquid" or "coolant" from now on.

Some coolant recovery systems are pressurized and have a *radiator pressure cap* instead of a normal cap. Some older vehicles have no coolant reservoir, so to check and add coolant you have to open the cap on the radiator.

WARNING

Never add coolant to a *hot* engine! If you need to add more liquid, wait until the engine has cooled down to avoid the possibility of being burned or cracking your *engine block.* Don't open the caps on either of these systems when the engine is hot; if you do, hot coolant may be ejected. Be sure to read up on safely removing pressure caps and checking and adding coolant in Chapter 12 before working on them.

>> **Coolant is usually red, green, blue, or yellow.** If it looks colorless, looks rusty, or has things floating around in it, flush your cooling system and add new coolant.

>> **If the coolant has a sludgy, oily surface, immediately take the vehicle to your mechanic to check for internal *head gasket* leakage.** The service facility has special equipment for performing this check.

>> **While you're messing around with your cooling system, feel the radiator hoses, too.** (They're the big hoses that go into the top and come out of the bottom of the radiator.) If they're leaking, cracked, bulgy, or squishy, they should be replaced. The next section tells you how to check all the hoses under the hood. For more information about replacing hoses, see Chapter 12.

# Check the Hoses

There are a variety of hoses under the hood. Some carry water or air; vacuum hoses have . . . well . . . nothing in them. Walk around the hood area and squeeze every hose you encounter. If you find any that are leaking, bulgy, soft and squishy, or hard and brittle, it's easy and inexpensive to replace them. You can find instructions for how to do so in Chapter 12.

**TIP**

It pays to replace hoses *before* they leak, collapse, or break; by putting it off, any savings in time or effort aren't worth the aggravation of having your trip come to an abrupt halt on the highway. Most tow trucks don't carry spare hoses (they'd have to carry too many different kinds, and they don't have the time to change hoses on the road), and you may end up paying an expensive tow charge for a couple of dollars' worth of hose that you could have replaced ahead of time in about ten minutes. When you replace a hose, keep the old one in the trunk so if you need one fast you won't have to wait for the proper one to arrive if the repair facility doesn't have it in stock. (You can replace the old, temporary hose with a fresh one when time allows.)

# Check the Dipsticks

Checking dipsticks is a major part of your under-the-hood check. It's easy to do and provides valuable clues, not only to whether the fluid levels are sufficient but also to the condition of several vital systems on your vehicle. The following sections deal with how to check each type of dipstick. If you have trouble locating a dipstick, check your owner's manual or ask a service station attendant to check it for you and watch closely to see where it is.

## Check the oil

Oil reduces the friction in your engine and keeps it running smoothly. You should check your oil at least once a month to make sure that there's enough oil and that it isn't contaminated.

**TIP**

Some European vehicles don't have an oil dipstick. If you can't find one on your vehicle, check the owner's manual for the proper way to check your oil.

To find out whether your vehicle needs oil, follow these steps:

1. **When the engine is cold (or has been off for at least ten minutes), pull out the dipstick (the one with a ring or other type of finger grip on the end of**

**it that sticks out of the engine), and wipe it off on a clean, lint-free rag.**

The location of the oil dipstick depends on whether your vehicle has an *in-line engine (rear-wheel drive)* or a *transverse* engine *(front-wheel drive),* as shown in Figures 2-8 and 2-9.

2. **Insert the stick back into the pipe.**

   If the dipstick gets stuck on the way in, turn it around. The pipe it fits into is curved, and the metal stick bends naturally in the direction of the curve if you put it back in the way it came out.

3. **Pull the dipstick out again and look at the film of oil on the end of the stick (see Figure 2-10). Note how high the oil film reaches on the dipstick and the condition of the oil, and add or change the oil as needed.**

   Oil turns black pretty quickly, but that doesn't affect the quality. Rub a little between your thumb and index finger, and if it leaves a dirty smudge, it probably needs to be changed.

If your oil looks clean enough but only reaches the "Add" level on the dipstick, you need to add oil. You can buy oil the next time you fill up with gas at the

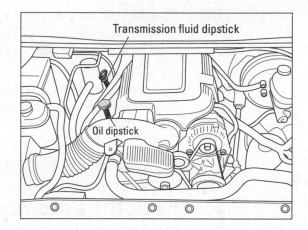

**FIGURE 2-8:**
Where to find the oil dipstick and transmission dipstick on an in-line engine.

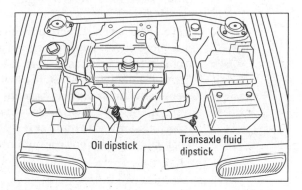

**FIGURE 2-9:**
Where to find the oil dipstick and transmission dipstick on a transverse engine.

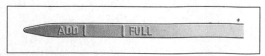

**FIGURE 2-10:**
Check the oil on the end of the dipstick.

service station or you can find it at auto supply stores, supermarkets, discount stores, and large drugstores. Chapter 13 can help you to determine the proper weight oil for your vehicle; it also provides instructions for locating the place to pour in the oil.

If the oil is dirty or smells of gasoline, it should be changed. You can pay a mechanic or an oil-change station to change it for you, but why not head to Chapter 13 to find out how to change the oil yourself? The task is easy and can save you a lot of money.

**4.** **Put the dipstick back into the pipe. You're done!**

## Check the automatic transmission fluid

To check your *automatic transmission* fluid, look for a dipstick handle sticking out of your transmission toward the rear of an *in-line engine* on vehicles with *rear-wheel drive* (refer to Figure 2-8) or sticking out of the *transaxle* if your vehicle has *front-wheel drive* (refer to Figure 2-9).

**REMEMBER**

If you have a vehicle with a *manual transmission,* disregard this part of the under-the-hood check. The fluid level in a manual transmission must be checked with the vehicle on a hoist to enable the technician to reach a plug in the bottom of the transmission. It's best not to monkey around with this yourself. The next time your car is in for service, have the technician check the *transmission fluid* level for you. It's a good idea to know what type and *viscosity* of fluid goes into your transmission and to make sure that's what the technician plans to use. Some newer manual transmissions use automatic transmission fluid; others use engine oil.

## WHY YOU SHOULD CHECK THE OIL YOURSELF

The problem with driving into a service station and allowing the attendant to check your oil is that the *dipstick* always reads a little low because so much of the oil is still inside the hot engine rather then in the *oil pan.* By adding more oil until it reaches the "Full" level on the stick while the engine is still hot, the attendant may overfill the engine and damage it. For this reason, *always wait at least ten minutes after you shut off the engine before allowing anyone to check the dipstick.* If you don't feel like sitting around at a gas station, the best time to check your oil is first thing in the morning, when the vehicle has been sitting all night and the engine is cold.

To check your automatic transmission fluid, follow these steps:

1. **With the gearshift in Neutral or Park and the *parking brake* on, let your engine run. When the engine is warm, pull out the dipstick. (Don't turn off the engine.)**

2. **Dip the tip of your index finger into the fluid on the dipstick and rub the fluid between your finger and the tip of your thumb.**

   The transmission fluid on the dipstick should be pinkish and almost clear. If it looks or smells burnt or has particles in it, have a mechanic drain and change the fluid.

3. **Wipe the dipstick with a clean, lint-free rag; then reinsert it and pull it out again.**

4. **If the transmission fluid is clear but doesn't reach the "Full" line on the dipstick, use a funnel to pour just enough transmission fluid down the dipstick tube to reach the line. Don't overfill!**

**WARNING**

There are several types of transmission fluid. Each is made for a specific type of automatic transmission. Newer transmissions from the major automakers require different fluid than older ones. Because so many different kinds of transmissions are around these days, check your owner's manual or dealership to find out which type of fluid your vehicle requires, and enter that type on your *Specifications Record* in Appendix B.

**TIP**

A faulty transmission and one that's just low on fluid share many of the same symptoms! If your vehicle hesitates when your automatic transmission shifts gears, check the transmission fluid level *before* you let any mechanic start talking about servicing or adjusting your transmission or selling you a new one. Obviously, adding transmission fluid is a lot cheaper than replacing the whole transmission system! See Chapter 20 for advice.

## Check the power-steering fluid

To check the *power-steering* fluid, locate the power-steering pump in your vehicle (see Figure 2-11). If you can't find it, your owner's manual should tell you where it is and

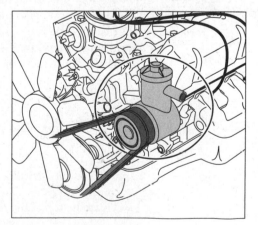

**FIGURE 2-11:**
The power-steering pump.

whether you need to check it and add to it with the engine running or turned off. Unscrew the cap on the pump and see whether the fluid reaches the "Full" mark on the dipstick. If the level is low, check your owner's manual or dealership to find out what kind of fluid your power-steering pump requires. Mark this on your *Specifications Record* in Appendix B for future reference.

# Check the Brake Fluid

The *brake booster* is on the driver's side of your vehicle, usually up near the *firewall*. Just in front of that, sitting on and connected to the brake *master cylinder* is the *brake fluid* reservoir, usually a plastic canister that contains (you guessed it) brake fluid (see Figure 2-12). Older vehicles don't have a plastic reservoir; instead, the master cylinder is a little metal box with a lid that you must remove to check the fluid level (see Figure 2-13).

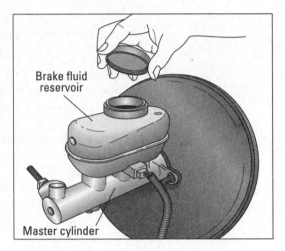

FIGURE 2-12:
The master cylinder on many popular cars.

TECHNICAL STUFF

When you put your foot on the brake pedal, the fluid in the master cylinder moves down the *brake lines* to the front and rear brakes. If there's insufficient brake fluid, air is introduced into the brake lines and your vehicle doesn't stop properly. Therefore, it's important to keep enough brake fluid in your brake fluid reservoir.

WARNING

If your vehicle has an *anti-lock braking system (ABS)*, consult your owner's manual before checking your brake fluid. Some ABS systems require you to pump the brake pedal approximately 25 to 30 times before opening and inspecting the fluid reservoir.

To check your brake fluid, do the following:

**1.** **Clean the top of the reservoir carefully.**

A small amount of dirt falling into the fluid can cause the internal seals of the master cylinder to fail. Your brakes will begin to lose effectiveness and ultimately fail completely.

2. **Open the top of your brake fluid reservoir.**

If you have the kind with a little plastic reservoir on top, just unscrew the cap of the reservoir shown in Figure 2-12. If you have a metal master cylinder that contains the reservoir, use a screwdriver to pry the retaining clamp off the top (see Figure 2-13).

**WARNING**

Don't leave the master cylinder uncovered or an open can of brake fluid sitting around for too long. Brake fluid soaks up moisture to keep it from settling in the hydraulic components and corroding them. If moist air gets to brake fluid for as little as 15 minutes, the fluid is ruined. So don't dawdle, and keep the can tightly closed until you're ready to use it.

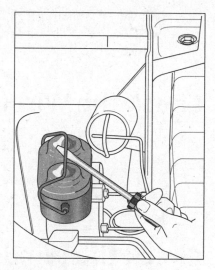

**FIGURE 2-13:**
Releasing the lid of a metal master cylinder with a screwdriver.

3. **Look to see where the fluid level lies between the "Low" and "High" marks on the plastic reservoir to make sure that the brake fluid level is within ½ inch or so of the cap.**

If the level isn't high enough, add the proper brake fluid for your vehicle. (You can find instructions for buying the proper brake fluid in Chapter 15.) If the brake fluid reservoir is empty when you check it, you may have to *bleed* the brake system. Turn to Chapter 15 for step-by-step instructions.

4. **Check the color of your brake fluid.**

Because brake fluid deteriorates with use, it should be replaced by a mechanic if it's dark in color.

**TIP**

Have your brake fluid changed every two years. Doing so protects the hydraulic components from internal corrosion and premature brake failure.

Also keep the following points in mind as you check the brake system:

**ECO-LOGIC**

>> **Brake fluid is toxic, so take any rags with more than just a couple of small spots of fluid on them and any partially used cans of fluid to a toxic waste center for disposal.**

>> **Don't get brake fluid on anything that's painted because brake fluid eats paint.** If you spill any, wipe it up immediately and dispose of the rag eco-logically!

>> Don't get grease or oil in your brake fluid; either one may ruin your hydraulic brake system.

# Check the Wiring

Feel the wires that you encounter under the hood. If they feel hard and inflexible, if bright metal wires show through the insulation, or if the wires look corroded or very messy where they attach to various devices, they may need to be changed before they short out. Have a professional do the rewiring work for you.

# Check the Windshield Washer Fluid

Under the hood of your vehicle is a plastic container that contains the fluid for your windshield wipers. Is it full of liquid? If not, you can fill it with any one of a variety of windshield washer solutions — you can even use a home window cleaner. Just *don't use detergent,* which can leave a residue that can plug up your lines. Plus, it isn't easy to drive with suds all over your windshield!

Pay attention to the kind of windshield washer fluid you use. Some are concentrated, which means that you need to mix them with water before adding them to the reservoir. If you live in an area that gets cold in the winter, consider a premixed washer solution that contains *antifreeze.* This solution comes in quart and gallon sizes and keeps your windshield clean while preventing the liquid from freezing up in cold weather.

# Check and Replace Windshield Wipers

If your wipers have been making a mess of your windshield, buy new blades or new inserts for them. The rubber wiper inserts are inexpensive and usually just slide into place. The metal blades into which the inserts fit are a little more expensive, but if your old ones look corroded or generally aren't in good shape, you should replace them as well. Consult your owner's manual or auto parts store for the type and size of blades you need and for instructions on inserting the blades if you can't figure out the instructions on the package. Be aware that some vehicles have different-sized wipers for the driver and passenger sides and that other vehicles have only one wiper. If your vehicle has a rear window wiper, don't forget to check that, too.

To avoid being caught in a downpour with no visibility, change your blades after a hot summer, before an annual rainy season, or at least twice a year.

**TIP**

# Check the Tires

Tires that are low on air pressure wear down faster, increase fuel consumption, and make your vehicle harder to steer. Tires with too much pressure may blow out or steer erratically. For these reasons, keep your tires inflated to within the manufacturer's specified range. Check the pressure in each tire regularly, and add or release air as needed. Chapter 17 has instructions for performing these easy tasks and checking your tires for signs of problems. Don't forget to check the sidewalls.

# Drive and Enjoy!

If you've done this monthly under-the-hood check, congratulations! You now know that your vehicle has what it needs in terms of fuel, oil, water, and other exotic beverages. You can be reasonably sure that it won't leave you stranded on the highway because of a faulty hose, wire, or belt, and you did it all yourself! Get in and drive around. It feels smoother, right? The pickup is better. Your vehicle knows that you care about it, and your efforts have drawn the two of you closer to one another. Silly romanticizing? Well, I have either an extremely affectionate car or a wild imagination.

# Chapter 3

# The Way to Your Car's Heart Is through Your Toolbox

Whether you're trying to cook up a decent meal, paint a picture, run an office, or work on your vehicle, you're only as good as your tools. Just as you can't slice tomatoes super-thin with a bent, rusty, dull knife, you can't do any kind of work on your vehicle if you lack the means to loosen or remove parts, clean them, reinstall them, adjust them, or replace them, and test the results.

Before you run off to return this book because you aren't prepared to spend a lot of money on tools that you'll probably never use again after you ruin your engine or cut off your thumb, let me tell you that all you really need are a few basic, inexpensive implements. (I'll deal with the engine and your thumb later.) In this chapter, I list and describe the basic tools you need for working on your vehicle. You may be surprised at how many of them you already own, and in the event that you need to buy a few, I give you pointers on getting value for your money.

**REMEMBER**

Whenever you encounter a term set in *this font,* you'll find it defined in the glossary in Appendix A.

# Shopping for Tools

TIP

Tool prices vary widely, but if you keep your eyes open and know where to go, whom to talk to, and what to look for, you can get a good value at a fair price. Here are some general pointers:

>> Shop for tools in a major auto parts chain store, and stick to well-known brands. Poor quality tools can break and cause injuries.

>> Watch the newspaper for sales; most chains have them regularly, and you can save a lot of money that way.

>> Buy each kind of tool in sets of different sizes rather than buying each size at random. You can save money this way.

>> Look for high-grade steel with no rough edges.

>> Pick out friendly-looking salespeople and ask them what kinds of tools they buy. Most are auto enthusiasts who are delighted that you're planning to do your own work (and be a future customer), and they're happy to point out the best buys.

REMEMBER

Buying everything at once isn't necessary to get started on your car; use the beg, borrow, and steal-from-the-family-toolbox methods if you must. Or, if as you read this chapter you're made painfully aware that you need to buy practically everything, consider prepackaged tool kits. Nearly every major supplier carries an inexpensive basic automotive tool kit that contains everything you need for maintenance and minor repairs. If you're totally tool-poor, such a kit may prove to be the best buy. Just make sure that you're getting good quality tools; it's better to have a couple of tools that work well than to have a large assortment of junk.

While I'm on the subject, empty toolboxes are inexpensive and worth buying. They keep tools clean, in good shape, and, most important, all in one place. Look for a lightweight, plastic toolbox that fits easily into the trunk of your vehicle. Although your tools are useful around the house, it's nice to have them handy if you get stuck away from home.

# Screwdrivers

There are two basic types of screwdrivers: *standard*, or *slot*, *screwdrivers* (the most common type) and *Phillips screwdrivers*. The difference between a standard screwdriver and a Phillips screwdriver is the shape of the head, as shown in Figure 3-1. You use Phillips screwdrivers with Phillips screws and standard screwdrivers with — you guessed it — standard screws.

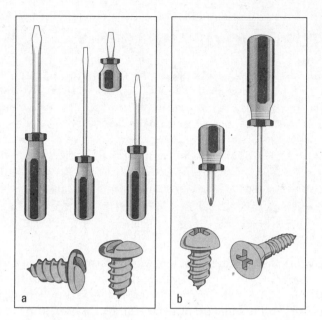

FIGURE 3-1:
Standard (a) and
Phillips (b) drivers
and their screws.

Offset screwdrivers, which are "S"-shaped and have different-sized tips at each end, also are very handy because they make it easy to get to screws that have little clearance over the head. Offset screwdrivers come in both standard and Phillips styles and some have one of each type of head at either end (see Figure 3-2).

WARNING

Using the wrong type or size screwdriver can damage the screw, the screwdriver, and even *you* if your hand slips while you're struggling to use the wrong tool. Always use a screwdriver with a tip that's the same width and type as the head of the screw you're working on.

Because you usually can't use a standard screwdriver on a Phillips screw or vice versa (although there are some exceptions), and because your vehicle is fitted with both types of screws in a variety of sizes, you need several of each type of screwdriver (not just for your vehicle, but for almost anything around the house).

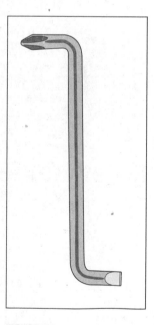

FIGURE 3-2:
An offset screwdriver.

# THE TURNING OF THE SCREW

If you find yourself confronted with a screw that's difficult to start unscrewing, try giving it a slight twist in the *opposite* direction (clockwise), as though you were trying to tighten it. Then loosen it (counterclockwise). If this trick doesn't work, tap the screwdriver on the head with a hammer, which may loosen the screw a bit. If strong-arm tactics don't get you anywhere, try squirting the troublemaker with penetrating oil. (Don't use penetrating oil on a running engine or on any really hot areas because it could ignite.) Remember to keep your temper with difficult screws; otherwise, you risk stripping the threads and turning a fairly simple job of replacing what you've loosened into a hair-puller.

Screwdriver shafts vary in length too, which is useful because a longer shaft provides greater access to "buried" screws that are sunk below the surface of some parts instead of level with them; a shorter shaft gets into tight places more easily. Handles also vary. It's important to have large, easy-to-grip handles to help you loosen tight screws.

**TIP**

You can get all the screwdrivers you need to work on your vehicle for relatively little money. Look for sales on plastic- or rubber-handled screwdrivers in sets of varying sizes. Also available are nice gadgets that contain assorted Phillips and standard screwdriver heads in a single, magnetized ratchet handle. You just pop the right-sized head on the shaft and twist the handle to turn the screwdriver automatically. This magnetized tool also serves as a *screwholder* (see the next section).

# Screwholders

Screwholders are perfectly marvelous for hanging onto screws that have to fit into tiny places. Instead of holding a screw in place with the fingers of one hand while wielding the screwdriver with your other hand, you simply fit the screw into the screwholder and use the screwholder instead of a screwdriver to insert and tighten the screw. One type of screwholder has a magnet to hold the screw; another (see Figure 3-3) has a little gizmo that grabs the screw when you twist the screwholder. Both are great and work equally well. They come in standard and Phillips versions.

**FIGURE 3-3:**
A screwholder helps you get into hard-to-reach places.

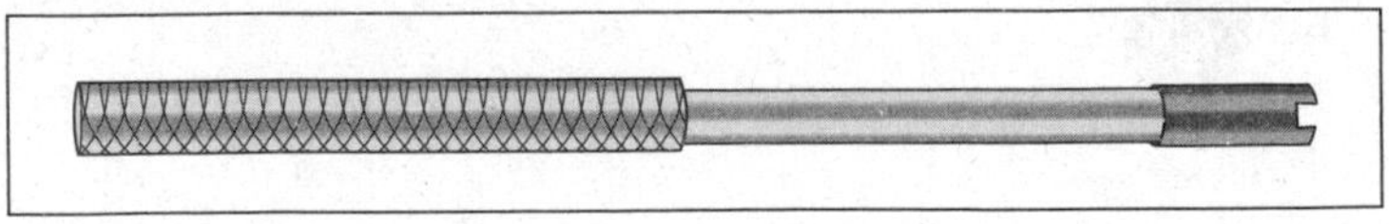

# Wrenches

Wrenches are probably the most basic tools for auto repair. You need a couple of different kinds in different sizes. There are several types of wrenches, and some have very specialized uses, but the following sections cover the kinds you need for most jobs. Look for sets made by well-known toolmakers, and try to buy them on sale. (For more pointers on buying tools, see the earlier section "Shopping for Tools.")

**TIP**

Most wrenches are available in both standard — also known as SAE (Society of Automotive Engineers) — and metric measurements. Before you go wrench-shopping, know which system of measurement your vehicle is based on. Originally, most foreign vehicles were based on the metric system (except British ones, which had their own thread standard), whereas domestic engines used SAE standards based on fractions of an inch. Today, most American vehicles have a mix of SAE and metric nuts and bolts. Foreign vehicles or foreign components used on American vehicles (a practice that's becoming quite common) use metric nuts and bolts — even the inch-based British. Check your *owner's manual* or ask your dealer to tell you whether your vehicle requires metric or standard SAE tools before you buy anything.

## Socket wrenches

A good set of *socket wrenches,* shown in Figure 3-4, can really make the difference between enjoying your work and killing yourself over it. Socket wrenches come in sets for a wide variety of prices, depending on quality and how many wrenches are in the set. Sets can include a mix of SAE and metric sockets, all SAE sockets, or all metric pieces. Unless you've decided to become a mechanic, you can buy an inexpensive set of basic socket wrenches suitable for your vehicle and home repairs. If you're not sure you're up for anything major, start with just a spark-plug socket, a *ratchet handle,* and an extension bar that lets you easily reach the

**FIGURE 3-4:**
A socket wrench set.

socket deeper into the engine compartment, as required for some spark plug changes (see Figure 3-5).

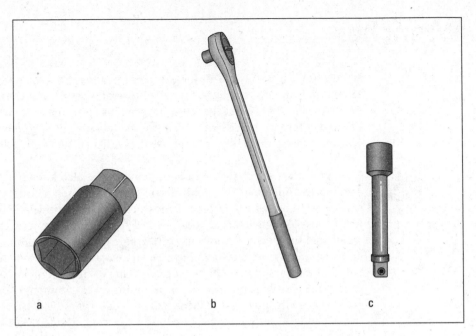

**FIGURE 3-5:**
A spark-plug socket (a), a ratchet handle (b), and an extension bar (c).

a  b  c

A good set of socket wrenches should contain the following basic items:

>> **A variety of ¼-inch, ⅜-inch, or ½-inch drive sockets.**

>> **A spark-plug socket:** This large socket has a soft lining to hold the *spark plug* securely without damaging its soft jacket when you remove and insert it. Spark plugs come in two sizes, so be sure to get the size that fits the spark plugs in your vehicle. Your owner's manual may note the spark plug size, or you can ask your dealership or service shop.

**TECHNICAL STUFF**

The word "drive" refers to the size of the square hole in each socket where it attaches to the ratchet handle. It's easy to remember that the smaller the drive, the smaller the job you use it for. You can use adapters to convert sockets of one drive to fit handles of another drive.

>> **At least one ratchet handle, which allows you to turn the socket as many times as you need to without having to remove the handle from the socket after each turn:** The ratchet handle should fit any of the sockets. Most sets have two or three handles with at least one adapter. You may want to add additional extensions to extend the handle to different sizes and adapt it to different drives.

>> **A flex-head handle:** Although not strictly necessary, a flex-head handle is very useful because it enables you to hold the ratchet handle at any angle when working in tight places — and engines are full of tight places!

>> **Socket extenders:** These indispensable items help you get your socket head way down into the bowels of your engine compartment to reach those almost-unreachable nuts and bolts.

**TIP**

The way to identify a good socket wrench set is by the number of teeth in the ratchet handle. Most have 20 to 30 teeth. The really good ones have up to 60 teeth. The more teeth the handle has, the better it can fit into tight places. With more teeth, you have to move the handle only a few degrees to turn the nut as much as a cheaper handle would in many degrees. In other words, a ratchet handle with 24 teeth must be moved 15 degrees to reach its limit, but a handle with 60 teeth has to be moved only 6 degrees to turn a nut as far. You can find instructions for using a socket wrench in Chapter 6.

## Combination wrenches

When shopping for wrenches, you'll come across *open-end wrenches* and *box-end wrenches*, but the very best kind to get are *combination wrenches*, which have both an open end and a boxed end (see Figure 3-6). These wrenches come in sets of several sizes, and each wrench is made to fit a nut of a specific size, whichever end you use. See the sidebar "Using a combination wrench like a pro" for details.

**TIP**

### USING A COMBINATION WRENCH LIKE A PRO

Here are a few tips for using a combination wrench:

- Always use the proper size wrench. If the wrench you use is too big, it can slip and round off the edges of the nut, which makes the nut harder to tighten later on. It also can round off the inside edges of the wrench, with the same results. (Of course, a wrench that's too small won't fit over the nut.)

- To use the open end of the wrench most effectively, place it around the nut you want to remove and then move the wrench to the right so that the nut moves in a counterclockwise direction. If the nut sticks, give it a squirt of penetrating oil.

- Use your free hand to keep the wrench down over the nut. This approach gives you some control and prevents the wrench from flying off the nut.

- When you move the wrench as far as it can go, you loosen the nut 15 degrees. (That's why the slot is at an angle.) By simply turning the wrench over so that the other surface of the same end is around the nut, you can move the nut another 15 degrees without having to place the wrench at a different angle.

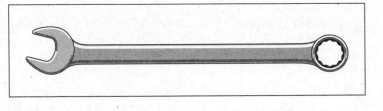

**FIGURE 3-6:**
Combination
wrenches have
one open end
and one
boxed end.

# Torque wrenches

A *torque wrench* (two types of which are shown in Figure 3-7) is designed to tighten a nut, bolt, or screw to an exact degree to avoid under-tightening or over-tightening things.

**WARNING**

If you're replacing a spark plug and you don't tighten it enough, it will work itself loose and fail to deliver a spark. If you over-tighten a spark plug, you can strip the threads or crack the plug. Similarly, parts that have *gaskets* can leak if the bolts that hold them aren't tightened enough. But if you over-tighten the same bolts, the gaskets will be crushed, causing the fluid to leak anyway.

Most really good torque wrenches are expensive, but a cheaper one is good enough to serve your purposes. If you'd rather not spend the money until you're sure that you really like working on your vehicle, borrow a torque wrench just to get the feel of how tight a nut, bolt, or other part should be. Or you can just forget the whole thing — I've never used a torque wrench; I use common sense.

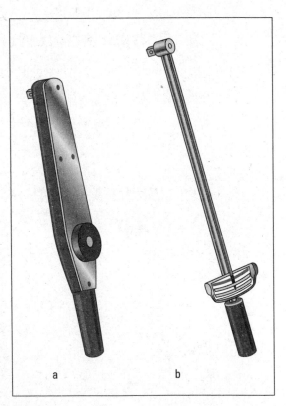

**FIGURE 3-7:**
A dial torque wrench (a) and a deflecting beam torque wrench (b).

If you use a torque wrench, keep the following in mind *(follow these tips when you're using any kind of wrench to tighten anything)*:

>> Grip a torque wrench well down the shaft (not up close to the dial), and operate it smoothly.

>> Tighten a series of nuts or bolts to the specified torque in the specified sequence, which will distribute the pressure evenly instead of in strict clockwise or counterclockwise order.

**TECHNICAL STUFF**

>> When tightening a series of bolts, tighten them all just until they're snug. Then go back and tighten them all a bit more. Then go back and tighten them all the way to the torque **specifications.** Doing so ensures that the entire part you're tightening is under even pressure, prevents leaky gaskets, and increases the life of the bolt and the part.

**REMEMBER**

>> Before using a torque wrench, make sure that the nut or bolt turns freely so that the torque wrench gets a true reading of the proper nut tightness. You can use a lubricant such as WD-40 on the threads and run the nut up and down a few times to free it before using the torque wrench on it.

## Adjustable wrenches

An adjustable wrench, sometimes called a *crescent wrench,* is a useful addition to your toolbox (see Figure 3-8). You probably already have one in the house, and you can adjust the jaws to fit a variety of nuts and bolts simply by turning the wheel. I like the very small and medium sizes because they fit into tight spaces easily.

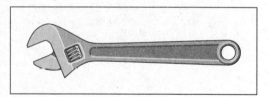

**FIGURE 3-8:**
An adjustable wrench.

# Pliers

Almost everyone has *needle-nosed* and *slip-joint pliers* (see Figure 3-9); if you rummage through the family toolbox, you'll probably discover that you have them, too. Both types of pliers are useful for auto repair.

If you have to buy pliers, the very best kind to get are *combination slip-joint pliers.* You can adjust this general-purpose tool to several widths with a sliding pin. If you're the only person on your block that doesn't possess combination slip-joint pliers, by all means rush out and buy one before dark. Again, it needn't be expensive. Just make sure that the tool works easily, is made of forged hardened steel, and seems to be well-finished.

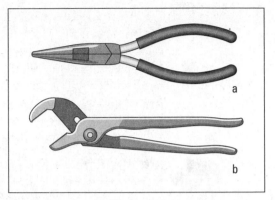

**FIGURE 3-9:**
Needle-nosed pliers (a) and combination slip-joint pliers (b).

If you're *really* into tools, you may also want to buy the following pliers, but you can easily get along without them:

>> **Robogrip pliers** are a useful variation of slip-joint pliers that automatically lock in position when you have a grip on the part that you want to manipulate.

>> **Adjustable vice-grip pliers** are useful for persuading recalcitrant stuff to loosen or twist, especially if, for example, you round off the edges of a nut so that normal tools don't loosen it. When set properly, the jaws lock onto a metal part very tightly, and you can pull, push, or twist almost anything with them.

## USING PLIERS SAFELY

Here are a couple of notes on the use of pliers:

● If you're working on electrical wiring and don't want to get shocked, make sure that the handles of your pliers are covered with rubber to insulate them. If the handles are naked metal, slip a length of rubber hose over each handle, leaving the hose in one piece. Doing so insulates the pliers, and the rubber straightens out when you release the pliers, causing them to spring open quickly.

● Never use combination slip-joint pliers on nuts and bolts — they round off the corners, making them harder to replace. Besides, nuts and bolts are the reason you have all your lovely wrenches.

# Gauges

Despite the simple principles behind how an engine works (for the lowdown, head to Chapter 4), many auto repair tasks require fairly precise adjustments: You put only so much oil into the engine. You add only so much air to tires. You tighten some nuts and bolts only so tight. And you leave a gap of a precise size between spark plug electrodes by using *feeler gauges*. Several tools are available to help you determine when enough oil, fluid, air, pressure, or whatever is enough. This section highlights those gauges that are most useful.

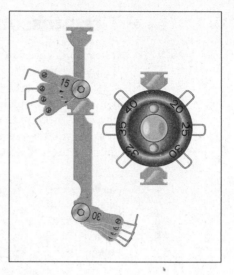

**FIGURE 3-10:**
Wire feeler gauges.

## Wire and taper feeler gauges

You use wire and taper feeler gauges for "gapping" spark plugs. These tools are very inexpensive — some stores even give them away free with other purchases. Although I usually discuss specialized tools in the chapters that call for them, I want to mention these gauges now so that you can pick them up while you're at an auto supply store buying other stuff.

**FIGURE 3-11:**
A taper feeler gauge.

You can use either a wire feeler gauge (see Figure 3-10) or a taper feeler gauge (see Figure 3-11) for gapping spark plugs. *Gapping* simply refers to sliding the proper-sized wire or taper gauge between the spark plug *electrodes* to make sure that the surfaces are the proper distance apart. Gapping ensures that the spark can jump across the *gap* with the proper intensity.

All cars sold in the U.S. since 1975 have been equipped with electronic ignition systems. So, unless you've got an even older model, the ignition timing never needs adjustment.

## Tire pressure gauges

If you never check anything else on your vehicle, make a habit of regularly check-ing the tire pressure; it's critical both for safety and good fuel economy. Tire pres-sure gauges come in several styles. The most basic, shown in Figure 3-12, looks like a big chrome pen, with a bulbous end that fits over the tire's valve stem and a plastic or metal rod, marked in pounds per square inch of pressure, that pops out to show you the pressure in the tire. You can find instructions on how to check your tire pressure in Chapter 17.

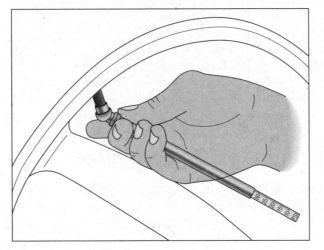

**FIGURE 3-12:**
A tire pressure
gauge.

## Compression gauges

You use *compression gauges,* shown in Figure 3-13, to check the pressure that builds up in each *cylinder* as your engine runs. These gauges also reveal worn or damaged *piston rings* and *valves.* If your vehicle is new, you probably won't have this problem for some time, but if you have an older or secondhand vehicle, this easy-to-use gauge is a good investment because it can help you spot trouble and save money. Chapter 8 has instructions for using a gauge to check compression. The screw-in kind shown on the right in Figure 3-13 is easiest to use but usually costs a bit more.

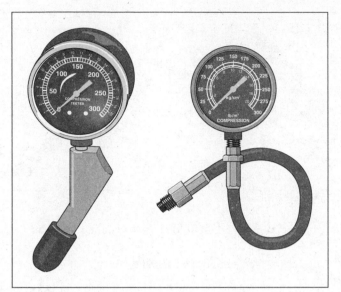

**FIGURE 3-13:**
Compression
gauges.

# Work Lights

Whether you plan to work on your vehicle at home in your garage, in your driveway, at the curb near your house, or in the auto shop at a local school, I can guarantee that the lighting will be inadequate once you get under the hood — or under the car, if you're that adventurous. A *work light* provides all the illumination you need and enables you to shine the maximum amount of light right on the work area and not in your eyes.

TIP

You'll find that a work light is useful for a variety of home repairs and for working outside after dark, but if you'll be working far from an electrical outlet, you'll need either a long extension cord for the work light or a 12-volt battery-operated fluorescent light. Fluorescent work lights can draw power from the car's battery or cigarette lighter or plug into a wall socket. They also come with changeable batteries, like flashlights.

REMEMBER

If you get a work light that gets its power from your vehicle's battery, it won't be useful for repairs in your home. Portable battery-powered fluorescent lanterns are useful for night work and for camping, but I don't recommend one because the batteries can go dead from disuse or if you need to work for a long time. Luckily, most extension cords and work lights are inexpensive, so you may want to get more than one type. Figure 3-14 shows two types of work lights.

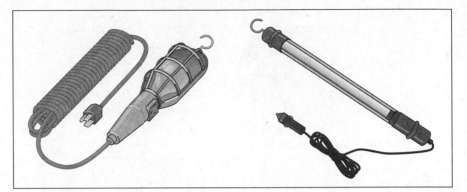

**FIGURE 3-14:**
Work lights.

When you shop for a work light, be sure to get one that has:

>> A protective cage around at least half the bulb.

>> A power cord that's long enough and properly insulated. Go for at least a 25-foot cord. Lights with shorter cords are cheaper, but if you need to buy an extension cord to get the light to your vehicle, you may end up spending more in the long run. (Battery-operated work lights are also available that don't require power cords.)

>> The Underwriter's tag, which ensures that you're getting quality equipment.

**WARNING**

The typical work light cage has a hook at the top so that you can hang the light from the inside of the hood or on a nearby part. The hook is very handy, but *don't hook the light to anything that carries electricity* or to anything that could be ripped from its moorings if the light cord gets yanked too hard!

# Jacks

Most new vehicles come with a *jack* to be used when changing tires. If you have a secondhand car, or if your jack has been lying around neglected, you may need to buy one. When shopping for a new jack, you can buy the scissor type, but I suggest that you invest in a *hydraulic jack,* which is faster and safer and not terribly expensive. Illustrations of different types of jacks appear in Chapter 1. Be sure to buy one that can handle the weight of your vehicle.

**TIP**

Whatever type you buy, make sure that the jack is suited to your vehicle's body design. To determine the type of jack you need and to find out how to use the jack that came with the vehicle, check your *owner's manual* or ask someone at an auto parts store.

**WARNING**

Check your jack periodically, never use it without the base plate, and never jack up your vehicle unless the wheels are properly blocked. You can find instructions and safety tips for using a jack and changing a tire in Chapter 1.

Your jack should be in the trunk of your vehicle at all times. There's nothing more depressing than knowing how to change a flat and realizing that you've left your jack in your garage when you get a flat tire on the side of the road.

# Jack Stands

If you plan to remove a wheel for any reason, you need a pair of *jack stands* as well as a jack. The stands hold the vehicle off the ground with less danger of slipping and enable you to jack up more than one side of the vehicle at a time. Chapter 1 shows you what they look like and how to use them. Remember to get two jack stands — you'll need them both.

**WARNING**

Substituting boxes, stones, or bricks for jack stands is very dangerous. They can slip out or break while you're under the vehicle. A jack can do the same thing, and when it really comes down to it, jack stands aren't all that stable, either. So I recommend that, instead of doing anything under your vehicle that involves more than just reaching under the vehicle for a few minutes (like opening and replacing the *oil drain plug* or changing an *oil filter*), you seriously consider paying a professional to put your vehicle on a hoist and do the job. If you can work under your vehicle without having to jack it up, you should also get a creeper.

# Creepers

A creeper is basically just a board with casters (wheels that can move in several directions) on the underside (see Figure 3-15). If you have an SUV with sufficient clearance under it to allow you to scoot around underneath without having to jack it up, a creeper comes in handy when removing mud and debris from the undercarriage.

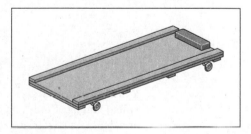

**FIGURE 3-15:**
A creeper.

TIP

If you have some carpentry skills, you can make a creeper from some plywood and a couple of old roller-skate wheels. If you're fed up with buying things and you don't want to make a creeper, try lying on an old bed board or a ratty old blanket instead.

If you're not yet game for a lot of under-the-car work and you just want to change your tires, change your oil, and be done with it, forget about the creeper. Get a jack and jack stands that work properly, and know how to use them safely (see Chapter 1).

# Fire Extinguishers

A fire extinguisher isn't really a tool, but it's a *must* for your vehicle. Get the 2¾-pound dry-chemical ABC-rated type.

An engine fire won't necessarily ruin your vehicle — if you can extinguish it quickly. A gasoline leak can be ignited by a stray spark from your spark plug wires. The resulting fire looks awful, but it's really burning on the *outside* of your engine. If you put it out quickly, your vehicle may suffer little or no damage.

WARNING

Cigarette butts may land on your backseat, causing a fire, and fires can be caused by ruptured *fuel lines* and faulty wiring as well, so an inexpensive fire extinguisher not only may save you money but also may save your life. If the flames are any- where near the *fuel tank,* forget the heroics; just run for it and throw yourself to the ground if you think that the tank may explode.

TIP

Because the fuel tank is usually located right under the rear of most vehicles, keep your extinguisher under the *front* seat so that you can get to it when you need it. It should be in a suitable bracket that will prevent it from rolling under the pedals.

# Funnels

You use funnels to fill your *coolant recovery bottle* and add *oil, brake fluid,* wind- shield washer fluid, and *transmission fluid.* Steal a large funnel from the kitchen and dedicate it to auto work, or buy one at an auto supply or hardware store. Either metal or plastic is fine as long as you clean it thoroughly after each use.

TIP

Some automotive funnels come with a short hose attached so that you can insert the hose directly into a narrow opening in a space that's too small for the funnel to fit into.

# More Things to Carry in Your Vehicle

You can pack your auto repair toolbox with the best tools that money can buy, but all those fancy gadgets and gizmos won't do you any good if they're at home when your vehicle breaks down 30 miles from civilization. Don't tempt fate: *Keep basic tools and materials onboard at all times.*

In addition to the tools mentioned earlier in this chapter, be sure to keep the following items on board (you probably have most of this stuff already, so there's no excuse for being unprepared):

**WARNING**

» **Rags:** Rags should be clean and lint-free. Keep a clean, lint-free rag in your vehicle to wipe your oil or transmission *dipstick* or to clean the inside of your windshield if it clouds up.

Get rid of gasoline-soaked rags, which are highly combustible. Never keep them in closed places. Don't use an oily rag on anything that isn't oily already. Because your vehicle contains a variety of substances that must be kept away from other substances, throw out or wash dirty rags, and use a clean one each time you start a job.

» **Spare parts:** If you replace your *spark plugs,* save the old ones if they're not too worn. Carry them in your trunk compartment toolbox for quick replacements if something goes wrong with the ones in your engine. If you have to use the old plugs in an emergency, be sure to replace them as soon as possible because they won't hold up well. The same goes for old, not-too-cruddy *air filters* and other minor gizmos. A couple of extra nuts, bolts, and screws also are useful to have on hand in case you lose the ones you have or strip them accidentally.

» **Emergency parts:** Carry a spare set of windshield wiper blades, an extra *radiator cap,* and extra *fuses.* If you plan to travel for a while in hot weather in remote regions, top and bottom radiator hoses might be a good idea. These items are inexpensive and could get you out of a lot of trouble on a long trip. Although they're more costly, it's good to carry extra *accessory belts,* too. Emergency road services may not replace these things on the road, and if the parts you need aren't available in the area, you'll have them on hand when you reach a repair facility.

» **Spare tire:** Check your spare tire often. It's humiliating to go through the work of changing a tire only to find that your spare is flat, too. If your spare is worn beyond belief, most garages will sell you a not-too-hideous secondhand tire at a low price. Make sure that it's the right size.

>> **Lug wrench:** A *lug wrench* is sometimes provided, along with a jack, on new vehicles (see Figure 3-16). You use it to remove the wheel or *lug nuts* when you change a tire. If you buy a lug wrench, get the cross-shaft kind, which gives you more leverage. If your vehicle has *alloy wheels* with lovely, shiny chrome lug nuts, be sure your wrench is the right size and type so that it doesn't scratch them. (Chapter 1 has instructions for using a lug wrench.)

>> **A can of inflator/sealant:** This item saves you the trouble — and possible danger — of changing a flat on the road. It attaches easily to the valve stem on your flat tire and inflates the tire with goop that temporarily seals the puncture. Choose a brand that enables you to drive at least 50 miles — that should get you to a repair shop. Be sure to tell them that you used inflator/sealant and ask them to remove it when they fix the flat.

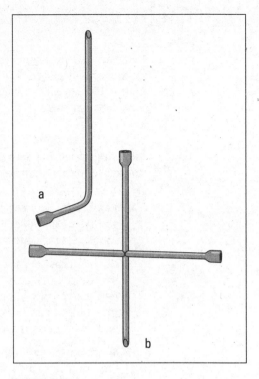

**FIGURE 3-16:**
Lug wrenches: Single-shaft (a) and cross-shaft (b).

>> **Jumper cables:** One of the most common automotive malfunctions is the loss of power to start the engine, either from an old or faulty battery or from leaving the headlights on by mistake. If you're in this situation, *and if your owner's manual indicates that you can jump a start without harming your onboard computer,* you can wait for AAA or CAA roadside assistance (if you're a member) or a nearby garage to come and bail you out; or, *if you're in a safe, well-populated area,* you can stop a passing vehicle, whip out your *jumper cables* (shown in Figure 3-17), attach them in seconds, and "jump a start" from the Good Samaritan's vehicle to your own. Many people are willing to lend their cars to this sort of operation because they lose nothing but a few minutes of their time, but it's up to you to decide whether you want to risk getting carjacked if the Good Samaritan turns out to be a devil in disguise. Your alternative, of course, is to use your cellphone to call roadside assistance or the highway patrol to send help. Chapter 23 has instructions for the proper way to jump a start.

You can buy a set of jumper cables for much less than you'd have to pay a garage to send someone to start your car. Good cables cost more because they have more strands of better-conducting wire, which let more juice flow between the vehicles with less loss of voltage.

TIP

Sometimes the success or failure of an attempt to jump a start depends on the quality of the jumper cables and their grips. If you get a cheap set, here's an easy way to make them work better: Get under the plastic sheath that covers the place where the cables meet the grips and squeeze the connection tight with pliers. Doing so improves the connection, and sometimes the cheap set of cables works beautifully — at least for the first few times. Ultimately, the best way to stay out of trouble is to pay a little extra for a quality set of cables.

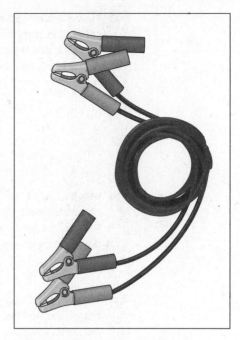

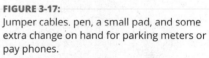

**FIGURE 3-17:**
Jumper cables, pen, a small pad, and some extra change on hand for parking meters or pay phones.

>> **Snow and ice equipment:** If you live in an area that's cold in winter, carry tire chains or a bag of sand in case of icy conditions. (Rock salt is no longer used for this purpose because it corrodes metal and is considered an environmental hazard.) A small shovel also may prove useful for digging your tires out, and a scraper allows you to clear your windshield of snow and/or ice. A can of de-icer is useful in icy weather.

>> **Flashlights and reflectors:** A flashlight in your glove compartment can help your kids locate dropped toys on the floor of the car, enable you to see under the hood if your vehicle breaks down, and serve as an emergency light for oncoming traffic if you have to stop on the road for repairs. (A flashlight with a red blinker is safest for the last purpose.) Of course, you have to put in fresh batteries now and then and carry a couple of extras.

TIP

An inexpensive set of reflector triangles can save your life by making your stopped vehicle visible on the road. Flares can be dangerous, and many states have rules regarding their use on highways.

>> **First-aid kit:** Keep a first-aid kit in your workshop and in your vehicle. Choose one that's equipped with a variety of bandages, tweezers, surgical tape, antibiotic ointment, something soothing for burns, and a good antiseptic. You can find inexpensive kits at drugstores and auto parts stores.

>> **Hand cleaner:** Most hand cleaners are basically grease solvents. They range from heavy-duty stuff that removes the skin along with the grease, to soothing, good-smelling creams that leave your skin feeling reborn, to precleaners that you use *before* you start working so that the grease slides off your hands easily afterward. Some of these cleaners can also be rubbed into work clothes to remove grease and oil stains before you launder them.

>> **Gloves:** Keep a pair of gloves in the vehicle for emergencies. Industrial rubber gloves, available at swimming pool supply stores, aren't affected by gasoline, solvent, or battery acid. They're your safest bet. Thin, tough, and comfortable dishwashing gloves are available at any discount store or supermarket. They cost little and keep the grease from under your fingernails. One problem, however, is that gasoline or solvent may melt them.

>> **Spare tools:** If you can't carry your toolbox in your vehicle all the time, or if it's too large or too heavy to waste fuel toting around, place a couple of screwdrivers, some standard-size combination wrenches, an adjustable wrench, and a can of penetrating oil in a lightweight toolbox in your trunk compartment.

**TIP**

Auto parts stores carry some very handy gizmos that combine a variety of basic tools into one all-purpose, weird-looking instrument that can save weight and space in your trunk compartment.

>> **Hat:** To keep the dust and grease out of your hair, and to prevent long hair from being caught in moving parts, wear a hat that you can afford to get dirty. A wooly watch cap or a baseball hat worn backwards works just fine. At the very least, keep a hair band in the glove compartment to tie back your hair. In this case, safety trumps vanity.

>> **Cellphone:** A cellphone literally can be a lifesaver when you're stuck on a road somewhere with a dead vehicle or when you have an accident. It enables you to call for help without having to rely on the kindness of strangers. (It's also handy for calling your loved ones or next appointment to tell them that you're going to be delayed.) Some cellphones have built-in AAA roadside assistance or 911 call buttons.

>> **Miscellaneous stuff:** Rolls of duct tape and electrician's tape, a sharp knife, and scissors come in handy. A disposable camera lets you collect evidence for insurance claims if you're involved in an accident. Keep a pen, a small pad, and some extra change on hand for parking meters or pay phones.

# Chapter **4**

# What Makes It Go? The Inner Secrets of Your Car Revealed!

One of the major events that marked the transition of early man from "wise monkey" to a more civilized critter was gaining the ability to get something else to do his work for him. Along with such major technological breakthroughs as the club and spear, the control of fire, and the invention of the loincloth was the eventual use of round logs (later cut into slices called "wheels") to move things and people. Wheeled carts of various types were pushed or pulled by humans and animals for centuries until some early science-fiction freak decided to invent a machine that could move itself, and the first engine appeared.

Today, most people possess vehicles that can move themselves. True, you have to tell your vehicle when to go and when to stop, and you have to steer it in the proper direction and keep it in good running order, but any vehicle is basically a set of wheels with an engine to turn them.

The *internal combustion engine (ICE)*, which still forms the heart of most vehicles, is a fairly efficient, relatively uncomplicated piece of machinery. It works on a mixture of fuel and air to produce enough power to turn a shaft that turns the wheels. The basic gizmos on your vehicle are simply the things that bring the fuel and air together in the proper quantities, ignite them, and channel the resulting power to the wheels. The rest of the stuff is there to make this happen with ease and efficiency, to provide you with some control over what's going on, and to give you a place to sit and to stow your groceries.

REMEMBER

Whenever you encounter a term set in *this font*, you'll find it defined in the glossary in Appendix A.

Because diesels and most *alternatively fueled vehicles* have pretty much the same basic systems as ICEs do — with the exception of the *fuel system* — and because ICEs still make up the majority of vehicles on the road (although I hope this will change given the dwindling supply of petroleum and the growing concerns about smog-causing emissions and *global warming!*), this chapter gives you a brief overview of how each of the basic automotive systems functions and how these systems work together to make your vehicle run. Don't worry about the type of vehicle you own; with the exception of the fuel system, every vehicle works on the same principles. (I cover clean diesels in Chapter 9 and alternatively fueled vehicles in Chapter 10.)

TIP

Because it's much easier to do any job if you understand what you're doing and why you're doing it, I advise you not to jump right into the instructions in this book for doing specific jobs before you get to know the system involved. Take it in easy stages. Reading this chapter will enable you to view your vehicle as a series of simple systems, each with a specific job to do, so you can stop seeing it as a dismaying collection of wires, hoses, and gizmos and be able to deal with it easily and confidently. When you have a general idea of how things work, the individual chapters in this book that explore each system in detail will be easier to understand. And when you're familiar with how a system functions, you'll be ready to tackle the chapter that shows you how to work on that system.

TIP

To get the most from this chapter, take this book out to your vehicle and try to find as many of the parts as possible. (If you don't know how to get the hood open, you can find instructions in Chapter 1 or in the owner's manual, which may also help you locate parts.) Just touching the weird-looking gizmos under the hood helps you get past any doubts and fears you may have about getting more intimately involved with your vehicle. But then, isn't it always that way?

# Keeping Your Owner's Manual Handy

Although you certainly don't need them to get through this book, it's good to have both an *owner's manual* and a *service manual* for every vehicle you own. If you don't have an owner's manual, ask your dealership to get one for you or to tell you how to get one from the manufacturer. If you have an older vehicle, you can find new or used service manuals or instruction books for it in bookstores. Public libraries often have surprisingly large collections of service manuals, too. Service manuals for many vehicles also are available from automotive publishers in paperback, on disc, or online.

I strongly suggest that you get the service manual because every auto repair facility can't stock a service manual for each year, make, and model of every vehicle, and if you lend your service manual to an independent service facility that's working on your vehicle, you can save money by reducing the time it would take them to figure out the proper way to make a repair. Also, if you get to the point where you want to do more than basic repairs, a service manual becomes indispensable. The drawings in service manuals show you where every little screw and washer fits so that you don't end up with a couple of "extra" parts at the end of the job; the manual also shows you how to do each job in the most efficient manner. The "How to Take Anything Apart — and Get It Back Together Again" section in Chapter 1 helps you to keep track of parts and get them back in the proper order.

REMEMBER

Every vehicle manufacturer makes sure to do something a little bit differently than the competition does so that it can get patents and say that its vehicles are the best. Also, the location and looks of the engine and *transmission* in rear-engine vehicles and *front-wheel drive* vehicles are different from those with traditional front engines and *rear-wheel drive*. Electric vehicles (EV) have electric motors instead of engines, and *hybrids* have both! Therefore, if any part on your vehicle isn't exactly where it is in the pictures in this chapter, or if a part doesn't look quite the same, don't panic. Believe me, all the parts are there — otherwise your vehicle wouldn't go.

TIP

If you have trouble finding something, your owner's manual should have a diagram (which was probably gibberish to you until you bought this book) showing the location of each principal part. You also can ask a friend who has a similar vehicle or your friendly automotive technician to point out these "missing" parts. I'm willing to bet, however, that if you read this chapter carefully with an eye on your own vehicle, you'll be able to locate almost all the parts yourself.

TIP

If you're planning to work on your vehicle and want instructions for making specific repairs, you can get a subscription for $19.95/year per vehicle that allows you to download instructions for specific tasks from Chilton, one of the major publishers of automotive service manuals. Visit www.chiltondiy.com for more information.

Enough about manuals. Get ready to take a quick trip through the basic parts and systems on your vehicle. When you finish this chapter, you'll truly know "What Makes It Go."

# Introducing the Engine Control Unit (ECU)

Meet the *engine control unit (ECU,* also called *Powertrain Control Module, or PCM),* which is the key player in virtually every system involved in running your vehicle. In an automotive sense, the ECU is the all-knowing, powerful "god" that makes it go. You'll find it plays a vital role in most of the systems explored in this chapter, so I thought I'd introduce you to it first.

The ECU is the most powerful computer on modern vehicles. It uses a variety of *sensors* to monitor and control most of the engine functions, including the *electrical, fuel,* and *emissions control systems.* Among other tasks, the ECU controls the *fuel injectors* on fuel-injected engines; fires the *spark plugs;* and controls *valve timing,* the *fuel/air mixture, battery charging,* and even the cooling *fan.* It's the key to the diagnostics that pinpoint problems and is primarily responsible for managing the fuel efficiency and performance of your vehicle. If the ECU malfunctions, it usually needs to be replaced.

# What Makes Your Vehicle Start?

Although people tend to think that most vehicles are totally powered by fuel, many parts — the radio, headlights, air conditioner, windshield wipers, power seats and windows, clock, and so on — actually function on electricity, which is provided by the *electrical system.* The electrical system includes several subsystems that provide your vehicle with that vital spark that makes it start, keeps it running, and powers all electrical devices. It's one of the many systems on a vehicle that's monitored and controlled by the *ECU* (see the previous section). Figure 4-1 shows you the electrical system.

The following is a blow-by-blow description of what happens from the time you activate the ignition until the engine is purring and ready to go:

1. When you turn the key in your vehicle's *ignition switch* to Start or activate the ignition by pushing a button, you close a *circuit* that allows the current to pass from your *battery* to your *starter* via the *starter solenoid switch* (see Figure 4-2).

2. The starter makes the engine *turn over* (that's the growling sound you hear before the engine starts running smoothly). Chapter 5 tells you exactly how it does this.

3. The electric current stops flowing to the starter but continues to flow through the *charging system* (which uses an *alternator* to generate power and charge the battery) and to the rest of the electrical system.

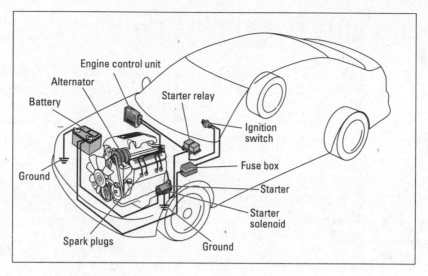

**FIGURE 4-1:**
The electrical system.

4. Now the *fuel system* comes into play (see Figure 4-3): If you drive a vehicle with an *internal combustion engine* (ICE), whether your vehicle is more than 20 years old or just 20 days old, has *fuel-injection* or a *carburetor,* it probably has the same basic parts in its fuel system with one exception: On modern vehicles, the fuel system — along with most other systems — is controlled by the *ECU.* Chapter 7 explores the fuel system in detail, and Chapter 8 tells you how to keep it in tune.

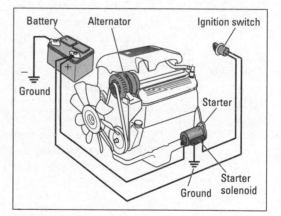

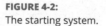

**FIGURE 4-2:**
The starting system.

5. When the engine is running, fuel flows from the *fuel pump* (usually located inside the *fuel tank* at the rear of the vehicle) through the *fuel filter,* to the *fuel injectors,* into the *intake manifold,* and then into the *combustion chamber.*

6. Each pound of fuel is mixed with 14.7 pounds of air to form a vaporized mixture, like a mist. Because fuel is much heavier than air, this mixture works out to something like 1 gallon of fuel to 2,000 gallons of air (which is the equivalent of a gallon of gas to a roomful of air). In other words, your engine really runs on air, with a little fuel to help it!

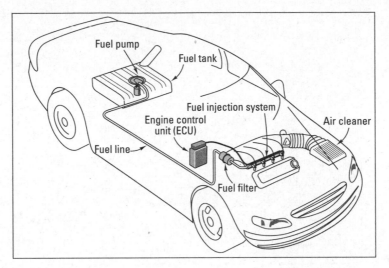

**FIGURE 4-3:**
The fuel system.

**7.** The ***fuel/air mixture*** passes into the ***cylinders*** in your engine. A cylinder, as shown in Figure 4-4, is a hollow pipe with one open end and one closed end. Inside each cylinder is a ***piston,*** which fits very snugly and moves up and down. The piston moves up, trapping the fuel/air mixture in the upper part of the cylinder and compressing it into a very small space.

**8.** A spark from a ***spark plug*** ignites the fuel/air mixture, causing it to burn and expand rapidly.

**9.** This expansion of gases forces the piston back down again, with more power than when it went up.

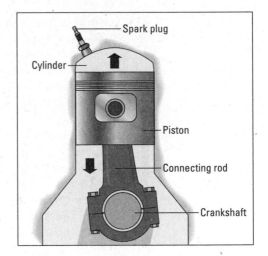

**FIGURE 4-4:**
A cylinder and piston.

**10.** Attached to the bottom of the piston is a ***connecting rod*** that's attached to a ***crankshaft,*** which leads, eventually, to the ***drive wheels*** of your vehicle. As the piston and the connecting rod go up and down, they cause the crankshaft to turn. As shown in Figure 4-5, this is pretty much the same motion you use to pedal a bike: Your knee goes up and down while your foot pedals around and around.

**11.** To the rear of the crankshaft is the *transmission,* called a *transaxle* on vehicles with *front-wheel drive.* If your vehicle has *rear-wheel drive* (see Figure 4-6), the transmission is under the floor ahead of the front seat. If it has a *transverse engine* and *front-wheel drive* (see Figure 4-7), the transmission is under the engine. On rear-engine vehicles, both the engine and the

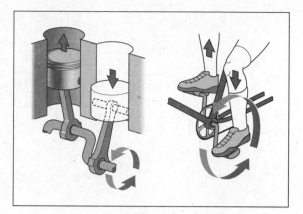

**FIGURE 4-5:**
The pistons and connecting rod move up and down to turn the crankshaft in circles.

transmission are under the rear deck lid, where the trunk ordinarily is found.

**12.** If your vehicle has a *manual transmission,* you'll also find the *clutch* located between the crankshaft and the transmission. The clutch connects or disconnects the engine from the rest of the *drive train.* Because the parts are all stretched out in a row and easy to see, Figure 4-8 shows you the drive train on a vehicle with rear-wheel drive and a manual transmission. Remember, in a car with an *automatic transmission,* the clutch action is done automatically.

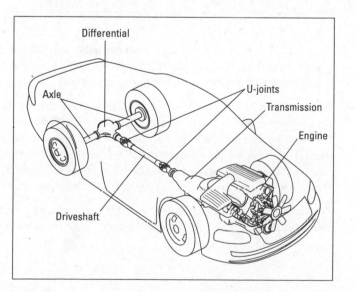

**FIGURE 4-6:**
Cutaway view of a car with rear-wheel drive.

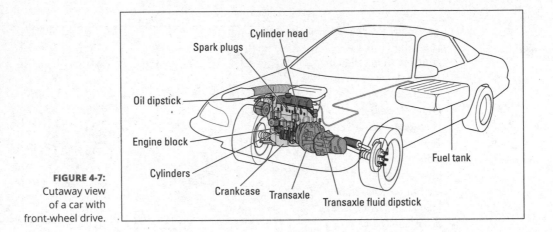

**FIGURE 4-7:**
Cutaway view
of a car with
front-wheel drive.

Cylinder head

Spark plugs

Oil dipstick

Engine block

Cylinders

Crankcase    Transaxle

Transaxle fluid dipstick

Fuel tank

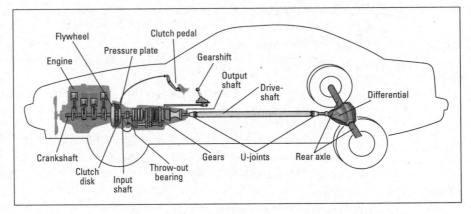

**FIGURE 4-8:**
The drive train in
a vehicle with
rear-wheel drive
and a manual
transmission.

Flywheel

Clutch pedal

Engine

Pressure plate

Gearshift

Output
shaft

Drive-
shaft

Differential

Crankshaft

Clutch
disk

Input
shaft

Throw-out
bearing

Gears

U-joints

Rear axle

**13.** When you shift into Drive (or First, if you have a manual transmission), a set of gears causes the rest of the crankshaft (which is called the **driveshaft** after it leaves the transmission) to turn at a particular speed.

**14.** The driveshaft runs to the rear wheels of conventional rear-wheel-driven vehicles and ends in another set of gears called the **differential.** The differential turns the power of the engine and the transmission 90 degrees into the **axles** that connect to **drive wheels** of the vehicle. Because on most vehicles the axle is set at right angles to the driveshaft, you can see that the differential is really changing the direction of the power so that the drive wheels can turn.

Chapter 18 looks at all types of drive trains and transmissions in detail, including **all-wheel drive, four-wheel drive,** and **continuously variable** *transmissions (CVT).* In that chapter, Figure 18-3 shows you how the differential changes the direction of the power 90 degrees.

**TECHNICAL STUFF**

Vehicles with ***front-wheel drive*** or with rear engines don't require a long driveshaft because the power source is located right between the drive wheels that drive the vehicle. On these vehicles, the transmission and the differential are combined into a single unit called the ***transaxle,*** which connects directly to provide power to the drive wheels. Figure 4-9 shows you how power flows through a transaxle.

**15.** The drive wheels turn and push the vehicle forward (or backward), and off you go. And all you had to do was turn on the ignition and step on the gas!

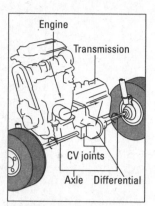

**FIGURE 4-9:**
The flow of power through a transaxle.

# What Makes Your Vehicle Run?

The following sections take a closer look at what various automotive systems do to keep your vehicle moving happily down the road. Because these systems work simultaneously and just keep on doing the same thing over and over, there's no need to take them step-by-step.

## The ignition system

After your engine has started running, the *ignition system* continues to provide high voltage to the *spark plugs* so that they can provide the spark that causes the fuel/air mixture to burn. To do so on modern vehicles with *distributorless ignition systems,* the ECU or a dedicated *ignition control module (ICM)* receives signals from *sensors* and controls when the spark plugs fire and ignite the *fuel/air mixture* in the *cylinders,* which provides the power to drive the engine. Figure 4-10 shows a distributorless ignition system.

Chapter 5 examines both distributorless electronic ignition systems and ones with distributors and explores the rest of the electrical system and subsystems in greater detail. Chapter 6 shows you how to keep the various parts of the electrical system working together in harmony.

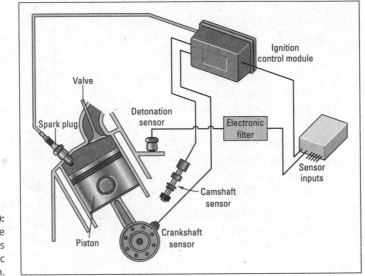

FIGURE 4-10:
The distributorless electronic ignition system.

# The cooling system

The *combustion* of fuel and air takes place at around 4,500°F, so the excess heat must be removed or the engine would melt down. This is accomplished by the circulation of liquid *coolant* through *water jackets* that surround the cylinders which carry the heat to the radiator, which dissipates it. A *water pump* keeps the coolant circulating while a cooling *fan* keeps the air flowing through the radiator when you're *idling* in traffic. You can see the entire cooling system in Figure 4-11. Modern vehicles also have a *transmission cooler* to keep the transmission from overheating.

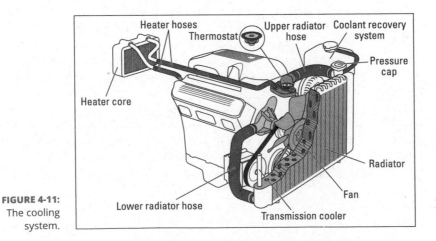

FIGURE 4-11:
The cooling system.

Chapter 11 explores the cooling system in greater detail, and Chapter 12 shows you how to do simple jobs like flushing the system and replacing the coolant. It also shows you what to do if your vehicle overheats.

## The lubrication system

*Oil* constantly circulates through your engine to keep its moving parts (pistons, connecting rods, crankshaft, and the like) lubricated to move freely and to reduce the friction that causes your engine to heat up. An *oil pump* keeps the oil circulating, and an *oil filter* keeps it clean. Figure 4-12 shows you what a lubrication system looks like.

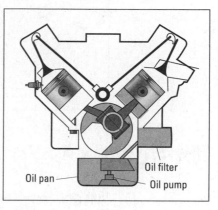

Chapter 13 tells you what oil does and how to change your oil and oil filter. For a close-up look at various steering and suspension systems, see Chapter 16.

**FIGURE 4-12:**
Oil cools the engine as part of the lubrication system.

## The exhaust system

The exhaust system, shown in Figure 4-13, is your vehicle's waste-disposal system. *Exhaust gases* from the burnt *fuel/air mixture* that was ignited in the *cylinders* pass through *exhaust pipes* to the *tailpipe* at the rear of the vehicle.

ECO-LOGIC

Because exhaust gases contain toxic substances and affect *global warming*, on the way to the tailpipe, *emissions controls* such as a *PCV valve*, various *sensors*, a *catalytic converter*, and other gizmos remove some of the harmful substances and recycle unburned fuel vapors before they can get into the air.

A *muffler* controls the noise of the escaping gases; if it fails, you can get a ticket, probably for disturbing the peace! A muffler also has an effect on the pressure required to pass the exhaust gases through it: It creates the "back pressure" that the engine requires to run efficiently and affects the temperature and therefore the efficiency of the catalytic converter.

You get a closer look at all the parts of the exhaust system in Chapter 7.

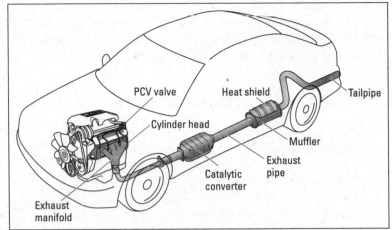

**FIGURE 4-13:**
The exhaust
system.

PCV valve     Heat shield     Tailpipe

Cylinder head

Muffler

Catalytic
converter     Exhaust
pipe

Exhaust
manifold

# What Makes Your Vehicle Stop?

Still with me? Good! Now all you need to know is what goes on when it's time for our vehicle to stop. This is the job of the *brake system* (but you knew that, right?).

Today, vehicles not only have *hydraulic* brakes — many have electronic brake systems, as well. Most modern vehicles come with *anti-lock braking systems (ABS)* that can prevent skids in slippery conditions and keep you in control of your vehicle until you can stop safely. *Electric vehicles (EV)* and *hybrids* feature *regenerative braking systems* that generate electric current to drive their electric motors.

For details on all the various braking systems and parts, including *power brakes* and *parking brakes,* check out Chapter 14. Chapter 15 has instructions on checking your brakes and doing other related jobs, and Chapter 10 has a section on regenerative braking systems.

Figure 4-14 shows you the major parts of a system with *drum brakes* at the rear wheels and *disc brakes* up front. Use it as you review the steps that follow, which give you a basic view of how a brake system operates.

1. To stop your vehicle, you step on the ***brake pedal.***

2. The brake pedal pushes against a piston in a cylinder located under the hood. This part is called the ***master cylinder,*** and it's filled with a liquid called ***brake fluid.***

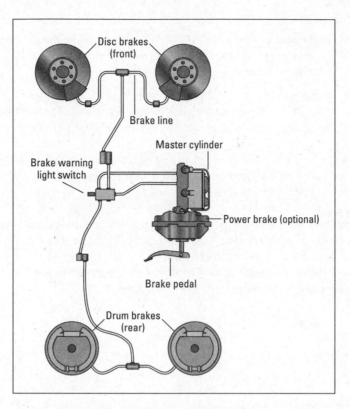

FIGURE 4-14:
A brake system.

3. When the piston in the master cylinder is pushed by your brake pedal, it forces the brake fluid out of the master cylinder into tubes called **brake lines,** which run to each wheel. (A power **brake booster** located between the brake pedal and the master cylinder increases the force applied to the piston in the master cylinder so that it takes less effort to stop your vehicle.)

4. Each wheel has either a **disc brake** or a **drum brake.** To keep it simple, I just look at disc brakes here. (Drum brakes work on the same general principles, as I explain in Chapter 14.) A disc brake is composed of a flat, iron disc (surprise!) sandwiched between a pair of **brake pads** by a **caliper,** as shown in Figure 4-15. The caliper contains one, two, or four pistons that force the friction material on the pads against the disc.

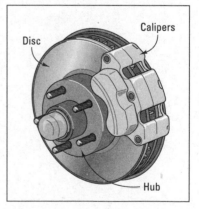

FIGURE 4-15:
A disc brake.

**5.** *Brake pads* located in the caliper on both sides of the disc grab the disc and force it to stop turning. This forces the wheel to stop turning. When the wheels stop turning, the vehicle comes to a stop.

**6.** When you take your foot off the brake pedal, the whole process is reversed: The brake pads release their hold on the disc, the fluid moves back up the brake lines to the master cylinder, and the wheels can turn freely again.

**TECHNICAL STUFF**

Four-wheel disc brakes are standard on most new vehicles. Other vehicles have disc brakes on the front wheels and drum brakes on the rear wheels. A few older vehicles have drum brakes all around.

Now that you have a general picture of how the various systems in your vehicle work together, don't stop here! The rest of this book goes into detail about each of the systems outlined in this chapter and what *you* can do to repair them and keep them running smoothly. *Be sure to read the chapter on how a particular system works before tackling the related instructional chapter.*

# 2

# Powering Up with Air, Fuel, and Fire

In Part 1 you get a quick look at how the different systems in a vehicle work together to get you moving and where you want to go. In this part, I give you a closer look at the electrical system and the fuel system. After you know the basics about each system, you get detailed instructions on what you can do to maintain them or to ensure that the professionals do their best to keep these systems in shape.

This part also covers a variety of innovative and ecologically sound alternatively fueled vehicles that increase fuel efficiency, reduce air pollution, and reduce the threat to our planet from global warming.

Chapter **5**

# The Electrical System: Your Car's Spark of Life

The *electrical system* includes several subsystems that provide your vehicle with that vital spark that makes it start and then keeps it running. It's one of the many systems on a vehicle that's monitored and controlled by a kind of "super computer" called the *engine control unit*, or *ECU* for short. You encounter this god-like critter in several chapters of this book, so you should meet it before you get to the various systems that form the electrical system.

**REMEMBER**

Whenever you encounter a term set in *this font*, you'll find it defined in the glossary in Appendix A.

## Introducing the Engine Control Unit (ECU)

The *engine control unit (ECU)* is the most powerful computer on a vehicle. It uses a variety of *sensors* to monitor and control most of the engine functions of the car, including the electrical, fuel, and *emissions control systems.* Among other tasks, the ECU fires the *fuel injectors* on fuel-injected engines, fires the *spark plugs,* and controls *valve timing, emissions controls,* the *fuel/air mixture,* and even the cooling fan. The ECU itself rarely malfunctions, is the key to the diagnostics that pinpoint problems, and is primarily responsible for managing the fuel efficiency and performance of your vehicle.

Moving on to the electrical system (see Figure 5-1), here are some of the services that the individual systems and major parts involved in the electrical system perform:

>> The ***starting system,*** unsurprisingly, provides the initial power to get your engine started.

>> The ***ignition system*** fires the ***spark plugs*** so they can cause the fuel and air to "combust" and drive your engine.

>> The ***charging system*** generates electrical power for the various systems in your vehicle that depend on electric current, and it regulates the power flowing to the battery to keep it from running down.

>> The ***battery*** stores excess current for future needs.

>> Various ***circuits*** run a mixed bag of electrical gadgets, like your vehicle's horn, headlights, and so on, most of which are protected by ***fuses.***

The following sections explore each of the basic subsystems that make up the electrical system.

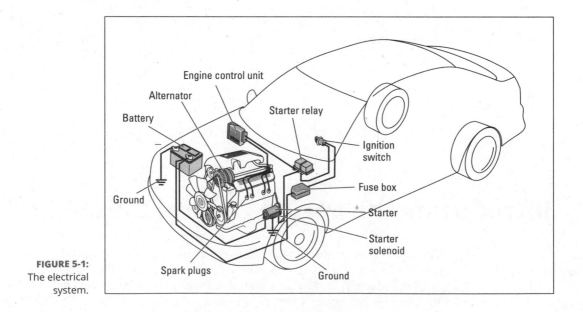

**FIGURE 5-1:**
The electrical
system.

# The Starting System

The starting system, shown in Figure 5-2, is the portion of the electrical system that gets your vehicle started. When you turn your key in the *ignition switch* to "Start" (or activate the ignition by pushing a button), the action closes a circuit that lets electrical current flow from your car's *battery* to its *starter*. On the way, the current passes through a device called the *starter solenoid*. Basically, all the solenoid does is pass the current along and move the starter gears into contact with the flywheel. You don't adjust or replace it unless it breaks down.

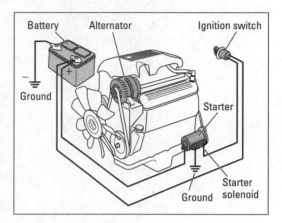

**FIGURE 5-2:**
The starting system.

**TIP**

Because actually seeing and touching something is worth a thousand words, it's a good idea to take this book out to your vehicle and trace the path of the electric current to each part in the system. Don't be shy now! (If you need them, you can find instructions for opening the hood in Chapter 1.) I know the area looks like a maze of wires, bottles, and boxes, but once you can identify the major parts, it won't be as scary anymore.

As you try to trace the wiring through the starting system, if you find a couple of parts that I haven't mentioned yet, just hang in there. Like the solenoid, you don't have to fuss with these parts unless they fail; and if they fail, they have to be replaced by a professional.

The following sections give you a closer look at each part of the starting system. Be sure to read them before undertaking any of the electrical work covered in Chapter 6.

## The battery

The battery is the big box that sits under the hood, usually up near the front of the vehicle. It's filled with acid, distilled water, and a set of plates that are combined into "cells" (see Figure 5-3) that produce electric current for starting the car, turning on the lights, and powering the ignition system. The battery also stabilizes the voltage in the electrical system and provides current whenever the electrical demands exceed the output of the charging system. Quite a helpful gadget!

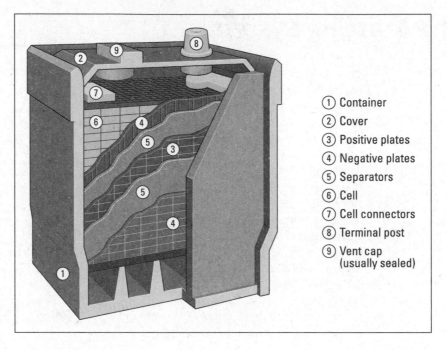

① Container
② Cover
③ Positive plates
④ Negative plates
⑤ Separators
⑥ Cell
⑦ Cell connectors
⑧ Terminal post
⑨ Vent cap (usually sealed)

**FIGURE 5-3:**
Cutaway view of a battery.

TECHNICAL STUFF

On the battery, attached to either the top or the sides of the box are two large metal terminals. One is a *positive terminal*; the other is a *negative terminal*. You can tell which is which because the positive terminal is usually larger and may have a "+," "POS," or the word "Positive" on or near it. The negative terminal usually has "−" or "NEG" on it.

TIP

On many vehicles, there's a red cap on the positive terminal, and the battery cable leading to it may be red as well. The cable to the negative terminal is usually black. The clamps on the cables that you use to jump-start a dead battery are usually colored red and black so that you can easily match them to the terminals. You can find instructions for jump-starting a dead battery in Chapter 21.

Most vehicles are *negative ground*, which means that the wire from the negative terminal is attached to the frame of the vehicle to ground it; the wire from the positive terminal leads to the starter, ignition, and so on.

Today, most batteries are sealed and don't require much maintenance. However, deposits do form on the terminals, and they can impede the flow of current. Chapter 6 tells you how to check your battery and remove these deposits.

## I KNOW *WHAT* THE PROBLEM IS; I JUST DON'T KNOW *WHERE* IT IS . . .

After I took my first class on the electrical system, I went out one morning and found that my car, Tweety Bird, wouldn't start. I remembered my instructor saying that if you hear a clicking noise (that's your solenoid) but your engine won't start running, you probably have a loose wire somewhere between the ignition switch and the starter. So I opened the hood (it was only the second time I'd gotten that far) and peeked in. Sure enough, I saw a cluster of wires on the *firewall* in front of my steering wheel. I could see where the wires ran along the frame of the car to the battery, but after that I got lost. I ended up calling the AAA.

When the AAA truck arrived, I proudly informed the technician that I knew what was wrong. "It's just a loose wire between my battery and my starter," I announced. "Then why didn't you fix it yourself?" he asked. "Because I don't know which gadget is the starter!" He was nice enough to keep from laughing, and I felt better when the problem *did* turn out to be a loose wire on the starter. He also pointed out the starter and showed me the wires that connected to it.

## The starter

After the battery sends the current to the *starter solenoid* (refer to Figure 5-2), the current goes to the *starter.* The starter is the device that makes your engine *turn over.* (Figure 5-4 shows what a starter looks like, and Figure 5-5 shows how a starter works.) It's an electrical motor with a gear called a *starter drive* at one end. The starter drive engages a *ring gear* on a *flywheel* that's bolted to the back of the engine *crankshaft.* When you turn your key in the *ignition switch* (or push the ignition

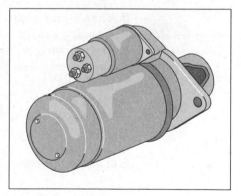

**FIGURE 5-4:**
A starter with a starter solenoid attached.

button on some vehicles), the starter drive slides down the shaft and engages the ring gear. This spins the flywheel, which starts the crankshaft turning so that the *pistons* can go up and down, the spark plugs can fire, and the engine can start running. As soon as the engine is started, the starter has done its job.

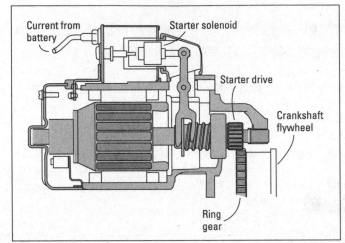

**FIGURE 5-5:**
Anatomy
of a starter.

TIP

If you use a key to start your vehicle, you should let go of the key immediately after the engine starts. As your key returns to the "On" (or "Run") position (where it stays until you shut off the engine), the starter drive disengages from the fly-wheel, and your engine continues running on the fuel and air that are being pumped into its *cylinders.*

WARNING

If you keep the ignition key in the "Start" position after the engine starts running, you'll hear a strange noise. That noise is the clutch in the starter drive that allows the engine to spin faster than the starter. Even though this one-way clutch prevents starter damage after the engine starts, it's not a good idea to hold the key in the "Start" position for more than ten seconds at a time when the engine is under its own power. If the vehicle doesn't start, allow the starter to cool down for one to two minutes before attempting to start it again. Failure to do so can overheat the starter and damage it. And *don't turn the key to the "Start" position when the engine is running.* If you do, you can damage the gear on the starter and the ring gear on the flywheel.

# The Charging System

After you start your engine, it (usually) runs at a nice steady rumble unless you have a *hybrid* or *electric vehicle (EV).* EVs run silently, and hybrids are silent when operating on the electric motor only (see Chapter 10). The rumble in a conventional vehicle is possible because as soon as the pistons in the *cylinders* start to go up and down, your engine begins to run on its usual diet of fuel and air (read all about it in Chapter 7). When you let go of the key and your *ignition switch* moves from "Start" to "On," the electric current stops flowing to the starter but continues to flow through the *charging system* (see Figure 5-6) and the rest of the *electrical system.*

# The alternator

The running engine drives a belt that enables your *alternator* to produce electric current for the rest of the trip. Here's how it does this: Your alternator (see Figures 5-6 and 5-7) replaces the electricity that was taken from the battery when you started the car. Then, every time your battery sends out some of its "juice," the alternator replaces it.

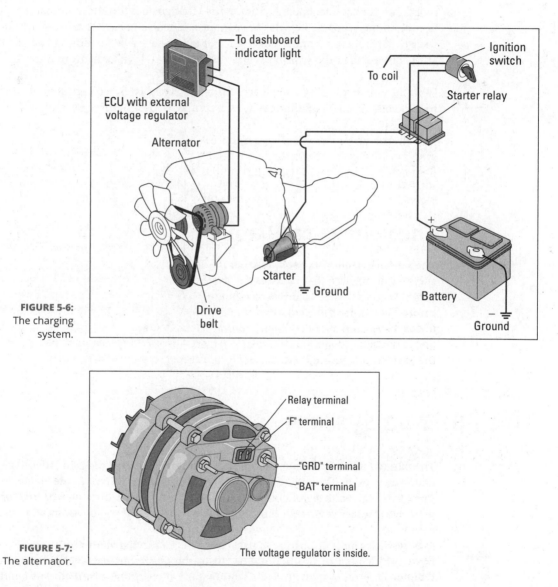

**FIGURE 5-6:**
The charging system.

**FIGURE 5-7:**
The alternator.

TECHNICAL
STUFF

An alternator produces *alternating* current (AC), which is internally converted to the *direct* current (DC) needed to drive various gadgets. You occasionally hear the alternator referred to as a *generator.* Generators are usually found on pre-1964 vehicles. They generate direct current (DC) and pass it on. Today's generators still generate electric current for other uses, but their automotive days are over.

When the alternator is generating electric current, it's said to be *charging.* Although most cars just have dashboard "idiot lights" that go on if the alternator isn't functioning properly, some vehicles have gauges called *voltmeters* that show whether the system is charging or discharging. They either have a "C" at one end and a "D" at the other end of the scale or a range of voltage levels (usually from 8 to 18).

TIP

With the engine running and all accessories off, the system voltage should be 13.5 to 14.5 volts. If not, something may be wrong with the charging system.

The alternator also supplies your electrical system with current to run the radio, headlights, and so on. I get to that equipment at the end of this chapter.

### The voltage regulator

The *voltage regulator* (see Figures 5-6 and 5-8) is a device that controls the *alternator.* On older cars, it's a little box mounted somewhere under the hood. On newer cars, it may be mounted inside the alternator or inside the *ECU.* If the voltage regulator fails, the alternator is literally "powerless."

**FIGURE 5-8:**
One type of voltage regulator.

# The Ignition System

The purpose of the *ignition system* is to *ignite,* or fire, the **spark plugs** in order to generate power to run the engine. To do so, the battery sends current to the **ignition coil.** Then that high voltage goes on to the spark plugs — either through a **distributor,** if you have an older vehicle, or directly to the spark plugs, if you have a newer one.

TECHNICAL
STUFF

Most vehicles built prior to 1974 use a non-electronic distributor ignition system. Most vehicles built from the mid-1970s to the late 1980s use an electronic distributor ignition system. Today's vehicles use an *electronic distributorless ignition system,* which, as the name implies, has no distributor at all. I discuss and illustrate both of these systems a little later in this chapter.

As later sections explain, both types of *electronic ignition systems* employ electronic parts. Unlike older systems, except for the spark plugs, their components don't need to be replaced unless they break down. The good news is that they tend to be relatively trouble-free. The bad news is that if they do break down, you have to pay a professional to replace them.

Because all types of ignition systems employ spark plugs, you get to explore them first. Read on!

## The spark plugs

*Spark plugs* are located in the **cylinders** of your vehicle (look ahead to Figure 5-17). They deliver the spark of voltage to the **combustion chamber** just when the *fuel/air mixture* is at the point of greatest compression. The resulting combustion provides the power to propel your vehicle. Chapter 6 tells you how to "read" your spark plugs for clues as to how your vehicle is running and provides instructions for removing, gapping, and replacing spark plugs. Figure 5-9 shows you the various parts of a spark plug. You need to get to know them if you want to work on them yourself.

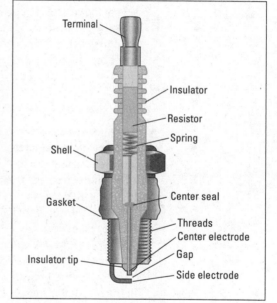

**FIGURE 5-9:**
Anatomy of a spark plug.

The location of the cylinders varies from one type of engine to another; the order in which the spark plugs fire the fuel in the cylinders differs from one engine to another as well. The next two sections tell you about *cylinder sequence* and *firing order.* It's good to know how this works because if the spark plugs aren't firing properly, your engine is as "out-of-tune" as an orchestra whose players aren't keeping time. (That's probably why they call it a *tune-up.*)

### Cylinder sequence

The cylinder sequence of an engine is the order in which the cylinders of the engine are numbered. This sequence varies from one type of vehicle to another, depending on whether it has *front-wheel drive* or *rear-wheel drive* and whether it has an *in-line engine,* with the cylinders lined up in one row, or a *V-type engine,* with the cylinders in two parallel rows.

Here are cylinder sequences for several types of engines:

>> Vehicles with *front-wheel drive* have *transverse engines.* On both in-line and V-type engines, the cylinders run from one side of the vehicle toward the other. Aside from being set cross-wise, they have the same sequence and firing order as their *rear-wheel drive* in-line or V-type counterparts (see Figure 5-10).

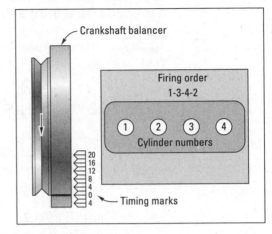

FIGURE 5-10:
The cylinder sequence and firing order of an in-line 4-cylinder transverse engine.

>> **In all U.S.-made in-line 4- and 6-cylinder vehicles with rear-wheel drive, the cylinder nearest the front is called the #1 cylinder.** The numbering for the rest of the cylinders (#2, #3, #4, and so on) runs in sequence back toward the *firewall* at the rear of the engine compartment (see Figure 5-11).

TIP

Some *foreign* automakers reverse the cylinder sequence. As you can see in Figure 5-12, the #1 cylinder is at the rear, near the firewall. If you have a foreign car and no owner's manual, ask your local dealer where your #1 cylinder is.

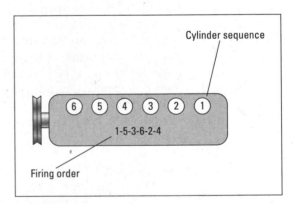

FIGURE 5-11:
The cylinder sequence and firing order of an in-line U.S. 6-cylinder engine with rear-wheel drive.

» **V-8 engines aren't as easy to figure out. Most Ford V-8s with rear-wheel drive have the #1 cylinder in the front on the passenger side of the car.** Then cylinders #2, #3, and #4 follow it toward the rear firewall. The #5 cylinder is up front on the driver's side, with cylinders #6, #7, and #8 in sequence going toward the rear (see Figure 5-13).

» **On most other vehicles with V-8 engines and rear-wheel drive, the #1 cylinder is up front on the driver's side, with cylinder #3, #5, and #7 proceeding toward the rear of the vehicle.** Then cylinder #2 is up front on the passenger side, with cylinders #4, #6, and #8 following (see Figure 5-14).

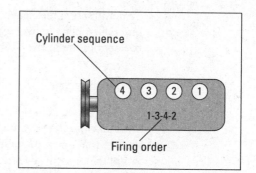

**FIGURE 5-12:**
The cylinder sequence and firing order of a foreign in-line 4-cylinder engine.

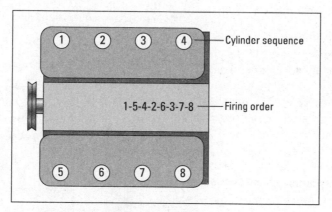

**FIGURE 5-13:**
The cylinder sequence and firing order of most Ford V-8 engines.

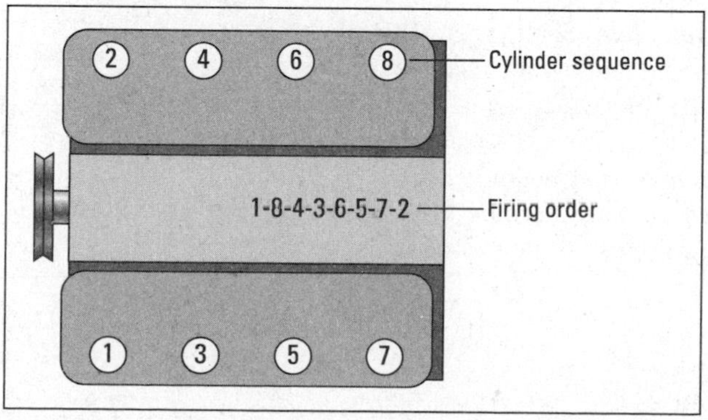

**FIGURE 5-14:**
The cylinder sequence and firing order of many other V-8 engines.

Transverse engines have the same cylinder sequence and firing order as in-line engines, and no matter what the engine configuration, the #1 spark plug is always the spark plug in the #1 cylinder (see Figures 5-10, 5-15, and 5-16).

## Firing order

Don't confuse cylinder sequence with *firing order.* Although your engine may have its cylinders in simple numerical sequence, if the cylinders were fired in that order, the engine would rock violently as first the cylinders on one side (or toward the front) fired in rapid succession, and then the other cylinders did likewise. To avoid this, the firing order is carefully arranged to distribute the shock of *combustion* evenly throughout the engine.

The cylinders fire in very swift sequence, and the result is a fairly stable engine. The firing order is printed inside each of the engines shown in Figures 5-10 through 5-16. Trace the path of combustion back and forth through each of these engines to see how the shock of combustion is distributed to avoid rocking the engine. And remember, the whole thing happens very rapidly.

Now that I've dealt with the basics, the following sections deal with the two types of elec-tronic ignition systems: the modern ones that no longer have *distributors,* and the older elec-tronic ignitions with distributors.

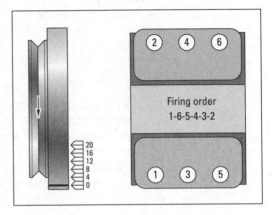

**FIGURE 5-15:**
The cylinder sequence and firing order of a transverse V-6 engine.

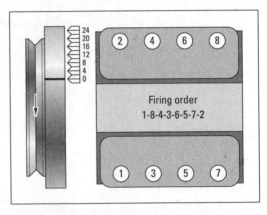

**FIGURE 5-16:**
The cylinder sequence and firing order of a transverse V-8 engine.

# Modern distributorless ignition systems

Found in most vehicles from the mid-1990s on, *distributorless ignition systems* (see Figure 5-17) have fewer moving parts and are much more fuel-efficient and less prone to breaking down than those with *distributors*. In all distributorless ignition systems, the *ECU* or a dedicated *ignition control module (ICM)* controls when the spark plugs fire and ignite the *fuel/air mixture* in the cylinders, which provide the power that propels the vehicle.

The following sections take a closer look at the electronic components found in modern distributorless electronic ignition systems (refer to Figure 5-17).

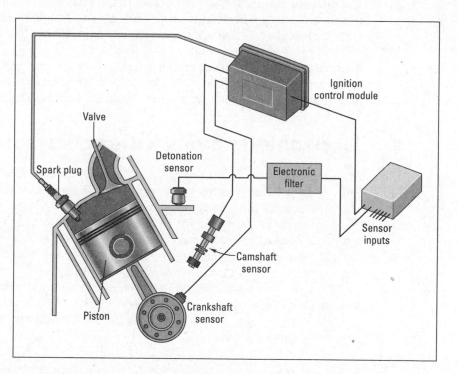

**FIGURE 5-17:**
A distributorless ignition system.

## The electronic coil module

The *electronic coil module* does the same thing in a much more sophisticated way as the ignition *coils* and distributor on older vehicles did: It transforms the relatively small amount of electrical *voltage* (12 to 14 volts) that it receives from the battery into a big enough jolt of voltage (15,000 to 60,000 volts) to jump the *spark plug gap*. On most vehicles, a set of *spark plug wires* (sometimes called *ignition cables*) carries the high voltage to each spark plug.

On these systems, instead of just one coil increasing the voltage and sending it to each of the spark plugs, each spark plug has its own little coil. As a result, if one should misfire, all the others can carry on the job until the system is repaired.

### Ignition system sensors

An electronic ignition system relies on a number of electronic sensing devices that feed information to the ECU, or a dedicated *ignition control module* (ICM) (see Figure 5-17), which sends the signals that fire the spark plugs at the proper time.

A *crankshaft position sensor* (refer to Figure 5-17) is mounted on the engine block and can read the position of, you guessed it, the *crankshaft.* It's one of the sensors that tells the ICM when to fire each spark plug by keeping track of where the crankshaft is and how fast it's spinning at any given time.

A *camshaft position sensor* found on *distributorless ignition systems* (refer to Figure 5-17) is another trigger device. It helps the *spark plugs* to fire at the right time, provides the data to synchronize the *fuel injectors,* and identifies misfiring *cylinders.*

## Electronic ignitions with a distributor

Although most more recent vehicles don't have *distributors,* many built from the mid-1970s to the mid-1990s still have them. (If your vehicle doesn't have one, you can disregard this section and bop on down to the sections "Warning Lights and Malfunction Indicator Lights (MIL)" and "Other Electrical Gadgets.") In an ignition system with a distributor, the distributor works in much the same way as the old-fashioned mechanical distributor that preceded it, but without all the moving parts that constantly needed adjusting. It still gets voltage from a coil and distributes it to each spark plug in turn. The good news is that electronic distributors are relatively trouble-free. The bad news is that if they break down, you have to pay a professional to replace them. They include the following parts, which can be seen in Figure 5-18:

>> The *distributor cap* (shown in Figure 5-19) sits atop the distributor to protect the parts inside from the elements. Current enters and leaves the distributor via the coil and spark plug wires that run through holes in the cap to each spark plug.

>> The *rotor* (refer to Figure 5-18) sits atop the distributor shaft inside the distributor. As the distributor shaft turns, the rotor rotates with it and points toward the terminal at the base of each spark plug wire so that each plug can fire in the correct order. For example, when the rotor's pointing at the terminal of the wire leading to the #1 spark plug, it directs the current to that spark plug at precisely the time when the *fuel/air mixture* in the #1 cylinder is waiting to be burned.

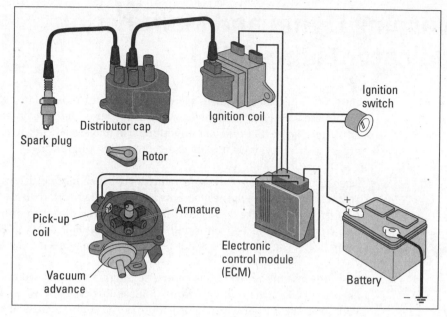

**FIGURE 5-18:**
An electronic ignition system with a distributor.

>> The *armature* (refer to Figure 5-18) sits inside the distributor, revolving past a *sensor* called the *pickup coil.* Each time one of the teeth on the armature passes the sensor, it creates voltage that signals an ***ignition control module (ICM)*** to shut down the primary circuit in the coil. This "fires" a jolt of high voltage to the secondary coil circuit, which shoots it out through the rotor to the proper spark plug. A circuit in the electronic module switches the primary circuit back on between each "firing."

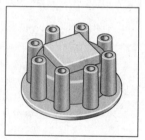

**FIGURE 5-19:**
A distributor cap for an electronic distributor.

>> The ***ignition control module*** is a transistorized component that triggers the ignition coil to fire high voltage. The module is a "non-wear" component that replaced the old-style "breaker" points in the early to mid-1970s.

>> A ***pick-up coil*** is a magnetic pulse generator that tells the ignition control module when to fire the spark plugs. Some vehicles use a *Hall-effect* switch or a photoelectric sensor to do the same thing. It probably doesn't make much difference which type your vehicle has because there's no need for you to develop a personal relationship with it.

# Warning Lights and Malfunction Indicator Lights (MIL)

Until fairly recently, vehicles were equipped with either dashboard gauges that monitored your vehicle's temperature, oil pressure, *charging system,* and fuel level; or *warning lights* that told you something bad had already occurred in one of these areas (which is why we usually called them "idiot lights").

The warning systems on today's vehicles are much more efficient. Warning lights still tell you how much fuel you have; whether the hood, trunk, or a door is open; or if the *parking brake* is engaged. They beep at you like a frustrated parent if you don't put your seat belt on. And *malfunction indicator lights* (MIL) check almost every system and warn you about problems that may need to be corrected.

The only trouble is that MILs can be so enigmatic about what's gone wrong — especially when the ominous words "Check Engine" appear — that they can be very unsettling. That warning can apply to the engine, emissions, or accessories, so at first you can't know if it's just that your gas cap is loose or if major surgery is required.

When I turn on Esmerelda's engine, a whole panel of little yellow symbols lights up. Many of these MIL are undecipherable. Others are initials that stand for . . . what? My owner's manual describes most of them, but because these lights only stay on for seconds, it's hard to keep track of them. And if one of them stays lit (bad news!), basically all the owner's manual advises is to head for the dealership. Because that means I have to pay someone to put the car on a scan tool and "read the codes," as a confirmed do-it-myselfer, I'm not happy.

However, because the MIL report the findings of the electronic sensors that constantly monitor your vehicle's airbags, *traction control, ABS system, ECU, transmission,* and other vital systems — all of which you can't work on yourself — if one of them stays lit after the others go out, it's probably a good idea to head for the car doctor. Failing to do so can void your *warranty* or really damage your vehicle.

**TIP**

There is one bright spot on the horizon: In some areas, there are now do-it-yourself service centers where you can drive into one of their bays, follow instructions for finding the place under your dashboard to plug in their diagnostic equipment, get a printout of the "codes," and look up what's wrong. There's a good chance that you'll need professional help, but if you just left your gas cap loose, you can save yourself a lot of time and money.

# Other Electrical Gadgets

In addition to what I cover in the *alternator* section earlier in this chapter, by keeping the battery charged, the alternator also indirectly supplies the electrical current for the sound system, headlights, taillights, directional signals, defroster/heater/air conditioner blower, and other electrical gadgets. Although most of these components require professional repair, the following parts are pretty easy to deal with yourself:

>> **Fuses** protect electrical component circuits the same way they do in a home. The fuses are located in a fuse box that's usually found under or near the dashboard and possibly under the hood. Your owner's manual should show you where the fuse boxes on your vehicle are, or you can crawl under the dashboard and trace the wires from your sound system until you reach the fuse box. See Chapter 6 for instructions on checking fuses and replacing a burned-out fuse.

>> **Windshield wipers** need to be checked and their blades replaced periodically. Chapter 2 provides tips on checking and replacing your windshield wiper blades and windshield washer fluid.

>> **Directional signal flashers** on your dashboard do more than tell you whether the directional signals themselves are flashing. They're also designed to provide clues to malfunctions elsewhere on your vehicle! Chapter 21 tells you how to decipher these clues and rectify the problems that they indicate. For information about replacing directional signals, flip to Chapter 6.

>> **Headlights and headlamps** have been considerably improved in recent years. Although vehicles with *sealed-beam units* and old-style light bulbs are still on the road, more modern vehicles have headlamps filled with halogen or Xenon gas. The Xenon headlamps are also known as *HID (high intensity discharge) lamps.* They're brighter and use less power than halogens do. Most of these are no more difficult to adjust and replace than sealed-beam units were (see Chapter 6 for instructions on how to replace headlights and headlamps).

**TECHNICAL STUFF**

Headlight development continues. Innovations that already exist and will become more widely available include *adaptive front lighting systems (AFS)* that can swivel to illuminate a corner and lightweight LED headlamps that have the potential to outlive your vehicle.

IN THIS CHAPTER

» **Knowing if it's time for a tune-up**

» **Reading, gapping, and changing spark plugs**

» **Replacing your vehicle's battery**

» **Finding and changing fuses**

» **Adjusting, aligning, and replacing headlights and directional signals**

# Chapter **6**

# Keeping Your Electrical System in Tune

U nlike older vehicles, which needed ignition tune-ups at least once a year, most vehicles on the road today have *electronic ignition systems* that are built to go for years without the need for them. The term "tune-up" is still used to refer to routine maintenance, which varies with a vehicle's make, model, and year, so check your owner's manual for scheduling recommendations.

**REMEMBER**

Although this chapter provides instructions for quite a number of jobs you can do yourself, because major tune-ups require electronic diagnostic equipment and sensitive *onboard computers,* they should be done by professionals at the dealership or a qualified service facility. And remember, if you fail to get a scheduled tune-up you could violate your vehicle's *warranty* or leasing agreement.

**TECHNICAL STUFF**

In case you're wondering what a modern tune-up includes, it generally involves doing an electronic diagnostic check, changing *spark plugs,* replacing *air* and *fuel filters,* and checking fluid levels. Other parts may not need to be replaced for the life of the car.

There are several jobs involving the electrical system that you can deal with yourself. The first involves checking, reading, and reinstalling or replacing spark plugs if your vehicle's performance suddenly drops and if your vehicle is configured so that you can work on the spark plugs without harming your engine. You also can troubleshoot and replace *fuses* and replace and adjust the headlights. In this chapter, the sections "Changing Your Spark Plugs," "Changing Fuses," and "Dealing with Headlights and Directional Signals" tell you what to do and whether you should do it yourself.

**REMEMBER**

If you haven't already done so, please read Chapter 5 before this one so that you understand what you're working on. Also, be sure to read the sections in Chapter 1 called "Following safety rules," "Buying the right parts for your vehicle," and "How to Take Anything Apart — and Get It Back Together Again" before you undertake *any* electrical work.

**WARNING**

Before you get down to work on your electrical system, please be aware that there are devices that you shouldn't attempt to deal with yourself unless you've worked on them before. If you have trouble with your defroster, heater, anti-theft devices, or stereo system, get professional help. Later, if you turn into a confirmed do-it-yourselfer, you can find books that deal with these repairs.

*Don't attempt to work on your air conditioner under <u>any</u> circumstances.* It contains refrigerant under pressure that can blind you if it escapes. For service or repairs, head to the dealership or to an automotive air-conditioning specialist. Now, let's get on to what you *can* do!

**REMEMBER**

Whenever you encounter a term set in *this font,* you'll find it defined in the glossary in Appendix A.

# Determining Whether Your Vehicle Needs a Tune-up

Tune-up intervals vary from one vehicle to another. Most older vehicles with non-electronic ignitions should be tuned every 10,000 to 12,000 miles or every year, whichever comes first. Newer cars with electronic ignition and *fuel injection* systems are scheduled to go from 25,000 miles to as many as 100,000 miles without needing a major tune-up.

**WARNING**

Refer to your *owner's manual* for recommended tune-up intervals, but be aware that even if it says that the vehicle doesn't require *scheduled* tune-ups very often, it's in your best interest to check periodically that your vehicle's working at peak efficiency. If you do a lot of stop-and-go driving or pull heavy loads (like a camper or boat), your *ignition system* may need to be tuned more often. Here are a couple of symptoms that tell you that your electronic ignition system may need to be tuned or adjusted:

>> **The car stalls a lot.** The *spark plugs* may be fouled or worn, the *gap* between the *spark plug electrodes* may need adjusting, or an *electronic sensing device* may need to be adjusted. Stalling also can be caused by problems with the *fuel system* (see Chapters 7 and 8).

If you're having trouble pinpointing why your vehicle is stalling, you can help your automotive technician diagnose the problem by paying attention to whether the engine stalls when it's hot, cold, or when the air conditioner is on.

**TIP**

>> **The engine is running roughly when *idling* or when you accelerate.** Chances are the vehicle needs a tune-up.

>> **The car gets harder to start.** The problem can be in the *starting system* (for example, a weak battery), in the fuel system (for example, a weak fuel pump), in the ignition system, or can be due to an electronic component, such as the *electronic control unit (ECU).*

# Changing Your Spark Plugs

How often you replace spark plugs depends on the type of plugs you have. You may have 30,000-mile plugs, or if the plugs have platinum tips, they may be good for up to 100,000 miles, although some professionals recommend replacement every 60,000 miles to avoid damage to the engine. (For detailed information about what spark plugs do, turn to Chapter 5.) However, if they become fouled with oil or become defective, spark plugs may need to be replaced ahead of schedule.

There are several ways to tell whether or not the spark plugs on your vehicle need to be changed or just need to be adjusted and replaced. This section tells you how to do that. Of course, before you can evaluate the condition of your spark plugs, you have to find them.

## Finding your spark plugs

To locate your spark plugs, look for a set of thick wires (or thin cables) that enter your *engine block* in neat rows — on both sides if you have a *V-type engine* or on one side if you have a 4- or 6-cylinder *in-line engine* (also called a *straight* engine). These spark-plug wires run from the *ignition coil* (or the *distributor* on older vehicles) to the spark plugs. You can see where the spark plug wires connect to the spark plugs on various types of engines in Figures 5-10 through 5-16 in Chapter 5. And, if you've never met one, Figure 6-3 later in this chapter provides a look at the anatomy of a spark plug.

Don't see your plugs? They may be hidden or hard to reach, which means that you need to reevaluate your plan to work on them. Be sure to read the following section before you do another thing!

## Deciding if you should do the job yourself

The first — and most important — thing to consider is whether or not you should change the spark plugs on your vehicle yourself. Because so many modern vehicles have crammed engine compartments that make access difficult, which can damage the spark plug wires and the threads in the cylinder heads, I honestly feel hesitant about even providing instructions. So take the cautions below seriously before deciding whether or not to proceed.

WARNING

Even if only *one* of the following conditions is true for your vehicle (and they're true for most modern vehicles), you should have a professional change your plugs. You don't want to risk having to replace a really expensive ECU just to save a few dollars on a job that only has to be done infrequently! So *don't* be a hero!

>> **There's so little space between the stuff under the hood that it's difficult or impossible to get at your spark plugs.** Remember, you need room to get a *socket wrench* in there to unscrew the plug and then replace it, and you need to have an unimpeded view of what you're doing. Not only that, but *if you don't get the wrench at the correct angle, you can cross-thread the plug or strip the threads it screws into.* Both are bad news. You could end up needing a multi-thousand dollar repair.

>> **The entire engine has to be dismounted and lifted out of the vehicle in order to reach at least one plug.** If you have one of these beasts, leave this job to the professionals.

ECO-LOGIC

Studies have found that many shops just don't bother to dismount the engine to get at difficult plugs. If left unchanged, that one funky plug can increase your fuel consumption, add to air pollution, and cause other problems. So, if your engine is one of these, when you bring your vehicle in for a tune-up be sure to confirm that the shop will do whatever's necessary to replace *every* plug.

>> **Your engine has an aluminum *cylinder head.*** Because the metal is soft, it's easy to strip the threads in the spark plug's hole. If you do, the head will probably have to be removed for repair, and that means more mega-bucks. Most modern engines have aluminum heads, so for most people, this fact should eliminate doing this job yourself.

>> **Your spark plugs are hidden.** On some vehicles, you can't get at the plugs until you remove other parts that are in the way. For example, on some *transverse engines,* you'd have to remove the top engine mount bolts in order to tilt the engine forward to replace the rear spark plugs. And on other engines, you can only get to some spark plugs from underneath or through the wheel well area.

Still other engines conceal the plugs beneath a metal shield that covers the engine. Removing this shield can require disconnecting cables that can seriously affect the ECU. That's why the shield is there! Some older domestic engines, most modern import engines, and an increasing number of modern domestic engines have systems that place an *ignition coil* directly atop each spark plug. There are no spark plug wires, and you can't see the spark plugs until you remove the aluminum cover that's bolted to the top of that engine.

If I were you, I'd leave all these vehicles to the professionals who have hoists and special tools that allow them to do the work safely and with relative ease.

Okay, with all this in mind, if you can get to your plugs easily and feel that you can do the job safely, proceed to the next section. Otherwise, skip it.

**REMEMBER**

Before you take care of your spark plugs, you must understand what the terms *cylinder sequence* and *firing order* mean. Chapter 5 has detailed explanations for these terms and illustrations of most of the major configurations, so if you haven't read them, stop for a moment and check them out.

## What you need to change and gap your plugs

If you've decided that you can get at your spark plugs without damaging your vehicle, assemble the items you need *before* you begin:

**TIP**

>> **An old blanket, mattress pad, or padded car protector to place over the fender where you'll be working to protect it from scratches:** Commercial car protectors often come with handy pockets that hold tools and little parts while you work. You can make such a pocket yourself by pinning up the bottom edge of your folded blanket or pad.

>> **Work clothes:** Wear something that you don't mind getting stained with grease, oil, and other stuff. Changing spark plugs may be simple, but it can get messy. Trust me.

>> **Hand cleaner:** Chapter 3 has suggestions for the best type to buy.

>> **Clean, lint-free rags:** You'll use these to wipe the spark plugs clean, wipe the cleaner off your hands, and generally tidy up after the work is done.

» **A work light (or flashlight, at least):** Chapter 3 describes the different types available.

» **A new set of spark plugs:** The next section helps you determine what type and how many spark plugs your vehicle needs. Buy one for each cylinder in your engine. And don't be shocked if you're told that you need eight spark plugs for your 4-cylinder engine. Some engines require two spark plugs per cylinder.

WARNING

Never change just a few plugs; it's all or nothing for even engine performance. If you're feeling especially wealthy, buy an extra plug in case you get home and find that one of them is defective, or in case you accidentally ruin one by dropping and cracking it or by cross-threading it when you install it. If you don't use it, keep it in your trunk compartment tool kit for emergencies. Spark plugs don't get stale.

» **Anti-seize compound and silicone lubricant (optional):** The threads of the spark plugs should be lightly coated with a dab of engine oil off the ***oil dipstick*** or with anti-seize lubricant before you install them in the engine. Also, if there are *rubber boots* on your spark plug wires, apply silicone lubricant to them to prevent them from sticking to the porcelain part of the spark plug. (Silicone boots don't need this.)

» **A wire or taper *feeler gauge:*** You use this to gap spark plugs. (I explain what ***gapping*** is in the later section "Gapping your spark plugs.") Chapter 3 shows you what these gauges look like and what they're used for.

» **A small set of basic socket wrenches that includes a *ratchet* handle and a *spark plug socket:*** If you need to buy a set of ***socket wrenches,*** Chapter 3 describes them and provides tips on buying good ones.

## Buying the right plugs

To buy the proper spark plugs for your vehicle, you must know its *specifications* (or "specs," as they're often called). Your owner's manual may have specifications for buying and gapping the spark plugs on your vehicle. If you don't have an owner's manual, or if yours lacks the necessary information, you can find the correct spark plugs and spark plug *gap* in a general "Tune-Up Specification Guide" (called a "spec sheet," for short) at an auto supply store. These guides are either in pamphlet form or printed on large sheets, like the one in Figure 6-1, that are displayed near the parts section of the store. If you can't find a spec sheet at the store, ask a salesperson to show it to you. For a sample spec sheet, see Figure 6-1. I've italicized the examples in the list of basic information below so you can find them on the figure.

To obtain the specs for your particular vehicle, you need some basic information. All this information should be in your *owner's manual,* and most of it is also printed on metal tags or decals located inside your hood. You can usually find these in front of the radiator, inside the fenders, inside the hood — anywhere the auto manufacturer thinks you'll find them. I know of one vehicle that has its decal inside the lid of the glove compartment. These identification tags also provide a lot of other information about where the vehicle was made, what kind of paint it has, and so on, but don't worry about that information right now.

Here's what you need to know to obtain the specs for your vehicle:

>> **The make of the vehicle** (*Toyota,* Chevrolet, and so on).

>> **The model** (*Prius,* Malibu, and so on).

>> **The model year** (*2004,* 1999, and so on).

>> **The number of *cylinders* and type of engine.**

>> **Whether the vehicle has an *automatic* or a *manual* (standard) transmission.**

>> **The engine *displacement:*** How much room there is in each **cylinder** when the **piston** is at its lowest point? (For example, a 3-liter 6-cylinder engine has a displacement of one-half liter, or 500 cubic centimeters — usually shown as 500 CCs — in each cylinder.) The bigger the displacement, the more fuel and air the cylinders in the engine hold.

The displacement of engines on older vehicles may be listed in cubic inches, such as 302, 350, 454, and so on. Modern vehicles are usually listed in liters (1.8, 2.3, 5.9) or cubic centimeters (2200, 3400, 3800).

>> **The kind of *fuel system:*** If your engine is **fuel-injected,** you may need to know whether your car has *throttle body* injection or *multi-port* injection. Carburetors, on the other hand, were distinguished by how many "barrels" they had. (Chapter 7 makes sense of this stuff.)

>> **Whether the vehicle has air conditioning:** It's not usually necessary to take this into account when buying most parts, but you never know when you'll need it.

If you haven't already done so, enter your vehicle's make, model, year, and number of cylinders on a copy of the *Specifications Record* in Appendix B. If your owner's manual has the model number of the plug you need and the size of the gap, enter that information, too. If not, take the record with you to the store and use their spec sheet to fill in the necessary information.

| IGNITION SPECIFICATIONS | | |
|---|---|---|
| 2004 Toyota Prius L4-1.5L (1NZ-FXE) (Hybrid) | | |
| **SERVICE DATA** | | |
| Spark plug<br>Recommended spark plug | DENSO<br>NGK | SK16R11<br>IFR5A11 |
| Electrode gap | Standard<br>Maximum | 1.0 to 1.1 mm (0.039 to 0.043 in.)<br>1.0 mm (0.047 in.) |
| Camshaft position sensor<br>Resistance | 1 (G+)-2(G-) | 1,630 to 2,740 Ω (Hot)<br>2,065 to 3,225 Ω (Cold) |
| Camshaft position sensor<br>Resistance | 1 (NE+)-2(NE-) | 965 to 1,600 Ω (Hot)<br>1,265 to 1,890 Ω (Cold) |

**FIGURE 6-1:** Ignition specifications for a 2004 Toyota Prius.

*Courtesy of ALLDATAdiy*

At the auto supply store, *don't* just ask a salesperson which type of plug you should buy — you have a very good chance of getting the wrong one. First look up the specifications yourself, and then ask for the plug by *number*. If you're unsure, have a salesperson double-check it for you.

Look up your vehicle by make and model under the proper year on the spec sheet at the store. (For example, for my first car, Tweety Bird, a "previously owned" 1967 Mustang, I looked under 1967, then under Ford, then under Mustang, then under "200 cu. in. 6 Cyl. Eng. (1 bbl.)" — which means that Tweety had an engine displacement of 200 cubic inches, a 6-cylinder engine, and a single-barrel carburetor.) Then write down the following information from the spec sheet in the appropriate columns on your *Specifications Record*:

>> **The spark plug gap:** This is the amount of space that there should be between the center and side electrodes of each spark plug.

>> **The part number for the spark plugs designed for your vehicle.**

## Removing old spark plugs

Before you undertake *any* of this work, re-read the section "Deciding if you should do the job yourself," and if your vehicle fits even *one* of those descriptions, don't try to do the work in this section. It's better to pay a professional than to risk damaging your engine or ECU!

One way to royally confuse yourself and turn the relatively simple task of changing spark plugs into a nightmare is to pull all your spark plugs out at one time. To keep your sanity and to avoid turning this job into an all-weekend project, work on one spark plug at a time: Remove it, inspect it, clean it, and — if it's salvageable — gap it. Then replace it *before you move on to the next spark plug in cylinder sequence order.* To maintain the proper *firing order,* each spark-plug wire must go from the spark source to the proper spark plug. Therefore, *only remove the wire from one plug at a time, and don't disconnect both ends of the wire!* This way, you won't ever get into trouble — unless a second wire comes off accidentally.

Follow these steps to remove each spark plug:

1. **Gently grasp a spark plug wire by the boot (the place where it connects to the spark plug), twist it, and pull it straight out.**

   Never yank on the wire itself (you can damage the wiring). The shiny thing sticking out of the **engine block** after you remove the wire from the spark plug is the *terminal* of the spark plug. Figure 6-3 later in this chapter shows you all the parts of a spark plug, including the terminal.

2. **Use a soft, clean rag or a small paintbrush to carefully clean around the area where the spark plug enters the block. You also can blow the dirt away with a soda straw.**

   Cleaning the area keeps loose junk from falling down the hole into the cylinder when you remove the plug.

3. **Place your *spark plug socket* (the big one with the rubber lining) over the spark plug; exert some pressure while turning it slightly to be sure that it's all the way down.**

   REMEMBER

   Like everything else in auto repair, don't be afraid to use some strength. But do it in an even, controlled manner. If you bang or jerk things, you can damage them, but you'll never get anywhere if you tiptoe around.

4. **Stick the square end of your *ratchet handle* into the square hole in the spark plug socket.**

   You may work more comfortably by adding a couple of extensions between the handle and the socket so that you can move the handle freely from side to side without hitting anything. Add them in the same way you added the socket to the handle. If a plug is hard to reach, the sidebar "Getting to hard-to-reach plugs" gives you additional tips.

5. **Loosen the spark plug by turning it counterclockwise.**

   To get the proper leverage, place your free hand over the head of the wrench, grasping the head firmly, and pull the handle, hitting it gently with the palm of your hand to get it going (see Figure 6-2).

   WARNING

   It's okay to exert some strength; just be sure your socket is securely over the plug and that the ratchet is at the same angle as the plug to avoid stripping the threads on the plug or in the spark plug hole in the engine head.

You may have some difficulty loosening a spark plug for the first time. Grease, sludge, and other junk may have caused the plug to stick in place, especially if it's been a long time since it was changed. If it feels stuck, try a little spray lubricant. You'll feel better knowing that after you've installed your new plugs by hand, it will be a lot easier to get them loose the next time. So persevere. I've never met a plug that didn't give up and come out, eventually.

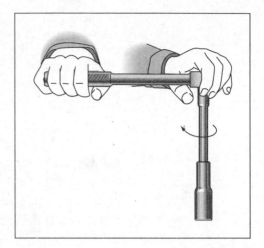

**FIGURE 6-2:**
Using a ratchet handle.

6. **When the ratchet turns freely, finish the job by removing the ratchet handle and turning the socket by hand until the plug is free from the engine.**

TIP

# GETTING TO HARD-TO-REACH PLUGS

With all the stuff crammed under the hoods of vehicles, it can be hard to get at some spark plugs and, even when you can reach them easily, they may be difficult to remove. Here are some tips on extracting these spark plugs:

- Almost every vehicle has at least one plug that's a miserable thing to reach. If you have one, and it's safe for you to deal with, save it for last. Then you can work on it with the satisfaction of knowing that, when you get the darn thing finished, you'll have finished the job.

- If you find that one or more plugs are blocked by an air conditioner or some other part, try using various ratchet handle extensions to get around the problem. There are *universal* extensions that allow the ratchet handle to be held at odd angles; *T-bar* handles for better leverage; and *offset* handles for hard-to-reach places (see Chapter 3 for examples). *Just remember that you must keep the ratchet handle right in line with the angle of the plug it's contacting to avoid stripping the threads.*

- If you absolutely can't reach the offending plug, you can always drive to your service station and humbly ask them to change just that one plug. They won't like it, but it *is* a last resort. If you get to that point, you'll probably be glad to pay to have it done.

## MASTERING THE MIGHTY RATCHET

**TIP**

Ratchet handles can be a bit tricky if you've never used one. When you figure out how yours works, it will make many jobs much easier. The little knob on the back of the ratchet handle causes the ratchet to turn the socket either clockwise or counterclockwise. You can tell which way the handle will turn the plug by listening to the clicks that the handle makes when you move it in one direction. If it clicks when you move it to the right, it will turn the socket counterclockwise when you move it, silently, to the left. If the clicks are audible on the leftward swing, it will move the socket clockwise on the rightward swing.

Every screw, nut, bolt, screw-on cap, and so on that you encounter should loosen counterclockwise and tighten clockwise ("lefty loosey, righty tighty"). If your ratchet clicks in the wrong direction, just move that little knob to reverse the direction. Figure 6-2 shows you the proper way to use a ratchet handle.

**REMEMBER**

After you remove the spark plug from the engine, remove the plug from the socket. But don't go on to the next plug until you've read the plug (see the section "Reading your spark plugs" and Table 6-1) and *gapped* and replaced it, following the instructions later in this chapter.

# Reading your spark plugs

You can (and should) actually *read* your spark plugs for valuable "clues" about how your engine is operating. To read your spark plugs, follow these steps:

1. **When you get the first spark plug out of the engine, remove the plug from the spark plug socket and compare the condition of the plug to the clues in Table 6-1.**

   Figure 6-3 can help you to identify the various parts of a plug mentioned in the table.

2. **Check the plug's shell, insulator, and gaskets for signs of cracking or chipping, which indicate that the plug should be replaced.**

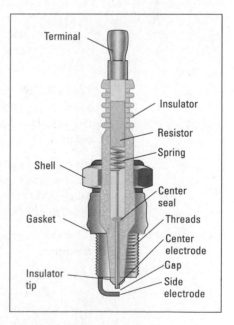

**FIGURE 6-3:**
The anatomy of a spark plug.

**TABLE 6-1**  　　**What Your Old Spark Plugs Tell You about Your Vehicle**

| Condition | Clues | Probable Causes | Remedies |
|---|---|---|---|
| Normal plug | Brown or grayish-tan deposit on side electrode | Everything's fine | Just clean and regap the plug. |
| Carbon-fouled | Black, dry, fluffy soot on insulator tip and electrodes | Overly rich fuel/air mixture, dirty air filter, too much driving at low speeds, or idling for a long time | Switch to "hotter" plug plugs. (The higher the plug number, the hotter the plug. |
| Oil-fouled plug | Wet, black, oily deposits on insulator tip and electrodes | Oil may be leaking into cylinders past worn pistons or poorly adjusted or worn valves | Clean and regap the plug, or replace it, but find out where the leak is coming from. |
| Burned plug | Blisters on insulator tip, melted electrodes, burned stuff | Engine overheating gap is too wide, wrong or loose plugs, overly lean fuel/air mixture, or incorrect timing | Replace the plug. |
| Worn plug | Severely eroded or worn electrodes | Plug has been in there too long | Replace the plug. |

3. **Look at the plug's *firing end* (the end that was inside the cylinder).**

   As you can see in Figure 6-3, the hook at the top is the *side **electrode,*** and the bump right under its tip is called the *center* electrode. The spark comes up the center of the plug and jumps the ***gap*** between these two electrodes. This gap *must* be a particular distance across for your engine to run efficiently.

4. **Take your *wire* or *taper feeler gauge* and locate the proper wire. (If your spark-plug gap *specifications* say .035, look for this number on the gauge.) Then slip that part of the gauge between the two electrodes on your old plug.**

   If the gauge has a lot of room to wiggle around, it may be because your old plug has worn down its center electrode, causing a gap that's too large. If the gauge can't fit between the center and side electrodes, the gap is too small, which means that the spark plug isn't burning the ***fuel/air mixture*** efficiently.

5. **Look at the center electrode bump again and use Table 6-1 to judge its condition.**

   Is it nice and cylindrical, like the center electrodes on your new spark plugs? Has the electrode's flat top worn down to a rounded lump? Or has it worn down on only one side? Chances are it's pretty worn because it's old. When the center electrode wears down, the gap becomes too large. (When you do this job yourself, you'll probably check your plugs more often and replace them before they get too worn to operate efficiently.)

**6.** **Clean the plug by gently scrubbing it with a wire brush.**

**7.** **Either gap or replace the old plug with a new one, following the instructions in the next two sections.**

Keep in mind that although you don't need to clean new spark plugs, you do need to gap them. Some plugs are sold "pre-gapped," but I recommend checking them with a *feeler gauge* anyway.

**8.** **Repeat the entire process for each additional plug.**

Work on only one plug at a time, and don't remove a plug unless the one you just dealt with — or its replacement — is safely back in the engine.

REMEMBER

TIP

To keep your engine operating efficiently, don't mix plugs in varying states of wear. Either replace *all* the plugs with new ones or clean and reinstall *all* the old ones. If you find that a few of your old plugs aren't too worn and are in fairly good shape but you need to replace the others, clean and regap the salvageable plugs and store them in your trunk compartment tool kit for emergencies.

Sometimes you can cure a problem — such as carbon-fouled plugs — by going to a hotter- or cooler-burning plug. You can identify these by the plug number: The higher the number, the hotter the plug. Never go more than one step hotter or cooler at a time.

TECHNICAL
STUFF

If your plugs indicate that something is seriously wrong with the way your engine is running, ask a professional for an opinion. If you're told that it requires extensive or expensive work, get a second opinion at another service facility without telling the technicians that you went to the first place. This is a good policy to follow whenever major repair work is suggested. You wisely get a second opinion when a doctor tells you that you need major surgery; why not give your vehicle the same thorough attention before incurring a major expense? Chapter 22 has plenty of tips for surviving automotive surgery.

## Gapping your spark plugs

As I mention in the preceding section, the space, or *gap*, between the center and side *electrodes* needs to be an exact distance across; otherwise, your plugs don't fire efficiently. Adjusting the distance between the two electrodes is called *gapping* your spark plugs.

REMEMBER

Gap new as well as old spark plugs, even if the package says that the new plugs are "pre-gapped." To avoid problems, work on only one plug at a time, in *cylinder sequence order*.

The following steps explain how to gap your spark plugs:

1. **If you're regapping a used plug, make sure that it's clean (gently scrub it with a wire brush). If you're using a new plug, it should be clean and new-looking, with the tip of the side electrode centered over the center electrode.**

   You shouldn't see any cracks or bubbles in the porcelain insulator, and the threads should be unbroken.

2. **Select the proper number on your feeler gauge, and run the gauge between the electrodes (see Figure 6-4).**

   If the gauge doesn't go through, or if it goes through too easily without touching the electrodes, you need to adjust the distance between the electrodes.

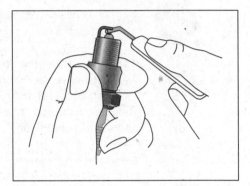

**FIGURE 6-4:**
Gapping a plug with a wire gauge.

3. **Adjust the gap as necessary.**

   If the wire didn't go through, the gap is too narrow. Hook the part of the feeler gauge that's used for bending electrodes under the side electrode and tug *very gently* to widen the gap.

   If the gauge goes through too easily without touching the electrodes, the gap is wide. Press the side electrode *very gently* against a clean, mar-proof surface until it's *slightly* bent down toward the center electrode.

4. **Run the gauge through the gap again.**

5. **Repeat Steps 3 and 4 until the gap is just right.**

   You want the gauge to go through fairly easily, just catching the electrodes as it passes.

If you keep adjusting the gap too narrow or too wide, don't feel bad. Everyone I know goes through the "too large–too small–too large" bit a couple of times for each plug, especially the perfectionists.

After you're done gapping your spark plug, it's time to insert it in the engine. The next section has the details.

# Installing a spark plug

To insert a spark plug into the engine, follow these steps:

1. **Clean the spark plug hole in the cylinder block with a clean, lint-free cloth.**

   **WARNING**

   Wipe *away* from the hole; don't shove any dirt into it.

2. **Lightly coat the threads of the spark plug with a dab of oil from the *oil dipstick, being careful not to get any on the center or side electrodes.***

3. **Carefully begin threading the spark plug into the engine by hand, turning it *clockwise.***

   This is called "seating the plug." You have to do it by hand or you run the risk of starting the plug crooked and ruining the threads on the plug or the threads in the spark plug hole in the engine.

   **TIP**

   If you have trouble holding onto the plug, you can buy a *spark plug starter* and fit it over the plug. Or, you can use just about anything you can wrap around or slip over the plug top, including an old spark plug wire boot, a finger cut from a vinyl glove, an old piece of thin plastic tubing, or a piece of vacuum hose.

4. **After you engage the plug by hand, turn it at least two full turns before utilizing the spark plug socket and ratchet.**

5. **Slip the spark plug socket over the spark plug, attach the ratchet handle, and continue turning the plug clockwise until you meet resistance.**

   **WARNING**

   Don't over-tighten the plug (you can crack the porcelain); just get it in nice and tight with no wiggle. The plug should stick a little when you try to loosen it, but you should be able to loosen it again without straining yourself. Tighten and loosen the first plug once or twice to get the proper feel of the thing.

6. **Take a look at the spark plug cable before attaching its boot to the plug. If the cable appears cracked, brittle, or frayed or is saturated with oil, have it replaced.**

7. **Before you attach the boot to the spark plug, apply some silicone lubricant to the inside of the boot; then push the boot over the exposed terminal of the new plug and press it firmly into place.**

   You've just cleaned, gapped, and installed your first spark plug. Don't you feel terrific? Now you have only three, five, or seven more to do, depending on your engine.

8. **Repeat the steps to remove, read, gap, and install each spark plug.**

   It's at times like these that owners of 4-cylinder cars have the edge on those who drive those big, expensive 8-cylinder monsters. Unless, of course, they have two plugs in each cylinder. . . .

## LEAVE YOUR DISTRIBUTOR TO A PRO

Most cars built after 1975 have *electronic ignition systems* that require no regular servicing. Some have no distributors at all. All testing and servicing of these systems should be left to trained professionals because they're easily damaged if hooked up improperly, and they employ high voltage that can also damage *you*. If you're curious, Chapter 5 explains what distributors do.

When you're done, start your engine to prove to yourself that everything still works. Then wash your hands with hand cleaner. If you've had a hard time with a hard-to-reach plug, get some rest before taking on additional work. And take comfort in the fact that, next time, the job should be a breeze.

# Replacing a Battery

No matter how well your vehicle is working, if your battery dies and can't be recharged, you're stranded in a vehicle that you can't drive in for service. A battery usually has a sticker on it that shows when you bought it and how long you can expect it to survive. To prevent being stuck on the road with a dead battery, enter that information in your *Specifications Record* in Appendix B and have the battery replaced *before* it comes to the end of its life expectancy.

REMEMBER

To extend its life, your battery should be checked and maintained regularly. You can find instructions in Chapter 2 for dealing with it as part of your monthly under-the-hood check. And if it has just run out of juice temporarily because you left the lights on, Chapter 21 tells you all about jumping a start.

## Deciding if you should do the job yourself

Unless your vehicle has a shield over the battery that's difficult or dangerous to remove, it shouldn't be hard to replace it yourself. However, if installation and disposal are included in the price of a new battery, there may be no advantage in undertaking the job.

To further assist you in deciding whether or not to do the job, open the hood of your vehicle (Chapter 1 tells you how) and find the battery. Figure 6-5 shows you where it's located and what it looks like. If the battery on your vehicle is concealed under a plastic shield, take a look at what's holding it in place. If you see just a few screws or bolts, you can probably unscrew them and remove the shield without much trouble. If it looks difficult to get the thing off, have the battery installed wherever you buy it.

## Buying the right battery for your vehicle

If you've decided to replace your battery yourself, the first thing to do is to buy the right one. Keep the following in mind:

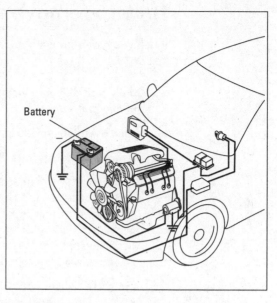

Battery

**FIGURE 6-5:**
Locating the battery under the hood.

>> **If you haven't already put the information on your *Specifications Record*, consult your *owner's manual* to find the *specifications* for the battery designed for your vehicle.**

>> **Buy a brand name battery at a reputable dealership, auto parts store, or battery dealer.** (Chapter 1 has useful tips on buying the right parts for your vehicle.)

TIP

Batteries are priced by their life expectancy. Most are rated for five years. Don't risk getting stranded by a poor quality battery that malfunctions, but if you don't plan to keep your vehicle longer than five years, don't spring for an expensive long-term battery that will vastly outlive your need for it.

>> **Take the new battery out to your vehicle and compare it with the original one.** It should be the same size, shape, and configuration. If it isn't, march right back in and return it for the right one.

TIP

While you're battery shopping, be sure you have all the stuff you need for the job. If you don't have an *adjustable wrench* (see Chapter 3), buy or borrow one. You'll also need a couple of clean lint-free rags, a pair of disposable latex gloves, some water and baking soda, and a battery brush. To protect your eyes from any deposits that can hurt them, invest in an inexpensive pair of safety goggles, too.

# How to remove and install a battery

When you have your equipment handy and you're ready to start, follow these easy steps:

1. **Make sure that your vehicle is in Park, with the engine shut off and the *parking brake* on.**

2. **Open the hood and place a blanket or pad over the fender to protect it.**

3. **Remove the cables from the battery terminals.**

   Look in your owner's manual to see whether your vehicle has *negative* **ground** (most do). If it does, use an adjustable wrench to first loosen the nut and bolt on the clamp that holds the battery cable on the **negative terminal.** (That's the post with the little "–" or "NEG" on it.) If your vehicle has *positive* ground, loosen the cable with "+" or "POS" on it first. Remove the cable from the post and lay it out of your way. Then remove the other cable from its post and lay that aside.

TIP

   If you have trouble loosening the bolt, grab it with one wrench and the nut with another, and move the wrenches in opposite directions. In this case, you don't want to remove the bolts; just loosen them enough to release the cable clamps.

4. **Remove whatever devices are holding the battery in place.**

TIP

   When you're removing a bolt or screw, after you've loosened it with a tool, turn it the last few turns by hand so that you have a firm grip on it when it comes loose and it doesn't drop and roll into obscurity.

5. **When the battery is free, lift it out of its seat and place it out of your way.**

6. **If the tray on which the battery was standing is rusty or has deposits on it, clean it with a little baking soda dissolved in water.**

   Wear your gloves because the battery stuff is corrosive and be sure the battery tray is completely dry before taking the next step!

7. **Place the new battery on the tray, facing in the same direction as the old one did.**

8. **Replace the devices that held the old battery in place. Try to wiggle the battery to make sure it's completely secure.**

9. **Replace the battery cables on the terminals in *reverse* order from which you removed them.**

   (If your vehicle has negative ground, the positive cable goes back first.) Make certain that the clamps holding the cables on the battery terminals are gripping the posts tightly.

**ECO-LOGIC**

**10.** **Take the old battery to a recycling center that accepts batteries.**

Batteries are filled with a toxic, corrosive liquid and must be disposed of properly. What's more, old batteries are usually **rebuilt** into new ones, so just throwing one in the trash is doubly bad for the environment. If you have your new battery installed when you buy it, the shop will recycle the old one for you. They'll probably want to charge a few dollars for this service, but try to negotiate it into the price. You also can call your local recycling center for a referral.

# Changing Fuses

If your stereo goes dead, your turn signals don't blink, a light goes out, or some other gadget stops working, it's often just the result of a blown fuse. You can change fuses yourself, easily and with very little expense. This section shows you how.

Many vehicles have two fuse boxes: one under the hood and one under the dash. A fuse box is easy to recognize (see Figures 6-6 and 6-7), and replacing burned-out *fuses* is a fairly simple matter. Changing a fuse is much cheaper than paying for new equipment or repairs that you don't need (even if you chicken out and have an automotive technician do it), so take a few minutes to find your fuse boxes. Your owner's manual can help you locate them.

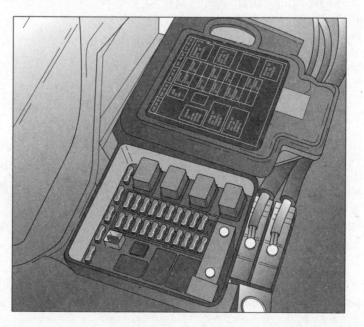

**FIGURE 6-6:** A fuse box located under the hood.

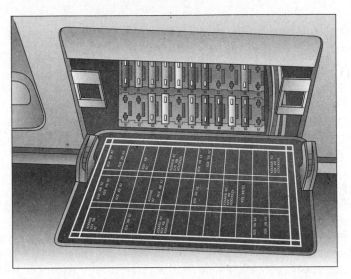

**WARNING**

Before you open or work on a fuse box, be sure that your vehicle's ignition is turned off.

**WARNING**

*Never replace a fuse with one that has different amperage than the original.* The new fuse has to be the same color and size as the one you're replacing. As you can see in the figures, the lid of each fuse box usually has a chart that shows you what each fuse is for and how many amps it is. If the fuse you're replacing has different amperage than the one on the chart, someone may have replaced it incorrectly, and that may be why it's blown.

After you've replaced all the burned-out fuses, test the part that malfunctioned to see if it's operating properly again. If it still doesn't work, have it professionally repaired or replaced.

## Blade-type fuses

Most modern vehicles have blade-type fuses with prongs that plug into the fuse box the same way that appliances plug into wall outlets (see Figure 6-8). They come in various sizes and are color-coded for amperage.

If you can't just yank a fuse out, you need a plug puller. If you're lucky, your automaker has provided one right in the fuse box. If not, try a pair of tweezers.

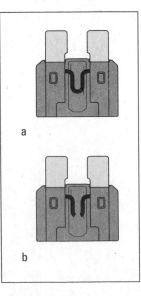

**FIGURE 6-8:**
A good blade-type fuse (a) and a blown one (b).

You can tell if the fuse has blown by looking at the filaments visible in its little window. If they're fused (no pun intended) or burned through, the fuse has had it.

## Tubular fuses

If you encounter tubular glass fuses, look for one that's black inside or no longer has its filaments intact (see Figure 6-9). To remove this blown fuse, *gently* pry it out with your fingers, a very small standard screw-driver, a small set of pliers, or, as a last resort, a bent paper clip.

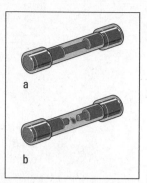

**FIGURE 6-9:**
A good tubular fuse (a) and a burned-out fuse (b).

TIP

To avoid breaking the fuse, try prying up one of the end caps first. If that doesn't work, gently pry it up from one end of the center area. Inspect the fuse to be sure it's burned out, and then *gently* press a new fuse into place.

# Dealing with Headlights and Directional Signals

Today's vehicles feature many kinds of illumination: Headlights, taillights, directional signals, and fog lights make it easier for you to see and be seen; overhead lights, map lights, lit glove compartments, and illuminated mirrors on sun visors all require attention periodically. In this section, I deal primarily with headlights and modern headlamps. If you experience problems with other lights, it's usually just a matter of changing the bulb or changing the fuse associated with the light. If that doesn't do the trick, seek professional help.

REMEMBER

Older vehicles have headlights with sealed-beam units (bulbs). Modern vehicles have headlamps filled with halogen or Xenon gas. In the interest of brevity, where I refer to both systems, I just call them headlights.

## Troubleshooting headlights

Here are some headlight problems and how to tell what may be wrong with them:

>> **If a headlight doesn't work on Low beam but does work on High,** you have to replace the whole sealed-beam unit or headlamp.

>> **If a headlight doesn't work on either High or Low beam,** you probably just have a bad connection in the wiring.

>> **If _both_ of your headlights go out at the same time,** chances are the units are okay but the fuse that controls them has blown and needs to be changed. The "Changing Fuses" section earlier in this chapter tells you how to do that.

**TIP**

It doesn't hurt to wash the outside of your headlights and taillights occasionally; clean lights provide better visibility at night. If you still have trouble seeing at night (and you've been getting enough vitamin A), check to make sure that both of your headlights are shining straight ahead rather than at the side of the road or into the eyes of other drivers. If they appear to be out of alignment, check out the "Checking headlight alignment" section later in this chapter.

## Determining which headlights you have

Before attempting to replace or adjust your headlights, you need to know whether you have halogen or Xenon headlamps or the old-style sealed-beam units. You can tell which type of headlights you have by looking at them when they're on at night.

Headlights with _sealed-beam units_ are quickly going out of style. The light they give off is just plain white. Many modern vehicles have halogen headlights. The newest models often come with _HID (high intensity discharge lamps),_ also called Xenon or bi-Xenon lamps. Light from Xenon lamps has a bluish cast.

If you're in doubt, check the clear outer cover of your headlamp assembly. If it's marked with D1R, D1S, D2R or D2S, you have HID lamps. (Those markings denote the type of bulb.) If the lens cover isn't marked and you still see a bluish cast to the light from the lamps, you either have an _aftermarket_ Xenon system or a halogen bulb that's been tinted. Your parts dealer or service facility can tell which type you need by looking at the bulb.

## Replacing and adjusting halogen and Xenon headlamps

Although they are far more powerful than sealed-beam units and enable a driver to see 20 percent farther, these modern units require less power to operate. Xenon are the brightest, have the longest life, and consume the least power. Halogen and Xenon headlamps have also allowed designers to get pretty creative with shapes because they use small, replaceable lamps that don't have to be contained in round or rectangular housings.

To replace a bulb on a halogen or Xenon headlamp, use Figure 6-10 as a guide while you take the following steps:

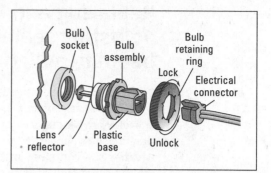

**FIGURE 6-10:**
Replacing a halogen or Xenon lamp.

1. **Make sure that your vehicle's ignition is off before you open the unit.**

2. **Open the hood and find the wiring leading to the electrical connector that plugs into the bulb assembly.**

3. **Remove the connector.**

   The connector can be held in place by a ring that unlocks by twisting it counterclockwise, by a little catch that you need to press down while pulling on the plug, or by a metal clip that pulls off (don't lose it!).

4. **Pull out the bulb assembly, remove the old bulb, and install the replacement.**

   *Don't touch the replacement glass bulb!* Natural oils from the skin on your fingers will create a hotspot that will cause the new bulb to burn out prematurely. Instead, handle the bulb by its plastic base or the metallic tip, if it has one. Also, these fragile bulbs are filled with gas under pressure, so be careful to avoid breaking them.

5. **Replace everything you removed and replug the connector.**

6. **Turn your headlamps on. If the bulb is still out and the fuse is okay, have a professional diagnose and fix the problem.**

Because HID headlamps are so intensely bright, it's most important that they be properly focused to avoid temporarily blinding other drivers, pedestrians, or animals. If you want to check that the beams are properly aligned, see "Checking headlight alignment" at the end of this section.

If you need to adjust the alignment of a halogen headlamp, it has two adjusting screws, as shown in Figure 6-11. The screw on the bottom will angle the beam higher or lower; the one at the top or side will focus the beam to the left or right.

# Replacing and adjusting sealed-beam headlights

Older vehicles have sealed-beam units, which are relatively easy to deal with. If one of your headlights ceases to shine, first consult your owner's manual to see whether it contains instructions for replacing the bulb. If it doesn't, the following steps should get you through the job with a minimum of hassle:

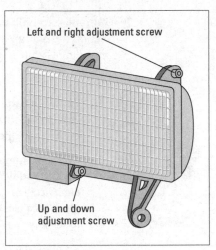

**FIGURE 6-11:**
Headlamp adjustment screws.

**WARNING**

1. **Make sure that the vehicle's ignition is off before you open the unit.**

2. **Remove any exterior rings or frames that surround the headlight.**

   If you need some exotic tool to do this, forget the job and have it done professionally.

3. **Carefully turn the *correct* screws to loosen the retaining plate that holds the unit in place.**

   The plate has several screws; round headlights have three screws that loosen the plate, and rectangular headlights have four. The other screws align the headlights by adjusting the angle of the bulb.

**REMEMBER**

   If you turn the wrong screws, your headlights go out of alignment, so check your owner's manual for details. If you think you've messed up the alignment, see the next section "Checking headlight alignment."

4. **Remove the bulb.**

   If the retaining screws stick, spray a little penetrating solvent (like WD-40) on them. Hold onto the bulb as you remove the screws so that it doesn't fall out and smash. Pull the wiring connector off the back of the old bulb and set the bulb out of the way.

5. **Scrape any corrosion off the connector, and check its wiring for wear.**

   If the connector is very corroded or the wiring looks bad, the problem with the light may be in the wiring rather than the bulb. You'll know for sure in a minute. . . .

6. **Plug the wiring into the new bulb, and insert the bulb into the receptacle.**

   Be sure to put the new bulb into its locking slots with the unit number at the top. Any small bumps you find on the back edge of the bulb should align with corresponding little depressions in the socket.

7. **Hold the bulb in place while you put back the retaining plate. Then replace whatever trim surrounded the headlight.**

8. **Turn your headlights on. If the bulb is still out and the fuse is okay, have a professional diagnose and fix the problem.**

## Checking headlight alignment

If you managed to goof up your headlight adjusting screws, or if you just aren't sure whether your headlights are properly aligned, you can perform a simple check. When you're driving on a fairly straight road at night, see if your headlights appear to be shining straight ahead and are low enough to illuminate enough of the road in front of you to enable you to stop safely if an obstruction appears. Be sure to check your headlights on both high and low beams.

TIP

You can also have headlights checked and aligned professionally. Auto repair facilities often have headlight-aiming equipment to check and set your headlights in accordance with state laws. Some are certified Motor Vehicle Bureau inspection stations. Note, though, that if you go to a repair facility that does MVB inspections just to see whether your headlights are aimed properly, you'll probably have to pay them for checking the lights and for an inspection certificate *whether or not they have to adjust your lights.*

A cheaper way to check out headlight adjustment is to contact a highway patrol station. The station may have the equipment to check your headlights for you or be able to tell you where their current highway checkpoints are so that you can check the lights yourself. Of course, if the highway patrol finds that your headlights aren't in focus or finds anything wrong with your vehicle's emissions, you'll have to get the problem fixed within a stipulated period or face a fine.

TIP

If you try to fix the alignment problem yourself by turning the adjustment screws on your headlights, go back to the checkpoint afterward for a certificate saying that the lights have been adjusted and meet the proper standards. This certificate is usually part of the price.

## Replacing directional signals

Directional signals are usually easy to replace. On some vehicles, you have to remove the frame from around the signal to reach the bulb. On others, you can access the bulb from the trunk. If any of your directional signals stop flashing or don't flash in synch, or if the directional signal indicators on your dashboard don't flash, the signal lights themselves may not be malfunctioning. You can find information about troubleshooting directional signals in Chapter 20.

Chapter **7**

# The Traditional Fuel System: The Heart and Lungs of Your Car

This chapter introduces you to a traditional fuel system. The fuel system shown in Figure 7-1 stores and delivers fuel to the combustion chambers of the engine so that it can be burned efficiently. Although most fuel systems have some basic components in common, fuel systems do vary. Most modern vehicles employ fuel injectors to get the fuel to the engine, whereas vehicles built before the mid-1980s usually relied on carburetors. Since many of the basic parts covered in this chapter either are common to both systems or do the same jobs as their counterparts on carbureted vehicles did, this chapter is relevant no matter which type of vehicle you have.

ECO-LOGIC

Today, in addition to vehicles that run on gasoline, there are a number of other fuel systems around. If your vehicle has a *diesel engine,* be sure to read Chapter 9, which helps you understand and maintain a diesel engine and covers eco-friendly *biodiesel* and *clean diesel* models. There are *hybrid* vehicles that generate their own power, so they can use electric motors to augment traditional gasoline engines when necessary and can even run on all-electric power at times. Other eco-friendly vehicles run entirely on alternative sources of power such as natural gas

*(NGV)* and hydrogen *(fuel cells).* You can discover more about these modern environmental marvels in Chapter 10.

In this chapter, I trace the flow of fuel from the *fuel tank* to the *engine block,* through the *exhaust system,* and out of your vehicle. When you know what each component does and where to find it, it's easy to see how all the parts work together to provide your vehicle with "GO power."

If a picture is worth a thousand words, actually looking at — and maybe even touching — something is worth a thousand pictures. So, if possible, take this book out to your vehicle, open the hood, and visit with the parts of the fuel system as you read about them.

Whenever you encounter a term set in *this font,* you'll find it defined in the glossary in Appendix A.

# Basic Fuel System Components

Whether your vehicle is more than 20 years old or just 20 days old, has *fuel injectors* or a *carburetor,* it probably has the same basic parts in its fuel system with one exception: On modern vehicles, the fuel system — along with most other systems — is controlled by the *engine control unit (ECU).* The ECU controls the *fuel/air mixture* and other fuel system operations based on inputs from a *mass air flow meter,* a *throttle position sensor,* and an *oxygen sensor.* As you can see in Figure 7-1, it's located under the hood.

## Fuel tank

The fuel tank is a metal or plastic composite container that's usually located under the trunk compartment (refer to Figure 7-1), although some vehicles have some fairly interesting alternative locations for it. If you're not sure where your fuel tank is and you can't find it just by looking under the car, your *owner's manual* or mechanic can show you where it's located.

Inside the fuel tank is a little float that moves up and down as the fuel level in the tank increases or decreases. The float is at its highest when the tank is full. Its position relative to the top of the tank is picked up by a *sensor* that sends an electronic signal from the tank to the *fuel gauge* on your dashboard so that you can tell when you have to buy more fuel. (Chapter 8 tells you why you should always try to keep your fuel tank full.) Although some vehicles run on *diesel fuel* or alternative fuels, the ones I talk about in this chapter are gasoline-powered, so I may refer to fuel as gasoline.

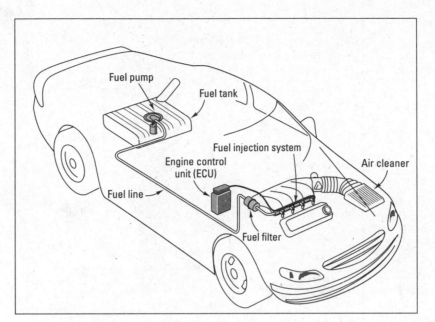

**FIGURE 7-1:**
A fuel system.

## Fuel lines and fuel pump

The *fuel pump* (see Figure 7-2) pumps fuel through the *fuel lines* that run under your vehicle from the fuel tank to the fuel injectors (or to the carburetor on older vehicles). Engines with *fuel injection* use an electric fuel pump that may be located in or near the fuel tank. (On most carbureted vehicles, a mechanical pump is under the hood.)

TECHNICAL
STUFF

If your vehicle is suffering from fuel-system problems, remember that a number of things can be the cause. Most fuel pumps are located inside the *fuel tank* or so far under the vehicle that you can't reach them easily without a hoist or crawling under your vehicle, so have a professional check it for you.

TIP

If your fuel pump *does* need replacing, ask your service facility to replace it with a new one, as their charges for rebuilding yours would probably be more expensive than for just installing a new one. Be sure that they guarantee the pump for at least a year. Hopefully, it will last much longer than that.

## Fuel filters

*Fuel filters* do exactly what their name implies — they filter impurities out of the fuel. As the fuel passes along the fuel line on its way to the fuel injectors (or carburetor), it passes through the principal fuel filter. A small screen inside this filter traps the dirt and rust that would otherwise foul up your injectors.

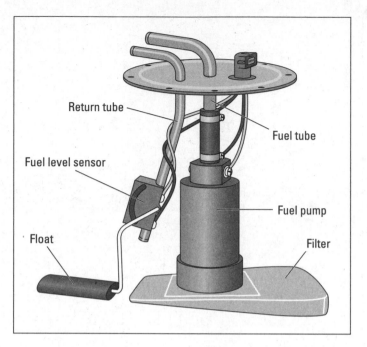

TECHNICAL
STUFF

If you drive around most of the time with a near-empty fuel tank, the water in the air inside the tank may cause rust to form, contaminate your fuel, and foul up your fuel filter and possibly the fuel injectors.

There's usually a filter screen inside the fuel tank, and some vehicles have additional fuel filters inside the fuel pump, between the fuel tank and the fuel pump, and at the entrance to the *throttle* body. Figure 7-3 shows two types of fuel filters.

WARNING

To avoid fouling up your vehicle as well as your vehicle's *warranty*, it's important to change your fuel filter(s) according to the manufacturer's maintenance schedule. Chapter 8 can help you tackle this task.

## Cold air collector box and air filter

Because gasoline engines run on a mixture of air and fuel, the air has to be cleaned before it's mixed with the fuel. The *air filter* removes dirt and dust particles before they can enter the combustion chamber. In the "olden days," most air filters were inside large, round *air cleaners* that sat on top of the *carburetor*. Today's fuel-injected engines have a rectangular air filter inside a *cold air collector box* located near the front of the engine compartment; see Figure 7-4.

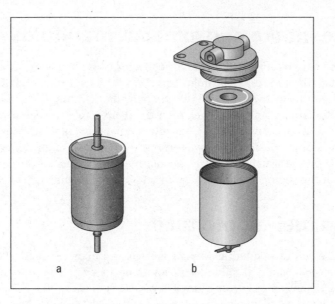

**FIGURE 7-3:**
External (a) and
spin-on (b) fuel
filters.

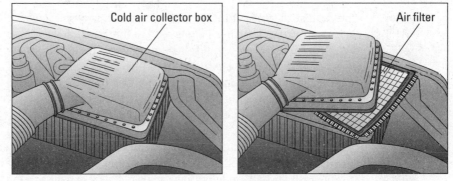

Cold air collector box

Air filter

**FIGURE 7-4:**
The cold air
collector box
houses the air
filter.

To find the rectangular cold air collector box in your vehicle, pop the hood and follow the large *air intake duct* away from your engine. If you have an older vehicle with a large round air cleaner, you can't miss it. If you don't know how to get the hood of your vehicle open, see Chapter 1 or your owner's manual.

REMEMBER

To keep your engine functioning efficiently, be sure to check your air filter regularly as part of the under-the-hood check that I cover in Chapter 2, and replace it at least once a year or every 20,000 miles, whichever comes first. (Replace the air filter more often if you regularly drive in a dusty or sandy area.) Chapter 8 helps you find your air filter, judge whether it needs to be changed, and change it yourself (it's a surprisingly easy job).

## The intake and exhaust manifolds

After being filtered in the cold air collector box, air bound for the engine flows through the air intake manifold. This chamber usually is found near the top of the engine; it holds the air under vacuum and admits it into the combustion chamber with the proper amount of fuel. After the fuel/air mixture is burned in the engine, another set of manifold pipes, called the *exhaust manifold,* carries carbon monoxide and other waste gases away from the engine through the *exhaust system* for disposal. You usually find the exhaust manifold either lower down on the same side of the engine as the intake manifold or on the other side of the *cylinder head.*

## The fuel/air mixture

In case you're wondering why air is such an important fuel system component, it's because liquid gasoline won't ignite on its own. The pressure caused by the rapid expansion of burning gases is what drives the engine. The only way to get gasoline to ignite is to mix it with air — hence the need for the *fuel/air mixture.*

**WARNING**

The explosive nature of fuel and air together is why so many accidents occur with near-empty gasoline cans. People tend to think that an almost-empty can of gasoline is harmless, but it couldn't be more dangerous! Gasoline in liquid form will burn but not explode. An air and gasoline vapor combination is more explosive than TNT! Even a seemingly empty can still contains gasoline vapor, and you need only one part of gasoline to 2,000 parts of air by volume to get a combustible mixture! Any kind of spark can set it off.

**WARNING**

Never carry gasoline in anything but a specialized fuel can, and *keep that can filled up.* What's more, unless you're going far from any source of fuel, don't carry (or store) gasoline at all, and get rid of any old cans you have around. (See the sidebar called "How to dispose of empty gasoline cans safely" in Chapter 1).

# Following Fuel through the Fuel Injectors

Just about every new vehicle is fuel-injected. (The last carbureted vehicles came off the assembly line in 1990.) Although they're more expensive to service than carburetors were, fuel injection systems with computerized *electronic sensing devices* have shown sufficient sensitivity, accuracy, and dependability to repay their cost with better performance, greater fuel economy, cleaner exhaust emissions, and more controllable power. Some of the newest models are reported to be

95 to 100 percent clean-burning! Innovations in design are constantly producing cheaper and more durable systems.

Basically, fuel injection systems inject fuel at precisely the right time and place for it to mix with air and form the fuel/air mixture that drives the engine. This section follows the fuel and air through the fuel injection system to the *cylinders.*

TIP

Fuel injection systems are too difficult to adjust or repair yourself, but if you know how they work, you can communicate with your technician more knowledgeably, which will save you time and money. Besides, it's really interesting!

Today's engines use *electronic fuel injectors* that are controlled by transistors in the ECU known as *injector drivers.* The *ECU* relies on feeds from a variety of *sensors* to tell it the following:

>> How much air is flowing in through the air intake system

>> The pressure of the air in the *intake manifold*

>> The engine *coolant* temperature

>> The engine speed

>> The *throttle* angle

>> The amount of oxygen in the exhaust gases

The ECU's injector driver uses all this information to figure out just how much fuel to spray into each cylinder to mix with the air to get the optimum power to drive the piston.

A *transistor* turns the injector on by completing a *circuit* to allow electric current to flow through a *solenoid* in the injector. A spring-loaded valve in the injector opens, and fuel is injected into the engine cylinders. The amount of time that the ECU keeps the current applied to the injector is known as the *injector pulse width.* The ECU controls the fuel/air mixture by controlling that pulse width, changing the pulse width to make the mixture richer or leaner based on the information it gets from the various sensors.

You can find fuel injectors (see Figure 7-5) in one of two places: Modern *multi-port injection* systems are located in the *intake port* just ahead of the

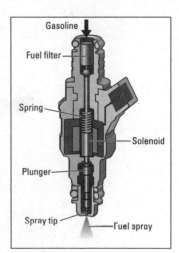

**FIGURE 7-5:**
Anatomy of a fuel injector.

*intake valve.* The earlier *throttle- body fuel injection* systems are located inside the throttle body assembly (surprise!), which is kind of like an electronically controlled carburetor. The following sections explore each of these injection systems in detail.

## Multi-port fuel injection

Most modern vehicles have *multi-port fuel injection* (MFI) with a separate fuel injector for each cylinder. This system mixes the fuel and air together right in the intake port for each engine cylinder just ahead of the intake valve.

Here's how multi-port fuel injection systems work:

**1.** **An electrical *fuel pump* pumps fuel from the *fuel tank* through a *fuel filter* to the *fuel rail assembly,* which carries fuel under pressure to the *fuel injectors* (see Figure 7-6).**

The fuel rail assembly also may contain the ***fuel pressure regulator,*** which maintains proper fuel pressure and meters unused fuel back to the fuel tank. Fuel injectors, one for each cylinder, are attached at one end to the fuel rail and at the other end to the intake port in the engine.

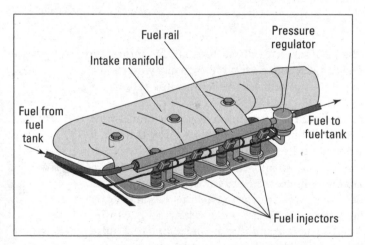

**FIGURE 7-6:** Fuel flows through the fuel rail to the injectors.

**2.** **A whole bunch of sophisticated *sensors* measure a variety of factors and send messages to the *ECU,* which decides how much fuel to inject at any given time.**

These sensors are so perceptive that they even check the weather; how much weight you're carrying in the vehicle; and whether you're starting up, speeding up, slowing down, or idling at a light. This information makes the system respond faster and results in greater fuel economy than older vehicles achieved with throttle-body fuel injection (described in a later section).

3. **The ECU completes the electrical circuit to the injector *solenoid* for the proper *injector pulse width,* and fuel under pressure is injected into the *intake port* just before the *intake valve.***

# Sequential fuel injection

More recent fuel-injected engines feature *sequential fuel injection (SFI)* in which the fuel injectors fire in *sequence* rather than all at once. Because each injector opens individually just before its intake valve opens, the fuel is always sprayed right into an open port and therefore stays in suspension. This type of system is more efficient than a system whose injectors fire simultaneously. (For example, if you have a six-cylinder multi-port fuel-injected engine that's simultaneously fired, three of the six injectors are pulsed together, and then the other three injectors are pulsed.) In addition, emission levels are lower in an SFI system, but the system requires a separate electrical circuit for each injector.

The upside is that using less metal, plastic, and rubber places less strain on the world's dwindling supply of raw materials. It also reduces the amount of energy consumed by production (as well as driving) and the number of disposal facilities required to process all the worn and broken stuff that gets thrown away. So let's hope that the trend continues, wizards and all.

# Gasoline direct injection

The *gasoline direct injection (GDI) system* is relatively new in the United States but is expected to grow more popular as time goes on. It resembles diesel technology (see Chapter 9) but uses gasoline instead of diesel fuel. Instead of being mixed with air to form a *fuel/air mixture* prior to injection, the gasoline is injected directly into each engine cylinder. The *ECU* uses data from various *sensors* to time the injection of the fuel into the cylinder and regulate the resulting fuel/air mixture for maximum efficiency under varying driving conditions.

Although a gasoline direct injection system is currently more expensive to build than a standard engine, it measures fuel so precisely that you get the most bang for the buck. However, to handle its higher emission of *NOx emissions* (nitrogen oxides), the GDI system requires a more costly *catalytic converter* than a standard engine does. Because of the greater fuel efficiency, automakers are currently working on gasoline direct injection systems to reduce their emissions and bring down the cost. As fuel becomes more expensive and the efficiency of these engines increases relative to the costs, they'll become more popular and more widely available.

# IMPROVEMENTS TO FUEL INJECTION SYSTEMS

Two exciting ways that fuel injection systems are being perfected is the replacement of moving parts with stationary ones and solid parts with intangible substances. By reducing the number of mechanical parts, car manufacturers hope to reduce production costs and create devices that are less susceptible to breakdown due to physical stress.

Now, I've been in favor of simplification ever since my mother taught me to always buy the washing machine with the fewest gadgets on the principle that the fewer parts involved, the fewer things there are that can break down. But I keep having this fantasy that if they continue to replace mechanical car parts with miniaturized and computerized equipment, eventually I may lift the hood of my vehicle and find nothing but a little black box! At that point, when things go wrong, I'll probably have to seek the services of a wizard rather than a technician!

## Throttle-body fuel injection

Throttle-body fuel injection (TBI) was the first fuel injection system to become popular as *carburetors* were being phased out. This system is less complicated than the multi-port fuel injection systems found on more recent vehicles (refer to the preceding sections), but it's also less efficient. Instead of using *individual* fuel injectors to pump the fuel into each cylinder, the TBI system mixes the fuel and air together right in the *throttle* assembly of the vehicle. Along the way, *sensors* monitor air flow, throttle position, temperature, and other factors and report back to the **ECU** *(engine control unit)*. You can see the parts of this system in Figure 7-7. Some of these systems use *solenoids* to spray the fuel into the airstream in the throttle through a fuel injector nozzle.

If you have a vehicle with throttle-body fuel injection, here's how it works:

1. An electrical ***fuel pump*** pumps fuel to the throttle body assembly. The throttle body assembly looks similar to a carburetor and houses the fuel injector(s) and a ***fuel pressure regulator.***

2. The fuel pressure regulator maintains proper fuel pressure and meters unused fuel back to the ***fuel tank.***

3. A computer controls one or two fuel injectors mounted in the throttle body assembly. The computer applies electrical current to the injector **solenoid** for the proper duration (called the ***injector pulse width***), and fuel under pressure is then injected and mixed with air as it passes through the throttle on its way to the engine.

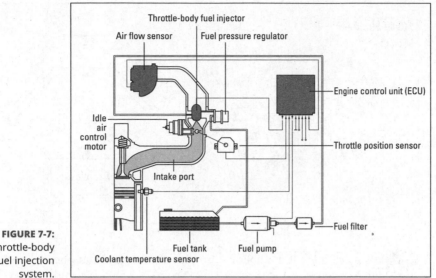

Throttle-body fuel injector

Air flow sensor     Fuel pressure regulator

Engine control unit (ECU)

Idle
air
control
motor

Throttle position sensor

Intake port

Fuel filter

**FIGURE 7-7:**
The throttle-body
fuel injection
system.

Fuel tank     Fuel pump

Coolant temperature sensor

# The Engine Block: Where the Fuel System and Ignition System Meet

Whether accomplished through a fuel injection system or a carburetor, after the air and fuel unite in the form of a vapor and the spark plugs are ready to provide that all-important spark of ignition, all that's needed is a spot for that passionate meeting to take place. The rendezvous occurs in your engine's *cylinders,* and it's truly a triumph of *timing* (as any successful rendezvous must be!).

In this section, I describe the major parts of the engine and explain how they create the power that drives your vehicle.

## Major engine components

Inside the engine are several fascinating parts, which you can see in Figure 7-8.

At the top are the *cylinder heads.* These contain the mechanisms that allow the *valves* to open and close, letting the *fuel/air mixture* into the *cylinders* and allowing the burnt *exhaust gases* to leave. Below the cylinder heads is the *engine block* itself. This piece contains the *cylinders,* which contain the *pistons.*

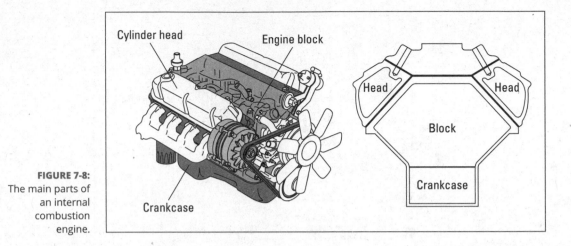

FIGURE 7-8:
The main parts of an internal combustion engine.

So what's a cylinder? It's a hollow iron pipe that's capped at one end and has a *spark plug* inserted into and through that cap so the plug's *electrodes* are available for action (see Figure 7-9).

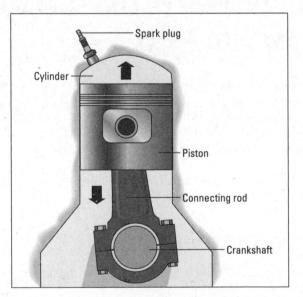

FIGURE 7-9:
Anatomy of a cylinder.

TECHNICAL
STUFF

The cylinders in the engines on vehicles with *rear-wheel drive* often run from the front of the engine back toward the *firewall* at the rear of the engine compartment. On other vehicles, particularly those with *front-wheel drive,* the cylinders in the engine are set sideways, parallel to the wheels. These engines are called *transverse* engines (see Figure 7-10).

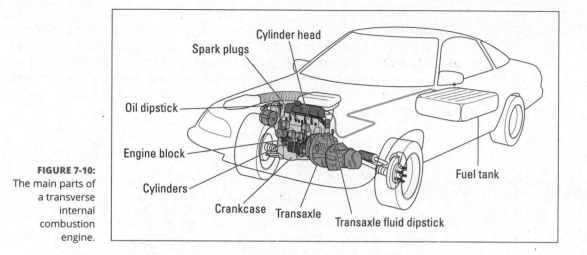

**FIGURE 7-10:** The main parts of a transverse internal combustion engine.

Labels in figure:
Cylinder head
Spark plugs
Oil dipstick
Engine block
Cylinders
Crankcase
Transaxle
Transaxle fluid dipstick
Fuel tank

Engines that have a single row of cylinders are called *in-line engines* (sometimes called *straight* engines). *V-type engines* have two parallel rows of cylinders set on an angle to each other. On *rotary engines* (found on some Mazdas), there's a single large internal chamber inside which a three-lobed, or triangular, rotor revolves. The rotor makes an eccentric or uneven revolution, continually forming smaller chambers in which occur the same *four-stroke power cycle* as in a conventional internal combustion engine (the next section describes the four-stroke power cycle).

**TECHNICAL STUFF**

Each cylinder has a number, determined by the particular engine's *cylinder sequence.* You can find descriptions and illustrations of the cylinder sequence for a variety of engines in Chapter 5.

Inside each cylinder is a metal *piston* that fits snugly against the walls of the cylinder so that nothing can get past it. On the outside of the piston are *piston rings* that ensure a snug fit. The cylinder also has other openings besides the ones for the *spark plug* and the piston. These are for the *intake valves* and the *exhaust valves.*

At the bottom of the engine is the *crankcase,* which houses the *crankshaft* and the *oil pan.* Coolant circulates throughout the engine to keep it cool, and oil circulates to keep the parts moving freely.

Now that you've met the "players," you're ready to get on to the main event in which they play their roles: the fiery meeting of air, fuel, and fire known as the *four-stroke power cycle.*

## The four-stroke power cycle

The piston rides up and down inside the cylinder on a *connecting rod* that attaches to the *crankshaft,* causing the crankshaft to turn. Each movement of the piston is called a *stroke.* Four strokes — down, up, down, up — complete the cycle that creates the power to drive the engine. This process is aptly called the *four-stroke power cycle.* The four-stroke power cycle varies slightly depending on whether your vehicle's engine is a conventional *internal combustion engine* or a *diesel engine.* I cover the conventional internal combustion engine in this section and the power cycle in diesel engines in Chapter 9.

Here's what happens on each stroke of the piston in a conventional internal combustion engine:

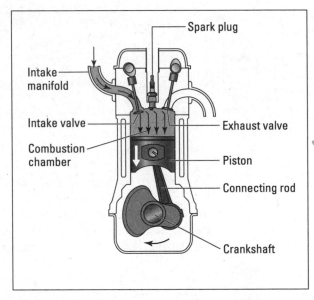

FIGURE 7-11:
The intake stroke.

1. **Intake stroke:** See Figure 7-11. When the piston moves *down,* it creates a vacuum in the top portion of the cylinder (where the piston was at the end of its last upstroke). Air can't get in from the bottom of the cylinder because the rings on the piston seal it off. Then the *intake valves,* conveniently located in the cylinder head, open up and let the ***fuel/air mixture*** into the cylinder. This mixture rushes in to fill the vacuum left by the piston.

2. **Compression stroke:** See Figure 7-12. The piston moves back *up,* compressing the fuel/air mixture into a tiny space between the top of the piston and the top of the cylinder. This space is called the ***combustion chamber*** and also happens to be where the end of the spark plug enters the cylinder. The difference between the total space inside the cylinder and the space inside the combustion chamber is called the ***compression ratio.*** It indicates that the pressure has been raised from normal air pressure of 15 psi (pounds per square inch) to hundreds of psi, which makes the resulting explosion much more intense.

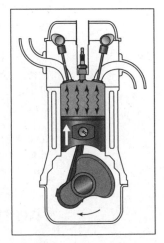

FIGURE 7-12:
The compression stroke.

At this point, the intake valves have closed, so the compressed mixture can't get out. (The intake and exhaust valves create airtight seals to ensure that nothing can get past them when they're closed.)

3. **Power stroke:** See Figure 7-13. The spark plug produces a spark across the **gap** between its **electrodes.** This spark ignites the compressed fuel/air mixture. Then the burning fuel/air mixture ignites, creating intense pressure that forces the piston *down* again. The power that pushed the piston down is transmitted, via the **connecting rod,** to the **crankshaft.** It then travels, via the **drive train,** through the **clutch** or **torque converter,** the **transmission,** the **driveshaft,** the **differential,** and so on to the wheels. (A quick overview of this process appears in Chapter 4.)

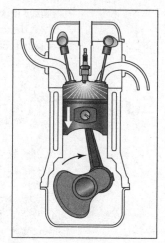

**FIGURE 7-13:**
The power stroke.

4. **Exhaust stroke:** See Figure 7-14. The piston moves *up* again, pushing the burned gases up with it. Then the **exhaust valve** opens and lets the burned gases out into the **exhaust manifold.** From there, the burned gases travel through the **exhaust system** (which includes antipollution devices), through the **muffler,** and out the **tailpipe** into the environment.

The cylinders don't fire all at once. To keep the engine properly balanced with all that action going on, they fire in a particular order called the *firing order.* So while one cylinder is going through the intake stroke, another will be at the compression stroke, and so on. The firing order varies from one engine to

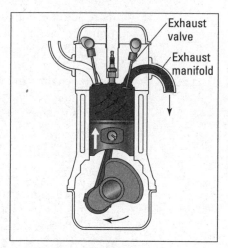

Exhaust valve

Exhaust manifold

**FIGURE 7-14:**
The exhaust stroke.

another, and Chapter 5 has descriptions and illustrations of the firing orders for a variety of engine types.

When you understand the four-stroke power cycle it's easier to see why the diagnostic inspectioins and service required by your warranty are so important. Spark plugs are checked and replaced because, if the spark is insufficient or the timing is off, the result is less power and incompletely burned fuel. Increased air pollution and fuel consumption are high prices to pay for stretching the intervals between spark plug replacements, especially because they're much less frequent than before! Chapters 6 and 8 show you what you can do to help keep your electrical system and fuel system in tune.

# Supercharging with Turbochargers

A *supercharger* is a pump that compresses the intake air and forces it into the cylinders of a gasoline-powered car. Because superchargers are usually belt-driven by the engine (instead of being driven by recycled exhaust gases as a turbocharger is), they consume engine power to increase engine power. Because they're not fuel-efficient, they're generally used only to increase the speed of "high-performance," low-efficiency vehicles. *Supercharging* shouldn't be confused with *turbocharging*.

*Turbocharging* means to use a turbine — powered by the engine's waste gases — to force greater amounts of air into an engine's cylinders. This process produces more power in both diesel and conventional vehicles because they run on a greater volume of air and fuel. The more air the engine can take in, the bigger the bang during the power stroke of the *four-stroke power cycle*. At first, cars were turbocharged to perform better on racetracks, but when automakers began to put smaller engines in larger vehicles to lighten their weight and conserve fuel, turbocharging provided a way to increase the engine's power so that these bigger vehicles wouldn't be sluggish on the road.

Here is how turbocharging works:

1. The hot **exhaust gases** leave the **exhaust manifold,** but instead of going directly through the **exhaust system** and out of the vehicle via the **tailpipe,** they first pass through a *turbine,* which is just a fan that's set in motion by the expanding gases.

2. A shaft connects the fan to a compressor, which blows fresh, filtered air into the cylinders. (On a carbureted vehicle, the compressor takes the fuel/air mixture and blows it into the cylinders.)

3. The excess and used exhaust fumes pass from the turbine to the exhaust system and continue on their way to the tailpipe and out into the air.

The more load on the engine, the hotter and faster the exhaust fumes that turn the turbine. The faster they turn it, the more air the compressor sends to the engine and the more power the engine can produce. This unique way of converting exhaust gas energy into mechanical power has a nice merry-go-round effect.

Sounds simple, doesn't it? Well, usually the first thing an engineer learns is "The simpler, the better," or as the Zen monks put it, "Less is more." (From engineering to philosophy in a couple of paragraphs! Maybe I ought to change the name of this book to *Zen and the Art of Auto Maintenance*.)

ECO-LOGIC

When it came to designing *diesel* cars, the pressing problem was how to change a car with a reputation of being noisy, underpowered, and smoky into a faster, quieter, more-efficient vehicle that could meet the requirements set by the U.S. Environmental Protection Agency (EPA). The results have been heartening indeed. A turbocharger can increase the power of a diesel vehicle by 50 percent while lowering its fuel consumption by 20 to 25 percent! What's more, because the turbine itself is powered by the hot gases that normally would go out of the exhaust pipe, you don't need to provide anything extra to drive it. What a wonderful example of recycling!

Check out Chapter 9 for more about diesels, especially the new environmentally friendly innovations that have turned diesel-driven vehicles from potential causes of cancer into efficient eco-friendly vehicles. The innovations also are turning overburdened garbage dumps into recycling opportunities.

# The Exhaust System

The *exhaust system*, shown in Figure 7-15, is the waste disposal system of your vehicle. When the fuel system brings the fuel and air together in the *cylinders* to drive the vehicle, waste products are formed, and some of them are toxic. This section deals with how the exhaust system works to detoxify or reduce these toxins before they're released into the environment.

ECO-LOGIC

Now that people all over the world are finally aware of how toxic exhaust gases can be for people and how drastically they affect *global warming,* it's really important to understand the system that works to detoxify these pollutants and disburse them as safely as possible.

As the *exhaust gases* pass from the *cylinders* in the engine through the *muffler* to the *tailpipe* at the rear of the vehicle and into the air, *emissions-control* devices — including the *PCV valve,* various *sensors,* a *catalytic converter,* and other components — work to reduce or remove the harmful substances and recycle unburned fuel vapors.

TIP

There's little you can do to maintain or repair most of the parts in the exhaust system except to check and clean your PCV valve and replace it, if necessary; and troubleshoot to see whether your catalytic converter needs to be replaced (Chapter 8 has instructions for both of these tasks). If the converter, the tailpipe, or the muffler needs to be replaced, have the job done by a professional.

The following sections explore each of the major parts of the exhaust system in . . . exhaustive? . . . detail.

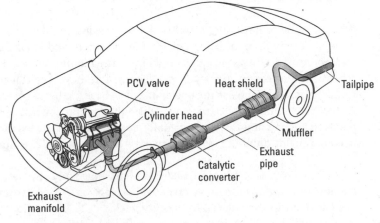

FIGURE 7-15:
The exhaust system.

PCV valve

Heat shield

Tailpipe

Cylinder head

Muffler

Catalytic converter

Exhaust pipe

Exhaust manifold

## The muffler

Exhaust pipes carry what's left of the exhaust gases through a *muffler,* which controls the noise of the escaping gases to the *tailpipe* and out of the vehicle (see Figure 7-16). If it fails, you can get a ticket, probably for disturbing the peace! Besides keeping the noise down, the muffler also has an effect on the pressure required to pass the *exhaust gases* through it, which

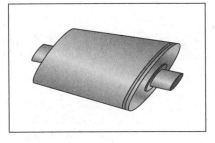

FIGURE 7-16:
The muffler.

creates the "back pressure" that the engine requires to run efficiently and affects the temperature and therefore the efficiency of the *catalytic converter.*

ECO-LOGIC

The next sections take a closer look at two *emissions control devices* that play a major part in cleaning up exhaust gases and have had a major effect on reducing air pollution.

## The PCV valve

The *PCV valve* (shown in Figure 7-17) is part of the *positive crankcase ventilation system,* which reroutes unburned gases, or *blow-by,* from the *crankcase* to the *intake manifold* and back to the engine, where they can be reburned in the *cylinders.* This process cuts the amount of pollution released into the environment. It also increases fuel economy because unburned fuel in the blow-by is consumed the second time around. The PCV valve also extends the life of the engine by reducing the water vapor and acid deposits that contaminate oil and form engine sludge. Figure 7-18 shows you how the PCV valve works.

## The catalytic converter

The catalytic converter (shown in Figure 7-19) is usually attached to the exhaust pipe just after the *exhaust manifold* pipes. It was developed to deal with smog by further reducing the toxic substances in the *exhaust gases* before they can pollute the air. The catalytic converter is basically a cylinder filled with either little ceramic beads or a honeycomb structure coated with minute amounts of expensive metal catalysts that interact with the pollutants:

**FIGURE 7-17:**
A PCV valve.

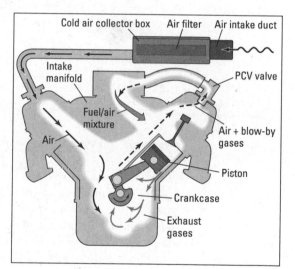

**FIGURE 7-18:**
How a PCV valve works.

>> **Reduction catalysts** (rhodium and palladium) turn the **NOx** (nitrogen oxide) *emissions* to oxygen and nitrogen, which exist in the air we breathe.

>> **Oxidation catalysts** (palladium and platinum) turn carbon monoxide and hydrocarbon into harmless carbon dioxide and water.

ECO-LOGIC

The use of catalytic converters brought about another development that has been of great benefit to the environment. Originally, the lead in gasoline fouled catalytic converters, rendering them less effective and eventually destroying them, so legislation was passed to remove lead from fuel. Because lead is toxic to humans and other animals, we've all benefited greatly from its removal from automotive fuel and its emissions.

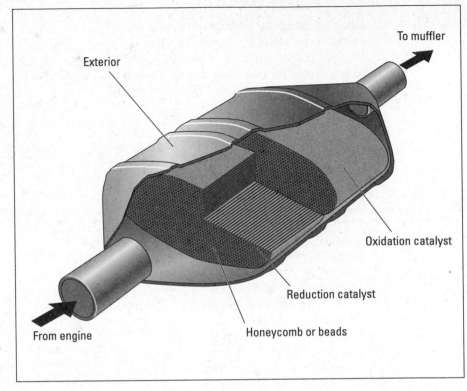

To muffler

Exterior

Oxidation catalyst

Reduction catalyst

From engine

Honeycomb or beads

**FIGURE 7-19:**
Interior and exterior views of a catalytic converter.

## Other emissions control devices

Other emissions control devices include an *exhaust gas recirculation system (EGR)*. An EGR valve on the *intake manifold* allows a small percentage of the *exhaust gases* back into the intake manifold, which lowers the peak combustion temperature in the *combustion chambers* and results in lower *NOx emissions*. Also, oxygen *sensors* tell the *ECU* about excess oxygen in the exhaust gases so that the ECU can correctly control the *fuel/air mixture*. Air injection systems and various other gizmos also help clean up the exhaust before it enters the air.

ECO-LOGIC

Engineers are developing new ways to clean up and reduce automotive emissions every day. All you need to know is that the parts and processes are there, and they're working to keep you healthy. But the healthiest thing you can do is drive the most-efficient vehicle possible, as little as possible! To get more specific, Chapter 9 tells you about new *diesel engines* and fuels that not only burn clean but also can reduce the burden on overflowing garbage dumps. Chapter 10 covers a variety of *hybrid* and *alternatively fueled vehicles* that may inspire you to trade in Old Faithful for a 21st-century set of wheels.

**IN THIS CHAPTER**

» **Checking and replacing fuel and air filters**

» **Checking the fuel pump and servicing the PCV valve**

» **Troubleshooting the catalytic converter**

» **Gauging compression in the engine cylinders**

» **Arming yourself with fuel system knowledge for a trip to the store**

# Chapter **8**

# Keeping Your Fuel System in Tune

Fuel system problems may occur for a variety of reasons. Some remedies, such as replacing a fuel filter, are relatively inexpensive. Others, such as replacing a fuel pump, are costly. Because unethical mechanics often try the more expensive solutions first and work backwards to the cheaper ones, you end up paying for all the time, labor, and parts involved. You can avoid the expense of repairs that don't solve the problem by using the instructions in this chapter to check things out before heading for professional help. If you can do the job yourself, great! If you can't, you will still be able to discuss the less-expensive possible solutions with your service facility and request that they try them first. If these work, they won't waste their time (and your money) on lengthy test drives and diagnostics. At the very least, try to do the simple adjustments and maintenance tasks (such as changing the air filter) yourself. Doing so will cost you little in time and money and may prevent major repair bills. Plus you can brag about doing it yourself!

If your vehicle has *fuel injection, air* and *fuel filters,* and *PCV valves,* they should be checked and replaced, if necessary, at the intervals specified in your owner's manual, or you may risk voiding your *warranty.* Otherwise, your fuel system should just hum along for years. If it breaks down, don't monkey with it; take it to a professional for repairs. If your vehicle has a *carburetor,* it requires periodic tune-ups to keep it operating at peak efficiency. Regardless of what kind of fuel system your vehicle has, it requires the basic maintenance (such as changing air and fuel filters and *PCV valves*) mentioned in this chapter. All the work in this chapter is under-the-hood stuff, so you don't need to jack up your vehicle, and you probably don't have to indulge in any acrobatics to reach the scene of the action.

TIP

Before you undertake any of the work in this chapter, be sure to read (or reread) Chapter 7. If you understand *where* the part you're dealing with fits into the system and *what* it does, you'll have a clearer idea of *why* the work you're doing is necessary and *how* it needs to be accomplished. This knowledge not only makes the job easier and more pleasant, but it also helps you locate each part and understand how it functions. Also check out the coverage of safety, buying parts, and taking things apart and putting them together again in Chapter 1. Believe me, the aggravation you can prevent with just a little preparation is well worth the time!

TECHNICAL
STUFF

If your vehicle isn't due for regular maintenance and it isn't starting right up in the morning, starts conking out at stoplights or running roughly, or is producing readings that indicate problems on the electronic diagnostic machine at your repair shop, it may be a good idea to try the work outlined in this chapter before opting for major surgery. Even if it turns out that the problem calls for more drastic measures, you'll still have taken care of maintenance that would have been necessary before too long.

REMEMBER

Whenever you encounter a term set in *this font,* you'll find it defined in the glossary in Appendix A.

# Maintaining Your Air Filter

On most modern vehicles, the *air filter* is under the hood inside a rectangular *cold air collector box* that's located up near the front of the engine compartment. Figure 8-1 shows you what it looks like. (Other vehicles, including those with carburetors, have big round metal *air cleaners* that are hard to miss.)

As you can see in Figure 8-1, the air cleaner has a large *air inlet duct* (also called the *air intake hose*) connected to it. Loosen the hose clamp that seals it to the box, and then undo all the screws, clamps, or wing nuts that hold the lid of the box in place. Put the fasteners you removed somewhere safe so that they don't roll off into oblivion. Open the lid of the box and . . . voila! . . . you should find the air filter inside (see Figure 8-1). Lift out the old filter (it isn't fastened down) and take a look at it.

Some older vehicles have permanent air filters, and some off-road vehicles have more-complex filters with wet and dry elements. Clean and replace these according to the instructions in your *owner's manual.* If you don't find a pleated paper, cotton, or gauze filter inside your air cleaner, you probably have one of these alternatives.

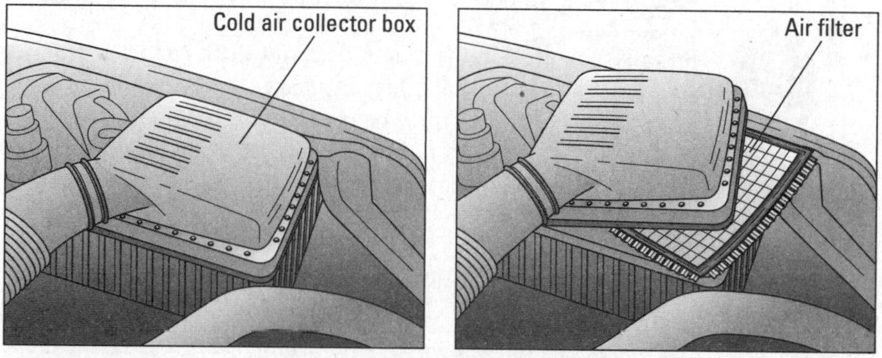

Cold air collector box

Air filter

**FIGURE 8-1:** The cold air collector box houses the air filter.

## Checking and cleaning your air filter and cold air collector box

To figure out whether your air filter needs to be replaced, just hold it up to the sun or to a strong light. Can you see the light streaming through it? If not, try dropping it *lightly,* bottom side down, on a hard surface. Doing so should jar some dirt loose. If the filter is still too dirty to see through after you've dropped it a few times and it looks as though it just needs a bit of cleaning, you can try to clean it following the directions below. If that doesn't work, you need a new one.

To clean a pleated air filter either use an air hose to blow the dirt off (not *through*) it or a vacuum to suck it out. For both methods, handle the filter gently to avoid crushing the pleats. Keep the nozzle of the air hose or vacuum cleaner several inches away from the filter — don't jam it up against it. And if you're using compressed air, do it away from the vehicle to avoid blowing the dirt around under the hood.

If the interior of the box is fouled with dust or sand, before you clean the box paste some duct tape over the open end of the air intake hose so that the dirt can't get in. Then either use the compressed air hose to blow the dirt out of the box or the vacuum cleaner to suck it out.

TIP

I prefer a "hand vac" for this job. You don't have to buy a compressed air gun or schlep the car to a service station to use theirs (and some of them are now *charging* for the air!). Also, with a hand vac, you run less risk of blowing the dirty air out of the cold air collector box and into something else. I keep a battery-powered hand vac in the trunk of my car to do stuff like this as well as to get the dirt off the floor mats and to clean the upholstery.

## Buying and replacing an air filter

REMEMBER

Because the air filter extracts dirt and dust particles from the air, you should change it at least once a year or every 20,000 miles, whichever comes first — unless yours gets very dirty before then. If you do most of your driving in a dusty or sandy area, you may need to replace your air filter every 5,000 miles or less. If a road trip takes you to such an area, it's a good idea to check the air filter right after you return.

When buying an air filter, keep the following points in mind:

>> **Look for well-known, quality-brand filters, especially if you're buying at discount stores.** Unknown brands sell for very little, but they aren't always of good quality, and if your air filter lets a lot of junk get into your fuel system, you may find that the cheap filter is very costly in the long run.

>> **If you need help determining which air filter you need, go to your local auto supply store or to the parts department at your dealership.** Give them your vehicle's make, model, and year, and they'll select the right part number for your vehicle.

REMEMBER

When you have the correct part number for the filter, enter it in the *Specifications Record* in Appendix B.

>> **To save yourself a trip back to the auto supply store, take the time to open your cold air collector box and check the filter you purchase against your current filter while you're still in the store parking lot.**

WARNING

Make sure that the filter you get matches your old filter in size and shape. It should look exactly like the old one. If it doesn't, you've bought the wrong filter. If the new filter looks right, replace the old filter with the new one, making sure that the rubber rim is facing up to create a seal between the filter and the box.

When the cleaned filter — or the new one — is in place, put the lid back on the box and replace all the stuff that held it on. Then, remove the duct tape from the open end of the air intake hose and use the hose clamp to reattach it to the box. Done!

# Replacing a Fuel Filter

Unless your vehicle suddenly starts to hesitate or run roughly, *fuel filters* on modern fuel-injected vehicles only need to be checked — and replaced, if necessary — during the tune-up inspections specified in your owner's manual. The likelihood of a fuel filter malfunctioning is significantly greater if you tend to ride around with an almost-empty *fuel tank.* (See the sidebar "Why you should keep the fuel tank full" to find out why this is a bad idea.)

If your vehicle starts to run roughly as soon as you fill it up with gas, contaminants in the fuel may have plugged up the filter. In that case, it should be replaced immediately. To decide whether you can do this job yourself, you need to know what type of fuel filter your vehicle has and whether you can tackle the job. Check your owner's manual or a *service manual* for your vehicle's make, model, and year to find the filter and see what's involved in changing it.

## WHY YOU SHOULD KEEP THE FUEL TANK FULL

Because the space in the fuel tank above the fuel level is filled with air, and because air contains quite a bit of water vapor, the water in the air tends to condense on the sides of the fuel tank and elsewhere on cool mornings. This water vapor can rust the insides of a metal fuel tank, it can mix with the fuel in any tank — metal or plastic — and it can act in a variety of pesky ways to keep your vehicle from operating efficiently. If you keep your fuel tank well-filled, there's less room for air and therefore less water vapor hanging around. This is an excellent reason for *not* driving around until your fuel gauge reads "Empty."

Another reason for making those extra trips to the gas station is that the rust formed by the water vapor in the air tends to sink to the bottom of the fuel tank. These sediments can do no harm as long as they're happily sloshing around in the bottom of the tank. But if you let the fuel level in the tank get too low, the fuel fed to your engine could be like the last bit of coffee in the bottom of the pot — full of sediment that tends to stick in the throat. Some fuel tanks have filters to prevent this junk from getting through to the engine, but the filters can get choked up if you consistently drive on an empty tank.

## Deciding whether to change a fuel filter yourself

Changing the filter on a fuel-injected vehicle can be tricky. On fuel-injected vehicles, you need to disable the *fuel pump* to relieve the pressure on the *fuel lines,* which may be secured to the filter with clamps, threaded fittings, or special quick-connect fittings. Lines with threaded fittings require a special flare-nut line wrench. Lines with special quick-connect fittings may require special tools to disconnect them. Ask the clerk at an auto parts store or the service department at your dealership which type of filter your vehicle has. If doing this infrequent job requires purchasing special tools, it's probably cheaper to have it done by a technician. If not, the first thing you need to do is find the filter.

## Locating the fuel filter

Your owner's manual should show you where your fuel filter is and whether there's more than one on your vehicle. If it doesn't, ask someone in the service department at your dealership or consult a *service manual* for your vehicle's make, model, and year. (Although it's a good idea to own one, you can usually find these manuals at your local library.)

If your engine has *fuel-injection,* your fuel filter is located somewhere in the high-pressure *fuel line,* either under the vehicle near the *fuel tank* (see Figure 8-2) or under the hood in the fuel line near the engine (see Figure 8-3).

Some vehicles also have a fuel filter in the *fuel pump* as well as a filter screen inside the *fuel tank.* If they get blocked up, only a professional should deal with them.

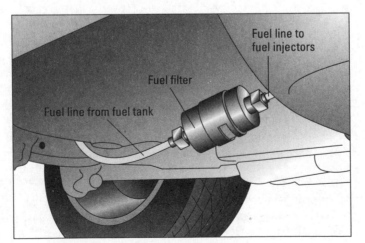

Fuel line to fuel injectors

Fuel filter

Fuel line from fuel tank

**FIGURE 8-2:**
A fuel filter located under the vehicle near the fuel tank.

**TIP**

On some vehicles, the fuel filter is found anywhere in the fuel line from the fuel tank to the fuel injectors and is held in place by metal clamps on either side of it. Some fuel filters on fuel-injected engines require special tools to disconnect the fuel lines in order to get to the filters.

**FIGURE 8-3:**
A fuel filter in the fuel line under the hood.

**WARNING**

Don't use a work light with an incandescent bulb when changing a fuel filter. Fuel that drips on the bulb can cause it to break and start a fire. Use a flashlight if you need to shed some light on the subject.

## Replacing a fuel filter

Here are step-by-step instructions for changing a fuel filter. Before you get started, read them carefully and make sure that you want to do this job yourself.

1. **Relieve the pressure in the fuel line before disconnecting it. To do so, you have to disable the electric fuel pump *before* you start the engine.**

   To disable the fuel pump, do the following:

   1. With the engine off, remove the fuel pump *fuse* from the fuse box (your owner's manual should show you where it is), following the instructions in Chapter 6.

   2. Make sure that the *parking brake* is on and that the vehicle is in Park or Neutral, and then start the engine. It won't run very long after you start it up, but the pressure in the fuel lines will be reduced.

   3. Turn off the engine. With the fuel pump disabled, you're ready to disconnect the fuel lines from the filter.

2. **Look at the old filter and the new one before disconnecting anything.**

   You should see an arrow stamped on both filters that shows in which direction the fuel flows through it. If the new one doesn't have an arrow on it, look to see in what direction the old filter is installed so that you can tell which end of the new filter goes where.

3. **Remove whatever is holding the old filter in place.**

4. **Put the new filter on with the arrow facing toward the engine or in the same position as the old one was.**

5. **Replace whatever holds the filter in place, and make sure it's secure.**

6. **Replace the fuse for the fuel pump in the fuse box.**

7. **Make sure that the parking brake is on and that the vehicle is in Park or Neutral, and then start the engine and check for leaks around the filter.**

## Replacing an insert in a fuel filter

If your vehicle has a fuel filter with an insert that can be replaced, follow Step 1 in the previous section to disable the fuel pump. Then open the cap on the filter, lift out the old insert, and drop in the new one facing in the same direction as the old one was (see Figure 8-4). Be sure to replace the cap securely. Then replace the fuse for the fuel pump, check to be sure the vehicle is in Neutral or Park with the parking brake on, start the engine, and check the filter for leaks.

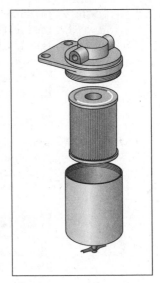

**FIGURE 8-4:**
Replacing an insert in a fuel filter that has one.

# Servicing the PCV Valve

The *PCV valve* (positive crankcase ventilation valve) is a vital part of the *emissions control system* on most vehicles. Chapter 7 tells you all about both the valve and the rest of the emissions control system.

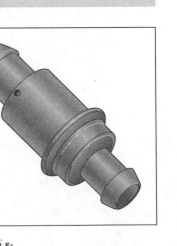

**FIGURE 8-5:**
A PCV valve.

Not every vehicle has a PCV valve, but most do. If yours has one, and if your engine has been *idling* roughly or a *malfunction indicator light* goes on, check the PCV valve (shown in Figure 8-5) to make sure that it isn't clogged with *sludge* from the contaminants in the exhaust fumes or stuck in the wide-open position.

Car manufacturers suggest that PCV valves be cleaned or replaced after somewhere between 20,000 to 50,000 miles of driving. Consult your owner's manual to see where the PCV valve is located on your vehicle and what the recommended service intervals are. The valve is usually replaced during scheduled *tune-ups,* but depending on its type and location, you may be able to check, clean, and replace it yourself. This section has instructions for doing all the jobs.

## Locating the PCV valve

The PCV valve is usually plugged into a rubber grommet in the *valve* cover (see Figure 8-6), although it may be located on or near the *intake manifold* (see Figures 8-6 and 8-7). A hose leading to the PCV valve is often kept in place by a clamp. Sometimes there's a little L-shaped housing on the end of the hose that covers the end of the valve.

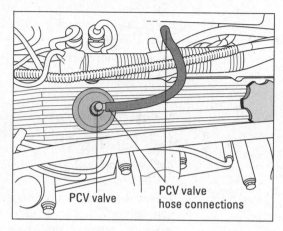

PCV valve

PCV valve hose connections

**FIGURE 8-6:**
A PCV valve located in the valve cover.

## Checking the PCV valve

TIP

There are several ways to check whether your *PCV valve* is functioning properly. Pick the one that seems easiest for you (the engine should be *idling* no matter which method you choose):

>> **Method 1:** Following the instructions in the next section, remove the PCV valve from the *valve cover* with the hose still attached. Then place your finger over the open end of the hose (see Figure 8-8). If the valve's working well, you will feel strong suction. Try shaking the valve. If it's unobstructed, it should rattle. If it's fouled, the rattle will be indistinct or non-existent.

>> **Method 2:** Remove the cap from the *oil filler hole* on the valve cover and place a stiff piece of paper over the opening. If your PCV valve is working properly, the paper should be sucked against the hole within seconds.

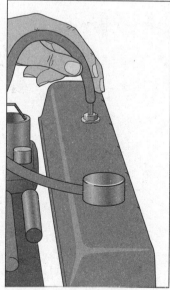

**FIGURE 8-7:**
A PVC valve located on the valve cover, with the hose that leads to it removed.

If the valve doesn't seem to be working properly, before you go to the trouble to replace it, try cleaning it to see if that makes a difference (see the later section that covers cleaning the valve). If that doesn't work, replace it with a new valve (following the instructions in the next section). The good news is a PCV valve isn't terribly expensive.

## Removing and replacing the PCV valve

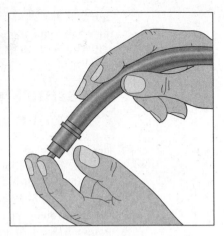

**FIGURE 8-8:**
One way to check your PCV valve.

Follow these instructions to remove your vehicle's PCV valve in order to check, clean, or replace it with a new one:

1. **Locate the PCV valve and loosen the hose clamp if there is one, or pull the little L-shaped housing off the end of the valve.**

2. **Remove the valve.**

   Some PCV valves are held in place with a rubber grommet and can just be pulled free. Others are threaded into place. If you can't unscrew the valve by hand, try to grasp its base with the open end of a combination wrench or a small crescent wrench. (See the "Wrenches" section in Chapter 3 for more on these tools.)

TIP

3. **While you have the PCV valve off, check the hose and the hose clamps or grommet. (You don't want to have to make two trips to the auto parts store!)**

   Remove the hose and blow through it. If the hose is dry, brittle, soft, spongy, or full of sludge or hard deposits, you should replace it. If the clamps are rusty or the grommet looks deteriorated, you should replace them, too. In Chapter 12, you find out about the various types of hose clamps available and which kind you should buy for your vehicle.

4. **If the new valve screws into place, do this by hand to avoid stripping the threads in the valve cover.**

WARNING

   Make sure that the valve is seated securely (it should stick just a little when you try to unscrew it again), but don't over-tighten it!

5. **Reconnect the hose to the PCV valve.**

6. **Start the engine, and check around the PCV valve for leaks.**

## Cleaning the PCV valve

If your vehicle's PCV valve isn't working, you can clean it yourself by immersing it in carburetor cleaner or solvent your auto supply store deems suitable. There should be no gummy deposits or discoloration on a clean valve. If your PCV valve must be replaced, buy a new one, remove the old valve, and insert the new one in its place (refer to the previous section for instructions on replacement).

# Troubleshooting Catalytic Converters

The *catalytic converter* is a very important part of the *emissions control system* on your vehicle. (Chapter 7 tells you what this part looks like and how it works.) It's usually good for the life of a vehicle, but occasionally it does fail. The best thing you can do is be alert for signs of trouble and head for a service facility if you suspect that the catalytic converter is malfunctioning. Technicians will put your vehicle on an electronic diagnostic machine to locate the source of the problem, possibly remove the oxygen *sensor* from the exhaust manifold or exhaust pipe ahead of the catalytic converter to see if that changes things, and replace the catalytic converter, if necessary.

TIP

Here are five ways to tell that something may be wrong with your catalytic converter:

>> Your vehicle's fuel efficiency suddenly drops.

>> Your vehicle doesn't accelerate when you step on the gas pedal.

>> Your vehicle may refuse to start.

>> Your vehicle fails an emissions test.

>> The *MIL* or Check Engine light comes on.

The most common cause of failure in a catalytic converter in an older car is that it becomes so clogged that the *exhaust gases* can't get through it to the muffler and out of the car. (If air can't get out the rear of the vehicle, it can't come in the front end, so the engine dies because no air is coming in to form the *fuel/air mixture.*)

Every car sold in the U.S. since 1996 has had an OBD (On-Board Diagnostic) II system that tests the catalytic converter (among many other things). If the unit allows too much pollution to escape from the tailpipe, it illuminates the *MIL* and produces a trouble code that can be read by a technician with what's called a "scan tool."

The catalytic converter is sensitive to changes in the contents and temperature of the exhaust gases, so another possible cause for failure is if the *cylinder head gasket* is damaged, allowing oil or *coolant* to get into the combustion chamber and be burned in the *cylinders.* Also, if your *ignition system* isn't operating properly, unburned fuel in the exhaust gases can cause the catalytic converter to wear out or break down. This is another good reason for going for tune-ups at specified intervals!

**REMEMBER**

It's against the law in many states to remove a catalytic converter and run a vehicle without one.

**WARNING**

Because the catalytic converter can become extremely hot, it's important not to park your vehicle over a bed of dry grass or dry leaves, which could catch fire and destroy not only your vehicle but also the surrounding area!

# Checking the Compression in the Cylinders

If your vehicle has been running roughly or seems to be losing power, it's possible that there's a lack of pressure in one or more of the *cylinders.* Without enough pressure, the *fuel/air mixture* doesn't ignite efficiently. If one or more cylinders has a good deal less pressure than the others, the engine doesn't run evenly.

**TECHNICAL STUFF**

So why wouldn't there be enough pressure? Because something is letting the pressure escape. Where can it go? Basically, three places: either out through one of the *valve* openings (because the valve is improperly adjusted or so worn that it doesn't close properly) or down past the *rings* on the *piston* or through a blown *head gasket.* These rings prevent the pressure at the top of a cylinder from escaping and the oil that lubricates the engine from entering a cylinder. When the rings get worn, oil gets in and pressure gets out.

To determine whether pressure's escaping from the engine, you need to check the compression in the cylinders. For this job, you need a *compression gauge* (see Figure 8-9). This device tests the amount of pressure that the piston exerts on the fuel/air mixture before the *spark plug* fires the mixture. Your compression gauge can tell you whether one or more of your cylinders isn't firing efficiently and whether your rings or valves are worn or out of adjustment. These gauges don't cost much, and they're quick and easy to use. Some gauges screw into the spark plug opening, and others have to be held in place.

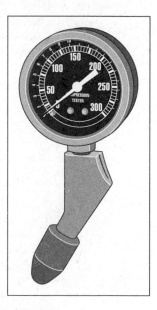

**FIGURE 8-9:**
A compression gauge.

## POOR MAINTENANCE RESULTS IN POOR PERFORMANCE

**WARNING**

Poor maintenance can cause the rings and cylinder walls to become thinner with wear, creating a gap between them that allows gases to bypass the rings. This reduces *compression* in the cylinders and, as you know from the section on the *four-stroke power cycle* in Chap-ter 7, you don't get as big a bang for your buck, so your vehicle loses power. Piston rings can be replaced, but it's an expensive job. Before you allow anyone to undertake a "ring job," check the compression to see whether your car really needs it and be sure that the vehicle's *blue book* value warrants such a costly investment. You may save money in the long run by trading in the old "fuel hog" for a more efficient vehicle.

**TIP**

Checking compression is easier if you have someone to assist you, especially if your gauge needs to be held in place (see Figure 8-10).

**WARNING**

If your engine is covered by a shield, carefully remove any dust on the surface of the shield before you remove it. If removing the shield involves removing other parts that may be damaged in the process, have a professional check the com pression for you.

Here's how to use a compression gauge:

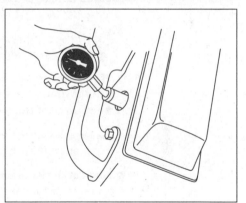

**FIGURE 8-10:**
Checking compression.

1. Unless you buy or borrow a remote starter switch, have someone sit in the driver's seat with the engine off, the gearshift in Park or Neutral, and the parking brake on.

2. The next step depends on the type of distributor you have:

   - **On vehicles with distributors:** Pull the big wire that leads to the coil from the center of the *distributor cap,* and lean the metal connector against an unpainted metal surface *as far away from the spark plugs as possible.*

   - **On vehicles with distributorless ignitions:** Disconnect the electrical connector at the *ignition control module.* If you're not sure what to disconnect, ask a mechanic.

**3.** For safety's sake, disable the fuel injection system so that gasoline mist won't spray out of the spark plug holes and possibly ignite. Remove the *fuse* labeled "Fuel Pump"; then start the car and let it run until it stalls from lack of gasoline. If you can't find the right fuse and you want to do a compression test anyway, be especially careful.

**4.** Before you remove them, label the boots that connect each spark plug wire and each spark plug so that you can remember which plug each boot was attached to.

If you get the plug wires mixed up, you can really screw up your engine.

**5.** Remove all the spark plugs and lay them down in a clean place.

Keep the labeled plugs in order to insure that you return each one to its original cylinder when the time comes.

**6.** If you have a remote starter switch, connect one clip to the battery's positive or "plus" terminal, and the other to small terminal of the *starter solenoid*.

**7.** Insert the compression gauge into the hole in the engine where the first spark plug screwed into the cylinder (refer to Figure 8-10).

**8.** If you *don't* have a remote starter switch, have a friend turn on the ignition until the engine cranks over about six times. Otherwise, press the button of the remote starter switch.

Be sure to keep the gauge plug firmly inserted while the engine is cranking. (The car won't run because the engine has been disabled.)

**9.** Look at the gauge and write down the reading, which will be in *psi* (pounds per square inch). Then reset the gauge.

**10.** Repeat Steps 6 through 8 for each of the other cylinders and don't forget to reset the gauge and crank the engine each time.

**11.** After you've tested each cylinder, look at the readings.

The highest and lowest shouldn't vary by more than 15 percent. If one or more of the cylinders reads well below the rest, use a trigger-type oil can to send a good squirt of motor oil down the spark plug opening, and retest the compression of that cylinder with the gauge. If the reading is the same, the **valves** either are worn (and letting pressure escape) or are out of adjustment. If the reading rises dramatically after you insert the oil, you probably need new **rings** on the **piston** in that cylinder. If the pressure recorded by the gauges is less than 100 psi, the cylinder definitely isn't mechanically sound.

**TECHNICAL STUFF**

After you know what's wrong, you have to decide whether the problem is worth correcting. If your vehicle was on its way out anyway, it's time to get rid of it. If it's otherwise in good shape, you may want to have the engine **rebuilt** or replaced with a new or **remanufactured** one.

**WARNING**

**12. Replace each spark plug in the cylinder it came from.**

Make sure that the ignition is off before you reconnect the spark plug wires, and be sure to put the correct spark plug wire boot back on each plug. Screw the plugs in by hand to avoid damaging the threads in the aluminum valve cover.

If the "Check Engine" warning light comes on after you perform a compression test and doesn't disappear in a couple of days, have it reset at the dealership.

# What to Do When All Else Fails

If you try all the fixes that I cover in this chapter and your vehicle still isn't *idling* properly, isn't starting up in the morning without a hassle, or is hesitating or stalling at corners or when you accelerate sharply, then you need extra help. *But you don't have to seek help like a lamb being led to the slaughter!*

**TIP**

If you want to drive into a service facility like someone who knows the score and is prepared to judge intelligently whether the proposed remedies are necessary, here's what to do:

**1.** **Ask the people at your service facility whether they intend to test your *ignition system* in case that's the culprit.**

**2.** **Ask whether they intend to test your *exhaust gases* to see whether you're running on a *fuel/air mixture* that's too lean or too rich or whether your *catalytic converter* may be at fault.**

**TECHNICAL STUFF**

Notice that I don't say "tell them" because if you do and the work turns out not to have been necessary, you'll get charged for it anyway. Just suggest that these *may* be the culprits to impress them with the fact that you're an informed customer (and no longer a dummy . . .).

**3.** **After they identify the problem, if the suggested remedy is costly or seems overly drastic, get a second opinion at another service facility.**

**ECO-LOGIC**

Even if your vehicle has a traditional *internal combustion engine,* you may want to brush up on newer and more fuel-efficient alternatives that await you when it's time to buy a new one. Chapters 9 and 10 tell you all about vehicles equipped with *diesel engines* and *alternative fuel* systems.

IN THIS CHAPTER

» Weighing the advantages and disadvantages of diesel-powered vehicles

» Exploring diesel fuel, electrical, and exhaust systems

» Troubleshooting and maintaining diesel engines

» Starting a diesel when it's cold outside

» Identifying a good diesel mechanic

Chapter **9**

# Diesels For Dummies

Think of this chapter as a mini-version of Auto Repair For Dummies devoted entirely to diesel-powered vehicles. It explores the new generation of clean diesel vehicles and explains how diesel engines work. It also provides instruc-tions for maintaining and troubleshooting diesel-powered vehicles and for finding a good diesel mechanic when your best efforts just aren't enough.

Whenever you encounter a term set in *this font*, you'll find it defined in the glossary in Appendix A.

REMEMBER

## Clean Diesels: Nontoxic Newcomers

Diesel-powered vehicles are popular in the large part of the world where gasoline is very expensive or almost unavailable. In the United States and Canada, up until recently diesel engines were found mainly in heavy equipment, large trucks, buses, heavy-duty pickup trucks, and boats. Diesel-powered passenger vehicles existed, but they had a reputation for being noisy, underpowered, smelly, and carcinogenic. For a short period in the 1980s people overlooked those negatives when fuel shortages made diesel-powered vehicles popular because they got 25 percent more miles per gallon than gasoline engines and *diesel fuel* was less expensive than gasoline. They soon fell out of favor because major carmakers dropped diesel engines into vehicles that weren't equipped to withstand the higher stress these engines imposed.

ECO-LOGIC

The good news is that growing concern about the environment and the disturbing news that emissions from high-sulfur diesel oil were contributing not only to air pollution and *global warming* but to cancer as well produced legislation that accelerated technological breakthroughs in diesel mechanics. The result is a new generation of clean diesel vehicles (see Figure 9-1) that not only perform efficiently but also have the potential to recycle waste products into clean-burning sources of energy. U.S. federal law mandated significantly lower emissions on diesel engines nationwide by late 2006, and modern federal standards have significantly reduced the levels of sulfur in diesel fuel.

As fuel prices rise and nations compete (sometimes violently) for dwindling sources of oil, efficiency and power are excellent reasons for replacing your gas-guzzler with a vehicle that saves you money because it goes farther on less fuel and gives you the satisfaction of knowing that you're doing your bit to protect the environment.

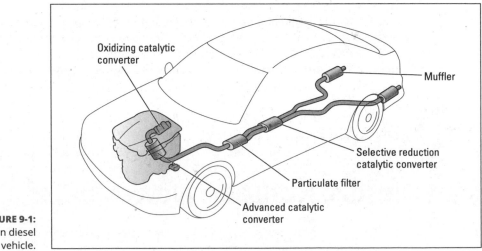

Oxidizing catalytic converter

Muffler

Selective reduction catalytic converter

Particulate filter

Advanced catalytic converter

**FIGURE 9-1:** A clean diesel vehicle.

# The Pros and Cons of Diesels

If you're considering buying a new set of wheels, take a good look at this chapter on the new clean diesels as well as the *alternatively fueled vehicles* that I cover in Chapter 10 before you decide what to buy. This section helps you weigh the advantages and disadvantages of diesel-powered vehicles.

**TECHNICAL STUFF**

To help you accurately compare diesel vehicles with traditional gasoline-powered and alternatively fueled vehicles, here are some commonly held positive and negative beliefs about diesels, plus some facts to consider:

**PRO:** Diesels get great mileage. This is true; they typically deliver 25 to 30 percent better fuel economy than similarly performing gasoline engines. Diesels also can deliver as much or more fuel economy than traditional gasoline-electric *hybrids,* depending on the models involved and whatever rapidly developing automotive technology achieves.

**CON:** Although diesel fuel used to be cheaper than gasoline, it now often costs the same amount or more. Diesel fuel is also used for commercial trucks, home and industrial generators, and heating oil, so as demand for diesel passenger vehicles grows, the price of diesel fuel is likely to continue to rise because of competition from those other users.

*BUT:* Even if the price goes up, diesel fuel would have to be 25 to 30 percent more expensive than gas to erase the cost advantage of a diesel engine's greater fuel efficiency.

**PRO:** Diesel fuel is one of the most efficient and energy dense fuels available today. Because it contains more usable energy than gasoline, it delivers better fuel economy.

**CON:** Although diesel fuel is considered more efficient because it converts heat into energy rather than sending the heat out the *tailpipe* as gas-powered vehicles do, it doesn't result in flashy high-speed performance. In some ways, a gasoline-powered engine is like a racehorse — high-strung, fiery, and fast — whereas a diesel engine is more like a workhorse — slower, stronger, and more enduring.

*BUT:* Because of the way it burns fuel, a diesel engine provides far more *torque* to the *driveshaft* than does a gasoline engine. As a result, most modern diesel passenger cars are much faster from a standing start than their gas-powered counterparts. Diesels with *manual transmissions* usually don't have to be *downshifted* to easily pass other vehicles on the highway, and although they don't reach the highest speeds of gasoline-powered cars, many diesels still can cruise quite handily at 100 miles per hour or more (providing you can find a place to do that legally!).

What's more, diesel-powered trucks, SUVs, and cars also can out-tow gas-powered vehicles while still delivering that improved fuel economy.

**PRO:** Diesels have no *spark plugs* or *distributors.* Therefore, they never need ignition *tune-ups.*

**CON:** Diesels still need regular maintenance to keep them running. You have to change the oil and the *air, oil,* and *fuel filters.* Cleaner diesel fuels no longer require you to *bleed* excess water out of the system, but many vehicles still have water separators that need to be emptied manually.

**PRO:** Diesel engines are built more ruggedly to withstand the rigors of higher *compression.* Consequently, they usually go much longer than gas-powered vehicles before they require major repairs. Mercedes-Benz holds the longevity record with several vehicles clocking more than 900,000 miles on their original engines! You may not want to hang onto the same vehicle for 900,000 miles, but longevity and dependability like that can sure help with trade-in and resale values.

**CON:** If you neglect the maintenance and the *fuel injection* system breaks down, you may have to pay a diesel mechanic more money to get things unsnaggled than you would to repair a gasoline system because diesel engines are more technologically advanced.

*BUT:* All types of vehicles need maintenance, and the increasing complexity of both traditional and alternative vehicles may require repair by specialized technicians that work at higher rates than the mechanics at your neighborhood garage.

Diesel technology is constantly being improved. Government pressure to produce low-emission diesel engines for passenger vehicles, trucks, buses, and farm and construction equipment has resulted not only in low-sulfur diesel fuels but also specialized *catalytic converters,* advanced filters, and other devices to cut down or destroy toxic emissions. There are also dual-fuel engines that run on natural gas but can switch to diesel if the gas supply runs out. To reduce dependency on dwindling supplies of petroleum, *biodiesel* fuels derived from agricultural and commercial sources are being developed. The section "Diesel fuel" later in this chapter tells you more about them.

## What Makes It Go?

The basic difference between a diesel engine and a gasoline engine is that in a diesel engine, the fuel isn't ignited by an outside power source like a *spark plug.* Instead, the fuel is sprayed into the *combustion chambers* through *fuel injector* nozzles just when the air in each chamber has been placed under such great pressure that it's hot enough to ignite the fuel spontaneously. (You can find more-detailed information about this process in the later section "The diesel four-stroke power cycle.")

**TECHNICAL STUFF**

Most conventional gasoline engines have *compression ratios* of around 8:1, which means that the volume of each *cylinder* is eight times larger when the *piston* is at the bottom of the cylinder than when the piston is at the top of the cylinder. Diesel engines may employ compression ratios of above 20:1. Because of this volume, and because the compressed air can reach very high temperatures, diesel engines must be built for greater strength and endurance.

Following is a step-by-step view of what happens when you start up a diesel-powered vehicle. In the later section "The diesel four-stroke power cycle," you take a closer look at each step of the power cycle that converts all this into power to drive the vehicle.

The following details may vary from one vehicle to another, but the action remains pretty much the same. (You may find it fun to compare this description with the short overview of how *internal combustion engines* work in Chapter 4.)

1. When you first turn the key in the ignition, you're asked to wait until the engine builds up enough heat in the cylinders for satisfactory starting. (Most vehicles have a little light that says "Wait," but a sultry computer voice may do the same job on some vehicles.) Turning the key begins a process in which fuel is injected into the cylinders under such high pressure that it heats the air in the cylinders all by itself. The time it takes to warm things up has been dramatically reduced — probably no more than 1.5 seconds in moderate weather.

**TECHNICAL STUFF**

Diesel fuel is less volatile than gasoline and is easier to start if the combustion chamber is preheated, so manufacturers originally installed little *glow plugs* that worked off the *battery* to pre-warm the air in the cylinders when you first started the engine. Better fuel management techniques and higher injection pressures now create enough heat to touch off the fuel without glow plugs, but the plugs are still in there for emissions control: The extra heat they provide helps burn the fuel more efficiently. Figure 9-2 shows a

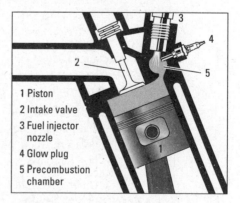

1 Piston
2 Intake valve
3 Fuel injector nozzle
4 Glow plug
5 Precombustion chamber

**FIGURE 9-2:**
Glow plugs provide extra heat to burn fuel more efficiently.

glow plug in a *precombustion chamber,* which allows the glow plug to heat a smaller amount of air more quickly and efficiently. Some vehicles still have these chambers, others don't, but the results are still the same.

2. When everything is warm enough, a "Start" light goes on. When you see it, you step on the *accelerator* and turn the ignition key to "Start."

3. *Fuel pumps* deliver the fuel from the *fuel tank* to the engine. On its way, the fuel passes through a couple of *fuel filters* (see Figure 9-3) that clean it before it can get to the *fuel injector* nozzles (see Figure 9-4). Proper filter maintenance is especially important in diesels because fuel contamination can clog up the tiny holes in the injector nozzles.

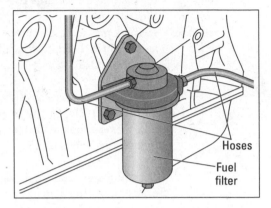

**FIGURE 9-3:**
A diesel fuel filter.

4. In the most common type of modern diesel fuel system, called *common rail direct injection* (CDI) and shown in Figure 9-5, the *fuel injection pump* pressurizes fuel into a delivery tube called a *rail* and keeps it there under constant high pressure of 23,500 pounds per square inch *(psi)* or even higher while it delivers the fuel to each cylinder at the proper time. (Gasoline fuel injection pressure may be just 10 to 50 psi!) The fuel injectors feed the fuel as a fine spray into the *combustion chambers* of the cylinders through nozzles controlled by the engine's *engine control unit (ECU),* which determines the pressure, when the fuel spray occurs, how long it lasts, and other functions.

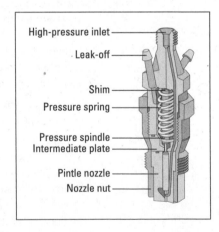

**FIGURE 9-4:**
Anatomy of a fuel injector.

Other diesel fuel systems use *hydraulics,* crystalline wafers, and other methods to control fuel injection, and more are being developed to produce diesel engines that are even more powerful and responsive.

**5.** At this point, the action moves to the *cylinders,* where the fuel, air, and "fire" meet. While the preceding steps get the fuel where it needs to go, another process runs simultaneously to get the air where it needs to be for the final, fiery power play.

On conventional diesels, the air comes in through an air cleaner that's quite similar to those in gas-powered vehicles. However, modern *turbochargers* can ram greater volumes of air into the cylinders and may provide greater power and fuel economy under optimum conditions. A turbocharger can increase the power on a diesel vehicle by 50 percent while lowering its fuel consumption by 20 to 25 percent!

**6.** Combustion spreads from the smaller amount of fuel that's placed under pressure in the precombustion chamber to the fuel and air in the combustion chamber itself.

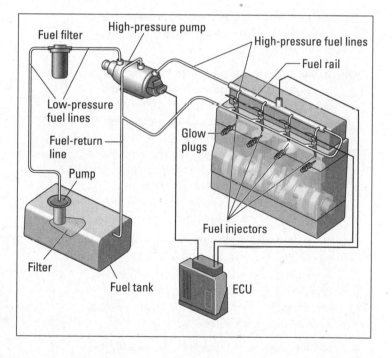

**FIGURE 9-5:**
A common rail fuel injection system.

# The Fuel System

The fuel system in a diesel engine performs the same functions as it does in gas-powered engines and consists of many of the same parts. After the fuel gets to the cylinders, however, there's a difference in the four-stroke power cycle that converts it into the power to drive the vehicle. The next section provides a closer look at that cycle.

## The diesel four-stroke power cycle

Although some smaller diesel engines (on motorcycles and marine engines, for instance) operate with two-stroke power cycles, most automotive diesel engines use a *four-stroke power cycle*, which is similar to, but not the same as, the power cycle of a gasoline engine (see Chapter 7). Here's how the diesel's four-stroke power cycle works:

>> **Stroke 1: Intake stroke (see Figure 9-6).** The *piston* descends, the *intake valve* opens, and air is drawn into the cylinder.

>> **Stroke 2: Compression stroke (see Figure 9-7).** The intake and *exhaust valves* are closed as the piston moves upward and places the air under extreme pressure. As the pressure increases, the air heats up to the *flash point* (the point at which it causes the fuel to undergo spontaneous combustion). Just before the flash point is reached, *fuel injectors* spray fuel into the *combustion chambers* at the precise instant when ignition is to take place.

>> **Stroke 3: Power stroke (see Figure 9-8).** With the intake valve and the *exhaust valve* closed, the fuel ignites, and combustion forces the piston down. This driving power is transmitted through the *transmission* and the rest of the *drive train* to the wheels, causing the vehicle to move.

>> **Stroke 4: Exhaust stroke (see Figure 9-9).** The exhaust valve opens as the piston rises and pushes the burned gases out of the cylinder.

**FIGURE 9-6:** Intake stroke.

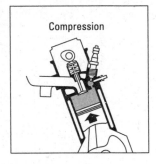

**FIGURE 9-7:** Compression stroke.

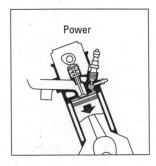

**FIGURE 9-8:** Power stroke.

# Diesel fuel

Diesel engines run on *diesel fuel,* which is more efficient than gasoline because it contains 10 percent more energy per gallon than gasoline. It's also safer than gasoline because its vapors don't explode or ignite as easily as gasoline vapors.

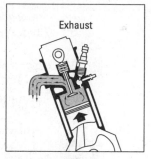

**FIGURE 9-9:**
Exhaust stroke.

ECO-LOGIC

When the exhaust from conventional diesel fuel was found to cause cancer, *clean diesel* engines were developed. Although thousands of conventional diesel fuel-burning vehicles are still on the road, public pressure and environmental organizations have prodded individual states and the federal government to enact legislation and fund replacement programs to take them out of use as quickly as possible.

## Standard diesel fuel

ECO-LOGIC

Much stricter diesel fuel standards have had a huge impact on cleaning up diesel exhaust. By 2007, the sulfur content of diesel fuels was restricted to 15 ppm (parts per million) compared to the dirty diesel previously in use that averaged something like 550 ppm. This ULSD (ultra low sulfur diesel) is derived by extra refining of the same high-sulfur petroleum diesel oil as before, but *biodiesel* fuels derived from agricultural and waste products are becoming more popular in North America. I cover biodiesel fuel in the next section.

Standard diesel fuel (sometimes called *diesel oil*) comes in two grades: Diesel #1 (or 1-D) and Diesel #2 (or 2-D). Just as gasoline is rated by its octane, diesel fuel is rated by its *cetane,* which indicates how easy it is to ignite and how fast it burns. The higher the cetane number, the more volatile the fuel. Most diesel vehicles use fuel with a rating of 40 to 55. You won't have to worry about which type to use because all diesel automakers specify Diesel #2 for normal driving conditions. Truckers use Diesel #2 to carry heavy loads for long distances at sustained speeds because it's less volatile than Diesel #1 and provides greater fuel economy.

REMEMBER

Don't confuse diesel fuel grade ratings with API (American Petroleum Institute) categories for oils used to lubricate diesel engines. The later section "Changing the lubricating oil" contains a guide to these API categories and more information about them.

Diesel fuel also is measured by its *viscosity,* which has to do with its thickness and ability to flow. Like any oil, diesel fuel gets thicker and cloudier at lower temperatures. Under extreme conditions, it can become a gel and refuse to flow at all. Diesel #1 flows more easily than Diesel #2, so it's more efficient at lower temperatures. The two types of oil can be blended, and most service stations offer diesel fuel blended for local weather conditions.

If you plan to drive in very cold weather, choose diesel fuel rated at least 10 degrees lower than the coldest temperatures you expect to encounter. Consult your owner's manual for specifics.

Because emissions from conventional diesel fuel have been found to be extremely toxic to humans and other living things, until safer forms of this fuel are developed, be careful not to inhale the fumes while pumping it into your fuel tank. (The same goes for gasoline!)

The diesel fuel sold at truck stops is often cheaper than at service stations, and the fuel is fresher, too. Freshness is important because diesel fuel can easily become contaminated by the water vapor that condenses in fuel tanks, and although it's rarely found in North America these days, really dirty fuel can contain fungus and other microbes that can clog filters and fuel injectors. If you find yourself at a station that arouses your suspicions, look for slimy stuff on the nozzle of the fuel pump. Try to fill up at a truck stop on a Saturday morning, when commercial trucking action is light. Weekday evenings are the worst times to buy because muscling a small vehicle into a crowd of big rigs isn't easy!

## Biodiesel fuel

Biodiesel fuels derived from agricultural materials have the potential to provide a clean-burning alternative to dwindling sources of petroleum.

Rudolph Diesel's first engine was designed to run on peanut oil, and Henry Ford envisioned plant-based fuel as the primary fuel for transportation and partnered with Standard Oil to develop biofuel production and distribution. However, as this book goes to press, the only type of biodiesel fuel that can be used in vehicles in the United States and Canada without violating manufacturer's warranties is B5, a blend of 5 percent biodiesel and 95 percent regular diesel. Most diesel engines run just fine on blends of up to 30 percent biodiesel.

For higher blends, the engine control unit's (ECU) electronic fuel "mapping" system, which regulates *timing, fuel/air mixture,* and so on, has to be reprogrammed to perform efficiently. The reason is that, although there's no mechanical difference between a diesel engine that runs on diesel oil and a biodiesel-burning engine, biodiesel has slightly different energy and burning characteristics than regular petroleum-based diesel.

## EMERGENCY SUBSTITUTES

Theoretically, diesel engines should be able to run on kerosene, certain airplane fuels, biodiesel in all blends between 5 percent and 100 percent, and home heating oil, but the key word here is "theoretically." *Do not use these oils in your vehicle except in absolute emergencies.* Standards of refining, filtering, and blending these oils differ widely, and they can ruin your engine, void your warranties, and create a whole lot of trouble for you.

If you find yourself low on fuel in a remote area, look for trucking companies, food-processing plants, electric plants, hospitals, and farms. These places usually have diesel engines on the premises, and some good Samaritan may take pity on you and let you have some.

If you absolutely can't find a source of diesel fuel, *as a last resort* borrow some home heating oil or buy some Jet-A fuel at a local airport. Diesel mechanics consider these substitutes to be like rotgut whiskey — it will get you there, but it's not the best stuff for your system! Drive on these fuels only long enough to get to the nearest source of proper fuel.

**WARNING**

Biodiesel vehicles in the U.S. have been modified by do-it-yourselfers and specialty shops so that they can use higher biodiesel blends and fuels made from a variety of substances. It's possible to make biodiesel from most any crop-based oil, and the news is filled with stories about modified vehicles that run on biodiesel made from french-fry oil and other restaurant grease, fresh-pressed cottonseed oil, you name it. But some of these oils contain compounds that can eat through *gaskets* and may be prone to going rancid if stored too long. Also, because biodiesel is a better solvent than standard diesel fuel, it can remove deposits in the *fuel lines.* That sounds like a good thing, but those deposits may foul up *fuel filters* and *fuel injectors* as they move through the fuel system. As a result, federal standards for the chemical composition of biodiesel fuel must be in place before it's available in widespread use and before automakers will permit its use under *warranty* in anything but very diluted amounts. This should happen very soon.

# The Electrical System

Diesels require more stored energy for starting than gasoline vehicles do, especially on cold days. Instead of just using the *battery* to enable the *starter* to crank the engine, a diesel must have sufficient power to enable the *glow plugs* to warm the *combustion chambers* and then must build up enough heat and *compression* in the *cylinders* to ignite the fuel. For this reason, diesels must possess considerably more battery capacity than conventional vehicles. Some diesels come equipped with two batteries; others feature a single oversized battery that may be more than 50 percent bigger than one found on a conventional vehicle. You can find instructions for jump-starting diesel batteries in the section "Caring for Your Diesel" later in this chapter.

Aside from this battery issue, electrical systems on diesels are pretty much the same as those on conventional vehicles; *alternators, solenoids,* and starters perform their usual functions. For information about these components, turn to Chapter 5.

# The Emissions System

Along with much cleaner fuel, automakers are transforming the old, toxic diesels into vehicles with clean exhaust emissions by making dramatic changes to their *emissions control systems.* As of 2007, all diesels sold in the U.S. were *clean diesels,* and they'll continue to get cleaner each year as new technologies for exhaust cleansing are developed. California has led the way in this area of change, and each year more and more states adopt its standards, which are stricter than those set by the federal government. Hopefully, the federal government will raise its standards as high as California's (or higher!) as time goes on.

The first innovations in cleaner diesel emissions systems were the additions of the following components (you can see them in Figure 9-1):

>> A diesel oxide *catalytic converter* that cleans hydrocarbons from the exhaust stream

>> A diesel *particulate filter* (see Figure 9-10) that scrubs sooty particles from the exhaust, trapping them in the filter material and regularly hitting the filter with a burst of superheated gasses to burn up the particles

A number of automakers have introduced additional emissions traps to their diesel passenger vehicles and light trucks. Here are two systems:

>> One system injects a mist of urea (a type of ammonia) that's nontoxic, odorless, and biodegradable into the exhaust stream, where it bonds to toxic **NOx emissions** (nitrogen oxides) and breaks them down to nitrogen and water. Then the exhaust flow carries the residue into a *selective reduction catalyst* (SRC) where it's burned away. The urea container must be refilled regularly, usually with each scheduled mechanical checkup.

>> The other system uses a new type of *plasma catalyst* to superheat and convert the NOx emissions into ammonia and then into harmless nitrogen gas.

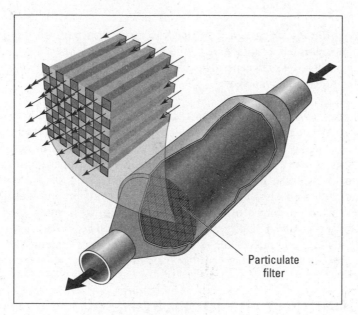

**FIGURE 9-10:**
A diesel
particulate filter.

Particulate
filter

# Caring for Your Diesel

Regular maintenance is absolutely imperative if you want a diesel engine to last, and every diesel owner will probably encounter some pitfalls and problems. This section helps you deal with maintenance and repair issues — whether or not you choose to do the work yourself.

Although diesel engines require no ignition *tune-ups* and tend to last longer without major repairs than gasoline engines, they do require regular low-cost maintenance, mostly in the form of frequent oil and filter changes. The urea injection systems that reduce *NOx emissions* (see the previous section) also need refilling, which is usually done as part of regularly scheduled maintenance.

**WARNING**

If you own a conventional gas-powered vehicle and you get sloppy about maintenance and don't change the oil often enough, you'll probably end up with an engine that has aged prematurely. If you own a diesel and do the same thing, you may end up with an engine that's prematurely dead. The same goes for changing filters: A dirty *fuel filter* can impair a conventional vehicle's performance, but dirty fuel can clog a diesel's *fuel injection system,* and you may need expensive professional help to get back on the road again.

**REMEMBER**

As a rule, you shouldn't try to clean or adjust a diesel's fuel injectors yourself, but if you maintain your vehicle according to the directions in the owner's manual, they can last 100,000 miles or more. After all, truckers have always preferred diesels because they find them to be tough, reliable, and cheap to run and maintain.

Most diesels are designed so that the owner can perform regular maintenance chores without an undue investment of time and money. The following sections cover these tasks in general terms; your *owner's manual* should contain the rest of the information you need.

TIP

If your owner's manual doesn't advise you on a specific maintenance task, or if you have no manual, amble on over to your dealership's parts department and ask to see a copy of the *service manual* for your vehicle (some bookstores and public libraries may also have them). A quick look at the proper sections should tell you whether you can do the job yourself. If you're not sure, ask one of the service advisors at your dealership to show you where the oil, air, and fuel filters are located and what's involved in changing or servicing them. Most service facilities are pretty nice about that kind of thing. If the job really is easy, they don't make enough on it to make lying to you worth the loss in customer goodwill; if the job isn't so easy, they figure you'll be happy to have them do it for you.

## Changing the lubricating oil

Because *diesel fuel* is sometimes called diesel *oil*, be aware that the *oil* you have to change is not the fuel oil but the oil that *lubricates* the engine. This job requires lubricating oil that's specially designed for diesel engines — not gasoline engines. After you understand that distinction, the actual work involved is the same as it is for conventional vehicles except that you have to do the task more often on a diesel.

TIP

Be sure to check your oil *dipstick* at least once a week (following the instructions in Chapter 2), and change the *oil filter* every time you change the oil (see Chapter 13 for instructions). Don't be surprised if you change the lubricating oil in your diesel, run the engine for two minutes, and check the dipstick only to find that the new oil has turned pitch black; this is normal and not a reason to change the oil again immediately.

TECHNICAL STUFF

Your owner's manual tells you the maximum interval you can wait between changes, but I believe that the more often you change the oil on *any* vehicle, the longer the vehicle will live and the healthier it will be. That goes double for diesels because extreme heat and pressure help to contaminate the lubricating oil more quickly. The cost of having a professional change the oil on a diesel engine can be from two to four times greater than on a gas engine. This may be extra motivation for doing this relatively simple job yourself.

Because the procedure is the same, all the instructions for changing oil and oil filters in Chapter 13 are relevant for diesels *except for the oil classification codes.* (The classification codes for automotive oils tell you which oil to use under a specific set of conditions.) Figure 9-11 shows what the API classification code symbol looks like on containers of diesel oil from reliable manufacturers.

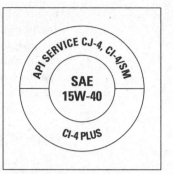

As new and improved oils appear on the market, these codes have changed from the original CA to CB to CC, and so on. Each new level can replace previous ones, and the earliest oils are considered obsolete. Unless your vehicle is several years old, your owner's manual will list the proper API category oil to use. The manual also specifies a *viscosity* grade in the form of a number preceded by the initials "SAE." This grade refers to the "weight" of the oil and the temperature conditions under which it will flow. Diesel lubricating oil comes in the same range of weights as oil for conventional vehicles, and you can find additional information on that in Chapter 13.

**FIGURE 9-11:**
The API symbol for diesel oil.

**TIP**

To be sure you're putting the most-improved diesel oil in your vehicle, check out the most recent API classification codes at your dealership or auto parts store, or go to the American Petroleum Institute (API) Web site at `new.api.org/certifi cations/engineoil/categories` and click on Engine Oil Guide.

## Changing the air filter

The *air filter* setup on most diesels is the same as on gasoline-powered vehicles, with the filter located inside the *cold air collector box* located under the hood. You can find directions for reaching the air filter in Chapter 8.

**WARNING**

You have to take one big precaution when you change the air filter on a diesel: *Always shut off the engine first.* Diesel engines produce exceedingly powerful suction, and the air intake goes directly to the engine. Because almost anything can fly or drop into it — from nuts and bolts to your favorite hairpiece — you risk serious damage to the engine if you open the cold air collector box with the engine running.

## Changing the fuel filters

Most diesels have two *fuel filters:* a "primary" filter located between the *fuel tank* and the engine, which cleans the fuel before it gets to the *fuel transfer pump;* and a "secondary" filter up near the engine, which gives the fuel a final cleaning before it gets to the *fuel injectors.* Both are usually easy to change, and your owner's manual should show you how to do this job. On some diesels, the job is much like changing the *oil filter* on a conventional vehicle: You unscrew the old one, moisten the *gasket* of the new one with fuel, and screw it into place. Others have filters with replaceable cartridges; you just remove the old one and pop in the new one. There's one catch to changing the fuel filter, however, and the next section has the details.

## Bleeding and priming the fuel system

When you change the fuel filter or run out of fuel in a diesel vehicle, you must *bleed* the air bubbles out of the *fuel system* and then prime it to get a new supply of fuel circulating. *Cranking* the engine does the job but also wears down the *battery*, so most diesels include a manual *primer pump* and an *air-bleed screw* for the purpose of bleeding the system and priming it. On many vehicles, you simply pump the primer's handle to get the fuel moving, and then you turn the air-bleed screw until a hissing noise tells you that the air is escaping. Just keep pumping until all the air leaves and the noise ceases; then tighten the air-bleed screw and replace the pump handle.

TIP

Because bleeding and priming the fuel system is something that you may need to do fairly often, I suggest that you check the equipment and procedure for any model you're interested in purchasing to be sure that you can do this job quickly and easily.

## Draining water separators

Diesel fuel can easily become contaminated by water because diesel fuel absorbs water more than gasoline does. For this reason, many diesel vehicles feature a gadget called a *water separator* that collects water from the fuel. It's usually located on or near the *fuel filter.* If your vehicle doesn't have one, I strongly suggest that you have one installed. The part shouldn't be terribly expensive, and it can save you a bunch of money on repairs.

Although a few water separators are self-cleaning, most need to be manually drained: You just turn a little drain valve called a *petcock* and empty the water from the collection chamber of the separator.

TIP

It's a good idea to check the water separator weekly at first to see how fast it fills up under normal conditions when you're driving on fuel from your usual source. If the fuel contains a lot of water, you may want to consider buying it elsewhere.

# Jump-starting diesel batteries

Even though diesel-powered vehicles can have dual batteries or one oversized battery (refer to the earlier section, "The Electrical System"), it's possible to jump-start a diesel from the battery on a conventional gasoline-powered vehicle.

**TIP**

To avoid confusion, in this section I call the vehicle with the dead battery the *disabled* vehicle and the one you're jumping the start from the *source* vehicle. Follow these steps to jump-start a dead diesel battery:

**1.** Make sure that both vehicles are in Park or Neutral with the *parking brakes* on.

**2.** Turn on the heater on the *disabled* diesel vehicle to protect the electrical system from surges in voltage.

**3.** Make sure that the lights and other electrical accessories on the *disabled* diesel vehicle are off.

**4.** A vehicle with dual batteries usually has thicker cables on one of the batteries. If *either* vehicle has dual batteries, always attach the jumper cables to the battery with thicker cables.

If either vehicle has dual batteries with cables of the *same* thickness, use either battery for the jump. If a vehicle has only one battery, just be sure to hook the cables up in the proper order.

**WARNING**

**5.** Connect the clamp on one of the jumper cables to the *positive terminal* of the *disabled* vehicle's battery.

The positive terminal should have a (+) or a red cover on it.

**6.** Connect the other end of the *same* jumper cable to the *positive* terminal of the *source* vehicle.

**7.** Connect one end of the other jumper cable to the *negative* terminal (-) of the *source* vehicle.

**8.** Here's the tricky part: Connect the other end of that jumper cable to an unpainted, metallic part of the *disabled* vehicle.

I often use the bracket that keeps the hood up, but any such part will do as long as it's not near the battery, belts, or any other moving parts of the engine.

**9.** Start the engine on the *source* vehicle.

**10.** Start the engine on the *disabled* vehicle, and let both engines run for a minute or two, more if the battery has been dead for a long time.

**11.** Turn off the engine of the *source* vehicle. (Leave the *disabled* vehicle's engine running.)

**12.** Remove the cable from the unpainted metal part of the *disabled* vehicle.

**13.** Disconnect the cable from the *positive* terminals of both vehicles.

**14.** Disconnect the cable from the *negative* terminal of the *source* vehicle.

**15.** The *disabled* vehicle should be driven around for at least 15 minutes to ensure that the battery is fully charged.

TIP

If you jump-start a dead diesel vehicle and the battery dies the next time you try to start the car, you probably need a new battery. Be sure to get the proper one for your vehicle's make, model, and year.

# Getting Started on a Frosty Morning

Diesel drivers everywhere are thankful that diesels have become easier to start in cold weather. Most turn over within 1.5 seconds of turning on the ignition.

Metal *cylinder* walls become very cold when the temperature drops, so most vehicles are harder to start in cold weather. Because diesel engines require much higher temperatures to fire the fuel, they've always been harder to start in cold weather than gasoline-powered vehicles. To warm things up before the engine can run, a variety of heaters have been developed that keep various parts of the vehicle warm and snuggly even when it isn't being driven. Some of these gadgets may be on the vehicle when you buy it; others you can buy and install later on if the need for them arises.

TIP

If you're planning to buy a diesel, be sure to ask which heating devices are included in the purchase price. If you live in a cold climate or do much traveling, consider having several devices available for extreme weather conditions. The following sections describe some of your options.

## Block heaters

Many diesels come equipped with built-in electric-powered *block heaters* to keep the *engine block* warm overnight. You just park the vehicle, plug the heater cord into a heavy-duty three-pronged extension cord, and then plug the extension cord into a 110-volt electrical socket that can handle a three-pronged plug. When shopping, don't skimp on the length of the extension cord — it can be 50 feet to a socket from a motel parking lot! I've been told that in Alaska, where a block heater is vital, electrical outlets are built right into some parking meters. I doubt that anyone tries to beat those meters, especially at −40°F!

If your vehicle doesn't have a block heater, you can buy one and have it installed. Various types are available, but *immersion*-type heaters are the most popular.

**WARNING**

When buying a heater, consult the charts at an auto parts store or dealership to match the wattage of the heater to the size of your engine and the range of weather you expect to encounter. When plugged in, a high-wattage heater will run up your electric bills unnecessarily if you have a small engine or don't expect the temperature to go below zero very often.

## Battery warmers

If your diesel doesn't start in cold weather and you remembered to plug in the *block heater,* your *battery* may be the culprit. Batteries can lose 35 percent of their power at 32°F and as much as 60 percent at 0°F. Because the battery has to supply the glow plugs with sufficient juice to get things warmed up (refer to the earlier section, "What Makes It Go?"), a frostbitten battery isn't of much use on an icy morning.

**TIP**

This problem has two remedies: You can buy a battery with greater capacity (providing that there's room for one under the hood), or you can buy a *battery warmer.* The two most popular models, both of which simply plug into a nearby 110-volt socket, are:

>> **The "hot plate" warmer,** which simply slides under the battery like a cookie sheet and warms its little toesies.

>> **The "electric blanket" warmer,** which wraps around the battery and uses more current than the hot plate version to deal with really frigid situations.

## Oil warmers

You can buy a heated *dipstick* to heat the oil in the engine *crankcase* (you just trade it for your normal dipstick and plug it into an electrical outlet) and a host of other gadgets to warm the *coolant* in the engine and the fuel in the *fuel lines.* (Most people don't need all this stuff, but for my readers in Alaska, Canada, and other cold climates, I want to cover the subject thoroughly.)

**TIP**

Here's a handy hint that may work in a pinch: On a day when your *block heater* isn't able to combat the cold effectively, if you have an electric hair dryer and a long enough extension cord to get it to the vehicle, try turning the dryer on and putting the nozzle into the car's *air inlet duct.* The warm air should help your engine warm up faster.

## What not to do on a frosty morning

**WARNING**

Never use engine-starting fluids to start your engine — no matter how eager you are to get underway. The ether in these fluids can ignite at such low temperatures that you risk a fire or an explosion, either of which can mean severe damage to both yourself and your precious diesel. Although the containers carry instructions, measuring the "safe" proportions required is just too hard. If you feel that you must use this stuff, I suggest that you have a starting-fluid injection kit installed instead; it's safe and effective. Just stay away from those spray cans!

# Finding a Reliable Diesel Mechanic

If you need professional diesel maintenance or repair and your vehicle is out of *warranty,* you may want to check around for a good independent diesel mechanic so that you can compare prices with those of the dealership or get a second opinion on major surgery. One way to find a good independent diesel mechanic is to look in your local yellow pages under "Automobiles, Repair" (or something similar) for a shop whose ad carries the logo of the Association of Diesel Specialists (ADS). The ADS authorization goes to repair facilities that send their mechanics to factory schools for instruction, maintain standards of cleanliness, and meet requirements for stocking the tools and parts to deal properly with a variety of diesel systems. (Chapter 22 is devoted to finding and maintaining a good relationship with a mechanic; it also tells you how to get satisfaction on complaints about labor or services.)

# Chapter **10**

# From Horses to Hybrids: Alternatively Powered Vehicles

In recent years, environmental concerns about the impact of automotive exhaust on air quality, health, and global warming — plus the fact that the rapidly diminishing world supply of fossil fuels has contributed to international conflicts and radically raised the price of fossil fuels — have motivated hundreds of thousands of drivers to replace gas-guzzling vehicles with more efficient ones. United States federal and state clean-air laws, rising fuel-economy standards, and growing public and auto-industry awareness have greatly accelerated the development of an ever wider variety of vehicles that run on alternative fuels. Although alternatively fueled vehicles may require different kinds of fuel tanks, regenerative brakes, and modified fuel injection and emissions control systems, the brakes, cooling, steering, suspension, lubrication, and safety systems are pretty standard on most of them.

This chapter covers alternative fuels and vehicles that will eventually supplant traditional gasoline-powered *internal combustion engines (ICE)*. However, it will be a while before ICEs are relegated to museums and classic car collections; improvements, particularly in *emissions control systems,* have made them cleaner and more efficient. The need for greater fuel efficiency has led to the development of ICEs that can shut down half their cylinders when power demand is light and then resume running on all cylinders when you need to "step on it." Engineers also are constantly working on fine-tuning ICEs to boost fuel efficiency and reduce emissions and low rolling resistance tires have improved fuel economy as well.

**WARNING**

Consult your owner's manual for maintenance instructions, but don't try to repair specialized systems yourself. They should be repaired by professionals with the experience and tools to deal with their components and the high voltages that may be involved. Although, at this writing, some alternatively fueled vehicles in this chapter are still in development, they're expected to be available within the next couple of years and may already be available by the time you read this book. Welcome to the new millennium!

# Ethanol

Alcohol fuels have been around for years, typically mixed with gasoline in a blend also known as *gasohol.* E10, with a ratio of 10 percent gasoline to 90 percent *ethanol,* can be used in *any* ICE, and many oil companies already blend their fuels that way. *Methanol,* mostly used in race cars, isn't popular for other vehicles because it isn't as clean and it also relies on fossil fuels. The use of these fuels in higher proportions requires modification to the fuel storage and delivery systems on cars and trucks. E85, a mixture of 85 percent ethanol to 15 percent gasoline, can be used in *flex-fuel vehicles,* and car enthusiasts have modified their vehicles to run on ethanol or methanol alone, with mixed results. One point that's commonly overlooked is that alcohol is about half as energy-dense as gasoline, so you can only go half as far on a tank.

**ECO-LOGIC**

Because *ethanol* is biodegradable, nontoxic, and dissolves in water, E85 has been praised by the U.S. Department of Energy (DOE) as producing emissions that contain less carbon dioxide and carbon monoxide than emissions from vehicles that run on gasoline or diesel oil. As the supply of gasoline diminishes, the current E85 standards that require the mix to contain 15 percent gasoline are being challenged to allow a greater proportion of ethanol.

## HOW TO FIND ALTERNATIVE FUELS

Although production has dramatically increased, making these fuels available in thousands of service stations nationwide is a slow process. You can use the Internet to locate filling stations that sell alternative fuels in your area and on road trips. Check out these Web sites:

- `www.eere.energy.gov/afdc/index.html`: To find a fueling station in any city or zip code, look under Quick Links to AFDC Tools for the Alternative Fueling Station Locater.

- `www.eere.energy.gov/afdc/fuels/stations_route_mapper.html`: Enter the start and end points of a trip for route maps showing the location of alternative fuel stations.

- `gasprices.mapquest.com/index.jsp`: This site helps you find stations selling a variety of alternative fuels in your area as well as the ones with the lowest price available.

The major controversy concerning ethanol fuel concerns the sources used to produce it. Corn-based ethanol has disastrous effects on the price and availability of corn for food and other products. It also doesn't produce as much energy as gasoline and requires fossil-fuels to grow, refine, and deliver it. Happily, *cellulosic ethanol* does not have those drawbacks. Because it is derived from the cellulose found in non-food agricultural and waste products such as switch grass — a fast-growing plant that has a high yield of energy and requires little in the way of fertilization and other high-energy production costs — old newspapers, and other substances, it can compete with gasoline for fuel efficiency and not affect the price and supply of grains and other vegetation vital to humans and livestock.

**TECHNICAL STUFF**

Although vehicles can run on pure alcohol, the addition of gasoline is usually justified because it helps with ignition in cold weather, and if the fuel catches fire, it burns with a visible, colored flame.

**TIP**

You can find out more about ethanol and whether your vehicle can run on E85 at `www.e85fuel.com`. To find E85 in your area, go to the "How to find alternative fuels" sidebar.

# Flex-fuel Vehicles

Vehicles that can run on two or more types of fuel are called *flex-fuel vehicles* (*FFVs*). (They're also known as *dual-fuel* or *multi-fuel* vehicles.) The most popular FFVs can run on either gasoline or ethanol or a mixture of the two. At least one major carmaker has a test fleet of vehicles that burn liquid hydrogen but can switch to gasoline if there's no hydrogen to be found. Many people drive FFVs and don't even know it! If you'd like to know whether your vehicle is an FFV, check your *owner's manual*, look for a sticker inside the little door you open to add fuel, call your dealership, or go to www.fueleconomy.gov, which has a list of available flex-fuel vehicles.

# Hybrids

Hybrid vehicles are called *hybrids* because they utilize both a small *internal combustion engine (ICE)* and an electric motor to obtain maximum power and fuel economy with minimum emissions. How they do this varies from one model to another, with varying success. What all hybrids have in common is the ability to generate electric current, store it in a large *battery,* and use that current to help drive the car. This is usually done in two ways: Hybrids can capture electrical energy produced by a *regenerative braking system* (described later in this chapter), and their engines can power a *generator,* too. Hybrids can also conserve energy by shutting down the ICE when the vehicle is in Park, *idling* at a light, or stopped in traffic; or when the electric motor's energy is sufficient to drive the vehicle without assistance from the ICE.

## Parallel hybrids

A *parallel hybrid* (see Figure 10-1) uses both an electric motor and an internal combustion engine (ICE) for propulsion. They can run in tandem, or one can be used as the primary power source with the other kicking in to assist when extra power is needed for starting off, climbing hills, and accelerating to pass other vehicles. Because both are connected to the *drive train,* they're said to run "in parallel."

The Toyota Prius uses a *power split device* that connects the ICE, the electric motor and the *continuously variable transmission (CVT)* (see Chapter 18). It allows the engine and the motor to operate together or separately, and enables either one to generate power for storage or immediate use. It's basically a parallel hybrid, but because of this unique feature, Toyota refers to it as a "series/parallel hybrid."

I drive a Prius (named Esmerelda) so here's as an example of how this type of parallel hybrid works:

1. When you press the ignition button, the electric motor uses energy stored in the high-voltage battery to start the car. (A 12-volt battery under the hood supplies power for lights, radio, and so on, as in conventional vehicles.)

2. Whenever the high-voltage battery needs charging, the ICE starts up to generate electricity for it, and once the vehicle is moving faster than around 15 **mph,** the ICE kicks in to provide additional power for accelerating, driving at high speeds, and going up hills.

3. When you step on the brakes, the **regenerative braking system** generates electricity to power the vehicle or be stored in the high-voltage battery.

4. When the vehicle stops, the ICE shuts off automatically so you don't waste fuel. Even though you're sitting there in a silent car, the radio, air conditioner, windshield wipers, and other electric features continue to work uninterrupted!

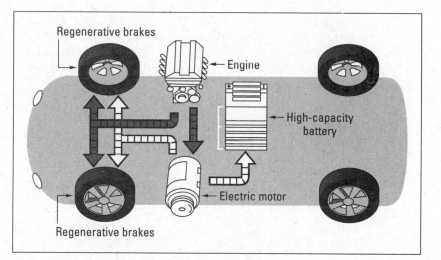

**FIGURE 10-1:**
How a parallel hybrid works.

## Series hybrids

A *series* hybrid (see Figure 10-2) uses a gasoline or diesel ICE, coupled with a *generator,* to generate electricity *but not to drive the car.* The engine can send the electric current directly to the electric motor or charge a large battery that stores the electricity and delivers it to an electric motor on-demand. The electric motor propels the vehicle, using its power to rotate a *driveshaft* or a set of drive *axles* that turn the wheels.

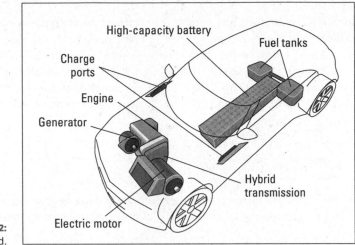

**FIGURE 10-2:**
A series hybrid.

## Plug-in hybrids

Because *plug-in* hybrids (see Figure 10-3) feature larger batteries that can be charged at any ordinary 110-volt electrical socket, they have the capacity to extend the ability of the electric motor to drive the car farther without the need for starting the *ICE* and therefore substantially increase the vehicle's fuel efficiency. Estimates have ranged as high as 100 mpg!

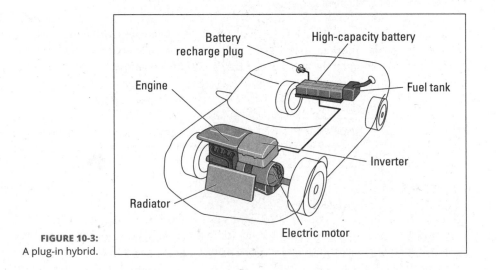

**FIGURE 10-3:**
A plug-in hybrid.

Some technologically savvy individuals have adapted their hybrid vehicles into plug-in hybrids, and automakers are in the process of developing and producing them (sometimes in cooperation with major utility companies). The development of new, smaller, high-capacity lithium-ion batteries that can be recharged many times is the key to making plug-in hybrids available to the general public. Estimates are that plug-in hybrids equipped with these more powerful batteries will have a range of as much as 125 miles before the charge is depleted and the vehicle reverts to standard hybrid mode.

ECO-LOGIC

The main environmental problem with plug-in hybrids is that the electric current they draw is usually generated by utility companies powered by fossil fuels. The good news is that some major chains have committed to establishing charging stations powered by solar panels or wind energy, and many hybrid owners are willing to install solar panels to recharge these vehicles at home. Plug-in hybrids charged by commercial sources of electricity or solar panels will be less dependent on the ICE, but will still need it for long trips, climbing hills, and so on. Future hybrids may use a small *fuel cell* to make electricity from hydrogen, which would mean the ICE would have to run even less frequently. There's more about plug-ins and fuel cells later in this chapter.

WARNING

Although instructions are available for converting conventional hybrids into plug-in hybrids, doing so yourself will void your car's warranty.

## Two-mode hybrids

*Two-mode* hybrids (see Figure 10-4) may be the key to a competitive place for the U.S. in the hybrid market. Instead of the large storage battery found on conventional hybrids, two-mode hybrids use smaller batteries and two electric motors located inside an *automatic transmission* with two sets of *gears* — one for the ICE and the other to amplify the power of the electric motors. The transmission can function as a *continuously variable transmission (CVT)*, as well. In one mode, at lower speeds, the vehicle can run with one or both electric motors, with or without the ICE, or on the ICE alone. At higher speeds, the second mode kicks in, and the ICE runs continuously in its higher gear ratios.

## Regenerative brakes

Hybrids and other energy-efficient vehicles have *regenerative braking systems* that generate electric power to help keep the batteries charged. When the driver applies the brakes, the electric motor turns into a generator, and the magnetic drag slows the vehicle down. For safety, however, there is also a normal *hydraulic braking system* that can stop the car when regenerative braking isn't sufficient. There's no difference in maintenance or repair except that the *brake pads* tend to last much longer because they don't get used as much. In fact, if you drive a hybrid in a moderate manner, you almost never actually use the *disc brakes* on the wheels and may be able to go the life of the car without changing *pads*. (Chapter 14 tells you about brakes.) The big difference is that regenerative brakes capture energy and turn it into electricity to charge the battery that provides power to an electric motor.

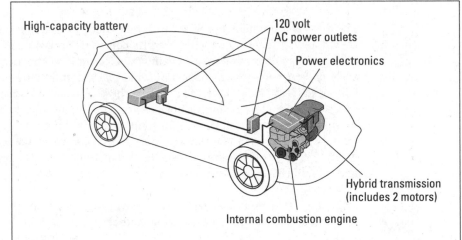

High-capacity battery

120 volt
AC power outlets

Power electronics

Hybrid transmission
(includes 2 motors)

Internal combustion engine

**FIGURE 10-4:**
A two-mode
hybrid.

# Electric Vehicles (EV)

Many people picture *electric vehicles (EVs)* as glorified golf carts powered by 12-volt batteries, with limited range and speed. They assume the vehicles are great for local driving but can't contend with traffic on busy streets or highways. However, as larger and more powerful EVs with a wider range appear, this image is no longer accurate.

Modern EVs accelerate more powerfully, have competitive top speeds, seat at least five passengers, and can be recharged easily by their owners. They can haul big loads and climb steep hills with relative ease. As with *plug-in* hybrids, storage-battery technology has been slow to achieve the breakthrough needed to let EVs store enough energy to give them the extended range to compete with vehicles powered by conventional engines and to recharge fast enough to compete with just driving into a filling station. Major efforts are being made to improve storage batteries and cold-weather performance. EVs powered by *fuel cells* have the potential to overcome these drawbacks. EVs are already popular in Europe, and EVs with enhanced performance are featured in car shows throughout the U.S.

Electric vehicles utilize a powerful electric motor and a large capacity battery to store the energy and deliver it to the motor on-demand (see in Figure 10-5). They also have the same 12-volt battery as other vehicles to keep electric devices working when the motor that drives the vehicle isn't in use. Otherwise, EVs have the same steering, suspension, and other gizmos as conventional vehicles and use the same *regenerative braking system* to generate electric current when the brakes are applied. Because EVs *don't* have a conventional *fuel system,* a dashboard display tells you when the vehicle is generating, storing, or using electricity and how far you can go without recharging the battery.

Except for a small fan that may kick in for a short time when you start the car, EVs are silent when you start, drive, and come to a stop. How hard you step on the *accelerator* tells a computerized *controller* how fast you want to go. The controller can shut down the motor to prevent it from operating at too high a speed and deliver just the right amount of energy to the motor. The more power the motor receives, the faster it can turn the drive *axle* that transmits the power to the wheels. The power is transmitted to the drive axle directly because an electric motor delivers full *torque* at all times, so a *transmission* isn't necessary. Despite this different configuration, you drive an EV in the same way as you do a conventional vehicle.

ECO-LOGIC

Recharging the battery on an electric car is usually cheaper *per mile* than buying gasoline, and because it's a *zero-emission vehicle (ZEV)* it doesn't pollute the air as vehicles that run on *fossil fuels* do. However, plugging into power from public utilities generated from *fossil fuels* presents the same problems as with plug-in hybrids. Happily, the positive developments for remedying this apply to EVs as well. *Fuel cells* (see the next section) may be the deciding factor in whether EVs become the "greenest" way to go.

## TRAGIC HISTORY OF THE EV

Although electric vehicles (EVs) were popular in the early 1900s, they were eclipsed by petroleum-powered cars. The first popular EV was the EV-1. General Motors produced and leased about 1,200 from 1997 to 1999. In 2004, when the last lease expired, although there was a waiting list of about 35,000, GM said that EVs weren't popular enough to continue production. Over the protests of the lessees, who were willing to buy them, GM recalled the EV-1 and destroyed most of them. For undisclosed reasons, the Smithsonian even took their EV-1 off display a few years later! The documentary film *Who Killed the Electric Car?* delves into this controversial story. The demand for *zero-emissions vehicles (ZEVs)* has now renewed interest in a new generation (pardon the pun) of affordable electric vehicles.

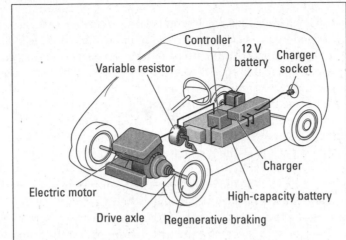

**FIGURE 10-5:** How an electric vehicle works.

# Hydrogen and Fuel Cell Vehicles

Although hydrogen is the element found in the greatest quantities in the universe, it doesn't exist in a purely natural state on earth as fossil fuels do. It is attractive as a fuel because, by a process called *electrolysis*, it can theoretically be derived from water, the air, and many other substances. Of course, until ways can be found to fill a vehicle's tank with water and have it produce its own hydrogen, there's still the problem of the fossil-fuel energy necessary to produce hydrogen in large quantities and deliver it to a vehicle as a liquid or gas. And because hydrogen is highly flammable and very cold in its liquid form (minus 453°F!), there are safety concerns about shipping it, pumping it into a vehicle's fuel tank, and storing it there under extreme pressure.

## How fuel cells work

A *fuel cell* creates electrical current from hydrogen and oxygen and may well be the best use of hydrogen as an alternative to fossil-fueled vehicles. When used in a hydrogen-powered *EV* called a *fuel cell vehicle (FCV)*, virtually the only *tailpipe* emissions that hydrogen produces are water molecules. Although there are many types of fuel cells, the ones using a *polymer exchange membrane* are the most popular for vehicles because they produce more power and operate at lower temperatures, which enables them to warm up faster than other, hotter, types of fuel cells. The resulting current is fed directly to the vehicle's electric motor.

As you can see in Figure 10-6, a fuel cell has a positive *anode* and a negative *cathode*. Hydrogen gas enters the cell and is sent to the anode, while oxygen in the form of air flows to the cathode. A thin plate of platinum particles serves as a catalyst to split each atom of hydrogen into positive and negative ions. The *polymer electrolyte membrane* lets the positive ions go through it to the anode. The negative ions can't get through and have to take another route to the cathode — on the way they create electrical current to drive the electric motor of the vehicle (represented as a light bulb in Figure 10-6).

When the positive and negative hydrogen ions are reunited at the cathode, they combine with the oxygen from the air into $H_2O$ and leave the cell as water vapor. On vehicles, hundreds of individual fuel cells are linked together into *fuel cell stacks* to increase the electrical output. Whether or not they become widely available depends on whether cheaper and more efficient alternative vehicles eliminate the need for them.

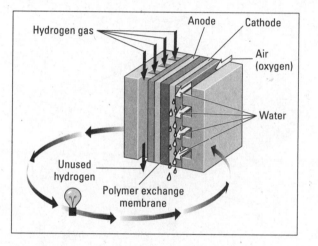

**FIGURE 10-6:**
How a fuel
cell works.

# Natural Gas Vehicles (NGV)

*Natural gas vehicles (NGV)* use *compressed natural gas (CNG)* rather than liquid natural gas (LNG) such as *butane* and *propane*. Because CNG burns cleanly with few emissions, NGVs are popular outside the United States. NGVs haven't been as popular in the U.S. because natural gas isn't as available as gasoline at filling stations, although it is a common fuel for shuttles, buses, and fleets that must meet government clean-air requirements.

**TECHNICAL STUFF**

The biggest differences between gasoline vehicles and NGVs are as follows (see Figure 10-7): Because CNG is compressed, it requires *fuel tanks* that can withstand such pressure. (The fuel is measured in units called *gasoline-gallon equivalents,* or GGE.) *Fuel lines* on NGVs also have to be high-pressure lines, and the *fuel injection* delivery system has to be specially made for CNG. But after the gas is mixed with air and injected into the engine's *combustion chamber,* the engine works the same as a gasoline *ICE.* A significant difference occurs at the *tailpipe,* however. CNG produces far fewer pollutants than either gasoline or diesel, which means that most NGVs meet low- to ultra-low-emission standards.

You can find stations that sell CNG in your area at `gasprices.mapquest.com/index.jsp`. Simply select CNG from the drop-down menu under the heading Find Gas Prices.

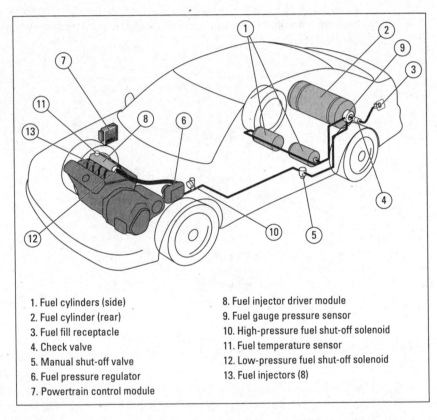

1. Fuel cylinders (side)
2. Fuel cylinder (rear)
3. Fuel fill receptacle
4. Check valve
5. Manual shut-off valve
6. Fuel pressure regulator
7. Powertrain control module
8. Fuel injector driver module
9. Fuel gauge pressure sensor
10. High-pressure fuel shut-off solenoid
11. Fuel temperature sensor
12. Low-pressure fuel shut-off solenoid
13. Fuel injectors (8)

**FIGURE 10-7:** A natural gas vehicle.

ECO-LOGIC

I hope that you will be so turned-on by the amazing advances in automotive technology that you will trade your less-efficient set of wheels as soon as you can for a vehicle that will get you there at less cost to you and to the environment. Until then, please see Chapter 26 for tips on driving and maintaining your vehicle to increase its fuel efficiency. This is something that *you* can do right now to — literally — "save the world!"

# 3

# Staying Cool and In Control

A cool head and good control of your vehicle are essential to driving safely, and your vehicle needs to stay cool, well-oiled, and capable of stopping quickly and efficiently, too. This part tells you how the cooling system works and how to maintain it, how to change your oil, and how the brake system works and what you can to do check it and maintain it. The results? A safer and longer life for both you and your vehicle!

Chapter **11**

# The Cooling System Up Close

With all that air, fuel, and fire stuff going on in its engine, your vehicle needs something to help it keep a cool (cylinder) head! Because water is usually cheap, plentiful, and readily available, auto manufacturers have found it to be the simplest answer to the problem. A few have found that air is even cheaper and more abundant; they designed the air-cooled engines on the old Volkswagens, but aside from some VW bugs and air-cooled Porsches that are still on the road, there are few air-cooled vehicles available in the United States these days.

Of course, nothing is as simple as it seems. Automakers have added some gizmos to keep the water in the engine from boiling too easily: a *water pump, fan, radiator, thermostat,* and *coolant.* There's also a transmission cooler to keep the transmission from overheating and an air-conditioner to keep *you* from overheating. Together they comprise your vehicle's *cooling system* (see Figure 11-1).

The cooling system is highly efficient. It usually requires almost no work to keep it operating — just a watchful eye for leaks and an occasional check or change of coolant. Of course, some vehicles have more complicated systems or variations on the theme, but in general, if you understand the way the basic cooling system works, you should have little trouble dealing with the one in your vehicle. Whether you do the work yourself or have it done professionally, keeping the cooling system in good shape will go a long way toward "keeping your cool" when things heat up on the road.

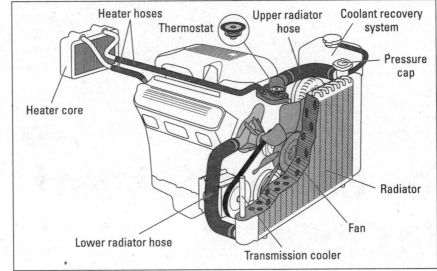

**FIGURE 11-1:**
The cooling
system.

This chapter explores the cooling system part by part. Chapter 12 shows you what to do if your vehicle overheats and how to maintain and troubleshoot the cooling system and make easy repairs. Chapter 21 helps you get out of trouble if your car overheats on the road.

Whenever you encounter a term set in *this font,* you'll find it defined in the glossary in Appendix A.

REMEMBER

# Coolant/Antifreeze

To keep the water in the cooling system from boiling or freezing, the water is mixed with *coolant* or *antifreeze.* In the interest of brevity, I just call it "coolant" throughout this book.

Most coolants contain about 95 percent *ethylene glycol*, a chemical that stops water from freezing or boiling even in extreme temperatures. (Ethylene glycol is toxic; there are nontoxic coolants that contain *propylene glycol* instead. See Chapter 12 for more.) In addition to the glycol, coolant also contains rust, corrosion, and foaming inhibitors, so coolant does more than just keep the water in the system in a liquid state: It also helps to prevent the formation of rust on the metal surfaces of the engine and the radiator, lubricates the water pump, and keeps the liquid from foaming as it circulates through the system. Since the early 1960s, auto manufacturers have designed the cooling systems of most vehicles for a 50/50 mixture of ethylene glycol and water, which is still generally considered the proper proportion of coolant to water for the cooling systems of most vehicles. (I often refer to the coolant and water mixture as "liquid" in this chapter.)

Today's engines require specially formulated coolants that are safe for aluminum components. There are long-life (sometimes called "extended life") coolants with organic acid rust and corrosion inhibitors that promise to last for as long as five years. Automakers use some of these coolants as original fluid in new vehicle radiators made of aluminum (they can't be used in anything except aluminum radiators).

Due to differences in Japanese, Korean, European, and American compounds, you can shorten coolant life by putting the wrong stuff in your vehicle's cooling system. So make sure that you use the automaker's recommended coolant to ensure the longest life and best protection for your vehicle.

If your cooling system is operating properly, you shouldn't have to keep adding liquid to it. Chapter 2 shows you how to check the level and condition of the liquid in the cooling system, and Chapter 12 shows you how to add liquid or flush the system and replace the liquid in it.

# The Radiator

When the *fuel/air mixture* is ignited in the *cylinders*, the temperature inside the engine can reach *thousands* of degrees Fahrenheit. It takes only *half* that heat to melt iron, and your engine would be a useless lump of metal in about 20 minutes if your vehicle couldn't keep things cool. Naturally, the *coolant* (and water) that circulates from the *radiator* through the top radiator hose to the *thermostat* and around the cylinders in the *engine block* gets very hot, so it's continually circulated back to the radiator via the bottom radiator hose, where it cools off before heading back to the scene of the action. The radiator's *pressure cap* keeps your car from boiling over, and the *coolant recovery system* holds extra coolant so it doesn't overflow onto the roadway.

# The hoses

The radiator is designed to cool the liquid quickly by passing it over a large cooling surface. The liquid enters the radiator through the *top radiator hose*, which is usually connected to (you guessed it) the top of the radiator (refer to Figure 11-1). As the liquid descends, it runs through channels in the radiator that are cooled by air rushing in through *cooling fins* between the channels. When the liquid has cooled, it leaves the radiator through the *bottom radiator hose* (surprise!). This hose usually has a spring inside it to prevent it from collapsing when the water pump draws coolant from the radiator. (If it collapses anyway, Chapter 12 has instructions for replacing it.)

Smaller-diameter hoses also lead from your engine to the *heater core* (see the later section, "The Heater Core"). Some vehicles have a small bypass hose near the *thermostat* as well (see the later section, "The Thermostat"). These hoses are an important part of the cooling system because they're designed to carry the liquid in it from one component to another.

## The coolant recovery system

A *coolant recovery system* is a plastic or metal container with two little hoses coming out of the cap (see Figure 11-2). One hose leads to the radiator, and the other serves as an overflow pipe for the container, which holds an extra supply of water and coolant in case the system loses any.

**TECHNICAL STUFF**

When your cooling system heats up and starts to overflow, the liquid pours back into the recovery system reservoir instead of pouring out of the radiator overflow pipe and onto the ground. When the system cools off, the pressure drops and the liquid is drawn out of the reservoir and back into the radi-

**FIGURE 11-2:**
A coolant recovery system.

ator. This process not only saves you coolant but also protects animals and children from sampling puddles of the toxic stuff.

Some of today's new vehicles have *pressurized* reservoirs. In these cases, you may find the *pressure cap* (which I get into in the next section) on the reservoir and not on the radiator. I've been told by radiator specialists that, on some vehicles, this system doesn't work very efficiently because, as the pressure builds up in the coolant reservoir, it forces the coolant out of the overflow pipe and onto the street. Not only is this overflow a toxic hazard, but as the coolant supply diminishes, the chance of the engine overheating increases, leading to a vicious circle.

Many recovery systems are considered "sealed" because you add water and coolant by opening the cap on the reservoir rather than on the radiator. You also check the level of liquid in the system by seeing whether it reaches the "Max" level shown on the side of the container rather than by opening the radiator and looking inside. (For instructions on adding liquid to a sealed system safely, see Chapter 12.)

## The pressure cap

To further retard the boiling point of the liquid in the cooling system, the entire system is placed under pressure. This pressure generally runs between 7 and 16 pounds per square inch *(psi)*. As the pressure increases, the boiling point rises as well. This combination of pressure plus coolant gives the liquid in your cooling system the capability to resist boiling at temperatures that can rise as high as 250°F or more in some vehicles.

To keep the lid on the pressure in the system and to provide a convenient place to add water and coolant, each radiator has a removable *radiator pressure cap* located on either its *radiator fill hole* or its *coolant recovery system*.

**TECHNICAL STUFF**

The pressure cap has two valves: a *pressure valve* that maintains a precise amount of pressure on the liquid in the system, and a *vacuum valve* that allows the liquid to travel back into the radiator from the recovery reservoir.

**WARNING**

Pressure caps are relatively inexpensive, but if you have a cap that isn't working properly, or if you have the wrong type of cap, you'll be amazed at the amount of trouble it can cause. For example, if the *gasket* inside the cap isn't working, the pressure in the system will escape, allowing the liquid to boil at a lower temperature. A modern cooling system that has been designed to operate normally at temperatures over 212°F, and that is filled with liquid and in perfect condition, will still continually boil over if the radiator cap isn't operating efficiently. That boiling liquid will be forced into the overflow system, and your vehicle's engine will overheat. An overheated engine can cause an inconvenient highway breakdown and possible danger to your engine.

If your vehicle overheats on the highway, Chapter 21 can get you cooled down safely. Chapter 12 offers remedies for other overheating problems.

# The Fan

Air rushing through the radiator cools things off when you're driving merrily down the highway, but a fresh supply of air doesn't move through the radiator fins when the vehicle is standing still or crawling its way through heavy traffic. For this purpose, the *fan* is positioned so that it cools the liquid in the radiator (refer to Figure 11-1). Today, most fans have a plastic shroud that funnels air through the radiator. Some vehicles have air dams that help force the air up through the radiator from below.

**TECHNICAL STUFF**

Originally, the fan operated in connection with the *water pump,* and they were both driven by a single *fan belt* that ran around a pulley connected to the *alternator.* This fan belt drove the fan as long as the engine was running. Almost all fans today are electric and thermostat-controlled, not hooked by belts to the engine or water pump. These fans only come on when they need to. Because the air rushing past them allows these fans to simply "coast" at high speeds, the engine doesn't have to work as hard or burn as much fuel to supply the power that the fans would normally consume.

Some vehicles now have two fans because styling changes that have lowered the profile of the hood area have caused radiators to get lower and longer, meaning that a single fan doesn't cover the entire surface. These two fans are sometimes run by electric thermostats that aren't connected to the water pump at all (I cover the water pump in the next section).

# The Water Pump

The *water pump* (see Figures 11-1 and 11-3) draws the cooled liquid from the radiator through the *bottom radiator hose* and sends it to the engine, where it circulates through *water jackets* located around the *combustion chambers* in the *cylinders* and other hot spots. Then the liquid returns to the radiator to cool off again. An *accessory belt* connected to the *crankshaft* drives some water pumps, while some *overhead cam* engines drive the water pump with the *timing belt.* Chapter 2 tells you how to check accessory belts, and Chapter 12 has instructions for adjusting and replacing them.

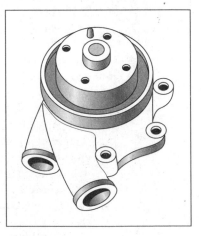

**FIGURE 11-3:**
A water pump.

If the timing belt drives your water pump, the water pump will be difficult to see unless you remove the plastic timing belt cover.

# The Thermostat

The *thermostat* is the only part of the cooling system that does *not* cool things off. Instead, it helps the liquid in the cooling system warm up the engine quickly.

The thermostat is a small, metal, heat-sensitive valve (see Figure 11-4) that's usually located where the upper radiator hose meets the top of the engine. (On a few vehicles, you find the thermostat where the bottom hose joins the engine. Your owner's manual should tell you where yours is.)

When it senses hot liquid, the thermostat allows the liquid to pass through. But when the thermostat senses that the liquid is cold (like when you first start your engine in the morning), it closes and doesn't allow the liquid to circulate through the radiator. As a result, the liquid stays in the engine, where it gets hot as the engine warms up, and in turn, the increasing heat of the liquid helps the engine to warm up more quickly. As a result, the vehicle runs more efficiently and burns less fuel.

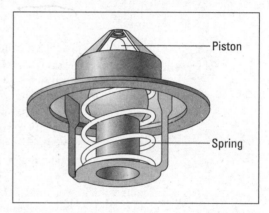

**FIGURE 11-4:**
A thermostat.

# The Heater Core

The *heater core* is located inside the vehicle between the instrument panel and the *firewall* (refer to Figure 11-1). It looks like a miniature radiator minus the fill neck and cap. The purpose of the heater core is to provide heat for the passenger compartment. The same liquid that the water pump circulates throughout the engine also circulates through the heater core when the engine is operating. When you get chilly, you can direct air across the heater core and heat the interior of your vehicle by turning on the inside fan. Because the heater core is relatively passive, it usually doesn't need attention unless it breaks.

# The Transmission Cooler

Vehicles with *automatic transmissions* have a *transmission cooler* located in or near the bottom or side of the radiator (refer to Figure 11-1). The *transmission fluid* circulates from the hot transmission to the cooler, which cools it and returns it to the transmission. If the transmission cooler on your vehicle is working properly, you don't need to monkey with it. If it leaks, have it repaired by a professional.

# Air Conditioning

Air conditioning is now standard equipment on most vehicles rather than an option. It uses *refrigerant* to remove the heat from the air (rather than cooling it) and a blower to send the cool air into the passenger compartment.

ECO-LOGIC

Until 1992, a refrigerant called CFC-12 (commonly called Freon) was standard on most vehicles. When it was found to contribute to the depletion of the ozone layer, CFC-12 was phased out and replaced by R-134a. Production of CFC-12 ceased at the end of 1995, and although the stuff can be recycled, supplies may be limited. The biggest improvements since the development of R-134a are better, less-porous hoses and seals so that the smaller R-134a molecules don't leak out like they used to. A new $CO_2$ refrigerant system that has been in the prototype stage since around 2002 may be the next major development in vehicle air conditioning systems.

WARNING

If your vehicle was built before 1992, you may have trouble getting Freon if you need to replace the refrigerant in your vehicle's air conditioner. Conversions to an alternative refrigerant (R-134a) are expensive, so think about this fact before buying a pre-1992 used vehicle or undertaking expensive repairs on an older vehicle that you already own; the vehicle may not be worth as much as it would cost to rebuild the air conditioning system. Chapter 12 tells you how to trouble-shoot problems with your air conditioner and provides tips on servicing it and finding out what it would cost to convert from CFC-12 to R-134a refrigerant.

IN THIS CHAPTER

» **Dealing with overheating problems and removing a radiator cap safely**

» **Checking your cooling system; and flushing, changing, or adding coolant**

» **Finding and repairing cooling system leaks**

» **Replacing hoses, hose clamps, the thermostat, and accessory belts**

» **Dealing with the air conditioner**

Chapter **12**

# Keeping Your Car from Getting Heartburn

E very vehicle has a cooling system to help it run efficiently and prevent it from overheating. Keeping it operating properly usually requires just an occasional check or change of coolant and a watchful eye for leaks. (Chapter 11 takes a close look at the parts of the cooling system; please review it before undertaking any of the work in this chapter.)

This chapter discusses the things you can do to help your vehicle keep its cool under normal circumstances. It tells you how to prevent overheating by checking and replacing the liquid in the system, how to flush the system and change the coolant, and how to deal with other common causes of overheating, such as a malfunctioning *pressure cap* or *thermostat*, deteriorated hoses, and coolant leaks.

**REMEMBER**

Whenever you encounter a term set in *this font*, you'll find it defined in the glossary in Appendix A.

# Overcoming Overheating

The first sign of overheating is either when the needle on the temperature gauge pushes its way into the ominous red zone or the "Check Engine" or "Temperature" *malfunction indicator light* on the dashboard casts a sinister glow. Left alone, the liquid in the *radiator* eventually boils over and steam rolls out from under the hood.

**WARNING**

If you ignore the problem, your vehicle eventually loses power, your engine grinds to a halt, and you end up with a giant repair bill. If you take action at the first indication of a problem, you probably can avoid this doomsday scenario. Even if you end up needing major repairs, at least you'll know that you explored all the cheaper options first.

## Addressing occasional overheating

**TIP**

Although overheating isn't the problem it once was — there was a time when most every vehicle overheated occasionally — it can still happen. Often the cause of the problem is nothing more than being stuck in stop-and-go traffic on a hot day. If your car overheats, Chapter 21 tells you what to do.

## Dealing with a chronic hothead

If your vehicle overheats often and constantly loses coolant, the problem may be caused by one or more leaks in your cooling system (see the sections "Finding Leaks in the Cooling System" and "Repairing Leaks in the Cooling System" later in this chapter). If your vehicle overheats in normal weather and traffic, you may need to add liquid to the system, replace the *thermostat,* adjust or replace the *accessory belt,* or check the *water pump.* You may be able to deal with most of these problems by following the instructions in later sections of this chapter.

The first thing to check if your vehicle overheats often is the *pressure cap.* Sometimes the *gasket* on the cap deteriorates and lets pressure escape, which causes the cooling system to malfunction. Most service stations can test your cap for you and tell you whether it's in good condition.

**TRUE STORY**

When I bought Tweety Bird, my first car, she sang when I shut off the engine! Her mysterious behavior was eliminated by a new pressure cap. Although I paid for some unnecessary (and unsuccessful) repairs before it occurred to me to ask the shop to test the cap, I was luckier than someone I met who paid big bucks for radiator rebuilding and a new water pump before discovering that all he needed was a cap that cost less than $10! Lesson learned: Professionals sometimes try the more profitable solutions first. Do-it-yourselfers try the cheapest solution first.

**WARNING**

If your vehicle is old and the cooling system isn't leaking, be sure the shop just pressure tests the cap. Pressure testing the entire system can sometimes cause leaks by blowing out any stuff that's plugging them up! The section "Locating leaks by pressure-testing the cooling system" later in this chapter tells you more about this process.

## Identifying other causes of overheating

**TIP**

Some overheating problems aren't related to the cooling system at all. Other circumstances that can cause a vehicle to overheat include lack of *oil*, a blown *head gasket,* and *transmission* problems. If the cooling system seems to be in good order after you check it and do the maintenance work covered in this chapter, investigate these possibilities:

>> **Late timing:** If your ignition system is malfunctioning, late *timing* may be causing your vehicle to overheat because the *spark plugs* are firing the *fuel/air mixture* *after* the *piston* moves back down from the top of its *stroke.* When the spark plugs fire too late to allow all the fuel to burn properly, more heat burdens your cooling system. Late timing alone doesn't cause an engine to overheat by more than a few degrees, but when coupled with other problems, it can bring the engine temperature to a critical point. The remedy is simple: Have a service facility place your vehicle on an electronic diagnostic machine to check your timing and adjust it if necessary.

>> **Plugged radiator:** Some radiators get so plugged up with rust, sediment, or small insects that even cleaning and flushing them doesn't get all the junk out. Because plugged passages cut down on the system's liquid circulation, the system can't cool efficiently. The remedy is to have a radiator specialist remove and inspect the radiator. If you're lucky, just steam-cleaning the radiator does the job; if you're not, the solution may be more expensive. Keep your fingers crossed. . . .

>> **Slipping accessory belt:** On many modern vehicles, the *accessory belt* is hidden by a plastic shield or dust cover that may be difficult to remove. However, if you can see and reach the accessory belt that drives the *water pump,* check to be sure that there's no more than about ½ inch of give. If the belt is looser than that, it may not be driving the pump properly, and that can impair circulation and overheat the cooling system. If the belt seems loose or very frayed, you can try to replace it by following the instructions in the section "Adjusting and Replacing Accessory Belts" later in this chapter. If you can't do the job, have a professional deal with it.

- » **Collapsing bottom radiator hose:** Occasionally, a bottom radiator hose begins to collapse under the vacuum that the water pump creates, and the impaired circulation causes overheating. The section "Check the hoses" later in this chapter tells you how to determine whether the hose is collapsing.

- » **Low oil level:** If you still can't find the cause of overheating, check your oil *dipstick.* A vehicle that's low on oil tends to overheat because the oil removes from 75 to 80 percent of the "waste heat" in your engine (in addition to doing its other job of cushioning the moving engine parts).

**TECHNICAL STUFF**

If you're one quart low in oil and your vehicle holds five quarts, the oil will carry away 20 percent less heat than it should. See Chapter 2 for instructions on checking the oil level and adding oil as part of a monthly under-the-hood check.

Under normal circumstances, you can prevent overheating by checking the level of liquid in the system and maintaining it properly. The next sections tell you how to do so.

# Checking and Adding Liquid to Your Cooling System

One of the quickest, easiest, and least expensive tasks you can perform to keep your cooling system cool is to check the fluid level in the system and, if necessary, add water and coolant. Before you attempt to do anything to your cooling system, be aware of two important safety rules:

**WARNING**

> NEVER REMOVE THE PRESSURE CAP WHEN THE ENGINE IS HOT. NEVER ADD COLD WATER TO A HOT ENGINE!

## Removing a pressure cap safely

**WARNING**

Before you can do anything involving your cooling system, you need to know how to remove the *pressure cap* safely. It's dangerous to remove the pressure cap from the radiator or *coolant recovery system* reservoir while the engine is still warm. Because it's hard to tell just how hot things are inside the engine, follow these guidelines when removing a pressure cap:

>> Keep your cool until your car regains its own! *Never* remove the cap from a radiator or coolant recovery system reservoir when the engine is hot. Because adding cold water to a hot engine can crack the *engine block,* you have no reason to remove the cap until the engine temperature drops to a safe level.

>> If your engine overheats on the highway, get safely to the side of the road, turn off the ignition, and then wait 15 to 20 minutes for things to cool down. If you can stay safely away from traffic, you can lift the hood to help the heat escape *but you should leave the pressure cap alone.*

>> If you're parked where traffic is zooming by, or if you're concerned about your security if you leave your vehicle, you're better off just waiting in the car until the engine cools. If it heats up again when you start driving, get to the nearest service station or a place where you can safely park, get out, and deal with the situation yourself. Chapter 21 has more tips about what to do if your car overheats on the road.

To remove the pressure cap safely, follow these steps *after the engine is cool:*

1.  **Don't remove the cap on the radiator unless your vehicle has no plastic coolant recovery reservoir. (These days, almost every vehicle does; Figure 12-1 shows you what one looks like.)**

2.  **If your system has a *safety* pressure cap, lift the lever on the safety cap to allow the pressure to escape.**

    To keep from burning your hand, place a cloth over the cap after you raise the lever (see Figure 12-1). Then turn the cap counterclockwise to remove it.

TIP

**FIGURE 12-1:**
A coolant recovery reservoir (a) and a cap being removed safely from a radiator (b).

**If your vehicle *doesn't* have a safety cap, place a cloth over the cap and turn it counterclockwise just to its first stop.**

Turning to the first stop allows some of the pressure to escape, but if you see liquid or a great deal of steam escaping, retighten the cap and wait for things to cool down. If nothing escapes, continue turning the cap counterclockwise to remove it.

3. ***Tilt* the cap as you remove it so that the opening points *away* from you (and anyone else nearby).**

   If there's still enough heat and pressure to spray hot stuff around, it lands on the engine or inside the hood, where it can do no harm. *Be particularly sure to follow this procedure if you don't have a safety cap.*

4. **When you finish, replace the cap by screwing it on clockwise. (If you have a safety pressure cap, push the lever down again.)**

Radiator safety caps cost very little, so if you don't have one, buy one! Almost every service station stocks them, but they're cheaper in auto supply stores. Check your owner's manual for the amount of *psi* (pounds per square inch) of pressure in your system and look for the proper number of psi on the new cap. These safety caps are well worth the money.

Of course, if the engine is completely cold, you face no risk at all, so get into the habit of checking your coolant level at least once a month in the morning before you warm up the engine, as part of the under-the-hood check in Chapter 2.

## Avoiding disaster when adding liquid to any type of cooling system

As you know from Chapter 11, most vehicles have *coolant recovery systems.* Some are pressurized and serve as the fill tank when you need to add coolant, but there are many vehicles still on the road that require you to add liquid directly to the radiator. The following cautions apply no matter which type of vehicle you have.

### Never add cold liquid to a hot engine!

Adding cold liquid to an engine that's hot can crack the *engine block* because the hot metal contracts sharply when the cold liquid hits it. If you *must* add liquid to an engine that's still *warm* (and I can't imagine why you should) always do so slowly with the engine running. This way, the cold liquid joins the stream of hot water that's circulating through the system rather than falling all at once into the system when you start the engine again. This technique isn't foolproof, however, so I advise patience instead.

Under normal conditions, a 50/50 mix of water and coolant is preferred for most vehicles. If the day is extremely hot or cold, a higher proportion of coolant/antifreeze may be necessary (see "Determining whether your coolant needs changing" later in this chapter).

## Don't overfill the system!

ECO-LOGIC

If you overfill the system, the extra liquid gets hot, expands, and flows out of the overflow pipe. That may not seem too terrible, but because coolant is toxic, it can harm animals or children, who love its sweet taste (see "Keeping coolant out of the mouths of babes and small animals" later in this chapter).

If you don't have coolant on hand and you just need to add a little liquid to the cooling system, plain old tap water will do. But try to maintain a good coolant level by adding a similar amount of straight coolant the next time you add liquid to the system.

WARNING

Several types of coolant are on the market. If your vehicle has an aluminum engine, make sure that the coolant container specifies that it's safe for aluminum engines. If you have extended-life coolant in the system, only add extended-life coolant to it.

TIP

Keep some coolant in your trunk to use in case you're driving in an area where you may not be able to find the brand of coolant for your system.

## Checking and adding liquid to a coolant recovery system

TIP

Many vehicles have a pressurized coolant recovery system called an *expansion tank* that makes opening the radiator unnecessary. These systems are considered "sealed" because the safety pressure cap is on the recovery reservoir rather than on the radiator. On these systems, you can check the level of liquid on the side of the plastic reservoir, and you just open the cap on the reservoir to check whether the coolant looks as though it needs changing or to add water and coolant.

You will probably never need to open the cap on the radiator, but *if* you have to open the cap for any reason, make sure to fill the radiator to the top with a 50/50 mixture of coolant and water before replacing the cap. This addition *bleeds* the system by forcing any air that may have gotten into the system into the reservoir and out through its overflow pipe when the engine heats up. Follow these steps when adding liquid to the coolant recovery system:

1. **Check the liquid level.**

   Look at the *outside* of the reservoir to see where the level of the liquid in it lies relative to the "MAX" and "MIN" lines embossed on the side (refer to Figure 12-1).

2. **If the liquid level is low, add equal parts coolant and water to the reservoir.**

   Follow the instructions in the earlier section, "Removing a pressure cap safely," to remove the pressure cap on the reservoir, and add equal parts coolant and water until the level reaches the "MAX" line on the side of the container.

## Checking and adding liquid to a radiator

If you don't have a pressurized coolant recovery system, you have to add liquid directly to the radiator. Here's how:

1. **Open the radiator cap, following the instructions in the earlier section "Removing a pressure cap safely."**

2. **Take a peek down the radiator fill hole to see how high the liquid level is inside.**

   If you're unsure about what the liquid level should be, just make sure that it covers the radiator tubes that are visible when you look down the hole, or that it reaches to within a couple of inches below the cap.

3. **Add water and coolant, or pre-diluted coolant, as necessary.**

   Be sure to follow the tips given in the earlier section "Avoiding disaster when adding liquid to any type of cooling system."

4. **When you finish, replace the cap by screwing it on clockwise. (If you have a safety pressure cap, push the lever down again.)**

# Flushing Your System and Changing Your Coolant

You should do three things to keep your cooling system in good shape:

>> Check for leaks.

>> Replace worn hoses before they split.

>> Flush the system and change the coolant at least once a year or every 20,000 miles, whichever comes first, unless your vehicle has the new extended-life coolant that lasts for five years.

I discuss the leak situation and how to change hoses later in this chapter. This section covers the proper way to flush your system and change the coolant in it.

## Deciding if you're up for the job

There are pros and cons to flushing your cooling system and changing your coolant yourself:

**PRO:** The difference in cost is tremendous: If you do it yourself, all you need to buy is a jug of coolant, which sells for less than $10. A professional job can cost as much as five times more. Remember, not only does your service station expect to make a profit on the coolant (they bought it and stocked it, didn't they?), but they also charge for labor and coolant recycling.

**CON:** In the "good old days," flushing the system and changing the coolant yourself was easy. You just hooked a garden hose to a little tee in the heater hose, opened the radiator cap, and let the coolant and water flow through the system and onto the ground until the system was clean. However, times have changed.

**ECO-LOGIC**

Coolant is highly toxic, especially to children and small animals, who love its sweet taste. If a small child, dog, or cat drinks the stuff, it will probably die. To protect your children, pets, and the animals in your area, see the section "Keeping coolant out of the mouths of babes and small animals" later in this chapter. Because of the need to keep the used coolant out of the environment, flushing and changing coolant has become more complicated. Service stations in most states must either meet stringent disposal requirements or purchase a machine that recycles the coolant by cleaning the coolant as it flows out of the vehicle, adding a shot of the chemicals that have been depleted by use, and putting the coolant back into your system. The good news is that this recycled coolant is every bit as good as the stuff you buy at the auto supply store.

**WARNING**

Although a flushing "tee" may be installed in one of the heater hoses on your vehicle, please don't try to use it yourself without following the instructions in "Flushing the system," later in this chapter, so that you can do the job and recycle the used coolant safely.

## Determining whether your coolant needs changing

There are several situations when the coolant in your vehicle definitely should be changed: if you haven't changed it in a year or in the past 20,000 miles; if your vehicle constantly loses liquid in the system and overheats easily; or if you've frequently added plain water to your cooling system to the point where it's probably lowered the proportion of coolant to less than half the required 50/50 mixture.

Even if none of the above is true, your coolant may still need a change.

**TIP**

Checking the coolant is especially important if you haven't changed the coolant recently or if you've been adding a lot of plain water. Coolant testers like the one shown in Figure 12-2 are cheap and easy to use; they tell you whether the protection level of the coolant in your system is adequate. They usually involve opening the pressure cap and drawing a little liquid out of the system and into the tester. Little balls or a float in the tester tell you whether you need to add coolant (the instructions are on the package). (While you're at it, you also can check the liquid in the tester for rust.) You can buy test strips that do the same thing as a tester by changing color.

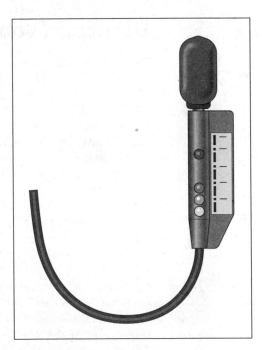

**FIGURE 12-2:**
A coolant protection level tester.

Here are a couple of things to consider in order to decide whether a change really is in order:

>> **The quality of the liquid in the system:** Unscrew the *pressure cap* and look at the liquid inside the reservoir or radiator, depending on the type of system you have. Coolant can be green, greenish yellow, orange, red, or blue, but is

the liquid clear, or is stuff floating around in it? Does it look rusty? (Don't mistake red coolant for rust; rusty water has particles floating around in it.)

>> **How frequently you've added water and how much you've added:** If you've been adding plain water every couple of days or weeks, your coolant protection level is probably low.

>> **What kind of climate you live in:** If the temperature gets very cold in the winter or very hot in the summer, be sure that you have enough **coolant/ antifreeze** in your system before extreme weather sets in. In most areas, a 50/50 solution is recommended for year-round use. If the weather turns *extremely* cold, you can add a slightly higher proportion of antifreeze without hurting your cooling system.

*Never exceed a 70/30 mixture of antifreeze to water.* Freeze protection actually worsens with too much antifreeze and not enough water. If the weather is extremely hot, exceeding the recommended proportions of water and coolant won't help prevent your vehicle from overheating; it may actually cause it to overheat more rapidly.

>> **How often you use your car's air conditioner:** Although the air conditioner does a fine job of keeping the interior of the car cool, it raises the temperature of your engine. So be sure to have a 50/50 mix of coolant to water during the warm months when you use your air conditioner most often.

If during a pre-summer check you find that the level of coolant is very low or that its protection level is weak, it may be a good time to flush your cooling system and start fresh. If you don't flush the system then, check the level again at the end of autumn to see whether you should flush it before the cold weather sets in.

## Figuring out how much coolant you need

You can consult your *owner's manual,* the back of the coolant jug, or the charts that coolant manufacturers supply to find out the number of quarts that your cooling system holds. Many coolants are now pre-diluted with water, but if you're buying straight coolant, divide that number by two and buy that amount of coolant. Adding an equal amount of water to straight coolant gives you a 50/50 water/coolant mixture, which is fine for everything but extremely cold weather.

Some auto manufacturers make coolant formulated specifically for their vehicles. At least one coolant manufacturer advertises its coolant as being safe for all vehicles. Whatever you buy, if your vehicle has an aluminum engine, make sure that the coolant is marked "Safe for use on aluminum engines." If you're adding coolant, always use the same brand and type as the coolant already in the engine.

# Keeping coolant out of the mouths of babes and small animals

Before you start to flush your cooling system yourself, it's really important to read this section in order to avoid endangering children and animals.

WARNING

Anyone who has raised kids through the crawling and toddling stages knows that they tend to pick up the most revolting stuff off the ground and put it into their mouths. Because coolant looks and tastes good, a puddle of the stuff can be hazardous to children. That goes double for thirsty cats, dogs, and wildlife. Most coolant contains ethylene glycol, which is poisonous when swallowed. According to the EPA (Environmental Protection Agency), this chemical causes depression followed by respiratory and cardiac failure, kidney damage, and brain damage.

ECO-LOGIC

Although no coolant is completely nontoxic, some coolants on the market contain propylene glycol instead of ethylene glycol to reduce their toxicity. At least one brand has received the Seal of Approval from the ASPCA (American Society for the Prevention of Cruelty to Animals). However, even if you use this type of coolant, be sure to take the following steps to protect your pets and small children from accidentally drinking coolant:

1. **Make it a habit to check under your vehicle for coolant leaks.**

   If you find a puddle of colored liquid below the under-the-hood area and it isn't oily, it's probably coolant.

2. **Clean up any spills thoroughly.**

   Sop up *all* of it with kitty litter or absorbent rags, and then hose down the area thoroughly until the surface is clean. (Don't just hose it without sopping it up — you'll just be spreading the stuff around!)

3. **Dispose of the contaminated rags or kitty litter safely by placing it in a plastic bag, sealing it, and putting it in the trash.**

4. **Store unused coolant safely.**

   The appropriate jugs have childproof lids, but you should still store them out of reach and away from heat, which can release toxic fumes.

5. **Store used coolant safely until disposal.**

   Pour used coolant into a container with a screw-on cap, label the container as "coolant" or "antifreeze," and place it well out of the reach of kids and pets until you can dispose of it, following the instructions in Step 6.

WARNING

   Don't put used coolant in containers that formerly contained beverages. They're too easily mistaken, and the sweet taste of the coolant can compound the error.

**6.** **Dispose of used coolant safely by taking it to a recycling center that handles toxic waste or a place that specifically recycles used coolant.**

To find a place to safely dispose of used coolant, visit the Web site for Earth 911, www.1800cleanup.org/default.asp, or call your city hall or your local toxic waste management agency.

TIP

Some auto supply stores accept used coolant as a public service. Call the major stores in your area to find out whether they do so. If not, try a service station, which can either run the coolant through its recycling machine or include it in the batch sent out for safe disposal. Be prepared to pay for this service, though, because the service station didn't get to flush your cooling system for you.

The EPA has this advice about coolant disposal (they refer to it as "antifreeze"): "If your home is connected to a sanitary or municipal sewer system, household quantities of antifreeze can be flushed down the drain *with plenty of water.*" However, the EPA warns that antifreeze can overwhelm the organisms in your septic system and damage the system, and it suggests that if your wastewater goes into a septic tank, you should dispose of antifreeze in a sanitary sewer system. The organization cautions, *"Do not pour antifreeze into storm sewer openings, sinkholes, or abandoned wells."*

REMEMBER

If your engine boils over, be sure to clean up the spill wherever you are. Wild animals are just as vulnerable to being poisoned by coolant as domestic pets are.

When you have your priorities in order regarding the safe handling of coolant, if you're still up for the job, the next section tells you how to flush a cooling system.

## Flushing the system

If your vehicle's owner's manual has instructions for draining the liquid from the cooling system, follow them. (This option is better than following the instructions in this section because air is less likely to be trapped in the system after you finish the job.)

ECO-LOGIC

If you don't have a manual, or if it lacks such instructions, follow these steps to flush your cooling system and change the coolant without endangering the environment:

**1.** **Park the vehicle in a safe place, away from children and small animals.**

Make sure that the engine is cold, the ignition is off, and the *parking brake* is on.

WARNING

**2.** **Place a bucket that can hold at least two gallons under the drain valve at the bottom of the radiator.**

**3.** **Open the drain valve and allow the liquid to drain into the bucket.**

Don't allow the liquid to drain onto the ground or into a storm drain or sewer.

**4.** **Close the drain valve!**

**5.** **Pour the used liquid into containers with tight-fitting lids. Label them clearly as "antifreeze" or "coolant," and place them away from kids and pets until you can dispose of them safely.**

A funnel and some old gallon water jugs do the job as long as you pour carefully to avoid spilling the liquid on the ground and label them prominently, as in Step 8.

**6.** **Open the radiator pressure cap and fill the radiator with water.**

**7.** **Run the engine with the heater control on High for about ten minutes.**

Keep an eye on the temperature gauge to make sure that the engine doesn't overheat. If your vehicle has an engine temperature warning light instead of a gauge, shut off the engine as soon as it lights up.

**8.** **Shut off the engine and allow it to cool down until the water in the radiator is cool enough to touch. Then drain the water out of the system into the bucket again, and transfer it from there into more closed containers for disposal.**

Label the containers "toxic water" to differentiate them from the others and to prevent someone from drinking their contents accidentally.

**9.** **Close the drain plug and refill the system with water and coolant.**

If you don't have pre-diluted coolant, mix sufficient equal parts of water and coolant to fill your system (see "Figuring out how much coolant you need" earlier in this chapter). The liquid should reach the "MAX" line on the coolant recovery reservoir or cover the fins in the radiator. If it doesn't, continue to add equal parts water and coolant until it does.

**10.** **To disperse the water and coolant evenly throughout the system, replace the pressure cap and run the engine with the heater on High until the temperature gauge reads in the normal range.**

**11.** **Shut off the engine.**

**12.** **Clean up any spills, place contaminated rags or kitty litter in sealable plastic bags and put them into the garbage, and store the unused coolant safely away from kids and pets.**

To clean up spilled coolant and properly dispose of the bottles of used coolant and toxic water, see the earlier section "Keeping coolant out of the mouths of babes and small animals."

**13.** After you've driven your car for a few days, check the liquid level in the recovery system reservoir again, adding equal parts water and coolant to the reservoir if the level is low.

If it's low again in a few more days, have the system checked at a service facility.

TIP

You can buy products for cleaning the cooling system during the flushing process. These products remove rust and sediment that flushing with plain water can't. If your cooling system has been cleaned regularly and you want to clean it yourself, buy a well-known brand and follow the instructions on the package carefully.

WARNING

If your vehicle's cooling system hasn't been cleaned for a few years, using a cleaner on a system that has years of built-up rust and sediment can free so much of the stuff that you run the risk of clogging your radiator or *thermostat* or possibly loosening the deposits that have prevented the system from leaking. Have the system flushed, cleaned, and refilled professionally.

# Finding Leaks in the Cooling System

In addition to keeping the water and coolant level where it needs to be, you can prevent trouble in your cooling system by keeping an eye out for leaks and replacing old or damaged hoses. Figure 12-3 shows the common trouble spots in the cooling system — the places where you should check for coolant leaks.

The following sections give you a few pointers on what types of coolant leaks to look for, and the section, "Repairing Leaks in the Cooling System," tells you what to do if you find them.

## Look under your vehicle

Look under your vehicle in the morning to see if there's any liquid on the ground below the under-the-hood area. If you see liquid, stick your finger in it and smell it. If it's coolant (green, red, blue, orange, or rust-colored), get a flashlight, look around under the hood at the parts of the car located over the puddle, and feel around for wetness. Be sure to check the hoses leading to the coolant recovery reservoir and the radiator.

TIP

If you're not sure what's leaking out of your vehicle, turn to Chapter 20 for an easy way to locate, troubleshoot, and deal with leaks of all types, including *coolant, oil, transmission fluid,* and *brake fluid.*

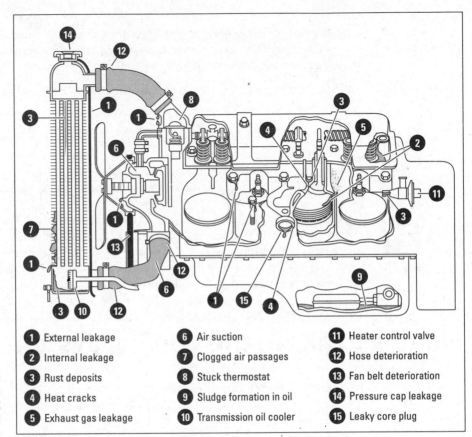

**FIGURE 12-3:**
Where to check for cooling system leaks and other problems.

| | | | | | | | |
|---|---|---|---|---|---|---|---|
| **1** | External leakage | **6** | Air suction | **11** | Heater control valve |
| **2** | Internal leakage | **7** | Clogged air passages | **12** | Hose deterioration |
| **3** | Rust deposits | **8** | Stuck thermostat | **13** | Fan belt deterioration |
| **4** | Heat cracks | **9** | Sludge formation in oil | **14** | Pressure cap leakage |
| **5** | Exhaust gas leakage | **10** | Transmission oil cooler | **15** | Leaky core plug |

## Check the radiator

Feel the underside of the radiator to see if it's leaking, and look around your radiator for whitish deposits or rust-colored stains. These indicate old leaks that have dried, but they may not be all that old; water tends to evaporate quickly on a hot radiator. If you find any deposits or stains, the "Radiator leaks" section later in this chapter tells you what to do. Also check the front end of the radiator to see whether the surface is befouled with dirt, leaves, and bugs. If so, wash them off with a brush and a garden hose.

TIP

If your radiator catches a lot of debris, to trap the stuff and keep it from getting stuck between the radiator fins you can attach a piece of nylon window screen over the front surface with twist-ties. You still need to check the screen periodically to be sure it isn't blocked, but it makes the stuff easier to remove.

## Check the pressure cap

If your vehicle overheats easily, the cheapest remedy is to buy a new safety cap — or ask a mechanic to pressure-test your cap to see whether it's functioning properly. If you need a new one, give the salesperson the make, model, and year of your vehicle and check the pressure limits *(psi)* on the new cap against your owner's manual to make sure that you're buying the proper cap for the amount of pressure in your cooling system.

**WARNING**

Never let an unfamiliar service station hook you into buying a new cap unless you watch them pressure-test your old one. You may want to have them test the new cap as well. I've been sold a faulty new cap to replace a faulty old one!

## Check the hoses

**TIP**

Regularly check all the hoses under the hood of your vehicle, whether you've been having trouble or not. For instant panic, there's nothing like having a hose burst while you're driving. If it's a radiator hose, the resulting shower of steam is frightening at best and dangerous at worst. If a vacuum hose goes, the sudden loss of vacuum can stop your vehicle in the midst of traffic. Checking your hoses and replacing the funky ones *before* they leak can save your nerves and your pocketbook in the long run.

If you find a hose that's soft and squishy, bulging, hard or brittle, cracked, leaking, or marked with a whitish deposit where stuff has leaked and dried, replace it immediately before it breaks. I show you how to do that in the "Buying and Replacing Hoses and Hose Clamps" section later in this chapter.

**TECHNICAL STUFF**

If you find a hose that's collapsed when the engine is cold but springs back when you remove the *pressure cap,* the cap or *coolant recovery system* — not the hose — is at fault.

If your car starts to overheat and you suspect that the bottom radiator hose is collapsing, park in a safe place away from traffic. Make sure that the car is in Park or Neutral with the *parking brake* on. Then open the hood *without shutting off the engine.* Take a look at the bottom hose (be careful not to get your hair or clothing caught in the *fan* or the *accessory belt*) and see whether the hose has collapsed. If it has collapsed and you have a spare hose with you, replace it (see the later section "Replacing hoses" for instructions).

**TIP**

If a radiator hose malfunctions while you're driving, no service facility is going to send a replacement hose out to you, so the vehicle will have to be towed. If you had a hose replaced because it looked like it was getting worn, or if you want to hedge your bets on the road, keep the old hoses or, better yet, new top and bottom radiator hoses in the trunk. Even if you don't want to change a hose yourself, you won't be stuck somewhere waiting for a new hose to be delivered to a service facility if they don't have one in stock.

While you're checking hoses, check the *hose clamps* that secure all the hoses under the hood, and tighten any that appear loose. Replace those that are rusty, corroded, or impossible to remove without special tools with screw-type hose clamps (see the next section, "Buying and Replacing Hoses and Hose Clamps").

# Buying and Replacing Hoses and Hose Clamps

If you've followed the instructions in the "Check the hoses" section and found one that's leaking or deteriorated, replacing it is usually pretty easy and inexpensive, with two caveats:

>> **Make sure that both ends of the hose are accessible.** Some heater hoses disappear through the *firewall* and under the dashboard. I'd much rather pay a mechanic than hang upside down in a cramped space while I locate and replace one of these hoses.

**WARNING**

>> **Never attempt to replace a hose connected to your air conditioner.** Air conditioners and their hoses contain *refrigerant* under pressure that can blind you. If you have *any* problems with your air conditioner or its hoses, seek professional help.

**TIP**

If your service facility doesn't have an air conditioner specialist on staff, consider going directly to the specialist to avoid paying for the time it would take your service facility to deliver your vehicle to the specialist and then pick it up.

## Buying the right hose

Before you can replace a hose, you need to visit the parts department at your dealership or an auto supply store to buy the proper type, diameter, and length of hose for your vehicle.

**TIP**

If possible, while you're still in the parking lot wherever you bought it, check the new hose against your old hose. If the hose doesn't seem to be the same size and shape as your old one, take it back in and exchange it. If you can't drive your vehicle to the store, remove the hose by following the instructions in the section

"Replacing hoses" and take it with you so that the parts department at the store can match it.

If you can't bring the vehicle or the hose with you, here's how to find the right replacement for the vehicle's make, model, and year without a sample on hand:

>> **If it's a *top* radiator hose:** *Don't get a radiator hose that has wire inside it.* Radiator hoses have to bend to fit properly between the radiator and whatever they lead to. Some hoses are straight tubes, with wire coiled inside the rubber casing. These are called *universal* hoses; they're designed to bend to fit many cars. Often, the wire breaks or works its way through the top covering of the hose, causing the hose to leak. The kind of hose to look for is called a *preformed* hose, shown in Figure 12-4, which is made with the proper bend already in it and no wire inside the rubber.

**FIGURE 12-4:**
A preformed top radiator hose.

The hose should be *squeezable* — another reason that you don't want a top radiator hose with wire inside. This way, if you have problems with your cooling system, you can squeeze the hose to see whether the system is operating under pressure.

**WARNING**

A dangerously pressurized hose that's hard to squeeze warns you not to remove the radiator cap until the car cools down and the pressure is reduced.

>> **If it's a *bottom* radiator hose:** The hose *must* have a wire coil inside it (see Figure 12-5) to help it keep its shape and withstand the vacuum caused by the water pump drawing water out of the radiator.

>> **If it's any other kind of hose:** Make a photocopy of the *Specifications Record* in Appendix B for each of your vehicles and enter the

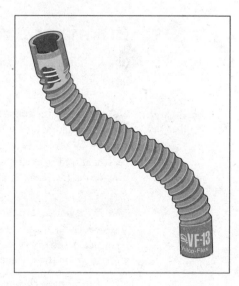

**FIGURE 12-5:**
A flexible bottom radiator hose with a wire insert.

following information on it. Then take it to the auto supply store whenever you have to buy hoses and other parts.

- **The make, model, and year of your vehicle:** The auto supply store may also need to know the size and type of your engine and whether the vehicle has air-conditioning.

- **The *type* of hose, if you know it:** For example, a heater hose or vacuum hose.

- **What part(s) the hose connects to**

- **The diameter, color, and length of the hose:** Most hoses are sold by their *inside* diameter (see Figure 12-6), so you may have to disconnect one end of the hose, measure the inside diameter, and reconnect it if you're going to drive to the store.

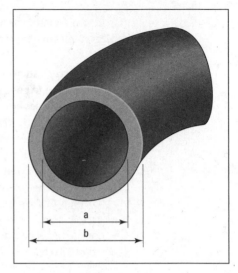

**FIGURE 12-6:**
How to measure the inside (a) and the outside (b) diameters of a hose.

## Buying and replacing hose clamps

When buying a new hose, don't forget to buy new hose clamps. They should be large enough to fit the *outside* diameter of the hose.

TIP

Clamps are so inexpensive that you should make it a habit to replace them whenever you change a hose. If you're changing a hose that was secured with *wire* hose clamps or screw-type clamps, replace them with *gear*-type clamps that can be removed and replaced easily. Figure 12-7 shows all three types of clamps. Here's how to deal with each kind:

>> **Wire hose clamps:** I hate these clamps because they are relatively hard to deal with. If you need to change a hose that has them, use a pair of ***slip-joint*** pliers (see Chapter 3) to pinch the wire ends together so that you can slip them off the hose, and then replace them with gear-type clamps.

>> **Screw-type clamps:** These clamps don't loosen easily, so they're often found on radiator hoses and the like to keep them in place. Unscrew the screw and remove it. Then slip your screwdriver under the clamp and loosen it. To avoid the hassle of reinserting the screw, replace with *gear-type clamps.*

>> **Gear-type clamps:** These clamps are my favorites. Just use a screwdriver to turn the screw counterclockwise to loosen the clamp, slip the clamp over the hose, slip the end of the new hose in place, and turn the screw clockwise to tighten the clamp. Easy!

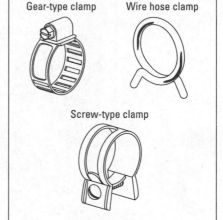

TIP

It's impossible to tell someone in a book how tight or loose a clamp should be. If the clamp is so tight that it appears to be cutting into the hose, loosen it. If you can hear or see air or liquid escaping from the ends of the hose, the clamp should be tighter. Give the hose a tug to see whether it's secure, and check it again after you run the engine, to make sure that it isn't leaking.

**FIGURE 12-7:**
Various types of hose clamps.

## Replacing hoses

The basic process of changing a hose is quite simple (see Figure 12-8), but there are differences, depending on the type of hose you're replacing.

>> **If the hose is a vacuum hose,** you'll find literally *nothing* in it. Just loosen the clamps, remove the hose, slide the new clamps on the new hose, slip the ends of the hose over whatever they connect to, and tighten the clamps.

WARNING

>> **If the hose is a fuel hose,** have a professional replace it. Fuel is not only highly flammable, but it's also toxic. The danger, effort, and time necessary to clean up any spills and to dispose of everything properly at a hazardous waste center just isn't worth trying to tackle this relatively inexpensive job yourself.

WARNING

>> **If the hose contains liquid under pressure,** before removing the hose, be sure that the engine is shut off and the liquid has been allowed to cool so the pressure is released.

To prevent leaks, some manuals suggest putting a water-resistant sealant on the ends of the fittings to which the hose connects. Because these sealants tend to make the hoses difficult to remove when you need to replace them again, I suggest that you try it without sealant first. In most cases, if the hose is the right one and the clamps are on tight enough, you should be able to get by without sealant. If the hose leaks, you can always go back and use the sealant as recommended.

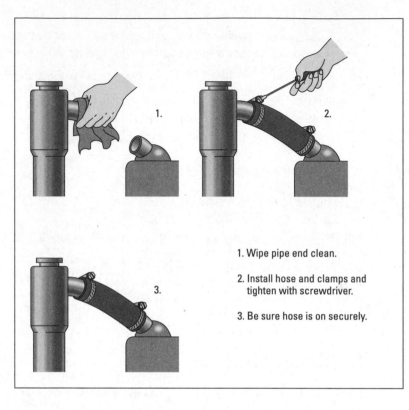

1. Wipe pipe end clean.

2. Install hose and clamps and tighten with screwdriver.

3. Be sure hose is on securely.

**FIGURE 12-8:**
How to install
a hose.

>> **If the hose is a radiator or heater hose,** to catch the coolant and water that will run out of the system, you'll need a bucket or pan that holds at least two gallons of liquid and will fit under the radiator drain valve (called the *petcock*) that drains the radiator.

**WARNING**

Never allow coolant to drain onto the ground (see "Keeping coolant out of the mouths of babes and small animals" earlier in this chapter).

If you haven't flushed your **cooling system** and replaced the coolant in the past year, do so at the same time you replace the hose. (See the "Flushing Your System and Changing Your Coolant" section for instructions.)

**TECHNICAL STUFF**

Some newer engines have cooling systems that need to be bled. If your engine falls in this category, the cooling system contains special *bleeder screws.* If you're not sure what type of system your vehicle has, check the **owner's manual** or ask a mechanic *before* you undertake this job. To do it properly, you need to follow instructions in the owner's manual or a **service manual** for your vehicle.

Follow these steps to replace a radiator or heater hose:

1. **Make sure that the *parking brake* is on and that the car is in Neutral or Park before you start work.**

2. Remove the *pressure cap* from the radiator or coolant reservoir, and place a bucket or drain pan under the radiator drain valve.

3. Open the drain valve, allow the coolant to drain into the container, and then close the valve.

4. Remove the clamps at both ends of the hose.

   As I say in "Buying and replacing hose clamps" earlier in this chapter, you're going to replace those clamps, so if you can't remove them easily, cut them off. (If you haven't read that section, do so before going any further.)

**REMEMBER**

5. Carefully twist the hose to remove it, and use the container to catch the liquid that drains from it.

   Be gentle when removing the hose. If you're not careful, you could damage the radiator.

6. Use any degreaser or just a damp clean rag to clean the fittings that the new hose will attach to, and install new clamps over the hose (refer to Figure 12-8).

7. Install the new hose, attaching and clamping one end securely in place before you tackle the other end.

   Make sure that the hose won't interfere with any moving parts or touch the engine when it's hot, and that the clamps are tight.

8. If the coolant that you drained is fairly new and your container was clean, pour the liquid back into the system; otherwise, refill the system with a 50/50 mix of fresh coolant and water.

   If you're replacing the coolant, see "Keeping coolant out of the mouths of babes and small animals" for instructions on disposing of the old stuff safely.

9. Start the engine and add more water and coolant as the level in the radiator drops.

**WARNING**

   Don't fill the radiator to the top of the neck or the coolant reservoir up to the "MAX" line until the ***thermostat*** opens. When the upper hose is hot, the thermostat has opened. Then it's okay to top off the radiator or the reservoir.

10. Replace the pressure cap.

    If your engine is the type that needs to be bled, do so now, following the instructions in the ***owner's manual*** or ***service manual*** for your vehicle.

11. Run the engine and double-check that the clamps are nice and tight so that no liquid leaks out.

# Repairing Leaks in the Cooling System

When you find a leak, you must decide whether you can handle it yourself or you need to see a professional. The following sections cover the different types of leaks and give you a few pointers to help you decide.

## Radiator leaks

**TIP**

If the radiator is leaking badly, I recommend going directly to a reliable radiator shop. If they say it's cheaper to replace it than to repair it, do so.

**REMEMBER**

At the radiator shop, ask the radiator specialists what they intend to do and request a written estimate *before* they do the work. If the estimate seems high, call another radiator shop (use the yellow pages to find one), tell them what needs to be done, and ask for an estimate.

### A WORD ABOUT SEALER

If you find a small leak in your radiator or **engine block** (a couple of drops a day, with no need to add water more frequently than once a week), you may want to try a **sealer,** or *stop-leak* as it's sometimes called, before you head for a repair shop.

You add sealer to the liquid in your cooling system. It circulates around with the water and coolant, and when it finds a hole where a leak is occurring, it plugs it up.

You can purchase several kinds of sealers. The trick is to choose the one that does the best job without gumming up the cooling system. Ask for advice at the dealership or auto supply store. It's especially important that the sealer be compatible with your coolant (the label should tell you).

Sealers are usually added through the **radiator fill hole.** Some coolants have a sealer built in, but these are rarely strong enough to deal with established leaks. If you try a sealer and the leaks recur in a couple of days, get professional help. On the other hand, if the leaks occur in any of the hoses, replacing the hoses yourself is quite simple. The section "Buying and Replacing Hoses and Hose Clamps" earlier in the chapter tells you how to do it.

# Leaks in the engine-block core plugs

On the sides of some *engine blocks* are little circular depressions called *core plugs,* or *freeze plugs* (see Figure 12-9). These plug the holes where sand was removed when the engine block was cast. If you see leaks or rusty streaks leading away from the core plugs on your engine block or signs that leaks from them have dried, and you've been losing liquid lately, you may need to have the core plugs replaced. Your best

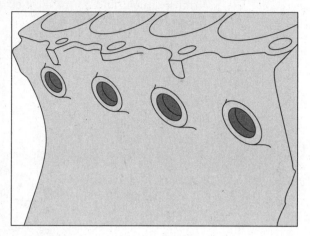

**FIGURE 12-9:**
Core plugs in the sides of the engine block.

bet is to seek professional help on this one. If replacing them is a high-ticket item, get a second estimate. If that's high, too, check the *bluebook* value of your vehicle's make, model, year, and accessories on www.kbb.com or www.edmunds.com to see whether it's worth putting the money into it.

## Internal leaks

Sometimes a leak right under the *cylinder head* can be the result of an ill-fitting *head gasket* or the fact that the bolts that hold the cylinder head on the *engine block* (see Figure 12-10) are too loose or too tight. If you try to tighten these bolts yourself, you may damage the gasket because the bolts have to be tightened to *specifications* and you probably don't have a *torque wrench.* The best thing to do is to get professional help here. If a mechanic only has to tighten the bolts, the cost should be minimal, whereas replacing the head gasket is more costly.

TIP

You're always ahead of the game if you go to a professional with a good idea of what's wrong and the possible ways to correct the problem. (If you're told that the head gasket has to be replaced before the technician has really checked the head, don't *tell* the technician what to do; just *ask* whether it would be wise to just try tightening the bolts first instead of replacing the gasket immediately.)

With today's aluminum cylinder heads, it's quite possible that your cylinder head may have small cracks that are allowing coolant to leak internally. If this is the case, usually you'll notice thick, white smoke from the *tailpipe* and/or engine oil that looks like a mocha milkshake when you inspect the oil *dipstick.* Also, vehicles with *automatic transmissions* have a transmission cooler inside the radiator that can leak. When it leaks, coolant mixes with the *transmission fluid,* making the transmission fluid on the dipstick look like a strawberry milkshake. Both problems require professional help.

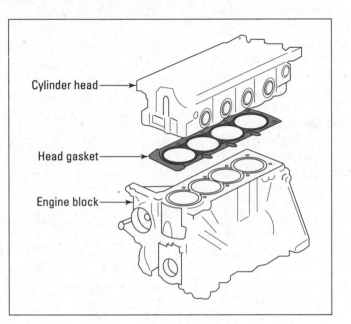

## Leaky water pump

Often, a *water pump* that's about to break down sends out noisy warning signals and then starts to leak before it fails completely. On some *overhead cam* engines, the water pump is behind the timing cover and is driven by the *timing belt,* making inspection difficult. Leave those to a professional. If the water pump on your vehicle is visible, you can check your pump by looking around it for leaks or signs of rust or corrosion around the seals.

If the pump is leaking in the front where it rotates with the belt, the pump probably needs to be replaced. If the leak is around the *gasket* that lies between the water pump and the engine, you may be able to stop it by tightening the bolts that hold the water pump in place. If tightening the bolts doesn't do the job, then you probably need a new pump.

TECHNICAL
STUFF

Originally, the water pump operated in connection with the fan and there was a single *fan belt* that ran around a pulley connected to the *alternator.* Almost all fans today are electric and thermostat-controlled, not hooked to the engine or water pump. These fans are mounted to the radiator and only come on when they need to, so they're not part of the water pump system anymore.

TIP

If your water pump needs to be replaced, instead of paying top dollar for a new one, ask your mechanic about installing a *rebuilt* or *remanufactured* pump (the glossary explains the difference between these two terms) *if* such a pump is available for your vehicle and *if* it's considerably less expensive than a new one. Professionals usually prefer to obtain these parts themselves so that they can make a little profit on the part, but if your mechanic is okay with you providing the pump, there are a few things to keep in mind: Make sure that the pump is designed for your vehicle's make, model, and year; comes with a gasket that matches the old one; and comes with at least a 90-day written *warranty* or *guarantee.* If the service facility provides the pump, they should be willing to guarantee it for the same amount of time.

## Locating leaks by pressure-testing the cooling system

If you can't locate the source of a leak and your vehicle is losing liquid from the cooling system on a regular basis, drive to your service station and ask the attendants to pressure-test your cooling system. The test involves very little time or labor, so a friendly technician may do the test free of charge. While you're at it, have the technician pressure-test the radiator *pressure cap* as well.

WARNING

If you have an old vehicle that hasn't had its cooling system serviced or *rebuilt* in a long time, pressure-testing the system may dislodge the deposits sealing the weak spots, causing the system to leak. Before the technician starts testing the system, ask whether the procedure is worth the risk.

# Adjusting and Replacing Accessory Belts

Chapter 2 tells you how to check *accessory belts.* Whether or not you can adjust or replace a belt yourself depends on the type of belt(s) you have.

On most modern vehicles, a single, long, flat belt called a *serpentine multi-accessory drive belt* (see Figure 12-11) drives all the engine accessories. This belt winds its way around every accessory pulley, and on the way winds tightly around a "tensioner" pulley that keeps the belt at the correct tension. In cases where it's possible to adjust the tensioner, you usually find a set of marks on the tensioner assembly that indicates the correct tension.

TIP

There are very few older vehicles still on the road that have an accessory belt that only drives one component. If your car has this setup, you can check the belt by following the instructions in Chapter 2 to see whether it has more than ½ inch of "play" and needs to be adjusted; or is cracked, frayed, or otherwise in need of replacement.

**TIP**

It isn't easy to figure out whether a belt is at the right tension just by looking at it, and often it's obscured by a shield or cowling. If the belt is loose, you'll hear squeaky noises when you accelerate sharply. With the hood up, the *gearshift* in Park or Neutral, and the *parking brake* on, have a friend accelerate the engine while you listen. *Be sure to keep your hair and clothing away from the belt.*

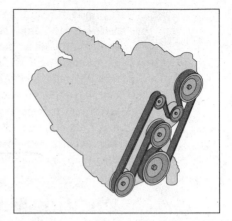

**WARNING**

Because tensioners are spring-loaded, they can be unsafe to deal with yourself. Check your *owner's manual* or a *service manual* for your vehicle's make, model, and year to see what's involved in adjust-ing your accessory belt. If you can't reach

**FIGURE 12-11:**
Serpentine multi-accessory drive belt.

the adjusting mechanism without removing other parts, if adjusting the belt requires special tools, or if it looks as though releasing the tension may be risky, you should have a professional deal with it.

If the belt squeaks, it may have been contaminated by water, coolant, oil, or another fluid. If it's just water, check around the *water pump* and the hoses to see where the leak is, and eliminate the cause of the leak. The water will dry up on its own. The belt needs to be replaced if the contaminant is coolant, oil, power-steering fluid, or some other substance or if the belt has broken, is frayed, or has large cracks or pieces missing.

**TECHNICAL STUFF**

If a belt needs to be replaced and you're dealing with a shop you know and trust, ask them to check the tensioner. Replacing a tensioner may be costly, so if it looks as though it may need to be replaced soon, you can avoid having to pay again for the time and labor to access it by having both jobs done at once.

# Replacing Your Thermostat

If your vehicle has been overheating or doesn't warm up properly and none of the things in the preceding section is the problem, you may need to replace your *thermostat*. This little gizmo simply stays closed and keeps the liquid in the *engine block* until the engine heats up. Although it's a simple device, it can malfunction.

If the thermostat sticks in the *open* position, it doesn't keep the liquid in the engine long enough, so you have trouble getting your car warmed up. If the thermostat sticks in the *closed* position, the liquid isn't allowed to get to the radiator, and overheating results.

Because replacing the thermostat is quite simple and thermostats are quite inexpensive, you may want to try this task before you take more drastic measures:

1. **Locate your thermostat if you haven't already done so.**

   Most thermostats are located where the top radiator hose joins the engine, so these steps deal with this type. If your thermostat is in the bottom radiator hose, the principle is the same.

2. **Buy a new thermostat.**

   Supply the usual information (vehicle make, model, year, and so on) to the auto supply store. If you've done other work on your vehicle and have filled out the *Specifications Record* in Appendix B, you should know the drill by now.

3. **Unscrew the clamp that holds the end of the radiator hose where your thermostat is located.**

4. **Pull off the hose.**

   Some fluid will escape, so have a *clean* two-gallon container handy to catch it, and return the fluid to the radiator when you finish the job. Or you can consider this a golden opportunity to flush your cooling system and change the coolant by following the instructions that I provide earlier in this chapter. Whatever you do, *avoid spilling the coolant where animals and small kids can get to it.*

5. **Remove the bolts that hold the thermostat housing in place, and lift out the old thermostat.**

   Compare the new thermostat and its *gasket* with the old ones. If the new thermostat and the gasket that's included with it aren't *exactly* like the old ones, go back to the store for the right ones.

   There's a gasket around the hole where the thermostat was located — take that off, too. Scrape off any pieces of gasket that may be stuck, but *be sure not to let these pieces fall into the hole!*

6. **Lay the new gasket in place.**

7. **Drop in the new thermostat, making sure to place the spring side *down* (see Figure 12-12); then replace the bolts.**

8. **Replace the hose, and screw down the hose clamp.**

   Screw it down tightly but not tight enough to cut into the hose.

9. **Replace whatever fluid ran out of the hose by pouring it from the container into the radiator fill hole or coolant reservoir.**

   Be sure not to pour it on the ground where children and animals can be endangered by it. If you accidentally spill fluid, wipe it up thoroughly before hosing down the area and place the rags in a sealed plastic bag before disposing of them.

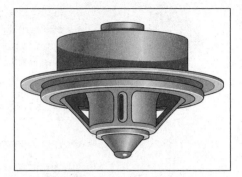

**FIGURE 12-12:**
Thermostats are replaced spring side down.

# Servicing Air Conditioners

Most people tend to run the air conditioner in their vehicles until it breaks. However, air conditioners should be serviced professionally each year.

Air conditioners contain refrigerant under pressure, which can injure or blind you if it escapes; *don't attempt to work on the air conditioner or its hoses yourself.*

If your vehicle was built prior to 1992, the air conditioner contains a refrigerant called Freon (CFC-12). Because Freon contributes to the breakdown of the ozone layer, manufacturers ceased production of it in 1995. Newer vehicles use an environmentally acceptable refrigerant called R-134a. It's possible that new types of refrigerants may be used as automotive technology changes.

If you have a pre-1992 vehicle and your air conditioner breaks down, you may find that Freon is hard to obtain. Your options are to run without air conditioning, have the air conditioner converted so that it can use R-134a, or get a newer vehicle.

To find out the cost to convert a vehicle's air conditioner from Freon to R-134a, consult the auto manufacturer or an authorized dealership or service facility, or call the EPA Stratospheric Ozone Hotline at 800-296-1996.

WARNING

Be alert to the following signs that your vehicle's air conditioner may be in trouble:

>> The air it puts out isn't as cold as it used to be

>> A funny smell is coming from the vents

>> The air conditioner's drive belts, compressor, or blower are noisier than they used to be

>> You hear a rhythmic clicking noise under the hood when you turn on the air conditioner or defroster

>> The defroster no longer defogs the windshield effectively

>> You find water on the floor of the passenger compartment

>> The cooling fan keeps cycling on and off

IN THIS CHAPTER

» **Understanding why oil is so important**

» **Picking the correct oil for your vehicle**

» **Getting the truth about additives**

» **Changing and recycling your oil and oil filter**

# Chapter **13**

# Oil: Keeping Your Car Young and Happy

W hen people think about the good life, they tend to think in terms of freedom from pressure, discomfort, and friction. If your car could talk, it would probably agree. When you consider that the temperature in your vehicle's combustion chambers can get as high as 4,500°F, with high pressures, the shock of combustion, and many metal parts rubbing and grinding against one another, you can see that a vehicle that's not adequately protected against heat and friction will swiftly come to an untimely death. Luckily, this kind of protection is cheap and easy to ensure. It's a simple matter of providing sufficient lubrication to keep things running smoothly and then making sure that your vehicle gets regular attention.

ECO-LOGIC

Changing the *oil* is the most essential thing you can do to give your vehicle a long and happy life. And changing the oil regularly is a gift that keeps on giving because an engine that keeps its cool and operates with less effort uses less fuel. So if you change your oil on a regular basis, you can cut fuel consumption, which in turn reduces the carbon dioxide emissions that contribute to *global warming*. Such a deal!

This chapter tells you how to choose the right kind of oil for your vehicle, how frequently you should change the oil for maximum performance, and how to do the job quickly and easily.

**REMEMBER**

Whenever you encounter a term set in *this font,* you'll find it defined in the glossary in Appendix A.

# How Oil Benefits Your Vehicle

To choose the proper kind of oil, you should know what that oil is expected to do. When your engine isn't running, the oil slops around quietly in a container called the *oil pan,* which is located at the bottom of the *crankcase* just below the engine (see Figure 13-1). When the engine is running, oil is pumped by an *oil pump* through holes and channels in the engine, where the oil helps to cool and clean the engine and provides a nice, slippery cushion that keeps moving parts from grinding one another into oblivion. The following sections explain in greater detail how oil benefits your vehicle.

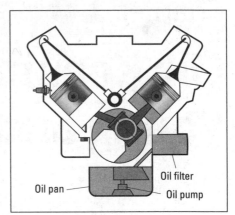

**FIGURE 13-1:**
Oil is filtered as it circulates through the engine.

## Oil cools the engine

Because the oil pan is located below the engine, where the air that rushes past the moving vehicle can cool it, the oil picks up some of the heat as it travels around inside the engine and then cools off when it circulates through the oil pan. Although this isn't enough to keep most engines sufficiently cool without a *cooling system,* it helps.

## Oil keeps your engine clean

Most engine oils contain some detergent, which helps flush out the muck that accumulates inside your engine. Not only does detergent remove and dissolve this old *sludge,* but it also helps prevent new gobs of the stuff from forming. Believe me, you have no idea of the meaning of any of those yucky words until you've looked into the engine of a vehicle that hasn't had its oil changed often enough. Masses of black slimy stuff, hunks of indefinable vileness, and pebble-like particles cling to everything. It's hard to see how these engines function at all. Even more depressing are the all-too-visible signs of wear on steel parts that have been eroded away by this ugly stuff or have succumbed to friction because the oil lost its ability to protect them. If your vehicle hasn't had its oil changed often enough, you can consider the growls coming out of its engine to be cries of pain!

## Oil cuts down on friction

By far the most important thing that the oil in your engine does is to form a cushion between moving parts to help them slide past one another easily. This lubrication cuts down *friction*, which in turn dramatically reduces the heat and wear that friction can cause.

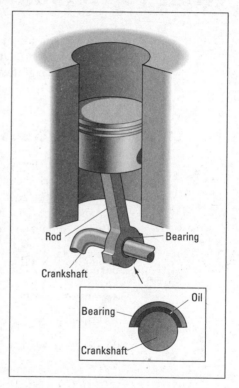

**TECHNICAL
STUFF**

Figure 13-2 shows you how oil cuts down on friction. As you can see, each *piston* is attached to a *connecting rod*. Each connecting rod has a hole in it with a *bearing* that the *crankshaft* fits through, enabling the crankshaft and the connecting rod to operate together. Now take a closer look at the enlarged portion of the figure: Notice that there's a space around the crankshaft that's always filled with oil. When the engine is running, the oil pressure forms a cushion that keeps the connecting rod bearings from ever touching the crankshaft. Instead, each bearing moves on its cushion of oil to prevent friction and wear, which is important because the rod exerts 4,000 pounds of pressure every time it moves down. This arrangement has additional benefits: If the bearings wear, replacing them is much less costly than replacing the connecting rod or the crankshaft. This same principle applies to other moving parts in your vehicle.

**FIGURE 13-2:**
Oil forms a cushion to keep your crankshaft and connecting rod from wearing each other away.

## Oil retards corrosion

Oil retards corrosion in your engine by enveloping the particles of water and acid that are present. These particles, plus the solid particles that the oil holds in suspension, contaminate the oil and thin it out. You must change the oil regularly to get rid of this stuff before it can build up to the point where the oil can't do its job properly.

# What You Should Know about Oil

Various types of motor oil are on the market, each designed for a particular purpose. This section helps you choose the proper type of oil for your vehicle by explaining the significance of the oil *additives, viscosity* ratings, and classification codes that you'll encounter at auto parts stores and service stations.

## Oil additives

To help the oil keep your engine cool, calm, collected — and clean and corrosion-free — refiners blend in various additives, which can account for as much as 25 percent of the cost of the oil. (Don't confuse these with the *aftermarket* additives sold at auto supply stores, described in the sidebar called "Using aftermarket additives: Should you or shouldn't you?")

The additives in oil help in the following ways:

>> They enable the oil to pour better in cold weather.

>> They prevent corrosion of the metal parts of the engine.

>> They cut down on friction between moving parts.

>> They dissolve impurities and prevent sludge from building up.

>> They prevent foaming at high temperatures.

## Viscosity ratings

Oil is rated and identified by its *viscosity*, which determines its ability to flow. In cold weather, oil thickens and becomes less able to flow through the engine. In hot weather, oil thins out, and although it flows well enough, it may become so thin that it can't prevent friction.

**REMEMBER**

# USING AFTERMARKET ADDITIVES: SHOULD YOU OR SHOULDN'T YOU?

You can buy three basic types of aftermarket additives in auto parts stores, each of which is designed to augment the additives in the oil itself. The first type thickens the oil. The second type loosens junk and dissolves gummy deposits. The third type acts as a friction lubricant to make the oil "tougher" under extreme temperatures and usage.

Remember that even though most oils don't advertise the presence of additives, they already have most of this stuff in them, and *no amount of additional additives can improve the performance of oil unless the oil you start with is of the best grade.* If you buy a well-known brand, you get all the protection you need in these categories if your engine is in reasonably good shape. If you use API-rated oil of the proper weight and classification and change it often, you can leave the rest of the additives on the store shelves. They may provide *temporary relief* if the engine is disintegrating, but they're not a *cure* for a worn-down, filthy, miserable old engine. And using aftermarket oil additives actually may void manufacturer's warranty on some engines.

**TECHNICAL STUFF**

Two types of oil are on the market: *single-viscosity* oil and *multi-viscosity* oil. (These are also called *single-weight* and *multi-weight* or *multigrade*.) For many years almost every vehicle has been designed to run on multi-viscosity oil. Automakers rate oil viscosity according to the temperature range expected over the oil change period. The lower the number, the thinner the oil and the more easily it flows. In 10W–40 oil, for example, the two numbers mean that it's a multi-viscosity oil that's effective over a range of temperatures. The first number, 10, is an index that refers to how the oil flows at low temperatures. The second number, 40, refers to how it flows at high temperatures. The W designation means that the oil can be used in winter.

To find out which viscosity to choose for your vehicle, look in your *owner's manual* for an oil viscosity chart. Just select the range of temperatures in any location where you plan to spend a good deal of time driving and the type of driving conditions you will operate under, and look on the chart for the grade of oil recommended for use. If you don't have an owner's manual, check with your dealership.

**TIP**

The "Choosing the Right Oil for Your Vehicle" section later in this chapter provides some surprising information on how your driving conditions affect the kind of oil you should buy and how often you should change it.

## Oil classification codes

The oil industry's American Petroleum Institute (API) has adopted a symbol to certify that a particular motor oil meets the latest industry requirements and codes for protection against deposits, wear, oxidation, and corrosion. The starburst symbol on an oil container label shown in Figure 13-3 means that the oil meets the current engine protection standard and fuel economy requirements of the International Lubricant Standardization and Approval Committee (ILSAC), a joint effort of U.S. and Japanese automobile manufacturers. The API donut symbols also shown in Figure 13-3 mean that the oil meets Energy Conserving requirements (it improves fuel economy by reducing engine friction). Oils without these symbols may not perform as well.

**FIGURE 13-3:**
API starburst
symbol (a), API
donut symbol for
gasoline engine
oil (b), API donut
symbol for diesel
engine oil (c).

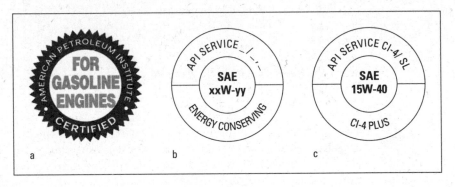

The classification codes for vehicles with gasoline engines started with SA in the early 1960s. As engines became more demanding and oil improved, the codes progressed alphabetically from SB onward. Any oil coded before SJ is no longer considered current. You can use SM (and any future grades that come along) in a vehicle of any age to make the engine run and feel better. All the major brands of oil with the API symbol are equally good.

At publication, CI-4 Plus oil is the latest, most advanced oil for diesel engines. Oils with CF (or higher) designations also are currently acceptable. For more complete classifications for diesel oils, see Chapter 9.

## Synthetic oil

A lot of claims have been made about synthetic oils: that they allow longer intervals between oil changes, result in less wear on engine parts, and are able to operate at higher engine temperatures. The longer interval claim has yet to be proven; in fact, one synthetic oil manufacturer that claimed a 20,000-mile oil change interval for its oil has retracted that claim and now suggests that its oil be changed at the normal frequency for mineral-based oils.

A *Consumer Reports* test found no difference in engine wear between vehicles that had mineral oils in their engines and those that had synthetic oils in their engines. There's no doubt, however, that synthetic oils do perform better than mineral oils at very low and very high temperatures. So if you live in a very cold or hot climate, or if your engine works very hard pulling a trailer or climbing steep hills, synthetic oil may be right for you. Just be forewarned that synthetic oil is expensive; it can cost three times as much as mineral-based oil.

A compromise between synthetic and mineral oil has been developed. This blend of mineral and synthetic oil sells for less than synthetic oil and more than mineral oil.

# Choosing the Right Oil for Your Vehicle

If all the preceding variables have you wondering how you're going to choose the right oil for your vehicle, ask yourself the following questions:

**WARNING**

**TIP**

>> **What kind of oil have you been using?** If your vehicle is running well, there's probably nothing to be gained by switching to another brand of oil. There's not a lot of difference between API-rated oils as far as performance is concerned, and you'd have to drain all the oil out of your engine before replacing it with another brand.

>> **What kind of oil does your owner's manual recommend?** Is your vehicle still under *warranty?* Be sure to use whatever weight of oil the owner's manual recommends. Using something other than the recommended oil may invalidate the warranty on a new vehicle.

Some car manufacturers now offer their own brands of motor oil specifically designed for their vehicles, and if you have a vehicle with that kind of oil in it, it's a good idea to continue to use it. Otherwise, stick with the same stuff you've been using as long as it bears the API symbols and is the proper weight for your vehicle.

>> **Do you live in a very cold or very hot climate? Is it mountainous? Are there sharp changes in temperature where you live or where you're going?** Multi-weight oils cover a range of temperatures. Consult a viscosity chart to be sure that the oil you use will flow properly under extreme conditions.

The lower the number after the "W," the better the oil works in cold weather; the higher the number after the "W," the better the hot weather performance. For example, the best oil for a Minnesota winter may be a 0W-20 and the best for a Florida summer 30W-50.

# WHAT TO DO WHEN NO AMOUNT OR TYPE OF OIL CAN HELP

**TECHNICAL STUFF**

If your vehicle has a worn, clanking workhorse engine, investigate the following alternatives to an oil change:

- **Find out how much it would cost to *rebuild* the engine.** A simple engine rebuild only replaces parts that are completely worn out, leaving you an engine with some new and some half-worn pieces. The price depends on how many parts have to be replaced and how much work is involved. Prepare to pay up to $2,000 to $4,000 for this service — perhaps more if you have a newer engine.

- **Buy a new engine or a good *remanufactured* one and have it installed.** This is a more expensive but often longer-lasting solution if you just have to keep Old Faithful or are restoring a ***classic car.*** The cost, including labor, can easily range from $2,500 to over $5,000 — perhaps more for modern engines with fancy electronic components. But that's still cheaper than a new vehicle, and you get all-new parts.

  Be sure to check your vehicle's current ***blue book*** value at www.kbb.com or www.edmunds.com to see whether a new or remanufactured engine is worth the expense, keeping in mind that other systems may be at the point of wearing out, as well.

  If rebuilding or replacing the engine will cost more than the vehicle's blue book value, it's not worthwhile (unless Old Faithful has sentimental value because your firstborn was conceived in the backseat).

- **Put Old Faithful out of its misery.** You'll both be happier in the long run. Either sell it to a wrecker who will resell some of its parts and recycle the rest, or donate it to a charity and put the tax deduction toward the purchase of a replacement vehicle.

**TIP**

If you're going to be driving your vehicle in an area where the conditions are very different from those at home and those conditions call for oil of a different viscosity than you usually use, drain all the oil from the engine before switching to the new viscosity, and drain it again before switching back to your usual weight oil after the trip is over.

>> **How old is your vehicle?** If you have a really old vehicle that has been running on single-weight oil for most of its life, it has built up quite a bit of sludge because some single-weight oils don't have detergent in them.

If you suddenly switch to multi-viscosity oil, the detergent in it will free all the gook in your engine, and the gook will really foul things up.

>> **How worn is your vehicle's engine?** If your vehicle has been logging a great many miles over several years and has been running on 30- or 40-single-weight oil, multi-weight oil isn't consistently thick enough to lubricate the worn engine parts that have become smaller while wearing down, leaving wider spaces between them. To keep the oil thick enough to fill these gaps, switch to heavier single-weight oil as your vehicle gets older and starts to run more roughly or burn up oil more quickly. If you've been running on 30-weight oil, switch to 40-weight at least during the summer, when oil tends to thin out. The manual for Tweety Bird (my faithful 1967 Mustang) called for 10W-40 oil, but when she had more than 80,000 miles to her credit, I put her on straight 40-weight oil. There's even 50-weight oil for the real oldies!

Whenever you buy oil, look for major brands or check *Consumer Reports*. Good brands of oil are often on sale in supermarkets and at auto supply stores, so if you want to save money and you spot a sale of a major brand with API certification, buy a case and stash it away.

No matter how cheap low-grade oil is, it will cost you money in lower fuel economy, poorer performance, and repair bills for wear and tear on your engine.

# How Often You Should Change Your Oil

Dirty oil just doesn't do the job as well as fresh oil does. The *additives* in dirty oil boil out, contaminants form in the *crankcase* and eat metal parts, and water collects over time and forms *sludge*. The oil holds more and more abrasive particles of metal suspended in it, and these particles wear away the parts of the engine that the oil is supposed to protect. That's why you should change your oil at regular, reasonable intervals. But what is a reasonable amount of time — or mileage — between oil changes?

All oil looks pretty black within a couple of days after an oil change, so the only way to avoid running on oil that's so dirty that it becomes a liability is to keep a record of when it was last changed and to change it frequently — as often as every 1,000 miles in extreme operating conditions (I get to what those are in a minute). By changing your oil frequently, you may get *twice* the mileage out of an otherwise good engine.

You'll be surprised by what some "extreme operating conditions" are: If you do a lot of stop-and-go driving in city or rush-hour traffic, make a lot of short trips each day and leave the car parked long enough to have your engine cool down between them, and don't often get up to high speeds on a highway, your engine rarely gets hot enough to evaporate the water that forms in the crankcase and builds up sludge in the engine. Other extreme conditions are if you drive in very hot weather or in areas with a lot of blowing dust or dirt, or tow or haul heavy loads all the time. In any of these circumstances, change the oil as often as every 1,000 to 3,000 miles on older vehicles. On new vehicles, follow the manufacturers' recommendations for extreme use.

Some manufacturers suggest that oil be changed every 7,500 miles or more, but that's based on optimum operating conditions, and the manufacturers are the ones who get to sell you a new vehicle if your old one wears out prematurely. Although new vehicles can run longer on the same oil than older ones can, and improvements in motor oil have extended its efficiency over longer periods of time, to be on the safe side, I now change my oil every 5,000 miles or every six months, whichever comes first. If you're a freeway driver who goes on a lot of long journeys at high speeds, you can probably extend the oil change interval, but on anything but the newest vehicles I wouldn't go longer than 5,000 miles between changes. And never, under any circumstances, go farther than the manufacturer's recommended maximum interval between oil changes.

# How to Change Your Oil Yourself

Changing oil is usually easy. In fact, unless it's impossible to reach your *oil filter* and/or *oil drain plug,* you have good reasons to change your oil and oil filter yourself: It's cheaper, you know that the job's being done right, and it requires little time or effort. (During one of my TV guest appearances, Regis Philbin changed the oil in a car in five minutes, and he didn't get a spot on his Italian silk suit!) All you have to do is unscrew a plug and a filter, let the oil drain out, replace the filter and plug, and pour in some new oil.

If you have a professional do it for you, you have to telephone the shop to make an appointment, drive the car in, either wait for it or find a ride home and back again to pick it up, and then wait until they write up your bill — all of which takes much longer than changing your oil yourself. If you go to one of those quickie oil change places, you don't know what *viscosity* and grade of oil they've *really* used, whether they really changed the filter, and whether the drain plug was secured properly. (If you don't think that's a problem, check out the nearby sidebar "A tragic tale"!) Most important, when you see how inexpensive and easy it is to do this job yourself, you'll change your oil as often as necessary rather than adding visits to the service station to your procrastination list!

## A TRAGIC TALE

Before I stopped being an automotive "dummy," my family car, Big Green Feller, resided for its first 35,000 miles in a commercial garage where professional mechanics looked after it. Whenever they said that the car needed the oil changed, I scheduled the work promptly. Yet when I took the engine apart in an adult-education automotive class, I found that the mechanics had never changed the oil! This lack of proper lubrication had led to big trouble: The dirty old oil had formed big, black pebbles, and the **camshaft** had practically worn away! When this happens, either you opt for major and expensive surgery or you get rid of the vehicle. As I sadly watched Big Green Feller vanish into the sunset, the major question on my mind was, "How did this happen?"

The answer, unfortunately, was that I'd depended on someone else for lubrication reminders and had trusted someone else to do the job properly. Not only had I been paying at least twice as much as it would have cost to do the job myself, but I ended up paying to replace a car that could have gone almost twice as far if it had been lubricated properly.

TIP

If you can't reach the oil filter or drain plug without having to crawl under your vehicle, or if you want to chicken out of the job for any other reason, most shops regularly offer low-priced specials for changing oil or include it in maintenance packages. Just be sure that they use the right grade of high-quality oil for your vehicle and that they change the oil filter, too. To be sure they've replaced the drain plug, drive the car off the spot where they've parked it and look for fresh oil on the ground that was under it. Paranoid? Maybe, but *if the oil drains out while you're driving, you could ruin the engine in a matter of blocks.*

## Get your supplies together

Before you start the job, assemble the following items:

>> **Oil:** Check your **owner's manual** to find the proper oil **viscosity** recommended for your vehicle and the number of quarts you need. (As a general rule, most vehicles require five to six quarts of oil, but you don't want to risk overfilling it.) If you have no manual, call a local dealer who sells your vehicle's make and model and ask someone in the service department. Or find the information at your local library in a **service manual** for your vehicle's make, model, and year.

>> **An oil filter:** Under the hood of most cars, sticking out of the engine is what looks like a tin can screwed into the **engine block.** This is the **oil filter** (see Figure 13-4). As the oil circulates from the **oil pan** through your engine, it passes through this filter, which cleans the oil and removes some of the

particles of metal and dirt. *Change the oil filter every time you change your oil,* especially if you do it less frequently than every 5,000 miles. Oil filters sell for very little at auto supply stores (at a service station, you'll usually pay more).

TIP

Check the price of an oil filter at your dealer's parts department. If it's within a dollar or two of the auto parts store price, buy it. It's probably a better filter. (Some of the auto parts store filters are very cheaply made, and they fail occasionally.) Make sure to get the right filter for your vehicle's make and model!

» **An oil filter wrench (optional):** Most oil filters screw on and off. If your old filter hasn't been changed in a long time, you may need an oil filter wrench, like the one shown in Figure 13-5, to unscrew your filter. *Always tighten the new filter by hand to avoid crushing the seal.*

» **An adjustable wrench:** Use this tool to unscrew the oil drain plug. If you're not sure what an adjustable wrench is, see Chapter 3.

» **A screwdriver:** Select one that's strong enough to punch a hole in an oil filter (you'll find out why later on).

» **An oil drain plug** *gasket:* If you buy your oil filter from a dealership, a new *gasket* may be in the package. If it isn't, get a gasket for your vehicle's make, model, and year.

WARNING

Some vehicles don't have drain plug gaskets, relying instead on a tapered metal-to-metal contact to prevent oil leakage. Don't try to use a gasket on one of these arrangements. It won't work, and you may end up with your new oil in a pool on the floor.

**FIGURE 13-4:**
An oil filter.

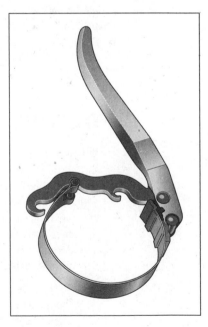

**FIGURE 13-5:**
An oil filter wrench.

» **A drain pan to catch the oil:** Find an old basin that's low enough to fit under your vehicle's drain plug without the necessity of jacking up the car, and large enough to hold all the old oil — usually about five quarts. Line the basin with a heavy-duty plastic garbage bag, opened so that it can catch the oil, leaving the basin clean.

You can buy a container made especially for catching old oil. These containers are reusable, but you have to wash them out and find a place to keep them, or throw them out and buy another one each time. More important, you can't recycle the oil that's drained into them.

» **A funnel:** Oil is sold in containers that have narrow necks to facilitate pouring the oil into the engine. If you're still worried about your aim, use a funnel to prevent messy spills. The funnel also comes in handy for decanting the used oil into containers for recycling. See the later section "Recycle your old oil and filter" for instructions on doing that.

» ***Thin* disposable plastic gloves to keep your hands clean:** You also can use dish detergent to easily remove oil from your hands.

» **Things to clean up oil:** You should have a clean, lint-free rag handy for wiping your oil dipstick and a dirty, old, thick rag that you don't mind throwing away to use on spills and tools. You can use paper towels to clean up spills and tools, but don't risk bits of paper getting into your engine by using paper to tidy it up. (If you own a cat, kitty litter is the best way to sop up spills on the ground, but not on the engine. See the later section "Clean up spilled oil thoroughly" for more instructions.)

» **A work light:** A work light helps you see better underneath the vehicle; a flashlight can be awkward if you have to hold it between your teeth!

## Do the job systematically

Always use a *system* when you do an oil change: *Do each part of the job in order, and don't change that order from job to job.* This may sound unduly restrictive if you like to improvise, but if you ignore this advice, you may find that you've added the new oil before replacing the *oil drain plug* or the *oil filter.* In either case, you wind up with your brand-new oil all over the ground and not enough oil in the engine to drive to the store for more. Also, the minute you replace the oil drain plug, *always* tighten it completely and — so that you won't forget it — put in the new oil immediately. (Don't laugh; people have forgotten and have ruined their engines in a couple of miles.)

Although the oil change process takes 17 steps to explain, it shouldn't take more than 15 minutes to accomplish after you buy the necessary stuff. Follow these easy steps to change your oil and oil filter:

1.  **Either park on level ground or in such a way that the oil drain plug is at the lower end of the oil pan.**

WARNING

    If you've chosen to disregard my suggestion that you not do the job if you have to jack up your vehicle, at least read Chapter 1 to be sure that you do so safely. Block the wheels, use jack stands, and don't jack the car up too high, or the oil may not drain out of the oil pan completely. If

    you can, jack up the vehicle so that the oil drain plug is at the lower end of the *oil pan*.

2.  **Before you begin work, be sure your *gearshift* is in Park or Neutral with the *parking brake* on, and set out all your tools and equipment.**

    Place all the stuff you're going to use within easy reach so that you don't have to jump up and run around to the other side of the vehicle in the middle of the job.

3.  **Warm up your engine for two or three minutes so that the gook gets churned up and can flow out of the engine easily.**

WARNING

    You don't want the engine so hot that you burn yourself. When it's *slightly* warm, shut off the engine.

4.  **Use a work light or flashlight to look under your car. You should be able to see and reach a large nut or plug located under the oil pan at the bottom of the engine (see Figure 13-6).**

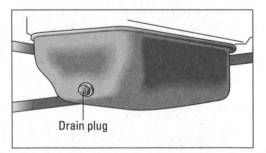

Drain plug

**FIGURE 13-6:**
The drain plug is located at the bottom of your oil pan.

    This is the *oil drain plug.* It unscrews with the aid of an adjustable wrench. If the plug is too hot to touch comfortably, let the engine cool off for a while longer.

REMEMBER

    If you can't reach your oil drain plug easily and you still want to do this job yourself, you'll have to either crawl under your car to reach the plug or jack up the car.

**5.** **Push the basin with the plastic bag opened inside it (or the oil-change container) under the oil drain plug so that it can catch the oil.**

The oil may not come down vertically to start with; it may come out sideways from the direction the drain plug is facing. Allow room for that when you place the drain pan.

**6.** **Use your adjustable wrench to unscrew the oil drain plug until it's _almost ready to come out_. Then protect your hand with the dirty rag or a disposable plastic glove, and give the plug a last quick turn by hand to release it. _Pull your hand away quickly so that you don't get oil all over yourself._**

If the plug falls into the container, you can retrieve it later. The oil should drain out of your engine into the container (remember to retrieve the **gasket** if, against my recommendation, you're going to reuse it). While the oil drains, get out from under the vehicle and take a look under the hood.

**7.** **Remove the cap from the _oil filler hole_ at the top of your engine.**

This large cap is easy to recognize: It lifts or screws right off, revealing a largish hole.

**8.** **Unscrew the oil filter using an oil filter wrench if you can't do it by hand.**

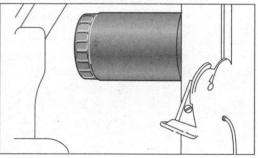
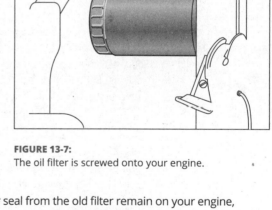

The oil filter looks like a tin can that's screwed onto the engine (see Figure 13-7). Like most other things you find on a vehicle, the oil filter unscrews if you twist it counterclockwise. _The old filter will have oil in it, so be careful not to dump it on anything when you remove it._

**FIGURE 13-7:**
The oil filter is screwed onto your engine.

If any remnants of the rubber seal from the old filter remain on your engine, scrape them off carefully, making sure they don't fall into the hole.

On some vehicles, you can easily reach the oil filter by leaning under the hood. Unfortunately, on other models the filter must be reached from under the vehicle. If your vehicle is one of these, you may have to jack the vehicle up to get at it.

**9.** **Empty the oil from the filter into the drain pan.**

Use a screwdriver to punch a hole in the dome of the can (which releases the pressure in the filter) and invert it in the drain pan to allow the oil to flow out. When the filter has drained _completely_ (this can take as long as 12 hours), wrap it in newspaper and set it aside to take to a recycling center with your old oil (see the section "Recycle your old oil and filter" later in this chapter).

10. **While the old oil drains out of the engine, open a new bottle of oil. Dip a finger in the new oil and moisten the gasket on the top of the new oil filter. Then screw the new filter into the engine where the old one was.**

**WARNING**

Follow directions on the filter, or turn it gently until it settles into place, and then turn it another three-quarter turn. Unless the filter manufacturer specifically recommends it or there isn't enough space to get your hand into the area, don't use an oil filter wrench to *tighten* the filter. It should fit tightly, but you don't want to crush the gasket or the filter will leak.

11. **Reach under the vehicle again and use your dirty rag to wipe around the place where the oil drain plug goes.**

12. **Replace the oil drain plug and use an adjustable wrench to tighten it. If your vehicle uses an oil drain plug gasket, make sure that the old one has been removed, and lay a new gasket on the pan before you replace the plug.**

13. **After you install the oil filter and replace the oil drain plug, use a funnel — or just good aim — to pour all but one quart of fresh oil into the oil filler hole.**

14. **Replace the oil filler cap and run the engine for 30 to 60 seconds while you check for leaks from the oil drain plug and around the filter.**

The oil pressure light on your dashboard should go out in 10 or 15 seconds (or if your vehicle has an ***oil pressure gauge,*** the needle should move off of "Low"). *Don't rev up your engine during this period.* Your oil pressure ranges from zero to low while the light is on and won't reach the proper pressure until your oil filter fills up. If the light doesn't go out, check under the vehicle and around the engine for leaks. Running the engine circulates oil into the new oil filter, and because filters hold from a half to a full quart of oil, you want to be sure that your filter is full to get an accurate reading on the oil ***dipstick.***

15. **Shut off the engine and wait five to ten minutes for the oil to settle into the oil pan. Then remove the oil *dipstick,* wipe it with a clean, lint-free rag, and shove it back in. Pull it out again and check it.**

Refer to Figure 2-10 in Chapter 2 if you don't know what an oil dipstick looks like. Your owner's manual should tell you where it is on your engine.

16. **Keep adding oil a little at a time and checking the stick until you reach the "Full" line on the dipstick.**

17. **Remove the drain pan from under the vehicle, drive around the block a couple of times, let the oil settle down again, and recheck the dipstick and the dashboard indicator.**

**WARNING**

*Never* keep running an engine or drive a vehicle that tells you its oil pressure is low. Because oil not only lubricates but also helps cool the engine, you can ruin your engine if you drive even a short distance with insufficient oil or with a defective ***oil pump.***

In Appendix B, enter the vehicle mileage and date of the oil change in the *Maintenance Record* and the oil filter make and part number, with the weight and amount of oil you needed, on the *Specifications Record.*

When you see how easy changing the oil is, you'll tend to change your oil more frequently, and your vehicle will perform better, last longer, burn less fuel, and cause less air pollution. You'll feel pretty happy with yourself, too!

## Clean up spilled oil thoroughly

You can't just hose off oil you've spilled on the ground — it will only rise to the surface of the water and spread to a larger area. The best way to clean up spilled oil is to cover the oil with a generous layer of kitty litter, let it soak up the oil for a few hours (it will even pull some up out of the concrete or asphalt), then sweep up and properly dispose of the oil-soaked stuff. Next, squirt some liquid dishwashing soap onto the stain and scrub with a stiff brush; or on unpainted concrete, scrub the area with a solution of half laundry soap and half bleach. Wipe up the dirty cleaning liquid with paper or cloth towels, and rinse the area well.

## Recycle your old oil and filter

WARNING

*Never dump oil onto the ground, throw it out with your regular garbage, or flush it down a drain.* It's a major toxic pollutant that needs to be treated accordingly. In many locales, putting oil filters into a landfill is against the law, so you may risk a fine.

So what do you do with your old oil? Decant the oil from the garbage bag that was in your collection pan into *clean* disposable containers with tight-fitting, screw-on lids — the bottles that the new oil came in or old, *washed* soda bottles work well. Place a funnel in the neck of the container, tie-off the bag, and hold it above the funnel. Then cut a tiny hole in a bottom corner of the bag and let the oil drain out of the bag into the funnel and container. You may want to cover the ground underneath the container with a thick layer of newspapers. (If you spill oil anyway, see the preceding section "Clean up spilled oil thoroughly.")

WARNING

Oil recyclers probably won't accept oil that's contaminated with another substance or in a dirty container, so take it to a toxic waste disposal center.

ECO-LOGIC

The Steel Recycling Institute says that if all the oil filters sold in the United States each year were recycled, enough material would be recovered to build 16 stadiums the size of Atlanta's Olympic Stadium! Many auto parts stores and some service stations accept old oil and oil filters for recycling. If you don't have one close by, look in your local yellow pages for the nearest oil recycling center or toxic waste disposal center, or visit www.earth911.org or www.filtercouncil.org and type in your zip code.

# Chapter **14**

# It's the Brakes!

This chapter deals with an automotive system that most people take for granted even though it may be the only system in your vehicle that can kill you if you don't keep it in good repair. As you've probably guessed — especially if you read chapter titles — I'm talking about your brakes.

As with the other basic automotive systems covered in this book, I deal with brakes in two parts: This chapter covers the general theory behind brakes and braking systems, and Chapter 15 tackles the hands-on information you need to repair and maintain them.

**REMEMBER**

Whenever you encounter a term set in *this font,* you'll find it defined in the glossary in Appendix A.

## Brake System Basics

One reason that today's vehicles are the safest in history is that, since 1968, all vehicles come equipped with *dual brake systems* to ensure that if one set of brakes fails, the other set can still stop your car (see the "Dual brakes" sidebar later in this chapter). Your vehicle also has a dashboard light to warn you if your brakes are malfunctioning. A growing number of modern vehicles not only are equipped with *hydraulic* brake systems but also feature *electronic* brake systems that operate even more safely and efficiently.

Because electronic brake systems employ most of the same hydraulic parts as hydraulic systems, I start with the basics and get to the more advanced systems later in this chapter.

Figure 14-1 shows a basic brake system with a *brake booster, disc brakes* on the front wheels, and *drum brakes* on the rear wheels. Your vehicle may have disc brakes all around, but the principle is the same in any case.

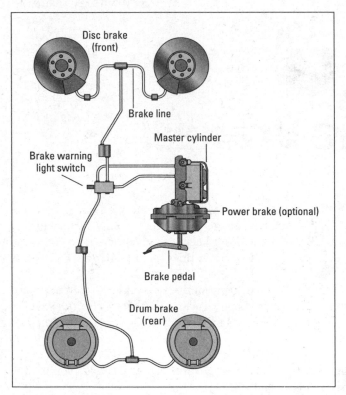

**FIGURE 14-1:** A brake system with drum brakes at the rear and discs up front.

The following sections take a look at each of the components of a basic hydraulic brake system, starting with the first point of contact between you and your brakes and working down the line to the brakes themselves.

## The brake pedal

The brake pedal in your vehicle is attached to a shaft that leads to the brake *master cylinder.* When you step on the brake pedal, small pistons in the master cylinder force *brake fluid* out of the master cylinder and into the *brake lines.* (I tell you how to buy the proper brake fluid and work with it safely in the "Flushing and Changing Brake Fluid" section in Chapter 15.)

**TIP**

If your brakes are working properly, the pedal should stop a couple of inches from the floor. It should push down easily, stop firmly at its lowest point without feeling spongy, and stay put instead of sinking down slowly when you put normal pressure on it. Chapter 15 shows you how to check the brakes on your vehicle.

## Power brakes

Today, most vehicles have *power brakes* with a *brake booster* located between the brake pedal and the master cylinder to increase the force applied to the pistons in the master cylinder so that your car can stop with less effort on your part (see Figure 14-2). The two most common types of power brake boosters are *vacuum-assisted boosters,* which use engine vacuum and atmospheric pressure to do the job; and *hydraulic-assisted boosters* (commonly referred to as *hydro-boost units*), which use hydraulic pressure from the car's power steering to accomplish the same thing. Some vehicles with *anti-lock braking systems (ABS)* have a hydraulic pump to generate pressure for booster operation. (You can find a section on ABS later in this chapter.)

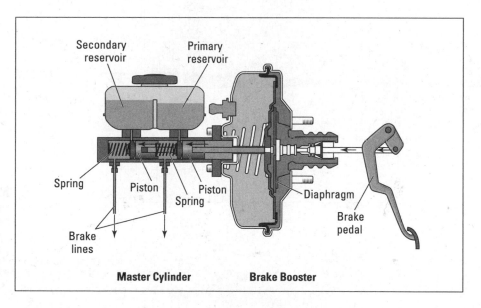

**FIGURE 14-2:**
When you step on the brake pedal, the brake booster activates the master cylinder.

Your owner's manual can tell you what kind(s) of brakes you have on your vehicle, in case you don't already know, but seeing for yourself is more fun. Later in this chapter, I cover each type of brakes in detail.

## The brake master cylinder

Under the hood of your car, usually up near the *firewall* on the driver's side, you should see either a metal box (see Figure 14-3) or, on most newer vehicles, a plastic container (see Figure 14-4). This is the brake *master cylinder* (refer to Figure 14-2). It's filled with *brake fluid* and is connected to your brake pedal, with *brake lines* leading from it to the four wheels of your vehicle. Stepping on the brake pedal activates the brake *power booster,* which activates the pistons in the master cylinder, forcing brake fluid out of the master cylinder into the brake lines. When you release the pedal, the fluid flows back into the master cylinder. In Chapter 15, I show you how to open and check the master cylinder safely. This task is also part of the monthly under-the-hood check in Chapter 2.

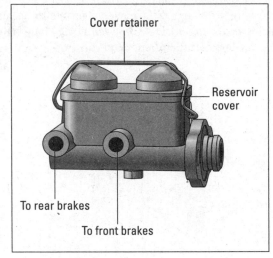

Cover retainer

Reservoir cover

To rear brakes

To front brakes

**FIGURE 14-3:**
A metal master cylinder.

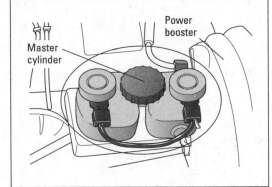

Master cylinder

Power booster

**FIGURE 14-4:**
A plastic master cylinder.

## DUAL BRAKES

A *dual* brake system simply means that the inside of the master cylinder is divided into *two* compartments, each filled with brake fluid. On a vehicle with ***rear-wheel drive,*** one compartment has brake lines that lead to the brakes on the front wheels; the other compartment has lines leading to the brakes at the rear wheels (refer to Figure 14-3). If a leak or a block develops in one set of lines, the fluid in that com-partment is lost or useless. But the other compartment and set of brakes can still stop your vehicle. It may not stop smoothly, but it will stop, and in such a case, that's all that counts! This simple modification has saved countless lives.

Most ***front-wheel drive*** vehicles have a diagonally split ***hydraulic*** brake system that ties the right-front wheel with the left-rear wheel and the left-front wheel with the right-rear wheel. That's because the front brakes on front-wheel drive vehicles do almost 90 percent of the braking. By diagonally splitting the hydraulic system, you always have one front brake and one rear brake operating in the event of a hydraulic failure.

## Brake lines

The brake lines run from the master cylinder along the frame of your vehicle to each wheel. The lines are made of steel except for the portions that lie right near your front wheels and your *rear axle*. These portions are made of rubber or syn-thetic material that's flexible enough to contend with the greater amount of movement that takes place in these areas as the *suspension system* works and the wheels turn when you steer.

## Brake fluid

Although electronic brakes using electric motors to do the work are in develop-ment, brake systems today still are activated by *hydraulic* fluid called, you guessed it, *brake fluid.* You can make your brake system work better and live longer if you change the fluid — or have it changed by your mechanic — once every 24 months, regardless of mileage. Brake fluid soaks up moisture from the atmosphere. As this water contaminates it, the boiling point of the brake fluid lowers until it can reach a point where it begins to boil as brake heat builds up. When that happens, the air bubbles in the boiling fluid cause the brakes to fail, a situation nobody wants. Chapter 15 tells you how to change brake fluid.

The parts discussed thus far are common to most hydraulic brake systems. Now for some of the major differences: When you press the brake pedal and force the brake fluid from the master cylinder into the brake lines, what happens next depends on the type of brakes you have. For many years, cars had *drum brakes* (see Figure 14-5) on all four wheels. As you can see in Figure 14-1, some vehicles have drum brakes on the rear wheels and *disc brakes* (see Figure 14-8) on the front wheels. Today, many vehicles have four-wheel disc brakes, and most have the *power brakes* described earlier in this chapter. *Anti-lock braking systems (ABS)* also have become popular, and I get to them shortly.

# Drum Brakes

*Drum brakes,* shown in Figure 14-5, are the oldest type of brakes still on the road. Their main advantage is that they require less *hydraulic* pressure to stop your vehicle because the *brake shoes* tend to screw themselves into the *brake drums* after the pistons in the *wheel cylinders* push them there. The following sections get you acquainted with what's inside drum brakes and how they work. Chapter 15 shows you how to access a drum brake and check its condition.

Even if your vehicle has *disc brakes* all around, you should read this section because they work on the same principles as drum brakes.

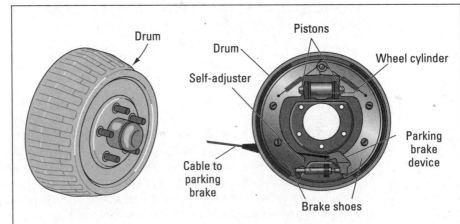

**FIGURE 14-5:**
Anatomy of a drum brake.

# Brake drums

*Brake drums* are hollow steel cylinders located in back of each wheel (refer to Figure 14-5). Because the *lug bolts* that go through them are the same as the ones that go through the wheels of your vehicle, the drums turn when the wheels turn. If you keep your brakes in good condition and replace your *brake linings* before they become too worn, your brake drums should last for the life of your vehicle. If drums become worn, they can be "reground" or "turned" to a smooth surface — unless they're worn more than their manufacturer's recommendation (usually more than .060 of an inch), in which case the drums must be replaced. Chapter 15 shows you how to inspect your brake drums and get a fair deal if they need work.

# Wheel cylinders

As you can see in Figure 14-6, *wheel cylinders* are small but powerful mechanisms located inside each brake drum on the *brake backing plate.*

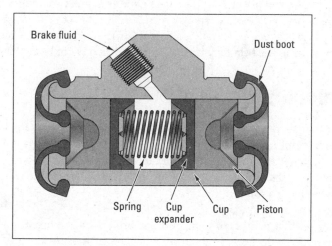

**FIGURE 14-6:**
Anatomy of a wheel cylinder.

The brake fluid that's forced through the brake lines by the piston in the master cylinder goes into the wheel cylinders. The fluid then activates the two small pistons located inside each wheel cylinder by forcing them farther apart. The pistons emerge from either end of the wheel cylinder and push against the *brake shoes.* Figure 14-7 shows how the wheel cylinders work.

**TECHNICAL STUFF**

Seals inside the wheel cylinder, called *cups,* keep the brake fluid from leaking out. *Dust boots* on each end of the wheel cylinder prevent dirt and dust from entering and fouling the cylinder.

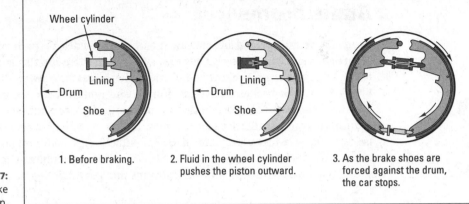

1. Before braking.

2. Fluid in the wheel cylinder pushes the piston outward.

3. As the brake shoes are forced against the drum, the car stops.

**FIGURE 14-7:** A drum brake in action.

## Brake shoes

As you can see in Figure 14-7, *brake shoes* are curved pieces of metal that stop the vehicle when the pistons in the wheel cylinders push them against the inside of the brake drum. The brake shoes are attached to a set of springs that draw them back into place when you take your foot off the brake pedal. Chapter 15 provides tips on getting the best deal if your brake shoes have to be replaced.

## Brake linings

Either bonded or riveted to the brake shoes are curved *brake linings* of tough, very heat-resistant material. As you can see in Figure 14-7, when the brake shoes are forced against the insides of the brake drum, the linings create friction, which causes the brake drum to stop turning. This in turn forces the wheels to stop turning, which stops the car.

TECHNICAL STUFF

The brake linings on front-wheel drum brakes have a larger surface than those on the rear wheels because the front wheels bear most of the pressure of stopping (the weight shifts from the rear to the front when you brake). Also, in a *front-wheel drive* vehicle, most of the weight of the *drive train* is up front to begin with. For these reasons, on each set of brake linings on *any* wheel, the lining toward the front of the vehicle is larger and often is a different color so that mechanics don't make a mistake when replacing them.

TIP

You should check your brake linings for wear every 10,000 to 20,000 miles. Chapter 15 shows you how.

## Adjusting devices

Drum brakes that could be manually adjusted used to be popular, but today's passenger vehicles have *self-adjusting* brakes. The self-adjusting device is located at the bottom of the brake backing plate. These devices are used to adjust the distance between the surface of the brake lining and the inside of the brake drum when you step on the brake pedal. As your brake linings become worn, the distance increases, and the adjustment compensates for that. If you didn't have a self-adjusting device and your linings became very worn, eventually the brake shoes wouldn't contact the inside of the drum and your car wouldn't stop. You can see the self-adjusting device on the drum brake in Figure 14-5.

# Disc Brakes

*Disc brakes* used to be found mainly on the front wheels of vehicles, with drum brakes at the rear (refer to Figure 14-1). Today most passenger vehicles have disc brakes all around. Each brake has a flat steel disc — you knew that, right? — sandwiched between a pair of *calipers* (see Figure 14-8) or a single caliper (see Figure 14-9). These calipers contain one or more pistons that force the *brake fluid* in the *brake lines* into the disc. Between the disc (sometimes called a *rotor*) and the pistons are *brake pads,* which operate in the same way that *brake shoes* do: They grab the disc with their friction linings and force the disc to stop turning, which in turn forces the wheel to stop turning and the vehicle to stop moving. The effect is the same as on a bicycle when the brakes grab the wheel directly to stop it from turning. Chapter 15 tells you how to inspect and troubleshoot disc brakes.

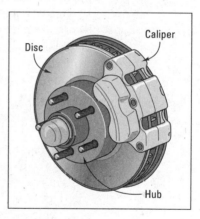

**FIGURE 14-8:**
A multiple caliper disc brake.

Older vehicles use *fixed-caliper* brake systems in which one or two pistons on each side of the disc push the pad against it. A *single-piston floating-caliper* disc brake system is becoming increasingly popular (see Figure 14-9). When you apply the brakes, the caliper moves from side to side and centers itself. Because these systems are self-adjusting, more reliable, and less expensive, they'll probably become the standard.

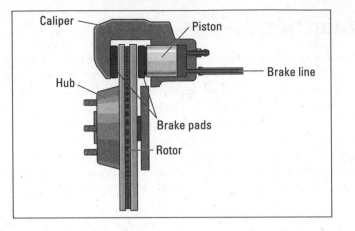

**FIGURE 14-9:**
Anatomy of a single-piston, floating-caliper disc brake.

Caliper
Piston
Brake line
Hub
Brake pads
Rotor

**TECHNICAL STUFF**

Disc brakes have advantages over drum brakes. Because they operate in the open air (instead of inside brake drums), they're less prone to overheating. They're also less affected by water because the leading edge of each brake pad scrapes the water away before it can get between the pads and the disc. (When drum brakes get wet, the brake linings may not grab the brake drum satisfactorily and the car may not stop.)

# The Parking Brake

The *parking brake,* or *emergency brake,* is usually attached to a car's rear wheels. On vehicles with rear *drum brakes,* the parking brake is usually attached with cables to the rear brakes, as shown in Figure 14-10. These are called *integral* parking brakes (see Figure 14-11). Although most newer vehicles have *self-adjusting systems,* if your vehicle doesn't you can easily adjust the cables, which run underneath the car, by turning a screw that controls the tension on the cable. Chapter 15 provides instructions on how to do so.

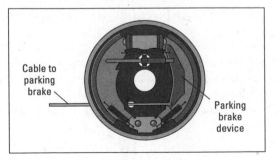

**FIGURE 14-10:**
A cable activates the parking brake system on a rear-wheel drum brake.

Cable to parking brake

Parking brake device

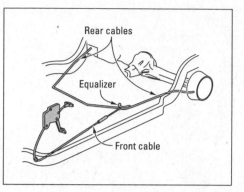

FIGURE 14-11:
An integral
parking brake
system.

On other vehicles with drum brakes, different devices do the same job. Some parking brakes on vehicles with *rear-wheel drive* are linked to the *transmission,* and rather than activating the rear brakes, they stop the *driveshaft* from turning the rear wheels. On these brakes, shown in Figure 14-12, the band and lining are attached to a drum on the transmission. When you pull the lever, the band squeezes the lining against the drum, and the driveshaft stops turning. When a transmission-type parking brake doesn't seem to be performing properly, have a professional check it.

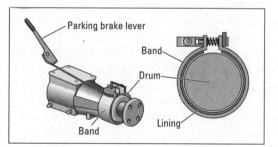

FIGURE 14-12:
A transmission-
type parking
brake system.

If you have rear *disc brakes* on your car, it may incorporate a parking brake that works like a mini-drum brake attached to the rear wheels (see Figure 14-13). Most parking brake systems for vehicles with rear disc brakes, however, employ the disc brake itself. Vehicles with disc brakes on both front and rear wheels use a cable to activate their parking brakes. You can see how it all hooks up in Figure 14-14.

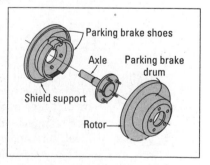

FIGURE 14-13:
A parking brake system on a rear-wheel
disc brake.

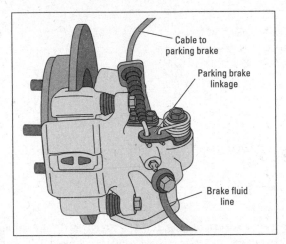

**FIGURE 14-14:**
A cable activates the parking brake system on some rear-wheel disc brakes.

# Anti-Lock Braking Systems (ABS)

*Anti-lock braking systems (ABS)* are designed to prevent skidding and enable you to keep steering control of your vehicle until you can stop safely. This system also often shortens the distance your vehicle takes to stop and can prevent the tire damage that would result if you had to stop with the wheels locked.

ABS comes in two types: two-wheel and four-wheel. Some light trucks and vans have a *two-wheel* anti-lock braking system on the rear wheels that maintains directional stability. Although the front wheels can still lock up, the vehicle continues to move in a straight line. With just enough pressure applied to the brake pedal, the driver can control the steering. You find *four-wheel* anti-lock braking systems on other light trucks and most cars. These prevent all four wheels from locking up, which enables you to maintain steering ability in emergency stopping situations. If no impending lockup occurs, the ABS stays in standby mode.

## How ABS works

**TECHNICAL STUFF**

Here's how an anti-lock brake system operates: A microprocessor called an *anti-lock brake computer* monitors the speed of each wheel with an electronic component called a *speed sensor.* When you apply firm pressure to the brake pedal, the system triggers electronic **solenoids** to trap or release *hydraulic* pressure to each wheel independently, thousands of times faster than if you pumped the brake pedal as you would with ordinary brakes. You can usually hear this happening and feel the brake pedal pulsing when the system energizes. *While the system is working, it's important to keep your foot pressed firmly on the pedal until the vehicle stops.*

Do not pump your brake pedal if your vehicle has ABS. Instead, use firm pressure on the brake pedal, keep steering, and let the microprocessor do the work for you.

If the anti-lock system has a problem, a warning light on the dashboard comes on and normal braking without anti-lock takes over. So if your amber anti-lock light illuminates, remember that you still have normal brakes. Just *pump* them and steer in the proper direction as though you'd never heard of ABS. And be sure to get the ABS fixed as soon as possible!

## What ABS doesn't do

WARNING

ABS can't prevent all skids, nor does it always stop your vehicle in a shorter distance. Although ABS does help you maintain steering, your vehicle may not turn as quickly on a slippery road as it would on dry pavement. A combination of excessive speed, sharp turns, and slamming on the brakes can still throw an ABS-equipped vehicle into a skid. On roads covered with loose gravel or freshly fallen snow, the locked wheels of a vehicle without ABS can build up a wedge of gravel or snow and stop faster than an ABS-equipped vehicle. Therefore, it's important to keep a safe distance between your vehicle and the one in front of you and to try to maintain a constant speed rather than jamming on the brakes at the last minute.

TIP

When you drive a new vehicle with ABS, it's a good idea to know what the brakes feel like when they're operating normally. Find an *empty* parking lot on a rainy or snowy day and slam on the brakes, noticing how your vehicle responds. Keep your foot firmly on the pedal and get a feel for steering while the brakes operate. Then you'll know what to expect in a panicky situation. Chapter 15 shows you how to check your anti-lock braking system; a professional must do adjustments and repairs.

# Other Electronic Braking Systems

Because the brake system is such a vital feature of every vehicle, the technology for creating safer and more responsive systems is constantly developing. Newer electronic braking systems now exist that provide additional advantages, often coupled with ABS. The following sections cover two that are in production now.

## Brake Assist (BA)

*Brake Assist* (BA) is like having a superhero in the car to save you in an emergency. It keeps an electronic eye on how you're braking, and if you suddenly get into an emergency and have to stop short, BA automatically boosts the power of the brakes to help you. When you're out of trouble and take your foot off the brake, the system automatically does so too and resumes its surveillance.

Originally offered as an option on high-end vehicles, often as part of a "precollision" package, BA is becoming available on more vehicles as the cost of the system goes down. You often find it combined with EBD, which I cover next.

## Electronic brakeforce distribution (EBD)

First popular on luxury vehicles and some SUVs, *electronic brakeforce distribution (EBD)* ensures that braking power is distributed proportionately among all the wheels. If a vehicle carries a heavy or unequally distributed load, ordinary brake function can be skewed to one area of the vehicle, causing it to pull to one side or even sending it into a skid. To ensure stability, EBD automatically distributes the force of the brakes proportionately to all the wheels so that the vehicle can stop safely.

TECHNICAL
STUFF

*Regenerative braking systems* that literally generate power to drive *hybrid* vehicles are discussed in Chapter 10. If you haven't read that chapter on alternatively powered vehicles yet, you're gonna love it!

# Chapter **15**

# Be a Buddy to Your Brakes and Bearings

As I explain in Chapter 14, all vehicles today are equipped with dual *hydraulic* brake systems. Many newer vehicles are also equipped with *anti-lock braking systems (ABS).* This chapter provides instructions for performing preventive maintenance on your brakes and doing checkups that help you to spot trouble before it occurs. If you need professional work done, this chapter also provides tips that enable you to deal with an auto mechanic or brake specialist knowledgeably.

**REMEMBER**

If you haven't read Chapter 14, or if you've forgotten what you read, please go back and review it before continuing with this chapter. Before you can troubleshoot or work on your brakes, you must be familiar with how the system on your vehicle works, what its principal parts do, and what *should* be happening when you step on the brake pedal.

# EXTENDING THE LIFE OF YOUR BRAKES

The best way you can "be a buddy to your brakes" is to extend their lifespan. You're also doing yourself a favor, and not just because repairing and replacing brakes is expensive: These techniques will help your brakes help *you* live longer, too!

- Riding your brakes (keeping your foot on the brake pedal when you drive) causes them to wear out prematurely. The excess heat also can warp brake ***rotors*** and ***brake drums.***

- Although being cautious is always a good policy, try to anticipate stopping situations well enough in advance to be able to slow down by releasing the pressure on your gas pedal and then using your brake pedal for that final stop. In slippery conditions or situations that call for slowing down rather than stopping, if you have traditional brakes, instead of jamming on your brakes and screeching to a halt, *pump* your brake pedal to reduce speed and avoid sliding. If the road is slippery and your vehicle is equipped with ABS, *don't* pump the brake pedal; simply apply firm, steady pressure and keep steering.

  Maintaining the speed limit so that you don't have to stop at every light also increases fuel efficiency, which reduces not only your expenses but also ***global warming!*** You can find more fuel-saving tips in Chapter 26.

**WARNING**

Although you can probably do most of the work in this chapter yourself, if you want to do *major* brake work, you should do it under supervision. If you don't get things back together properly, you risk losing much more than you gain! However, if after reading this chapter you simply can't stand the idea of exposing your brakes to a total stranger, get yourself to a good community auto class at a local high school or dealership and do the work under an instructor's watchful eye. In such a setting, you have access to the hydraulic hoists, brake lathes, and other expensive equipment needed to do a really good job. So even if you're sure that you need no further instruction after reading my enlightened and crystal-clear prose, having the equipment and the instructor's expertise available is still worth the price of enrollment.

**REMEMBER**

Whenever you encounter a term set in *this font*, you'll find it defined in the glossary in Appendix A.

# Checking Your Brake System

It's best to start by going over the brake system in your vehicle and checking each part for wear and proper performance. If it's safe for you to do the necessary work, I tell you how to do it in this section. If you need professional help, I tell you what the work should probably entail so that you don't end up paying more than is necessary.

Check your brakes every 10,000 to 20,000 miles, depending on your vehicle's age, type, braking system, and how much stop-and-go driving you do. If you tend to ride your brakes, they get more than normal wear and should be checked more frequently. If it's taking longer, your vehicle pulls to one side, or your brakes squeal when you try to stop, check them immediately. (After one of those breath-taking emergency stops on the freeway, I always say "Thanks, pals" and promise myself that I'll peek at my brakes and *brake lines* soon and make sure that they're in good shape.)

**WARNING**

Use extreme caution when checking vehicles with *anti-lock braking systems (ABS)*. Some ABS are pressurized by an electric pump, and there may be more than 2,000 *psi* pressure in certain parts of the system! The "Checking Anti-Lock Brakes" section in this chapter tells you what you can do and what should be done by a professional.

## Checking your brake pedal

If you're like most people, you're usually aware of only one part of your brake system: the *brake pedal*. You're so familiar with it, in fact, that you can probably tell if something's different just by the way the pedal feels when you step on the brakes.

To check your brake pedal, you simply do the same thing you do every time you drive: You step on the pedal and press it down. The only difference is that you should pay attention to how the pedal feels under your foot and evaluate the sensation. The following steps tell you what to feel for:

1. **Start your engine, but keep it in Park with the *parking brake* on. (If your vehicle doesn't have *power brakes*, it's okay to do this check with the engine off.)**

2. **With the vehicle at rest, apply steady pressure to the brake pedal.**

    Does it feel spongy? If so, you probably have air in your *brake lines.* Correcting this problem isn't difficult; unless your brakes have *ABS* or other sophisticated brake systems, you can probably do the job yourself with the help of a friend.

The "Bleeding Your Brakes" section later in this chapter tells you whether you can **bleed** the system on your vehicle and provides instructions for doing the job.

Does the pedal stay firm when you continue applying pressure, or does it seem to sink slowly to the floor? If the pedal sinks, your **master cylinder** may be defective, and that's unsafe.

3. **Release the parking brake and drive around the block, stopping every now and then (but without driving the people behind you crazy).**

   Notice how much effort is required to bring your vehicle to a stop. With power brakes, the pedal should stop 1 to 1½ inches from the floor. (If you don't have power brakes, the pedal should stop more than 3 inches from the floor.)

   If your vehicle has power brakes and stopping seems to take excessive effort, you may need to have the **power booster** replaced.

4. **If you feel that your brakes are low (meaning that the pedal goes down too far before the vehicle stops properly), pump the brake pedal a couple of times as you drive around.**

   If pumping the pedal makes the car stop when the pedal's higher up, either a brake adjustment is in order or you need more **brake fluid.** Check the brake fluid level by following the instructions in the next section, "Checking your master cylinder."

TIP

   If the level of brake fluid in the **master cylinder** is low, buy the proper brake fluid for your vehicle (see "Flushing and Changing Brake Fluid" later in this chapter for tips) and add fluid to the "Full" line on your master cylinder. Check the fluid level in the cylinder again in a few days. If it's low again, check each part of the brake system, following the instructions in this chapter, until you find the leak, or have a brake specialist find it and repair it for you.

   If you find that you're *not* low on fluid, drive *carefully* to your friendly service facility and ask them to remedy the situation. When they've worked their magic, the pedal shouldn't travel down as far before your vehicle stops.

   *Disc brakes* self-adjust and should never need adjusting. *Drum brakes* also have *self-adjusting devices* that should keep the drum brakes properly adjusted. If any of the self-adjuster components on drum brakes stick or break, the drum brakes won't adjust as they wear out, resulting in a low pedal. Chapter 14 tells you more about self-adjusting devices.

TECHNICAL
STUFF

5. **As you drive around, notice how your total brake system performs, and ask yourself these questions:**

   • **Does the vehicle travel too far before coming to a stop in city traffic?**
     If it does, either your brakes need adjusting or you need new **brake linings.**

- **Does the vehicle pull to one side when you brake?** On vehicles with front disc brakes, a stuck *caliper* and brake fluid leak can cause this problem. On vehicles with front drum brakes (antiques), a *wheel cylinder* may be leaking or stuck, or the *brake shoes* may be wear-ing unevenly. I explain how to check disc and drum brakes in the section "Getting at Your Brakes" later in this chapter.

- **Does your brake pedal pulsate up and down when you stop in a *non*-emergency situation?** A pulsating brake pedal usually is caused by excessive *lateral run-out* (mechanic-speak for wobbling from side to side), which causes a variation in the thickness of the discs. This can happen because your brakes are overheating from overuse.

**REMEMBER**

*ABS* brakes sometimes pulsate when you need them to stop quickly, so don't confuse that with a braking problem (read "Checking Anti-Lock Brakes" at the end of this chapter). Make sure that your rear brakes are working; if not, they could be causing your front brakes to work too hard and overheat.

- **Does your steering wheel shake when you brake?** If it does and you have *disc brakes,* your front *brake discs* need to be professionally machined or replaced.

- **Do your brakes squeal when you stop fairly short?** The squealing is a high-pitched noise usually caused by vibration. Squealing can occur when the *brake linings* are worn and need replacement, the *brake drum* or disc needs to be machined, the front disc *brake pads* are loose or missing their anti-rattle clips, the hardware that attaches the brake *calipers* is worn, or inferior brake linings are in use.

    Properly functioning disc brakes are sometimes a little noisy, and totally eliminating a squeal can be difficult. When you open your brakes to check them, make sure that your brake discs or drums aren't badly scored or worn and that plenty of lining material is left. Also, the brake pads on disc-type brakes should fit properly into the caliper. Some disc brake pads require special *shims* to eliminate squeal.

**WARNING**

- **Do your brakes make a grinding noise that you can feel in the pedal?** If so, stop driving *immediately* and have your vehicle *towed* to a brake repair shop. Further driving could damage the brake discs or drums. Grinding brakes are caused by excessively worn *brake linings;* when the lining wears off, the metal part of the *brake pad* or *brake shoe* contacts the brake disc or drum and can quickly ruin the most expensive mechanical parts of the brake system.

- **Does your vehicle bounce up and down when you stop short?** Your *shock absorbers* may need to be replaced. Chapter 16 has information about shock absorbers.

Never put off brake work. If any of the checks in this chapter show that you have a problem, *take care of the situation immediately.* If your brakes fail, you (and other people) may be in serious trouble. Other kinds of automotive trouble may keep your vehicle from moving, but brake trouble keeps it from *stopping.* The rest (and you) may be history.

## Checking your master cylinder

*Brake fluid* is stored in the *master cylinder.* When you step on the brake pedal, fluid goes from the master cylinder into the *brake lines;* when you release the pedal, the fluid flows back into the master cylinder. Essentially, when you check your master cylinder, you're making sure that you have enough brake fluid.

If your vehicle has *ABS*, consult your *owner's manual* before checking the master cylinder. Failure to do so may result in under- or over-filling the reservoir. And remember that some ABS are under extreme pressure and should be handled professionally.

To check the brake fluid in your master cylinder, follow these steps:

**1.** **Open the brake fluid reservoir on top of your master cylinder.**

If you have the kind with a little plastic bottle on top, just unscrew the cap on the little plastic bottle that sits on top of the master cylinder (see Figure 15-1). (Some master cylinders have a cap for each chamber.) If you have a metal reservoir, use a screwdriver to pry the retaining clamp off the top (also shown in Figure 15-1).

Don't let any dirt fall into the chambers when you open the lid. If your hood area is full of grime and dust, wipe the lid before you remove it.

**FIGURE 15-1:**
Unscrew the plastic reservoir cap (a) or use a screwdriver to release the lid on your master cylinder (b).

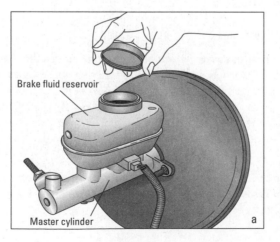

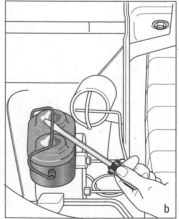

Brake fluid reservoir

Master cylinder

a

b

## 2. Take a look at the lid.

Attached to the inside surface of the lid is a protective diaphragm with rubber cups (see Figure 15-2). As the brake fluid in your master cylinder recedes (when it's forced into the brake lines), the diaphragm cups are pushed down by air that comes in through vents in the lid. The cups descend and touch the surface of the remaining brake fluid to prevent evaporation and to keep the dust and dirt out. When the fluid flows back in, the cups are pushed back up.

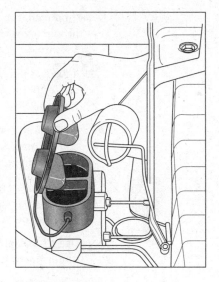

**FIGURE 15-2:**
Rubber cups inside the lid of a master cylinder.

**TIP**

If your brake fluid level is low, or if the cups are in their descended position when you remove the lid, push them back up with a clean finger before you replace the lid.

**WARNING**

If the cups seem very gooey or can't be pushed back to their original position, the wrong brake fluid may have been used. Because some *power steering fluid* reservoirs are the same shape as the brake fluid reservoirs in master cylinders, there have been cases where power steering fluid was accidentally installed in the master cylinder. If this happens, everything but the steel *brake lines* must be *rebuilt* or replaced, includ-ing the master cylinder!

## 3. Look inside the master cylinder.

The brake fluid should be up to the "Full" line on the side of the cylinder or within ½ inch of the top of each chamber. If it isn't, buy the proper brake fluid for your vehicle and add it until the level meets the line.

**WARNING**

Be sure to read the "Flushing and Changing Brake Fluid" section in this chapter to ensure that you buy the proper kind of brake fluid. Also remember to close the brake fluid reservoir as quickly as possible so that oxygen or water vapor in the air doesn't contaminate the fluid. And try not to drip it on anything — it eats paint!

A low brake fluid level may not mean anything if it's been a long time since any fluid was added and if your vehicle has been braking properly. If you have reason to believe that your brake fluid level has dropped because of a leak, use this chapter to check the rest of your system very carefully for leaks.

4. **If both chambers of your master cylinder are filled with brake fluid to the proper level, close the master cylinder carefully, without letting any dirt fall into it.**

   If dirt gets into your master cylinder, it will travel down the brake lines. If it doesn't block the lines, the dirt will end up in your *wheel cylinders* and damage your brakes.

5. **Brake fluid evaporates easily, so don't stand around admiring the inside of your master cylinder. Close it quickly, and be sure that the lid is securely in place.**

**WARNING**

   Because most master cylinders are pretty airtight, you shouldn't lose brake fluid in any quantity unless it's leaking out somewhere else. If your fluid level was low, you'll find the cause as you continue to check the system.

6. **Use a flashlight or work light to look for stain marks, wetness, or gunk under the master cylinder and on whatever is in its vicinity.**

   If your master cylinder is — or has been — leaking, you'll see evidence of it when you look closely.

**TIP**

It's a good idea to check your master cylinder at least every couple of months — more often if it was low in fluid when you last checked it. This task is part of the regular under-the-hood check that I describe in Chapter 2.

## Checking your brake lines

If the fluid level in your master cylinder remains full (see the preceding section), chances are that you don't need to check for leaks in the *brake lines* that carry the fluid to each *wheel cylinder.* However, if you find that you're losing brake fluid, or if the inner surfaces of your tires are wet or look as though something has been leaking and streaking them, it could be a leak in the wheel cylinders or the brake lines — or a visit from a neighbor's dog!

The easiest way to check brake lines is to put the vehicle up on a hydraulic hoist, raise it over your head, walk under it, and examine the lines as they lead from the hood area to each wheel. Leaks may be coming from holes in the lines where the steel lines become rubber ones or where the brake lines connect with the wheel cylinders.

**TIP**

If you don't have access to a hoist at the auto repair class at your local school or at a friendly garage, you have to jack up your vehicle, one end at a time, and get down on the ground with a flashlight or work light to look at your lines. Before you do so, be sure to check Chapter 1 for instructions and safety tips on jacking up your car!

To check your brake lines, do the following:

1. **Check carefully along the brake lines for wetness and for streaks of dried fluid.**

2. **If you see rust spots on your lines, *gently* sand them off and look for thin places under those spots that may turn into holes before long.**

3. **Feel the rubber parts of the brake lines for signs that the rubber is becoming sticky, soft, spongy, or worn.**

TIP

Your brake lines should last the life of your vehicle. If they look very bad, have a professional take a look at them and tell you whether they should be replaced. If the vehicle is fairly new and the brake lines look very bad, go back to the dealership and ask them to replace the lines free of charge.

4. **Look at the inner surfaces of your tires for drippy clues about leaking wheel cylinders.**

# Getting at Your Brakes

Checking your brakes to see whether they're in good condition isn't as scary as it sounds; in fact, it's quite simple — with two qualifications: Don't fiddle with anything unless I tell you to, and be sure to disassemble the stuff that covers your brakes in the proper manner so that you don't have trouble reassembling it. For details on this foolproof technique, see the section in Chapter 1 called "How to Take Anything Apart — and Get It Back Together Again."

Keep the following in mind for any major work your brakes may need:

>> **Don't attempt to replace brake shoes or discs, linings, or wheel cylinders yourself unless you do so under the eye of an auto shop instructor.** If you choose to go this route with proper supervision, the money you save more than pays for your tuition! The job is neither difficult nor complicated. It just needs supervision.

>> **If you'd rather have the work done for you, find a reliable brake specialist rather than taking your vehicle to the corner garage.** If you have an exotic system, go to your dealership. If not, get an estimate from the dealership, and then have the mechanic at your local service station recommend a brake specialist or try the yellow pages or the Internet to locate brake shops in your area. Call a couple of places and ask for estimates on ***rebuilding*** your brakes. Eliminate the cheapest place as well as the most expensive! Chapter 22 is filled with advice on finding good service facilities and dealing with them successfully.

# Things to do and not to do when working on brakes

**WARNING**

Here are a couple of "nevers" to remember when working on your brakes. *Doing any of these things can cause serious damage and huge headaches:*

>> **Never step on your brake pedal when you have the *brake drum* off your brakes.** The pistons can fly out of the ends of the ***wheel cylinders*** because the drum won't stop the ***brake shoes*** from moving outward. (If this makes no sense to you, Chapter 14 tells you how wheel cylinders work.)

>> **Never use anything but the correct *brake fluid* in your brakes.**

>> **Never get oil anywhere near your brake system.** Oil rots rubber and will destroy the cups in the master cylinder reservoir and the dust boots on your wheel cylinders. If it gets on your ***brake linings,*** they won't grab the brake drum.

>> **Never get brake fluid on a painted surface. Brake fluid will destroy the paint.**

>> **Never remove wheel cylinders or brake shoes, or tamper with the self-adjusting device on your brakes, without supervision.**

Now, here's what you *can* do: Most modern vehicles either have disc brakes on the front wheels and drum brakes on the rear wheels or disc brakes all around. Your owner's manual should tell you what the configuration is on your vehicle. When you know, follow the instructions in the following sections that deal with the type of brakes on your vehicle.

**TIP**

When you check your brakes, check one of your front brakes first because the linings wear faster on the front brakes than on the rear ones. If the first set of brakes you look at seems to be in good condition, and if your vehicle has been braking properly, there's probably no need to check the other three. Just remember to check the other front wheel first the next time. If your brakes haven't been behaving properly, check each set of brakes until you find the culprit.

Before you start to check your brakes, scan the instructions later in this chapter (including the "Checking and Packing Wheel Bearings" section) to be sure that you have the necessary tools and products on hand. You don't want any last-minute surprises when your vehicle is up on jack stands with at least one wheel off! If you're unfamiliar with the tools you need for the job, see Chapter 3 for descriptions.

**REMEMBER**

I provide separate sections for checking and reassembling drum brakes and checking disc brakes, so just read the ones that relate to the type of brakes you have. The section on checking and packing *wheel bearings* applies to both drum and disc brakes, but if you have disc brakes, do these jobs only under supervision at an auto class.

A *front-wheel drive* vehicle doesn't conform exactly to the following description. You can still check the brakes, but you can't repack the wheel bearings. Brakes in vehicles with *ABS* and other brake-related safety systems are linked to sophisticated electronic control systems and have wheel *speed sensors* mounted on the *axles* near the brakes, so if your brakes don't feel right, see the brake specialist at your dealership or a reliable brake shop.

## Checking drum brakes

As you can see in Figure 15-3, you have to remove a bunch of stuff to get to a drum brake. The steps in this section explain how to do so and what to look for when you finally get to your brakes.

**WARNING**

Arrange to do this work in a well-ventilated area, wear an inexpensive but protective paper mask, and be very careful not to inhale the dust from the brake drum. If you have an older vehicle, it probably contains asbestos. If you get asbestos in your lungs, you run the risk of serious lung disease. Even asbestos-free brake dust is nasty stuff when inhaled.

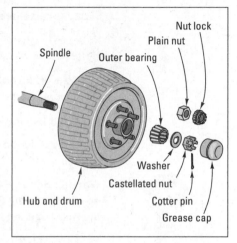

**FIGURE 15-3:**
The things you have to remove to get at your drum brakes.

Follow these steps to check drum brakes:

1. **Jack up your vehicle.**

   For instructions, see Chapter 1. Be sure to observe safety precautions with that jack!

**TECHNICAL STUFF**

   Brake drums are classified as either *hubbed* or *floating* (hubless). Hubbed drums have wheel bearings inside them; floating drums simply slide over the **lug nut** studs that hold the wheels on the vehicle.

2. **If you have a hubbed drum, pry the grease cap off the end of the hub using a pair of combination slip-joint pliers (see the tool in Chapter 3) and lay the grease cap on a clean, lint-free rag.**

   **If you have a floating drum, skip Steps 3 through 7 and just slide the drum off the hub.**

**TIP**

   You sometimes need to strike floating drums with a hammer to break them loose from the hub.

**3.** **Look at the *cotter pin* that sticks out of the side of the castellated nut or nut-lock-and-nut combination.**

Notice in which direction it's placed, how its legs are bent, how it fits through the nut, and how tight it is. If necessary, make a sketch.

**4.** **Use a pair of needle-nosed pliers to straighten the cotter pin and pull it out.**

Put it on the rag that you're using to hold all the parts you've taken off, and lay it down pointing in the same direction as when it was in place.

**5.** **Slide the castellated nut or nut-lock-and-nut combination off the *spindle*.**

If it's greasy, wipe it off with a lint-free rag and lay it on the rag next to the cotter pin.

**6.** **Grab the brake drum and pull it toward you, but *don't slide the drum off the spindle yet;* just push the drum back into place.**

The things that are left on the spindle are the *outer* wheel bearings and washer.

**7.** **Carefully slide the outer bearing, with the washer in front of it, off the spindle.**

TIP

**8.** **Whether or not you want to repack your wheel bearings, check them now by following the instructions in the "Checking and Packing Wheel Bearings" section later in this chapter. Then resume with Step 9.**

As long as you're removing your bearings, you should check them for wear. If they're packable, it's a good idea to repack them while you have everything apart. (All this task involves is squishing wheel-bearing grease into them, a wonderfully sensual job.)

**9.** **Carefully slide the drum off the spindle, with the inner bearings inside it.**

WARNING

Inhaling brake dust can make you seriously ill. For safety's sake, *never* attempt to blow away the dust with compressed air. Instead, put your mask on and saturate the dust completely by spraying the drum with brake parts cleaner according to the instructions on the can. Wipe the drum clean with a rag; then place the rag in a plastic bag and dispose of it immediately.

**10.** **Take a look at the inside of the drum.**

You can probably see grooves on the inner walls from wear. If these grooves look unusually deep, or if you see hard spots or burned places, ask your service facility to let you watch while they check out the drums with a *micrometer* (see Figure 15-4). If the drums aren't worn past legal tolerances (0.060 of an inch), they can be *reground* (or *turned*) rather than replaced. A special machine called a *brake-lathe* does this job in a relatively short amount of time. It shouldn't be a major job in terms of expense. You could do it yourself, under supervision at a school auto shop; most classes have the machine.

If you need new drums, have a professional install them for you because the brake shoes must be adjusted to fit. Make sure that the shop orders drums for your *exact* make, model, and year and that they specify drums for *front* or *rear* wheels. Brake drums must also be replaced with drums of the same *size* for even braking performance. The new drums should look *exactly the same* as your old ones.

**11.** **Look at the rest of your brakes, which are still attached to the brake *backing plate* (see Figure 15-5).**

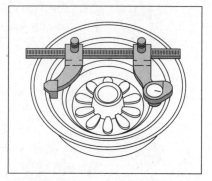

**FIGURE 15-4:**
Checking drum wear with a micrometer.

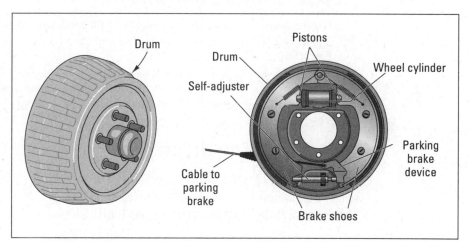

**FIGURE 15-5:**
Anatomy of a drum brake.

Here are the parts you should look at, what you should find, and what to do if they need to be repaired or replaced:

- **Wheel cylinders:** The **wheel cylinders** should show no signs of leaking **brake fluid.** If they're leaky, consult a brake shop.

- **Brake shoes and linings:** These should be evenly worn, with no bald spots or thin places. The **brake lining** should be at least 1/16 inch from the steel part of the **brake shoe** or 1/16 inch from any rivet on brake shoes with rivets, preferably more. The linings should be firmly bonded or riveted to the brake shoes. Most brake shoes and linings are built to last for 20,000 to 40,000 miles; some last even longer. If yours have been on your vehicle for some time, they'll have grooves in them and may be somewhat glazed.

If your brake drums have been wearing evenly and your vehicle has been braking properly, disregard the grooves and the glazing unless your linings look badly worn. If your linings are worn, have them replaced at once. This job involves replacing the brake shoes with new ones that have new linings on them. For even performance, always replace brake shoes in sets (four shoes for two front or rear wheels is a set). Replacing them all at once is even better.

If your brake shoes need to be replaced, remember that almost all "new" brake shoes are really *rebuilt* ones. When your brake shoes are replaced, your old brake shoes are returned to a company that removes the old linings, attaches new ones, and resells the shoes.

**12.** **Take a look at the *self-adjusting devices* on your brakes. (Figure 15-5 shows one of the most common self-adjusters.) Trace the cable from the anchor pin above the wheel cylinder, around the side of the backing plate, to the adjuster at the bottom of the plate.**

Is the cable hooked up? Does it feel tight? If your brake pedal activates your brakes before it gets halfway down to the floor, the adjustment is probably just fine. If not, and if the cylinders, linings, shoes, and so on are okay, the adjusting devices may be out of whack. Making a couple of forward and reverse stops should fix them. If this approach doesn't work, you may need a professional to adjust them. Don't attempt to fiddle with these parts yourself.

## Reassembling drum brakes

After you finish inspecting your brakes, you're ready to reassemble everything. Refer to Figure 15-3 to make sure that you get everything back in the proper order and direction. The following steps tell you how:

**1.** **As you did with the drums (see the previous section), saturate the dirt on the brake backing plate with brake parts cleaner; then wipe it off with a clean, *grease-free* rag.**

Don't blow the dust around — it can cause serious lung damage.

**2.** **Wipe the dirt off the spindle and replace the wheel hub and brake drum on the spindle. If you have a floating drum, skip Steps 4 through 8 and slide the drum back over the lug nut studs until it contacts the hub.**

Be gentle so that you don't unseat the grease seal.

**3.** **If you haven't already cleaned the inside of the drum, spray it with brake cleaner and wipe it out with a grease-free rag.**

**4.** **Replace the *outer* wheel bearing (smaller end first) and the washer.**

Don't let any dirt get on these parts!

**5.** Replace the adjusting nut by screwing it on firmly and then backing it off half a turn and retightening it "finger tight."

Another way to complete this step is to back the adjusting nut off one full notch (60 degrees) and, if the notch doesn't line up with the hole in the spindle, back it off just enough until it does. Then spin the wheel by hand to be sure that it turns freely. If it doesn't, loosen the nut a bit more.

**6.** Insert the *cotter pin* into the hole in the castellated nut.

The cotter pin should clear the outer grooves and go all the way through. Make sure that it's pointing in the same direction as it was when you took it off (refer to your sketch if you made one in Step 3 of the previous section).

**7.** Bend the legs of the cotter pin back across the surface of the nut to hold it in place.

**8.** Replace the grease cap.

**9.** Follow the instructions in Chapter 1 to replace your wheel, lug nuts, and hubcap, and lower the vehicle to the ground.

**10.** Don't try to detoxify the contaminated rags you used on this job by laundering them! Place them in a sealable plastic bag, zip it closed, and dispose of it immediately.

## Checking disc brakes

Today, most vehicles have four-wheel *disc brakes.* Others have disc brakes on the front wheels and *drum brakes* on the rear wheels.

You should check disc brakes (see Figure 15-6) and disc brake linings every 10,000 miles — more often if your brakes suddenly start to squeal or pull to one side, or if your brake pedal flutters when you step on it. Don't confuse the fluttering with the normal pulsing of *ABS* brakes when they're applied in an emergency stop.

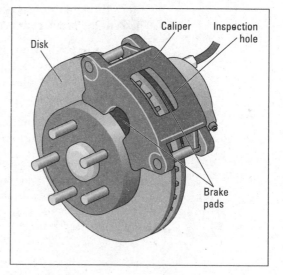

**FIGURE 15-6:**
A disc brake.

**TIP**

When you check your disc brakes, measure the thickness of the linings on the pads so that you can tell whether the linings on your brakes are badly worn. If the lining is down to the thickness of the steel backing plate, the pads should be replaced.

To check disc brakes, follow these steps:

1. **Jack up your vehicle and remove a *front* wheel.**

   You can find instructions for how to do this safely in Chapter 1.

2. **Look at the *brake disc* (also called a rotor), but *don't attempt to remove it from the vehicle.***

   The brake *caliper* has to be removed before you can remove a brake disc, and the good news is that there's no need to do so. If you're working alone, just check the visible part of the disc for heavy rust, scoring, and uneven wear. Rust generally is harmless unless the vehicle has been standing idle for a long time and the rust has really built up. If your disc is badly scored or worn unevenly, have a professional determine whether it can be *reground* or needs to be replaced.

3. **Inspect your brake caliper (the component blocking your view of the entire brake disc).**

   **WARNING**

   Be careful. If the vehicle has been driven recently, the caliper will be hot. If it's cool to the touch, grasp it and gently shake it to make sure that it isn't loosely mounted and its mounting hardware isn't worn.

4. **Peek through the inspection hole in the dust shield on the caliper and look at the brake pads inside (refer to Figure 15-6).**

   If the linings on the *brake pads* look much thinner than the new ones you saw at the supply store or dealership parts department, they probably have to be replaced. If the linings have worn to the metal pads, the disc probably has to be reground or replaced as well.

5. **Follow the instructions in Chapter 1 to replace your wheel, lug nuts, and hubcap, and lower the vehicle to the ground.**

   If the disc and pads seem to be in good condition and your brake pedal doesn't flutter when you step on it, you don't need to do anything else.

**REMEMBER**

Relining, caliper maintenance, and disc grinding should be left to a professional unless you do the job under supervision at an auto class.

# Checking and Packing Wheel Bearings

As you can see in Figure 15-7, *wheel bearings* usually come in pairs of *inner* and *outer* bearings. They allow your wheels to turn freely over thousands of miles by cushioning the contact between the wheel and the *spindle* it sits on with friction-less bearings and lots of nice, gooey grease. This grease tends to pick up dust, dirt, and little particles of metal, even though the bearings are protected to some extent by the hub and the brake drum or disc.

Usually, only the *non*-drive wheels (that is, the front wheels on *rear-wheel drive* vehicles and the rear wheels on *front-wheel drive* vehicles) have repackable wheel bearings. Vehicles with front-wheel drive have sealed front bearings, but some have packable rear ones. The bearings on four-wheel drive vehicles are quite complicated and should be repacked professionally.

**TIP**

Before you check your bearings, consult your owner's manual or dealership to find out whether the bearings on your vehicle are *sealed.* If they are, you can't repack them.

>> **If you have *drum brakes,*** it's important to check the bearings when you check your brakes to make sure that the grease hasn't become fouled. If it has, the particles act abrasively to wear away the very connection the bearings are designed to protect, and the result is a noisy, grinding ride. In extreme cases, you could even lose the wheel! If the bearings look cruddy, either repack them yourself or get a professional to do it.

**WARNING**

>> **If you have *disc brakes,*** you have to remove the ***caliper*** to get at the bearings. Although this task isn't terribly difficult, certain aspects of the job can create problems for a beginner. Because your brake system can kill you if it isn't assembled properly, I strongly suggest that if you want to do it yourself, you do the job under supervision at an auto class.

**TIP**

If you don't want to — or shouldn't — check your bearings right now, try the process I outline in the later section "A quick way to tell whether your bearing's wearing." If they are, have your wheel bearings repacked immediately. If you need other brake work, have it done at the same time so that you don't have to pay for any duplicate labor involved.

## Inspecting and repacking your wheel bearings

If you have *disc brakes* and you have to remove the *caliper* to get the disc off the *spindle* in order to get at the inner bearings, I think that you should inspect and pack them only under supervision at an auto class or under the eye of an experienced mechanic. It's not a difficult job; it's just that you may not get the calipers back on right, which could cause your brakes to malfunction. Otherwise, if you have *drum brakes,* go right ahead and do the job yourself. Figure 15-7 gives you a detailed look at what you'll encounter. Follow these steps to repack your wheel bearings:

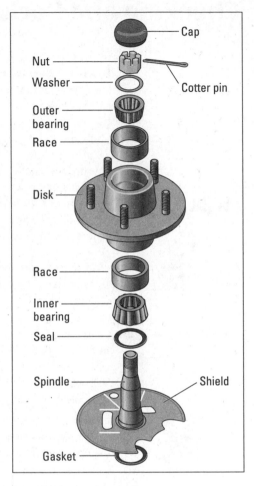

1. **If you have drum brakes and your bearings *aren't* sealed, to get at the bear-ings follow the instructions in the earlier section "Checking drum brakes."**

   When you get to Step 7, where you slide the outer wheel bearings off the spindle, return to this section.

2. **If you haven't already done so, carefully slide the *outer* bearing, with the washer in front of it, off the spindle.**

   As you can see in Figure 15-7, the bearings are usually tapered *roller* bearings, not *ball* bearings.

**FIGURE 15-7:**
Getting at wheel bearings.

3. **Take a good look at the grease in the spaces between the bearings. *Don't wipe off the grease!***

   ⚠️ **WARNING**

   If the grease has sparkly silver slivers or particles in it, or if the rollers are pitted or chipped, you must replace the bearings. If the outer bearings are damaged, the inner bearings probably are, too. In this case, either replace the bearings in an auto class under the instructor's guidance or have a repair facility do the job for you.

4. **If you *don't* intend to repack your outer bearings at this time but you want to continue your inspection, *don't* attempt to wipe any grease off them, no matter how icky they look.**

Just put them in a little plastic bag and lay them on your rag, pointing in the right direction. The bag will keep dust from getting into them. A speck of dust can wear out a bearing quickly.

**If you *do* intend to repack your outer bearings, clean them thoroughly in solvent or kerosene with an old paintbrush.** *Don't smoke when cleaning the bearings!*

You need to get rid of all the old grease in order to inspect the bearings properly. Also, when you repack the bearings with fresh grease, you don't want any old grease spoiling the new stuff.

5. **When the bearings are shiny and clean, rinse them off with water and dry them, or use brake cleaner to remove the solvent.**

WARNING

If you pack new grease over the solvent, the grease will dissolve and you'll ruin your bearings.

6. **When the bearings are clean and dry, look at the rollers for signs of wear.**

If the rollers are gouged or bluish in color, or if you can almost slip the rollers out of their place, replace the bearing and its *race,* which is pressed into the hub. You can see the race in Figure 15-7.

7. **To repack the outer bearing, take a gob of wheel-bearing grease (which is different from most chassis-lube grease) and place it in the palm of your left hand (if you're a righty).**

TIP

You may want to invest in a pair of thin, disposable plastic gloves for this job. However, there's something kind of nice about fresh, clean grease, and if you use gloves, you miss one of the more sensual aspects of getting intimately involved with your car. In any event, hand cleaner gets the grease off easily.

8. **Press the bearing into the gob of grease with the heel of your other hand (see Figure 15-8).**

Doing so forces the grease into the bearing and out the other end. Make sure that you work the grease into every gap in the bearing. You want it to be nice and yucky. Then put your bearing down on your clean rag.

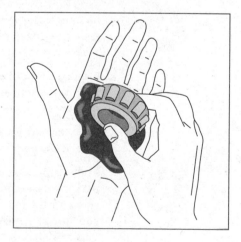

**FIGURE 15-8:**
How to pack bearings with your bare hands.

**Another set of bearings is in the center hole of the drum or disc.** These are your *inner* wheel bearings. At this time, you have to decide whether you're going to remove the inner bearings to check and pack them. The following will help you decide whether to remove the inner bearings:

- **You can't remove the inner bearing from its seat in the hub unless you have a new *grease seal* for it.** So if you're just checking on this occasion, leave the inner bearings alone until you're sure from the condition of the outer bearings that repacking is in order.

- **Generally speaking, if the outer bearings look okay, the inner ones are okay, too.** Just check each wheel and put everything back according to the instructions for reassembling drum brakes earlier in this chapter.

9. **If you're not planning to repack the *inner* bearings, *do not* attempt to take them out of their seat in the drum or disc. Skip Steps 10 through 13 and continue with Step 14.**

   **If you *are* repacking the inner bearings, slide the brake drum or disc toward you, with the inner bearings still in place, but *do not slide the drum completely off the spindle*. Instead, screw the adjusting nut back in again, pull the drum toward you, and push it back.**

   The adjusting nut should catch the inner bearing and its grease seal and free them from inside the hub.

10. **Clean and pack the inner bearings using the technique described in Steps 5 through 8.**

11. **Take a rag and wipe out the hole in the hub of the drum where the inner bearing was; then take a gob of grease and smooth it into the hole.**

   Be sure that the grease fills the *races* inside the hub where the bearing fits. Wipe off excess grease around the outside of the hole so that it doesn't fly around when the car's in motion, possibly damaging your brakes.

12. **Insert the inner bearing into the hub with the small end first. Take the new grease seal and spread a film of grease around the sealing end (the flat, smooth side).**

13. **To fit the new grease seal into place properly, slide it in evenly; otherwise, it will bend or break and you'll lose your grease.**

   Find a hollow pipe or a large socket from a **socket wrench** set that has roughly the same diameter as the seal. With the flat, smooth side of the seal toward you, place the seal in the hub opening, and use the pipe or socket to move it into the hub gently and evenly. The new seal should end up flush with the outside of the hub or slightly inside it.

14. **Return to the earlier sections "Checking drum brakes" or "Checking disc brakes."**

You'll be glad to know that your rear wheels have no wheel bearings to pack (unless your vehicle has *front-wheel drive* and the manual says that you can repack the rear bearings). You do have *axle* bearings, but you must replace these if they wear out; you can't repack them.

**TIP**

If your vehicle is quite old and you hear a clicking or grinding noise from the vicinity of your rear wheels, have these bearings checked and replaced if necessary. It's easier to hear worn *axle* bearings when you drive down an alley or a narrow driveway because the noise echoes loudly.

## A quick way to tell whether your bearing's wearing

If you just want to check your wheel bearings for wear without removing the wheels, do the following:

**1.** **Jack up your vehicle and support it on jack stands.**

If you've been checking your brakes, your car is already jacked up; if not, instructions in Chapter 1 show you how to do this task safely.

**2.** **Without getting under the vehicle, grasp each wheel at the top and bottom and attempt to rock it.**

There should be minimal movement. Excessive play may indicate that the wheel bearing is worn and needs adjustment or replacement.

**3.** **Put the gearshift in Neutral if you have an *automatic transmission,* or take your *manual transmission* out of gear.**

**4.** **Rotate the wheel, listening for any unusual noise and feeling for any roughness as it rotates, which may indicate that the bearing is damaged and needs to be replaced.**

**5.** **Shift back into Park (for an automatic transmission) or gear (for a manual transmission) before lowering the vehicle to the ground.**

# Flushing and Changing Brake Fluid

After checking your *brake system,* if you find that you have a leak or you have to *bleed* your brakes (see the section "Bleeding Your Brakes" for more information), you'll have to restore the *brake fluid* in your *master cylinder* to its proper level. Here are some things that you should know about buying and using brake fluid:

>> **Always use top-quality brake fluid from a well-known manufacturer.** Many vehicles call for either D.O.T. 3 or D.O.T. 4 fluid. D.O.T. 5 is now available, too; it's

a great improvement because it doesn't eat paint or absorb moisture. The downside is that because D.O.T. 5 doesn't absorb it, water that gets into your brake system can form little pools that can corrode your brakes.

Sometimes the type of brake fluid you should use is listed on the master cylinder reservoir cover or cap. If not, check your owner's manual or ask the service department at your dealership for the proper type for your vehicle.

WARNING

>> **Exposure to air swiftly contaminates brake fluid.** The oxygen in the air oxidizes it and lowers its boiling point. Brake fluid also has an affinity for moisture, and the water vapor in the air can combine with the brake fluid, lowering its boiling point and, in cold weather, forming ice crystals that make braking difficult. Adding fluid contaminated with water vapor to your brake system can rust the system and create acids that etch your *wheel cylinders* and master cylinder and foul your brakes, causing them to work poorly — or not at all. It can also destroy vital parts of *ABS* and other expensive braking systems.

TIP

If you're just going to add brake fluid to your system, buy a small can of the correct type, add the fluid to your master cylinder, and *either throw the rest away or use it only in emergencies.* The stuff is pretty cheap, and your vehicle shouldn't need more fluid after you fix a leak. If you keep a can with only a little fluid left in it, the air that fills up the rest of the space in the can contaminates the fluid no matter how quickly you recap it.

WARNING

>> **Keep brake fluid away from painted surfaces — unless it's D.O.T. 5, *it eats paint.*** (If this stuff seems scary, remember that the same statements can be made about turpentine and nail polish remover.)

You should flush and replace the fluid in your brake system every two years. Service facilities now do this with brake flushing machines. If you want to do it yourself, follow these steps:

1. **Use a cheap, plastic turkey baster to remove the old, dirty fluid from the *master cylinder* reservoir.**

2. **Use a lint-free cloth to wipe out the reservoir — if you can get in there.**

3. **Pour new brake fluid into the reservoir just until it reaches the "Full" line, replace the cap on the reservoir, and then follow the steps in the next section, "Bleeding Your Brakes."**

As you bleed the brakes, the new fluid pushes the old fluid out of the system. Continue to bleed the brakes until you see clean, clear fluid exiting the bleeder screw.

# Bleeding Your Brakes

If your vehicle has squishy-feeling brakes, the way to get the air out of the lines is to *bleed* the brakes. To do the job, you need either a *brake bleeder wrench* or a combination wrench that fits the bleeder nozzle on your vehicle, a can of the proper *brake fluid,* a clean glass jar, and a friend.

**WARNING**

To avoid getting air into the *actuator* of *ABS, EBD, BA,* or other sophisticated brake systems, a professional should bleed the brakes for you.

Follow these steps to bleed your brakes:

1.  **Find the little nozzle called a *brake bleeder screw* (see Figure 15-9) that's located behind each of your brakes.**

    Reaching this bleeder screw may be easier if you jack up the vehicle (see Chapter 1 for instructions and safety tips). If you're going to crawl underneath, lay down an old blanket or a thick layer of newspapers first. If you really want to be comfortable, beg or borrow a *creeper* to lie on and slide around with easily (I describe creepers in Chapter 3).

2.  **Special wrenches called *bleeder wrenches* fit the bleeder screw and can prevent rounding the screw's hex-head. Find the proper wrench or socket that fits the screw, and loosen the screw.**

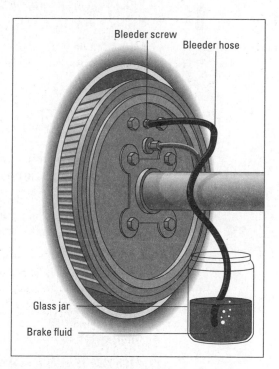

**FIGURE 15-9:**
Using a bleeder hose to bleed your brakes.

Be careful not to break the screw off or you'll need professional repairs. If it's stuck, spray some penetrant like WD-40 around the screw. After you loosen the screw, tighten it again (but not too tight).

3. **If you have a small piece of flexible hose that fits over the end of the bleeder screw, attach it and place the end of the hose in the jar. Then fill the jar with brake fluid to cover the end of the hose (see Figure 15-9). If you don't have anything that fits over the bleeder screw, just keep the jar near the nozzle so that any fluid that squirts out lands in the jar.**

4. **Have your friend slowly pump your brake pedal a few times (see Figure 15-10). Have your friend say "Down" when pressing the brake pedal down and "Up" when releasing it.**

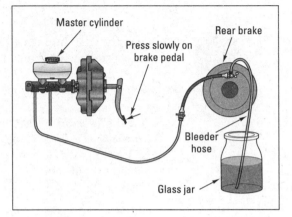

FIGURE 15-10:
How to bleed your brakes.

If the vehicle is jacked up, before you let your friend get into it with you underneath it, make sure that the wheels are blocked in the direction in which the car would roll and that it isn't parked on a hill. Leave your tires in place so that the vehicle will bounce and leave you some clearance if it falls.

5. **When your friend has pumped the pedal a few times and is holding the pedal *down*, open the bleeder screw.**

   Brake fluid will squirt out (duck!). If there's air in your brake lines, air bubbles will be in the fluid. Seeing these bubbles is easiest if you're using the hose-in-the-jar method, but you can also see them without it.

6. ***Before* your friend releases the brake pedal, *tighten the bleeder screw.***

   If you don't, air is sucked back into the brake lines when the pedal is released.

7. **Tell your friend to release the pedal, and listen for him or her to say "Up." Then repeat Steps 2 through 6, loosening the screw and tightening it again and again until no more air bubbles come out with the fluid.**

8. **Open your master cylinder and add more brake fluid until the level reaches the "Full" line.**

   If you neglect to do so, you run the risk of draining all the fluid out of the master cylinder and drawing air into the lines from the top. If that happens, you have to go back and bleed your master cylinder until you suck the air out of that end of the system. Who needs the extra work?

If you goof and have to bleed the *master cylinder*, it's the same deal as bleeding your brakes (friend and all). Just bleed it at the point where the brake lines attach to the cylinder or at the master cylinder's bleeder nozzle if you have one (see Figure 15-11).

9. **Repeat Steps 2 through 8 with each brake until the air is out of each brake line. Don't forget to add brake fluid to the master cylinder after you bleed each brake.**

10. **After you finish the job and bring the brake fluid level in the master cylinder back to the "Full" level for the last time, drive the vehicle around the block.**

   The brake pedal should no longer feel spongy when you depress it. If it does, check the master cylinder again to be sure that it's full, and try bleeding the brakes one more time (this situation isn't unusual, and it doesn't take as long as it sounds).

**FIGURE 15-11:**
Bleeding a master cylinder: If you have a bleeder nozzle, use the hose and jar method (a). If not, bleed the cylinder at the brake line connections (b).

If you know that no air is left in the brake lines but the brakes still don't feel right, you may need a new master cylinder. Unless you have one of the few Japanese vehicles that integrate the *ABS* actuator in the master cylinder, you should definitely consider installing it yourself — at an auto class. All it involves is disconnecting the old master cylinder (a bolt or two and the hoses leading to the brake lines), removing it without spilling brake fluid on anything painted, installing the new one, filling it with brake fluid, and bleeding it. If your vehicle has ABS, the new fluid is pumped through the actuator as well as the master cylinder when you bleed the system, using up a bit more brake fluid than bleeding a non-ABS system, so plan ahead and buy an extra can or two.

If the job seems like too much of a hassle, have a professional do the work. You shouldn't have to pay for much labor, and if you choose a brake shop wisely, the whole deal shouldn't cost too much. Whatever you do, just be sure that when the job is finished, they (or you) bleed the brakes and the master cylinder to get all the air out of the lines.

When I bought Tweety Bird, my first car, I had her master cylinder replaced professionally for about $60. (It would cost *sooo* much more now!) A few months later, I helped a friend replace a master cylinder with a *rebuilt* one. The rebuilt master cylinder cost about half of what I'd paid for a new one, and there were no labor charges (naturally). What are your time and trouble worth to you?

# Adjusting Your Parking Brake

These instructions for adjusting your parking brake work only if you have *drum brakes* on your rear wheels. If you have a *manual transmission*, you may have a transmission-type *parking brake*, which should be adjusted professionally, and parking brakes on rear-wheel disc brakes should be left to professionals, too. Your *service manual* may tell you which kind you have, or you can crawl under the vehicle and see for yourself. (Chapter 14 describes both *integral* and *transmission*-type parking brakes and shows you what they look like.) Because most people have *integral* parking brakes, that's the type I deal with in this section. Figure 15-12 shows you several types of integral parking brakes. They may look different, but you adjust them all the same way.

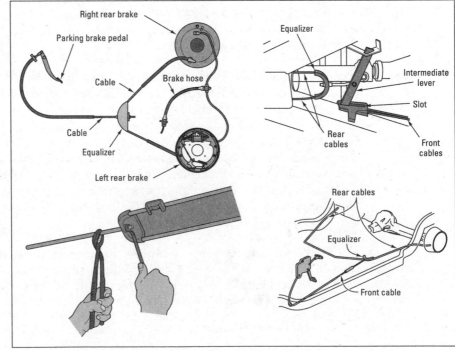

**FIGURE 15-12:** Integral parking brakes.

**TIP**

You shouldn't have to pull or push the parking brake handle to the most extreme level to make the brake work. (As the cables loosen up, you have to pull the handle up higher to engage the brake.) Also, you shouldn't be able to drive the vehicle with the parking brake on. If you can, the brake needs to be adjusted or repaired.

To adjust your parking brake, do the following:

**1. Jack up the car (a hoist would be lovely) and make sure that it's secure (see Chapter 1 for instructions). Be sure to leave your parking brake *off*.**

If you don't want to jack the car up, you can slide underneath it armed with a work light.

**2. Trace the thin steel cables that run from each of your rear wheels until they meet somewhere under the backseat of the vehicle.**

Where they meet there should be a device (usually a bar and a screw) that controls the tension. Compare what you find with the parking brakes in Figure 15-12 to see which type you have. If you can't find the system on your vehicle in that illustration, you probably need professional help.

**3. Turn the screw (or whatever else you have) until the cables tighten up, and then tighten the screw nuts to hold the screw in place.**

You may have to hold the cable to keep it taut (the illustration at bottom left of Figure 15-12 shows you how).

**4. Get out from under the vehicle and test-drive it to see whether the parking brake is working.**

**5. Pay attention to whether the parking brake warning light on your dashboard comes on when the parking brake is engaged. If it doesn't, check or replace the bulb or fuse.**

You can find instructions for checking fuses in Chapter 6. If changing the bulb or fuse doesn't work, get someone to check the connection between the warning light and the brake; there may be a short in it.

# Checking Anti-Lock Brakes

**WARNING**

*Anti-lock braking systems (ABS)* vary from one vehicle to another, and most require no special maintenance. (Chapter 14 tells you how ABS brake systems work and how to operate them properly.) Manufacturers install a *warning light* — usually yellow or amber in color — in the instrument panel that, under normal circumstances, goes on briefly during engine startup and turns off in a short amount of time. If it goes on while you're on the road, the ABS system isn't working properly and your vehicle is using only the normal brake system. In this case, get the ABS repaired as soon as you can.

REMEMBER

If you want to test the operation of your anti-lock brakes, find an *empty* parking lot on a rainy day. While traveling on a slippery surface at about 30 mph, with no obstacles in front of you, firmly press the brake pedal. You should hear some clicking and feel some pulsing of the *brake pedal* while the vehicle comes to a stop without sliding. If the warning lamp stays on, or if you suspect that the ABS isn't working properly, take your vehicle to a professional who specializes in brake systems.

# 4

# Smoothing the Ride: Steering and Suspension, Tires and Transmissions

Drivers of the first horseless carriages were delighted to find that the ride was smoother (although sometimes noisier) than when the horse was attached and they had to steer with reins. Over the years, rubber tires have replaced rattling wooden wheels; flexible suspensions now cushion the bumps; and new types of transmissions enable you to smoothly change speed. Put simply, "rattle-traps" have evolved into comfortable forms of transportation.

This part shows you how each of these wonderful systems works and what you can do to maintain and troubleshoot it. Enjoy the ride!

# Chapter **16**

# Steering and Suspension Systems Smooth the Way

Except for the steering wheel, you probably consider the steering and suspension systems on your vehicle to be unknown territory, and up until now, you've probably been content to leave it that way. But these systems are the unsung heroes that smooth out the driving process and keep you headed exactly where you want to go. This chapter can help you get a good idea of how the type of steering and suspension your vehicle possesses works so that you can deal intelligently with a technician if something goes wrong.

**REMEMBER**

Whenever you encounter a term set in *this font*, you'll find it defined in the glossary in Appendix A.

## The Steering System

The *steering system* consists of a series of linkages and gears that link the driver to the wheels. On most vehicles only the front wheels turn in response to the steering wheel, while the back wheels just follow along. When you make a turn, each of the front wheels has to turn at a different angle because one wheel is closer to the direction you're turning in than the other one is (think of the "snap the whip" game).

There's a difference between how far you turn your steering wheel and how far the wheels of your vehicle turn during one rotation of the steering wheel. This is called the *steering ratio*. The more you have to turn the steering wheel to get the wheels to respond, the higher the steering ratio. To find the steering ratio, you divide one complete rotation of the steering wheel (360 degrees) by the amount of degrees the wheels turn. The steering ratio in most cars is between 12 and 20:1. For example, if the wheels on your car turn 20 degrees during one rotation of the steering wheel, the steering ratio would be 18:1 (360 divided by 20).

## The steering linkage

The *steering linkage* is composed of all the parts of the steering system that connect the steering wheel to the front wheels (see Figure 16-1). When you turn your steering wheel, the steering linkage causes your front wheels to respond by moving in the proper direction. The principal parts of the steering linkage are the *tie rod* ends, *ball joints,* and *control arms.*

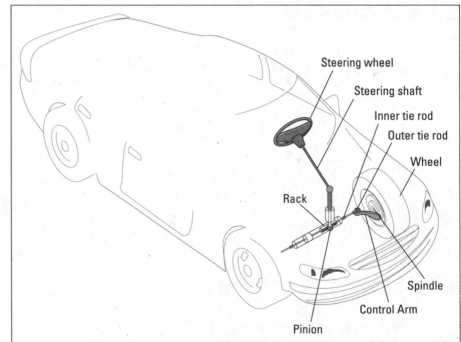

**FIGURE 16-1:**
A rack-and-pinion steering system.

### Tie rod ends

As you can see in Figure 16-1, the tie rod ends are a type of ball socket assembly located where the steering linkage connects to the wheels. As the two parts of the linkage move against each other, the grease in the tie rod ends cushions them. The grease keeps the parts moving freely and prevents friction that would wear them away.

### Control arms

The steering linkage actually connects to the wheels, which are held in place by a *spindle* that goes through the wheel and is attached to one or two *control arms,* or steering arms that allow the wheels to turn in any direction. To keep things moving freely, ball joints are located at points where movement takes place.

### Ball joints

*Ball joints* are important parts of the steering systems on all vehicles. A ball joint is a ball socket assembly that attaches the *steering knuckle* to the *suspension system.* The ball joint allows for pivotal and rotational movement of the wheel as it moves up and down and is steered left to right. You can see where ball joints are located in Figures 16-6, 16-10, and 16-15, which show various configurations.

**TECHNICAL STUFF**

Some steering system components are filled with grease to cut down on friction and keep the parts they protect from wearing away prematurely. In the past, these components needed the grease replenished at regular intervals. Almost all of today's vehicles (with the exception of a few SUVs, trucks, and specialty vehicles) have *lifetime lubrication systems* that are designed to operate for the life of the vehicle without the need for additional lubrication.

## Power steering systems

When *power steering* was first introduced, it was intended to help driversof large or heavy vehicles to steer more easily when parking or heading around curves. Then it became a luxury option for passenger vehicles. Today, virtually every vehicle on the road comes equipped with a power steering system. This section describes the most popular types of power steering.

Three types of power steering systems are in use today, or are scheduled to make their appearance in a very short time: *rack-and-pinion, recirculating-ball,* and *steer-by-wire.* The following sections take a closer look at each of them.

## Rack-and-pinion steering

Rack-and-pinion steering is found on most modern passenger vehicles (refer to Figure 16-1). The pinion is a gear that connects to the shaft of the steering wheel. The rack has notches cut in it that engage the teeth on the pinion gear. Each end of the rack connects to an inner and outer *tie rod*, which connect to the control arm, which connects to the spindle on the wheel at that side of the vehicle. As the steering wheel turns, the gear turns, moving the rack, which moves the tie rods, which cause the wheels to turn.

A *rotary valve* senses whether the driver is turning the steering wheel or just driving straight ahead. It does this via a *steering shaft* that connects to the steering wheel at one end and to the pinion gear at the other. As the steering wheel turns, the torsion bar twists, and the pinion gear responds accordingly.

Rack-and-pinion power steering is powered in two basic ways. Other steering systems described in this chapter may work on the same principles, but the clearest way to view them is to relate them to rack-and-pinion systems:

>> *Hydraulic* **power steering systems** incorporate a *power-steering pump* that's connected to the engine by a belt wrapped around a pulley (see Figure 16-2). As vanes inside the pump turn in response to the speed of the engine, they force power-steering fluid under hydraulic pressure into a piston located at the center of the rack. As you can see in Figure 16-2, the hydraulic piston has an opening on either side of it that allows the fluid to enter. The direction in which the steering wheel is turned forces the fluid into one side of the piston or the other. This causes the piston to move the rack in that direction, which moves the tie rods and the wheels accordingly.

>> **Electronic power steering systems,** also called *electronically assisted steering,* use an electric motor or motors instead of hydraulics to drive the steering mechanism (see Figure 16-3). An **ECU** controls the operation of the system. If the electronic system fails, the rack-and-pinion system continues to operate as unassisted (or unpowered) steering.

## Recirculating-ball steering

Another type of steering system most often found on trucks and SUVs is called *recirculating-ball steering* because it features a recirculating-ball gear (see Figure 16-4). The outer part is a block that has a hole in it and gear teeth on the exterior. A rod with threads at one end screws into the threads inside the hole. The threads in the rod are filled with ball bearings that reduce friction between the threads in the rod and the threads in the hole and keep the rod moving firmly in place.

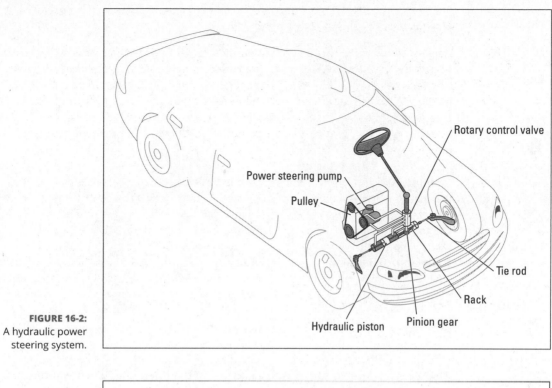

FIGURE 16-2:
A hydraulic power
steering system.

Rotary control valve

Power steering pump

Pulley

Tie rod

Rack

Hydraulic piston

Pinion gear

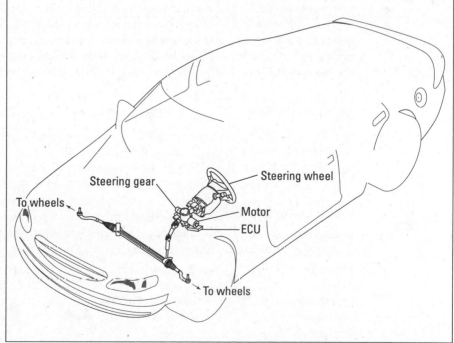

FIGURE 16-3:
An electronic
power steering
system.

Steering gear

Steering wheel

To wheels

Motor

ECU

To wheels

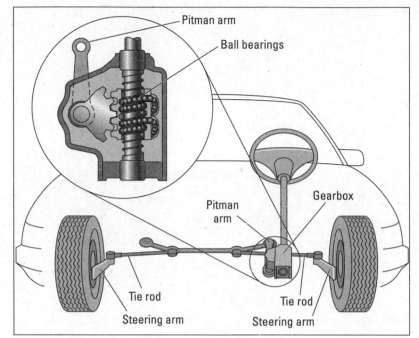

**FIGURE 16-4:**
Recirculating-ball
steering.

The rod is connected to the steering wheel at the other end. When you turn the steering wheel, it turns the rod, which turns the block it's screwed into. The gear teeth on the outside of the block move the wheels in whatever direction the block is turning in response to the steering wheel. If the system is power assisted, the power-steering pump sends hydraulic fluid under higher pressure to one side of the block or the other, depending on which way the steering wheel is turned.

## Steer-by-wire

*Steer-by-wire* is a new and innovative steering system that's controlled electronically. It senses the direction, force, and speed with which the driver is turning the steering wheel and conveys that information to a motorized steering system. Figure 16-5 shows a prototype steer-by-wire system. Because this system eliminates the pumps, hydraulic lines, pulleys, and other mechanical gizmos that connect the steering wheel to the wheels in rack-and-pinion and recirculating-ball systems, it steers more smoothly, frees up room under the hood, reduces the possibility of mechanical failure, lightens the weight of the car, and increases fuel economy. Such a deal!

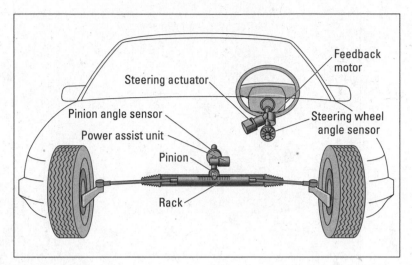

**FIGURE 16-5:** Steer-by-wire.

# Checking your steering

Checking your steering is easy. Just stand outside your vehicle, near the door on the driver's side. Stick your hand through the open window and move the steering wheel, with your eye on the left front tire. If you can move the steering wheel at all before the tire starts to move, then you need to have both your steering and alignment checked. There should be no "play" in the steering wheel before the signal is transmitted to the tires.

WARNING

As you drive your car, be alert to signs that it isn't handling as easily as before. If the vehicle seems to have a mind of its own and begins to resist you on turns (and when you're pulling out of turns), take a good look at your tires for signs of wear caused by misalignment.

# Suspension Systems

Underneath your vehicle are the main elements of the suspension system, which supports the vehicle and keeps the passenger compartment relatively stable on bumpy roads. This section deals with the most important parts involved in these systems and then with the major types of suspension systems. Figure 16–6 shows you a typical suspension system.

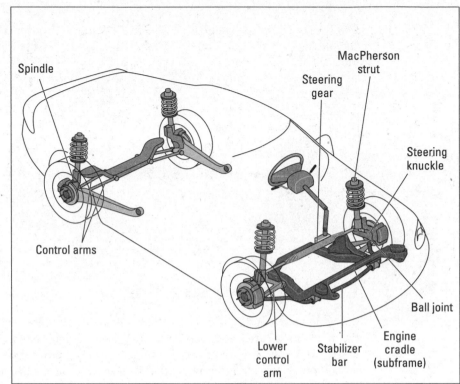

FIGURE 16-6:
A typical
suspension
system.

The figure shows a typical suspension system with labeled parts: Spindle, MacPherson strut, Steering gear, Steering knuckle, Control arms, Ball joint, Lower control arm, Stabilizer bar, Engine cradle (subframe).

## Major parts of the suspension system

You'll understand the different types of suspension systems best if you're familiar with the major parts involved.

### Control arms

*Control arms* are sometimes referred to as *A arms, A frames, I arms,* or *links* (look ahead to Figure 16-15). Ever hear the term *multi-link suspension?* It means that more than one link is holding the wheel to the frame or body.

### Stabilizer bars

*Stabilizer bars* (see Figure 16-7) are designed to prevent a vehicle from swaying and lurching on sharp curves and turns and when the wheels are traveling over uneven ground (a better solution than the legendary mountain goat that had shorter legs on one side than on the other for traveling along slopes!). These stabilizers (or *anti-sway bars*) also improve high-speed stability. Most vehicles have a *front* stabilizer bar and some also have a *rear* stabilizer bar. The stabilizer connects one side of the suspension to the other through the frame. As your car begins to dip on one side, the stabilizer bar restricts that side's movement, depending on the diameter of the bar. Larger-diameter stabilizers restrict more than smaller ones do. More and more modern vehicles are offering *stability control systems* that perform more efficiently. Chapter 19 tells you how these work.

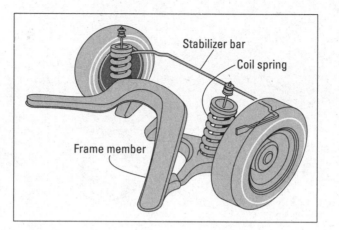

**FIGURE 16-7:**
A typical stabilizer bar and linkage.

## Springs

*Springs* are the core of the suspension system. Various types of springs are used to carry the weight of the vehicle and keep it off the tires, absorb the bumps, and keep your car at its proper trim height. These can be *leaf springs, coil springs, torsion bars,* or *air springs* (see Figure 16-8). Most cars use either coil or leaf springs; SUVs use coil springs, torsion bars, or leaf springs.

Here's a rundown of each type of spring:

>> **Leaf springs,** still found on pickup trucks and pickup-based SUVs, are usually made up of several relatively thin metal plates, called *leaves,* piled one on top of the other. The reason for using these layers instead of one thick metal bar is that, as a bar bends, the top of the bar has to stretch a little. Unlike a single, thick bar, which, if bent too far, would split from the top down, leaf springs are more flexible; each leaf bends independently, and the leaves can slide on one another instead of breaking (see Figure 16-9).

Each end of a set of leaf springs is attached to the *frame* at the rear of the car with fittings that allow the springs to bend and move freely. These fittings usually have rubber **bushings** that allow the fittings to bend and twist freely; they also absorb some of the vibration and prevent it from reaching the passenger compartment.

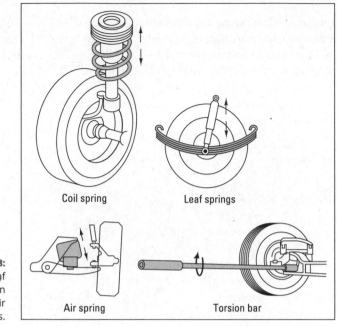

**FIGURE 16-8:**
Coil springs, leaf springs, torsion bars, and air springs.

Coil spring

Leaf springs

Air spring

Torsion bar

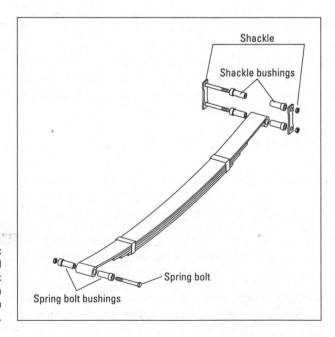

**FIGURE 16-9:**
Leaf springs bend but don't break because they can slide flexibly on one another.

Shackle

Shackle bushings

Spring bolt

Spring bolt bushings

» **Coil springs** look like old-fashioned bed springs. They're usually found at the front of the car, although they can be at both the front and the rear. At the front end, coil springs also help cushion the bumps, vibrations, and steering movements. Front coil springs can sit on either the upper or lower *control arms.* They're cushioned by *ball joints* (see Figure 16-10). At the rear, they're often suspended between control arms that have rubber bushings. Figures 16-10, and 16-16 through 16-18 show the location of coil springs on a variety of suspension systems. If the coil springs are making noise, you may be able to lube them with spray-on grease at the points where they connect at the top and bottom. However, I recommend that you check with the service department at your dealership before undertaking the job yourself.

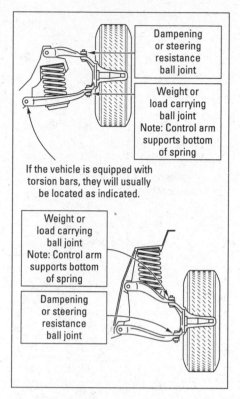

**FIGURE 16-10:**
Bushings and ball joints on front coil springs.

» **Torsion bars** are used mainly in SUVs and trucks. They're located at the front of the vehicle, connected at one end to a control arm. What they connect to at the other end differs from one vehicle to another. (Figures 16-10 and 16-11 show some configurations.) Torsion bars twist to accommodate differences in the load that the vehicle may be carrying, which allows the front wheels to move up and down freely. Think of torsion bars as coil springs that didn't get wound into a spiral.

» **Air springs** are usually found on luxury vehicles. A rubber air spring can be filled with the right amount of compressed air to control the ride and maintain the proper height. With this type of system, a computer monitors the ride height and signals an onboard air compressor to pump more air into the air springs when weight is added to the vehicle. When the weight is removed, the computer turns on an exhaust solenoid to let air out of the air springs (refer to Figures 16-8 and 16-12).

Usually, there's nothing to lubricate with air springs. But check with the dealer to find out whether it's okay to apply a rubber conditioner to the air bags to prevent them from wearing out prematurely.

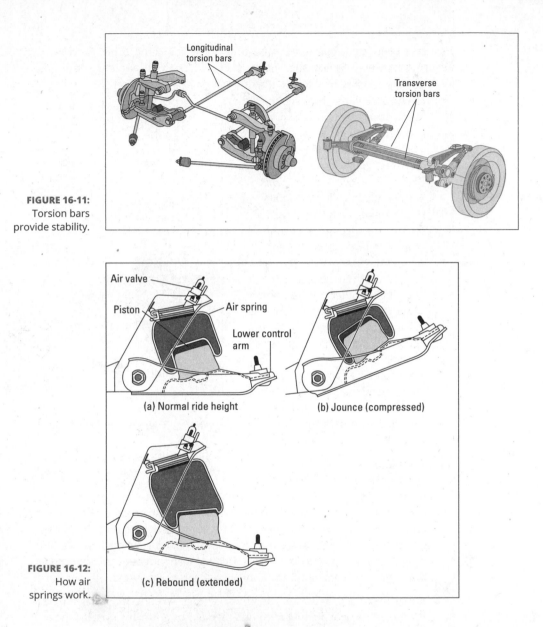

**FIGURE 16-11:**
Torsion bars
provide stability.

**FIGURE 16-12:**
How air
springs work.

## Shocks and struts

*Shock absorbers* and *MacPherson struts* (see Figures 16–13 and 16–14) do most of the work of protecting the passenger compartment from bumps. One or the other is located near each wheel. The way they cut down on vertical movement is interesting. When a wheel hits a bump, the wheel tends to keep bouncing up and down long after the bump has been left behind unless the movement is controlled. The bouncing effect is due to the inflated rubber tire on the wheel and also to the fact that a coil spring that's pulled or compressed doesn't just snap back into its former shape but keeps moving up and down for some time afterward. Shock absorbers and struts allow the springs to compress freely and to return or rebound slowly — like the door check on a storm door that opens quickly and easily but closes gently.

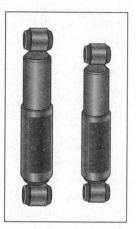

**FIGURE 16-13:**
Standard shock absorbers.

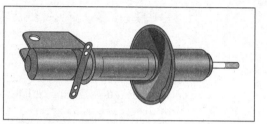

**FIGURE 16-14:**
A MacPherson strut.

Here are some points to keep in mind regarding your shocks and struts:

WARNING

>> **Shock absorbers that are faulty or worn increase tire wear and can cause you to lose control of the steering if you go over bumps and dips at high speeds.**

TIP

>> **There are a couple of ways to tell whether your vehicle needs new shock absorbers.** One is by leaning heavily on a fender or placing your weight on a bumper and then releasing it suddenly, watching to see whether the vehicle returns slowly to its original position. If the vehicle continues to bob up and down, you need new shocks. Another way is to stop fairly short. If your car dips up and down a couple of times before coming to rest, you need new shocks if your vehicle has them. If it doesn't, a professional should troubleshoot the suspension system to identify the problem.

TECHNICAL
STUFF

>> **MacPherson struts do more than shock absorbers do.** Both shocks and struts control the ride, but a strut is also a structural member of the suspension system.

>> **Electromagnetically adjustable shocks contain a *hydraulic* fluid whose *viscosity* can be altered by electromagnetic current. *Sensors* determine** how stiff or soft the shocks need to be. Some are driver-controlled by a switch in the cabin that usually offers "sport" and "comfort" settings, and sometimes "tow" or "load" settings, as well.

Although replacing *standard* shock absorbers isn't hard, the job can be brutal because you have to jack up your vehicle and crawl under it. Unless you can replace them under supervision on the lift at an auto class, I strongly recommend having a professional do it for you.

TIP

Within limits, you have a choice as to the type of shocks you use on your vehicle: "Heavy-duty" shocks provide a slightly harder ride; other shocks may not do as well with the entire family and two Great Danes in the car, but they give a softer ride. Some shocks even provide automatic level control for vehicles that carry loads ranging from very heavy to almost weightless. Suit yourself.

# Types of suspensions

Several types of suspension systems have been developed to make riding in your vehicle safer and more comfortable. Most cars have *independent* front suspension systems in which each front wheel is attached separately and can move independently of the others. Some vehicles also have independent rear suspensions, hence the term *four-wheel independent suspension*. Older *rear-wheel drive* vehicles and many of today's trucks use a *dependent* type of rear suspension that incorporates the rear drive-axle assembly.

Traditionally, *double-wishbone* suspensions and *strut* suspensions have been the most common suspension systems found on consumer vehicles. But *air suspensions* are becoming more popular, and *electromagnetic suspensions* are coming into play.

## Double-wishbone suspension

Double-wishbone suspension systems use a shorter upper *control arm* and a longer lower control arm that hold the wheel to the frame. The control arms allow the wheel to move up and down, kind of like a hinge allows a door to swing open and closed. The lower arm is larger because it bears most of the load when the vehicle moves up and down. There are rubber *bushings* at the inboard end of the control arms, and a *ball joint* at the outboard end of the control arm allows the wheel to rotate and pivot (see Figure 16-15).

## Multi-link suspension

Multi-link suspension (see Figure 16-16) is a more sophisticated version of double-wishbone suspension, and it comes in a variety of configurations. The main advantage of all of them is greater flexibility that enhances a vehicle's ability to adjust to changes in driving conditions on the road. Although multi-link suspension systems still have "wishbones," each of the arms connect to the spindle separately rather than as one solid unit. As a result, each can pivot independently in response to the movement of the steering wheel.

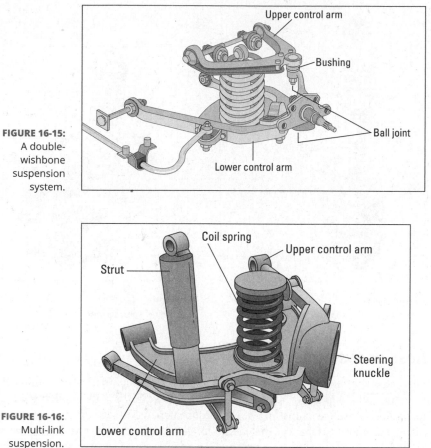

## Strut suspension

There are two types of strut suspensions: *conventional* and *modified* (see Figures 16-17 and 16-18). Conventional struts have the coil spring wrapped around the strut cartridge, and modified strut suspensions have a remotely mounted spring. Strut suspensions use no upper control arm. The upper strut mount is what holds the wheel in place. You can find more information about different types of shocks and struts in the earlier section, "Shocks and struts."

## Air suspension systems

Air suspension is found on some luxury cars and SUVs. It employs air-filled bags or tubes controlled by *sensors* that determine when the suspension needs to be softened or stiffened and pumps air into them or lets air out of them accordingly. Some air suspension systems are controlled by the driver, whereas others are automatic.

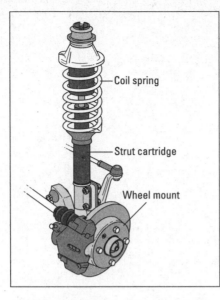

**FIGURE 16-17:**
Conventional strut suspension.

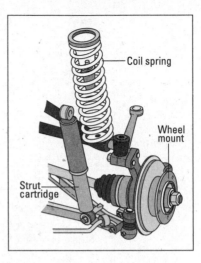

**FIGURE 16-18:**
Modified strut suspension.

## Bose acoustic suspension

Bose acoustic suspension is a product of the same company that builds those sensitive and expensive sound systems and earphones. By applying acoustic technology Bose has come up with a unique suspension system that represents a major automotive advance. Instead of conventional springs, shock absorbers, or hydraulics, Bose suspension employs an electromagnetic motor at each wheel. As the movement of the vehicle compresses and expands the system, amplifiers send electricity to boost the power at each of the wheel motors, enabling them to adjust the suspension much faster than conventional systems can. This sophisticated and sensitive system of controlling the motion of each wheel enables the rest of the vehicle to remain level when the driver steps on the accelerator or the brake pedal or makes a sharp turn, and it virtually eliminates vibrations in the passenger compartment. Bose expects to have this system available — at least on high-end vehicles — by 2009. Hopefully, as has happened with other significant advances in automotive technology that have enabled vehicles to operate more efficiently and safely, the system will swiftly become more widely available.

IN THIS CHAPTER

» Understanding the anatomy of a tire

» Deciphering the data on the sidewalls

» Choosing the right tires for your vehicle

» Maintaining your tires: Checking air pressure, rotating, aligning, and balancing

» Examining your tires for wear and getting compensated for defective tires

Chapter **17**

# How to Keep Your Car from Getting Sore Feet: Tires, Alignment, and Balancing

I f you think about *tires* only when it's time to buy new ones, you need to think again. The right tires in the right condition can enhance your driving experience and make it safer. In fact, your brakes and your tires have a two-way relationship: Poor braking action results in increased tire wear, but properly balanced and aligned wheels and properly inflated tires in good condition can help stop your car up to 25 percent faster!

Worn tires can cause your vehicle to skid or hydroplane in wet weather even if the treads aren't down to the legal tolerances. So checking your tires can save your life! There's also a strong correlation between tire inflation and tire wear. If your tires are *underinflated*, the outer treads wear out faster. If your tires are *overinflated*, the centers of the tread areas go. And if the wheels get out of **alignment**, your tires can wear out in as little as one day of hard driving! So, to get more mileage from your tires plus better braking action and a smoother, quieter ride, you ought to know a bit about buying, checking, and maintaining the tires on your vehicle.

In this chapter, I tell you about the kinds of tires available. (You can buy different types and grades, and just as you wouldn't wear your finest shoes to the beach, you don't want to put the most expensive, long-lasting, high-speed set of tires on an old car that just goes back and forth to the shopping center.) I also tell you how to check your tires and how to read your treads for clues about how well your vehicle is performing — and how well you're driving. If these clues show that you need to have your tires and wheels balanced or aligned or your tires replaced, I provide enough information for you to be sure that the work is done the right way for the right price.

You don't have to do much (in terms of physical labor) with this chapter, so just find a comfortable place to read, relax, and enjoy. For information about how to change a flat tire, see Chapter 1.

Whenever you encounter a term set in *this font,* you'll find it defined in the glossary in Appendix A.

# Tire Construction

Every tire has several major parts (see Figure 17-1). You find out more about them in the next section, "The Secrets on Your Sidewalls, Revealed!," which decodes all the useful data molded into the sidewall of a tire. But to start, here's a brief description of each part:

>> **The sidewall** is the part of the tire between the *tread* and the *bead.* It keeps the air in, protects the components inside the tire, and keeps it stable.

>> **The tread** is the part of the tire that gets most of the wear and tear. It used to just be made of rubber (hence the phrases, "where the rubber meets the road" and "burning rubber"). Today, the tread can be made from natural rubber, synthetics, or both. The tread patterns help the tire grip the road and resist puncturing. These patterns also are excellent indicators of tire wear and have built-in treadwear indicators that let you know when it's time to replace your tires. I get into reading these clues later in this chapter, in the section called — unsurprisingly — "Checking your tires for wear."

>> **The bead** is a hoop of rubber-coated steel wire that's shaped to help hold the tire onto the rim of the wheel. Most tires have several beads grouped into a *bead bundle.*

>> **The body** of the tire is located beneath the tread and the sidewalls. It helps the tire keep its shape when inflated instead of blowing up like a balloon.

>> **The plies** make up the body of the tire. They're rubber-coated layers of various materials (the most popular is polyester cord). The more plies, the stronger the tire. The innermost belt is called a *liner;* it provides a stable base for layering all the plies. High-speed tires sometimes have *cap plies* on top of the regular ones to keep the plies and belts in place.

>> **The belts** are located between the body and the tread. They provide longer wear, puncture resistance, and more directional stability and are usually made of rubber-coated steel. Belts also can be made of aramid (which is harder than steel), fiberglass, polyester, rayon, or nylon. But steel is the most popular type of belt material.

>> **The tire valve** lets air into and out of the tire. The valve core prevents air from escaping. Each valve should have a valve cap to keep dirt and moisture from getting into the tire.

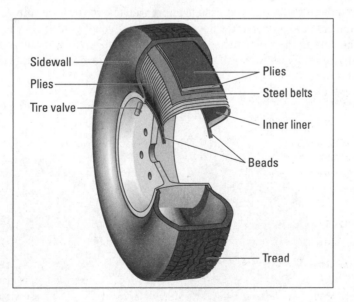

**FIGURE 17-1:** Anatomy of a tire.

TECHNICAL STUFF

For many years, tires came in a variety of constructions. There were *bias-ply* tires that featured cords wrapped around the beads at overlapping angles. These were superseded by *bias-belted* tires, which were constructed in the same manner as bias-ply tires but featured belts of another material that wrapped around the tires' circumference. Today, all vehicles come fitted with *radial* tires with belts that run at right-angles to the tread. Also available are *run-flat* tires, *puncture-proof* tires, and other new types, which are covered later in this chapter.

Radial tires have become the standard because they provide better handling, especially at high speeds; they tend to grip the road more efficiently, especially when cornering; and they can deliver twice the mileage of bias-ply and belted tires. Radial tires run cooler because they have less internal friction. Wear varies; some high-performance cars with tire treads made of a relatively soft compound that provides better road grip get only a few thousands miles per set if driven hard. But for most vehicles, tires last from 25,000 miles and up, depending on the belt material used. Top-of-the-line steel-belted radials can last from 40,000 to as many as 100,000 miles under average driving conditions. To decide what type of tire is right for your vehicle, see "Tips for Buying Tires," later in this chapter.

# The Secrets on Your Sidewalls, Revealed!

Many people are willing to spend extra dollars for tires with names like MACHO WILDCATS or TOUGH GUYS embossed in large white letters on the sidewalls, but did you know that the wealth of information that is embossed on those sidewalls in quiet little black letters can be more valuable in the long run? And this information is *free* — if you know how to decode it. Even if you're not the inquisitive type, the data in the following sections can help you when you buy and maintain tires. Figure 17-2 shows you all the different types of codes you can find on the sidewall of a tire.

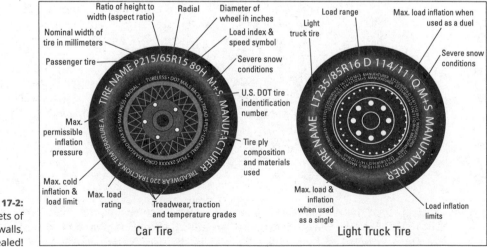

**FIGURE 17-2:**
The secrets of your sidewalls, revealed!

*Adapted from the NHTSA (www.safercar.gov)*

# Tire codes

Until around 1978, tire sizes were indicated by alpha-numeric codes, such as D78-14. With the adoption of the metric system, the codes changed drastically, and now modern codes provide more information. Tire dealers are required by law to have leaflets available that explain tire grades and ratings. The leaflets also tell you which metric codes replace the old alphanumeric designations. For example, here's a breakdown of the information provided by a common "P-metric" tire code, P215/65R15, as shown in Figure 17-2:

>> **P = Type of vehicle.** In this case, P means passenger. Other codes include LT for light truck and T for temporary or spare tire. Small pickup trucks and RVs often come with P-rated tires because they aren't expected to carry heavy loads.

**TIP**

   If you're planning to do any heavy hauling, look for a vehicle equipped with LTs. (Also check the load index information farther down this list.)

>> **215 = Tire section width.** This is measured across the tread, from one sidewall to the other, in millimeters. In this case, the tire width is 215 mm. Remember, the wider the tire, the higher the number.

>> **65 = Aspect ratio or tire series.** This is the ratio of the tire's sidewall height to its width. In this case, the tire's sidewall height is 65 percent of its width. Tires with a low aspect ratio (less than 70) are referred to as *low-profile* tires and usually are found on the *touring tires* or *high performance tires* described in the later section "Passenger vehicles."

>> **R = Tire type.** For tire type, R means radial and LT means light truck. Most tires on passenger vehicles are radials.

>> **15 = Diameter of the wheel.** The diameter is measured in inches. In this case, the diameter is 15 inches. Buying new wheels with larger diameters (and 18- to 20-inch wheels aren't uncommon these days) requires buying new tires with diameters to match.

>> **89 = Load index.** This number refers to how much weight the tire can carry. This information is especially important if you carry heavy loads (including several obese passengers), haul a lot of gear on camping trips, or if you're moving your kid to a college dormitory! There's no law that requires the manufacturer to put load index information on the sidewall, but your **owner's manual** may have it. If not, consult a tire dealer.

>> **H = Speed rating.** The speed rating of the tire is described in the next section. Providing this information on the sidewall isn't required by law.

>> **M+S or M/S = Mud and snow codes.** If you live in or drive through areas with extreme conditions, look for these codes on the sidewall.

**REMEMBER**

Codes may differ slightly from one tire to another. In addition to the P-metric code, there are European metric codes, which can be as simple as 155SR13 or as complex as 185/70R14 88S, but the data they disclose is pretty much the same.

## Speed ratings

Sometimes an additional letter appears between the load index and tire type, such as P215/65R15 89**H** in Figure 17-2. The letter **H** refers to the *speed rating*, which represents the safest *maximum* speed for the tire. It tells you nothing about a tire's construction, handling, or wearability but rather measures the tire's ability to dissipate heat so that it can endure the high temperatures that high speeds create.

Here's a list of what the most common speed rating letters mean:

» Q = 99 mph

» R = 106 mph

» S = 112 mph

» T = 118 mph

» U = 124 mph

» H = 130 mph

» V = 149 mph

» W = 168 mph

» Y = 186 mph

» ZR = Sometimes used for tires that can go over 149 mph; always used for tires that can go over 186 mph

Tires with the most common speed ratings, T and H, can go well over the speed limit. They're usually good buys because tires with higher speed ratings are more durable. However, if you usually drive at low speeds on local streets and rarely drive on the highway, the extra expense may not be worth it.

## DOT identification and registration

The Department of Transportation (DOT) identification number on the sidewall (refer to Figure 17-2) has a wealth of information. Here's what the letters and numbers of the DOT code mean:

>> **DOT** indicates that the tire meets or exceeds United States Department of Transportation safety standards.

>> **The next two numbers or letters** identify the plant where the tire was made.

>> **The next numbers or letters** are marketing codes provided by the manufacturer. They serve as a registration number that identifies the tire in case of a recall. (You can find more information on recalls in the later section "Dealing with Defective Tires.")

>> **The last four numbers** are the week and year the tire was produced. For example, 2408 would mean the tire was made during the twenty-fourth week of 2008.

WARNING

*Be sure to check this code to see how old the tires on your vehicle really are!* In some cases, it can only be found on the *inside* sidewall, but it's worth getting down there with a flashlight. A 2008 exposé by ABC's *Underground 20/20* found that, despite the fact that tires over 6 years old could suffer blow-outs that had resulted in a considerable number of fatal accidents, supposedly new tires were for sale at tire dealerships and major chains with codes showing that the tires were 12 years old or more! In 2008, NHTSA ruled that this date code had to appear on the *outside* of the tire where owners could easily check them on their own vehicles.

Under federal law, the dealer is required to put the tire's DOT number and the dealer's name and address on a form that's sent to the manufacturer. Although tire outlets owned by manufacturers and certain brand-name outlets must send them in to the manufacturer, independent tire dealers can simply fill out the forms and give them to customers to mail to the manufacturer. For more ideas about buying tires, see "Tips for Buying Tires" later in this chapter.

WARNING

When you buy new tires, make sure that they're properly registered. Unlike *guarantees* and *warranties,* in case of a recall you aren't eligible to receive replacements unless your tires have been properly registered and you respond to the recall within 60 days!

## Tire quality grade codes

The Uniform Tire Quality Grading System (UTQGS) rates tires for *treadwear, traction,* and *temperature,* but although the federal government requires that ratings be determined on most passenger car tires, they're set by tire manufacturers and not by an objective testing service. Personal driving habits, type of vehicle, road conditions and surfaces, and tire maintenance all have a huge impact on a tire's longevity and performance.

TIP

To find the tire rating for tires required to use them (many light truck and SUV tires aren't), go to www.safercars.gov/tires/pages/TireRatings.cfm and enter the brand of tire that you're interested in. You can then sort the tires by wear, traction, and temperature, all of which I describe in the next section. Your dealer also should have this information on hand.

Look for the tire quality grades shown in Figure 17-2 on the sidewalls of the tires on your vehicle or on stickers affixed to the treads of tires at a dealership. Here's what they mean:

>> **Treadwear:** This comparative number grade is based on carefully controlled testing conditions. In the real world, a tire rated 200 would have twice the treadwear of one rated 100 — *if* all other wear factors were equal.

>> **Traction:** This AA, A, B, or C grade represents the tire's ability to stop on wet pavement under controlled conditions (with AA being the best possible rating). The grades are based on straight-ahead braking only, not on cornering or turning. The higher the grade, the shorter distance it takes to stop the vehicle. A tire with a C grade just meets the government's test, whereas tires with B, A, and AA (in ascending order) exceed government standards.

>> **Temperature:** This A, B, or C grade represents heat resistance and the tire's capability to dissipate the heat if the tire is inflated properly and not over-loaded. Grade C meets U.S. minimum standards, while grades B and A exceed government standards.

## Other sidewall information

Check the sidewalls shown in Figure 17-2 and on your own vehicle for the follow-ing safety data:

>> **MAX LOAD:** How much weight the tire can bear safely, usually expressed in both kilograms (kg) and pounds (lbs)

>> **MAX PRESS:** The *maximum* air pressure the tire can safely hold, usually expressed in pounds per square inch *(psi)*

WARNING

MAX PRESS is *not* the proper pressure to maintain in your tires! To find the amount of psi the tires should normally hold, look for the *manufacturer's recommended pressure* for the best handling and wear on the tire decal on the door, door pillar, console, glove box, or trunk of your vehicle.

You can find instructions for checking tire pressure, reading treads for clues, and other work that you can do on your tires in the "Caring for Your Tires" section later in this chapter.

# Types of Tires

As I explain earlier in this chapter, if you use the proper type of tires on your vehicle, they will wear better, provide better traction, provide the best braking action, and are safer than the wrong tires. Here are some of the types of tires that you may want to consider.

## Passenger vehicles

The following types of tires are suitable for passenger vehicles, which include everything except trucks and SUVs (covered in the following section), race cars, construction equipment, and other specialized vehicles:

» **Basic all-season tires** are standard equipment on most popular vehicles because they usually provide a comfortable ride and good treadwear. The speed rating (see the "Speed ratings" section earlier in the chapter) is usually T or H. If "M+S" is printed on the *sidewall,* the tire meets standards for mud and snow, but if you live in an area with really inclement weather, you'll probably need snow tires instead.

» **Touring tires** are generally more expensive than basic all-season tires and can be found on sportier vehicle models because the tires are supposed to handle better and grip the road at higher speeds in dry conditions. Whether they're worth the money depends on the individual product. Touring tires have higher speed ratings, lower profiles (sometimes called lower *aspect ratios*), and may not be as durable as all-season tires.

» **Performance tires** are designed for people who drive aggressively. They perform better in terms of braking and cornering in dry conditions but usually are noisier and wear out more quickly than all-season tires. They're usually speed-rated at least at H and have a wide, squatty, low profile.

» **Ultra-high-performance tires** have both the positive and the negative aspects of performance tires to a greater degree: They go faster and brake and handle better in both wet and dry conditions, but they ride less comfortably and wear out even faster. They may have profiles as low as 25 and usually are speed-rated V through ZR.

**WARNING**

As a rule, low-profile tires such as touring tires and ultra-high-performance tires may not be as durable as all-season tires because they're more easily damaged by potholes and other road hazards and are more sensitive to underinflation than tires with higher profiles. There also have been many reports of damage to *alloy wheels,* especially the larger diameter, *aftermarket* wheels, when low-profile tires are used because the tires don't absorb as much of the shock from bumps and potholes as do tires with higher profiles.

# Tires for trucks and SUVs

SUVs, small pickup trucks, and vans may come with passenger-rated tires or truck tires. What you need depends on where you usually drive and how much you carry. Here are the categories for truck tires:

>> **Light-truck tires** are intended for use on light trucks and SUVs. They come in a variety of styles designed for normal conditions, driving on- or off-road, or both. The thicker treads on the off-road variety offer better traction on unpaved surfaces. Light-truck tires also vary for carrying normal, heavy, and extra-heavy loads.

>> **Street/sport truck** tires are pretty much the same as all-season tires except that they have a sportier look and are supposed to handle better.

>> **Highway tires** are useful if you drive a larger van or pickup truck because they can carry heavier loads.

>> **Off-road** tires have treads designed to deal with really difficult terrain. Because they're noisier and not as comfortable or fuel-efficient on paved roads as street/sport or highway tires, forget these tires unless you really plan to head for the hills or desperately want to project a more macho image enough to pay bigger bucks for tires and fuel. However, a compromise may be *all-terrain* off-road tires, which may not get you quite as far off the beaten path but are more comfortable and quieter than these heavy-duty beauties.

>> **Snow tires** may be better than all-season tires for driving in areas with heavy snowfall or muddy roads. Their treads usually have wider grooves and protuberances called *lugs* to provide better traction, but they're noisy, don't handle as well on dry roads, and are generally less fuel-efficient than all-season tires, so use them only when necessary.

# Specialized Tire Systems

Some tires are so sophisticated that they require a special system to enable them to communicate with the driver and/or other automotive systems. The following tires and systems fall into this category.

## Run-flat tires

Run-flat tires can be driven on without *any* air pressure inside the tire! This means that you don't face the stress and danger involved in having a blow-out or changing a tire at the side of the road. Run-flats can be constructed in two different ways:

>> **Self-supporting run-flat tires** have stronger sidewalls to keep the tire from collapsing if the air pressure inside the tire drops. Layers of rubber and heat-resistant cord, and sometimes support wedges, are used in the sidewall.

>> **The PAX system** designed by Michelin allows you to drive up to 55 mph for up to 125 miles with zero air pressure inside a tire! The system includes a tire, a tire-monitoring system that measures the temperature and the pressure of the air in the tire, and a wheel with a strong inner ring that supports the tread if the tire loses half its air pressure. Unlike most other tires, the system also features a special anchoring mechanism that keeps the tire on the wheel if the air pressure in the tire drops.

Michelin claims that PAX system tires wear longer and get better fuel economy than traditional tires because of reduced rolling resistance. If the tread area is punctured, the tire can be repaired and the support ring reused. You can read more about this system at www.michelinman.com/difference/innovation/paxsystem.html.

Under normal circumstances, properly inflated run-flat tires should last the same 30,000 to 40,000 miles as many ordinary tires. You can drive run-flat tires with no air pressure in them for 50 to 125 miles at speeds up to 50 or 55 mph without further damaging the tire. Although run-flats are durable, running on them without air at high speeds for a long period can damage them. Because the driver often can't feel any difference when a run-flat goes flat, automakers incorporate *low-pressure warning systems* to alert the driver that a tire has lost pressure and to drive more slowly and get the tire repaired as soon as possible to avoid further damage to the tire or wheel. See the next section for more details on these warning systems.

TIP

*Some run-flat equipped vehicles may not even come with a jack or spare tire!* Although run-flats are durable, there's always the chance that one can be disabled by a defect or accident, so if your vehicle lacks this equipment and has room to carry it, I strongly suggest that you buy yourself a jack (see Chapter 3) as well as a small, temporary spare tire in the correct size for the wheels on your vehicle. By being prepared, you save yourself a tow and/or a long wait if the dealership doesn't have the proper tire in stock. Forewarned is forearmed!

WARNING

Although you can have run-flat tires installed on a vehicle that didn't come with them, you also need to purchase a warning system designed for the new tires, and if the rims on your current wheels aren't sturdy enough to accommodate run-flats, you may have to replace those, too.

Also be aware that vehicles that come equipped with run-flats have *suspension systems* that are tuned to the rigidity of the sidewalls. So if you replace the tires on a vehicle with a standard suspension with run-flats, there may be a difference in the way your vehicle handles, and the ride may be a bit harder and noisier.

Be sure to purchase run-flats and have them installed at a car or tire dealer that knows how to do it properly. There's a good case to be made that the expense is well worthwhile compared to the possible consequences of blow-outs and flat tires.

## Low-pressure warning systems

TIP

Both run-flat and self-inflating tires (see the next section) require low-pressure warning systems, and the federal TREAD Act mandates that *all* vehicles built in the 2008-model year and after must come equipped with this safety feature. If your vehicle is an earlier model that doesn't have such a system, to save your tires — and yourself — from damage caused by running on flat tires, you may want to have such a system installed.

You can find two types of low-pressure systems on modern vehicles:

>> **Direct systems:** The only option for vehicles that didn't come equipped with run-flats. They employ a **sensor** on the wheel that usually is placed opposite the valve stem. The sensor sends a signal to a unit that usually activates a warning light on the instrument panel (some systems have warning chimes). The sensors are powered by small, five-year batteries that usually are replaced with each new set of tires.

>> **Indirect systems:** The least expensive option and therefore the type that automakers often prefer to use. They employ the same sensors as are used on **ABS** systems to measure the speed of the wheels. However, when used with run-flats, an indirect system needs to be specially tuned to be sensitive enough to the very slight differences between an inflated run-flat and one that's flat.

## Self-inflating tire systems

TECHNICAL
STUFF

Self-inflating tires aren't due to be generally available for several years, but you should be aware that they're in the works. Michelin, in partnership with several other companies, is developing TIPM (Tire Inflation Pressure Management), a tire inflation system for passenger cars and light trucks that will include a compressor that automatically adjusts the pressure in each tire while the vehicle is in operation to suit the actual driving conditions of the vehicle, taking into account load, weather, and speed. TIPM will automatically compensate for natural leakage as well as slow-leak punctures. The driver will be able to select comfort, sporty, all-terrain, or over-obstacle driving modes and adjust the pressure accordingly.

# Tips for Buying Tires

Tire wear is affected by a number of factors: the condition of the vehicle's *brake system* and *suspension system*, inflation and *alignment*, driving and braking techniques, driving at high speeds (which raises tire temperatures and causes them to wear prematurely), how great a load you carry, road conditions, and climate. So, before you rush out and buy a set of tires, you have several things to consider:

ECO-LOGIC

**How important is fuel-economy?** Some types of tires are more fuel efficient than others. The bottom line is that the narrower the tread width and the higher the inflation pressure *(psi)*, the less rolling resistance and thus the most fuel economy from the tire. However, the way any tire performs is most affected by road and weather conditions and, of course, the way you drive!

**Are you hard on tires?** If you tend to "burn rubber" when cornering, starting, and stopping, you know where that rubber comes from. A pair of cheaply made tires will wear out quickly, so buy the best quality you can afford. And learn not to be such a lead-foot!

**Do you drive a great deal and do most of your driving on high-speed highways?** A tire with a harder tread compound will take longer to wear out under these conditions. See the "Tire quality grade codes" section earlier in this chapter for more information about *treadwear* ratings.

TECHNICAL
STUFF

## RETREADS: BARGAINS OR BLOWOUTS?

Millions of tires are discarded every year, and an entire industry has developed to put them back in service by replacing the worn tread areas with new ones. The retreading process involves grinding the tread off an otherwise sound old tire and winding a strand of uncured rubber around the tire. Then the tire is placed in a mold, where the rubber is cured under heat and pressure and the tread itself is shaped. Finally, the tire is painted.

For many years, retreads had a reputation of being unreliable, and most consumers assumed that the strips of tread they saw littering the highways came from retreaded tires that had disintegrated on the road. But today, advances in retreading have raised their quality. Although they are now hardly used on passenger vehicles, and high-performance vehicles are probably better off with new tires, most large commercial trucks (such as semis) use them, as do virtually all the world's airlines. Retreaded tires are also used on school buses, racing cars, taxis, trucks, and federal and U.S. military vehicles.

You can find out more about retreads at www.retread.org.

**Do you drive a lot on unpaved rocky roads, carry heavy loads, or leave your vehicle in the hot sun for long hours?** If so, you need higher-quality tires that have the stamina to endure these challenges. Look for *extra load-rated* or even *LT* (light truck) tires. A tire dealer can tell you which tires are rated for extra loads.

**What's the weather like in your area?** Today, *front-wheel drive* vehicles with high-tech *all-season* tires get better traction than the old snow tires, which you had to replace when warm weather set in. However, if you drive under extreme conditions, you may want to check out tires designed for them.

**Do you drive mostly in local stop-and-go traffic, with many turns?** Softer tires with wider treads will suit you best.

REMEMBER

**How long do you intend to keep your vehicle?** Putting expensive tires on a car that you intend to get rid of in 10,000 or 20,000 miles is foolish. On the other hand, if you intend to keep your vehicle for several years, you'll save money in the long run by opting for more expensive, longer-lasting tires over *cheapos* or tires rated for less than 40,000 miles. Cheap tires wear out more quickly and cost more in the long run if you figure in the cost of buying, mounting, and *balancing* that second set. What's more, if you suffer a blowout, or if your tires fail to grip the road, you'll pay a great deal more if your vehicle — or you — is injured.

WARNING

If you drive only a couple of thousand miles a year, don't expect a pair of 60,000-mile radials to last forever. Rubber treads tend to rot eventually because of the ozone in the air, which causes cracks and hard spots in the sidewalls (it's a condition called *ozone checking*). For this reason, if your tires have more than 40,000 miles of wear and tear, even if the treads are in good shape, have the tires checked to make sure that deteriorating rubber hasn't made them prone to blowouts and leaks.

**Do you feel vulnerable on the road?** If you worry about having a blow-out, don't feel that you can change a flat yourself, or are afraid that you'll be car-jacked or injured if you stop to change a tire, *run-flat tires* (described earlier in the chapter) are well worth owning.

In addition to knowing which kind of tire is best for your vehicle and understanding the tire codes (explained in the section called "The Secrets on Your Sidewalls, Revealed!"), keep the following tips in mind when you shop for tires:

>> You can find the proper tire size for your car in your **owner's manual** or on a sticker affixed to the vehicle. If neither exists, ask your dealer.

>> Although you should never buy tires that are smaller than those specified for your vehicle, you often can buy tires a size or two larger (if the car's wheel clearance allows it) for better handling or load-carrying ability.

**WARNING**

However, *buy these larger tires in pairs and place them on the same **axle.*** Ask your mechanic or a reputable tire or auto dealer for advice about the proper size range for your vehicle. Sometimes buying larger tires also requires larger wheels, which can quickly get expensive.

>> Never use two different-sized tires on the same axle.

>> If you're replacing just one or two tires, put the new ones on the front for better cornering control and braking (because weight transfers to the front tires when you brake). Of course, if you have a sports car or performance vehicle with rear tires that are larger than the front tires, you have to make sure you keep the proper sizes on each axle.

>> You have to "break in" new tires, so don't drive faster than 60 mph for the first 50 miles on a new tire or spare.

>> Store tires that you aren't using in the dark, away from extreme heat and electric motors that create ozone.

# Caring for Your Tires

Tires don't require a great deal of maintenance, but the jobs in this section will pay off handsomely by increasing your tires' longevity, handling, and performance as well as providing you with a more comfortable ride.

## Checking tire inflation pressure

The single most important factor in caring for your tires is maintaining the correct inflation pressure. True, most newer vehicles have the built-in *pressure-monitoring systems* described earlier in this chapter, but there are still many vehicles on the road without them.

**TIP**

If your vehicle doesn't have a pressure-monitoring system, you should check your tires at least once a month and before every long trip to see that they're properly inflated. Tires that are correctly inflated tend to wear properly in spite of minor weather ups and downs. *Underinflated* tires wear out faster, create excessive heat, increase fuel consumption, and make the vehicle harder to handle. *Overinflated* tires can blow out more easily, wear out faster, and make the vehicle unstable and unsafe to handle. The section "Checking your tires for wear," later in this chapter, helps you check for signs of these problems and tells you what to do about them.

Check tire pressure in the morning before you start out or when you've driven less than a mile. If you drive more than that, your tires will heat up and the air will expand, so you won't get an accurate reading.

If the weather has changed radically, it's time to check pressure again. In hot weather, the pressure in your tires rises by one pound per square inch (*psi*) of pressure for every 10°F as the air in them heats up and expands. This can result in *overinflation.* Conversely, in cold weather, the pressure falls by one degree for every 10° drop as the cold air contracts, so your tires can end up *underinflated.* Therefore, if the weather gets very cold — and it looks as though it will stay that way for some time — and if you get a low reading, you may want to add a bit of air to your tires to bring the pressure back up.

Here's how you check the air pressure in your tires:

**1.** **Buy an accurate tire gauge at a hardware store or auto supply store.**

Figure 17-3 shows you what one type of tire gauge looks like.

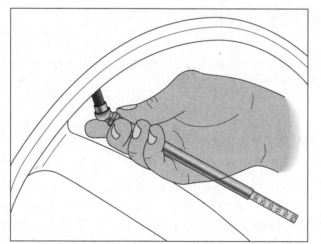

**FIGURE 17-3:**
The number on the tire gauge indicates air pressure in psi.

**2.** **Determine the proper air pressure for your tires by looking for the proper inflation pressure on the tire decal.**

You can find the tire decal on one of the doors, door pillars, glove box, console, or trunk. Sometimes the tire decal specifies one pressure for the front tires and a different pressure for the rear tires.

*Don't* consult the tire's ***sidewall*** for the proper inflation pressure. The sidewall lists the *maximum* pressure that the tire is capable of handling, not the pressure that's best for performance and wear (unless you're carrying heavy loads).

3. **Remove the little cap from the tire valve that sticks out of your tire near the wheel rim.**

   You don't have to remove your wheel cover or hubcap for this step.

4. **Place the open, rounded end of the tire gauge against the valve so that the little pin in the gauge contacts the pin in the valve.**

5. **Press the gauge against the valve stem.**

   You'll hear a hissing sound as air starts to escape from the tire. At this point, a little stick will emerge from the other end of the tire gauge valve (see Figure 17-3). It emerges partway almost as soon as the air starts to hiss and stops emerging almost immediately.

6. **Without pushing the stick back in, remove the gauge from the tire valve.**

7. **Look at the stick without touching it. There are little numbers on it; pay attention to the last number showing.**

   The last number is the amount of air pressure (in psi) in your tire, as shown in Figure 17-3. Does the gauge indicate the proper amount of pressure recommended on the decal?

   If the pressure seems too low, push the stick back in and press the gauge against the valve stem again. If the reading doesn't change, you need more air.

TIP

   Instead of a stick, some tire gauges feature a dial on the face of the gauge that shows the air pressure, and digital tire pressure gauges are becoming increasingly common. If you have one of these, just check to see if the needle on the dial — or the digital readout — shows the correct psi. If it doesn't, you need to add air to the tire until the reading is correct. But you knew that, right?

8. **Repeat Steps 3 through 7 for each tire.**

REMEMBER

   Run-flat tires and little temporary spare tires can lose pressure over time, so be sure to check them, too.

9. **Add air, if necessary, by following the steps in the next section, "Adding air to your tires."**

## Adding air to your tires

If your tires appear to be low, check the pressure according to the steps in the preceding section and note the amount that they're underinflated. Then drive to a local gas station.

TIP

Be sure to bring some change (usually quarters) with you for the air dispenser. (Forget about things being "as free as air" — at many stations it isn't!)

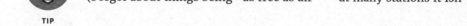

Follow these steps to add air to your tires:

1. **Park your vehicle so that you can reach all four tires with the air hose.**

2. **Remove the cap from the tire valve on the first tire.**

3. **Use *your* tire gauge to check the air pressure in the tire and see how much it has changed since your last reading (tests have shown that tire gauges on the air hoses at many gas stations are inaccurate).**

   The pressure will have increased because driving causes the tires to heat up and the air inside them to expand. To avoid overinflating the tire, no matter what the second reading indicates, you should only add the same amount of air that the tire lacked before you drove it to the station.

4. **Use the air hose to add air in short bursts, checking the pressure after each time with *your* tire gauge.**

5. **If you add too much air, let some out by pressing the pin on the tire valve with the back of the air hose nozzle or with the little knob on the back of the rounded end of the tire gauge.**

6. **Keep checking the pressure until you get it right.**

   Don't get discouraged if you have to keep adjusting the air pressure. No one hits it on the head the first time!

## Rotating your tires

People have differing points of view on tire rotation. Some say that you can get up to 20 percent more wear if you rotate your tires. Others caution against rotating them because rotation may hide the distinctive treadwear patterns that provide the clues to poor *alignment,* worn *shock absorbers,* and defective brakes found in the "Checking your tires for wear" section later in this chapter. If your tires seem to be wearing evenly and you haven't had any of these problems, then it's a good idea to rotate them — but check them first for signs of problems that may have arisen since the last time they were rotated.

For uniform tire wear, the tires on most vehicles should be rotated approximately every 6,000 miles, unless they show the signs of irregular wear in Table 17-1 and Figure 17-9 later in this chapter. There are a few other exceptions to this rule: Vehicles that have larger wheels and tires in the rear and vehicles that have different wheels front to back can't undergo tire rotation. And if you have unidirectional tires or tires with asymmetric tread designs, you can't rotate them in the patterns shown in Figure 17-4.

When you rotate tires, you simply move each tire from one location to another. However, where you move the tires depends on the type of tires and vehicle you have (see Figure 17-4). If you're not sure where to move the tires on your vehicle, consult your owner's manual (usually it has a diagram showing how the tires should be rotated), call the tire manufacturer, or ask the dealership.

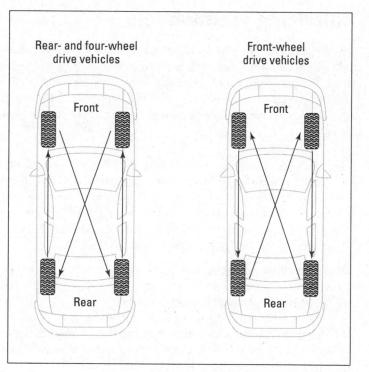

**FIGURE 17-4:**
How to rotate
your tires.

*Adapted from the NHTSA (www.safercar.gov)*

To save the enormous amount of effort involved in jacking up your vehicle and changing each tire, you can always just drive to a service facility and have them rotate the tires for you. Many shops include free tire rotation and *wheel balancing* in oil change and other special service promotions, and most tire dealers include periodic tire rotation and wheel balancing in their warranties. (I explain wheel balancing in the next section.)

**REMEMBER**

The tires on the front and rear wheels may require different air pressures. After the tires are rotated, remember to adjust the air pressure on each tire to whatever is indicated on the tire decal on your vehicle or in your owner's manual.

If you have a matching, full-sized spare, you can include it in the rotation process by starting it out in the right rear position and using the tire that would have been moved to the right rear as the spare tire until the next rotation. Obviously, you don't include a "Temporary Use Only" spare tire (those teeny little ones) in any rotation pattern.

## Balancing your wheels

*Wheel balancing* does a lot to eliminate some of the principal causes of tire wear, and an unbalanced wheel and tire can create an annoying vibration on smooth roads. Because balancing is a job that should be done with the proper equipment, and because that equipment is costly, get the job done for you at a service facility or tire store. Just remember that there are two kinds of wheel balancing: *static* and *dynamic.*

>> **Static balancing** deals with the even distribution of weight around the **axle.** You can tell that you need to have your wheels statically balanced if a wheel (or more than one wheel) tends to rotate by itself when your vehicle is jacked up. It rotates because one part of the wheel is heavier than the rest. To correct this problem, a technician finds the heavy spot and applies tire weights to the opposite side of the heavy spot to balance it out.

>> **Dynamic balancing** deals with the even distribution of weight along the **spindle.** Wheels that aren't balanced dynamically tend to wobble and wear more quickly. Because imbalance can be detected only when the tire is rotated and centrifugal force can act, correcting dynamic balance is a relatively complex procedure. Most service stations have computerized balancers that not only balance the wheels but also locate the places where tire weights are needed and decide how much weight to add.

Having your tires balanced both statically and dynamically shouldn't be terribly expensive and may be included in a service or *warranty* package. As with any general service, it pays to check around for the best deal.

If you plan to have your wheels balanced professionally, rotating your tires yourself beforehand is a waste of time. The technicians have to remove the tires to balance them anyway, so they may as well rotate them, too.

## Aligning your wheels

A cheap and easy way to substantially improve your vehicle's handling and extend the life of your tires is to be alert to signs of misalignment and to have your wheels aligned immediately if the signs appear.

**TRUE STORY**

I learned this lesson the hard way when I wore out a tire that was almost new in one day of highway driving because it was out of *alignment!* If I'd known enough to check my tires, I'd have seen that the tread on this tire was worn down one side, a sure sign of misalignment.

This job is sometimes called *front-end alignment* because the front wheels get out of line most often. They get that way because of hard driving with dramatic get-away starts and screeching stops, hitting curbs hard when parking or cornering, accidents, heavy loads, frequent driving over unpaved roads or into potholes, and normal wear and tear as the car gets older. Occasionally, the rear wheels need realignment as well. Vehicles with independent rear suspensions and *front-wheel drive* vehicles require four-wheel alignment. I used to think that alignment involved taking a car that had been bashed out of shape and literally pulling it back into line. Untrue. All the technicians do is adjust your wheels to make sure that they track in a nice, straight line when you drive. To do so, they use special equipment to check the following points:

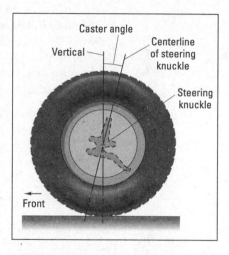

**FIGURE 17-5:**
Caster.

» *Caster:* Has to do with the position of your *steering knuckle* as compared to a vertical line when viewed from the side (see Figure 17-5). If properly adjusted, it makes your wheels track in a straight line instead of weaving or shimmying at high speeds. Caster also helps return the steering wheel to a straight-ahead position after completing a turn.

» *Camber:* The inward or outward tilt of the top of the wheels when viewed from the front/rear of the vehicle — in other words, how "bow-legged" or "knock-kneed" they are (see Figure 17-6). If the wheels don't hang properly, your tires wear out more quickly, and your car is harder to handle.

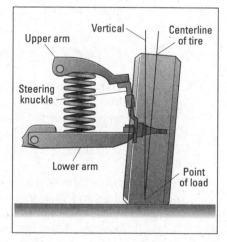

**FIGURE 17-6:**
Camber.

CHAPTER 17 **How to Keep Your Car from Getting Sore Feet: Tires, Alignment, and Balancing** 337

» **Toe-in** and **toe-out:** Involve placing your tires so that they're properly positioned parallel to the frame when driving down the road. Some cars call for a little *toe-in* (tires pointing inward, as in Figure 17-7), whereas others are set with a little *toe-out* (tires pointing outward). The result should be a nice, straight track when the car is moving quickly. On some front-wheel drive vehicles, the manufacturer may set the rear tires with a little toe-in and the front tires with a little toe-out so that the tires are parallel to the frame when the vehicle is in motion.

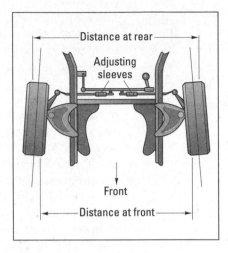

**FIGURE 17-7:**
Toe-in.

» **Turning radius:** The relation of one front wheel to the other on turns. If you turn to the right, the right front tire needs to turn at a slightly greater angle than the left front tire (see Figure 17-8). Your vehicle's steering arms accommodate this feat. If your tires squeal sharply on turns, one of your car's steering arms may be your problem.

TIP

How do you know if your wheels need aligning? Look at your tires to see whether they show any of the treadwear patterns that I discuss in the next section, and pay attention to how your car steers and handles. Does it pull to one side? Does the steering feel loose and sloppy? Is your vehicle hard to handle after a turn? If your tires show any unusual wear patterns and/or you answered yes to any of these questions, your car probably needs an alignment.

## Checking your tires for wear

TIP

You should check your tires for wear at least once a month and before and after long trips. To determine whether you need to (a) buy new tires, (b) have your wheels balanced, (c) have your wheels aligned, or (d) change your driving habits, simply read your tire treads for clues. Table 17-1 and Figure 17-9 show you what to look for.

REMEMBER

Underinflated tires wear out faster, create excessive heat, increase fuel consumption, and make your car harder to handle. Overinflated tires can "blow out" more easily, wear out faster, and make the vehicle unstable and unsafe to handle. And a new set of tires on wheels that are out of alignment can wear out completely in as little as one day of hard driving!

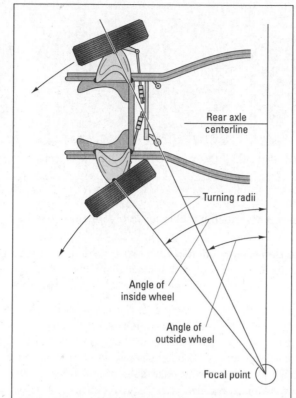

**FIGURE 17-8:**
Turning radius.

**TABLE 17-1**   **How to Read Your Treads**

| Clue | Culprit | Remedy |
|------|---------|--------|
| Both edges worn | Underinflation | Add more air and check for leaks |
| Center treads worn | Overinflation | Let air out to manufacturer's specifications |
| One-sided wear | Poor alignment | Have wheels aligned |
| Treads worn unevenly, with bald spots, cups, or scallops | Wheel imbalance and/or poor alignment | Have wheels balanced and aligned |
| Erratically spaced bald spots | Wheel imbalance or worn shocks | Have wheels balanced or replace shocks |
| Edges of front tires only worn | Taking curves too fast | Slow down! |
| Saw-toothed wear pattern | Poor alignment | Have wheels aligned |
| Whining, thumping, and other weird noises | Poor alignment or worn tires or shocks | Have wheels aligned or buy new tires or shocks |
| Squealing on curves | Poor alignment or underinflation | Check wear on treads and act accordingly |

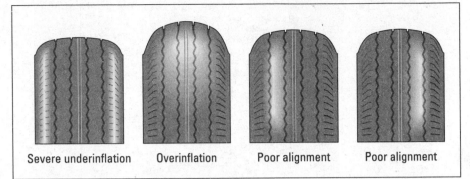

**FIGURE 17-9:**
What the signs of poor treadwear mean.

Severe underinflation    Overinflation    Poor alignment    Poor alignment

To determine what's causing problems with your tires, try the following:

**WARNING**

>> **Look for things embedded in each tire.** Do you see nails, stones, or other debris embedded in the treads? Remove them. *But* if you're going to remove a nail, first make sure that your spare tire is inflated and in usable shape.

If you hear a hissing sound when you pull a nail, push the nail back in quickly and take the tire to be fixed. If you aren't sure whether air is escaping, put some soapy water on the hole and look for the bubbles made by escaping air. If you're still not sure whether the nail may have caused a leak, check your air pressure and then check it again the next day to see whether it's lower (for help, see "Checking tire inflation pressure" earlier in this chapter). Tires with leaks should be patched by a professional. If the leak persists, get a new tire. These instructions apply to any sharp object that may have penetrated through the tread.

>> **Look at the sidewalls.** Check for deeply scuffed or worn areas, bulges or bubbles, small slits, or holes. Do the tires fit evenly and snugly around the wheel rims?

>> **Look at the treads.** Most tires have built-in *treadwear indicators* (see Figure 17-10). These bars of hard rubber are normally invisible but appear across treads that have been worn down to $\frac{2}{32}$ of an inch of the surface of the tire (the legal limit in most states). If these indicators appear in two or three different places less than 120 degrees apart on the circumference of the tire, replace the tire.

**FIGURE 17-10:**
It's time for new tires when treadwear indicators appear.

**TIP**

If your tires don't show these indicators and you think that they may be worn below legal tolerances, place a Lincoln penny head-down in the groove between the treads. If you can see the top of Lincoln's head, your tire probably needs to be replaced.

To measure treadwear more precisely, place a thin ruler into the tread and measure the distance from the base of the tread to the surface. It should be more than ²/₃₂ inch deep. (**Note:** If your front tires are more worn than your rear ones and show abnormal wear patterns, you probably need to have your wheels aligned.)

WARNING

Sometimes ²/₃₂ inch of tread isn't enough to keep you safe. If you live in a rainy area, measure the depth of your treads with a quarter rather than a penny, using Washington's hair to see if your tires have at least ⁴/₃₂ inch of tread remaining, which reduces the distance and time it takes for the car to stop.

>> **Pay attention to leaks.** If you keep losing air in your tires, have your local service station check them for leaks. Sometimes an ill-fitting rim causes a leak. The service facility has a machine that can fix this problem easily.

TIP

If the facility can't find a leak, your rims fit properly, and you're still losing air, you probably have a faulty *tire valve* that's allowing air to escape. If a tire valve needs to be replaced, be sure that the replacement provided by the service facility has the same number molded into its base as the valve it's replacing.

# Dealing with Defective Tires

Tires, like vehicles, can turn out to be *lemons*. But these lemons can put your life on the line. Defective tires should be replaced by the manufacturer, but you may need proof before you file a complaint. If you discover that one of your tires is defective, go to www.safercars.gov/tires/pages/TireDefects.htm for links that enable you to check for recalls; check for complaints by make, model, and year; and search to see whether a safety investigation is underway into defects found on a particular tire (there may be fees for this search, however). You can file a complaint at www-odi.nhtsa.dot.gov/ivoq/index.cfm.

If you prefer, you can call the Vehicle Safety Hotline toll free at 1-888-327-4236 to report safety defects and to obtain information on cars, trucks, child seats, and highway or traffic safety.

Chapter **18**

# Take the Drive Train: Understanding and Maintaining Your Transmission without Losing Your Mind

The *transmission* system in your vehicle is probably its most complex system in terms of automotive mechanics. But take heart: You don't have to be a genius to understand it (or I wouldn't be writing about it!). For starters, think of the transmission as a communication system that takes messages from you about whether you want to go forward or backward — and at what speed — and passes them on to the wheels.

Transmission systems vary from one vehicle to another. With a *manual transmission* (sometimes called a *standard* transmission), you shift into the proper *gear* at the proper time *yourself*; with an *automatic transmission,* the shifting is done *for* you. Some newer vehicles feature a *continuously variable transmission (CVT).* But the result is the same: Every transmission transmits power from the engine and directs it to the wheels. However, it doesn't do the job alone; it's part of a system that has several components, commonly known as the *drive train.*

This chapter takes you for a ride on the drive train. By the end of the line, the transmission and its related parts should no longer be a mystery. All *aboooard!*

After you get familiar with the *drive train,* your next mission (if you care to undertake it) is to establish a closer relationship with it. Because most of the parts related to your drive train are either electronic or require special tools and a hoist to deal with, you really can't do much to *repair* it yourself. However, you have no reason to feel helpless because there are lots of things you *can* do for your drive train, such as troubleshooting, simple maintenance, undertaking repairs wisely, and driving in ways that don't abuse it. This chapter covers it all. If you maintain it properly, the transmission and other parts involved will glide you along smoothly for the life of your vehicle. If it isn't performing well, being able to troubleshoot the symptoms can save you hundreds — even thousands — of dollars.

**REMEMBER**

Whenever you encounter a term set in *this font,* you'll find it defined in the glossary in Appendix A.

# The Drive Train

When your vehicle changes direction from forward to reverse, the *drive wheels* that actually drive the car (you find out which ones they are later in this chapter) don't just have to be told which way to rotate. They also must know how fast to turn, and they must be supplied with extra power for starting, climbing hills, and pulling heavy loads. All these things are accomplished via the *drive train.* By knowing what each part does and how it relates to the other parts of the drive train, you can trace the flow of power from the *engine* to the wheels.

Here's an interesting way to look at how the drive train functions: Imagine that you're the captain of a ship. You have a lovely set of engines down in the engine room that manufactures power to move your ship. You're up on the bridge, surveying the ocean with your binoculars, when suddenly you see an iceberg dead ahead. Instead of running down to the engine room and personally reversing the propellers so that the ship moves backward, you pick up the intercom and call the engine room. "This is the captain speaking. Reverse engines!" The person in the engine room hears you and does what's necessary. The ship is saved.

In a car, you're still at the wheel giving orders, but you're giving them to a vehicle that can't hear you. You need a piece of machinery to communicate with other machines. In this case, that piece is your *gearshift.* By moving the gearshift with your hand, you tell the transmission what to do. Then the transmission tells the wheels via the *driveshaft.*

**TECHNICAL STUFF**

With the aid of the drive train, you can tell your wheels not only to go forward or backward but also how fast to go. When you step on the *accelerator,* you compel the engine to produce power, but that power has to get to the wheels in the proper way for the wheels to respond most efficiently. There are ways to convey that extra power to the wheels by controlling how fast they turn in relation to the engine's speed when you're going up a hill, pulling a heavy load, or just trying to overcome inertia so the vehicle can start moving. To do this, your transmission has more than just forward and reverse gears; it has low and high gears, too. Some transmissions have as many as seven forward gears to control power and speed efficiently. Continuously variable transmissions glide from one end of the spectrum to the other without separate gears. In all cases, the *lower* gears provide *more power* at *lower speeds.* The *higher* gears provide *less power* but allow the vehicle to move at *higher speeds* because the wheels can turn faster in these gears at any engine speed. The following section shows how power flows through traditional drive trains; because you'll understand them better when you're familiar with the basics, we get to the more exotic versions later on.

# How Power Flows through the Drive Train

Most vehicles come with two basic types of drive trains: *front-wheel drive* and *rear-wheel drive.* The names are self-explanatory: With front-wheel drive the power flows from the *engine* to the *front* wheels, which *drive* the car. With rear-wheel drive, the power flows to the *rear* wheels, and they're in charge. Surprise! (There are *all-wheel drive, four-wheel drive,* and other variations, but I keep it simple for now.) On almost all vehicles, the front wheels respond to the steering system, which directs the vehicle around curves and turns.

**TIP**

On rear-wheel drive vehicles, all the parts involved run like the cars on a train, from the engine in the front to the wheels at the rear. (That's probably why they called it the "drive train.") Although today more vehicles have front-wheel drive — which combines the *transmission* and other parts into one neat package called a *transaxle* — in order to get a good look at every part involved in a drive train, it's easier to follow the power through a rear-wheel drive vehicle with a manual transmission. When you know what each part does and whether or not it's done manually, automatically, or combined into some exotic new mechanism, you'll stay on track through the more detailed descriptions of each type of vehicle found in separate sections of this chapter.

To make your ride smoother, Figure 18-1 shows all the components as they're located on a vehicle with rear-wheel drive and a manual transmission. If your vehicle has front-wheel drive, Figure 18-2 shows you the way the power flows through a transaxle. The principles and parts are pretty much the same in each type of drive train.

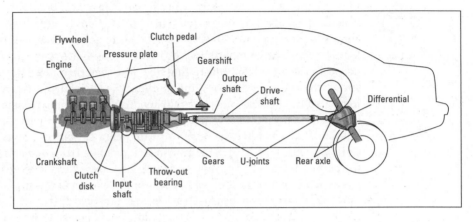

**FIGURE 18-1:**
The drive train in a vehicle with rear-wheel drive and a manual transmission.

Use Figure 18-1 to trace the flow of power from one part of the drive train to the next, as described in the following steps:

1. The running *engine* produces power that causes the *crankshaft* to turn at a particular rate of speed. The faster the engine runs, the more power it produces and the faster the crankshaft turns.

2. At the end of the crankshaft is the *engine flywheel.* This disk-shaped plate turns at the same rate and in the same direction as the crankshaft.

3. Facing the flywheel is the first part of the *clutch.* When you step on the *clutch pedal,* the clutch disconnects the engine from the *transmission* to allow the car to change gears.

4. After you move the *gearshift* to the proper gear, when you take your foot off the clutch pedal, the clutch allows the engine and transmission to resume contact and turn together at a new speed.

5. On the other side of the clutch, the drive train continues, with a separate shaft. It's not called the crankshaft anymore; it's now called the *transmission input shaft* because it carries the power via the turning shaft *into* the transmission. It rotates at the same speed and in the same direction as all the parts I've covered up to now.

6. Inside the transmission is a group of gears that can move together and apart, in various combinations, to determine how fast and with how much power the vehicle's wheels turn and whether they go forward, backward, or stop.

7. The next part of the drive train emerges from the other side of the transmission. It's now called the **transmission output shaft** because it transmits the power that the transmission is putting *out* to the driveshaft.

8. The driveshaft of a **rear-wheel drive** vehicle with a conventional engine has a *U-joint* (short for **universal joint**) at either end. The U-joints enable the driveshaft to move freely without affecting the more rigid transmission shaft at one end and to absorb the vertical movement of the rear axle and wheels at its other end.

   On vehicles with **transverse engines** (see Figure 18-2), ball-and-socket fittings called **constant velocity joints (CV)** transmit engine power from the axles to the wheels. You can find them where each axle joins the **transaxle** and where each connects with the vehicle's drive wheels. Like U-joints, they can turn and move in any direction — up, down, and from side to side.

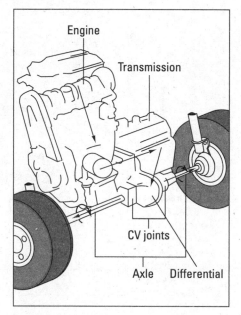

**FIGURE 18-2:**
The flow of power through a transaxle on a front-wheel drive vehicle.

9. The **differential** is another box of gears that, in a rear-wheel drive vehicle (see Figure 18-3), takes the movement of the spinning driveshaft through a 90-degree angle to the axle that turns the **drive wheels.** It also allows each side of the axle to rotate at a different speed. This ability is necessary because, when you go around a sharp curve, the outside wheel travels farther than the inside wheel and has to move more quickly than the inside wheel, just like the ice skater at the end of a snap-the-whip line.

10. The differential also provides the drive wheels with extra power by using its gears to convert varying numbers of revolutions of the driveshaft into one revolution of the drive wheels. This is called the **gear ratio.** I get into details about gear ratios in the later section "Manual Transmissions."

On a *front-wheel drive* vehicle the *transaxle* is in line with the center hubs of the front wheels (refer to Figure 18-2). The axles (sometimes called *half-shafts*) emerge from each end and run straight to the wheels. The differential changes the direction of the power coming out of the engine and into the transaxle.

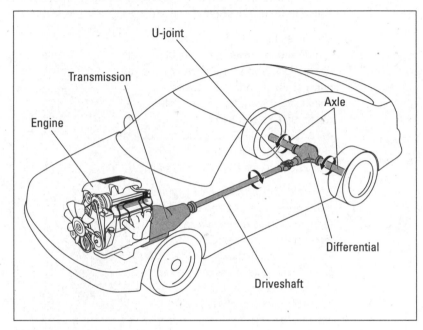

**FIGURE 18-3:**
The differential on a rear-wheel drive vehicle makes the axle and the rear wheels move at right angles to the spinning driveshaft.

# Four-wheel drive

If you own a sport-utility vehicle (SUV) that features *four-wheel drive* (as shown in Figure 18-4), your drive train includes a *transfer case* (see Figure 18-5). The transfer case controls the power to the front and rear drive *axles.* When you switch from two- to four-wheel drive with either a dash-mounted switch or a floor-mounted shifter, a gear in the transfer case engages the front driveshaft along with the rear driveshaft so that all four wheels get power from the engine. In two-wheel drive, only the driveshaft connected to the rear wheels gets power from the engine, and the front wheels are disengaged.

The transfer case also usually has settings for low and high gears. Low geardelivers a lot of *torque* (pulling and pushing power) to the wheels for traveling in very rugged, muddy, snowy, or slippery terrain at slow speeds. High gear is for traveling at moderate speeds on normal roads in wet or moderately slippery conditions. (Your owner's manual can tell you how fast your vehicle's system will let you drive without damaging it.)

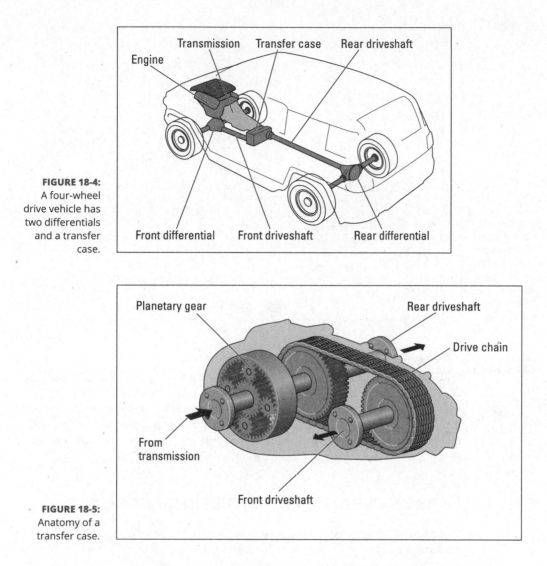

**FIGURE 18-4:**
A four-wheel drive vehicle has two differentials and a transfer case.

Transmission   Transfer case   Rear driveshaft

Engine

Front differential   Front driveshaft   Rear differential

**FIGURE 18-5:**
Anatomy of a transfer case.

Planetary gear   Rear driveshaft

Drive chain

From transmission

Front driveshaft

## All-wheel drive

*All-wheel drive* (AWD) vehicles are different from *four-wheel drive* (4WD) vehicles in that AWD vehicles send power to all four wheels *all* the time. As shown in Figure 18-6, AWD vehicles usually employ three differentials: one between each set of drive wheels and one in the center. They must split the power from the engine to the front and rear wheels for two reasons: because each set travels differently through a turn, and because many systems use computers that sense the amount of traction needed by each wheel and send different amounts of power to each wheel, if necessary.

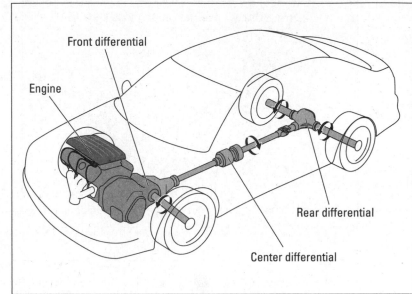

# Manual Transmissions

Even if your vehicle doesn't have a manual (sometimes called *standard*) transmission, you should understand how a *manual transmission* works. The principles involved are fairly simple, and *automatic transmissions* do basically the same things, just without a manual *clutch* and with less manual shifting.

## What a manual transmission consists of

This section takes a closer look at each major part of a manual transmission. You encounter most of them in the drive train section earlier in this chapter, but this section puts them into closer perspective.

REMEMBER

Figure 18-1 shows you where each part is located on the *drive train* of a manual transmission. Figure 18-7 shows a five-speed manual transmission.

### The gearshift

You use the *gearshift* to select and change *gears.* It's usually found on the floor in front of or between the front seats. Older cars used to have shifts with three forward speeds located on the steering column. Then sportier models with four forward speeds emerged. The gearshift in those vehicles was located on the floor, which gave rise to the phrase "four on the floor." Today, vehicles with manual transmissions have as many as seven forward speeds! Gearshifts also have positions for Reverse and Neutral (so the vehicle can *idle* out of gear).

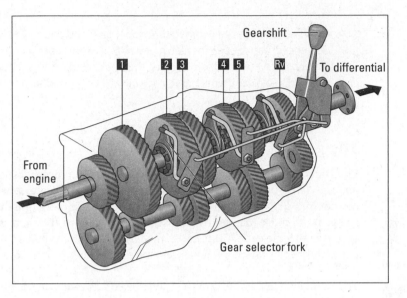

**FIGURE 18-7:**
Five-speed
transmissions are
standard on
many vehicles.

## The clutch

You use the *clutch* when you start, stop, and shift gears. In each case, you step on the *clutch pedal* with your left foot to disengage the *clutch disk* from the *engine flywheel* so that the engine's *crankshaft* can turn independently of the *transmission input shaft* (the turning shaft that carries the power from the *engine* into the *transmission*). If you attempt to shift gears without using the clutch, the gears in the transmission will rotate at different speeds and could clash and injure the transmission. The clutch consists of the following major parts, shown in Figure 18-1:

» The ***clutch pedal*** is located on the floor of the vehicle to the left of the brake pedal. The clutch pedal is connected to a clutch release lever via linkage. Sometimes a cable is used; most newer cars use ***hydraulic*** components.

» The ***clutch disk*** faces the flywheel. This disk-shaped plate moves back and forth to connect and disconnect the engine from the transmission.

» The ***clutch pressure plate*** is next to the clutch disk. This mechanism forces the clutch disk against the flywheel or allows it to move away from the flywheel when it's time to change gears. When you're *not* stepping on the clutch pedal, a coating of friction material causes the disk and the flywheel to adhere to each other, which forces them to turn at the same speed.

» The ***throw-out bearing*** is linked to the clutch pedal and activates the release levers that move the pressure plate back and forth. When you step on the clutch pedal to disengage the clutch and disconnect the engine from the transmission, a *clutch release arm* forces the throwout bearing into the pressure plate's release levers. As a result, the pressure on the clutch disk is released and the disk can turn independently of the flywheel.

>> After you move the gearshift to the proper gear and the engine is going at its new speed, you release the clutch pedal. This causes springs in the pressure plate to force the clutch disk against the flywheel again. The friction material on the disk causes them to grab each other lovingly and turn at the same rate once more.

## The gears

The transmission contains the *gears* and responds to messages from the *gearshift* and the *clutch*. On manual transmissions, the gears are metal wheels with notches on the rims that allow them to mesh with one another (see Figure 18-7). Originally, the gears in most manual transmissions were moved into and out of mesh with each other by the gearshift lever. In modern vehicles, the gears are always in mesh and only the *synchronizers* move, causing a change in power flow.

**TECHNICAL STUFF**

The number of gear wheels in the transmission depends on the number of forward speeds the vehicle has. An additional gear reverses the direction of power so that your car can move backward. Because you must bring a vehicle to a stop before you back up and because you rarely want to hit high speeds in Reverse, this gear works in conjunction with the lowest gear because it can provide the power to overcome inertia and get the car moving backwards.

## How a manual transmission works

**TECHNICAL STUFF**

Generally speaking, the faster your engine runs, the more power it puts out. If you need extra power to get up a hill — or to overcome inertia and just get that heavy monster moving in the first place — your engine must run faster than it runs when it's just maintaining a steady speed. Low gears supply that power by making your wheels turn at a slower rate than your engine does.

On the other hand, if you drive faster than the range of speed provided by a gear, your vehicle will "red line" — go beyond the maximum numbers of *rpm* (revolutions per minute) your engine is capable of — and damage the engine. That's why you have to shift up to the next higher gear as your speed increases. The ratio between how fast your engine turns and how fast your wheels turn is called the *gear ratio.*

Here's how the gear ratio works: As you can see in Figure 18-8, a large gear is placed next to a small gear so that their teeth mesh. If the large gear has 30 teeth and the small gear has 10, the large gear turns once to every three turns of the small gear. In other words, the large gear turns only a third of the way around for every complete revolution of the small gear. The gears in your transmission work on this principle, which, in this case, is called a 3:1 gear ratio. As you can see in

Figure 18-7, the turning drive train brings a gear into contact with other gears of different sizes. That's why the *transmission input shaft* that runs between the engine and the transmission turns at the same rate of speed as the engine but the *transmission output shaft* that leaves the transmission and carries the power via the *driveshaft* and *differential* to the rear wheels turns at a different rate, depending on which gears in the transmission are engaged.

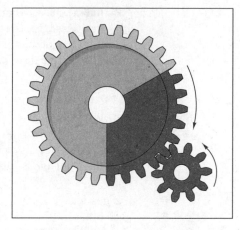

**FIGURE 18-8:**
A 3:1 gear ratio: A gear with 10 teeth will have rotated completely when a 30-tooth gear has traveled only a third of the way around.

If you're feeling mind-boggled, reread Steps 5 through 10 in "How Power Flows through the Drive Train" earlier in this chapter.

Now take a closer look at what goes on when you shift from one gear to the next.

>> **In First gear** (the lowest gear), the gears in the transmission make the driveshaft (and therefore the wheels) turn *more slowly* than the engine. In fact, the driveshaft may turn only once for every four engine revolutions (a 4:1 gear ratio). All the power of the swiftly running engine is channeled into those few turns. The wheels turn more slowly, but they have more power to put into each turn, so your vehicle can start, climb a hill, or pull a trailer. Not only does the engine run faster in First gear, but you also have the mechanical advantage of the big gear providing more leverage by turning slowly, but with more force.

>> **In Second gear,** the engine turns more slowly than it did in First, putting out less power but more speed because the wheels can turn more quickly. In this gear, the driveshaft may turn once for every two engine revolutions, or twice as fast as in First gear.

This process continues through each successive gear until the highest one. Every model of vehicle has its own set of gear ratios designed to provide the best combination of power and economy.

>> **Around Fourth gear,** the gear ratio can drop to around 1:1, which means that the engine and the driveshaft turn at relatively the same rate of speed. The wheels can go very fast; yet the engine doesn't put out additional power to produce that speed. Because you've overcome inertia by the time you shift into Fourth gear and generally have nothing more to contend with than wind resistance and the surface of the highway, you don't need much power to keep moving at a good clip after you get there.

REMEMBER

Some vehicles now have as many as *seven* gears! Although the ratio may be the same in a seven-speed transmission as in a five-speed, the greater number of gears provides a more precise range of ratios. The more forward speeds, the more precisely power can be applied to the drive wheels and the more fuel-efficient the vehicle becomes.

# Automatic Transmissions

Did you know that today's *automatic transmissions* are computer-controlled *hydraulic* systems? Previous automatic transmissions were mechanically controlled. This section covers the basic features of several popular automatic transmission systems.

An automatic transmission works on the same basis as a manual transmission does, with a *gear selector* on the steering column, dashboard, or floor to allow you to tell your vehicle to park, *idle,* go into Reverse, go forward at varying speeds, or move into lower gears. But instead of a manual *clutch,* an automatic transmission uses a *torque converter* and hydraulic pressure to change gears automatically.

A torque converter replaces the standard transmission's clutch. The torque converter is a fluid coupling that uses hydraulic pressure to control the amount of engine power transmitted through the converter to the *transmission input shaft.* It allows the vehicle to idle with the gear selector in Drive, provides a smooth transfer of power, and at highway speeds can be locked up to reduce slippage and improve fuel economy.

Shifting in an automatic transmission is controlled by a hydraulic system that's usually electronically controlled. Most hydraulically controlled transmissions consist of an intricate network of valves and other components along with hydraulic pressure to control the operation of sets of planetary gears (see Figure 18-9). These gearsets can be fashioned to generate three or more forward speeds. *Continuously variable transmissions (CVT)* don't use planetary gears (I get to them later in this chapter).

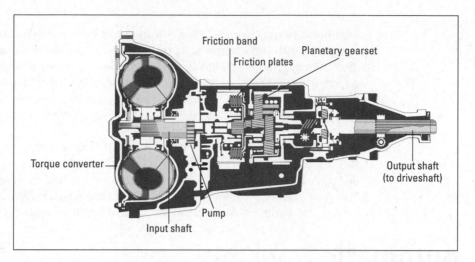

FIGURE 18-9:
A cutaway view
of a modern
hydraulic
automatic
transmission.

A very thin oil called *transmission fluid* fills the transmission system and generates hydraulic pressure. As the engine speed changes, the pump that pumps the transmission fluid to develop hydraulic pressure also changes speed. The transmission fluid responds to the changes in pressure by flowing through the transmission at different rates. When the vehicle is moving slowly, the pressure is low and only the low gears respond. As the car's speed increases, so does the pressure, and higher gears are brought into play.

The hydraulic pressure drives the transmission gears by means of *friction bands* and *plates.* These bands and plates function like the clutch on a manual transmission, pulling various gears into and out of action. When mechanics tell you that your bands need adjusting, these are the bands they're talking about. They usually can make this adjustment without taking the transmission apart.

*Electronic* transmission systems use a computer called a *transmission controller* to keep track of engine speed, acceleration, *load* (as when you're driving up a hill), and braking. It uses this information to send electronic messages to *solenoids* that control shifting.

ECO-LOGIC

Because of their ability to make more precise adjustments as you speed up, climb hills, take turns, and employ *ABS* brakes, electronic systems are more efficient than hydraulic systems and can increase fuel economy.

## Dual-clutch transmissions

Originally, prospective car-buyers had two basic options when choosing a transmission: manual or automatic. Now there's a third type that offers the driver the best features of both in a single vehicle! You can kick back and let your vehicle shift gears automatically, or you can manually select them yourself without the need to operate a clutch pedal. These nifty transmissions are known by a variety of names: dual-clutch, automated manual, semi-automatic, even "clutchless" (which makes no sense since they have two clutches instead of one!). To stay sane, I call them *dual-clutch transmissions,* or *DCT* for short. DCTs operate more smoothly than ordinary automatics or manuals, and they can deliver better fuel economy, as well.

As you can see in Figure 18-10, the most significant structural difference is that a DCT has two clutches (hence the name "dual-clutch"). One clutch operates the odd-numbered gears, and the other clutch controls the even-numbered gears. The result is that the flow of power to the transmission from the engine isn't interrupted as the transmission shifts from one gear to another.

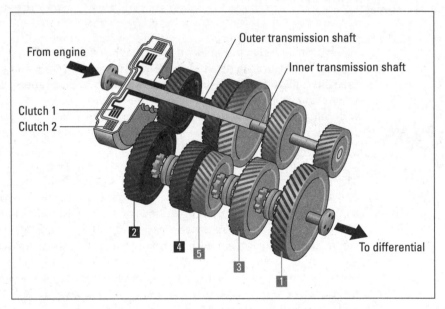

**FIGURE 18-10:**
A dual-clutch transmission has two clutches and two transmission shafts.

The DCT also has two *transmission input shafts,* one inside the other. The hollow outer shaft contacts the even-numbered gears, and the shaft inside it contacts the odd-numbered gears.

DCTs don't use *torque converters;* instead, most of them use "wet" clutches to hydraulically operate the gears, as most automatic transmissions do. This also lubricates them to cut down friction and heat. "Dry" clutches similar to the ones in manual transmissions will probably be available, too.

Don't confuse the more common sport mode found in many conventional automatic transmissions with a dual-clutch transmission. Automatics with sport mode enable the driver to shift manually by electronically locking each forward gear until the driver uses the gear selector to change gears. To keep the engine from blowing apart under stress if the driver fails to shift properly, many only allow the driver to lock into a gear until the engine hits red-line, at which point an electronic engine shutoff device kicks in. Others simply shift themselves if the *rpms* get too high.

## Continuously variable transmissions

Newer vehicles are now available with *continuously variable transmissions* (or *CVT*, for short) that have no physical gears at all! Instead, they move seamlessly from one *gear ratio* to the next by means of a pulley system that not only provides for smoother shifting but also results in higher fuel efficiency.

It's interesting to note that the CVT isn't a new concept. In 1490, Leonardo da Vinci designed a CVT, and Subaru brought the first production model to the United States in 1989.

CVTs aren't complicated systems. They may use hydraulic pressure, springs, or centrifugal force to adjust gear ratio in response to information collected by *sensors* and sent to a computer. Most of them consist of an *input drive pulley* that's connected to the engine *crankshaft* and brings energy into the transmission from the engine. An *output pulley* (or *driven pulley*) sends the energy out of the transmission to the *driveshaft*. (It's called "driven" because the input pulley drives it.)

As you can see in Figure 18-11, each pulley consists of two cones and a belt that rides in a groove between them. As the distance between the cones changes, the belt rides higher or lower in the groove. Where it's riding changes the radius of the belt's loop around each pulley, and its position on each pulley (its radius) determines the gear the vehicle is in.

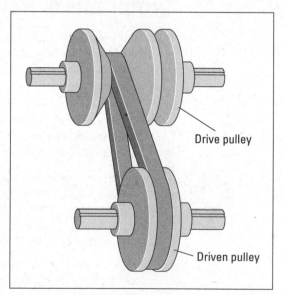

**FIGURE 18-11:**
A continuously variable transmission system consists of two pulleys and a belt.

CVTs are constantly evolving. Newer versions employ quieter and longer-lasting flexible metal belts that connect butterfly-shaped metal pieces and systems that use disks and power rollers, but the advantages remain the same: faster response time, greater power, smoother shifting, higher efficiency, and fuel economy. CVTs currently may be more expensive than traditional transmissions, but they're worth it.

# Troubleshooting Your Drive Train

Did you know that a low *transmission fluid* level or a malfunctioning, inexpensive gizmo may cause the same symptoms as a faulty transmission? Who knows how many unsuspecting customers have paid big bucks to *rebuild* or replace transmissions when they could have corrected the problems themselves with very little money or effort! This section shows you how to troubleshoot your transmission and try the cheapest remedies before paying professionals to do major surgery.

If you have to take the problem to a specialist, be sure to read the section called "Undertaking Transmission Repairs Wisely" later in this chapter. If you're lucky, your transmission may need only a simple adjustment. If you're not so lucky, your transmission may need to be rebuilt or replaced. But in any event, you'll know that you're getting the proper service.

## Symptoms of a sick transmission system

If weird things start happening on the road, how can you tell whether the transmission or one of the other parts of the drive train is in trouble? If this is the case, continuing to drive may make the situation worse. Here are ways your vehicle tries to tip you off:

**TIP**

>> **If light grey smoke is coming out of the tailpipe,** this can mean you're low on *transmission fluid* and the engine could be burning. Check the following section to beat "Those low-transmission-fluid blues."

In some pre-1990 vehicles, the smoke may also be due to a faulty *vacuum modulator* that's siphoning the fluid out of the transmission and into cylinders of the hot engine. Consult a service manual for your make, model, and year to see if Old Faithful has a vacuum modulator; if it's easy to reach, try unscrewing it and replacing it before you consider more costly remedies.

In most post-1990 vehicles with *automatic transmissions,* the vacuum modulator has been replaced by an electronic *solenoid.* It does the same job but is controlled by the *electronic control unit (ECU)* rather than engine vacuum, so there's no siphoning problem.

>> **If thick, black or tan, oily liquid is coming from under the vehicle,** gear oil may be leaking from a ***manual transmission,*** the ***differential,*** an ***axle,*** or the steering gears. Any of these leaks needs immediate attention.

>> **If the engine speeds up when you step on the accelerator but your vehicle doesn't; or if it hesitates before responding when you shift gears (or doesn't respond at all); or if shifting suddenly becomes awkward or noisy,** the cause depends on whether you have an automatic or manual transmission. If you have an ***automatic transmission,*** you may just be low on ***transmission fluid,*** have a disconnected hose or plugged filter, or your ***transmission controller*** may be out of whack. If you have a ***manual transmission,*** the trouble could be in the ***clutch*** or another component. In any case, it's a job for the car doctor.

>> **If you hear a clunking sound,** it can mean transmission trouble or just a low fluid level. If a loud clunking suddenly comes from under the hood, it could be just a broken ***accessory belt.*** In either case, pull to the side of the road and call for a tow.

## Those low-transmission-fluid blues

If your *automatic transmission* seems to be acting up by hesitating when you change gears or by shifting with a "clunk," first check your transmission *dipstick.* Your *transmission fluid* may be low or dirty. Chapter 2 tells you how to find and check your transmission dipstick and how to buy the proper kind of transmission fluid for your vehicle.

**TIP**

It's a good idea to check transmission fluid fairly often as part of the monthly under-the-hood check in Chapter 2. A good many "*band* jobs" have been bought and paid for when a quart of transmission fluid would have solved the problem for pennies. Before emptying your wallet, check your transmission fluid level and try the following remedies:

>> **If your fluid level is low,** with the ***parking brake*** on and the ***gearshift*** in Neutral or Park, use a funnel to add a *teeny* bit of fluid at a time down the dipstick hole until the fluid level *just* reaches the "Full" line on the stick.

**WARNING**

*Do not fill beyond the line!* Driving with too much transmission fluid can damage your transmission. Check the stick again in a couple of days; if the level is low again, you either have a leak or may need to have a seal replaced.

To check for a leak, before you drive off in the morning look at the ground under the vehicle for a greasy red, pink, or reddish-brown leak around the transmission area — or on the transmission itself, if you can see it easily.

(If you have a *rear-wheel, four-wheel,* or *all-wheel drive* vehicle, to get a look at the transmission you'll probably have to jack up your vehicle or have a professional place it on a hoist.)

>> **If your fluid level is fine but your transmission isn't working well; or if your fluid keeps disappearing and no leaks are evident,** you probably need transmission work.

>> **If the transmission fluid on the dipstick looks or smells burned or dirty,** you may want to consider having the fluid, filter, and the pan *gasket* changed.

**WARNING**

Transmissions should be serviced every 25,000 to 30,000 miles, but if your vehicle has more than 100,000 miles on it and the transmission fluid has never been changed, don't change it unless there are really serious reasons for doing so. The old transmission fluid has formed a deposit around the front transmission seal. If this fluid is totally replaced with fresh fluid, the new stuff may dissolve the deposit and cause the old seal to leak. In this case, I'd add just enough new fluid to bring the level up to the "Full" mark on the dipstick or as close to it as possible. Then, when the poor, neglected beast dies, have the transmission *rebuilt* (unless the rest of the vehicle is dying, too). This does *not* mean that you shouldn't have the transmission *serviced.* Because you'll probably lose only three quarts in the process of servicing, replacing the lost fluid shouldn't disturb the seals.

**TIP**

If you have no mechanical problems but want to replace *all* the fluid in your vehicle's transmission, check into one of the several transmission services available now though repair shops and dealerships that use suction pumps to flush virtually all the old fluid out of a transmission, circulate a cleaning agent through the system, and refill it — all without having to take the transmission apart.

**REMEMBER**

If you have an *all-wheel drive* or *four-wheel drive* vehicle, don't forget to check the fluid level in the *transfer case,* too.

**TECHNICAL STUFF**

Your manual or automatic transmission system will work better and live longer if you have the *U-joints* in your drive train checked and replaced with new ones if they're loose, and if you have your *differential* lubricated at regular intervals.

# Taking Care of Your Clutch

Most drivers can expect their clutches to last 40,000 to 60,000 miles but your clutch can be good for as little as a few thousand miles or as long as the life of your vehicle depending on the type of vehicle you drive, the way you drive it, and how much maintenance it receives.

Most newer vehicles with *manual transmissions* have self-adjusting clutches that require no adjustment, but if you have an older model without self-adjustment, you can cut down on the wear on your *clutch disk* by keeping your *clutch pedal* properly adjusted. (If you've forgotten, the "What a manual transmission consists of" section earlier in this chapter tells you what these parts are and what they look like.)

TECHNICAL
STUFF

Your clutch pedal should move down ¾ inch to 1 inch without effort and then require a good deal more effort to travel the rest of the way down to the floor. This *pedal free-play* ensures that when you release the pedal, the clutch disk is fully engaged. Too much free pedal play isn't good, either, because too much pedal travel is used up doing nothing: There's not enough movement left at the bottom of its travel to compress the clutch springs and allow the *engine flywheel* and the clutch disk to separate. With this excessive pedal play, the gears clash whenever you shift into First or Reverse from a stopped position.

If there's no free pedal play on your clutch pedal, another problem can occur, even if there's enough play to allow the clutch disk to engage. In this case, the *throwout bearing,* which responds to pressure on the clutch pedal by causing the disk to disengage, may go on spinning. If the throwout bearing is allowed to revolve constantly in this way, it will wear out, which makes getting into or out of gear difficult.

TECHNICAL
STUFF

*Don't ride the clutch.* Riding it can wear out the throwout bearing, too. You can tell that something is wrong because the bearing makes whirring, whining sounds. If the sounds disappear when you release the clutch pedal and resume when you step on it, you have a bad throwout bearing. If you think that you have one, or if your clutch misbehaves in other ways, go to a reliable mechanic and have the clutch checked out.

TIP

If you have a clutch disk replaced, have the entire clutch checked at that time to be sure that other parts aren't going to need work soon. Here's what should probably be done in each case:

>> **If the flywheel is worn, have a professional resurface it.** This procedure involves grinding it down to a new, flat surface and then polishing it to a mirror-like finish. If you fail to have this work done, the worn flywheel can wear out the facing of the new clutch disk very quickly. And if you've already had the disk replaced, chances are that it managed to score the flywheel by the time you recognized the trouble signs and had the disk attended to.

>> **If the pressure plate is excessively worn, scored, or glazed; or if the springs on the pressure plate become loose, you should have them replaced, as well.**

**TIP**

Because excessive wear on any part of your clutch results in wear on the other parts, it's generally a good idea to have the clutch assembly, levers, clutch disk, and throwout bearings checked and, if necessary, replaced at the same time. You also can have the *pilot bearing* (located where the *crankshaft* meets the flywheel) checked then, too, which saves you money on labor charges by eliminating the necessity of getting into your clutch and putting it back together a second time.

# Undertaking Transmission Repairs Wisely

Your first line of defense against unnecessary transmission work is to have your *automatic transmission* serviced periodically, according to the manufacturer's recommendations (usually around every 24,000 miles). Your second line of defense is to understand what the basic kinds of transmission work involve. Here are the various types of work that your vehicle may require and what each of them entails:

>> **If your transmission needs servicing:**

- The ***transmission fluid*** should be changed, if necessary.

- The ***bands*** on a hydraulic transmission should be adjusted, if this job can be done externally.

- The transmission filter should be replaced.

- The ***gasket*** around the transmission pan should be replaced, and the fluid in the pan should be changed.

>> **If your transmission is leaking:**

- If the *front seal* is bad, the technician must remove your transmission to replace it, but he or she doesn't have to take the transmission apart. Front seals usually have the biggest leaks.

- If the problem is the *rear seal,* the technician must remove your ***driveshaft,*** but your transmission can stay in place.

>> **If your transmission must be *overhauled:***

- The transmission should be removed and disassembled.

- The seals, clutches, bands, and ***bushings*** that are worn or defective should be replaced.

**TIP**

>> **If your transmission must be *replaced:*** The old transmission must be removed and a new one installed. You do have an option as to whether you replace it with a used, ***rebuilt,*** or new transmission. I make the distinction between *used* and *rebuilt* because you can buy a transmission from a wrecking

yard that has salvaged one designed for your vehicle's year, make, and model. This option is cheap, but risky. Your other option is to find a rebuilt transmission that has been salvaged and then completely refurbished and comes with at least a three-month *guarantee.* These cost a bit more, but you get a chance to make sure that the thing is in good working order.

Occasionally, *gearshifts* may become hard to move. This problem can happen if the *gearshift linkage,* which connects the shift lever to the rods that go to the transmission, needs adjustment, lubrication, or minor repair. These repairs aren't expensive and should certainly be investigated before you let anyone talk you into major transmission work.

*Front-wheel drive* vehicles have a transmission and *axle* assembly all in one, called a *transaxle. All-wheel drive* and *four-wheel drive* vehicles usually have an additional component called a *transfer case.* Expect to pay more for transaxle repairs and transmission repairs on a vehicle with a transfer case.

**REMEMBER**

As you can see, knowing what kind of transmission work is necessary can save you from paying for more work than you need. A number of other things can go wrong and seem to indicate that you need major transmission work to correct them; yet these problems often can be fixed for very little money. An unscrupulous mechanic can diagnose one of the problems as a major transmission breakdown and charge you hundreds of dollars when the real solution could be achieved for much less (see "Those low-transmission-fluid blues" earlier in this chapter).

**TIP**

When your transmission needs work, you have to rely on professionals, but that doesn't mean that you have to blindly accept whatever they tell you. Transmission repairs can range from regular service, which is relatively simple and inexpensive, to highly complicated and *very* expensive *rebuilds* and replacements. The best way to get an accurate diagnosis and the repairs that your vehicle really needs is to follow the advice I give in the section called "Getting the Best Possible Deal" in Chapter 22. If you get ripped off anyway, the chapter also tells you how to get satisfaction on complaints.

**TIP**

Here are some additional guidelines:

>> **For transmission repairs, take your vehicle to the dealership or to a reputable transmission specialist.** Ask the technician to diagnose the trouble and give you an estimate of the costs.

>> **Don't let the technician take the transmission apart.** When your transmission is in pieces, you're a sitting duck! Have the specialist drive the vehicle, listen to it, ask you questions about its history and its symptoms, and give you his or her ideas. The technician may say, "You may just need your transmission serviced, or you may need a new transmission; I can't tell until I open it

up." Fine. Ask for estimates for both jobs, and if the prognosis is expensive, get additional estimates. You'd get a second opinion before going through major surgery, wouldn't you?

# How to Keep from Driving Your Transmission Crazy

Driving your vehicle with expertise can prevent many of the most common causes of transmission failure. If you have a *manual transmission,* you should shift into the proper gear at the proper time to reduce the strain on the engine and the transmission and should not ride your clutch. To do this, a good driver with a manual transmission learns to watch the *tachometer,* or just "feel" the vehicle's need for more power or more speed, and then shift into the proper gear for each occasion.

Many drivers with *automatic transmissions* just shift into Drive and go up steep hills, carry heavy loads, and bounce into jackrabbit starts, happily oblivious to the fact that even automatic transmissions have *gear selectors* that provide one or two lower gears for these occasions. On the other hand, if you stay in a low gear unnecessarily, you're transmitting excessive power to your rear wheels, and your transmission feels the strain. If you attempt to speed in a low gear, you strain the transmission even more. On the other hand, if you attempt to climb hills in high gear, you force the engine and transmission to make the effort in a gear that lacks the power for the job. The result: more strain.

**TIP**

To avoid unnecessary wear and tear and to extend the life of your transmission if it's manual or a traditional automatic, use the following shifting strategies:

>> **When you need a sudden burst of speed, use *passing gear.*** On vehicles with an automatic transmission, passing gear provides the same kind of increased power as *downshifting* a manual transmission. You use passing gear when you're already in high gear and need an extra burst of power to pass a car or enter a freeway. If you've been traveling at less than 50 mph, suddenly flooring the *accelerator* makes your car downshift automatically to the appropriate lower gear to provide more power by speeding up the engine.

>> **Use *Overdrive* (or the highest gear on a manual transmission) when you're traveling steadily at a high speed.** With Overdrive or "top" gear, you have an extra, higher gear that allows your rear wheels to turn even faster while maintaining the same engine speed. After you're really moving, shifting into Overdrive means that you can move at the same speed while the engine turns more slowly and consumes less fuel.

>> **Shift manual transmissions to higher gears as soon as your speed enters their range.** There's no need to supply extra power when it's not needed. Your owner's manual should tell you the range of speed for each gear. Automatic transmissions shift for you.

>> **If traffic slows and you feel the engine straining (called *lugging*), shift manual transmissions into a lower gear.** Downshifting enables the engine to turn faster and carry you along with less strain. After you're moving freely again, return to a higher gear.

>> **With both types of transmissions, select lower gears for heavy loads and steep hills.** If you come to a steep hill — or if you're carrying four kids, two dogs, and everything you'll need for a month in the country — go for the lower gears instead of trying to haul the whole mess as fast as you can. Then shift back up again to coast down the hill. This way, the power goes toward carrying the load rather than toward maintaining speed.

**TECHNICAL STUFF**

*Continuously variable transmissions (CVT)* move smoothly from one speed to another without any physical gears at all. They respond to all road situations faster and more efficiently. You may want to ask Santa for a vehicle that has one.

# 5
# Staying Safe and Dealing with Emergencies

Today's vehicles are not only more efficient and responsive, but they also provide innovative features that can protect you and your passengers from harm. This part shows you what you can — and can't — expect from the safety systems on your vehicle and what else is out there so that when it's time to buy a new vehicle, you can choose the safest one available.

Despite your best efforts, your vehicle may break down while you're on the road. Maybe it will overheat. Maybe a tire will blow. Maybe you won't know what the problem is, but you'll know that it sounds — or smells — bad. This part also shows you how to troubleshoot the symptoms, sees you through these traumas, and helps you make your way out of them safely. Because fixing many problems is beyond your capabilities as a do-it-yourselfer, I also tell you how to locate, evaluate, and work with a good repair facility.

IN THIS CHAPTER

» Understanding how air bags and side-impact systems protect you during accidents

» Adjusting seats, head restraints, steering wheels, and pedals

» Buying and installing the proper safety seats for children of every age

» Seeing what's behind you and into blind spots

» Avoiding accidents with traction control, stability control, and rollover protection

» Navigating, getting roadside help, and recovering stolen vehicles with telematic systems

Chapter **19**

# Staying Safe on the Road

With the growing emphasis on fuel economy, it's easy to forget that the most important issue for everyone who owns, drives, or is a passenger in modern vehicles is *safety*. Getting there efficiently is not as important as getting there in one piece! As prospective buyers and state and federal government have made reducing road injuries and fatalities a major priority, automotive technology has responded with a variety of improvements and innovations. Many safety systems that were introduced as optional features on luxury vehicles a few years ago have become available either as an option or as standard equipment on an increasing number of models because research and testing by *NHTSA* and the *IIHS* has prompted government legislation to make an increasing number of them mandatory.

This chapter describes the most important safety features that are currently available or will be in the near future. I hope that it will inspire you to keep up-to-date on what's out there and make these protective systems a priority when choosing your next vehicle.

**TIP**

Every one of the safety features in this chapter is important, so the order in which they appear shouldn't affect the amount of attention you pay to each of them. Although buying a vehicle with highly rated protection systems may cost a bit more, ask yourself what the health — and lives — of you, your family, and friends is worth. If you're driving an older vehicle that lacks many vital safety features, you should definitely consider replacing it with a newer, safer, model.

**TECHNICAL STUFF**

Besides the systems in this chapter, rain-sensing windshield wipers, self-defogging side mirrors, night-vision enhancement, headlamps that can swivel to illuminate corners, and other innovations are becoming popular. Keeping up-to-date on what's available is easy. Several organizations and agencies have Web sites that rate vehicles and safety systems. At the NHTSA site, www.safercar.gov, you can type in a vehicle's make, model, and year and see its rollover and crash-test ratings. The IIHS lists the Ten Safest Vehicles along with ratings for air bags on www.iihs.org and offers a free brochure called "Shopping for a Safer Car" that you can view and download from the Consumer Brochures link. In addition, publications such as *Consumer Reports* feature the results of their tests and ratings on a regular basis.

**REMEMBER**

Whenever you encounter a term set in *this font,* you'll find it defined in the glossary in Appendix A.

# Air Bags

Air bags have been around for quite a while and are credited with saving tens of thousands of people from injury and death. Air bags also have been accused of causing injuries when they deploy with too much force. As a result, they're constantly being upgraded to be more sensitive and versatile, and they're designed for several locations to provide protection in a wider variety of accidents. This section tells you about the types of air bags found on many modern vehicles and what should be available over the next few years. It also tells you how to position yourself (and other passengers) to avoid being injured by them if they deploy.

## Traveling safely with air bags

The most important way to protect yourself from being injured by an air bag is to maintain a space of at least ten inches from the area where it's located. If you're the driver, this does *not* mean that you have to scoot the entire seat back ten inches from the air bag if that makes it difficult to steer and reach the *gearshift* and pedals. Instead, recline the seat back and raise the seat until you're a safe distance from the bag and still can see and drive comfortably.

Because the driver's front air bag (often called the *frontal* air bag) is located in the center of the steering wheel, if your steering wheel can be adjusted, tilt it downward so that the air bag area is aimed at your chest rather than at your head and neck. Figure 19-1 shows ways for the driver to reach the proper distance from the front air bag.

a) Move your seat so you're 10" away from the steering wheel.

b) Tilt your seat away from the wheel.

c) Tilt the steering wheel downward.

**FIGURE 19-1:** How to achieve the correct position.

*Adapted from the NHTSA (www.safercar.gov)*

If you don't wear a seat belt, or if you're wearing it improperly, you not only risk hitting whatever's in front of you if the car stops abruptly, but you also can end up on top of an inflating air bag and be injured by it.

**WARNING**

If necessary, don't be afraid to jam on the brakes. Air bags aren't deployed unless you hit something that the *ECU* senses as a moderate or severe *crash.* Just tapping an adjacent vehicle or curb or nudging the stanchion in a parking lot shouldn't trigger the air bags in your vehicle.

**TIP**

## How air bags work

Basically, an air bag system is made up of one or more air bags, the crash *sensors* that detect that a crash has taken place (or in some cases, may be about to happen), and the mechanisms that inflate and deploy the bags. Air bags usually are inflated with a harmless gas (usually nitrogen or argon). To keep you from suffocating and give you room to move around, the gas escapes through vents in the fabric and the bag deflates in less than a second after deployment.

If you notice something that looks like smoke after an air bag deploys, it's probably starch or talcum powder that's sometimes used to lubricate the action of the air bag. The substance is usually harmless, but it may contain a little sodium hydroxide, which could irritate your eyes or throat for a little while but won't cause injury.

Air bags are placed in several locations. The *frontal air bag* on the driver's side is usually located in the center of the steering wheel, and the passenger-side air bag can be found on the dashboard. A variety of *side-impact air bags* may be found on or over the doors, on the roof of the passenger compartment, or on the sides or backs of the front seats. There are even new seat belt systems that contain air bags to protect passengers from . . . air bags! I cover each type of air bag later in this chapter. Here's what's involved in order to deploy an air bag:

>> **The crash *sensors*** measure how fast the vehicle is decelerating or how badly it's crushed, if hit on the side. Frontal-crash sensors may be located in the passenger compartment, near the engine, or inside the **ECU.** Side-impact sensors can be located in the door, the pillar between the doors, the doorsills, or the ECU.

>> **The ECU** uses information from the sensors to decide whether or not to deploy a particular air bag.

>> **The air bag inflator** receives a signal from the ECU if the vehicle has crashed severely enough to warrant air bag protection. This signal starts a chemical reaction that produces the gas that inflates the air bag (see Figure 19-2). In frontal collisions, all this happens in less than $\frac{1}{20}$ of a second, and side air bags inflate even faster because there's usually less space between the potential victim and the site of impact.

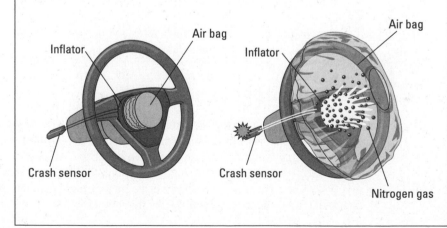

**FIGURE 19-2:**
How air bags work.

>> **ON-OFF switches** that can disable air bags when they're potentially more dangerous than protective may be found on some vehicles because the speed with which an air bag inflates can injure someone it's meant to protect. Modern sports cars and trucks that lack rear seats usually come equipped with these switches.

TIP

To ensure that children are placed in the rear seats of vehicles that have them, those vehicles aren't allowed to have an ON-OFF switch as standard equipment. If you want to have a switch installed in a vehicle with rear seating, you have to apply for it and explain why it's necessary. Because the driver and passenger air bags operate independently, turning one off doesn't affect the other. To decide whether your vehicle should have an ON-OFF switch, you can read a copy of NHTSA's brochure, "Air Bags and On-Off Switches: Information for an Informed Decision" at `www.safercar.gov/airbags/Brochure/index.html`. If you decide to request a switch, you can download the proper Request for Air Bag On-Off Switch form.

Many newer cars also equip the front passenger seat with a *pressure sensor* that deactivates the passenger-side air bag when it determines that a small-statured person, such as an infant or toddler, is in the seat. A "Pass Air Bag Off" warning will light up somewhere on the dashboard. These systems aren't perfect, though, and are no substitute for an ON-OFF switch.

## Replacing air bags

WARNING

When an air bag is deployed, it can't be reused, and you shouldn't drive your vehicle until it has been replaced. Be sure to go to an authorized repair center for this job; a "black market" exists for unused air bags recovered from vehicles that have been scrapped. Unless an air bag was designed especially for your vehicle's make, model, and year, it won't work properly — or possibly at all — when it's needed the most. You can find out whether a particular vehicle's air bags have been deactivated by going to `www.safercar.gov/airbags/VINs/Find_VIN.html` and typing in its *VIN (vehicle identification number)*.

REMEMBER

Having an air bag doesn't mean that you can do without your seat belt. Each safety measure has a job to do to keep you from being injured in an accident.

The following sections describe each type of air bag you may find on a vehicle. Some are standard equipment required by law, whereas others are optional. If you're shopping for a new set of wheels, air bag equipment should be a major factor.

# Frontal air bags

Originally, the only air bags found on most vehicles were frontal air bags designed to protect drivers and passengers in front-end accidents. The driver's air bag and the passenger's air bag are in different locations and have different shapes (see Figure 19-3). Because sensors can tell whether someone is in the passenger seat, each is deployed independently of the other.

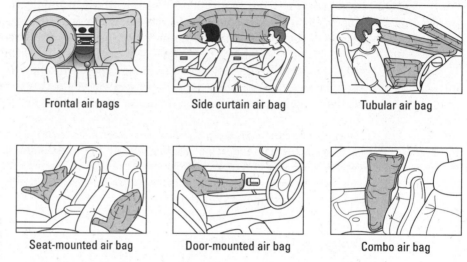

Frontal air bags     Side curtain air bag     Tubular air bag

Seat-mounted air bag     Door-mounted air bag     Combo air bag

**FIGURE 19-3:** Different types of air bags.

Because the speed and force with which air bags deployed sometimes caused injuries, over the years, frontal air bags have constantly been improved to increase their efficiency. Two such types found on more recent vehicles are *advanced* frontal air bags and *dual-stage* air bags.

## Advanced frontal air bags

All passenger cars, SUVs, and light trucks manufactured after September 1, 2006, are supposed to come equipped with *advanced* frontal air bags designed with sophisticated *sensors* that enable the *ECU* to regulate how powerfully the air bag will inflate depending on each occupant's size, whether the seat belt is worn, the position of the seat, and the force of the crash. Some can even sense how much you weigh! Advanced frontal air bags can minimize the risk of air-bag injury for children and adults of small-stature or fragile health either by not allowing the air bag to deploy when it's potentially more dangerous than the crash itself or by inflating the air bag with less force.

Because advanced frontal air bags can be turned off automatically if the sensors detect a child or very small person in a front seat, they must be equipped with an indicator light. Often in the center of the dashboard where everyone can see it, it says "DRIVER AIR BAG OFF" or "PASS. AIR BAG OFF."

**WARNING**

Having an advanced frontal air bag system does *not* mean that kids can travel safely in the front seat. They're still much safer in the rear of the vehicle, as mandated by law. For information on what to do if you can't avoid putting a child in a front seat, see the child safety seat section later in this chapter.

**TIP**

You can tell whether a vehicle has advanced frontal air bags by looking at the label on the reverse of each sun visor for the phrase, "EVEN WITH ADVANCED AIR BAGS."

### Dual-stage air bags

In order to protect riders from bags that inflate too forcefully, dual-stage air bags (sometimes called *multi-stage* air bags) have inflators that go off in one, two, or more stages depending on the severity of the crash. Variable output inflators do the same thing using a range of pressures rather than in stages. In the United States, dual-stage air bags are now required by law on both the driver and passenger sides of the vehicle.

## Side air bags (SAB)

Because frontal air bags don't protect individuals during side-impact crashes or rollovers, a variety of side air bags (SAB) have been designed to do the job (refer to Figure 19-3). They come in a variety of shapes, sizes, and locations. Designed to protect the head, chest, and body from hard objects and structures in the interior of the vehicle as well as from intrusions by exterior objects, SABs often stay inflated longer than frontal air bags in case of repeated impacts. Many SABs are designed to sense how severe a crash is and to "decide" whether or not to deploy and with how much force to use if they're needed. According to the *IIHS,* automakers have agreed informally to have side air bags as standard equipment on cars, pickups, and SUVs by around 2010; they're already included as standard or optional equipment on a growing number of vehicles.

**TIP**

If you're shopping for a vehicle, the type and number of side air bags should be a serious factor in your choice. Not only do they keep you safer on the road, but the more prospective buyers demand them, the sooner they'll become standard equipment.

The basic types of SABs are each designed to protect different areas from injury (refer to Figure 19-3):

>> **Curtain and tubular air bags protect your head.** Both types of air bags are usually located above the side windows of a vehicle and are designed to protect people seated in both the front and the rear. Besides protecting you from impacts, *curtain air bags* may keep you from being thrown out of the vehicle during a rollover. *Tubular air bags* stay inflated for about five seconds (rather than about $\frac{1}{20}$ of a second) to protect your head from repeated impacts and during rollovers. Because of their smaller size, tubular air bags are designed to work in tandem with standard side air bags, not to replace them.

>> **Seat-mounted air bags are located on the outer side of seats to protect the chest (or torso) when a vehicle is hit from the side.**

>> **Door-mounted air bags protect your torso from side impacts and in rollovers.**

>> **Combo air bags protect both the head and the chest.** They're especially protective in rollovers. Larger than the other types, combo air bags usually are installed on the side of the seats.

**TIP**

You can watch videos that show how each type of air bag is deployed at the NHTSA's Safer Car Web site, `www.safercar.gov/airbags/pages/ABTypesSAB Curtain.htm`, and you can find out whether a particular vehicle has side air bags at `www.iihs.org`.

# Side Impact Protection Systems (SIPS)

For additional protection in the event that a vehicle is hit from the side, side impact protection systems (SIPS) are now mandatory on American cars, utility vehicles, passenger vans, and pickup trucks. SIPS feature a variety of structural design elements as well as the side air bags and curtains described in the previous section. SIPS can include crash-resistant door pillars with top portions that are more rigid than the lower portions in order to transfer the force of the impact away from the head as the lower part of the pillar moves inward. Other SIPS components can include *safety cages* incorporated into the body structure of the vehicle and *crumple zones* that absorb some of the impact by crumpling in a way that doesn't endanger the occupants. Steel beams reinforce the doors and sides of the vehicle to prevent them from crushing those seated inside. Some vehicles have side-impact tubes that transfer the thrust of the crash to a steel box located in the center of the vehicle; the box collapses to absorb the impact. Others have increased padding in doors and other areas.

# Adjustable Devices

Although the ability to adjust side- and rear-view mirrors and seat-back angles has been standard for many, many years, an increasing number of other devices now can be tailored to fit each driver, and sometimes passengers, as well. The more comfortable a driver is — and the better he or she can reach and operate the steering wheel, pedals, and gearshift — the more efficient and less distracted and fatigued that driver will be, especially on long or difficult trips.

Here are some of most important adjustable features currently available:

>> **Adjustable seats:** The ability to adjust a seat's height, angle, and distance from the steering wheel is now standard equipment, and many models offer *power seats* that not only do this with little effort but also have a built-in memory that enables them to automatically adjust to the needs of each person who uses the vehicle on a regular basis.

>> **Adjustable steering wheels:** According to *Road & Track,* "researchers suggest that 40 percent of women driving larger vehicles do not sit at a safe distance from the steering wheel." Now, steering wheels whose tilt can be adjusted and that can telescope toward or away from the driver are increasingly standard. Some steering wheels can even be swung to the side without affecting the settings to allow the driver to enter and exit the vehicle more easily.

>> **Adjustable pedals:** A switch or keypad that simultaneously adjusts the height of both the accelerator and the brake pedals, as well as their distance from the driver, is now available. If you're below or above average height, this feature is worth serious consideration.

>> **Adjustable head restraints:** In 2007, according to the IIHS (the only agency that tests seats and head restraints dynamically to see how well they prevent whiplash injuries), about 200,000 whiplash injuries out of around 2 *million* claims filed annually caused serious long-term medical problems. They stress that the design of the seat and the head restraint must work together for effective protection.

**TIP**

The IIHS advises that "head restraints should be positioned high enough to protect the head so as to minimize neck distortion. Ideally the top of the head restraint should be positioned even with the top of the head and at least level with the top of the ears or about 3.5 inches below the top of the head . . . . The distance from the back of the head to the restraint should be as small as possible, *preferably less than 3 inches.* On seats without horizontally adjusting head restraints, this can be adjusted by adjusting the seatback recline angle." Figure 19-1 shows you the ideal position for both the seat and the head restraint.

WARNING

Vehicles should have head restraints that automatically adjust when the angle of the seat back is changed. But to avoid whiplash injuries, people who are not of average stature may need to adjust their head restraints manually to the safest position, and this definitely includes rear-seat passengers! In this case, the tallest people are at greatest risk, although short people are also affected.

Many vehicles don't have adjustable rear seat head restraints, and some have no head restraint for the center rear seat. If you're looking for a new vehicle, check to see whether passengers in the rear of the vehicle will be able to travel safely.

# Child Safety Seats and Booster Seats

According to research by *NHTSA*, in the first 20 years, approximately 7,000 lives were saved by the proper use of child restraints. As safer seats are developed and facilities made available to insure safe installation, the yearly figures are improving.

TIP

NHTSA suggests replacing child safety seats after five years or after an accident, and sending the registration card to the manufacturer so that you're notified in case of a recall.

## Child safety seat requirements

Even with all the publicity, the sad fact is that many parents remain ignorant about the proper way to seat their children in a vehicle, and research has found that thousands of child safety seats are improperly installed. *No single seat can carry a child safely from infancy through childhood* and children need special seating much longer than many would assume. Figure 19-4 shows you the four steps and types of seats that are necessary to seat a child safely at different stages of growth.

WARNING

Children should be placed far enough away from the side of the vehicle so that they can't open the door or window.

TIP

Ideally, *all* young children should be placed in the center of the back seat. Obviously, it's impossible to place more than one child in that position, but children are still better off in the rear than in the front passenger seat. With two kids, place the younger one in the center of the back seat and the other on the passenger side of the back seat so that you can see both of them clearly in the rear-view mirror. If you're concerned about keeping an eye on children in the back seats, *aftermarket* wide rear-view mirrors are available to give you a good view. Instead of turning around while you're at the wheel, learn to "talk to the mirror," and if pandemonium ensues, pull over and park at the side of the road before dealing with it face-to-face.

Here are NHTSA's recommendations for insuring that your children will have the best chance to travel safely on the road at each stage of their growth and development (refer to Figure 19-4):

» **Infants up to at least 1 year old and less than 20 pounds need special rear-facing safety seats.** Place an infant in the back seat of the vehicle in a rear-facing child safety seat for as long as possible, up to the height or weight limit of the particular seat you use. *Be sure that the seat can be adjusted so the infant's head is supported and doesn't bobble around.*

» **Until children reach around age 4 and at least 40 pounds, they must ride in the back seat in forward-facing child safety seats.**

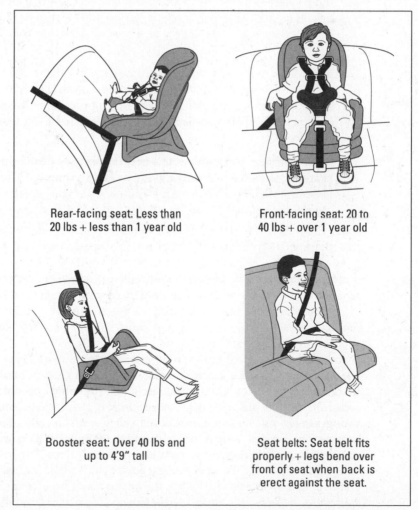

Rear-facing seat: Less than 20 lbs + less than 1 year old

Front-facing seat: 20 to 40 lbs + over 1 year old

Booster seat: Over 40 lbs and up to 4'9" tall

Seat belts: Seat belt fits properly + legs bend over front of seat when back is erect against the seat.

**FIGURE 19-4:** Seating children safely.

*Adapted from the NHTSA (www.safercar.gov)*

There are convertible seats on the market that will take a child from toddler age until they need a booster seat, and some seats can be used as part of a stroller, on dining chairs, and in airplanes. Be sure to check that whatever type you'd like to buy is rated properly for the entire age range.

>> **Children who weigh at least 40 pounds and are at least 4'9" tall (usually between the ages of 8 and 10) should ride in a booster seat.** The booster seat is used to elevate the child high enough for the adult seat belt to fit properly, with the lap belt laying across the upper thighs and pelvis (rather than the stomach) and the upper strap going over the shoulder (not the neck) and down across the chest.

Some booster seats have backrests, some are backless, and others convert from one form to the other. If your child is old enough to sit up straight in the booster seat with his or her back against the back of the rear seat and the seat belt fits properly, unless your vehicle has low seat backs or no rear headrests, a backless booster is fine. Otherwise, a backrest is a good choice until the child's head is higher than the backrest.

Don't give in to pressure from your kids to get out of "babyish" booster seats prematurely. It's better to have an angry child than an injured one. If your child will be riding in someone's vehicle without your supervision, it pays to find out how and where he or she will be placed. If necessary, send the proper seat along.

>> **Children are ready to get out of a booster seat and just use the vehicle's seat belt when the following conditions are present:** Both the lower and upper belts fit properly (see the preceding booster seats bullet) and their legs are able to bend at the knees against the edge of the seat when they sit up straight against the seat back without slouching. Figure 19-4 shows you what that placement should look like.

Children should only be placed in the front seat of a vehicle if the vehicle has no rear seat, if there are too many children for all to fit on the rear seat, or if a child is so sick that you have to be able to reach him or her immediately in an emergency.

If you *must* place a child in the front passenger seat on occasion, make sure that the seat is shoved back as far as possible, that the child is in a safety seat that keeps him or her in an upright position, and if the vehicle has an air-bag ON/OFF switch, the "How airbags work" section in this chapter tells you how to disable the passenger-side air bag. If you have to choose which child to put in front, pick the one who can best remain restrained in the proper position, even if it isn't the oldest or largest child.

# Choosing child safety seats

Here are some tips for selecting the best seat for your child and testing it out to be sure it's the proper one:

>> **Buy a new seat.** Secondhand seats may be worn or defective.

>> **A child safety seat must have a label that says it meets or exceeds Federal Motor Vehicle Safety Standards.**

>> **Read the current child seat ratings for safety, durability, and ease of use.** Select from among top-rated seats listed at www.nhtsa.dot.gov/CPS/ CSSRating/Index.cfm or in the most current listings in *Consumer Reports.* At www.aap.org/family/carseatguide.htm, the American Academy of Pediatrics also provides an extensive and detailed amount of information on this vital topic.

>> **Take your child along when shopping for a seat so that you can see whether you can work the buckles easily while the kid is squirming around.** Tension adjusters to lengthen or tighten the straps should be easy to use, and straps should go into the buckles and be released easily (but not so easy that "even a child can do it!").

>> **Make sure that your child is comfortable.** If you have an infant, the seat should adjust to recline so that his or her head is supported.

>> **There should be room in the seat for the child to grow into and to accommodate layers of heavier clothing.** If you choose wisely, your kid is going to be in that seat for at least four years.

## Considering types of harnesses and anchoring systems

Child safety seats come with a variety of harnesses to keep your child securely buckled in place. Some have a *three-point* harness with straps that come over the child's shoulders and connect with a buckle close to the bottom of the seat. *Five-point* harnesses have five straps, one for each shoulder, one for each hip and one at the child's crotch. Some seats feature a padded or triangle-shaped *T-shield* that's attached to the shoulder straps and the front of the seat. Still others have a shield that drops down from overhead to keep the child in place.

TIP

The five-point harness is generally considered to be the safest and most comfortable for a child, so you may want to look at seats with a five-point harness first.

Any child seat or booster seat is only as effective as the way it's anchored to the vehicle. There are two anchoring systems available to ensure that your child's seat is safely anchored, and compatibility with these should definitely be a vital consideration when choosing a seat:

>> **The LATCH system:** LATCH is an acronym for "Lower Anchors and Tethers for Children." Since September 1, 2002, every new vehicle and child safety seat has been required to have this system, which eliminates the need to use seat belts to secure the seat. As shown in Figure 19-5a, the system includes anchor hardware on the vehicle and hooks and straps on the seat that attach to them. You can find more information on LATCH and how to use it to install child seats at www.chop.edu/consumer/jsp/division/generic.jsp?id=77978.

**WARNING**

Unless both your vehicle and the child seat have the LATCH system, you will still need to use seat belts to install the seat! Before installing it, inspect the seat belts to be sure that they are not frayed, are securely anchored to the vehicle, and that the latches work properly. If you spot any problems, have new seat belts installed throughout the car. And be sure the seat can be securely anchored using seat belts alone.

>> **ISOFIX connections:** ISOFIX has been the worldwide standard in child-seat safety and convenience since 2004. It's available as standard equipment or as an option. This rigid interface between the child seat and the body of the vehicle enables the seat to be installed easily and to stay safely in place. With ISOFIX installed, instead of fussing with seat belts or hooks and straps, you just click the seat into the anchor points in the car, as shown in Figure 19-5b.

**FIGURE 19-5:**
The LATCH car seat system (a) and an ISOFIX car seat system (b).

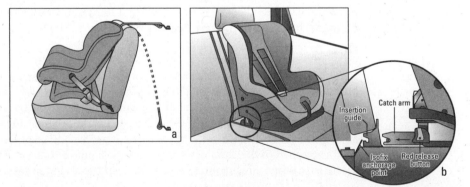

*Adapted from the NHTSA (www.safercar.gov)*

## Testing the candidates before you purchase

After you select the best candidates, take the seats out of the store to the parking lot and try them out in the rear seat of your vehicle to see whether they're easy to handle and whether your child is comfortable in them. Because you aren't going anywhere, there's no need to install each one — just place it on the seat and set your child in it.

TIP

If a store won't let you try seats out in your vehicle, offer to buy the one that looks the most likely to work for you and tell the clerk that you're going to try it out in the parking lot and may be returning immediately to exchange it for another — and another — until you find the one that satisfies your needs. At that point, the department head or store manager will probably give you permission to test the seats out without going through all that rigmarole.

TECHNICAL
STUFF

Check to see whether your child will be able see out of the window. Obviously this isn't a requirement for tiny infants, but a seat that sits high enough to afford visibility will cut down on the complaining as time goes on and the baby grows up.

TIP

Have the seat installed professionally at the store (if you feel that they're capable of doing that properly) or at your dealership, or locate a child-seat fitting station and have it installed there. To find local, professional assistance with correctly installing a child safety seat, go to www.nhtsa.gov and click on Locate a Child Seat Fitting Station in the left-hand column. The site also contains valuable information on child seats and a place to file complaints.

# Smart Seat Belts

Although seat belts have been mandatory on passenger vehicles for years, the technology to create "smart" seat belts that are safer, more efficient, and significantly adaptable to each individual is just hitting its stride.

Currently available are seat belts with *pretensioners* that detect a crash and increase the tension of the seat belt to literally haul you into a safer position on the seat. Although how these smart seat belts do this varies from one model to the other, most use the same *sensors* that activate the air bags in response to a crash. And there are seat belts on the road today that have built-in *load limiters* that lengthen the belt a bit if it constricts too forcefully during a high-speed crash.

BFGoodrich has a smart belt that inflates a little air bag that runs the entire length of the seat belt. It deploys along with the other air bags to protect you from them by pushing away from you rather than toward you. These are expected to become standard on personal vehicles, school buses, trains, and airplanes, too. The newest smart seat belts can *anticipate* a possible accident and react before it happens! Most of them are connected to sophisticated air-bag *sensors* and to the *anti-lock braking system (ABS)* described in Chapter 14. Currently in the works is an ultrasound finger scanner on the dashboard that can "read" the bone density of the individual and use it to determine how much tension that person's bones can handle! This could be especially important for seniors and children.

No matter how smart seat belts become, unless drivers and passengers are smart as well, the belts can't be truly safe and effective unless you wear them! They also need to be properly adjusted. A well-fitting seat belt should allow you to move around enough to look out the side window and run your vehicle efficiently. If the seat belts in your vehicle seem to have been designed for basketball players or dwarves, consult your dealership or a reliable auto parts store for gadgets that keep them from cutting into your neck or strangling you. Be sure your passengers in the rear seat are belted in, too. The Center for Transportation Injury Research at the University of Buffalo, New York, found that unbelted passengers sitting behind the driver tripled the odds that the driver would be killed in an accident because, if the unbelted passengers hurtle forward, they quadruple the maximum force to the driver's head and chest.

TIP

Pregnant women should always wear seat belts that are positioned correctly in order to avoid injuring themselves and their unborn children. The lap belt should be as low as possible around the hips rather than across the stomach, and the shoulder belt should rest across the breastbone rather than the stomach. NHTSA advises against deactivating air bags; its tests have shown that there's risk for greater injury without an air bag because it helps spread the force of the crash, which would be concentrated by the seat belt, over a larger area.

REMEMBER

One last reminder for expectant parents: Don't forget to bring an infant safety seat along with you to the hospital so your newborn can ride home safely.

# "Eyes" in the Back of Your Vehicle

When parking a vehicle or backing out of any parking space or driveway, most of us wish we had eyes in the back of our heads. What scares us when it's difficult to see what's behind us is not simply the possible damage to our vehicles — or to someone else's if we collide with them; the really tragic risks involve hitting a human being or an animal. Unfortunately, small children and pets are all but invisible in rear-view mirrors, and thousands have been killed or injured by vehicles that backed over them. *Back-up warning devices*, also called *rear sensing systems*, and *parking sensing devices* are being developed in a variety of configurations and are increasingly found as standard or optional equipment on passenger vehicles.

# Back-up beepers and sensors

For many years, the Occupational Safety and Health Administration (OSHA) has required construction equipment and other industrial vehicles to be equipped with back-up beepers that sound a warning to everyone within earshot when the vehicle is in Reverse, and this has probably saved many lives. Some passenger vehicles, particularly SUVs, are equipped with audible back-up alerts. Because kids and animals probably don't know enough to respond to audible alerts, the sensors and back-up cameras and monitors described in the following sections are probably a better solution.

*Sensors* that can be mounted at the rear of a vehicle are available on the *aftermarket,* as optional equipment on some vehicles, and as standard equipment on many luxury models (especially SUVs). Sensors use sonar to detect objects behind the vehicle and beepers or warning lights to alert drivers when they detect something dangerously close behind them.

# Back-up cameras and monitors

*Back-up cameras* that offer a view of what's behind the vehicle are now becoming popular options on newer models and are expected to become standard equipment on many models before too long. A variety of back-up cameras are already available on the automotive aftermarket, all of which require a monitor to view what they record. Cameras mount on the rear panel, on or under the rear bumper, or inside the vehicle, and monitors may be incorporated into rear-view mirrors, can be placed on the windscreen or the dashboard, or can hook into a navigation system. This safety device is definitely a worthwhile investment!

# Blind-spot information systems (BLIS)

The area where drivers can't see vehicles in adjoining lanes behind or to the side when using their side and rear-view mirrors is called the *blind spot.* Collisions and near-misses when changing lanes because the blind spot rendered a vehicle invisible are a daily occurrence on most highways and busy streets. As a result, Volvo has led the way in developing a *blind-spot information system* (BLIS) that employs a little camera mounted on each side mirror (see Figure 19-6) to alert drivers who are planning to change lanes to vehicles in those lanes that they may otherwise not be able to see. It also tells drivers when there is sufficient space to change lanes safely.

When a vehicle appears in a blind spot, the camera on that side activates a light on the door panel near that mirror. When there's enough room to change lanes safely, the light goes off. Drivers testing this system report that the light isn't distracting when they aren't looking to change lanes and that checking to see whether the light is on before changing lanes quickly becomes as natural as checking the mirrors.

**FIGURE 19-6:**
A blind-spot information system.

**WARNING**

It's a well-known fact that most side mirrors distort how close the vehicles coming up in adjacent lanes are, and I carefully adjust my side mirrors and rear-view mirror so that the moment a vehicle coming up behind me in the next lane disappears from view in the rear-view mirror its front-end becomes visible in the mirror on that side. I believe that modifications to side mirrors should be a priority for automakers. Until we all have BLIS-equipped vehicles, I urge you to never make a lane change unless you turn and take a swift peek out the side window to see whether there's someone dangerously close to you.

Drivers are warned about extensive blind spots on large trucks that make smaller vehicles all but invisible to truck drivers. Hopefully, BLIS will help to rectify that situation, especially if the federal government sees fit to mandate it for use on commercial vehicles. Until then, watch for BLIS systems to appear on a growing number of passenger vehicles. I hope every driver can be in a state of BLIS before long!

**TIP**

A system is becoming increasingly popular on up-scale pickups, SUVs, and large sedans that automatically tilts your side-view mirrors downward when you back up to park so that you can see the curb or whatever else is alongside the car. After the car is parked, the system automatically returns the mirrors to their original positions.

# Brake-Shift Interlocks

A *brake-shift interlock* is a device that prevents the *gearshift* from being accidentally shifted out of the Park position, which could allow the vehicle to accidentally roll into danger. The device makes it impossible to move the gearshift without simultaneously stepping on the *brake pedal*. Although many vehicles already come with this as standard equipment, in 2006, in response to a growing number of accidents involving children injured while playing with gearshifts, NHTSA and 19 automakers agreed to have brake-shift interlocks on all new vehicles by 2010.

# Traction Control Systems (TCS)

*Traction control systems (TCS)* have been around, in one form or another, for years (see Figure 19-7). The system senses when one or more wheels is spinning faster than the others and attempts to prevent the vehicle from going out of control. The problem can be due to a slippery surface but also can occur when a vehicle with *front-wheel drive* is driven so hard that the *drive wheels* don't steer properly and lose traction.

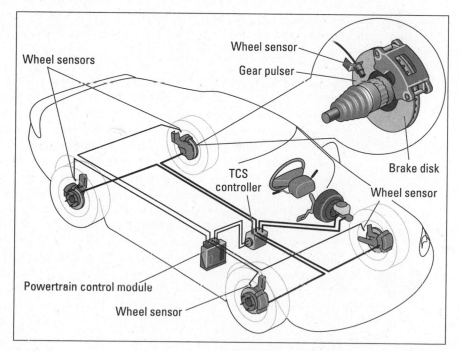

**FIGURE 19-7:** A traction control system.

Electronic traction control systems use the *anti-lock braking system (ABS)* to sense and compare the speed of each wheel and automatically pump the brake on a wheel that's spinning faster than the others. (You can read about ABS in Chapter 14.) Some TCS also decrease the power supplied by the engine to the wheel or wheels that are slipping. On systems like these, the *accelerator* pedal pulsates, much as the brake pedal does when ABS is employed. Other forms of traction control that involve *throttles* and *turbocharging* exist, and more are being developed.

REMEMBER

Traction control is no substitute for snow tires or chains in icy or snowy weather because it doesn't *increase* traction — it just tries to keep wheels that *lose* traction from spinning out of control.

# Electronic Stability Control (ESC)

Making emergency maneuvers to avoid obstacles, taking turns at high speeds, and cornering too sharply or too fast are some of the situations that can cause your vehicle to veer from the path you expect to follow when you turn the steering wheel. As a result, your vehicle either *oversteers* (turns more radically because it's sliding or spinning) or *understeers* (turns less than you planned because it loses traction). *Electronic stability control (ESC)* keeps your vehicle on the straight and narrow to prevent it from skidding sideways, spinning out, or rolling over.

As you can see in Figure 19-8, ESC uses the wheel-speed *sensors* that enable *ABS* and *TCS*. It also has a sensor that monitors the *steering angle* (the position of the steering wheel) and compares it with the data from a rotation sensor that monitors the *yaw angle* (how much the vehicle is rocking from side to side) to see where the vehicle is actually going. Other sensors can measure additional types of movement. With all this input, the vehicle's *ECU* can monitor how well your vehicle is responding to the position of the steering wheel and, by activating the brakes on the proper wheels and modulating power, correct the course of your vehicle so that you can go on your way safely. Figure 19-9 shows how ESC works to correct understeering and oversteering.

TIP

To find out whether a particular vehicle is equipped with ESC, just enter the make, model, and year at www.iihs.org/ratings/esc/esc.aspx. Because many automakers have trademarked their own names for their ESC systems, you can find a list of them at money.cnn.com/2006/06/12/Autos/esc_names/index.htm.

**WARNING**

Don't think that having an ESC-equipped vehicle means it will take care of you if you drive carelessly. ESC doesn't prevent accidents in normal stop-and-go driving or at low speeds; it's designed to go into action to help keep you from losing control at high speeds or on slippery roads. And "help" is the key word: ESC can't prevent loss of control in *every* situation, especially if you're driving too fast! The terrible toll caused by vehicles going out of control has made ESC a feature that drivers shouldn't do without (see the nearby sidebar).

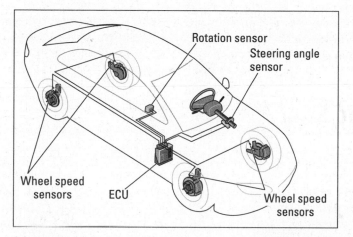

**FIGURE 19-8:**
Electronic stability control uses several sensors.

Rotation sensor

Steering angle sensor

Wheel speed sensors

ECU

Wheel speed sensors

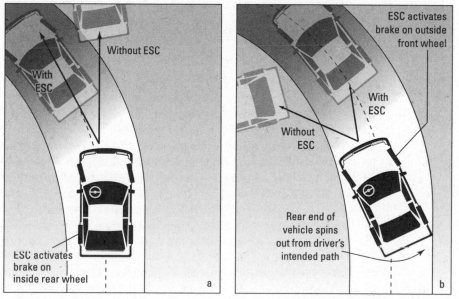

**FIGURE 19-9:**
How ESC corrects understeering (a) and oversteering (b).

Without ESC

With ESC

ESC activates brake on inside rear wheel

a

ESC activates brake on outside front wheel

With ESC

Without ESC

Rear end of vehicle spins out from driver's intended path

b

*Adapted from the NHTSA (www.safercar.gov)*

## RESEARCH MAKES A STRONG CASE FOR REQUIRING ESC ON *ALL* VEHICLES

When it comes to advocating ESC on all vehicles, the following quote from the Insurance Institute for Highway Safety (IIHS) says it all:

"In Institute studies, ESC has been found to reduce fatal single-vehicle crash risk by 56 percent and fatal multiple-vehicle crash risk by 32 percent for cars and SUVs. Many single-vehicle crashes involve rolling over, and ESC effectiveness in preventing rollovers is even more dramatic. It reduces the risk of fatal single-vehicle rollovers by 80 percent for SUVs and by 77 percent for cars. If all vehicles were equipped with ESC, as many as 10,000 fatal crashes could be avoided each year.

"Federal studies also show large benefits. The National Highway Traffic Safety Administration (NHTSA) estimates the installation of ESC reduces single-vehicle crashes of cars by 26 percent and single-vehicle crashes of SUVs by 48 percent. NHTSA estimates that ESC has the potential to prevent 64 percent of the passenger car rollovers and 85 percent of the SUV rollovers that would otherwise occur in single-vehicle crashes."

The IIHS requires a vehicle to have ESC to earn their "Top Safety Pick" status. Although a growing number of vehicles already come equipped with ESC as standard or optional equipment (by 2007, the percentage of vehicles with ESC was ten times higher than in 1998), *all* cars, SUVs, pickups, and minivans built by the 2012 model year will have to have it.

# Rollover Stability Control (RSC)

The tendency of SUVs to roll over under conditions that were previously thought safe has prompted the development of *rollover stability control* systems (RSC) that identify situations where a vehicle that is taking a turn too sharply or too fast could roll over, and then help to prevent this from happening. RSC employs the *sensors* and other components found on ABS, TCS, and ESC, along with a *roll-rate sensor* and other modifications. To be effective, RSC has to be sensitive enough to differentiate between critical situations and relatively harmless instability caused by variations in the surface of the road or roadside shoulders, or by uneven loads.

If the system senses a potentially hazardous situation, it applies pressure to the brakes on the wheel or wheels on the vehicle closest to the outside of the turn, which helps keep the inside wheels on the ground. First introduced as an option on higher-priced vehicles, RSC is becoming available on more vehicles as time goes on.

# Adaptive Cruise Control (ACC)

Cruise control has been around for quite a while and is standard on most passenger vehicles today. However, *adaptive cruise control* (ACC) transforms cruise control into a system that can be programmed to maintain a safe distance between your car and the vehicle in front of you and to provide protection if a crash seems imminent.

Adaptive cruise control is available on a growing number of vehicles, and systems vary from one automaker to another. Variations include the ability to not only set the distance but also the minimum time gap to the vehicle ahead. Some systems employ a laser-based system called *lidar* (an acronym for "light detecting and ranging") and others use radar sensors to detect a slower vehicle in front of you and adjust your speed accordingly. Each system has its advantages and drawbacks: Lidar is less expensive but has a shorter range and doesn't operate as well in wet weather conditions that require windshield wipers or if the vehicle ahead is too dirty to reflect light properly. Radar is more expensive but doesn't have these problems. At pres-ent, radar seems to be more popular.

On ACC systems with forward collision warning (sometimes called *collision mitigation* systems), if the driver ahead brakes suddenly, a flashing red light can appear on your windshield along with an audible alarm. ACC systems also may include *collision warning with brake support* (CWBS) that will prepare your brakes for a panic stop. Additional features of ACC systems can tighten seat belts and deploy air bags in critical situations.

Because of the high percentage of rear-end accidents, there's strong support for mandating that vehicles be equipped with ACC and other collision prevention systems until your vehicle does most of the driving for you, staying in lane and changing lanes at safe distances from surrounding vehicles and obstacles and responding faster to critical situations than human drivers can. I can hardly wait!

# Telematics: How Cars Communicate

*Telematics* (a term derived from combining the terms "telecommunication" and "informatics") is the technical term for the wireless systems that enable your vehicle to communicate with the outside world. The information exchanged often involves GPS (global positioning systems) and can include where you are and the best way to get where you want to go, your vehicle's speed and condition, where other vehicles in the vicinity are and how fast they're going, the nearest restaurant or gas station, instant traffic reports, Bluetooth and other phone and instant messaging systems, music downloads, and other vital stuff. This section describes the most popular ways that telematic systems can make driving easier and safer. Services provided by individual systems overlap, so the telematic system in a particular vehicle may combine the features of one or more of the following systems.

# Navigation systems

*Navigation systems* have become increasingly popular as standard or optional equipment and also are available as stand-alone *aftermarket* units that can mount on the dashboard or above the windshield, and as part of in-dash aftermarket stereo and DVD systems with pop-up or fixed display screens.

All navigation systems are based on GPS technology that receives satellite signals that determine your exact longitude and latitude. When you enter the address of your destination or the name of a place of interest on a touch keypad, a CD that's loaded with street maps and installed in your vehicle enables the system to determine the best route. Most systems allow you to modify the suggested routes by stipulating that you don't want to take freeways, go over bridges, or drive on unpaved roads, and offer you a choice of the shortest, fastest, and other alternative routes.

These are the types of navigation features you may encounter:

>> **Built-in navigation systems** provide spoken turn-by-turn directions through the vehicle's audio system as well as a choice of map displays that enable you to zoom in or out, orient by the compass or the direction in which your vehicle is traveling, and so on. Most built-in systems will locate a variety of establishments in a specific area, including restaurants, service stations, hospitals, police stations, parks, and other places of interest.

>> **Aftermarket navigation systems** vary from some that are little more than a basic GPS to others that will provide oral directions and a full spectrum of information.

>> **Navigation services** have been incorporated into cellphones, PDAs, computers, and other electronic devices.

# Tracking systems

*Tracking systems* employ a combination of GPS, cellular, and other electronic technologies to enable a vehicle to communicate its location and condition to an outside source. Tracking systems are used to locate stolen vehicles; monitor the location of every vehicle in a commercial fleet; and enable worried parents to keep track of where their kids are driving, how fast they're going, and whether seat belts are engaged.

Tracking systems have been criticized for "spying" on people, just as every device that incorporates GPS technology (including cellphones) has come under suspicion that it may be used by "Big Brother" to keep an eye on everyone's whereabouts. At least this invasion of privacy is currently optional and can help you keep track of your kids and recover a stolen car! Following are good examples of the range of telematic tracking services available. I'm not endorsing them, as they each have competent competitors. For a comparison of the features of various telematic services go to www.edmunds.com/media/editorial/telemetrics/popout.html.

## OnStar

OnStar was the first widely available telematic system in North America. It uses a combination of GPS, cellular technology, voice recognition, and MapQuest data to connect you with its Call Center and provide you with a variety of services. OnStar enables you to communicate verbally with live and virtual advisors, get directions, report an accident or a flat tire, or announce that you need the doors unlocked for you. In an emergency, your vehicle can communicate its position and condition with no human assistance at all! Sensors that report that air bags have been deployed activate an automatic message that the vehicle has been in an accident, and even if nobody in the vehicle is able to communicate verbally, the service can call 911 and send help. Additional options can include automatic diagnostics and hands-free access to e-mail, weather reports, and stock quotes. Most major domestic and international automakers now offer systems similar to OnStar, so factor this in when deciding which vehicle best satisfies your needs and budget.

## LoJack

LoJack is a tracking system that offers two packages that can work together or separately. If you report that your vehicle has been stolen, LoJack's *Stolen Vehicle Recovery System* inaudibly transmits a unique code connected to the vehicle's unique *VIN* as well as the present location of the vehicle to police cruisers with tracking computers within a 25-mile range. LoJack claims a 90 percent recovery rate, and the system qualifies for a deduction on some insurance policies. LoJack's *Early Warning Recovery System* alerts you when your vehicle is being moved without your permission by sensing that someone who isn't carrying LoJack's Key Pass is at the wheel.

Chapter **20**

# Troubleshooting Leaks, Squeaks, Smells, and Strange Sensations

As you work on your vehicle, you'll get to know it better. Before long, you'll become more sensitive to its signals. If something sounds funny or smells funny or just doesn't feel right, you'll soon sense it. This can help you forestall expensive repairs because you'll be able to prevent trouble or deal with it before it becomes a major problem. And if something does need repair, being able to report symptoms accurately will save your mechanic time — and you money.

**TECHNICAL STUFF**

If you really want to diagnose symptoms professionally, you can buy an electronic diagnostic code reader, or, better yet, a scan tool that plugs into a Diagnostic Communications Link (DCL) mounted under the dashboard of most modern vehicles. Do-it-yourself versions cost from $60 to about $400. They read any trouble codes the on-board diagnostic program (OBD) has recognized and translate the codes into problems you can look up in a repair manual for your vehicle to see what's involved in buying the part and replacing it yourself.

For those of us who aren't that ambitious, this chapter shows how to use your eyes, ears, and nose to sense automotive symptoms, and it tells you how to deal with them.

REMEMBER

Whenever you encounter a term set in *this font,* you'll find it defined in the glossary in Appendix A.

# Sounds

You probably know how your vehicle sounds when it's running properly, and your ears can alert you to anything that sounds strange. Well, tune in to what your ears are telling you! If you hear a strange or different sound, pay attention to it and react accordingly.

>> **If a *fan belt* or *accessory belt* "sings" (you hear a high-pitched squeal that stops when you shut off your engine),** readjust or replace the belt. These belts should have about ½ inch of play and shouldn't be frayed, cracked, or glazed on the underside. Some belts tend to sing more than others. You can find instructions for adjusting and replacing belts in Chapter 12.

WARNING

*Don't drive with a broken belt.* If you carry a spare belt, you may be able to save yourself towing charges *if* you know how to replace it. Replacing a serpentine belt at roadside is difficult. You'd need a tow, but at least you wouldn't be stranded until a new belt could be obtained.

>> **If your *radiator* "sings" (you hear a continuous high-pitched sound that *may* continue after the engine's shut off),** check the radiator *pressure cap.* The rubber *gasket* may be worn, and steam from the hot engine may be escaping past it. Chapter 12 tells you how to remove a radiator cap safely.

>> **If something ticks rhythmically while your engine *idles,*** shut off the engine, wait ten minutes for the engine to cool down and the oil to settle in the *oil pan,* and then check the oil level, following directions in Chapter 2. The *hydraulic* lifters that operate the *valves* in your engine can make these ticking noises if you're down as little as a quart of oil. If the level is low, add oil up to the "Full" line on the oil *dipstick* and check it again in a couple of days. If you have enough oil, have a mechanic check the valve adjustment if your car has adjustable valves (some don't). Faulty valves can seriously affect your vehicle's performance and fuel consumption.

WARNING

>> **If you hear a loud tapping or knocking sound in your engine,** pull to the side of the road *immediately* and call for road service. The source may be just a loose *rocker arm* or carbon buildup inside the engine, but if it's a loose *bearing* or a faulty *piston,* letting it go unheeded can destroy the whole engine.

Mild knocking or "pinging" may be the result of using fuel with the wrong *octane rating.* Check your owner's manual to see whether your vehicle needs low-octane or premium fuel. Most newer vehicles can automatically adjust to a higher or lower octane than they were designed for. But even though you may not hear pinging if you put regular gas in a vehicle that's supposed to use premium, you probably won't get the best performance. And putting premium in a vehicle designed for regular fuel only makes the oil company wealthier.

» **If you hear the engine running after you turn off the ignition,** your engine is *dieseling.* This condition only happens to cars with carburetors. It is usually caused by an idle speed that's set too high or excessive carbon in the combustion chamber that ignites unburned fuel in the cylinders.

» **If you hear a whistling noise coming from under the hood,** check the hoses for vacuum leaks. If the whistling comes from *inside* the vehicle, there's probably a leak in the weatherstripping. Patch the weatherstripping according to the directions in Chapter 24.

» **If the engine *idles* with an offbeat rhythm,** it isn't displaying musical talent; it's probably *misfiring,* and one of the *spark plugs* or spark plug wires may be at fault. Try the following:

- *With the engine off,* check the *spark plug* cables for breaks or shorts in the wiring.

- *With the engine off,* remove the spark plugs one at a time and check to see if they're clean and properly *gapped.* Replace any that are fouled or burned. Chapter 6 shows you how to do all this spark plug work.

If attending to the spark plugs doesn't help, have a technician check the *ignition system* with an electronic engine analyzer. (People used to check spark plugs by holding the end of the spark plug cable close to a metal surface to see whether a spark jumped across when the engine was cranked, but the high voltage in most ignition systems now makes that procedure extremely dangerous.)

» **If the *idling* is rough but even,** have a technician put your vehicle on an electronic diagnostic machine to check it, or check the *compression* in each *cylinder* yourself, following the instructions in Chapter 8. If the engine needs to be *rebuilt,* you may prefer to get another engine — or another vehicle.

An easy way to determine whether your engine is *idling* evenly is to place a stiff piece of paper against the end of the *tailpipe* while the vehicle is idling (with the *parking brake* on, please). Doing so amplifies the sound and enables you to hear the rhythm. A misfiring *cylinder* comes through as a pumping or puffing sound. An even but rough *idle* is a clue that you may need to have your *fuel injection* system checked out by a mechanic with electronic diagnostic equipment.

» **If your car sounds like a "Mack truck" or makes some other loud, abnormal sound,** a hole in the *muffler* is probably the cause. Replace it immediately: Traffic cops hate noisy mufflers, and carbon monoxide hates people!

» **If the horn is stuck,** your vehicle is producing what may be the worst noise it can make. *Before* this happens, have someone honk your horn until you can locate it under your hood. There are usually two horns, and each one has a wire leading to it. If your horn gets stuck, pull these wires to stop the noise (see Figure 20-1) — sometimes you have to pull only one. When you take your car to a service facility to have the horn fixed, tell the mechanic that you pulled the wires, and find out why the horn got stuck. If you can't get at the horn wires, pull the *fuse* that goes to the horn to stop the noise. Another way to quiet things down fast is to disconnect one *battery* terminal. Of course, your vehicle won't run with the battery terminal disconnected, so this is just a short-term measure until you can fix the horn or help arrives.

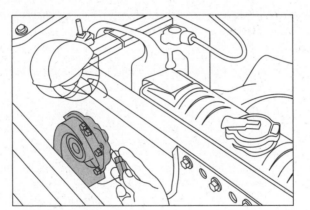

**FIGURE 20-1:**
If your horn gets stuck, pull a wire to silence it.

TIP

» **If you hear a sound but can't locate the source,** get an old stethoscope from a medical supply house or your family doctor. As shown in Figure 20-2, take off the rubber disc and insert a piece of tubing in its place (about 1½ inches will do). Then put the plugs in your ears, run the engine, and move the tube end of the stethoscope around the hood area. The stethoscope amplifies the sound as you near the part that's causing it.

TIP

A wooden broomstick works the same way. Place one end on the bone behind your ear and place the other end on the parts that seem to be the source of the noise.

» **If your tires squeal on curves (and you aren't speeding),** check their inflation pressure, treads, and *alignment* by using the instructions in Chapter 17.

» **If you hear whining or humming sounds on curves,** your *wheel bearings* may be wearing. Chapter 15 turns you on to the sensual thrill of repacking them with your bare hands.

» **If your tires "tramp" (they make a weird, rhythmic sound as you drive),** check inflation, tire wear, and *wheel balancing* (see Chapter 17).

» **If you hear squealing when you step on the brake,** you've probably worn the *brake pads* down too far. Get them replaced immediately. Some *disc brakes* are naturally noisy, and others have built-in wear *sensors* that squeal when it's time to replace the pads. But if the sound gets louder, have the brakes checked or follow the instructions in Chapter 15 and check them yourself.

TIP

If you have *drum brakes, brake linings* that are glazed or worn can cause them to squeal, as well.

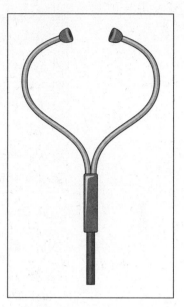

**FIGURE 20-2:**
A piece of tubing and an old stethoscope make an efficient troubleshooting device.

» **If you hear rumbling noises coming from under or toward the rear of the vehicle,** the trouble could be a defective exhaust pipe, *muffler,* or *catalytic converter;* or it could be coming from a worn *universal joint* or some other part of the *drive train.* Have a service facility put the car up on a hoist and find the problem.

» **If you hear clunking under your vehicle,** especially when you go over a bump, check the *shock absorbers* and *suspension system.* If the sound is toward the rear, your *tailpipe* or muffler may be loose.

# Squeaks, Rattles, and Vibrations

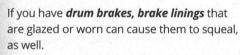

If you hear suspicious squeaks, rattles, or vibrations, you may be able to save yourself some money by checking and tightening the following items before seeking professional help:

» **Loose screws and bolts:** Check both inside the vehicle and under the hood.

» **Rearview and side mirrors**

» **Dashboard knobs and trim**

>> **Sound-system speaker grills**

>> **Window and door cranks and locks**

>> **Ashtray and other storage compartments:** Are they empty? Do the lids fit snugly?

>> **Glove box:** Is the door shut tight? Is anything in the glove box rattling around?

>> **Wheel covers or hubcaps:** Remove them and check inside for pebbles.

>> **Outside trim**

>> **Trunk:** Is something you've stashed in there moving around?

If none of these is the culprit, or if the noise persists, have a repair facility find the cause. Often, something inside the vehicle vibrates sympathetically because another part of the vehicle is running roughly.

If your car squeaks like an old taxi, especially when you drive it on a bumpy road, it may just need lubrication. However, the problem may be worn *shock absorbers* or struts, suspension *ball joints,* or broken *stabilizer* links (see Chapter 16).

WARNING

You may get used to the squeaks and groans, but because they're caused by parts rubbing together or moving without the proper lubrication, they indicate wear that can damage your vehicle. Obviously, action is required.

# Smells

The only odors you should smell inside your vehicle should come from smelly things that you've put in it: the takeout lunch that you bought at a drive-through, the perfume that your 6-year-old squirted all over herself, your not-so-freshly groomed dog who's pressing his nose against your recently washed windows. You can get rid of persistent odors easily by using a spray that eliminates odors rather than masking them. But if you smell any of the items in the following list, take immediate action to correct it:

>> **Do you smell rubber burning under the hood?** One of your hoses may have come loose and landed on a hot part of the engine. Rescue it before it melts through.

>> **Do you smell something burning with the hood closed?** Feel your wheels. If one is hot, a *brake shoe or pad* may be dragging, or you may have left the *parking brake* on. If neither of these checks out, an overheated *clutch* of a manual transmission car may be the cause.

» **Do you smell oil burning (a thick, acrid odor)?** First check the oil *dipstick* by following the directions in Chapter 2. Your *oil pressure gauge* may be lying, and you may be running out of oil. Or your engine may be overheating, and your temperature gauge may be broken. If neither is the case, look around the engine for oil leaking onto the engine block or exhaust manifold. If the oil situation seems to be okay, check the *transmission fluid* dipstick. Sometimes a faulty *vacuum modulator* can siphon the fluid out of the transmission and feed it to the engine, where it's burned. Also, if the transmission fluid is very low, it can be burned in the transmission because the gears aren't lubricated enough and are getting very hot.

» **Do you smell oil or exhaust fumes in the passenger compartment?** The cause could be burned oil from the engine area, but it also could be a faulty exhaust pipe under the car that lets *exhaust gases* into the vehicle through the floorboards.

**WARNING**

Exhaust fumes contain carbon monoxide, so if you smell oil or exhaust inside the car, be sure to keep your windows open at all times and have the problem checked out as quickly as you can. People have died from inhaling carbon monoxide or from passing out at the wheel because of it. Although the exhaust of most post-1995 vehicles is so clean that a bad headache is probably the worst you can get, have it checked anyway. It never pays to take chances.

» **Do you smell something sweet and steamy?** Take a look at the temperature gauge or light on your dashboard to see whether your engine is overheating. Chapter 12 tells you how to cool things down.

» **Do you smell rotten eggs?** The smell is probably coming from the *catalytic converter,* which is part of the *exhaust system.* The converter may be malfunctioning, or you may have a problem with your engine.

» **Do you smell burned toast (a light, sharp odor)?** Unless you've brought breakfast with you, it may be an electrical short circuit, or the insulation on a wire may be burning. Check around under the hood. Driving is a bit risky, so either get to the nearest service station or have roadside service come to you.

» **Do you smell that "new car smell" in your new vehicle?** It may be due to toxic emissions from the materials and adhesives used in the passenger compartment. If your vehicle smells strongly of these, until the odor dissipates, consider opening the windows or running the air conditioner while you drive.

» **Do you smell gasoline?** If you just had trouble starting the car, the engine may be flooded. Wait a few minutes and try again. If the smell comes from under the hood, check your *fuel injection* system or *carburetor* to make sure that it isn't leaking fuel. Also check your *fuel pump* (if it isn't hidden inside your fuel tank). Leaking gasoline will wash a clean streak across it, which can be seen with the naked eye. Then check all visible *fuel lines* and *hoses* that lead to the *fuel tank.* If they've rotted or are disconnected, you'll smell fuel vapors without seeing any leaks. Taking a look under the vehicle after it has been parked overnight may help, but remember that fuel evaporates quickly, so the clues may be stains rather than wet spots.

WARNING

Obviously, you shouldn't smoke while you check for a fuel leak! But then, you *never* should smoke when you're working on your vehicle. Gasoline ignites easily, and gasoline vapors can explode, so if you smell gasoline — and you didn't just fill your tank — find the source of the leak and have it repaired immediately. If your usual repair facility isn't close by, either drive to the closest garage and have them repair it or call your auto club and have them tow the vehicle to a repair facility.

# Smoke

If you see smoke coming from your *tailpipe,* pay attention to the color for clues to the cause of the problem:

>> **If you see white vapor on a cold morning,** disregard it if it stops after the vehicle warms up. If it continues after the engine is warm, a cracked *engine block* or *cylinder head* or a leaky *head gasket* may be letting coolant into the engine. You need professional help with this one.

>> **If you see black smoke and you drive an older vehicle with a *carburetor*,** the *fuel/air mixture* may need to be adjusted to a leaner setting or the carburetor float may have absorbed gasoline and is flooding the engine.

WARNING

Black smoke from a vehicle with *fuel injection* usually requires special diagnosis and should be left to a repair facility.

Check to see whether the fuel/air mixture on either type of vehicle is too rich by running your finger around the inside edge of the tailpipe (first make sure that it's not hot). If carbon comes off on your finger, the mixture is probably too rich.

>> **If the smoke is light or dark blue,** the vehicle is burning oil, which can indicate that oil is leaking into the *combustion chambers* and you may need to have your *valve stem seals* replaced or your engine *rebuilt* or replaced.

>> **If the smoke is light gray,** the car may be burning automatic *transmission fluid.* Check the transmission *dipstick* following the instructions in Chapter 2. Is the fluid dark and burned-looking? Does it smell burned? If so, changing the fluid may solve your problem.

A faulty ***transmission vacuum modulator,*** as found on very old cars, also can suck transmission fluid into the engine, where it's burned in the ***cylinders*** and causes light gray smoke to come out of the tailpipe. Have the mechanic check the problem.

There is hope . . . being low on transmission fluid can cause the same symptoms as a transmission that needs servicing, repair, or replacement. To avoid paying for work that your vehicle may not need, be sure to read Chapter 18 before you opt for major transmission surgery.

# Leaks

Pay close attention to leaks. Running a vehicle that's drastically low on a vital fluid can cause severe damage. After you find the source of the leak, the following information will help you decide whether you can handle it yourself or you need professional help.

If water is getting into your vehicle's passenger compartment, check the rubber *gaskets* and weatherstripping around the windows, doors, and sunroof, and refer to Chapter 24 for instructions on how to fix it.

Unless your vehicle has a protective shield under the engine area, here's an easy way to see whether anything is leaking out from under your vehicle and a few pointers to help you decide what to do about it:

1.  **Park your vehicle overnight on a clean patch of pavement or a large, clean piece of white paper.**

    Either tape some sheets of paper together or buy a roll of plain white commercial wrapping paper. Newspaper is too absorbent and can change the color of the stains.

2.  **Place marks on the paper to show where each of the four wheels is resting, and indicate the front and rear ends of the vehicle.**

3.  **In the morning, move the vehicle and look for small puddles or traces of liquid on the ground or paper. Touch and smell each puddle or trace of liquid.**

Here's how to decipher the evidence:

>> **If it's clear, watery, and under the air conditioner,** it's probably just normal condensation if you've used the air conditioner recently.

>> **If it's black or dark brown, greasy, and located under the engine area,** it's probably *oil.* Figure out which part of the vehicle was over the spot: Look under the hood around the *oil filter* and the engine and under the vehicle for leaks around the *oil drain plug,* the *crankcase,* and the *oil pan* below it.

>> **If it's thick, black or tan oily liquid,** gear oil may be leaking from a *manual transmission,* the *differential,* an *axle,* or the steering gears. Any of these leaks needs immediate attention.

>> **If it's red, pink, reddish-brown, and greasy and you have an *automatic transmission,*** it's probably *transmission fluid.* Check the transmission *dipstick* (see Chapter 2), and if the level is low, top it off with the proper transmission fluid. Then check the dipstick again in a day or two. If it's low again, have a professional check the transmission to make sure that the seals are intact.

>> **If it's watery or slippery; green, red, blue, or yellow; and is coming from under the radiator or engine,** it's probably *coolant.* To check the radiator, *pressure cap,* engine, and hoses for leaks, turn to Chapter 12.

**WARNING**

Coolant is toxic to children and animals, so leaks need to be remedied quickly. If you can't locate the source of the leak or your vehicle is losing coolant on a regular basis, consult a mechanic.

>> **If it's oily; pink, red, or clear; and you find it toward the front bumper (usually on the driver's side),** it's probably *power-steering* fluid. The power-steering system is sealed and shouldn't lose fluid. Chapter 2 tells you how to check the dipstick. If the level is low, add more and check again in a couple of days. If it's low again, have a mechanic check things out. The good news is that electronic *power steering* systems eliminate the need for fluid entirely; Chapter 16 describes them.

>> **If it's a light-colored or clear fluid,** it may be *brake fluid.* Even if the leaks have dried, the stains should be visible. Depending on which part of the car was parked over the puddle or spot, check for brake fluid leaks around the *master cylinder* and around the *brake lines.* If the leak is where a wheel was standing, check down the inside surface of that wheel. If you find stains or wetness there, the *brake cylinder* could be leaking — or a dog could have "marked" your tires!

**WARNING**

Leaky brakes are too dangerous to leave unattended. Have a professional repair any brake fluid leaks immediately.

>> **If it smells like rotten eggs,** it's *battery* acid. Avoid getting it on your hands or clothes and have the battery replaced.

>> **If it smells like gasoline,** it probably is! (If you drive a *diesel,* get to know what *diesel fuel* smells like so you can identify it.) If the smell is coming from under the hood, check around the *fuel pump* and the *fuel injectors* — or the

*carburetor* if your vehicle still has one. If the leak seems to be under the center of the vehicle, check the *fuel lines.* If it's under the rear end, check the *fuel tank.* (Don't smoke while you do this!)

**WARNING**

Gasoline ignites easily, and gasoline vapors can explode, so if you smell gasoline — and you haven't just filled your tank — find the source of the leak and have it repaired immediately. If your usual repair facility isn't close by, either drive to the closest service station and have them repair it, or call your auto club and have them either fix it on the spot or tow the car to a repair facility.

If you can't locate the source of the leak and your vehicle is losing liquid from the radiator on a regular basis, Chapter 12 can help you find the leak and check your radiator *pressure cap.*

# Strange Sensations

This is a catchall category for those things that just "feel funny." Use the process of elimination to check anything that may cause your vehicle to run roughly: hoses, tires, brakes, *oil* levels, *spark plug* connections, the *cooling system, clutch, gearshift,* and *steering linkage.* (The book's index can steer you toward the chapters that include instructions for checking these things.)

Here are a few specific sensations that you may encounter:

» **If steering is difficult and you have *power steering,*** see "Check the power-steering fluid" in Chapter 2 for information about checking the power-steering *dipstick.* If it's low again soon after you fill it, check for leaks in the hoses leading from the unit to the front wheels.

» **If your car starts wandering instead of running in a straight line,** the cause may be worn steering components or wheels that are out of *alignment.* If the vehicle starts pulling to the left or right, one of the tires may be underinflated or faulty, or the front end may be out of *alignment.* Look for the solutions to these problems in Chapter 16.

» **If your car pulls to one side when you step on the brake pedal,** Chapter 15 tells you how to check your brakes.

» **If your vehicle vibrates at highway speeds, the wheels may need to be balanced.**

» **If the engine speeds up but your vehicle doesn't accelerate when you step on the gas pedal; if there's a delayed response (or none at all) when you shift gears; or if shifting suddenly becomes awkward or noisy,** check the transmission (see Chapter 18). If you have an **_automatic transmission,_** you may just be low on **_transmission fluid,_** or you may have a disconnected hose or plugged filter.

If you seek professional help, make sure that they check the problems that are cheapest to remedy before deciding that you need major transmission work!

If you notice anything strange when your vehicle's running, I strongly suggest that you do the under-the-hood check in Chapter 2. This easy, 15-minute monthly checkup can prevent 70 percent of the problems that could cause your vehicle to break down on the highway. By checking for symptoms of trouble in advance, you can save yourself time and money that otherwise would go to towing and repairs.

# Directional Signals

Directional signals are vitally important for communicating your intentions to other drivers. If the signals malfunction, they should be fixed immediately — hand signals just don't do the job. Here's what to do in a variety of situations:

>> **If _all_ your directional signal lights don't go on,** check the fuse. Chapter 6 has instructions for finding your fuse box and replacing **_fuses._**

>> **If _all_ your directional signal lights go on but don't blink,** your flasher unit is bad. This unit usually plugs directly into the fuse box, so look for trouble there first. After you replace the bulb or fuse that's defective, the dashboard flashers go back to normal. Isn't that lovely?

>> **If both signal lights on one side don't go on,** check to see whether the bulbs need replacing. If they don't, the signals may not be grounded properly. Your mechanic can tell you whether this is the case.

>> **If there's no light on your dashboard when you move your directional signal lever,** either the bulb on your dashboard flasher is out or the unit is malfunctioning.

>> **If one signal light is flashing faster or slower than the others,** check to see whether the bulb is the proper one for your vehicle. A heavy-duty bulb will flash faster than a standard bulb. Also check for loose connections or corrosion around the socket the bulb fits into.

Be sure to replace burned-out bulbs at once. They usually cost very little, and changing them involves little labor. Headlights are more expensive because they have to be replaced as a unit (see Chapter 6 for instructions).

**IN THIS CHAPTER**

» **Moving safely to the side of the road**

» **Figuring out what caused the problem**

» **Cooling down an overheated vehicle**

» **Dealing with a car that won't start**

» **Jump-starting safely**

Chapter **21**

# What to Do If Your Car Drops Dead or Won't Start

Whether your vehicle dies on the road or in front of your house, it's always a time of unrivaled panic and stress. But an informed, well-organized approach to diagnosing your sick monster's ills can pay off by getting you moving again with a minimum loss of time, money, and composure.

Whenever you encounter a term set in *this font*, you'll find it defined in the glossary in Appendix A.

**REMEMBER**

## Getting Off the Road Safely

If you have reason to believe that your vehicle is having a problem, try to get to the right-hand shoulder of the road as soon as possible, especially if you're on a high-way. Very often, if a vehicle is going to do its swan song while in motion, it will give you a couple of hints first. If you can recognize those hints as signs of impending disaster, you'll be able to get out of traffic before the car dies completely.

All the following symptoms are good reasons to head for the side of the road immediately:

>> Your vehicle experiences a sudden loss of power, or you suddenly have to floor the accelerator to maintain speed or to keep moving at all.

>> A warning light comes on.

>> Your engine suddenly runs roughly.

>> The engine is misfiring.

>> You hear unfamiliar noises.

>> Your vehicle is pulling to one side.

>> The pavement hasn't changed but your tires are no longer rolling along smoothly.

>> You have a flat tire.

WARNING

As you pull your vehicle off the road, keep the following safety procedures in mind:

>> **Try to coast along the shoulder until you're well away from any curves in the road behind you.** This placement pays off when you're ready to get back onto the road because you can spot oncoming traffic before it's on your tail. And if you're on a narrow road, try to park away from curves ahead as well so that you'll see what's coming at you when it's time to drive away.

>> **If the engine dies right on the highway and you can't get off the road, *don't get out of the car!*** I know that sitting in a dead vehicle with traffic piling up behind you is unnerving, but attempting to cross a high-speed freeway on foot is suicide.

Just think good thoughts and surround the car with white protective light (every little bit helps!), and, most importantly, stay calm. If it's after dark, put the interior light on so that you're more visible. If the engine is operable, keep it running so that you don't run the battery down.

Most heavily traveled highways are also heavily patrolled, and a nice highway patrol officer will be along before you know it. When the officer is on the scene, it's a simple matter of stopping traffic long enough to push your vehicle to the right-hand shoulder.

WARNING

Whether you've managed to park at the side of the road or you're stuck in a traffic lane, take these additional safety precautions:

» **Roll down the window on the driver's side, hang out a white cloth or piece of paper, and roll the window back up to secure it in place.** The cloth or paper alerts drivers that your vehicle is in trouble and that they should proceed around you. If you can easily reach the passenger-side window without getting out of the car, do the same on that side. Just try not to obstruct your ability to see out the windows.

» **If you know that you're going to need roadside assistance, use your cellphone to call your auto club or the highway patrol.** If you're reading this and you don't have a cellphone, resolve to get one immediately; it's the best protection against getting stuck in these situations and against carjackers. If you don't otherwise need a cellphone, get a low-cost one without a contract that lets you just pay as you go.

If you have no phone, you're *not* stuck in a highway traffic lane, and you can see an emergency call box only a few feet away, use the call box to call for help, get right back in the car, and lock the doors. If no call box is nearby, you're probably better off just hanging the white cloth or piece of paper out the window and waiting for the highway patrol to spot you.

In these days of daytime carjacking, walking along the highway alone can be dangerous. So is opening the door to what appear to be good Samaritans. If someone stops to help, just roll down the window an inch or two, thank them for their help, and ask them to phone the highway patrol or the AAA or CAA (if you're a member) and report your location.

» **To avoid being hit by a passing vehicle, never work on your vehicle from the side that's exposed to traffic.** If you can, drive farther off the road to a safe, well-traveled place, and try to reach into the trouble area from the front or the side that's away from traffic.

» **If it's *daylight,* put on your emergency blinkers or your left-turn signal to alert oncoming traffic to the fact that your vehicle isn't moving.** This is *not* a good idea at night because motorists coming up behind you may think that your vehicle is still rolling along the highway and run right into the rear end of your car. (Drunk drivers are especially prone to this sometimes fatal error.)

» **If it's *nighttime and you're not stuck in traffic,* quickly place warning lights or reflective markers about six feet behind the vehicle to alert traffic, and then get back in the car.** If you don't have lights or markers, either turn on the interior lights manually or leave the car door that's away from traffic open so that the interior lights stay on. Don't worry about running down the battery; the tow truck will either haul you away or jump a start if you need one.

**TIP**

» **To alert oncoming traffic, always carry reflective markers, a large battery-operated light, or a couple of milk cartons filled with wax and a wick in the trunk of your vehicle.** (I don't suggest carrying flares because they can be dangerous.) Forewarned is forearmed!

**WARNING**

>> **If you get a flat tire, *do not* attempt to change it unless you can get to the side of the road and the tire is on the side of the vehicle that's safely away from traffic.** Even then, I'd think twice about exposing myself to possible carjackers.

Because driving on a flat tire for any longer than it takes to park safely can destroy the tire, you need to replace it close to where it went flat. This is another reason subscribing to roadside service is a good idea!

If you have a flat tire in a place where no help is available, or if you're in your driveway or garage, you can find complete instructions on how to change a flat tire in Chapter 1.

## Troubleshooting the Problem

If you've managed to get off the road and into a safe area, and you want to try to deal with the situation yourself, it helps to view what happened in "dietary" terms: Your vehicle lives on a mixture of air, fuel, and fire — if it won't go, it's not getting one of those ingredients.

### Air

Air is simple — and probably not the problem. Your vehicle gets its air through the *cold air collector box,* or air cleaner. Unless the *air filter* inside it is totally clogged, your engine should be getting enough air to keep it going. In a worst-case scenario, something has gone amiss with your *engine control unit (ECU)* and it's keeping air from mixing properly with the fuel. If that's the case, a "Check Engine" light should be glowing on your dashboard and the best you can do is call a tow truck and get to a repair shop. But the problem is most likely something else: One of the vacuum hoses may have become disconnected, or your *PCV valve* may be malfunctioning, either of which could keep your car from breathing properly. To troubleshoot the problem, do the following to check the hoses and the PCV valve:

>> **Look at all the hoses under the hood.** Have any of them become disconnected or broken? Do you hear air whistling while the engine idles — if it can? One strategic lost hose can slow or stop your engine. If this is the case, reclamp the wanderer or tape the hole and you'll soon be on your way. Of course, if you make a habit of checking and replacing worn hoses *before* disaster strikes (see Chapters 2 and 12), you can avoid this trouble completely.

>> **Check your *PCV valve* to make sure that it's clear and functioning.** The "Servicing the PCV Valve" section in Chapter 8 can help you to do so.

# Fuel

Whether your vehicle runs on gasoline, has a *diesel* engine, or is a *hybrid* or an *alternatively fueled vehicle,* it may not be getting whatever fuel it needs to keep it going. Therefore, if the engine *turns over* but doesn't start running, the first question you need to answer is whether your *fuel tank* is empty. Even if your *fuel gauge* says that you still have some fuel, the gauge may be on the blink. When did you last fill the tank?

**WARNING**

No matter how nervous you are, never smoke when working on a vehicle, especially if you're dealing with the fuel system!

**WARNING**

Sometimes the problem is *too much* fuel. If you open the hood and find that everything is covered with gasoline, *don't try to start the engine!* Gasoline is too flammable to monkey around with. Just hoist that white flag and get help.

If you're not out of fuel and your vehicle lost power before it died, fuel is probably not getting to the engine. The following sections offer additional reasons that specific types of vehicles may not be getting enough fuel.

## Gasoline- and diesel-powered vehicles

If you have a modern vehicle with a multiport or sequential *fuel injection* system, either the *fuel pump* isn't pumping fuel or the *ECU* isn't triggering the fuel injectors. In either case, a professional will have to troubleshoot it.

## Ethanol, methanol, and flex-fuel vehicles

The potential problems are the same whether the vehicle is running on pure gasoline or on gasoline mixed with alcohol in one form or another: Either you're out of fuel no matter what the fuel gauge tells you, or the fuel pump or fuel injectors aren't working properly. In any case, there isn't much you can do but call for help and be patient until it arrives.

## Electric vehicles

**If an electric vehicle suddenly stops running,** the battery that drives it (the big one, not the little guy under the hood) has run out of juice. Either you've driven too long without recharging it or the system is malfunctioning. Dashboard *malfunction indicator lights* should alert you to this problem before the vehicle stops completely.

**If a cable that conducts the current from the battery to the motor has discon-nected,** don't try to deal with it yourself. You can't trace the cable to or from the motor to the battery, and the voltages are so high that you could put yourself in danger if you try to reconnect any loose cable or wire you find. Get the vehicle towed to a repair shop that can handle battery-powered electric cars and trucks, and let them do the job.

## Hybrids

Hybrids combine a gasoline engine and an electric motor. If a hybrid vehicle sud-denly stops running, the systems are too sophisticated to try to troubleshoot yourself, and don't expect the tow truck operator to be able to troubleshoot or repair it. Because being pulled by a tow truck can damage your hybrid, request a *flat-bed* tow truck to get the vehicle to the nearest dealership that sells your vehi-cle and let them deal with it.

## Natural gas, hydrogen, fuel cells, and other exotica

Natural gas and hydrogen are stored under great pressure and are definitely too dangerous to monkey with yourself. If your vehicle operates under any of these systems, request to be towed by a *flat-bed* truck to your nearest dealership because most service stations aren't able to deal with these fuel sources either.

## Fire

If you think that your engine is getting enough air and fuel, you're probably having *ignition system* trouble. As I explain in Chapter 4, on traditional vehicles the "fire" is really electric current that's stored in the *battery,* replaced by the *alterna-tor,* monitored by *sensors,* and directed by the *ECU* to the *spark plugs* in the *cylinders* at the proper time. If something along the way goes wrong and the spark fails to reach the plugs, all the air and fuel in the world won't produce *combustion* in the cylinders, and the vehicle won't go. Because the engine was running before it died, it's probably not the fault of the battery, *solenoid,* or *starter.*

If just one spark plug suddenly malfunctions, the engine will continue to run on the other cylinders. It won't run smoothly, but it will get you off the road and into a repair shop.

**If your car has an** *electronic ignition system,* the *ignition module* may have gone bad. Because these vehicles have high-energy ignition systems that operate at 47,000 volts or higher, *the old technique of pulling a distributor or spark plug cable to test for a spark is unsafe.* Whether the vehicle has a *distributorless ignition system* or has an *electronic ignition,* you need to have a professional check it out. The good news is that these systems aren't prone to breaking down, so they probably aren't the problem. Chapter 5 gives you a good view of how both systems work.

**TECHNICAL STUFF**

**If your vehicle is an older model with a *non-electronic ignition system,*** you can check the *distributor cap* to see whether the spark is getting from there to the *coil* and on to the *spark plugs.*

As you can see, unless you're out of fuel, most modern vehicles that drop dead on the road just can't be dealt with on the spot. In addition to the causes I've already addressed, sometimes part of your engine has given out. If it's the *transmission,* or some other part that's really expensive to replace, you may be saying good-bye to Old Faithful if its *blue book* value is less than the cost of parts and labor. On the bright side, the sophisticated systems in most modern vehicles are relatively trouble-free; you usually have plenty of warning before they give up the ghost. Of course, if you haven't checked and maintained your vehicle properly — if you've ignored the *malfunction indicator lights,* the knockings, the smoke from the *tailpipe,* the hesitations, and the other symptoms that I cover in Chapter 20 — well, you asked for it.

# Handling a Vehicle That Overheats on a Hot Day

It's rare with modern vehicles, but even the happiest, most beautifully tuned vehicle can overheat (nobody's perfect). If you find yourself in stop-and-go traffic or climbing a steep grade on an extremely hot day, and your dashboard temperature indicator starts to rise or a *malfunction indicator light* comes on, here's how to help your vehicle regain its cool:

>> **At the first sign of overheating, shut off your air conditioner and open your windows.** Doing so decreases the load on the engine and helps it cool off.

>> **If you continue to overheat, turn on the heater and blower.** Doing so transfers the heat from the engine to the passenger compartment of the vehicle. (This does wonders for your overheated engine but very little for you!)

>> **If you're stopped in traffic and the temperature gauge is rising, shift into Neutral or Park and rev the engine a little.** Doing so makes the *water pump* and the *fan* speed up, which draws more liquid and air through the *radiator.* The increased air and liquid circulation helps cool things off.

>> **Try not to ride your brakes.** In stop-and-go traffic, crawl along slowly, on little more than an *idle,* rather than moving up and then braking repeatedly. Brake drag increases the load on the engine and makes it heat up. If traffic is

crawling, move up only when the gap between you and the vehicle in front of you gets too large.

>> **If you think that your vehicle is about to boil over, drive to the right-hand side of the road, open the hood, and sit there until things cool off.** Remember, *don't open the radiator cap* under these circumstances, and if your engine has boiled over, don't add water until the engine is quite cool again.

If you must add water when the engine is still a *little* warm, add the water *slowly* while the engine is running in Neutral or Park. Follow the instructions at the beginning of this chapter to park where you can safely get out and open your hood. Then, to avoid the possibility of burning yourself, follow the instructions in Chapter 12 for opening a radiator **pressure cap** and adding liquid to the system safely.

# Overheating When It Isn't Hot Outside

Although hot weather is the most common cause of overheating, many other factors can cause the same problem. If your vehicle overheats in traffic in normal weather, one of the following may be the culprit:

>> **The water and coolant level in the radiator is low.** If you haven't checked your fluid level in a while (or ever), check it now, either by looking at the level through the side of the **coolant recovery system** or by following the instructions in the "Check the Coolant" section in Chapter 2.

>> **There's a leak in the *cooling system*.** Chapter 12 has an entire section that explains where to look for leaks in various parts of the cooling system and what to do after you find them.

>> **If you can't locate any leaks, your *thermostat* may be malfunctioning.** Obviously, you can't replace the thermostat at the side of the road, but Chapter 12 has instructions for doing so cheaply and easily when you're safely back home. In the meantime, if you can park and get to the thermostat *safely*, you can eliminate this malfunction as a possibility. Wait until the engine cools down *completely*, and use those instructions to remove the old thermostat and reconnect the hoses without it. If the engine starts up and runs well without the thermostat, the old one was probably screwing up the works.

Get a new thermostat immediately if you find that your old one isn't working. Driving for long distances without a thermostat can damage your engine.

>> **If none of these seems to be the problem and your vehicle continues to overheat, check out Chapter 12 for other possible causes and their solutions.**

# If Your Vehicle Won't Start

Consider those panicky times when your vehicle won't start (they're definitely on my "Top Ten List of Lousy Situations!"). If you left your lights, heater, radio, or some other electrical gizmo on after you parked the car and turned off the engine, you know what the trouble is: Your *battery* is dead. The last section of this chapter, "Jumping a start," explains the safest way to jump-start your vehicle.

Of course, there are other possible reasons that your vehicle won't start. The next section lists them.

## Won't-start symptoms

Your conventionally fueled vehicle may not start for a number of reasons. The following list outlines the most common circumstances and tells you what action you can take to try to remedy each situation:

>> **The car is silent when you turn the key in the ignition.** Check the *battery* terminal cable connections (see Chapter 2). If they look really corroded, you need to clean the battery posts and cable connectors or replace the cables, following the instructions in Chapter 2. Reattach the cable connectors to the battery, making sure they are firmly in place. Now try again to start the engine.

>> **The car makes a clicking noise but won't start.** This sound usually means a dead battery. If not, check the wiring to and from the *starter* for a loose connection.

>> **The engine cranks over but won't start.** You may be out of fuel, or the fuel isn't getting to your engine (see "Fuel" earlier in this chapter). If it's not a fuel problem, the electrical spark isn't getting through to the spark plugs (see "Fire" earlier in this chapter).

>> **The engine starts but dies.** If you have *fuel injection,* you need professional help.

>> **The car won't start on rainy days.** If you have a *non-electronic ignition system* or an *electronic ignition* with a *distributor cap,* check inside the cap for dampness.

**WARNING**

Be sure the ignition is off and the vehicle is in Neutral or Park before you raise the hood and remove the distributor cap.

If you find moisture, get some mechanic's solvent from your friendly service station — they use it to clean car parts — or buy an aerosol can of it at an auto supply store. To evaporate any dampness inside the distributor cap, turn the cap upside down and pour or spray some solvent into it. Swish it around and pour it out. Then dry the cap as best you can with a clean, lint-free rag, and replace the cap.

**WARNING**

Use only *clean* solvent; even a tiny speck of dirt can foul the points. Gasoline won't do because a spark can ignite gasoline fumes and cause an explosion or a fire.

>> **The car won't start on cold mornings.** If you have *fuel injection,* you need to have a professional diagnose the cold-start problems.

>> **The engine misses while *idling.*** The *spark plugs* may be misfiring (see Chapter 6), the *fuel pump* may be malfunctioning, or the *fuel filter* may be clogged (see Chapter 8).

>> **The engine misses or hesitates during acceleration.** There are several reasons why this may happen: It could be faulty *spark plugs,* dirty *fuel injectors,* or a malfunctioning *ECU.* Some do-it-yourselfers buy diagnostic computers and learn to read the trouble codes, but chances are it will turn out to be something you won't want to undertake yourself. It's easiest to have a service facility put the vehicle on the "scope" and deal with it.

>> **The engine is *knocking* or pinging.** In older gasoline-powered vehicles, this usually was caused by using fuel with the wrong *octane rating.* In modern vehicles, the *ECU* senses engine noise and adjusts the *timing, fuel/air mixture,* and other factors to handle octane differences. Still, because using fuel with the wrong octane rating can affect your vehicle's health and performance, if you aren't sure whether it should be running on regular unleaded or premium gasoline, check your owner's manual. If you have the right fuel and you want to track the problem down yourself, checking the *cooling system* (see Chapter 12) and doing a *compression check* on the engine *cylinders* (see Chapter 8) may reveal the answer.

## Jumping a start

If your battery has died, you *may* be able to use *jumper cables* to jump a start from some good Samaritan's vehicle — with some important exceptions.

**WARNING**

If either vehicle has an *electronic ignition system* or is an *alternatively fueled vehicle,* the use of jumper cables *may* damage it. If your vehicle is one that may be damaged in this way, you may find a warning to that effect in the *owner's manual* or on a decal under the hood. Even if you don't find a warning, it pays to be safe, so call the service department at your dealership and ask about your vehicle's make, model, and year.

**WARNING**

If you can safely use jumper cables on your vehicle, make sure that the battery on the good Samaritan's vehicle has at least as much voltage as your own. As long as you hook up the cables properly (and the proper way is the same in every case), it doesn't matter whether your vehicle has negative *ground* and the GS's vehicle has positive ground, or your vehicle has an *alternator* and the GS's vehicle has a *generator.*

To safely jump a start, follow these steps:

**1.** **Take out your jumper cables.**

It's a good idea to buy a set of jumper cables (see Chapter 3 for tips) and keep them in the trunk compartment. If you don't have jumper cables, you have to find a good Samaritan who not only is willing to assist you but who has jumper cables as well.

**2.** **Place both vehicles in Park or Neutral, with their *ignition switches* shut off and their *parking brakes* on.**

**3.** **Connect the cables.**

The positive cable has red clips at either end, and the negative cable has black clips. *It's important to attach them in the proper order:*

**1.** Attach one of the red clips to the *positive* terminal of *your* battery (it has "POS" or "+" on it, or it's bigger than the negative terminal).

**2.** Attach the other red clip to the *positive* terminal of the GS's car.

**3.** Attach one of the *black* clips to the negative terminal on the GS's battery.

**4.** Attach the last black clip to an *unpainted* metal surface on your car that *isn't* near the battery. (I usually use one of the metal struts that holds the hood open.)

Figure 21-1 shows how both the positive and negative cables should be connected.

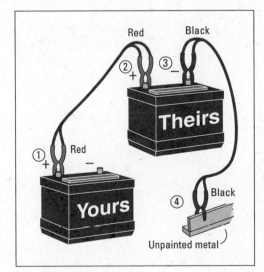

**FIGURE 21-1:**
Make sure to connect jumper cables in the proper order.

**4.** **Try to start your vehicle.**

If it won't start, make sure that the cables are properly connected and have the good Samaritan run his or her engine for five minutes. Then try to start your car again. If it still won't start, your battery may be beyond help.

**5.** **Disconnect the cables, thank the good Samaritan, and resume your life.**

*If the jump works and your car starts, don't shut off your engine!* Drive around for at least 15 minutes to recharge your battery. If the car won't start the next time you use it, the battery isn't holding a charge and needs to be replaced.

TIP

If your *alternator* warning light stays on or the gauge on the dashboard continues to point to "Discharge" after your car has been running, make sure that your *fan belt* or *accessory belt* is tight enough to run your alternator properly. If your battery keeps going dead, have a professional check both the battery and your alternator.

In any case, never drive around with a *malfunction indicator light* on or a gauge that reads in the danger zone; have the vehicle checked out immediately — that's why those lights and gauges are there!

IN THIS CHAPTER

» **Choosing the type of service facility that's right for you**

» **Paying attention to the certification of the mechanic and/or shop**

» **Evaluating automotive service facilities and deciphering a mechanic's invoice**

» **Maintaining a good relationship with a repair shop**

» **Getting satisfaction on any complaint**

Chapter **22**

# When All Else Fails: Finding and Dealing with a Good Mechanic

ou just moved and your trusted former repair facility is too far away. Or you bought a new set of wheels, and your old shop doesn't work on that particular type of vehicle. You haven't the faintest idea of where to go when your vehicle requires service that's beyond your abilities, or where to get help in an emergency. The phone book is full of ads, but how can you tell which shops are reliable and which are just waiting to take advantage of you? Relax, dear friend; you've come to the right place for advice.

In this chapter, I tell you how to find a good service facility, give you tips for establishing a good relationship with one, and provide you with a winning strategy for getting satisfaction on *any* type of consumer complaint.

Whenever you encounter a term set in *this font*, you'll find it defined in the glossary in Appendix A.

# Choosing a Service Facility

Several kinds of shops repair and service vehicles: dealerships, chain stores, specialists, and independents. How do you decide which is the right shop for you? Each has its drawbacks as well as its advantages. The following sections describe each of these service options so that you can choose the type that's best for you.

Of course, the type of facility you select may vary depending on the kind of specialized service your vehicle requires. If you drive a *hybrid* or other *alternatively fueled vehicle,* it's probably best to stick to the dealership. If you drive a traditionally powered vehicle, you may be able to depend on an experienced independent for the best deal on reliable, competent service at a good price. You may find the best buys on tires at a major chain and the best brake or transmission work done at shops that specialize in them. See the section "Finding a Reliable Service Facility" for more information.

## Dealerships

When they buy a new vehicle, many people assume that they have to use the dealership's service facilities, at least until the *warranty* period is over. Be aware that, in most cases, you can have warranty service (but not repairs) done by any licensed independent mechanic as long as all the service requirements in your *owner's manual* are fulfilled and you've kept the invoices for service and maintenance to prove it. (There are some exceptions, so read your warranties before going elsewhere for specialized work.) Of course, you may want to stay with the dealership that sold you the vehicle because dealerships may offer the following advantages:

>> **They often provide extra services to ensure goodwill.** These can include notification of any maintenance that's due, special sales on service and optional equipment, and so on.

>> **They usually have a variety of factory-trained specialists on the premises.** The advantage is that you may be able to have brake work, transmission work, and sometimes even bodywork done at the same place.

>> **They stock a wide variety of original parts and equipment *(OEM)* made specifically for your vehicle.** This not only assures you of satisfaction if parts fail, but original parts may increase the resale value of your vehicle.

>> **If you have a complaint, you're dealing with an established company that's financially able to reimburse you and that's insured to cover any major lawsuits that may result.**

However, dealerships have disadvantages to consider as well:

>> **Dealerships may be more expensive than other types of service facilities.** Independent shops usually have a lower overhead to support.

>> **The sales and service departments of a dealership often operate as separate entities.** The attitude may be, "We have more work than we can handle, so if you're not happy here, you can go somewhere else." If you feel that's the case, complain to the dealership.

>> **You probably won't receive the personalized service that you may get from an independent repair shop.** At the dealership, you generally deal with a service writer who assigns your vehicle to the next technician available when its number comes up. Of course, if you build a good relationship with the service writer, he or she may honor your request for a specific technician who's familiar with your vehicle and its quirks.

## Chain and department stores

Large chain stores and department stores that have automotive service departments offer their own set of pros and cons. Some advantages include:

>> **They can be less expensive than dealerships.**

>> **They usually stock a wide variety of parts, many of which are made to their specifications and carry their brand name.** How these parts compare in price and quality to the original equipment supplied by the car manufacturer varies, depending on which chain you deal with.

**TECHNICAL STUFF**

The only time you absolutely *don't* want to use anything but original equipment is when you're restoring a classic car or if there are no *reliable* aftermarket parts available.

>> **They usually provide good guarantees on parts and labor.** And if you have a complaint, they're generally motivated to keep your goodwill.

>> **Large chain stores maintain branches nationwide that honor their warranties and guarantees.** If you move or travel frequently, this feature can be very beneficial.

Chain and department stores also have their disadvantages, including the following:

>> **They use service writers, and the work tends to be impersonal, with a new technician working on your vehicle each time.**

>> **Technicians at some chains get a commission on the parts they sell.** This may motivate them to sell you a new part instead of repairing an old one, or to perform work that your vehicle may not really need.

Here's a feature of large chains that has both positive and negative aspects: They're good training grounds for inexperienced technicians who are just out of school and are working at their first professional jobs. If it falls into incompetent hands, your vehicle may turn out to be a guinea pig as well as a gas hog. On the other hand, it may be lucky enough to be tended to by bright, enthusiastic young people with all the latest knowledge and techniques at their fingertips.

## Independents

An independent service facility can offer the best — or the worst — alternative. Consider these points:

>> **Honest, reliable, and experienced independents can provide personalized service based on high standards of excellence.** They can offer you the opportunity to communicate directly with a professional who knows you, knows your vehicle, and cares a great deal about maintaining a good reputation because most independent business comes from referrals.

>> **Many independent shops are less expensive than dealerships.** Others, especially those that service only luxury cars or high-performance sports cars, may offer the finest workmanship at relatively exorbitant rates. A cherished few provide fine workmanship at low prices — these people are probably saints disguised in greasy coveralls!

WARNING

>> **Check carefully to be sure that the shop is reliable and able to do the job.** Expertise, the ability to stay current by attending classes held by automakers (who sometimes bar independents from enrollment), the availability of specialized tools and *service manuals,* and the variety of parts in inventory may vary from one independent shop to another. A good independent knows where to find the proper talent, borrow the tools, and buy *OEM* parts at a good price. An unreliable one patches things together, uses cheap parts, and hopes for the best.

# Specialists

There are two types of specialists: One type is a specialized chain store or independent facility that deals with a specific kind of repair, such as brake work, transmission work, bodywork, or muffler replacement. The other type of specialist is an independent shop that works only on specific makes or vehicles, such as Ferraris, Volvos, motorcycles, or classic cars.

Here are the pros and cons to consider:

>> **A reliable specialist can provide the experience, specialized tools, and extensive inventory that may be unavailable at a shop that handles everything in general and nothing in particular.** If you know that the trouble with your vehicle resides in a particular automotive system, you may want to look for a well-established specialist who focuses on that type of work.

WARNING

>> **Some specialized chains that sell and install cheap parts may be more interested in selling new parts than in repairing old ones.** Their lifetime guarantees may keep you coming back to pay more for the labor to install those "free" replacement parts than you'd spend initially on higher-quality parts that last longer.

Check out national chains that specialize in the type of repair you need in consumer publications such as *Consumer Reports* (www.consumerreports.org) to be sure that the one you choose has a good reputation for durable parts and quality service.

# Finding a Reliable Service Facility

Several organizations test, rate, and certify good service facilities or individual technicians. If you're unsure about a particular shop, you can feel pretty secure if you see a sign posted in the shop or a patch on a technician's uniform that indicates that the shop or the individual has achieved recognition from one of the following programs:

>> **AAA (American Automobile Association) or Canadian Automobile Association (CAA) Approved Repair Facilities:** Both the AAA and the Canadian Automobile Association have rating programs for auto repair shops. Representatives from these organizations visit and evaluate service facilities to make sure that they meet high standards for reliable work at a fair price, willingness to resolve complaints, and a history of few complaints. To qualify, shops must provide customers with written estimates of all costs and offer a

minimum warranty on parts and labor of 12 months or 12,000 miles (12 months or 20,000 kilometers in Canada).

In most cases and with some exceptions, both the AAA and the CAA are willing to arbitrate disputes between members and approved shops if negotiations between the shop and the member aren't successful.

To find an Approved Repair Facility in your area, look for the AAA or CAA logo on display at a shop, contact your local or regional association office, or visit www. aaa.com or www.caa.ca to find contact information for national headquarters.

If you're a member of one of these clubs and you have an unresolved complaint about an approved shop, contact the Approved Auto Repair Service Program at your local auto club or its national headquarters.

» **ASE (National Institute for Automotive Service Excellence) Certified Technicians:** The ASE certifies technicians (not individual shops) by testing them on a variety of automobile repair specialties, including brakes and transmissions. ASE-certified automotive technicians and other service professionals can be identified in several ways: the blue and white ASE Blue Seal of Excellence sign displayed by a facility, the ASE certificates earned by their technicians displayed in the office or waiting room, or the ASE shoulder patch on a technician's uniform. To obtain a list of ASE-certified technicians and/or Blue Seal businesses in your area, visit www.asecert.org.

» **ADS (Association of Diesel Specialists):** If you own a diesel-powered vehicle that's out of *warranty* and you're looking for a reliable diesel mechanic, look in your local yellow pages under "Automobile Repair & Service" for a shop that displays the ADS logo. ADS-authorized shops must send their technicians to factory schools to keep abreast of new parts, techniques, and systems; must meet high standards for cleanliness; and must stock sufficient tools and parts to deal efficiently with most diesel repair and maintenance jobs. To obtain a list of authorized shops, visit www.diesel.org.

» **ASA (National Automotive Service Association):** The ASA advances professionalism and excellence in the automotive repair industry through education, representation, and member services. For a list of ASA member shops, look for the ASA logo in your local yellow pages under "Automobile Repair & Service" or visit www.asashop.org.

» **Service and achievement awards:** Check out the framed certificates hanging in the facility manager's office. Reliable facilities often receive awards for customer service excellence. Also look for certificates awarded to individual technicians who have completed factory-training programs that qualify them to operate specialized electronic equipment and for grateful letters from satisfied customers.

- » **Better Business Bureau:** Check with your local Better Business Bureau (www.bbb.org) to find out whether a shop has been the subject of numerous consumer complaints.

- » **Referrals:** I've always felt that the best way to find a good mechanic is the same way you find a doctor, lawyer, or plumber — through referrals. Ask people who drive the same make vehicle as you do where they go for repairs, and then check out the shops that are conveniently located.

# Evaluating a Facility

TIP

A quick way to do a preliminary check on an auto repair facility is to call a shop and ask for its basic prices on regular maintenance jobs for the make and model vehicle you drive — ask about flushing the cooling system and changing the oil and oil filter, for example. Also ask what the hourly labor rate is and whether the shop uses *OEM (original equipment manufacturer)* parts for your particular vehicle.

Before you need service, follow up a positive phone interview with an unannounced visit to gather answers to the following questions:

- » **Is the place clean and well-organized or filthy and cluttered?** Auto repair is a trade that calls for patience and precision. If the shop is sloppy and disorganized, the work may be, too.

- » **Does the shop have *modern* electronic diagnostic and testing equipment?** Up-to-date machines save time (and your money) by pinpointing trouble areas and checking adjustments and tolerances. Ask if shop technicians attend factory schools and seminars run by manufacturers to learn how to use the more sophisticated analyzers and if they keep up-to-date on new systems.

WARNING

Modern vehicles require sophisticated, specialized, diagnostic computer equipment, sometimes specific to the make and model of vehicle. Find out whether your vehicle is in that category. If it is, you may have to take it to your local dealership for any work involving computer-controlled functions.

- » **Does the shop have the necessary tools to do your job?** Ask whether any part of the job will have to be sent out to a specialist. If so, ask if the shop will only charge you what the specialist billed them, or if the shop will increase the charge to compensate themselves for the time and effort involved in delivering the vehicle to the specialist and picking it up afterward.

**TIP**

If the entire job has to be done by an outside specialist, consider taking the vehicle there directly instead of having your shop serve as a middleman. Avoid conflicts with your service facility by saying that you want another estimate.

>> **What form of payment does the shop accept?** The advantage of using a credit card is that in the event of a dispute, you can withhold payment until the credit card company investigates the situation.

>> **How long does the shop guarantee its repairs?** Guarantees usually range from one month to one year. If a shop doesn't think that its work will endure for at least three months, go elsewhere.

>> **Can the shop provide references?** Most shops allow you to call a few of its customers who have the same vehicle to see whether they were satisfied with service.

**TIP**

Find out how the shop determines the price you pay for repairs. The answer has a great impact on your wallet as well as on the quality of the work.

>> **By the clock:** Any type of automotive repair facility may determine the cost of a job by multiplying a fixed hourly labor rate by the time it took to complete the work. This simple system encourages technicians to take the time to do their best work. However, this system makes it difficult to accurately estimate what the job will cost because unexpected technical problems can raise the price significantly.

>> **Pre-established price lists:** Specialists and major chains such as brake, muffler, and transmission shops often set fixed prices for specific jobs. Sometimes several basic services are combined into one package. Prices are easy to understand and usually are competitive. You don't pay more if the job goes slowly.

>> **Flat rates:** Most shops base their prices on the *Flat Rate Manual,* which lists every job that can be done and the amount of time it should take to accomplish the job on a specific vehicle. Estimates are accurate because they aren't affected if a job takes longer than normal. However, you may be charged for the amount of time listed in the manual no matter how little time the work actually takes. Few shops will keep a technician who can't "beat the book" by a substantial amount of time, so mechanics may skimp and cut corners to complete repairs as quickly as possible.

>> **Variable flat rates:** Some dealerships price jobs not only by the *Flat Rate Manual* but also by the level of skill necessary to do the work properly. Maintenance jobs usually are priced at a lower rate than more sophisticated repairs. You aren't penalized if the job takes longer than expected.

>> **Flat rates and parts commissions:** At many chains or department stores, the mechanic shares in the profits on the sale of parts. You aren't penalized if the job takes longer than expected, but you may have to pay more for a new part that could have been repaired cheaply and easily, or for parts that you never needed in the first place.

# Getting the Best Possible Deal

**TIP**

A big repair job is like major surgery: Not only do you want the best possible surgeon, but you also want to be sure that the surgery is necessary and that it's done under the best possible terms. Consumer laws in many states hold the repair facility responsible for failing to provide a written estimate, failing to notify the customer if the estimate increases radically because more problems have been uncovered, and failing to turn over parts that have been replaced when the customer has asked that they be saved. Because this may *not* be the case in your state, follow these guidelines whenever you bring your vehicle in for maintenance or repair, or to a shop you haven't patronized before:

>> **If you're dealing with a new shop or you're faced with major repairs, get at least a second opinion and an estimate of costs from another repair shop.** If there's a big discrepancy, or if it's a very costly job, get a third estimate and discard any that are much higher or lower than the others.

>> **Ask for detailed, *written* estimates and updates.** Require the shop to call you *before* they start the repairs if they find that the job will cost more than originally estimated. Beware of general statements; try to get as detailed an estimate as possible.

>> **If major work is underway, ask to be notified about what they find right after they open the vehicle up to diagnose the problem.** Will it be a simple adjustment or a major *rebuild?* Ask to be called if that estimate changes because the shop uncovers other problems during the course of the estimated repairs.

>> **Save yourself from paying for unnecessary R&R (which means "removal and replacement," not "rest and relaxation!").** If the technicians have to open the transmission or the *cylinder head* or get into the engine or any other hard-to-get-at area in order to make a repair, ask them to check the whole area for any other parts that look as though they're about to need repair or replacement. A good chunk of the cost for labor is usually associated with just taking stuff apart and putting it back together again, so if the shop has to do removal and repair only once, you save money.

>> **Don't give the shop *carte blanche* to replace anything they please.** Tell them that you will want to see how badly the parts are wearing before they proceed with any unauthorized work, and call around for estimates before you agree to additional major surgery if you feel that the price the shop quotes is out of line. (However, keep in mind that you'll have to pay the new shop for R&R, as well.)

>> **Ask that all the parts that are replaced be returned to you, regardless of whether the laws in your state require it.** That way you can be sure that you're getting what you pay for.

>> **Ask for credit for the *core charge* on any rebuildable part that's going to be replaced.** Always ask what the shop will do with your old part. If they're going to rebuild and resell it or sell it to a rebuilder, the core charge should be deducted from the price of the part that you buy to replace it.

Now go home, cross your fingers, and wait for the operation to be over. Of course, you may still be ripped off, but you'll know that you've done everything possible to prevent that from happening. And because you've been so diligent and are so familiar with the parts and systems involved, you just may scare a potential cheat into doing a good job and charging you properly for it.

If, despite all your precautions, you end up getting ripped off anyway, the "Complaining Effectively" section later in this chapter shows you how to get satisfaction on *any* type of complaint.

## Always check the invoice carefully

When you bring a vehicle into a service facility, you receive an original invoice with information identifying your vehicle, listing the work they plan to do, and an estimate of what it will cost. When the work is finished, they will give you a final copy of this invoice that lists the actual work done and the cost of the labor and parts it required. This section tells you what to look for when you receive the original, estimated invoice and how to understand the final bill.

Make sure that the original invoice for the job includes a written *guarantee* on parts and labor, and find out whether any of the parts installed comes with its own *warranty.* (This is especially important if it's a big job that involves expensive parts.) Knowing just where the responsibility lies in the event of a dispute or a malfunctioning part always pays off.

A standard mechanic's invoice is divided into separate areas, each of which serves a different purpose. To decipher an invoice, match the number preceding each of the following items with the corresponding number on the invoice shown in Figure 22-1:

**❶ Description of the work:** This area should list each job that needed to be done. When you pick up your vehicle from the shop, check this area item by item to see that everything was taken care of.

**❷ Labor charges:** These charges are shown in fractions of an hour. If a job seems to have taken an excessively long time, ask to check the *Flat Rate Manual,* which is a listing of every job that can be done on a vehicle, with the amount of time it should take to accomplish it.

If the hours seem right, multiply them by the shop's hourly rate to make sure that the math is correct. Then check that the labor total is the same as that shown in the Totals column ❺.

**❸ Parts used:** Each part should be listed with its price. Make sure that the costs have been added correctly and that the total is the same as that shown in the Totals column ❺.

**❹ Subcontracted repairs:** This area should show all the work that was sent out of the shop to be done by a specialist. The total costs should be repeated in the Totals column ❺.

**❺ Totals:** All the charges in the previous sections are repeated and totaled separately in this column. You pay the final figure.

In addition, every invoice should have a space for a written estimate ❻ and a phone number ❼ where you can be reached if necessary. You'll be asked to sign the estimate on the signature line ❽ when you receive the original estimated invoice, before the work begins.

Be sure to read the small print above the signature line before you sign. The small print should cover only your approval of the estimate and the fact that you're willing to allow the technicians to drive your vehicle in order to test, diagnose, and repair it.

**TIP**

The reverse side of the invoice often contains information about the shop's *warranty* and the *mechanic's lien,* which allows service facilities in some states to sell your vehicle if you refuse to pay for services. For this reason, if a dispute occurs, you should always pay your bill and then seek restitution. As I mention earlier in this chapter, credit cards really come in handy in these situations. To find out how to get satisfaction regarding a dispute, turn to the "Complaining Effectively" section later in this chapter.

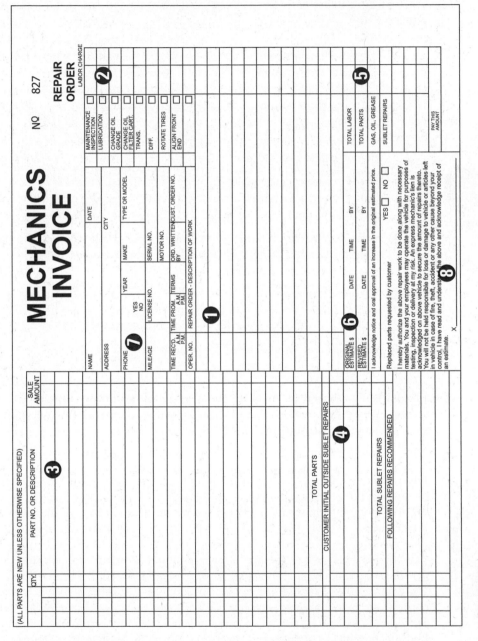

**FIGURE 22-1:**
A standard mechanic's invoice.

# Establish a good relationship with your service facility

Finding a mechanic who's reliable, honest, intelligent, efficient, and relatively inexpensive isn't enough. You should aim for "most favored customer" status. After you discover an outstanding automotive shop, the ball is in your court when it comes to establishing a good and lasting relationship that will have them going out of their way to make you happy. Even though most small businesses are struggling to stay alive these days, a good independent service facility is an exception. Every outstanding one that I've encountered has had more business than time to deal with it.

**TRUE STORY**

When I moved to a new city and needed someone I could trust to do major work or emergency surgery on Honeybun, my precious little classic car, I had to beg a highly recommended specialist in classic Mercedes to take me on as a customer. Only the facts that I had restored Honeybun myself and promised never to bother him with maintenance got him to agree. We became good friends, in no small part because I faithfully followed these guidelines:

>> **Call for an appointment.** Don't just show up and expect the shop to drop everything and take care of you.

>> **Get your vehicle into the shop early (by 8:30 or 9:00 a.m. at the latest) if you hope to get it out the same day.** Allow sufficient time to give the technician or service writer a full account of what you want done or what you've found to be wrong with the car.

>> **Bring along a written list of the things you want serviced or repaired.** Include a phone number where you can be reached if questions arise or if the work is going to cost more than the original estimate.

>> **On your list of what should be serviced or repaired, be as specific as possible about the symptoms you've experienced.** This is of great use to the technicians who work on the vehicle. Help them out even more by clarifying *what* is happening, *when* it happens, and *where* the trouble seems to be located.

**TIP**

To give you an idea of what kinds of things to look for, important symptoms include:

- Warning lights and abnormal gauge readings

- Abnormal changes in acceleration, braking, mileage, steering, and fluid levels

- Drips, leaks, odors, vibrations, and smoke signals

- Any change in the sounds the vehicle makes when starting up, on the road, or coming to a stop

- Unevenly or prematurely worn belts, tires, and hoses

If you can provide enough information to help the shop diagnose the trouble easily, you won't have to pay for test drives and electronic diagnostic procedures that may cost more than the simple adjustments or repairs that are necessary.

**WARNING**

>> **Provide the clearest information you can regarding all the symptoms, but *do not diagnose the problem yourself!*** If you tell a shop that your vehicle needs a specific job done on it, then that's the work that will be done, and you'll pay for it *whether the vehicle needed it or not.* If you want to inquire whether the trouble *might* be caused by a malfunction in a specific part, then do so but keep it in the form of a question. The final diagnosis must be up to the repair shop so that it can be responsible if the diagnosis turns out to be wrong.

>> **Keep a maintenance record on your vehicle and bring a photocopy for the shop's records if it didn't perform the past maintenance.** I provide a blank *Maintenance Record,* as well as a *Specifications Record* for basic information about a vehicle that will come in handy when shopping for parts, in Appendix B at the back of this book.

>> **Don't press to get the job done fast unless you're really in a bind.** A great way to take the pressure off everyone is to ask whether the shop has a spare vehicle, or *loaner,* that you can borrow until you get yours back.

>> **Call to make sure that your vehicle is ready before you make the trip to pick it up.** If it isn't ready, try to be understanding (unless the shop is chronically slow about getting work done). If it's a matter of parts that were ordered but not delivered on time, there's little that the shop can do about it. If there's a delay simply because the shop is overbooked with work, be polite but firm about your need to get the vehicle back as soon as possible.

>> **When the vehicle is ready, ask what was wrong and what was done to repair the problem.** Enter the details on your *Maintenance Record* for future reference. These records are also assets when you sell your vehicle.

>> **Be prepared to spend a little time test-driving to be sure that the job has been done to your satisfaction.** You're better off returning immediately with your complaints than showing up several days later, after any number of things may have happened to mess things up.

>> **Show your appreciation for a job well done.** A phone call to the manager means a lot to a service facility, but a letter that the shop can display, praising a technician's work, is even better.

**TIP**

If you know that your favorite independent technician likes a particular beverage or snack, arrange your pick-up for the end of the day, and bring that treat along in a paper bag. If you're lucky, you may be invited to stay and share it. I've received some of my most valuable tutoring strolling around a shop after working hours, cold beverage in hand, while my mechanic expounded on the secrets of his art.

# Complaining Effectively

Even if you follow all my advice about finding good service facilities and staying on the best of terms with them, there's still a chance that someday you'll get into a dispute. If you've maintained a good relationship with a shop, they're likely to be cooperative about redoing work that fails to correct a problem, replacing defective parts that they've installed, and the like.

**REMEMBER**

If you approach the shop assuming that the people there are going to treat you fairly and honestly, chances are that they will. If you attack immediately on the assumption that they're out to get you, you put them on the defensive and make things much harder for yourself.

## Getting satisfaction on <u>any</u> complaint

I learned the following technique from an excellent human-potential trainer, and I pass it on to you. It's based on this "Golden Rule":

**WARNING**

> THE BEST WAY TO GET WHAT YOU WANT IS TO MAINTAIN A FRIENDLY ATTITUDE IN ALL DISPUTES — AND REFUSE TO BE SWAYED FROM YOUR PURPOSE!

Follow these steps to get satisfaction when dealing with *any* kind of dispute:

1. **Before you contact anyone, decide exactly what you want done.**

   Presenting a specific plan for remedial action is much more powerful than waiting passively for someone else to decide what they're willing to do for you.

2. **Time your campaign carefully.**

   Don't call just before lunchtime or closing time. Someone who's hungry or eager to get home won't want to spend a lot of time trying to help you.

**TIP**

   Try calling 24-hour customer-service numbers in the middle of the night. Chances are they'll be grateful for a bit of diversion.

3. **Approach the proper person in a friendly way, assuming that he or she wants to do everything possible to settle the issue fairly.**

   To find out which person to approach, see the next section, "Climbing the complaint ladder."

**REMEMBER**

**4.** **Open with a bit of friendly conversation.**

The key is to establish a relationship as human beings. If possible, get on a first-name basis. Most complaint personnel have been trained to deal with suspicion, anger, and aggression. Very few are taught to expect friendliness, trust, and compassion. When they encounter it, the battle tactics they've been taught are useless.

**5.** **Clearly state the problem and what you'd like the person to do about it.**

Tell your story as though you were talking to a sympathetic friend, without blaming anyone. Keep it as short as possible, and don't cloud the issue with unnecessary details.

**6.** **Be prepared to back up your request with as much documentation as possible.**

**WARNING**

This is why it's so important to keep maintenance records, invoices, guarantees, and warranties. If you're asked to document your case, *never part with your originals; just send copies.* It's foolish to place your strategic weapons in the hands of a company that has everything to gain by "losing" them!

**7.** **Listen patiently to the person's responses without interrupting.**

If he or she gives you a hard-luck story to explain negligence or inability to give you satisfaction, be sympathetic. Showing that you care about the person's problems will encourage him or her to care about yours.

**8.** **In a friendly fashion, keep reiterating your problem and what you want done to rectify the situation.**

Say things like, "Gee, that's really a problem. I know how hard it must be to deal with something like that — *and* what can you do to help me?" Be reasonable. If the person can't do exactly what you suggest, be willing to consider other alternatives *as long as the problem is resolved.*

**9.** **Encourage the other person to see the problem through your eyes.**

Say, "Jim, put yourself in my place. How would you like to schlep yourself to work on the bus for a week only to find that your car still doesn't work when you pick it up and won't be ready for another ten days?"

**10.** **If the person says that he or she can't help you, ask who has the authority to do so, and get your call transferred.**

**11.** **If you're told that it's company policy not to provide a remedy for your problem, stay cheerful — but refuse to accept it.**

Kid the person out of it. ("Oh, come on, Charlotte, there has to be someone who can take this load off your shoulders. I'm sure your company wants to deal fairly with its customers, so who has the power to 'temper justice with mercy?'")

**12.** **Repeat the process with every person you're referred to. Keep repeating it until you get satisfaction.**

This combination of friendliness, sympathy, and inflexibility really pays off. I've seen people go out of their way to help me after they realized that I expected them to be compassionate and creative people who could remedy the situation and that I cared about the difficulties they may have in doing so. So try it. What can you lose? You can always bring out the big guns as a last resort!

TIP

Instead of calling Customer Service, go directly to the Cancellations department. Most companies arm Customer Service agents with many ways to deny you what you want, but they give the charmers in Cancellations every opportunity to keep your business. That's why Cancellations is sometimes called Retentions.

## Climbing the complaint ladder

It's usually good policy to take an auto repair complaint first to the person you dealt with and then work your way up to higher levels of power, if necessary. Going over someone's head rarely pays off unless that person has proven to be unsympathetic or unable to help you.

TIP

However, if the lower echelons fail to give you satisfaction, it pays to jump to the highest authority you can. Even if "The Big Boss" sends your complaint back down the ladder, it will have come from the Executive Suite — and the "underlings" must deal with the chance that the boss will follow up to see how well your complaint has been dealt with.

Here's a list of the steps to climb if you're working your way up the automotive complaint ladder (you can adapt it to deal with the hierarchy involved in other kinds of complaints):

**1.** The *technician* who did the repairs

**2.** The *manager* of the shop, or the service manager if it's a dealership or large chain

**3.** The *owner* of the shop or dealership

4. **The *factory representative* at the car manufacturer's nearest regional office**

   Write to the representative and explain what happened and what you want in order to resolve the issue. Be sure to include the following information:

   - The name and address of the service facility

   - The names and titles of the people you've already dealt with while trying to get satisfaction

   - The make, model, and year of your vehicle and its ***vehicle identification number (VIN).***

   - Copies (not originals) of any documentation that you think is required, such as invoices, warranties, previous correspondence, and so on

5. **The *president* or *CEO* of the corporation that built the vehicle**

   Some people suggest going to the corporate public relations department first, but I disagree. I've found that both the chief executive and the PR department often send the matter back to the regional office for action, so I'd rather have the president's or CEO's initials on the letter when it shows up at regional headquarters again.

6. **If you still "can't get no satisfaction" or you have problems with an independent shop that refuses to settle the matter properly, write to your local *Better Business Bureau,* your local *Bureau of Automotive Consumer Affairs* (if there is one), and your state's *Consumer Protection Agency.***

   These organizations may suggest taking the matter to a mediation service, or they may apply pressure of their own. Some states have special bureaus dedicated solely to handling auto repair disputes. If you live in Canada, contact the Canadian Motor Vehicle Arbitration Plan (CAM/VAP) at 800-207-0685 or www.camvap.ca.

7. **If the shop has AAA, CAA, ASE, ASA, or ADS accreditation, write to those organizations with the full specifics of your complaint.**

8. **If your problem is with a dealership, visit the National Automobile Dealers Association (NADA) Web site at www.nada.org to see whether your state has a *mediation service* (these services have no clout with independents, however).**

9. **Consider taking either an independent service facility or a dealership to *small claims court.***

   In many states, new laws have raised the maximum of small claims settlements to levels that cover all but the most expensive auto repair disputes. The fees involved are generally negligible, and you don't need a lawyer. From my experience, small claims procedures are usually swift and fair and aimed at allowing "the little guy" to bring a case of litigation without the need for legal or technical expertise or for great amounts of time and money. Be sure to bring all your documentation and, if possible, a witness who can testify on your behalf. "Expert" witnesses, like other automotive technicians, can be especially useful.

**TIP**

Many establishments would prefer to settle a dispute personally than to lose valuable time in court and have the fact that they've been sued by dissatisfied customers known to the general public and the Better Business Bureau. So it may be good to make these intentions known to the shop before you actually pursue these options.

**10.** If you're really riled, you can complain to the *Federal Trade Commission* (FTC) (or one of its regional offices) at www.ftc.gov/bcp/consumer.shtm.

**11.** To register complaints about defects and to obtain data on recalls, fuel, tires, child seats, seatbelts, and other safety-related issues, call the *Department of Transportation's Vehicle Hotline* at 888-327-4236.

**12.** Another excellent guide to obtaining satisfaction is the *Consumer Action Handbook.* It's full of valuable information on a variety of topics. Request the handbook by visiting www.consumeraction.gov.

**13.** Contact the *Consumer Federation of America* at www.consumerfed.org. This group of some 300 nonprofit organizations represents consumer interests through advocacy and education.

**WARNING**

No matter which line of recourse you decide to follow, paying the disputed bill first is always a good policy *if your state honors the mechanic's lien mentioned earlier in this chapter.* If you use a credit card, you may then be able to have the credit card company withhold payment until the disputed matter is investigated and resolved. Even if you lose, it's better than having your vehicle towed away and sold for a fraction of its value. So pay up first, and then go get 'em!

# 6

# Helping Your Vehicle Look Its Best

Presumably, you take care of yourself: You bathe regularly, you keep your fingernails neatly groomed, you treat bumps and bruises with bandages and the appropriate salves and ointments. You probably also take care of your home: You sweep, mop, dust, vacuum, and clean out the gutters occasionally. So why wouldn't you also take care of your vehicle? Like anything else, it will last longer and remain "healthier" if you do. Washing, waxing, removing small dings, cleaning the interior, you name it — this part covers everything you need to keep your vehicle looking great.

IN THIS CHAPTER

» **Cleaning your vehicle's exterior efficiently**

» **Keeping the environment safe from chemical cleaners**

» **Getting rid of dirt and grime under the hood**

» **Waxing and polishing your car to protect and beautify it**

» **Caring for glass, chrome, vinyl, leather, and more**

» **Cleaning and repairing upholstery, carpeting, headliners, and more**

Chapter **23**

# Keeping Your Vehicle Clean and Beautiful

A vehicle is more than a collection of parts and systems. When you drive it, try to trade it in, or sell it, it's judged on its appearance as well as its performance. Contrary to popular belief, the main reason for washing your car often and keeping a good coat of wax on it isn't to keep it looking good but rather to wash away the salt, mud, and chemical-laden dust and dirt that provide breeding grounds for rust and accelerate paint deterioration.

If you live in an area near the seashore, where a lot of salt is used on the roads in the winter, or where there's industrial air pollution, it's imperative that you wash your vehicle at least once a week. If you have no access to a hose or a place to wash your car, or if the weather in your area gets so cold that the water freezes on the windshield, drive to a coin-operated do-it-yourself car wash and use its facilities. The steamy hoses keep both you and your vehicle warm enough to wash away the mud and salt in the winter and can do an even better job than you could do at home, especially if your water pressure is low.

# THE LAZY PERSON'S GUIDE TO "GOOD HOUSEKEEPING"

**TIP**

If you have no time or inclination for cleaning your vehicle yourself, hire someone to do it for you. The expense more than pays off in the increased life of your car. At the very least, take it to a car wash every week or two and be sure that the interior gets cleaned and vacuumed as part of the deal.

Car washes vary considerably in efficiency and reliability. Be aware that your vehicle will probably respond to the rather rough and impersonal scrubbing it will receive from the machines at some car washes by acquiring scratches and losing a bit of paint around the edges. Spinning car-wash brushes are especially lethal for vehicles with clear-coat finishes. To keep the damage to a minimum, find a low-cost "brushless" or "touch-free" car wash that uses curtains of jiggling strips or one that washes vehicles by hand.

Forget about the optional hot-wax sprays offered by car washes. They're simply not strong enough to provide sufficient protection. Unless the car manufacturer warns that waxing will mar a special finish, most vehicles need a good coat of wax or one of the new polymer products to protect it from rust and fading. If you don't want to wax the car yourself, hire someone to do it by hand.

If you drive a convertible or a luxury or classic car and you can't keep it clean yourself, hire someone to wash it by hand at least every couple of weeks. Running such a special vehicle through a commercial car wash is tantamount to murder!

**WARNING**

If you use a do-it-yourself car wash with high-pressure hoses, be sure to adjust them so you don't damage the paint and protective coatings on your vehicle.

**TIP**

Always clean the interior of your vehicle before you wash the exterior. For advice on how to deal with each of the materials you may find inside your car, see the "Cleaning the Interior" section later in this chapter.

In this chapter, you discover the best ways to keep your vehicle clean and in good condition — inside and out and even under the hood!

**REMEMBER**

Whenever you encounter a term set in *this font,* you'll find it defined in the glossary in Appendix A.

# Environmentally Safe Ways to Clean Your Vehicle

**ECO-LOGIC**

Washing a vehicle can require a fair amount of water and produces some nasty runoff. A major advantage of using a car wash is that, rather than allow the dirty water to run into natural bodies of water via storm drains, most of these facilities are required to either remove contaminants like chemical cleaners, soap, oil, and grease and recycle the water to wash additional vehicles; or send the runoff to the sewage treatment plant so it can reenter the environment harmlessly. Because the price of water is rising, many car washes are recycling it whether or not they're required to.

When washing your vehicle at home, use *biodegradable* cleaning products to minimize environmental pollution. Try to do the job on a grassy or graveled area where the water can be absorbed and filtered by the dirt below, or do your washing near a drain connected to your home's sewer system. Do *not* just let the water run down the street and into a storm drain.

No matter where you wash your car, conserve water. Don't let the hose run while you work. Use it only to wet and rinse the vehicle, and shut it off when you don't need it. Car Wash Association studies have found that people often use as much as 140 gallons for a single car wash, which isn't surprising when you consider that a ⅝-inch hose can deliver 14 gallons of water *per minute.*

**TIP**

A good way to save water by not having to wash your vehicle as often, but also to preserve the finish of your vehicle, is to protect it with a car cover. The sidebar entitled "Car covers" later in this chapter tells you what you need to know in order to buy the right kind of cover for your vehicle.

# Cleaning the Exterior

Keeping the exterior of your vehicle clean isn't a matter of being a fanatic who spends every second of free time washing and waxing and dusting; just spending an hour or two each week can keep your new set of wheels young or brighten up Old Faithful.

# De-bugging your vehicle safely

**WARNING**

Getting rid of the bird–poop, tree sap, and other icky stuff on the body, windows, chrome, and wheel covers of your vehicle requires special treatment, often with harsh chemicals. Here are some precautions to take:

» **Don't scratch at hard-to-remove dirt.** *Soak* it loose by placing a wet rag on it. Wash off bird droppings and sap *immediately* with mild soap and water. If left to harden, they're much harder to remove and can permanently damage the finish.

» **Before you use a product designed to get rid of tar, dead bugs, and other hard-to-remove substances, read the label to make sure that it won't damage the finish.** Test specialized commercial solvents first on a door jamb or other hidden painted surface.

» **Be sure to remove intense cleansers thoroughly and wash the surface with soap and water immediately afterward.**

# Washing your vehicle's body

Most people think that there's nothing special to know about washing the outside surface of a car, but this isn't the case. Doing the job efficiently saves you time and effort and ensures that the vehicle's body comes out looking great. If you work in a haphazard way, the task takes much longer, and you run the risk of scratching the finish, streaking the surface, and leaving the body vulnerable to rust.

**WARNING**

## SAFETY TIPS FOR USING COMMERCIAL PRODUCTS

A commercial product can be just the thing you need to keep your vehicle in great shape, but with any store-bought cleaning supply, it's in your car's — and your — best interest to pay attention to a few common-sense and safety rules:

- **Always read and follow the directions on the package.** Some products can damage your skin or your car's surface if left on too long or if applied and removed improperly.

- **Never use a spray in an unventilated area.** And never get your face close enough to inhale it or risk getting it in your eyes.

- **Don't smoke when using chemicals or petroleum products.** As a matter of fact, don't smoke, period! Protecting the surface

Most modern vehicles are painted in a two-step process that produces a *clear-coat* finish, which can far outlast the acrylic lacquer or enamel used on older vehicles. Although a clear-coat finish protects and enhances the paint, it's extremely sensitive to abrasion and chemicals. If it wears away, the paint beneath it will deteriorate rapidly.

## Protecting the surface

Whether your vehicle has a clear-coat finish or not, to wash its body efficiently and preserve its sensitive "skin," follow these guidelines:

>> **Never wipe or dust the body with a dry cloth.** The tiny particles of dust and grit on the surface can scratch the paint, leaving it looking cobwebby wherever the sun hits it.

>> **Never wash a vehicle in the hot sun.** The cool water will cause the hot body to contract, which can crack the paint and ruin the finish. Park in the shade or wait until morning or evening.

>> **Be sure the windows and sun roof are closed before washing.** (Don't laugh, it can happen to anyone!) If you've never washed the vehicle with a hose before, spray lightly around the edges of the windows, sunroof, and rear deck lid for a short time and then check to see if the weatherstripping leaks. If it does, consult the instructions in Chapter 24 for patching or replacing weatherstripping, and try to avoid spraying these areas until you remedy the problem.

>> **Before you wash the car, hose it down to get rid of the surface dust, and then clean and polish such exterior surfaces as vinyl hardtops, convertible tops, glass windows and sunroofs, chrome bumpers and trim, side mirrors, wheel covers, whitewalls, and tires.** Then, when you wash and rinse the whole vehicle, you'll be sure to get off the last residue of all the substances you used for those jobs. Later sections of this chapter explain how to clean and restore some of those special surfaces.

>> **Use cold or lukewarm water and a hose rather than a bucket of water to wet and rinse the car.** A bucket holds a finite amount of water. As you rinse out your rag or sponge, the dirt is transferred to the water and back to the rag, where it can scratch or streak the paint. A hose with a spray nozzle can project a stream of water forceful enough to loosen the mud, bugs, bird waste, and other baddies that stick to the surface.

Blasts at extremely high pressure may loosen and chip paint and parts.

>> **Use a sponge, soft rag (old terrycloth towels, T-shirts, or cotton diapers are wonderful), or a cotton wash mitt.** Cotton swabs and an old toothbrush will help you get into small areas.

>> **To avoid cobwebby scratches, follow the contours of the surface rather than going in circles.** Rinse the rag often to get rid of grease and dust particles. Be thorough but gentle; vigorous scrubbing can scratch and remove the paint.

WARNING

>> **Don't use the hose under the hood because the water can damage electronic circuits.** I explain what you can and can't do in this area in the "Cleaning under the Hood" section later in this chapter.

>> **Use gentle cleansers.** Your vehicle's sensitive skin requires gentle cleansers just as your own body does. Use a commercial car-washing product, not laundry or dish soap or detergent, which can remove the wax and other protective finishes from the surface. If you have a unique paint job or other special surfaces on your vehicle, check your *owner's manual* for instructions on how to deal with them.

## Doing the job methodically

Every job goes more smoothly and efficiently if the work you do is organized properly. The following tips help you wash your vehicle in an order and manner that will get you the best results:

TIP

>> **Always wash the body of a vehicle from the top down so that soap scum and sludge don't muck up freshly washed areas.**

>> **Remember to get to all the corners where dirt can collect and rust can form: behind the wheels, inside the fenders, and behind the bumpers.** Don't forget the underbody — this is usually the muddiest and greasiest place of all and the most prone to rust. It's okay to use a more powerful jet of water under here to dislodge the mud, salt, or grime.

>> **Wash one section of the vehicle at a time.** Hose it down, soap it up, and rinse it off. When you finish the entire vehicle, hose it all down again to get off every last bit of soap. Remove the spray nozzle from the hose and use a medium stream of water that flows off in sheets and makes drying the car easier.

Make sure that no water collects in the tiny rust-prone spaces around the trim and behind the bumpers.

WARNING

>> **Towel-dry the car immediately with terry towels, cotton diapers, or a synthetic chamois to get rid of water spotting that can mar the surface.** Chamois are good for this purpose and can be washed, rinsed, and used for years. But they're more expensive, and I find that old, dry terry towels and diapers work pretty well, too. Don't rub hard, and if the towel-drying rag you're using gets dirty, switch to a clean one to avoid scratching the surface.

>> **At regular intervals, apply a coat of wax or sealer.** A high-quality polymer sealant provides the best protection because it binds with the paint. The slippery surface retards water spots and makes it easier to remove bugs and tree sap. A good sealer can last up to six months. Carnuba wax gives a deeper shine but lasts only a couple of months. Follow the instructions in the later section, "Clear coat and other delicate finishes," to get the best results.

If your vehicle has a clear-coat finish, use a product designed for it and don't use power buffers or polishers on it. These are too intense for your vehicle's sensitive skin. The sidebar "Electric buffers" later in the chapter explains why.

## Restoring visibility to windows and mirrors

Just as "the eyes are the windows of the soul," the windows are the eyes of your car. In both cases, clarity is important! Employ the same products you use to clean glass in your home to clean your car's glass windows and mirrors. Many of these products simply spray on and wipe off without rinsing. Just keep the following in mind:

>> **Be sure to use a lint-free soft rag or sturdy paper towels to avoid scratching the glass.** Newspaper also does a pretty good job.

>> **Wait to clean the inside surfaces of the windows and sunroof until you do the interior of the car.** The "Cleaning inside the windows" section has tips on how to clean these properly.

>> **Use vertical strokes on the outside of the windows and sunroof, and horizontal strokes on the inside, so that you can see at a glance which side the streaks are on when you're wiping off the cleaner.**

>> **Lift your windshield wipers away from the glass to clean under them, and don't forget to wipe the wipers, too.** A dirty blade can streak or scratch the glass. Handle the wipers gently to avoid bending the mechanism. Remove dead leaves that may have accumulated in the well under the wipers. Chapter 2 has instructions for checking and replacing windshield-washer fluid and wiper blades.

>> **Carry a package of pre-moistened glass cleaner wipes and a clean soft rag in your car to spruce up the windshield when visibility gets cloudy.**

If you have a convertible with a plastic rear window, that window may become cloudy from oxidation, especially if the hot sun shines on it constantly. Excellent conditioners designed to keep plastic windows clear and supple without scratching them are available. If your convertible's rear window is already clouded beyond visibility, I've found that Meguiar's Mirror Glaze Clear Plastic Cleaner polishes the cloudy stuff right off the window, leaving it relatively clear again. If you must park your vehicle where the sun can shine directly on its plastic window for long periods of time, cover the outside of the window with an old towel to protect it from the sun.

## Polishing metal trim and chrome

Consider its shining trim to be your vehicle's jewelry and keep it protected and looking good. Several excellent polishes are designed specifically to clean chrome without scratching the delicate layer of plating. These preparations also retard rust and leave the surface bright and shining. You can use chrome polish on other metal surfaces, too. Here are some tips for polishing metal trim and chrome:

>> **Try not to get the polish on the surrounding paint.** The polish can discolor it.

>> **Be sure to do the *inside* surfaces of a metal bumper, too, if you can reach it.** And don't forget the metal frames around the lights and side mirrors.

>> **Use a special glaze on black metal or plastic trim around the windows, on bumpers, or as side-protector strips.** The glaze, usually liquid, restores some luster to the blacked-out trim. As with metal polishes, avoid getting the glaze on the vehicle's paint.

WARNING

>> **If you find rust on any metal area, get rid of the stuff immediately!** For instructions, rush directly to the section on rust removal in Chapter 24.

>> **After you clean metal surfaces, wax them to prevent rust from forming.** Use a special wax designed for chrome bumpers and metal surfaces because these areas require more protection than painted surfaces do. Other types of wax may prevent the chrome from getting the oxygen it needs to preserve its shine.

## Caring for wheels and tires

Wheels come in a variety of styles and metals these days. They can be chrome-plated or made of aluminum or magnesium alloys or steel. Choose a wheel cleaner designed for the wheels on your vehicle, and apply it gently (your soft old toothbrush or a clean *soft* paintbrush comes in handy here). Clean one wheel at a time and rinse it immediately before the cleaner dries in order to avoid staining the metal.

Clean the sidewalls of your tires whenever you wash your car. (You wouldn't take a bath without washing your feet, would you?) Use mild soap or dish detergent to remove dirt and grease. A brush or scratchless kitchen scouring pad removes the stubborn stuff, but before you go at it like you're scrubbing your bathroom grout, be sure to wet the tires.

**WARNING**

Never use gasoline or kerosene to clean tires. If your vehicle has whitewalls that are extremely dirty or greasy, you may have to resort to a special whitewall cleaner to restore them to their original pristine good looks.

**TIP**

If you want your tires to look extremely shiny and spiffy and preserve the rubber as well, spray them with a tire protectant. It will leave them shining and retard *ozone checking.* You can usually use the same stuff for other black vinyl or rubber exterior surfaces.

# Cleaning and repairing convertible tops

A convertible is a joy to drive with the top down, but if you don't take care of it properly, you may find yourself cold and wet when the time comes to put it back up. This section deals with cloth tops (affectionately known as *ragtops*) and vinyl-covered hardtops.

## Ragtops

If you have a convertible with a cloth top, keep that top clean by vacuuming it often or by using a whisk broom to get the dust out of the areas around the trim. This isn't just a matter of cleanliness; the dirt can cause the fabric to rot away if it's allowed to remain there. Do the following to keep your ragtop in good shape:

>> **Check the top occasionally to make sure that it's not getting caught in the mechanism that raises and lowers it.** This can leave greasy streaks on the fabric, weaken it, and cause it to tear. If your top has a plastic rear window, make sure that it isn't getting scrunched by the mechanism when the top is down, and follow the instructions in the earlier section, "Restoring visibility to windows and mirrors," to clean it without scratching it.

>> **Inspect the metal mechanism that raises and lowers the top and polish it occasionally to keep it shiny and beautiful.** Put a coat of wax on the metal to retard rusting, and oil the hinges now and then to keep things working smoothly. Use the oil sparingly to avoid staining the top.

>> **Remember to dust or vacuum the well into which the top folds and to keep it free of objects that can puncture or mar the top.** I remember a friend who had a convertible with a glass rear window. The top was up for most

of the winter, and that well seemed like an ideal place to stash her umbrella and other paraphernalia. Then one day the sun shone, and she happily pressed the button to automatically lower the top. Crunch! End of story.

>> **Check for weak spots or tears, and check the seams for threads that are beginning to break.** Seams that are loosening up can be restitched by hand before they become major problems. Try to use the same holes as the original stitches, stitching right on top of them, and use strong thread in the same color as the original.

>> **If you see a weak place or a small hole, reinforce it by placing a patch on the *inside* of the top, and glue it in place with a good adhesive or stitch it down securely.** Convertible tops are under considerable tension, and a tiny rip can swiftly tear right across the top.

## Vinyl hardtops

Vinyl tops usually clean up easily with water and mild soap or dish detergent. If the top is very dirty, you may want to try a commercial product made especially for vinyl tops. Use a fairly soft brush to get the dirt out of the tiny crevices in the finish (a recycled toothbrush or nail brush easily gets into the areas around the trim). Brush in circles because the crevices run in every direction, and rinse often to wash the dirt away. Vinyl hardtops respond nicely to a light coat of wax or the proper silicone preservative.

TIP

Here are a few more tips:

>> **If you find that your vinyl hardtop has bubbles in it, prick the areas with a pin and try to press the air out.** If any adhesive comes out of the holes, wipe it off the vinyl immediately. When the air is out, press the vinyl against the roof to reseal it. If the adhesive has dried out, you can use a glue injector to insert a tiny amount of vinyl adhesive under the surface. Air bubbles can create holes in the vinyl if something catches them.

>> **If you find holes or rips in the vinyl, use a vinyl repair kit to correct them.** You can find different types of kits on the market. Before you buy anything, read the instructions to be sure that you select the simplest kit that suits your purposes.

>> **If your vinyl top has faded and become discolored, excellent sprays are available that can renew the color for you.** Before you use these sprays, be sure to mask the surrounding areas of the car. Always choose the same color or a slightly darker shade to cover up spots.

## ELECTRIC BUFFERS

**WARNING**

You may have seen professionals use electric buffers to apply cleaners and wax and to shine a car to a high gloss. Although buffing pads are available that can be attached to the shaft of an electric drill, don't use these or any other high-speed gadgets to buff or polish your vehicle. Professional buffing equipment works gently at slow speeds to avoid scratching or grinding the paint right off the surface. Low-speed buffers also are available, but most of this equipment can burn the finish if not used properly. So unless you have the light, experienced touch of a professional, I suggest you employ one.

# Cleaning and polishing your vehicle

Let me be clear on the distinction between *washing* and *cleaning and polishing* the exterior of a vehicle. Washing, which I cover earlier, gets rid of the dirt on the surface. Cleaning and polishing goes a little deeper. As a vehicle gets older, especially if it's exposed to the sun and other elements, the top layers of paint or *clear coat* begin to fade and *oxidize,* giving the body a hazy or smoky-looking surface. Regular washing and waxing usually retards this process, but an occasional good cleaning and polishing actually removes tiny scratches and dead paint.

## Clear coat and other delicate finishes

**WARNING**

If your car is a dark color or has a delicate lacquer or clear-coat finish, you want to avoid removing the thin outer layers. Look for a polish or wax/cleaner designed for these finishes that contains chemicals rather than abrasives because scratches really show up on these finishes. Don't use an abrasive cleaner on chrome or plastic unless the label specifically says that you can. If you do, you run the risk of scratching the surfaces and removing the chrome plating. *Do not use rubbing compound or electric buffers or polishers on clear-coat finishes; these products and tools can ruin the finish.* The sidebar "Electric buffers" provides the details.

## Acrylic or enamel finishes

When you clean and polish a vehicle that's been painted with acrylic lacquer or enamel, you use special products that actually remove a very thin layer of paint. When this layer goes, so do the scratches, oxidation, and thin coat of grime that regular washing doesn't get rid of, leaving even a well-kept vehicle shining with unusual brilliance.

**WARNING**

## RUBBING COMPOUNDS

Most polishes have a mild abrasive action, but the abrasives in rubbing compounds are designed to dig a bit deeper into the surface, discard the top layers of paint, and get down to the fresh stuff underneath (assuming that there is any). As a general rule, avoid any polishing preparation that contains such strong abrasives because it can go right through your vehicle's painted finish.

Some cars are painted with acrylic lacquer or enamel that has a hardener in it, which helps protect the finish and keep the color from fading for a long time. However, if your vehicle is in really sad shape, with paint that has faded and dulled to the point that it has little shine, you may want to try using a **rubbing compound** to restore the finish before you spring for a paint job or dump Old Faithful for a better-looking set of wheels.

Rubbing compounds come in fine, medium, and coarse grades. Always try the fine grade first because the others may be too harsh. The coarse grade removes so much paint that it's usually used for prefinishing jobs in which the surface is taken down, restored, and repainted. *Use rubbing compound sparingly. Follow the directions on the package and don't bear down too hard.* Go easy at first to avoid removing patches of paint that have loosened from the surface, bubbled, or chipped around the edges. You can always apply a bit more elbow grease if your initial efforts prove to be too gentle. *Always wax the car after using a rubbing compound* — unless, of course, you're going to paint it.

To clean and polish a lacquered or enameled vehicle, follow these steps:

1. **Wash the car and all its surfaces, as explained in the earlier section "Washing your vehicle's body."**

2. **Use car polish to remove the scratches.**

   If the finish is in such bad shape that just using car polish doesn't shine up the dull surface or eliminate scratches, try using a rubbing compound, *carefully* following the advice in the nearby sidebar, "Rubbing compounds." If the finish is somewhere between perfect and really bad shape (that is, if it feels slightly gritty to the touch but doesn't have scratches and a lot of oxidation to grind out), try using detailing clay. You rub the clay over the paint surface after applying a spray-on lubricant that comes with the clay bar; it grinds away surface contaminants without taking off any paint. A well-clayed car finish can feel as smooth as glass.

3. **Protect your vehicle from the elements by waxing it; instructions are in the next section, "Waxing your vehicle."**

A variety of cleaning and polishing products are available to you, including some that combine wax with a car cleaner to reduce the number of steps you have to go through. These combination products are easy to use and work well if the vehicle isn't too filthy, but they can't substitute for a thorough waxing when it comes to long-term protection.

Some commercial car-polishing products contain fine particles of abrasive, which effectively remove an infinitely small top layer of paint and grime. For this reason, *don't use these products more than once a month. Don't use them at all on clear-coat finishes.*

## Waxing your vehicle

If washing removes the surface dirt, and cleaning and polishing removes the dead layers of paint, waxing a vehicle preserves that clean and shiny finish and seals its "pores" against dirt, water vapor, and rust. If water doesn't bead on the surface of the vehicle when it rains or when you hose it down, it needs waxing badly. *Don't neglect this step.* Even if you use a car-washing product that has wax in it, you must still give most vehicles a thorough waxing at least twice a year, in the spring and fall, to protect them from heavy weather. Nothing is more vital than a thorough wax job if you want to keep your vehicle rust-free and looking young for years to come.

To avoid scratching the surface and trapping minute particles of dust, always be sure to wash the vehicle before you wax it, no matter how clean it looks. After applying wax or polymer sealant, use a terry cloth towel to break up the hazy surface by rubbing in one direction. Then switch to a soft, lint-free cloth (a cloth diaper works best) and rub in the other direction to bring out the shine.

If you drive a dark-colored vehicle or one with a clear-coat or sensitive lacquer finish, make sure that the cleaners and waxes you use have no abrasives in them. If you're unsure as to whether the finish on your vehicle requires special handling, check your owner's manual or call your dealership for instructions.

Unless your vehicle came with specific instructions from the manufacturer, you can choose from a variety of waxes, ranging from combination products that have both cleaners and wax together, to liquid, soft, and hard waxes. Or you can use a polymer sealant. Here's a closer look at your options:

> » **Liquid waxes:** Generally speaking, liquid waxes are very easy to use but don't last as long as soft or hard waxes, although some of the abrasive-free liquid wax/cleaners specially formulated for vehicles with delicate finishes are quite effective. Liquid wax is excellent to replace the wax you lose if you wash your car with a wax-free detergent or soap, or for a touch-up between professional waxings.

>> **Soft waxes:** These are my favorites. Soft waxes are light and fluffy and are very easy to apply and remove. Some are mixed with a light cleaner, but be sure to wash the car thoroughly first anyway to remove particles that can scratch it. Apply soft wax with the applicator pads provided or with a soft terry cloth rag. Simply wipe on the wax, *following the contours of the surface*; allow it to dry to a haze; and wipe the haze away.

Because the waxes that contain cleaners usually contain abrasives, don't use them for every car wash or more often than once a month. In between, use a liquid car cleanser that contains a little wax.

>> **Hard or paste waxes:** These types of waxes provide the most protection and should be used for your semi-annual major wax job. They last longer than anything except polymer preservatives. Hard or paste waxes are harder to apply and require rubbing and buffing to bring up a high-gloss shine. *Always do a small area at a time to avoid letting the wax harden to a point where it's hard to remove.* Apply the wax according to the directions on the can with an applicator or soft, lint-free rag.

>> **Polymer preservatives:** Products that contain polymer substances claim to protect a vehicle more effectively than wax and for longer periods of time. They literally bond with the surface and prevent it from fading and oxidizing. At the auto supply store, you can buy poly-sealants that are easy to apply and are supposed to protect your vehicle for six months to a year.

>> **Polyglycotes:** Professionals and auto manufacturers offer silicon-based polyglycotes that are supposed to last from two to five years, but the jury's still out on whether they can live up to their promises; most have to be freshened and buffed periodically to maintain the shine, which isn't much different than waxing. If you still want to use one of these products, wash the vehicle thoroughly and give it a good cleaning and polishing first (see the earlier sections in this chapter). Some polyglycotes products say that they can be applied over wax, but I prefer to get all the wax off the vehicle before applying them. When the surface is really clean, shiny, and dry, apply the protective coating, following the directions on the label. Make sure that it gets into all the little crevices around the trim and on the painted metal inner surfaces of the doors and deck lid. I recommend that you regularly inspect your vehicle for rust to make sure that this miracle stuff is really doing its job.

**TIP**

# Cleaning under the Hood

Many car owners never bother to deal with the dirt under the hood on the assumption that what they can't see can't hurt them. Although it's true that only people who exhibit show cars or are compulsively fastidious set much store by having the engine area constantly at its pristine best, there are practical reasons for removing a gross accumulation of grease, oil, fuel, and dirt from under the hood and for making an effort to keep things under control from then on.

Most engines are made of metal and depend on rubber hoses, *gaskets,* and wiring, if they're to work properly. Because all the aforementioned baddies can seriously deteriorate nonmetal parts and wiring, keep the under-the-hood area as clean as possible. If it's beginning to look grubby, get a rag and wipe off as much of the dirt and grease as you can without removing or moving hoses and wiring.

WARNING

*Never use a hose to wash under the hood — the water can ruin the electronics.* If the situation has reached the unspeakable stage, I strongly urge you to have a professional clean the area. Although engine degreasers are available at auto supply stores and coin-operated steam-cleaning facilities at do-it-yourself car wash centers, I don't recommend that you try either of these alternatives and instead have your engine cleaned professionally if it's too dirty to wipe clean yourself. When the job is done, you should be able to keep it in good condition by simply wiping off the area every now and then.

TECHNICAL STUFF

If you're planning to sell your vehicle, think twice about having the area under the hood cleaned. Although cleaning certainly spiffs it up, potential buyers may assume that it was done to obliterate signs of unsuccessful surgery on the engine.

REMEMBER

Whenever you clean under the hood, make sure that you clean the *blow-by* on the inner surface of the hood, too, and that you remove the mud and dirt that have accumulated on the *inner* walls of the car's body and near the wheel wells.

TIP

If you find that oil accumulates very quickly on your engine, first check the *PCV valve* to see whether it's plugged up. This little gadget is responsible for rerouting the exhaust fumes from the *crankcase* back to the engine, where they're burned again and then released through the *exhaust system.* If the valve gets plugged, pressure can build up in the crankcase and create oil leaks around the engine. A PCV valve can be checked and replaced very easily (read all about it in the section "Servicing the PCV Valve" in Chapter 8).

Oil also may seep from under the *valve cover* gasket if the cover needs to be *torqued* down properly or the gasket needs to be replaced. If this seems to be your problem, check with a mechanic.

TRUE STORY

If you think that cleaning your engine is compulsive, my uncle sprayed the under-the-hood area of his secondhand Cadillac with gold paint so that he could impress the service station attendants!

# Cleaning the Interior

The interior of your vehicle is like your living room at home: It's "decorated" with carpeting, paint, fabric, plastic, vinyl, and glass. Some cars have rubber, leather, and wood as well. Unlike the interior of your home, your car stands out in public and reflects your personal habits (and you certainly don't want everyone to think that you're a slob!). Keeping the interior clean is more than a matter of pride; because dirt contains grit and chemicals that can eat away the surfaces of your automotive "furniture," it's vital to practice the same good housekeeping techniques on your vehicle that you would on your home in order to keep it in decent condition for a long, long time.

Generally speaking, the same procedures and products that you use at home work quite well in your car. If you're an old hand at housework, read the following sections just to make sure that you don't forget anything. If good housekeeping has never been your bag — or if you've spent your life in hotels — the following sections tell you how to clean and care for the interior of your vehicle.

**TIP**

When you're ready to go on your cleaning campaign, pick a day when you have time to putter about. Arm yourself with a portable hand vacuum cleaner; line up all those groovy bottles of special cleaners; festoon the area with clean terry cloth rags or other softies, an old toothbrush, and cotton swabs for getting into little spaces; and tackle the entire interior in one glorious effort. Unless you habitually drive out into the wilderness, chauffeur a horde of wild kids armed with ice cream cones, or the weather gets really terrible, you probably won't have to go through this task more often than once a month — less often if you're very fastidious and don't travel around a lot.

## Keeping things tidy

Clean the interior before you do the exterior. The most effective thing you can do is vacuum the seats first, remove and clean the floor mats, and then vacuum the carpets. Dust the dashboard, rear window shelf, and other surfaces, and use the swabs or toothbrush to get into A/C vents, around dashboard knobs, and other tight places. Aerosol cans of air used for cleaning cameras and computers can force dust from tiny apertures.

**WARNING**

Never use a dry rag or paper towels to clean the plastic lenses on instrument panel gauges. Small, dry particles of dust and grit can scratch the surface. The lens-cleaning cloths or tissues you use on your eyeglasses or camera do a good job. If the lenses are clouded, use a plastic cleaner sparingly with a clean, *damp* terry cloth rag or sponge. Excess moisture can damage electronic instruments.

Here are a few other ways to maintain order and cleanliness in your vehicle:

>> **Keep the clutter under control and the seats free of everything but you, your passengers, and the seat belts.** Objects left lying on seats may rip or stain them as people enter, leave, and move about. Maps and guidebooks belong in the glove box. Store the flashlight, tools, and a copy of this book in the trunk; or store them under the passenger seat, if you can secure them there adequately.

>> **Your fire extinguisher takes precedence over any other candidate for under-the-driver's-seat storage.** You have to be able to reach it quickly in case of an emergency (and the trunk is right over the fuel tank). Store the fire extinguisher securely so that it can't roll out from under the seat and interfere with your driving.

**WARNING**

>> **Don't keep objects on the rear window ledge or dashboard.** If you have to stop suddenly, they can obscure visibility or fly around and hurt someone. Small objects like pencils and coins can fall behind the dashboard and damage the air vents, so find a better place for them as well. Shiny items will reflect on the windshield and obscure vision.

To reduce sun damage and keep the vinyl, plastic, or leather surfaces from cracking and fading, apply a conditioner with UV protection (that doesn't leave a shiny surface) to the dashboard regularly.

>> **If you have children who require a supply of toys, store the toys safely.** Keep them on the floor in an open carton that fits snugly between the rear seat and the back of the front seat, and make putting them away a regular part of each driving experience.

>> **If your car doesn't have a cup holder, buy one at your dealership or auto parts store.**

>> **Don't allow old food and drink containers to clutter up your vehicle.** They attract ants and other insects that can "bug" your vehicle's equipment and wiring, and they stink.

>> **Follow the instructions in your owner's manual when cleaning seat belts.** Ordinary household cleaners, ammonia, and solvents can weaken the webbing.

>> **Remember to vacuum and clean the trunk compartment.** It's part of the vehicle's interior, too!

# Cleaning upholstery and carpeting

You can use the same products to clean car upholstery and carpeting that you use to clean your chairs, sofas, and rugs. Keep the following in mind:

TIP

>> **Avoid using large quantities of water; you don't want to get the padding under the fabric wet or rust the upholstery buttons, if there are any.** Avoid sponges, working instead with damp rags wherever possible. If you think that you've gotten things too wet, use a portable hair dryer to dry the padding quickly and evaporate water from around buttons and seams.

>> **The best products for fabrics and rugs are the ones that spray on, turn to powder, and are removed by vacuuming.** Stain-repellent sprays are excellent if the fabric is clean and new; otherwise, they simply preserve your stains forever. See the later section "Fighting stains and odors" for more information.

>> **To keep upholstery from fading and deteriorating, park the vehicle facing in a different direction as often as possible so that the sun doesn't keep hitting the same surfaces.** During dry seasons, keep a window or the sunroof open a crack to prevent heat from building up inside. It can dissolve fabric adhesives and crack vinyl seat covers.

## Vinyl and plastic

Vinyl seats and interiors and plastic surfaces such as dashboards, steering wheels, and interior moldings usually respond well to water and a mild soap or dish detergent, but you may have to resort to special vinyl-cleaning products if you've allowed things to get out of hand. You can use a soft brush on vinyl to get at the dirt in the graining, along the welting, and around upholstery buttons, if there are any.

Protect all vinyl and plastic surfaces from sunlight and heat with products designed for those materials. While you're at it, use them or a spray silicone lubricant on dashboards, weatherstripping, vinyl or rubber floor mats, and tires, too, to prevent them from cracking and drying out and to keep them supple. Avoid oil- and petroleum-based products that can damage vinyl and leave it brittle.

## Leather

If you're lucky enough to have leather seats in your vehicle, take care of them. If properly cared for, leather can last a long time but, like all skin, it dries out and ages prematurely if it's not kept clean and moisturized. Follow this advice for caring for leather upholstery:

>> **Use a high-quality product like saddle soap to clean and preserve leather seats.** Neatsfoot oil waterproofs, softens, lubricates, restores, and preserves leather that has been cleaned first.

>> **If you must park where the sun can get at your leather seats, lean them forward or drape something over them to protect them.** If conditions are severe, think about installing window film that blocks UV rays. If this is impossible, take comfort from the fact that leather seats don't get as hot as vinyl ones, so you can probably sit down on them without screaming.

## Fighting stains and odors

Stains are caused by a wide variety of substances and can be enlarged or set permanently if you try to remove them improperly. In the interest of brevity and because I believe in leaving specialized areas to the specialists, I suggest that you refer to a stain-removal guide before tackling stains on fabric upholstery or carpeting. These stain-fighting tactics may also help:

TIP

>> **Be sure to attack the stain while it's fresh; the older a stain gets, the harder it is to remove.** You may want to stow a small spray container of stain remover in the trunk so that you can attack stubborn stains before sunlight and heat set them, but test the remover on a hidden spot first.

>> **Avoid drastic measures that can harm the upholstery.** I prefer to consult the experts on things like chewing gum, tar, blood, and other hard-to-remove substances.

>> **To avoid spreading a stain, work from the edges in toward the center.** Use a minimum of liquid and dab rather than scrub. When the stain is gone, dry the surface with a portable hair dryer.

>> **You *may* be able to cut the stains off high-napped carpets and then camouflage the resulting bald spots with loops cut from a hidden area and glued in with clear adhesive.** Try this trick on an area that doesn't show first to see whether your handiwork would look better (or worse!) than the original stain.

>> **Odors are considered stains, too — even though they assault your nose rather than your eyes.** Odor removal sprays encapsulate odors, lift them out of the fabric, and destroy them, rather than masking them with stronger fragrances, as most air fresheners do.

## Repairing tears and holes

Auto seats get considerable wear and tear, and reupholstery is very expensive. If you catch small tears and holes early, you can save yourself a lot of money. Try the following:

>> **Sew up tears in fabric seats with strong matching thread or use patch kits that allow you to put the patch under the fabric and seal the wound with a colorless adhesive.**

>> **For vinyl upholstery, check out the various vinyl repair kits available and choose the simplest one that can do the job.** If you have to patch an area where the vinyl no longer exists, be sure that the patch is at least ½ inch larger than the hole so that when you slip it under the hole, the adhesive doesn't contact the padding. If your seats need major corrective surgery, go to a professional who can do the work properly.

## Caring for headliners

**WARNING**

The *headliner* is the covering for the inside of your vehicle's roof; it's usually cloth or vinyl on older models and a form-fitting felt-covered plastic on many newer vehicles. Many vinyl and cloth headliners are held in place by adhesives that can be dissolved by cleaning materials or pulled away by strong vacuuming, causing the headliner to sag. For this reason, treat it gently. If the headliner is badly stained or torn, either spend the bucks to have it professionally repaired or replaced, or live with it until you get a new vehicle.

## Cleaning floor mats

The vinyl floor coverings that substitute for carpet on many new vehicles don't look very sturdy to me. Floor mats are useful for protecting them and are easy to remove and clean. You can also use mats to protect existing carpets, especially in rainy or muddy areas, and to hide carpeting that's stained or torn.

Clean vinyl and rubber floor mats with cold water and soap. You can take them right out of the car and hose them down as you wash the car. Use a brush or scratchless kitchen scouring pad to gently remove caked-on dirt. Be sure to rinse mats thoroughly, and don't replace them until they're dry on both sides. Clean mats made of carpet with a carpet cleaner or shampoo.

TIP

Place old or worn mats or throw rugs on the floor of the trunk or hatchback area to reduce the noise level and protect the interior.

## Cleaning inside the windows

REMEMBER

Clean the interior surfaces of your windows and sunroof and the rearview mirror to remove the films caused by smoke and by the vapors that vinyl, plastic, and adhesives give off. Wash them the same way you wash your windows at home, or refer to the earlier section "Washing your vehicle's body" for general instructions. When washing windows, remember to use horizontal strokes on the inside and vertical ones on the outside so that you can tell which side of the glass the streaks are on.

WARNING

Avoid products with ammonia, which can damage tinted window film, and don't get dedicated glass cleaners on synthetic surfaces because it can stain them.

# Remembering Those Final Touches

Just to cover all the bases: Oil the hinges of the doors, hood, and rear deck lid now and then; and spray the door and trunk locks with graphite to keep them working smoothly. Be happy that you don't have to put fresh flowers in a little crystal vase in the passenger compartment, as some chauffeurs used to do! (But if you're lucky enough to have one of the modern Volkswagen Beetles — complete with dashboard bud vase — stop by the florist on your way home and pick up one of your favorite blossoms.)

# CAR COVERS

**TECHNICAL STUFF**

After you have your vehicle looking wonderful inside and out, it pays to keep it that way. If you have no garage and you must park outdoors, you may want to invest in a cover to protect your vehicle from the sun and keep the dirt and dust off it. The first thing you should realize is that you don't buy a cover to protect a vehicle from *moisture.* People who purchase vinyl or waterproof covers to keep their vehicles dry innocently cause more trouble than they prevent: Moisture gets under the cover anyway — from underneath — and is trapped there and prevented from evaporating quickly. So, a vehicle that's covered with a waterproof cover remains damp longer than one that's been unprotected and has dried quickly in the air and sunlight following a storm.

Now that you know *not* to buy a vinyl or waterproof car cover, here's what to look for when you're shopping for a cloth cover:

- The best covers on the market are cotton or cotton and polyester, woven so closely that they keep out the sunlight, prevent a good deal of moisture from getting through, dry out quickly, allow any moisture to evaporate easily, and are durable enough to last a couple of years. The fabric is also soft enough to avoid scratching the finish. The best covers come in shapes and sizes designed to fit specific vehicles, and you order them by year, make, and model. These can cost up to a couple of hundred dollars, but they save you money in the long run if you have an expensive vehicle to protect.

- Some covers come with cables that slide under the car and lock onto the cover to keep it from being stolen. You may want this option, especially if your vehicle sits unattended for long periods of time.

- The cheaper car covers designed for small, medium, and large models work fairly well. If you buy one of these, make sure that it has no metal cleats or grommets that can scratch the car and that it will stay on securely in gusting, windy weather. Mail-order ads in car magazines have some of the best buys.

IN THIS CHAPTER

» Ridding your vehicle of rust

» Getting rid of small dents, dings, and other imperfections

» Touching up paint

» Repairing damage to weatherstripping and windshields

» Obtaining the best deal on professional bodywork

# Chapter **24**

# Bodywork: Getting Rid of Dings, Dents, and Other Hard Knocks

Your vehicle's body is subject to the same ravages of time and hard knocks as your own. If you want Old Faithful (or the new pony) to stay forever young, you must keep a careful eye on it and forestall major damage by taking care of the minor stuff as soon as possible. Earlier chapters in this book deal with proper nutrition and regular maintenance for your vehicle's innards and how to keep it clean inside and out. This chapter deals with the dings and dents that your vehicle may suffer, and America's number-one car killer: *rust*. You also find out how to touch up paint, replace worn weatherstripping, deal with windshield damage, and, if all else fails, get the best possible deal from body shops. So get out there and spruce up your vehicle — it will love you for it!

The following word of warning applies to all the tasks outlined in this chapter:

WARNING

> **NO MATTER HOW OPTIMISTIC AND AMBITIOUS YOU ARE, DO NOT TACKLE ANY BODY DAMAGE LARGER THAN A COUPLE OF INCHES IN SIZE.**

Repairing a small area is relatively easy. But if your vehicle has suffered fairly extensive body damage, such as major rusting or large holes, dents, creases, or tears in its metal or fiberglass skin, I advise you to forget about trying to fix it yourself unless you have considerable skill in working with your hands and you really enjoy challenging and time-consuming jobs with less-than-perfect results. Amateur attempts usually give themselves away with uneven surfaces or color, and the filler or paint may wear away prematurely if the surface isn't prepared properly. Instead, rely on a professional body shop for appropriate major surgery. (You wouldn't try to set a broken leg yourself, would you?) I cover body shops and ways to get the best work for your money in the section, "Turning to the Pros for Larger Repairs," later in this chapter.

REMEMBER

Whenever you encounter a term set in *this font,* you'll find it defined in the glossary in Appendix A.

# Getting Rid of Rust

Rust, the "heavy" of this chapter, should probably be called *car cancer.* It arrives unheralded, eats corrosively into the car's body in unsuspected nooks and crannies, and — if you're foolish enough to simply paint over it — goes right on with its deadly work unseen. This imagery may seem excessively grim, but I honestly believe that over the years more fine vehicles have given way to the ravages of rust than have been demolished in accidents. The good news is that many modern vehicles have aluminum or plastic pieces, hoods, trunk lids, fenders, and bodies that aren't subject to rust.

TIP

The first line of defense against rust is to wash and wax your vehicle regularly. See Chapter 23 for tips on doing these and other cleaning chores.

## Checking for rust

WARNING

If you live in an area where the streets are salted in winter, where it rains or snows a great deal, or near the seashore — in other words, anywhere your vehicle is exposed to moisture and/or salt — you must be especially vigilant about detecting and getting rid of rust quickly. However, even if you live in a dry climate, you must still make a habit of checking carefully every few months. If you find rust forming, get rid of it before it can do major damage.

The paint on your vehicle is there not only for beauty but for protection as well. Paint and *clear-coat* finishes help retard rust and, on aluminum parts, corrosion and pitting. As long as your paint job is unmarred, metal body surfaces are safe. But something as seemingly innocuous as a small scratch can spell the beginning of trouble. Check the following trouble spots:

>> **Small scratches, nicks, and spots where the paint may have flaked off:** Touch up the paint in those areas before rust or corrosion can form on the bare metal (see "Touching Up Your Paint Job" later in this chapter).

>> **Dark spots in the paint, which may indicate that the metal is rusting underneath:** If you find these spots, read the next section to find out how to take care of the problem.

>> **Pitted places in the paint and on the chrome and metal trim:** Treat these spots with rust remover, following the directions on the package. Look for a rust remover that's safe to use on painted surfaces, and test the stuff on a small, hidden area first to make sure that it doesn't affect the color — no matter what the package says.

TIP

Another prime breeding ground for rust is any place on a vehicle where grime, dirt, or salt can accumulate. These areas are usually around fenders, under trim, and so on. Pay special attention to the following tips when you look for rust:

>> **Each time you wash the car, take a flashlight and check around the fenders, in the wheel wells, and behind metal bumpers.**

>> **Shine a light into the little crevices between the car body and all the trim and moldings that are affixed to it.** Look all around the lights, windows, side mirrors, sunroof, and antenna, too.

>> **If you live in a damp area, check the metal surfaces *inside* the vehicle, and don't forget to check around the window frames.**

>> **One of the most insidious places rust forms is under your vehicle, where you can't see it.** The next time you bring your car in for service, have the shop put it up on the hoist and check its underbody thoroughly. If you're afraid that the shop won't be thorough enough, ask them to let you have a look around while it's up there. Some shops won't allow this because of liability issues, but if you've built up a good relationship with an independent technician or service writer, they may be willing to sneak you in.

**REMEMBER**

Even if you have a vehicle with plastic or aluminum (and therefore rust-proof) body parts, the underbody is steel and therefore still the most sensitive area where rust is concerned. I've ridden in venerable old cars where the floorboards had rusted through so completely that I could see the road flash by below. And if rust attacks the frame, Old Faithful can be on its way to the Great Car Lot in the Sky before you know it.

## Dealing with any rust you find

Okay, the worst has happened: You find some rust spots on your car. Don't panic: You still have time to save the patient — unless the rust has gone too far. If the rust is underneath the vehicle, on the underside of the body or bumpers where it doesn't show, or still confined to very small areas that can be touched up easily, you can probably take care of the matter yourself. Here's what to do:

1. **Gently scrape away the rust with a single-edged razor blade or *fine-grain* sandpaper.**

    For slightly larger painted areas, use a brush with stiff (but not metal) bristles. Use coarse sandpaper to grind the rust off large areas that are out of sight and not surrounded by paint. Rust remover can make this job easier if you apply it after you get the crusty stuff off the surface.

**TIP**

    Always work *inward* from the edges to avoid extending the area by damaging the paint. Don't turn a small job into a large one by carelessly damaging the surrounding paint!

2. **After you've removed all the rust, apply some rust arrestor to keep the rust from spreading further.**

3. **As soon as the area is dry, prime and paint it to protect the surface and restore it to its former beauty.** See the "Touching Up Your Paint Job" section later in this chapter for details.

**WARNING**

If you see large rust holes in the body of the vehicle, or if the frame has been badly weakened by rust, get a couple of estimates from reliable body shops on what repairing the damage would cost. Then check those estimates against what your vehicle is worth by looking up the *blue book* value by make, model, and year at the Kelley Blue Book site (www.kbb.com) or Edmunds' site (www.edmunds.com). If you're not computer savvy, call your local bank, insurance company, or loan agency or look in the Classified section of your newspaper to see what vehicles of that make, model, and year are selling for these days. If your vehicle seems worth the effort and money, and is mechanically sound, bite the bullet and get it fixed professionally. Otherwise, it's time to get yourself another set of wheels.

# Undercoating to prevent rust

Special *undercoating,* which prevents rust from forming on the undersurface of a vehicle, works quite well if the vehicle is so new that absolutely no rust exists. Thankfully, most modern vehicles have already been dipped, frame and all, in rust inhibitors before being primed and painted. So if I were offered undercoating as a dealer option on a new vehicle, I'd refuse it. However, if you drive a much older model and are considering having it undercoated (or doing it yourself), consider these points:

WARNING

>> **If rust is already present on the underbody, undercoating simply locks the rust away, where it continues its insidious work unseen.** Have all the rust removed and a rust arrestor used to destroy any rust that may have been overlooked, and then have the undercoating applied.

>> **Spray undercoatings designed for amateur use are probably better than nothing, but continue to watch closely for rust after applying them.** If you decide to try one of these, *work in a well-ventilated area.*

>> **Don't spray the undercoating (or anything else, for that matter) on any cables, pipes, or parts that get hot.** Otherwise, they'll smell awful when the heat hits them.

# Removing Small Dents and Dings

Although you need special tools and equipment to yank, hammer, or otherwise coax large dents in damaged steel body parts back into place, taking care of little dents and dings is another matter. This type of damage responds to simple measures and may not require much work at all, even on aluminum and plastic parts. Here are some situations that you may want to tackle:

TIP

>> **If the paint has simply flaked or has been scratched off the surface,** follow the instructions for touching up paint later in this chapter.

Before you prime and paint the vehicle, take care of any rust, dings, or dents that you find. By taking care of all these things at once, you can then put a final coat of paint on all of them at the same time and have a car that looks wonderful.

>> **If a steel surface has been pushed in and hasn't been badly creased,** you can try to pop it back into place with a rubber plunger (the kind they call a *plumber's helper*). Just moisten the edge of the rubber, place the plunger over the dent, establish suction by pressing down on the handle, and then pull it

toward you. It may take a couple of tries before the metal pops back to normal. This technique works especially well on large expanses of metal, such as doors and fenders, if they have only been bent inward. It may work on aluminum as well as steel, depending on the size of the dent, but it doesn't work on plastic body parts.

>> **If you have small dents in a steel part,** you can attempt to hammer them out by placing a flat piece of metal (with a rag wrapped around it to protect the paint from scratching) on the outer side of the vehicle and banging the dent from the underside with a *flat-ended* hammer. Be very careful to bang only the underside of the dent and not the surrounding area, or you'll end up with a couple of new bumps to deal with. Work from the shallow sides of the dent toward the deeper areas and avoid overworking the metal, which stretches it.

Don't try this with aluminum, which can stretch, or plastic, which is likely to crack.

>> **If you have very small dings or places where the paint has chipped,** you can fill them in with glazing putty, which is very easy to handle. Use a putty knife to apply it, following the directions on the package, and then prime and paint the area. If the damaged area is larger than a very small, shallow ding, you need to resort to a body filler designed specifically for a steel, aluminum, or plastic body. The next section tells you how to use this material.

TIP

There are inexpensive specialty shops that just fix dents and dings. Many of these "paintless" dent-repair specialists are mobile and will come to you. *Always get an estimate before you commit to doing any bodywork yourself.* Having the work done professionally may cost you so much less in time and effort than struggling through a learning process that it will be cheaper in the long run!

# Filling Small Dents and Holes

Dents and holes can be repaired in one of two ways. As I mention earlier, you should have large damaged areas repaired by having a professional replace or straighten the body panels. You can fill smaller indentations with body filler.

TECHNICAL
STUFF

Many people refer to the process of using plastic body filler as *bondoing.* Although "bondo" has become a synonym for all car body fillers, Bondo is really the commercial name of a wide variety of auto body-repair products manufactured by one company; each product is designed for a specific body material.

Many compounds are on the market for filling small holes, dents, and creases in the surface of your car. Buy a good-quality product designed for the type of material your vehicle's body is made of (the cheap stuff may break loose or flake away) and follow the directions on the package closely.

Most kits contain at least two substances: the filler and a hardener that you mix with the filler before you use it. Check carefully at the auto supply store to find the kit with the easiest instructions that can do the job for you as simply as possible. The salespeople should be helpful if you tell them that this is your first attempt at bodywork.

To give you an idea of how to apply body filler, here are a few general instructions that suit most situations (but be sure to read and follow the directions on the product you buy):

1. **Clean the body area thoroughly to remove all traces of dirt, wax, or rust.**
   (See Chapter 23 and "Getting Rid of Rust" earlier in this chapter.)

2. **Sand the area using #180 or #220 aluminum oxide sandpaper or the type specified for your vehicle's plastic or aluminum parts.**

**WARNING**

   The salespeople at the auto supply or auto paint store can help you make the right selection. Because body fillers don't stick to paint, you must sand the area. When sanding, be sure to *feather-edge* (blend) the paint edges to prevent the old paint from chipping up through the new paint in the future and to ensure a good bond. Gently work inward from the edges of the dent to avoid enlarging the damaged area.

3. **Mix only as much hardener-filler as you're going to use right away.**

4. **If there's a *hole* in a metal vehicle's body, place fiberglass screening or fine aluminum chicken wire beneath the hole (on the underside of the body) to keep the filler from falling out. If you have a fiberglass or plastic part, use the appropriate patch kit available at your local auto supply or auto paint store.**

   Be sure to clean the area under the edges of the hole thoroughly to get rid of any dirt or paint that may be present. Then mix a very small proportion of filler and hardener and apply it to the edges of the screen and the edges of the area to be patched in order to hold the screen in place. If the kit contains no applicator, use a putty knife or plastic pot scraper to apply the filler. Let the screen patch dry for several hours before moving on to the next step.

5. **Apply the plastic filler, working slowly and carefully to avoid spreading the filler outside the dent or hole and marring the surrounding area.**

   After you finish, the filled portion should be slightly higher than the surface of the car around it.

6. As soon as the filler starts to harden (about to the consistency of hard cheese), use a perforated file to bring the level down almost to the level of the paint.

7. Wait at least 20 to 30 minutes until everything is bone dry; then sand the area with medium-grain sandpaper until it conforms perfectly to the surrounding body surface.

8. When everything is smooth and even, prime the area and touch up the paint.

   You can use primer as a last layer of filler to fill tiny holes or irregularities. Apply several layers of primer, sanding each layer with a sanding block, until the area appears perfectly smooth. (To check that it's smooth, wet the primer and look at the way light reflects off the surface.)

# Touching Up Your Paint Job

**WARNING**

The techniques used to paint the body of a vehicle can vary depending on the size of the area you're working on and the original paint and finish. Unless you have an experienced and steady hand (and the car's original paint hasn't faded or changed color since it was new), it's almost impossible to conceal the fact that you repainted anything larger than a small area. Larger areas require spray-painting, which must be done in a well-ventilated area that's free from dust and dirt. So if the area you need to paint is large, it will probably cost you less in time, money, and effort to have the job done by a professional who can match the paint and do the job right.

**REMEMBER**

Never attempt to do a major paint job on a good vehicle without trying your hand on an old wreck first. If you practice on a junker, you can afford to make mistakes — because even a *bad* paint job can increase the resale value of a car that's practically worthless to begin with.

**TIP**

If you want a cheap but decent job that will last a year or so, find out where local car dealers take the used cars they get as trade-ins to have them spiffed up before resale. To save money, you can remove any rust, spot-fill, and paint the small areas yourself, and then have the rest of the job done professionally.

On the other hand, touching up a *small* spot with a little bottle of touch-up paint is easy. Before you start the job, mask the surrounding area well and use even, sweeping strokes to apply the paint. (Follow the directions on the can carefully.)

Practice on a piece of scrap metal before you tackle the car, and don't expect the results to look terrific. Follow these steps:

1. **To find the right paint color you need, look on the *firewall* of your vehicle — you should see a little plate with the body number and paint code number on it.**

   If you can't find the paint code number, consult your owner's manual or ask your local dealership where to find it.

2. **At the dealership's parts department, buy a little bottle of touch-up paint that matches the code number.**

   If that's not possible, your local auto supply store should have a chart that indicates the proper paint to match your vehicle's make, model, and year. If you can't find the right paint at either source, call a professional auto paint supply store. They're also often good sources for semiprofessional advice.

   Touch-up bottles of paint usually come with a brush or applicator in them. You also need a small bottle of primer unless the paint specifies that it isn't required.

REMEMBER

3. **Make sure that the area is rust-free.**

   If the damage is only a deep scratch or a tiny spot, you may need just a dab of rust arrestor to stop the rust from continuing to form under the new paint. If the area is any larger, you must remove all the rust carefully, following the directions in the earlier section, "Dealing with any rust you find."

4. **Sand the spot carefully with a small piece of #220 sandpaper to rough up the surface so that the primer adheres properly.**

5. **Wash the area thoroughly to remove any rust arrestor, dust, dirt, filler residue, and wax; then let the area dry completely before you apply the primer.**

   Primer is used to seal a metal surface against rust and to provide a surface for the paint to adhere to. Primer also fills in tiny holes and imperfections in the surface.

WARNING

   If you're dealing with a surface scratch or a chip that isn't down to the bare metal, you can probably get away with simply applying the paint. But never apply paint to bare metal or plastic. If a bare spot is exposed, or if the spot is larger than a fraction of an inch, prime the area first.

6. **Use a tiny brush or a matchstick to apply the primer sparingly.**

   You shouldn't need more than a drop to cover the damaged area. *Avoid getting primer on the original paint.* If you do, wipe it off immediately. Let the primer dry thoroughly before moving on to Step 7.

7. **Mix the paint in the touch-up bottle thoroughly to blend the color pigments properly.**

   Unless your vehicle is very new, the color probably won't match exactly (which is another reason for keeping the area as small as possible). The paint on new models doesn't fade as quickly or badly as old paints did.

8. **Apply the paint, covering the surface of the spot completely and working inward from the edges.**

**WARNING**

   If you're painting a scratch or a very small area, you can cut down the brush or use a matchstick or toothpick instead. The paint should be no thicker than the surrounding surface or it will show, run, bubble, or peel off.

9. **Wait several days for everything to dry completely, and then polish the whole vehicle to blend in the painted area and bring everything to a high gloss.**

10. **Give the car a coat of wax or polymer to protect your hard work (see Chapter 23).**

# Installing New Weatherstripping or Patching the Old

Whistles and leaks inside your vehicle are usually the result of worn, torn, or faulty *weatherstripping* (the *gaskets* that you find around the doors, windows, the sunroof, and the trunk opening). If the interior or trunk gets wet when you wash the car or when it rains, use a garden hose to locate the areas on the weatherstripping that let the water in. If the windows whistle when you drive with them closed, check the weatherstripping for the cause of the sound effects. (If you notice leaks *under* the vehicle, see Chapter 20 for ways to find the source and eliminate the problem.)

**TIP**

If your old weatherstripping is in pretty good shape but is admitting air or water in one or two small areas, try applying weatherstripping adhesive under the loose portions, or use a clear silicone sealer (which comes in a tube) to seal around the areas that leak.

If the weatherstripping is old, dried, cracked, or worn, you can probably buy a whole new piece designed for your vehicle's make, model, and year at your dealer's service department.

To install new weatherstripping, follow these steps:

1. **Check to see whether the new weatherstripping is the same as the old piece you're replacing.**

   The piece should be the same shape and thickness and should have holes, channels, and rubber studs on the inner side that match the ones on the original.

2. **Remove any screws and gently peel off the old weatherstripping, prying any rubber studs out of the holes they're inserted into without damaging the paint or scratching the surrounding trim.**

   If the weatherstripping is hard to remove, spray weatherstripping remover around the area and wait until the adhesive softens before continuing.

3. **Use weatherstripping remover to remove any old adhesive that remains on the frame after the seal is gone.**

4. **Insert the new weatherstripping into the frame to make sure that it fits the holes and contours of the frame. Then gently remove it.**

5. **Make sure that the new weatherstripping is clean.**

   Either rinse it off and dry it thoroughly or use fine-grain sandpaper to remove any unauthorized bumps and rough spots.

6. **Apply weatherstripping adhesive (it comes in a tube)** *sparingly* **to the strip and to the surface of the frame.**

7. **Before the adhesive dries, replace the new weatherstripping, making sure that every rubber stud or other fastening device is in its hole securely.**

8. **Replace any screws that you removed, and make sure that the ends of the weatherstripping meet and are glued down securely.**

TIP

A quick and easy way to patch things up if you don't care how they look is to get a roll of black household weatherstripping about ½ inch wide with an adhesive back and simply stick small pieces of it onto or under the weatherstripping in the trouble areas. This stuff is also useful for keeping camper hatches and sunroofs from leaking or banging if they don't fit quite perfectly and for keeping rain from coming past the rubber sleeve where the camper shell meets the cab of a truck. You can always use it around the house, too!

# Dealing with Damaged Windshields

Windshields can easily collect pits and cracks from flying pebbles and other debris. It's vital that these be repaired immediately — no matter how small — because, as you continue to drive, they will inevitably grow in size, obscure or distract your vision, and ultimately destroy your windshield. How you deal with windshield damage depends on the size of the crack or pit. This section discusses your options.

**TIP**

Generally speaking, if the windshield damage is less than one inch in diameter, it usually can be repaired. If it's much larger, you're probably better off getting a new windshield installed instead of paying a professional to repair it, only to have the weakened area give way at a future date.

If the damage is really tiny, you can try one of the windshield glass repair kits on the market, but their durability and whether they render the site irreparable by a professional is still under debate.

**WARNING**

If any damage is right in your line of vision, repairing it may not be the safest way to go. Have the windshield replaced with a new one as quickly as possible. It's not a great idea to get a used windshield from a wrecker because it may have tiny flaws, and it must be installed professionally anyway. Because airbag deployment creates stress on windshields and is designed with a specific windshield in mind, don't risk a part that isn't *OEM*. That bargain could cost you your life in an accident. For this reason, have the work done by a windshield specialist you can trust. In many areas, mobile windshield replacement companies will do the job right in your driveway.

If you can't get to a repair facility right away, *gently* put some transparent tape over the damage to keep it from spreading and try to drive as little as possible. Don't touch the damage, try not to get it wet, and don't run the air conditioner, heater, or defroster because moisture and changes in temperature can accelerate its growth.

# Turning to the Pros for Larger Repairs

If, for any reason, you feel that it's wiser to have a professional make repairs, in order to ensure that you get the best work at a reasonable price, you must be able to choose the right shop, make the best decision about the type of parts you feel are acceptable, and check to be sure the job's been done properly. This section helps you accomplish all these tasks efficiently.

## Evaluating body shops

Body shops run the gamut from small back-alley paint booth operations to high-tech specialists with space-age lasers, computerized sonar, electric eyes, and robots that scan, measure, and repair auto damage and alignment electronically. Some shops still mix colors by eye and formula, and others use computers and scanners that match even faded colors perfectly.

ECO-LOGIC

To protect the environment, find a shop that filters, recycles, and disposes of waste materials in an ecologically sound manner even though some states and provinces still don't require it. If you need to locate a reliable body shop, consult the sections in Chapter 22 on finding and evaluating a good service facility. Then use the following tips to pick the best one:

>> **Take a look around the shop to see whether they remove — or at least properly mask — chrome, trim, rubber, locks, door jambs, and handles to prevent paint from getting on them.**

>> **Look along the sides of finished vehicles.** The light reflected off the restored surfaces will reveal whether they're smooth and shiny. Does the color match the rest of the vehicle exactly?

>> **Get at least three estimates.** Each estimate should include a list of all the parts that need to be replaced or replated.

>> **Ask the owner or manager the following questions:**

- **Do you have the latest high-tech equipment?** If your vehicle has been damaged extensively and is covered by insurance, go for the most sophisticated setup you can find. If damage is relatively minor and you're paying for it yourself, a good job done with more traditional equipment at a lower price may suffice.

- **Do you do all the work in-house, or do you send some of it out?** Tell them that you'll want to see invoices for any new parts and outside labor involved. If trim must be sent out for plating, you may save money by arranging to take it there and pick it up yourself.

- **What *guarantees* or *warranties* apply for parts and labor?** Unless your insurance company guarantees the work it authorizes for the life of the vehicle, make sure that you'll be covered by the shop, if problems occur.

- **How do you prepare the surface of the vehicle before you paint?** If steel body panels (*not* aluminum, fiberglass, or plastic) are to be replaced, will the new ones be galvanized to protect them from rust? If old paint is stripped away from steel surfaces, will the bare metal be treated if the galvanized zinc layer has been stripped away? What kinds of primers does the shop use to ensure that new paint will adhere properly, especially if parts being painted are aluminum, fiberglass, or plastic?

- **Which sealants, coatings, catalysts, and hardeners do you use to protect the newly restored surfaces?** They should be the same, or at least as good, as those on the rest of your vehicle, or the restored areas will age prematurely when exposed to the elements.

## Choosing parts

Unless your insurer specifies that only *OEM* parts be used, body shops should offer you several options on the type of parts they buy for your vehicle. Used parts of all kinds can cost half as much as OEM equipment, but if you have to pay for the parts and labor to replace low-quality parts often, they can end up costing you more. As an environmentalist, I favor anything that can be reused, so here are the pros and cons for each type of part that may be available:

» *OEM (original equipment manufacturer)* **parts are supplied by the original automobile manufacturer.** They may cost more, but they're under *warranty*, designed for your vehicle, and often are more durable.

» *Replacement parts* **are made by independent companies called** *aftermarket* **suppliers.** They can range from poor quality to as good as OEM. Discuss with your body shop the origin of any aftermarket parts they propose to use and their warranties.

» *Rebuilt* **parts are used parts that have been taken apart, cleaned, and readjusted — often by hand from kits — until they're "as good as new."** Be sure that these parts are *guaranteed* and are from a reputable source.

» *Remanufactured* **or factory rebuilt parts usually have been rebuilt on an assembly line by a major company and repackaged for resale like new parts.** How good they are depends on the standards of the remanufacturer. Entering the brand name into your favorite Internet search engine to do a bit of research can help here.

ECO-LOGIC

» **Recycled parts can range from used parts of questionable quality fresh from a junkyard to higher quality parts in good condition.** They're always cheaper but usually come with a limited warranty or none at all. If you have a reliable mechanic who knows how to choose wisely, and you want to save money and be environmentally responsible, the risk may be worth it. Recycled parts decrease not only what ends up in landfills but also the energy and toxic materials used for rebuilding or reconditioning.

» **Reconditioned parts usually are used for old vehicles whose manufacturers no longer provide OEM parts.** Quality depends on the source, but the parts should be in spiffy condition with worn components replaced or rebuilt and all the rust removed. Warranties, if they exist, are limited and usually don't apply to labor.

# Checking bodywork

When the work on your vehicle is finished, check it carefully before you leave the shop:

>> **Check light reflected along the repaired surface for ripples, bumps, or depressions.**

>> **Make sure that the edges of the hood, rear deck lid, sunroof, and doors are smoothly aligned with the body of the vehicle.**

>> **Check whether the inside edges of the doors, hood, and trunk are neatly painted, or whether the old paint shows through.**

>> **Look for unpainted spaces around the edges of door handles, chrome, and other fittings.** For painting, these parts should be removed rather than masked so that the paint extends under them and protects the area from rust. If inadequate masking has allowed the paint to overspray these and other unpainted surfaces, refuse to pay until the unwanted paint has been completely removed.

>> **Compare newly painted parts to other areas to be sure that the color matches the older paint exactly.**

TIP

Because bodywork requires such expertise, buying a new bumper or piece of trim (or locating an unflawed one at a wrecker's) is often less expensive than restoring the damaged part. Many modern vehicles have thin body panels that are designed to be replaced rather than repaired. They crumple so easily that they're as difficult to straighten as tinfoil, and it's cheaper and easier to have a new panel installed and painted.

If extensive areas of a metal car body need to be repaired, have those damaged body panels replaced rather than filled in with body fillers. It's a good idea to ask each body shop you consult whether they plan to replace large, damaged areas with sheet-metal body panels welded in place of the old ones or if they plan to straighten the old panels and finish them with a thin skin of filler. Many vehicles are still made primarily of steel with plastic bumper covers and trim pieces, but a growing number use aluminum for door skins and hoods, and a few have all-aluminum or all-plastic (including fiberglass) bodies. A good shop will have no difficulty working with plastics or with aluminum body parts. But if you have an all-aluminum vehicle and have sustained underbody or frame damage, make sure that the shop is certified to work on aluminum.

# 7

# The Part of Tens

Want to know about the ten most important preventive maintenance measures for your vehicle? Want to find out the ten most powerful ways to save fuel — and be a little kinder to the environment in the process? You can find this helpful information in this part.

This part also contains two appendixes that I hope you'll find yourself referring to again and again as you explore your vehicle and take on the work it needs. Appendix A is a glossary that puts automotive jargon into easy-tounderstand terms. Appendix B contains *Specifications* and *Maintenance Records* for you to fill in; they'll help you keep track of your car's "specs" as well as the work it receives.

Chapter **25**

# The Ten Most Important Preventive Maintenance Measures

The major goals of preventive maintenance are to keep your vehicle from breaking down on the road, to catch minor problems before they become major expenses, to prevent premature wear and tear by keeping parts from wearing each other away and by removing objects that could damage your vehicle's interior and its occupants, and to safeguard warranties and guarantees on your vehicle and its parts. The tips in this chapter tell you what you need to do and refer you to more information in this book that will keep your vehicle running better, longer.

**REMEMBER**

Whenever you encounter a term set in *this font,* you'll find it defined in the glossary in Appendix A.

# Change the Oil Frequently and Regularly

**TIP**

Oil reduces the friction in your engine and keeps it running smoothly. Most automakers recommend much longer intervals between oil changes, but I believe that the most important thing you can do to extend the life of your vehicle is to change the oil every 5,000 miles or six months, whichever comes first, and as frequently as every 3,000 miles if you drive mostly in stop-and-go traffic or on dusty or wet roads. Chapter 13 helps you decide how often to change your oil and provides instructions for doing that job. It can be easier than cooking dinner!

# Do a Monthly Under-the-Hood Check

If you take 15 minutes to do the under-the-hood check in Chapter 2, you can prevent 70 percent of the reasons your vehicle might break down on the road! At least be sure to check the following fluid levels once a month: *oil, coolant,* automatic *transmission fluid, brake fluid, power steering* fluid, and windshield washer fluid. Refill or replace these fluids as necessary.

# Check the Tire Inflation and Alignment

Underinflated tires wear out faster, create excessive heat, increase fuel consumption, and make your vehicle more difficult to handle. Tires that aren't properly balanced or that are out of *alignment* wear out rapidly, increase wear and tear on the *steering* and *suspension systems,* and may take you for a bumpy or unsafe ride. Check the air pressure in your tires and look for signs of wear and misalignment at least once a month and before every long trip. Chapter 17 shows you how easy this is to do.

# Keep the Interior Clean

The cleaner you keep the interior of your vehicle, the longer the upholstery and carpets will remain in good condition. Remove the mats and vacuum them along with the upholstery, *headliner,* and carpeting when they start to get dirty or every time you wash your vehicle. Wipe up spills and get rid of stains as they occur, *before* they have a chance to set and become permanent. If it's too late to prevent stains, consult a stain-removal guide for the ways to avoid making the stain bigger or permanent. Use an odor remover to keep the interior of your vehicle smelling fresh. Chapter 23 offers advice for cleaning your vehicle's interior and dealing with nasty stains and odors.

TIP

Keep trash and personal effects in receptacles, and keep kids' toys stashed in a box that fits snugly on the floor behind the front seat. If you have to stop short, these things can become lethal projectiles. Unsecured objects on the floor or under the driver's seat can wedge under brake and accelerator pedals.

# Wash the Vehicle Frequently and Keep It Out of the Sun

TIP

Wash your vehicle once a week to protect paint and prevent rust. Work in the shade; sunlight on cleaners can ruin the finish of the paint. If water doesn't bead up on the car when it rains or when you hose it down, it needs waxing. Wax at least twice a year, in the spring and fall, to protect your car from weather extremes and preserve its finish. Chapter 23 tells you how to keep your car clean and protect it from the elements.

# Get Rid of Rust

WARNING

Rust can start out as a small spot in an inconspicuous nook or cranny and then spread like cancer through the vulnerable metals on your vehicle. Chapter 24 has tips on checking for and removing rust, preventing the formation of more rust, and restoring your vehicle's finish.

# Change the Filters

Changing your air, fuel, and oil filters regularly can help extend the life of your vehicle, increase its fuel efficiency, and improve its performance.

ECO-LOGIC

>> *Air filters* keep dirt out of *fuel injection systems* and *carburetors.* Your vehicle runs on a mixture of fuel and air, so if air can't flow freely through a dirty filter, you pay the price in fuel consumption and performance. Change the filter every 20,000 miles, and more frequently if you drive in dusty areas like

deserts or near construction sites. Chapter 8 shows how to check and replace air filters.

>> **Fuel filters** help prevent rust and sediment from entering the engine. Change the fuel filter at every **tune-up** — more often if you regularly drive with an almost-empty **fuel tank.** (Not a good idea!) Chapter 8 tells you how to check and replace a fuel filter.

>> **Oil filters** clean the oil and remove metal and dirt that, in circulating through an engine, create friction between moving parts, damage the engine, and wear it out prematurely. Change the oil filter every time you change your oil. Chapter 13 tells you how to do this.

# Change the Coolant

*Coolant* helps your vehicle keep its cool, and changing it is a job that you can handle yourself if you do it in an environmentally safe manner. Change the coolant at least once a year or every 30,000 miles, whichever comes first. Do it more often if your engine has been losing coolant or overheats easily. Chapter 12 has instructions on checking and changing coolant.

# Lubricate the Moving and Rubber Parts

A *lube job* involves applying grease and oil to some parts of your car to keep them moving freely and to keep rubber parts supple. Modern vehicles have sealed joints that don't need to be refilled with grease, but *all* vehicles still have *transmissions* and other parts that need to be checked and serviced regularly. Many service facilities include this as part of oil changes or other scheduled maintenance packages.

TIP

To prevent friction that can wear parts away prematurely, investigate and eliminate all squeaks and rattles as soon as they occur. Chapter 20 helps you troubleshoot strange sounds and other symptoms.

# Get Scheduled Maintenance
# to Keep Warranties Valid

Performing scheduled maintenance prolongs the life of your vehicle, ensures that your warranties remain valid, and may improve resale value when you're ready to part with the vehicle. Check your *owner's manual* or ask the dealership for your vehicle's maintenance schedule and *warranty* information. Appendix B contains a *Maintenance Record* to help you keep track of what you did and when you did it. Maintain a copy for each vehicle you own.

**TIP**

You don't have to have scheduled maintenance done at a dealership. Licensed independent shops can do the work without voiding the warranty as long as they use parts supplied by the original manufacturer of your vehicle (commonly known as *OEM*) or *aftermarket* parts that meet your automaker's specifications.

Chapter **26**

# Ten "Eco-Logical" Ways to Save Fuel

**W**ith rising fuel costs, increased emphasis on global warming, and the economic and political impact of dependency on fossil fuels, increasing fuel efficiency has become a major goal for federal and state governments and for most drivers, even if just to save money. The best way to avoid wasting fuel and dumping the unburned residue into the environment is to drive efficiently. But it doesn't end there: How well you maintain your vehicle has a major impact on its fuel economy because the more efficiently it operates, the less fuel it will burn and the less pollution it will add to the air. And there are other factors to consider, as well.

**ECO-LOGIC**

This chapter gives you ten very important ways to do your part for the environment by saving fuel. I call it "eco-logical" because it makes sense to view your vehicle and your driving techniques from an environmental perspective as well as from an automotive point of view. I've also used "Eco-Logic" icons like the one on this page throughout this book to alert you to issues and tasks that are directly related to the environment.

**REMEMBER**

Whenever you encounter a term set in *this font,* you'll find it defined in the glossary in Appendix A.

# Take a Look under the Hood

For your vehicle's best fuel economy, follow these recommendations to make sure that parts of your vehicle are in good condition and functioning properly:

>> **If your *air filter* is dirty, you can lose one mile per gallon at 50 *mph*.** Cleaning or replacing your air filter can cut your fuel consumption, and if you cut it by only 10 percent, you can save an average of 77 gallons a year! Chapter 8 tells you how to check and replace your air filter.

>> **If your *PCV valve* isn't functioning properly, your engine runs less efficiently, and you may be burning and polluting your oil and the air, as well.** Chapter 7 tells you what the PCV valve does, and Chapter 8 shows you how to check and replace it.

>> **If your *spark plugs* are misfiring because they're dirty or improperly gapped, the problem can cost you up to 25 percent in gas mileage.** Find out about spark plugs in Chapter 5 and how to check, adjust, and replace them in Chapter 6.

>> **Consult your *owner's manual* for how often your vehicle needs a *tune-up*, and if it's overdue, have it done immediately.** A simple tune-up can reduce carbon monoxide and hydrocarbon exhaust emissions by 30 to 50 percent. It also saves fuel and improves your vehicle's performance.

>> **If the *accessory belts* that connect your *fan, water pump, alternator*, air conditioner, and a variety of other devices are too loose or too tight, a serious loss of efficiency can be the result.** A belt should have about ½ inch of "give" and shouldn't be frayed or badly worn. Chapter 2 shows you how to check these belts, and Chapter 12 provides instructions for adjusting and replacing them.

>> **If a *brake* is poorly adjusted, it may "drag" while the vehicle is in motion. Moving the wheel against the dragging brake takes more power, which means that your *brake linings* and the fuel in your tank don't last as long.** To check for dragging brakes, jack up each wheel (see Chapter 1) and spin it. If a *brake shoe* or *brake pad* is dragging, you can feel it as you try to turn the wheel on the hub. Chapter 15 tells you everything you need to know about brakes. If you have a *hybrid* vehicle with *regenerative braking,* a professional should check your brakes.

>> **If you hear a rumbling sound while driving or when spinning the jacked-up wheel, your *wheel bearings* may be worn and may need to be replaced.** The wheel bearings are in there to prevent friction, and if they're worn, it takes extra energy (think fuel) to turn the wheels and move the vehicle down the road. Chapter 15 has instructions for checking and repacking wheel bearings.

# Start Up without Warming Up

When you start your car in the morning, do you warm it up before you drive off? If you do, stop! Modern vehicles don't need much (if any) warm-up, and experts caution you not to indulge in lengthy warm-ups because they waste fuel, pollute the air, and increase wear on your vehicle.

TIP

If your vehicle doesn't start up immediately, try the following:

» **Have a professional check for a computer malfunction.** Vehicles with *fuel injection* may have problems starting up because of a computer malfunction. A professional who deals with your model will have to set things right. Check out the section called "What to Do When All Else Fails" in Chapter 8.

» **Check your *thermostat* and replace it, if necessary.** The thermostat initially keeps the water in the engine from circulating, which helps the engine to quickly reach and maintain the proper temperature. If you have trouble starting your vehicle on cold mornings, Chapter 11 can help you locate your thermostat, and Chapter 12 shows you how to check and replace it if it's no longer properly regulating the flow of water through the engine.

# Drive Eco-Logically

Evaluate your driving techniques in terms of fuel consumption. For example, if you're driving at 55 mph and accelerate to 65 mph but then have to brake after a block or two, you've wasted the fuel it took to accelerate the vehicle because you returned to the original speed so soon.

TIP

Before putting on extra speed, check to be sure that you won't have to waste the effort by slowing for a blinker, crossroad, or curve ahead. Remember, every time you step on the brake pedal, you cancel the speed that you used fuel to achieve!

Here are some other driving techniques that can help you save fuel:

» **Adjust the driver's seat as comfortably as possible.** Research has shown that a comfortable driving position helps you tread more lightly on the *accelerator,* and a light foot saves fuel. By driving at 50 mph instead of 70 mph, a "feather-foot" can cut fuel consumption by 20 percent! Increased wind resistance at the higher speed also causes your vehicle's *chassis* to age twice as fast.

>> **Start and accelerate slowly and smoothly.** Moving a vehicle from a stationary position takes power. You can apply that power efficiently by starting and accelerating slowly, or you can blow the whole thing by slamming on the gas pedal for a quick getaway. A fast start may cost you eight miles per gallon for the first four miles. A slow start can carry you 50 percent farther on the same amount of gas. So try not to speed — at least for the first mile!

>> **Obey the speed limits, especially in city traffic.** Traffic lights are set for the local speed limit, so if you maintain a nice, steady, legal speed, you'll find that the lights magically turn green as you approach them. The result is less work for you and 15 percent less fuel consumed. My Prius has a lovely animated display that shows how my driving affects fuel consumption. It has taught me to drive more efficiently!

>> **Try to stay in your lane.** Each time you change lanes to pass another car on the highway, you waste fuel because you have to accelerate to pass and then you usually have to step on the brake to avoid hitting the vehicle in front of you when you get back into the lane. The result is up to 30 percent more fuel *wasted* than if you were to stay in your lane.

>> **Set a steady pace.** Anticipate slowdowns and halts in traffic so that you don't have to stop short. If you're not speeding, you may be able to account for a lot of slowdowns just by taking your foot off the accelerator; by decelerating rather than braking, you don't wear out your brakes as quickly, and you save fuel.

>> **Build up speed slowly *before* you get to a hill.** The extra momentum will carry you at least part of the way up. Don't accelerate to maintain your speed while you're climbing unless you're holding up traffic. Keep the gas pedal steady, and never crest the top of a hill at a high speed because you'll only have to brake on the way down, wasting the fuel that got you up there so quickly in the first place.

>> **Try coasting down hills, using the weight of your vehicle and its momentum to carry you down, with your foot off the accelerator.** If you're holding up traffic by coasting down a hill, accelerate *gently* to the legal speed limit.

>> **If you have an *automatic transmission* with an *overdrive* option, use it.** Doing so can save you another 10 percent in fuel.

>> **If you have a *manual transmission,* shift into higher gears as soon as possible.** Practice doing so at the lowest speed the vehicle can handle without laboring or lugging the engine.

# Structure Trips to Save Fuel

A one-mile trip on a cold engine can cut fuel economy by as much as 70 percent, so consider these recommendations when you need to go out to shop or run errands:

>> **Walk, ride your bike, or take public transportation.**

>> **If your trips take you farther afield and you need to drive, conserve fuel by combining lots of little trips into one longer one.**

>> **Shop locally.** Slightly higher prices are likely to be balanced by what you save in time, effort, and fuel.

>> **If you can, skip the trips altogether and shop by phone or online.**

>> **Consider putting together carpools, which are great fuel-savers and often result in new friendships as well.**

TIP

Believe it or not, it takes more fuel to make a left turn than a right turn because, for a left turn, you usually have to wait, idling at zero miles per gallon, until traffic clears and then overcome inertia to get the vehicle moving again. For the same reason, a trip around the block can use less fuel than a U-turn that involves a lot of stopping and starting.

# Fill 'Er Up Eco-Logically

Fuel economy involves more than altering driving techniques. How you pump gas affects your fuel consumption and can save you money as well. (Chapter 1 tells you how to fill 'er up yourself.) Keep the following points in mind the next time you fill up at a service station:

>> **In hot weather, fill up in the early morning or evening when the air is cooler and before gasoline is delivered to the station.** Like everything else, gasoline expands with heat. An increase of only 30 degrees can cause ten gallons of gas to expand by as much as four-fifths of a quart — that's as much as a bottle of whiskey! This expansion reduces its energy content, so you pay more for less when the fuel is hot.

WARNING

>> **Never overfill the tank.** When the filler hose clicks off automatically, resist the temptation to squirt in that extra little bit. An overfilled tank will run over and spill gasoline on the ground if you drive up a hill or park in the heat of the sun. Not only does this spillage waste fuel and dissolve asphalt on driveways and roadways, but the fumes also contribute substantially to air pollution.

# Keep Your Side Windows Shut and the AC Turned Off

Open side windows increase wind resistance, which reduces fuel efficiency. Use the interior vents or the sunroof instead. You may think that turning on the air conditioning in your vehicle is a good alternative to opening side windows, but it costs you mileage because your engine has to put out extra power to make the air conditioner work. Some air conditioners can consume an extra 2½ miles per gallon! So if you live in a fairly cool area, you may not want (or need) to use your vehicle's air conditioning at all.

# Keep Your Tires Properly Inflated

Underinflated tires consume about one mile per gallon of extra gasoline. They wear out faster, too, so make sure that your tires get all they need. Chapter 17 shows you how to "read" your tires' treads to see whether they're properly inflated and how to find the proper pressure range on the sidewalls of your tires.

**TECHNICAL STUFF**

After a car has been driven for a while, the tires heat up and the air in them expands. Therefore, to get an accurate reading, always use your tire gauge in the morning before you drive the car, and if you need air, head to the nearest air pump and let the tires cool down before adding the proper amount of air, following the instructions in Chapter 17.

**TIP**

Snow tires consume a lot more fuel than regular tires. If they aren't mandatory in your state in winter, take them off the car as soon as weather permits and consider all-weather tires instead. Ask a trusted tire dealer what's best for your driving situation. You may need just one set of tires, or you may be better off with one set for summer and another for winter.

# Clean Out the Junk

Every 500 pounds you carry costs you from two to five miles per gallon, so it pays to keep your vehicle as light as possible. Clean all but the essentials out of the trunk and interior, and consider how much fuel you'd save if *you* lost some extra pounds, as well! Turn to Chapter 23 for advice on cleaning your vehicle's interior.

# Keep Your Vehicle Waxed

Did you know that a highly waxed vehicle cuts wind resistance dramatically? And it looks good, too. Chapter 23 shows you how to wash and wax your vehicle properly.

# Use a Trailer Instead of a Roof Rack

Those light–looking roof racks are deceptive. They create quite a bit of drag, especially when fully loaded, and the ensuing wind resistance substantially interferes with the air flow around your vehicle. As a matter of fact, a small trailer loaded with the same gear is less of a liability because trailers travel in the wake of the vehicle and meet with less air resistance. Of course, they weigh more, too, but once underway, they follow along easily if you don't speed. Besides, you always disconnect the trailer when you don't need it, but you tend to carry the empty roof rack around even when you have no load to put on it.

# Appendix A

# A Practical Glossary of Automotive Terms

## DICTIONARY OF ACRONYMS

If you've encountered an acronym in this book and need a quick refresher as to what it refers to, this listing tells you the glossary term it stands for. If you want details, look up that term in the glossary.

- **ABS:** anti-lock braking system
- **ACC:** adaptive cruise control
- **ADS:** Association of Diesel Specialists
- **BA:** brake assist
- **CNG:** compressed natural gas
- **CV joint:** constant velocity joint
- **CVT:** continuously variable transmission
- **DCT:** dual-clutch transmission
- **EBD:** electronic brakeforce distribution
- **ECM:** electronic control module
- **ECS:** emissions control system
- **ECU:** engine control unit
- **ESC:** electronic stability control
- **EV:** electric vehicle
- **HID:** high intensity discharge lamps
- **ICE:** internal combustion engine
- **ICM:** ignition control module

*(continued)*

*(continued)*

- **IIHS:** Insurance Institute for Highway Safety

- **MIL:** malfunction indicator lights

- **mph:** miles per hour

- **NGV:** natural gas vehicles

- **NHTSA:** National Highway Traffic Safety Administration

- **NOS:** new old stock

- **OEM:** original equipment manufacturer

- **OHC:** overhead cam

- **PCM:** powertrain control module

- **PCV:** positive crankcase ventilation

- **psi:** pounds per square inch

- **PZEV:** partial zero-emission vehicle

- **R&R:** removal and replacement

- **RSC:** rollover stability control

- **TCS:** traction control system

- **U-joints:** universal joints

- **VIN:** vehicle identification number

- **ZEV:** zero-emission vehicle

**TIP**

Words appearing in ***this font*** are defined elsewhere in the glossary.

**accelerator:** The gas pedal.

**accessory (or drive) belt:** A V-shaped or flat serpentine belt that's driven by a ***crankshaft pulley*** and transmits this drive to various accessories, such as the ***alternator,*** air conditioning compressor, ***fan,*** power-steering pump, and ***water pump.***

**adaptive cruise control (ACC):** Transforms cruise control into a system that can be programmed to maintain a safe distance between your car and the vehicle in front of you and to provide protection if a crash seems imminent.

**additives:** Substances that may be added to gasoline, ***diesel fuel, coolant,*** or lubricating oil. Popular additives clean gasoline and diesel ***fuel injectors,*** add ***water pump*** lubricant and corrosion preventers to coolant, and add ***viscosity*** extenders to lubricating oil.

**aftermarket:** Any product or part *not* installed on or provided with the vehicle at the time of purchase (stuff you buy *after* you buy the vehicle, usually from a source other than the automaker).

**air bag:** An inflatable bladder that pops out of the dash, steering wheel, and/or side panels during a collision to protect the vehicle's occupants.

**air cleaner:** A container, called the **cold air collector box** on modern vehicles, that's located on or in the **air inlet duct** to the **fuel injection** system or **carburetor**. It contains an **air filter,** which removes dust and dirt from the air before it enters the engine. (This container also acts as a flame arrester in case of backfire.)

**air filter:** The element in the **air cleaner** that removes impurities from the air. Most air filters are disposable, although some **aftermarket** types can be cleaned and reused.

**air inlet duct:** The passage through which air travels to the **air cleaner** and the **intake manifold.** Also called the *air intake duct* or *air intake hose*.

**air intake hose:** See **air inlet duct.**

**air springs:** Rubber bladders filled with air that are computer controlled to cushion the bumps and vibrations of driving. See also **suspension system.**

**air-cooled engine:** An engine that uses air instead of water for its **cooling system.**

**alignment:** The position of the car wheels relative to the car body. Proper wheel alignment improves handling and performance and reduces **tire** wear. The front wheels — and on some cars, the rear wheels — have adjustments to allow the alignment to be changed. See also **camber, caster, toe-in, toe-out, steering-axis inclination,** and **turning radius.**

**Allen wrench:** An L-shaped rod designed to remove certain screws and fastenings with hexagonal holes in their heads. These wrenches come in sets of assorted sizes and are sometimes called **hex wrenches.**

**alloy wheels:** Ornamental wheels usually made of an aluminum or other metal alloy and typically consisting of spokes radiating out from a central hub to the outer rim.

**all-wheel drive:** A vehicle on which the **drive train** delivers power to all the wheels rather than just to the front or rear wheels. Full-time all-wheel drive operates constantly and improves handling even on dry pavement. Selectable all-wheel drive is engaged manually at the driver's discretion. See also **four-wheel drive** and **traction control.**

**alternative fuel:** A substance other than gasoline or **diesel fuel,** such as electricity, **compressed natural gas (CNG),** liquid hydrogen for vehicles with **internal combustion engines (ICE), ethanol,** and gaseous hydrogen for **fuel cells.**

**alternatively fueled vehicles:** Vehicles designed to replace or augment the **internal combustion engine (ICE)** so as to reduce air pollution and **global warming,** as well as to reduce demands for **fossil fuels.** These include **hybrids, clean diesels,** vehicles with ICE powered by **ethanol** and hydrogen, **natural gas vehicles (NGV)** powered by **compressed natural gas (CNG),** and **electric vehicles (EV)** powered by batteries recharged from the commercial power grid or by electricity produced onboard by **fuel cells.**

**alternator:** Generates electric current that's stored in the *battery* and used to start the car and run the electrical equipment. Alternators generate alternating current (AC), which is converted to direct current (DC) before being fed to the battery. Alternators have replaced *generators* that produced DC but otherwise performed the same functions on older cars.

**antifreeze:** See *coolant.*

**anti-lock braking system (ABS):** Have become increasingly popular because they enhance traction in slippery conditions and allow you to keep steering control of a vehicle, even in a skid. There are two-wheel and four-wheel anti-lock systems.

**automatic transmission:** A *transmission* that selects *gears* automatically, either by means of a *hydraulic* converter and a system of *bands* and *clutches,* or with an electronic *transmission controller.* Automatic transmissions come in three to seven speeds to provide more control over engine performance and fuel economy. See also *continuously variable transmission (CVT), dual-clutch transmissions,* and *manual transmission.*

**axle:** A solid metal shaft to which the wheels of a vehicle are attached.

**backflushing:** See *flushing the cooling system.*

**balancing:** See *wheel balancing.*

**ball joint:** A movable joint found on the *steering linkage* and *suspension system* of a vehicle that permits rotating movement in any direction between the parts that are joined. See also *boot* and *constant velocity joints (CV).*

**bands:** Older *automatic transmissions* rely on *hydraulic* pressure to change *gears* by means of a system of friction *bands* and *clutches.* These bands can be adjusted externally without taking the *transmission* apart. Adjusting the bands is part of normal transmission service.

**battery:** A box filled with a solution of water and acid called *electrolyte.* The box contains metal plates that store current generated by the *alternator* and deliver it to the parts of the car that operate electrically. See also *ground, negative terminal, positive terminal,* and *electrical system.*

**bearings:** Antifriction devices that are usually found between two moving parts. For example, the babbit bearings found between the *connecting rod* and the *crankshaft* are lubricated and cushioned with *oil,* and, although the front *wheel bearings* on *front-wheel drive* vehicles don't need servicing, on some vehicles they must be repacked with lube grease at regular intervals. Bearings can be ball- or roller-type.

**biocide:** A product that kills any fungus or microbes that may have contaminated *diesel* fuel.

**biodiesel:** *Diesel fuel* derived from agricultural and other waste products. It doesn't produce carcinogenic emissions and can help reduce human dependence on crude oil. See also *clean diesel.*

**bleed:** To remove air bubbles from a *brake system,* a *fuel injection* system, or a *cooling system* so that they don't impede the flow of liquid through that system.

**block heaters:** Devices that keep the engine warm when a vehicle isn't used in very cold weather. These are especially important for starting *diesel engines* at extremely low temperatures.

**blow-by:** Combustion products that blow past the *piston rings* during the piston's power *stroke.* These products form acid and *sludge* in the *crankcase* and, if excessive, can cause smoking from the *oil filler hole.*

**blue books:** Listings of the current prices for new and used cars based on age, condition, and optional equipment; published in the Kelly Blue Book, the NADA Used Car Guide (published by the National Automobile Dealers Association), and the Red Book (published by National Market Reports). Blue books are available at bookstores, auto supply stores, banks, loan offices, libraries, insurance companies, and on the Internet at www . kbb . com or www . edmunds . com.

**boots:** The rubber or plastic covers located at either end of a spark-plug cable to insulate the connections between the cable ends and the *spark plug* and *distributor* terminals; always grasp the cable by the boot when removing it. Also the protective cover of *ball joints* and *constant velocity joints* that holds the *grease.* See also *grease fitting.*

**bore:** The width or diameter of the *cylinder* hole. See also *stroke.*

**brake assist (BA):** A system that electronically boosts braking power.

**brake backing plate:** A metal plate, located inside the *brake drum,* on which the *wheel cylinder, brake shoes,* and other brake parts are mounted.

**brake booster:** In a vehicle with *power brakes,* a brake booster is located between the brake pedal and the *master cylinder* to increase the force applied to the pistons in the master cylinder. There are two common types: the vacuum booster, which uses engine vacuum and atmospheric pressure; and the hydro-boost unit, which uses *hydraulic* pressure from your car's *power steering* system. Some vehicles with *anti-lock braking systems (ABS)* have *hydraulic* pumps to generate pressure for booster operation.

**brake discs:** Also known as rotors, these are used universally on front braking systems and on some rear braking systems. *Brake fluid* under pressure pushes pistons in brake *calipers,* which clamp a set of *brake pads* against the rotating disc and slow it down, thus slowing down the car. See also *brake drums, brake fluid, brake pads,* and *brake system.*

**brake drums:** Metal drums mounted at the rear wheels on some cars. The *brake shoes* press against the inner surfaces of the drums to slow or stop the car. See also *brake system.*

**brake fluid:** The liquid used in the *hydraulic* brake system to stop or slow the car. See also *brake discs* and *brake lines.*

**brake lines:** A system of hoses and metal tubes through which the *brake fluid* flows from the *master cylinder* to the brakes at each wheel. See also *brake system.*

**brake lining:** A high-*friction* material that's attached to the *brake pad* or *brake shoe.* When the pad is pressed against the disc, or the shoe is pressed against the *brake drum,* the lining grabs the disc or the inside of the drum, which stops the wheel and thus the car.

**brake pads:** *Friction* material on a metal *backing plate* that, during braking, is clamped around a *brake disc* by brake *caliper* pistons to slow down the wheel to which it's attached. See also *brake system* and *brake fluid.*

**brake shoes:** Curved pieces of metal on which are bonded high-friction *brake linings* that are forced against the *brake drums* to slow or stop the car.

**brake system:** A system that uses *hydraulic* pressure to enable your car to slow and stop safely. Consists of the *master cylinder, brake lines,* and *disc brakes* or *drum brakes* at each wheel. See also *brake discs, brake drums, brake fluid, brake lines, brake lining, brake shoes, parking brake, power brakes, regenerative braking,* and *wheel cylinder.*

**bushing:** A protective liner that provides a cushion between moving metal parts.

**calipers:** Devices on *disc brakes* that hold the *brake pads* and use *hydraulic* pressure to force them to squeeze, or grip, the disc to stop or slow the car.

**cam:** A metal disc with irregularly shaped *lobes* used in the *camshaft* to activate the opening of the *valves* and, in a pre-1975 *distributor,* to force the points to open.

**cam lobes:** The bumps on a *camshaft* that contact and activate *cylinder head intake* and *exhaust valves,* either directly or via such devices as camshaft lifters or *push rods.*

**camber:** A wheel *alignment* adjustment of the inward or outward tilt on the top of the wheel when viewed from the front of the car. The correct camber is critical to handling and cuts tire wear.

**camshaft:** A shaft with *cam lobes* that causes the *valves* to open and close. See also *cam, overhead camshaft, push rods,* and *rocker arms.*

**camshaft sensor:** A trigger device found on *electronic ignition* systems that allows the ECU to synchronize fuel injector operation with the proper cylinder spark plug firing sequence.

**carburetor:** A device that *vaporizes* fuel and mixes it with air in proper quantities to suit the varying needs of the engine. Carburetors have been replaced by *fuel-injection* systems on most vehicles built since 1990.

**caster:** A wheel *alignment* adjustment that positions the wheels correctly so that the *tires* follow naturally in a forward straight line. On a turn, the wheels will tend to straighten out when the steering wheel is released.

**catalytic converter:** A pollution-control device that acts like an afterburner to consume unburned gas in the *tailpipe* and to reduce *NOx emissions.*

**cellulosic ethanol:** See *ethanol.*

**cetane rating:** A method of rating *diesel fuel* by measuring the time lapse between *fuel injection* and ignition to determine how easily the oil ignites and how fast it burns. See also *octane rating.*

**charging system:** A system that, using an *accessory belt* driven by the engine, enables the *alternator* (or *generator*) to generate electrical current, which is stored in the *battery* and delivered to the electrically operated parts of the vehicle.

**chassis:** The parts of a truck or SUV that are left when the body and fenders are removed.

**cherry condition:** A popular term for a vehicle that has been kept in — or restored to — perfect condition.

**circuit:** The path of electrical current through an *electrical system.*

**classic car:** A car that's generally considered to be one of the finest models ever built. Unlike antique cars, classic cars don't have to be extremely old; for example, Ford Mustangs and Volkswagen Beetles built in the late 1960s have long been referred to as classics. In a few years, these classics will be antiques as well!

**clean diesel:** A *diesel engine* that has been modified to run without producing many toxic emissions. Also refers to *diesel fuel* that burns clean, such as *biodiesel* and low-sulfur diesel.

**clear coat:** A finish on modern vehicles that protects the paint and retards rust. See also *polymer coating* and *rubbing compound.*

**cloud point:** The lowest temperature at which *diesel fuel* tends to thicken and cloud up.

**clutch:** In a *manual transmission,* a device that disconnects the engine from the *transmission* to allow the driver to change *gears* and then allows the engine and transmission to resume contact and turn together at a new speed. In an *automatic transmission,* a clutch performs a similar function. See also *clutch disk, clutch pedal, engine flywheel, pedal free-play, pressure plate,* and *throw-out bearing.*

**clutch disk:** In a *manual transmission,* a spinning plate located at the end of the *driveshaft* facing the *engine flywheel* and covered with an asbestos surface. When the *clutch* is engaged, the clutch disk is forced against the flywheel, causing the engine and the *transmission* to turn at the same speed.

**clutch pedal:** A pedal located on the floor of the car to the left of the brake pedal on cars with *manual transmission.* When the clutch pedal is depressed, it disengages the *clutch* so the engine and the *crankshaft* can turn independently of the *transmission* and the driver can change *gears.*

**coil:** See *ignition coil.*

**coil springs:** Large metal coils like bed springs that support the weight of a vehicle off the tires, and cushion and absorb the shocks and bumps as a car is driven. Coil springs are usually found near the front wheels, but many cars have them in the rear as well. Often the *shock absorbers* run up the center of the coil springs. See also *suspension system.*

**cold air collector box:** A rectangular box that contains the *air filter.* It performs the same function as the *air cleaner.*

**combustion:** The intense burning of the *fuel/air mixture* in the *combustion chamber.*

**combustion chamber:** The part of the *cylinder* where the *fuel/air mixture* is compressed by the *piston* and ignited by a spark from the *spark plug.*

**common rail fuel injection:** A fuel system found in *diesel engines. Diesel fuel* is pumped at high pressure into a distributor tube called a *rail*, which delivers fuel to all the *fuel injectors.*

**compressed natural gas (CNG):** An *alternative fuel* designed to replace gasoline as a source of automotive power. See also *natural gas vehicles (NGV).*

**compression gauge:** A device used to check the amount of pressure created in a *cylinder* when the *piston* is at its highest point and is squeezing the *fuel/air mixture* into the smallest possible space. A poor compression-gauge reading can indicate the need for repairs such as a *valve* job or new *piston rings.*

**compression ratio:** A measure of the amount of pressure applied to the *fuel/air mixture* in the *combustion chamber.* It's determined by comparing the volume of the combustion chamber when the *piston* is at its highest point to the volume of the *cylinder* when the piston is at its lowest point.

**connecting rod:** The metal rod that connects the *piston* to the *crankshaft* and converts the up-and-down motion of the piston into the circular motion of the spinning crankshaft. The phrase "throwing a rod" refers to a broken connecting rod breaking through the side of the *engine block*.

**constant velocity joints (CV):** The ball-and-socket fittings that transmit engine power from the *transaxle* to the wheels. Found mostly at either end of the *drive shafts* in *front-wheel-drive* cars and on the drive shafts of some *rear-wheel-drive* cars with independent rear *suspension systems,* these joints are specially designed to transmit engine *torque* while allowing full steering and suspension movement. They allow movement combinations and angles that U-joints are incapable of handling. See also *universal joints.*

**continuously variable transmission (CVT):** A computerized *transmission* with an infinite range (rather than a definite set of physical *gears*) that provides optimum performance and fuel economy with less wasted energy from the engine.

**control arms:** The upper or lower A-shaped suspension components that are mounted on the frame and that support the *ball joints* and *steering knuckles.* See also *suspension system.*

**coolant:** An ethylene glycol or propylene glycol solution that raises the boiling point and lowers the freezing point of the water in the *cooling system,* prevents rust and corrosion, and lubricates the *water pump.* Also called *antifreeze.*

**coolant recovery system:** A plastic bottle or metal tank that acts as a reservoir for liquid expelled from the *cooling system* through the *overflow pipe* and then returns the liquid to the system when it cools down. This requires a special *radiator pressure cap.* The system is sometimes called a *closed cooling system* when it's part of the original equipment.

**cooling system:** A system that stores, circulates, and cools a mixture of water and *coolant* that flows through *water jackets* in the *engine block* and cylinder heads and through the *radiator* in order to keep the engine from overheating as you drive. See also *coolant recovery system, fan, pressure cap, thermostat,* and *water pump.*

**core charge:** "Core" is an acronym for "cash on return." A sum of money that's refunded for a rebuildable part that's exchanged for a *rebuilt* part of the same type. A common core charge is for an alternator or starter.

**core plugs:** Metal plugs in the sides of the *engine block* that can pop out because of excessive pressure from ice formation and can prevent the engine block from cracking. These plugs sometimes develop leaks and should be replaced. Also called *freeze plugs.*

**cotter pin:** A locking device shaped like a pin but split up the center. It's usually inserted in a hole drilled through a nut and bolt and is intended to lock the nut in place so that it can't unscrew. After insertion, the legs of the cotter pin are bent around the nut to keep it in place.

**crankcase:** The lower portion of the engine where the *crankshaft* is located. The *oil pan* is located at the bottom of the crankcase.

**cranking:** The act of engaging the *starter* by turning the key in the *ignition switch,* which makes the engine *turn over.* Originally, a hand crank was used to do this, hence the term *cranking.*

**crankshaft:** The main rotating shaft in the engine. The *connecting rods* transmit power from the *pistons* to the *crankshaft,* which in turn transmits power to the *transmission,* then to the *driveshaft,* and eventually to the *drive wheels.*

**crankshaft position sensor:** A *trigger device* that tells the *powertrain control module* the position of the crankshaft. This input allows for proper timing of ignition and fuel injection, among other things.

**crankshaft pulley:** A grooved wheel attached to the front end of the *crankshaft.* The pulley is connected by *accessory belts* to the *fan, alternator, power steering pump, water pump, air conditioning compressor,* and other devices so that the rotating crankshaft can drive these other parts as well. The crankshaft pulley usually has *timing* marks located on it, and these are necessary for checking and adjusting timing with a timing light on older vehicles. Also called a *harmonic balance wheel.*

**creeper:** A platform on wheels that allows you to move around easily while lying on your back when you work under your vehicle.

**cross-shaft lug wrench:** See *lug wrench.*

**cruise control:** An optional feature that keeps your car cruising at a preset speed unless overridden by the brake pedal.

**cylinder:** A hollow, tube-shaped pipe in the *engine block.* The *piston* rides up and down in the cylinder to compress the *fuel/air mixture* that drives the engine.

**cylinder block:** See *engine block.*

**cylinder head:** The part of the engine above the *engine block* that contains the *combustion chambers* and the *valves.* The *spark plugs* screw into the top or side of the cylinder head. On most cars, a *valve cover, camshaft* cover, or *rocker-arm cover* is located on top of the cylinder head.

**cylinder sequence:** The order in which the *cylinders* are located on a particular vehicle. It's necessary to locate the #1 cylinder to check and adjust *timing* with a timing light. The #1 cylinder may be at the front of the engine on a United States-made straight 4- or 6-cylinder engine or at the rear of the engine on a foreign-made car. See also *firing order.*

**diesel engine:** An *engine* that burns *diesel fuel* instead of gasoline. The diesel fuel is injected directly into the *combustion chamber,* or a *pre-combustion chamber* on some vehicles, where it's ignited by the heat caused by intense compression rather than by a spark from a *spark plug.*

**diesel fuel:** Fuel for cars with *diesel engines.* It's similar to home heating oil, kerosene, and jet fuel. Also known as *diesel oil.* See also *biodiesel, clean diesel,* and *cetane rating.*

**dieseling:** An engine on older, carbureted vehicles that continues to run after the *ignition switch* has been turned off is said to be dieseling.

**differential:** A "box" of gears, situated in *rear-wheel drive* cars between the rear wheels, that turns the power of the rotating *driveshaft* at right angles to drive the rear *axles* and rear wheels. In *front-wheel drive* cars, the differential is located in the *transaxle.* The differential also allows each of the *drive wheels* to turn at a different speed when cornering.

**dipstick:** A metal stick that's inserted into a reservoir to check the level of the fluid in the reservoir by means of markings on the stick. The most common dipsticks check the levels of engine *oil, transmission fluid,* and *power-steering fluid.*

**disc brakes:** Brakes that have *calipers* with high-friction *brake pads,* which grab a *brake disc* (sometimes called a *rotor*) attached to the wheel and force it to stop turning, thus stopping the car. Older cars have disc brakes on the front wheels and *drum brakes* on the rear wheels. Many other cars have disc brakes on the front and rear wheels.

**displacement:** The volume of the inside of the *cylinders.* The amount of fuel and air that the cylinders can hold before compression takes place.

**distributor:** The part of the *ignition system* that distributes the proper amount of electrical voltage to each *spark plug* in the correct sequence. This task is now performed electronically on *distributorless ignition* systems. See also *engine control unit (ECU)* and *electronic ignition system.*

**distributor cap:** A cap that covers the *distributor.* It has an outlet for each *spark plug* wire, plus an outlet where the wire from the *ignition coil* enters the cap to conduct high-voltage electrical current to the *rotor.* The cap keeps dirt and moisture from getting into the distributor.

**distributorless ignition system:** An *electronic ignition system* that doesn't contain a *distributor* and contains multiple *ignition coils.*

**downshifting:** Shifting manually to a lower gear to accelerate, provide more power to climb a steep hill, or use engine drag to slow down on a grade.

**drive train:** The path of power from the engine to the *drive wheels.* Consists of the *clutch, transmission, driveshaft, differential,* and the *axle* on which the drive wheels are situated. On front-wheel drive vehicles, the transmission and differential are combined into one unit called a *transaxle,* which connects directly to the drive wheels.

**drive wheels:** The set of wheels that are connected to the *driveshaft* or *transaxle* and actually drive the vehicle forward and backward while the other set of wheels may simply turn in response to the car's motion. Vehicles are now identified as having *front-wheel drive, rear-wheel drive, four-wheel drive,* or *all-wheel drive.*

**driveshaft:** In *rear-wheel drive* cars, the spinning metal shaft that transmits power from the transmission to the *differential,* the rear *axle,* and the rear wheels. In *front-wheel drive* cars, two shorter driveshafts transmit power from the *transaxle* to the front wheels.

**drum brakes:** Brakes that use *hydraulic* pressure to force curved *brake shoes* against the inner walls of a hollow metal drum attached to each wheel. See also *brake system, disc brakes,* and *anti-lock braking system (ABS).*

**dual-clutch transmissions (DCT):** *Transmissions* that offer the driver the choice of shifting *gears* manually or letting the vehicle do it automatically.

**electric vehicle (EV):** An *alternatively powered vehicle* designed to use an electric motor as an environmental improvement over the *internal combustion engine.*

**electrical system:** A system that generates, stores, and distributes the electrical current required to start and run your vehicle and such electrically operated equipment as the radio, headlights, power seats, windows, air conditioner blower, and *engine control unit (ECU).* See also *charging system, ignition system,* and *starting system.*

**electrodes:** Metal rods attached to the center and side of the *spark plugs* to conduct current and create a *gap* across which the spark must jump.

**electrolyte:** The mixture of sulfuric acid and water that's found in the *battery.*

**electronic brakeforce distribution (EBD):** A system that distributes brake power proportionately among the four wheels.

**electronic control module (ECM):** A generic term for an on-board computer that is responsible for controlling the operation of one or more electronic systems. The earliest example replaced the *points* in mechanical distributors in the mid-1970s.

**electronic ignition system:** A computer-controlled *ignition system* that transmits electrical current to the *spark plugs* by electronic means, eliminating the need for *gap*ping and replacing *distributor* parts and frequent *tune-ups.* Modern *distributorless ignitions* have *ignition control modules (ICM)* or are controlled by the *ECU.* Older electronic ignition systems with distributors controlled by an *electronic control module (ECM)* are still on the road but are disappearing fast.

**electronic sensing devices:** See *sensors.*

**electronic stability control (ESC):** A system designed to help prevent a vehicle from skidding, spinning, or rolling over and to help return it to its intended path when it goes out of control. Using the *sensors* and computers that enable *ABS* and *TCS,* it monitors how the vehicle is responding to the steering wheel and helps you keep control of your vehicle by activating individual brakes and reducing power.

**emergency brake:** See *parking brake.*

**emissions control system (ECS):** Parts on a vehicle that reduce or remove harmful substances from the *exhaust* gases and recycle unburned fuel vapors before they get into the air and contribute to pollution and *global warming.* These parts include the *PCV valve,* various *sensors,* a *catalytic converter,* and other components. See also *exhaust system.*

**engine:** The part that produces power to drive a vehicle. It's usually fueled by gasoline or *diesel fuel* but may be powered by *alternative fuels.*

**engine block:** The cast iron, aluminum, or ceramic block in which the *cylinders* and the *crankshaft* are located. Also called the *cylinder block.*

**engine control unit (ECU):** The most powerful computer onboard a modern vehicle, also called a *powertrain control module (PCM).* Controls most engine functions including spark and valve *timing, emissions controls, air/fuel mixture,* fuel delivery, and even the cooling *fan.* The ECU also processes signals from all the various engine, emissions, and related *sensors.* See also *electronic sensing devices, onboard computers,* and *transmission controller.*

**engine flywheel:** A spinning plate located at the end of the *crankshaft* on vehicles with *manual transmissions* that engages the *clutch disk,* causing the engine and the *transmission* to turn at the same rate of speed. Also helps to dampen engine vibration. The starter turns the flywheel in order to start the engine. See also *clutch.*

**engine management computer:** See *engine control unit (ECU).*

**EPA estimates:** Estimates of the average amount of fuel consumed in city and highway driving by a particular vehicle, based on tests administered by the Environmental Protection Agency (EPA). These estimates should be used for comparison only because they vary with the driver, the load, and road conditions.

**ethanol:** An alcohol fuel distilled from plant materials such as corn and sugar. *Cellulosic* ethanol based on non-food agricultural products such as switch-grass and waste products offers the potential of fueling vehicles without negatively affecting the world's food supply. Fuels made from a blend of gasoline and alcohol fuels like ethanol or *methanol* are also known as *gasohol.*

**exhaust gases:** The burned residue of the *fuel/air mixture* that must be processed by the catalytic converter and expelled from the vehicle via the *exhaust system.*

**exhaust manifold:** A set of pipes that carry exhaust gases from the engine to the *exhaust system* and out of the vehicle through the *tailpipe.* See also *intake manifold.*

**exhaust port:** The opening in the cylinder head that enables the *exhaust valve* to allow the *fuel/air mixture* out of the *combustion chamber.*

**exhaust system:** The system that conducts *exhaust gases* from the *exhaust manifold* away from the passenger cabin to the tailpipe and into the air. Along the way, devices in the *emissions control system (ECS)* burn off or remove harmful substances, and a *muffler* (and *resonators* in some cases) controls the noise of the escaping gases. See also *catalytic converter, PCV valve,* and *resonator.*

**exhaust valve:** The *valve* that opens to allow the *exhaust gases* to pass from the *combustion chamber* to the *exhaust manifold.*

**fan:** Electrically driven and mounted in front of the *radiator* — or, in older vehicles, driven by an *accessory belt* and situated between the radiator and the engine — the fan draws air through the radiator to cool the liquid in the *cooling system* when the car is standing still or operating at low speeds, or when the air conditioner is running. Electrically driven fans are controlled by a thermal *sensor* in the cooling system.

**fan belt:** On older vehicles, a single flexible rubber belt that connects the *fan,* the *water pump,* and the *alternator* on some older vehicles. The operation of the engine turns the fan, which turns the belt, which drives the alternator, enabling it to generate electric current. See also *accessory belt.*

**feeler gauge:** A device for measuring the distance, or *gap,* between two surfaces. Use a wire or taper feeler gauge to gap *spark plugs.*

**firewall:** The insulated partition that runs from the windshield down between the interior of the vehicle and the engine compartment. Protects the driver and passengers from engine fires, noise, and fumes.

**firing order:** The sequence in which the *cylinders* fire on a particular engine to distribute the shock of *combustion* evenly and to reduce engine vibrations. This shouldn't be confused with *cylinder sequence,* which refers to the location of the #1 cylinder on a specific vehicle and where the other cylinders are located in relation to #1.

**flash point:** The temperature at which *diesel fuel* ignites.

**flat rate manual:** A listing of almost every repair and maintenance job that can be done on a particular vehicle with the average time required for a technician to complete it. Used by service facilities to estimate labor charges. Unscrupulous shops require their mechanics to "beat the book" yet charge their customers for the full time suggested by the flat rate manual.

**flex-fuel vehicles:** Vehicles that can operate on more than one type of fuel. Also called *dual-fuel* or *multi-fuel* vehicles.

**flushing the cooling system:** Circulating water through the *cooling system* to remove old liquid and clean the system of rust and dirt. *Backflushing* means circulating the water from the engine to the *radiator* (reversing the normal direction of flow) in order to clean the system more efficiently. Flushing is easy to do but requires recycling of the old *coolant,* which is toxic to animals and small children.

**fossil fuels:** Fuels derived from petroleum, such as gasoline and *diesel fuel.* Because fossil fuels are in dwindling supply and are a major cause of *global warming*, vehicles that run on it now are being replaced by *alternatively fueled vehicles.*

**four-stroke power cycle:** Refers to the four movements of the *piston* — down and up, down and up — that draw the *fuel/air mixture* into the *combustion chamber* (intake *stroke*), compress the mixture (compression stroke), transmit the power created by the *combustion* to the *crankshaft* (power stroke), and expel the *exhaust gases* from the *cylinder* (exhaust stroke).

**four-wheel drive:** Allows a driver to adjust a vehicle to operate in difficult terrain; how this is accomplished differs from one model to another. Four-wheel drive should be used only when needed because it doesn't work efficiently under normal road conditions. See also *all-wheel drive.*

**freeze plugs:** See *core plugs.*

**friction:** The rubbing of two moving parts against each other. Friction creates heat and wears down moving parts. The *lubrication system* uses *oil* to reduce friction and to increase the life of your vehicle. Friction is used between *brake pads* and *brake discs* and between *brake shoes* and *brake drums* to slow down and stop your car.

**front-end alignment:** See *alignment.*

**front-wheel drive:** A vehicle that's "pulled" by its front wheels rather than "pushed" by its rear wheels has front-wheel drive. This arrangement eliminates the long *driveshaft* and the center floor hump found on cars with *rear-wheel drive.* See also *transverse engine, transaxle,* and *constant velocity joints.*

**fuel/air mixture:** A vaporized, mist-like combination of fuel and air that's compressed in the *cylinders* and ignited to produce the power that drives the engine and the vehicle.

**fuel cell:** A power plant that creates electrical current from hydrogen and oxygen that's passed over a catalyst, usually a microscopically thin sheet of platinum. The electrical current then is fed directly to the vehicle's electric motor for propulsion. See also *alternatively fueled vehicles.*

**fuel filter:** A device that removes impurities from the fuel before it gets to the *fuel injection* system. In fuel-injected cars, the filter is found either in the fuel line under the car, or mounted on the firewall.

**fuel gauge:** A dashboard device that indicates the amount of fuel in the *fuel tank.*

**fuel injection:** A fuel system without a *carburetor* that employs an electronic fuel management system to deliver a specific amount of fuel to each *combustion chamber* in response to changes in engine speed and driving conditions. See also *engine control unit (ECU)* and *fuel injectors.*

**fuel injection pump:** Found mostly on *diesel engines,* it sends fuel under high pressure to the *fuel injector nozzles.* See also *fuel rail assembly* and *fuel transfer pump.*

**fuel injector:** A device that receives fuel at a constant pressure and is controlled by the *ECU,* which adjusts the amount of fuel sprayed into each *combustion chamber* by varying the length of time it holds the injector open.

**fuel lines:** The hoses or pipes through which the fuel passes from the *fuel tank* to the *fuel injectors.*

**fuel pressure regulator:** A spring-loaded diaphragm that maintains proper fuel pressure and meters unused fuel back to the *fuel tank.*

**fuel pump:** A pump that draws the fuel from the *fuel tank* and sends it through the *fuel lines* to the *fuel injectors.*

**fuel rail assembly:** A pipe in a *fuel injection* system that supplies fuel to the set of *fuel injectors* connected to it.

**fuel supply pump:** See *fuel transfer pump.*

**fuel system:** A system that stores, cleans, and delivers the fuel to the engine in proper quantities to meet the varying needs that arise as you drive. Consists of the *fuel tank, fuel lines, fuel pump, fuel filter,* and *fuel injectors* (or the *carburetor* on older vehicles without fuel injection).

**fuel tank:** The storage compartment, under the trunk in most cars, that holds the fuel for the vehicle.

**fuel transfer pump:** One of a series of mini-pumps on *diesel engines,* each of which is responsible for delivering fuel from the *fuel injection pump* to one of the *fuel injector nozzles* at a pressure of more then 1,000 *psi* (pounds per square inch). Also found on gasoline engines.

**fuses:** Fuses protect the electrical components and wiring on your vehicle the same way they do in your home. They're located in a **fuse box** (or boxes) that usually are found under or near the dashboard or under the hood. Your *owner's manual* can help you locate yours.

**gap:** The space between the *spark plug electrodes.* Adjusting this space is called "gapping." See also *feeler gauge.*

**gapper:** See *feeler gauge.*

**gas gauge:** See *fuel gauge.*

**gas tank:** See *fuel tank.*

**gasket:** A rubber, cork, paper, or metal plate that's inserted between two parts to prevent leakage of gases, fluids, or compression.

**gasohol:** See *ethanol.*

**gear ratio:** The speed of the engine compared with the output speed of the *transmission* and/or the *differential* in a given *gear.*

**gear selector:** A *gearshift* for vehicles with *automatic transmissions.* It can be located on the side of the steering column, in a console, on the dashboard, or on the floor between the front seats.

**gears:** Devices that enable the *transmission* to move a vehicle forward and backwards at a variety of speeds. See also *automatic transmission, manual transmission, gear ratio, gear selector,* and *gearshift.*

**gearshift:** The stick often located between the front seats on vehicles with *manual transmissions* that the driver uses to select and change *transmission* gears. See also *gear selector* and *stick shift.*

**generator:** See *alternator.*

**global warming:** An environmental crisis brought on by the unrestricted use of *fossil fuels,* carbon emissions, and a variety of other manmade conditions, which results in the heating of the Earth's atmosphere and oceans, weather changes, melting of glaciers, decline of species, and other natural disasters. See also *alternatively fueled vehicles.*

**glow plug:** An electrical element located in the ***combustion chamber*** of a ***diesel engine*** that helps to heat up the air in the chamber so that the ***diesel fuel*** is ignited more quickly.

**governor:** On ***diesel engines,*** it controls the exact amount of fuel that's sent to the ***fuel injector*** nozzles and makes sure that the engine doesn't go so fast that it damages itself with excessive heat and pressure.

**grease fitting:** A device that seals in ***grease*** to cushion two moving parts, allowing them to move freely and preventing them from wearing each other away. See also ***ball joint, steering knuckles,*** and ***tie rods.***

**grease seal:** A circular, metal-backed, rubber device, that keeps ***grease*** from leaking out and protects ***wheel bearings*** and similar parts from dust and water.

**ground:** An object that makes an electrical connection with the earth, to safely complete an electrical circuit. For example, one terminal of the ***battery*** is wired to the metal frame of the vehicle to utilize the frame as a path for returning electric current to the battery and thus completing the electrical circuit. All vehicles made in the U.S. are *negative ground* because the ***negative terminal*** is wired to the frame. In some countries, this is called *negative earth.*

**guarantee:** A promise by the manufacturer to fix or replace a specific part if it doesn't last for a specific time period or distance. See also ***warranty.***

**harmonic balance wheel:** See ***crankshaft pulley.***

**head gasket:** The seal between the ***cylinder head*** and the ***engine block.*** This ***gasket*** keeps the ***coolant*** out of the ***cylinders*** and free from contamination by ***exhaust gases.*** A "blown" head gasket causes a serious loss of compression.

**headliner:** Fabric or vinyl upholstery on the interior of the roof of a vehicle.

**heater core:** A device that heats the passenger compartment. Hot ***coolant*** and water circulate through it from the engine and heat air that's then blown by an interior fan into the vehicle

**hex wrench:** See ***Allen wrench.***

**high intensity discharge lamps (HID):** Headlamps filled with halogen or xenon gas that are brighter and use less power than the ***sealed beam units*** they've replaced.

**horsepower:** The energy required to lift 550 pounds one foot in one second — or 33,000 foot-pounds per minute.

**hose clamps:** Adjustable metal rings placed around a hose where it connects to another part to prevent leaks and to keep the hose in place.

**hubcap:** See ***wheel cover*** and ***alloy wheels.***

**hybrid:** An ***alternatively fueled vehicle*** that combines a small ***internal combustion engine*** and an electric motor to get maximum power with minimum emissions and maximum fuel economy.

**hydraulic:** A system that uses fluids under pressure to transmit force or power. Hydraulic devices on a vehicle may include *automatic transmission, power steering,* and *brake systems.*

**hydrometer:** A device to determine the specific gravity of a liquid. It's used to test *battery electrolyte* and the percentage of *coolant* in the *cooling system.*

**idiot lights:** Popular term for the dashboard indicators that light up only when your car is already in trouble from lack of *oil,* overheating, and so on (as opposed to gauges, which indicate levels of oil and engine temperatures, thus enabling the driver to prevent breakdowns and damage). See also *malfunction indicator lights (MIL).*

**idling:** The engine speed when a vehicle isn't moving.

**ignition coil:** The part of the *ignition system* that receives a small amount of electrical voltage from the *battery,* amplifies it into a big jolt of voltage, and sends it to the *spark plugs* via the *distributor* (if the vehicle has one). On electronic *distributorless ignition systems,* each spark plug may use its own coil.

**ignition control module (ICM):** A computer on an electronic system that receives data from *sensors* and controls the firing of the *spark plugs,* sometimes controlled by the *engine control unit (ECU).*

**ignition switch:** The means by which you activate a vehicle's electrical circuits and start the engine. On many vehicles, it's a slot in which you insert the key to the car. When the key is turned to Off, the electrical circuits are disconnected from the *battery.* Other vehicles may have an ignition button to push instead. See also *keyless ignition* and *keyless entry.*

**ignition system:** A system that provides the high-voltage electric current used to ignite the *fuel/air mixture* in the *combustion chambers* of the *cylinders.* Its parts include the *ignition coil,* which amplifies the voltage it gets from the *battery* and sends it to the *distributor,* which directs the current to each *spark plug* at the proper time. In cars with *distributorless ignitions,* the *engine control unit (ECU)* directs low-voltage current to the spark plug coils and then to the spark plugs*.*

**ignition timing:** The timing of the *spark plug* spark in the *combustion chamber* during the *piston*'s compression *stroke*. This timing is preset by the auto manufacturer and rarely needs to be adjusted in vehicles with *electronic ignition systems.* In vehicles with *engine control modules* or *distributorless ignitions,* no manual adjustment can be made.

**injector driver:** A transistor that is located in, and controlled by, the *ECU.* It controls how much fuel to spray into each *cylinder* to mix with the air in order to get the optimum explosion to drive the *piston.*

**injector pulse width:** The amount of time that the *engine control unit (ECU)* maintains the electrical circuit to a *fuel injector.* Using information it receives from a variety of *sensors,* the ECU changes the pulse width and controls the *fuel/air mixture.*

**inlet valve:** See *intake valve.*

**in-line engine:** An engine in which the *cylinders* are set in a single row with the *crank-shaft* running along the bottom. Also called a *straight engine.* See also *V-type engine.*

**intake manifold:** This chamber is found near the top of the engine; it routes the air needed for combustion to the *cylinders.* See also *exhaust manifold.*

**intake port:** The opening in the *cylinder head* containing the *intake valve*, and through which the air and fuel passes into the *combustion chamber.* See also *four-stroke power cycle.*

**intake valve:** A *valve* that opens to allow the *fuel/air mixture* to enter the *combustion chamber.* Also called the *inlet valve.*

**integral equipment:** Any device or system that's designed for, and installed in, a vehicle by the manufacturer rather than added to a finished vehicle at a later date.

**internal combustion engine (ICE):** An engine that works on power released by *vaporized* fuel and air burning inside the engine itself, rather than on an outside source of *combustion* as, for example, a steam engine does.

**jack:** A device for lifting all or part of a vehicle off the ground to facilitate repairs. The most popular jacks are tripod, scissors, and *hydraulic* jacks.

**jack stand:** A safety device that keeps the vehicle from falling to the ground if the jack is removed or faulty. Most jobs require two jack stands for safety.

**journal:** The area on the *crankshaft* that fits into the bearings in the engine block and the lower portion of the *connecting rod(s).* A layer of *oil* and metal *bearings* cushions the movement of the journal to prevent premature wear.

**jumper cables:** Cables used to jump a start by conducting current from one *battery* to another, allowing a vehicle whose battery has run down to start and begin to generate its own power. Jump-starting can injure onboard computers on some vehicles. Before using jumper cables, consult your owner's manual for instructions. See also *negative terminal* and *positive terminal.*

**keyless entry:** A feature that allows you to open a vehicle's door without a key because the vehicle recognizes a chip in a remote device. Some keyless entry systems require you to click the remote, whereas others can sense its presence without "seeing" or "hearing" it. See also *keyless ignition.*

**keyless ignition:** A feature that allows you to start and run a vehicle with no need to place a key in the ignition switch. This feature often is combined with *keyless entry.*

**knocking:** A sound that occurs in the *cylinders* when the *fuel/air mixture* is ignited too soon and the subsequent explosion hits the *piston* as it travels up the cylinder on the compression *stroke.* Also called *pinging, detonation,* or *pre-ignition.* Usually, it's due to faulty *timing,* gas with a low *octane rating,* or a build-up of carbon in the cylinders. Knocking sounds like marbles rattling in a can and can be heard best when accelerating up hills. The term is also used to describe the sound a worn-out *bearing* or *piston* pin makes. See also *four-stroke power cycle.*

**leaf springs:** A series of flexible steel plates, placed one on top of the other, that carry the weight of the vehicle and bend to absorb the bumps and shocks of driving. They're most often used in the rear suspensions of trucks and some sport-utility vehicles. See also *suspension system.*

**lubrication system:** A system that stores, cleans, cools, and recirculates oil through the engine to lubricate and cool its moving parts. The system components are the *oil pan, oil pump, oil filter,* and dashboard *oil gauge or warning light.* You can check the level of oil in the system with the oil *dipstick.*

**lug nuts:** The nuts that hold the wheel onto a vehicle. You remove them with a *lug wrench* in order to change a tire. Some vehicles use *lug bolts* instead.

**lug wrench:** A wrench used during tire changes to remove the *lug nuts* that hold the wheel onto the car. The *cross-shaft* type of wrench provides the best leverage. Carry one in your trunk.

**malfunction indicator lights (MIL):** Dashboard alerts that are activated by various electronic control modules which check many automotive systems and alert drivers to conditions that need checking and possible adjustment or repair. Also known as *warning lights* or *"Check Engine"* or *malfunction indicator lamps.*

**manifold:** See *exhaust manifold* and *intake manifold.*

**manual transmission:** A *transmission* system in which *gears* are selected by the driver by means of a hand-operated *gearshift* and a foot-operated *clutch*. Also called a *standard transmission.* See also *automatic transmission* and *gear selector.*

**master cylinder:** A device that stores *brake fluid* and hydraulically forces it through the *brake lines* to the brakes when you step on the brake pedal. *Hydraulic clutches* have master cylinders, too.

**mechanic's lien:** Recourse available to repair facilities in some states by which they can confiscate and sell your vehicle to compensate themselves if you don't pay your bill.

**misfiring:** The failure of the *fuel/air mixture* in one or more *cylinders* to undergo *combustion* while the vehicle is running. Misfiring can be due to poor compression caused by worn or improperly adjusted *valves,* worn *piston rings,* or a faulty *head gasket.* Or it can be caused by poor ignition due to worn, dirty, or improperly gapped *spark plugs,* poor fuel delivery, or faulty ignition wiring. Misfiring can be detected by placing a stiff piece of paper at the end of the *tailpipe* and listening for an irregular puffing sound.

**motor mounts:** The brackets that hold the engine and *transmission* to the frame of the car and have rubber or polyurethane elements that cushion vibrations.

**muffler:** A device for controlling the noise of the *exhaust gases* before they're released into the air through the *tailpipe.* Mufflers also help control exhaust gas pressure. Some innovative systems use specially designed piping, sometimes combined with electronics, to cancel out loud exhaust tones and to muffle the noise without an actual muffler, thus allowing the exhaust to flow more freely, which improves engine performance and fuel economy. See also *resonator.*

**natural gas vehicles (NGV):** Vehicles powered by *compressed natural gas (CNG).*

**negative ground:** See *ground.*

**negative terminal:** The *battery* terminal that conducts electric current back to the battery. The negative terminal usually has either "NEG" or "–" on it.

**non-electronic ignition system:** An *ignition system* found on older vehicles with *carburetors* that needed frequent *tune-ups* involving the gapping and replacing of *distributor* parts.

**NOS (new old stock):** New parts made in the past for out-of-production vehicles that are used in their *restoration.* See also *OEM (original equipment manufacturer).*

**NOx emissions:** A familiar term for the toxic oxides of nitrogen that pollute the air if they aren't reduced or removed from exhaust emissions.

**octane rating:** A method of rating gasoline by measuring its ability to resist *knocking* in *internal combustion engines.* Engines with higher *compression ratios* require higher-octane gasoline. See also *cetane rating.*

**odometer:** A dashboard device for measuring and indicating the number of miles a vehicle has traveled. Some vehicles also have a trip odometer that can be set to zero in order to register the mileage on a particular trip.

**OEM (original equipment manufacturer):** Parts supplied by the original manufacturer of a particular vehicle. See also *NOS (new old stock), rebuild, replacement parts,* and *remanufactured.*

**oil:** A substance that lubricates and cools the moving parts of the engine and reduces the formation of rust and corrosion. Oil comes in varying weights suitable for efficient operation in cold and hot weather and for engines in varying states of wear. See also *viscosity.*

**oil drain plug:** The plug that secures the drain hole in the *oil pan.* In many (but not all) vehicles, an oil plug *gasket* lies between the plug and the hole and should be replaced if leakage occurs. In some vehicles, there's no gasket because the metal-to-metal connection between the drain plug and the oil pan is tapered and leak-free.

**oil filler hole:** A hole at the top of the engine through which new oil can be added after the filler hole cover is removed.

**oil filter:** A can-like device that screws onto the outside of the *crankcase* and cleans the *oil* as it circulates through the *lubrication system.* Oil filters should be replaced as part of every oil change.

**oil pan:** The chamber at the bottom of the *crankcase* that stores *oil.* The *oil drain plug* at the bottom of the oil pan can be removed to allow old oil to flow out of the car during an oil change.

**oil pressure gauge:** A dashboard device that indicates the oil pressure as the oil is pumped through the engine. If this gauge shows a sharp drop, reads "Low," or lights up, stop the car immediately and find the reason for your loss of oil pressure before driving any farther. Without oil pressure, you can burn out your engine in a very short time. A low indication doesn't necessarily mean that you're low or out of oil in your oil pan; among other things, it could mean that the oil pump is defective or has failed. See also *malfunction indicator light (MIL).*

**oil pump:** A small pump located in the *crankcase* that circulates the *oil* from the *oil pan* to the moving parts of the engine.

**onboard computer:** One of many computers that may control *ignition systems, fuel systems, heating, ABS,* airbag deployment, *electronic stability control, traction control, rollover stability control (RSC),* seat belt pre-tensioning, and other systems. See also *ECU (engine control unit), electronic sensing devices, sensors, system management computers.*

**optional equipment:** Any equipment or feature of a new vehicle that isn't included in the basic price and is provided only if the purchaser requests it. Beware of new car deals that force you to buy a vehicle equipped with options you don't need.

**original condition:** Refers to an older vehicle that has all its original paint and equipment and hasn't been restored or modified.

**overdrive:** A special gear that allows the rear wheels to turn faster at the same engine *rpm.* Overdrive lowers fuel consumption during sustained high-speed driving on highways.

**overhaul:** See *rebuild.*

**overhead cam (OHC):** A *camshaft* located above the *cylinder head.* Overhead camshafts eliminate the need for *push rods* to activate the *valves.* Double overhead cam (DOHC) engines have two overhead camshafts: One operates the *intake valves,* and the other operates the *exhaust valves.*

**owner's manual:** A handbook provided by the car manufacturer to give the owner basic instructions for operating the various devices on a vehicle. Many owner's manuals contain *specifications* for items associated with maintenance, but very few offer instructions for doing it yourself. See also *service manual.*

**ozone checking:** Cracks or hard spots usually found on the sidewalls of *tires.* Caused by the action of the ozone in the air on the rubber, this condition is normal but could be dangerous on tires that are more than 40,000 miles old or that have been exposed to ozone for a long time.

**parking brake:** An auxiliary brake, usually attached to a rear wheel or to the *transmission,* that keeps the vehicle from moving accidentally. Also called an *emergency brake.*

**partial zero-emission vehicles (PZEV):** Vehicles with *internal combustion engines* that are so clean-running that they almost meet California's zero-emission standards. See also *zero-emission vehicles.*

**passing gear:** A gear on *automatic transmissions* that shifts a vehicle into a lower gear for a short burst of extra power to pass other vehicles on the highway. This gear is engaged by sharply depressing the gas pedal. When the pedal is released, the car returns to a normal driving gear.

**PCV valve:** Part of the positive crankcase ventilation system, which routes *crankcase blow-by* to the *intake manifold* and back to the engine where it's reburned in the *cylinders* as part of the *fuel/air mixture.* This action cuts emission pollution and increases fuel economy because unburned fuel in the blow-by is consumed the second time around. It also keeps the blow-by and water vapor from fouling the *oil* in the crankcase, thus reducing the formation of engine *sludge.*

**pedal free-play:** The distance the *clutch pedal* can be depressed before it begins to disengage the *clutch.* About ¾ to 1 inch of pedal free-play is normally required to assure that the clutch will be fully engaged when not in use. Without pedal free-play, the *throw-out bearing* and/or the clutch would wear out.

**Phillips screwdriver:** A screwdriver with a pointed tip that's shaped to fit the crossed slots in the heads of Phillips screws.

**pinging:** See *knocking.*

**piston:** A cylindrical part, closed at the top, that moves up and down inside the *cylinder* to compress the *fuel/air mixture* and drive the engine by means of a *connecting rod* that's attached to the piston at one end and to the *crankshaft* at the other. See also *journal* and *piston rings.*

**piston rings:** Metal rings located in grooves on the outside of the piston that keep the *fuel/air mixture* from leaking past the piston into the *crankcase* during compression and that keep *oil* from going up into the *combustion chamber.* Faulty rings can cause poor compression, severe *blow-by,* and excessive smoking from the *tailpipe.*

**planetary-gear system:** A set of *gears* used in some *automatic transmissions* that features a central gear, called a *sun gear,* surrounded by two or more smaller planetary gears that mesh with a ring gear.

**polymer coating:** A coating that prevents paint from oxidizing, protecting a car from premature fading and rusting. Do-it-yourself polysealants last for six months to a year; professionally applied polyglycotes are touted as lasting from two to five years but haven't really been around long enough to prove this. See also *clear coat.*

**positive terminal:** The *battery* terminal that leads to the *electrical system* on vehicles with negative *ground.* The positive terminal usually has "POS" or "+" on it. *Jumper cables* and other devices that connect to the battery usually have red clips for the positive terminal and black clips for the *negative terminal* and ground*.*

**power booster:** See *brake booster.*

**power brakes:** A *brake system* that uses a *power booster* to make braking easier.

**power steering:** A device that uses *hydraulic* power to help the driver steer more easily. Vehicles with power steering usually have a reservoir in the power-steering pump, which requires the occasional addition of power-steering fluid (sometimes automatic *transmission fluid*).

**powertrain control module (PCM):** A computer that controls the operation of the fuel, ignition, and *emissions control systems* on newer vehicles. Also called an *electronic control module (ECM).*

**precombustion chamber:** A small chamber located outside the *combustion chamber* of some vehicles in which a small amount of rich *fuel/air mixture* can be ignited to start the combustion process to increase fuel efficiency and cut emissions. It's found principally on *diesel* engines and certain older gasoline engines. Also called *prechambers.*

**pre-ignition:** See *knocking.*

**pressure cap:** A radiator cap on a *coolant recovery system* or radiator that allows the cooling system to operate under pressure at higher temperatures for greater efficiency. *Safety* pressure caps can be used to help release the pressure before the cap is removed in order to prevent injuries due to escaping steam or hot coolant.

**pressure plate:** A disc that's forced by springs against the *clutch disk,* which forces the disc and the *engine flywheel* against each other, causing the engine and the *transmission* to turn at the same rate of speed. See also *clutch.*

**psi:** The abbreviation for *pounds per square inch*, a measurement of pressure. The term is used to measure the amount of air pressure in *tires* and the amount of compression of the *fuel/air mixture* in the *combustion chamber,* etc. In the metric system, pressure is measured by kilograms per square centimeter.

**pulse width:** See *injector pulse width.*

**push rods:** The rods that run between the *camshaft* lifters and the *rocker arms.* The lifters and the push rods are pushed up by the *cam lobes,* causing the rocker arms to make the *valves* open and close. Engines with *overhead cams* don't need push rods because the camshaft cam lobes contact the valves or rocker arms directly.

**race:** A metal ring surrounding the balls or rollers of a *wheel bearing,* allowing them to turn against its smooth surface.

**radial tires:** See *tires.*

**radiator:** A device that cools the liquid in the *cooling system* by allowing it to circulate through a series of water channels that are exposed to air ducts.

**radiator cap:** See *pressure cap.*

**radiator fill hole:** An opening at the top of the radiator through which a 50-50 mix of water and coolant can be added if there's no *coolant recovery system.* The *pressure cap* seals the fill hole.

**radiator pressure cap:** See *pressure cap.*

**R&R:** A common term used by service facilities for "removal and replacement" of parts in order to access the site of needed repairs.

**ratchet:** A device that allows you to turn a screw or bolt in one direction and then move the handle of the wrench or screwdriver back, without force, in the opposite direction to prepare for the next stroke without removing the tool from the screw or bolt. See also *socket wrench.*

**rear axle ratio:** The number of times the rear wheels turn compared to a particular *transmission* speed. The higher the rear axle ratio, the slower the engine can run and still allow the vehicle to achieve a given speed.

**rear-wheel drive:** A vehicle that's pushed by its rear wheels rather than pulled by its front wheels has rear-wheel drive. See also *front-wheel drive, all-wheel drive,* and *four-wheel drive.*

**rebuilt:** See *rebuild.*

**rebuild:** To disassemble a device, clean it thoroughly, replace worn parts, and reassemble it. *Engines, clutches, carburetors,* and *brakes* are sometimes rebuilt as part of the maintenance or *restoration* of older vehicles. You can rebuild certain parts yourself with a kit containing instructions and part replacements, or you can buy a *rebuilt* part and turn in your old part for a *core charge.* Rebuilding is sometimes called *overhauling.* See also *remanufactured.*

**regenerative braking system:** Brakes found on *EV*s and *hybrid* vehicles that generate energy and feed it to the *battery* that powers the electric motor. See also *brake system.*

**remanufactured:** A part or engine that has been completely refurbished with new parts—as opposed to a *rebuild,* where only worn or defective parts are replaced.

**replacement parts:** Parts made by independent companies called *aftermarket* suppliers. These parts can range from poor to as good as *OEM (original equipment manufacturer).*

**reproduction:** A vehicle or part that has been duplicated by other manufacturers because the original is no longer widely available. See also *NOS (new old stock)* and *OEM (original equipment manufacturer).*

**resonator:** A small auxiliary *muffler* found on some vehicles that further reduces the noise of the escaping *exhaust gases,* or "tunes" the exhaust tone, to make a four-cylinder engine sound more like a V-8, for instance.

**restoration:** Restoring a vehicle to its original condition (including original parts, paint, rechroming, and so on) rather than merely *rebuilding* or repairing one. See also *NOS (new old stock), OEM (original equipment manufacturer), reproduction, rebuild,* and *cherry condition.*

**retreads:** Used *tires* that have been refurbished by grinding the tread off and replacing it. Not used much on passenger vehicles. The quality of retreads can vary; to be safe, only buy retreads from well-known manufacturers.

**rings:** See *piston rings.*

**rocker arm cover:** A metal lid located on top of the *cylinder head* on vehicles that have *valves* activated by an *overhead cam* or *rocker arms.* See also *valve cover.*

**rocker arms:** Curved levers, each of which has one end contacting a *push rod* and the other end bearing on a valve stem in order to make the *valves* open in response to the pressure of the *cam lobes* on the spinning *camshaft* and close from the pressure of the valve spring. Cars with *overhead cams* don't always require rocker arms because the valve stems may have lifters that contact the cam lobes directly.

**rollover stability control (RSC):** A safety system that identifies situations in which a vehicle that's taking a turn too sharply or too fast could roll over, and then helps to prevent the rollover.

**rotor:** A device on vehicles with *ignition systems* with *distributors* that sits on top of the distributor shaft and rotates with it to conduct electric current to each *spark plug* terminal in turn. The discs on *disc brakes* are also referred to as rotors, as is the triangular device inside a rotary engine that revolves, creating smaller chambers where the ***four-stroke power cycle*** takes place. See also ***ignition system.***

**rpm:** The abbreviation for *revolutions per minute.*

**rubber:** All the rubber seals, mats, and pads that cushion and protect car windows, trim, handles, bumper sections, carpets, and so on. A ***restoration*** should include replacement of all damaged or missing rubber with ***OEM (original equipment manufacturer)*** rubber parts or exact ***reproductions.***

**rubbing compound:** A polish that contains abrasives harsh enough to remove layers of dead paint. Useful in radical ***restoration*** procedures, rubbing compounds shouldn't be used on new vehicles with ***clear coats*** or delicate finishes.

**safety pressure cap:** See ***radiator pressure cap.***

**sealed beam unit:** A headlight that contains high- or low-beam filaments or both, a reflector, and a lens. It is sealed to keep out dirt and moisture. When the headlight fails, you replace the entire unit. Sealed beam units usually are found on older vehicles. Newer vehicles have small bulbs or ***high intensity discharge lamps (HID)*** filled with halogen or xenon gas.

**sealer:** A substance added to the liquid in the ***cooling system*** to seal small leaks; also called *stop-leak.* Other kinds of sealing compounds are used to coat surfaces before installing hoses or ***gaskets.*** These are effective in preventing leakage but usually make the hose or gasket hard to remove.

**sensors:** Electronic devices that monitor conditions such as fuel pressure, intake air temperature, ***throttle*** position, wheel speed with ***anti-lock braking systems (ABS), electronic stability control, rollover stability control (RSC),*** and ***traction control*** systems, engine speed, and load. This data is fed to the ***engine control unit (ECU),*** which controls a variety of ***system management computers.***

**serpentine belt:** See ***accessory belt.***

**service manual:** A handbook published by a car manufacturer or a specialized publishing company that contains instructions and ***specifications*** for the maintenance and repair of specific vehicles. Most deal with only one make, model, or year. Although intended for professionals or very experienced amateurs, service manuals are useful for locating various parts on your vehicle and for parts specifications. It's good to carry one in case of a breakdown in an area where local technicians may be unfamiliar with your vehicle. If you don't want to buy one, ask your local library to find one you can borrow. See also ***owner's manual.***

**service writer:** The person responsible for receiving vehicles brought to the service department at dealerships. He or she estimates the nature and cost of repairs and when the work will be completed.

**shims:** Thin pieces of metal used between parts to fill gaps or level them.

**shock absorbers:** Devices located near each wheel to cut down the vertical bouncing of the passenger compartment on the ***springs*** after the wheels go over a bump or the vehicle stops short. Shock absorbers also improve handling on rough road surfaces. See also ***suspension system*** and ***stabilizing system.***

**sludge:** A combination of oxidized *oil,* gasoline, *coolant,* and *blow-by* that can foul an engine. Modern engine oils have detergents to break down sludge.

**socket wrench:** A wrench that completely covers the head of a bolt rather than fitting around its circumference. A socket set usually consists of a variety of sockets, at least one handle (usually a *ratchet* handle), a couple of extenders, and sometimes a *spark plug socket* as well.

**solenoid:** A device connected to electrical current that induces mechanical movement in another device. See also *starter solenoid.*

**spark plug:** A device that delivers the electrical spark to the *combustion chamber.* The spark ignites the *fuel/air mixture* and produces the power that drives the engine. See also *ignition system,* and *spark plug gap.*

**spark plug gap:** The space between the center and side spark plug *electrodes,* across which the spark must jump to ignite the *fuel/air mixture* in the *combustion chamber.* Adjusting this *gap* is a major part of the basic *tune-up* because the width of the gap affects the intensity of the spark. See also *feeler gauge.*

**spark plug socket:** A metal cylinder with a rubber lining that fits over the exposed end of the *spark plug* to make it easy to remove the plug without damaging its porcelain surface. This socket can be purchased separately or as part of a *socket wrench* set.

**specifications:** The size, description, or part numbers for various items needed to maintain or repair a vehicle; often referred to as *specs.* See also *owner's manual* and *service manual.*

**speedometer:** A dashboard device that measures and indicates how fast the vehicle is going. If a vehicle has a speedometer cable, it should be lubricated when the needle starts to move erratically or if the cable begins to make noise. Electronic speedometers on many modern vehicles don't have cables.

**spindle:** The small shaft located at each front wheel on which the front wheels revolve on *rear-wheel drive* vehicles.

**splash shield:** A removable device found on *disc brakes* that helps to keep water and dirt from fouling the brakes.

**springs:** Devices to cushion and absorb shocks and bumps and to keep the vehicle level on turns. A vehicle can have *air springs, leaf springs, coil springs,* or a combination of these. See also *suspension system.*

**stabilizers:** A variety of devices used to keep the passenger compartment of a vehicle from swaying and lurching on sharp curves and turns. Also known as sway bars. See also *suspension system.*

**standard transmission:** See *manual transmission.*

**starter:** A small electrical motor that causes the engine *crankshaft* to begin to turn, which starts the engine running and so starts the car. See also *starting system.*

**starter solenoid:** A device that uses electrical current to start and engage the *starter.* See also *solenoid.*

**starting system:** The portion of the *electrical system* that starts the car. Consists of the *ignition switch,* which closes the circuit and allows current to flow from the *battery* to the *starter* via the *starter solenoid* and in some cases a relay. It's also called the *cranking circuit.*

**steering-axis inclination:** An *alignment* adjustment that allows the steering wheel to return to the straight-ahead position when the vehicle comes out of a turn.

**steering knuckles:** A type of *ball joint* located at the ends of the *tie rods* on the *steering linkage.* See also *grease fittings.*

**steering linkage:** The system that connects the steering wheel to the front wheels and allows the wheels to change direction in response to commands from the driver. It contains *grease fittings* to cushion against wear and friction. See also *alignment.*

**steering ratio:** The relationship between how far you turn the steering wheel and how far the wheels actually turn.

**steering system:** A series of linkages and gears that link the driver to the wheels.

**stick shift:** See *gearshift.*

**straight engine:** See *in-line engine.*

**stroke:** The vertical distance that the *piston* moves as it travels from the top to the bottom or from the bottom to the top of the *cylinder.* See also *bore* and *four-stroke power cycle.*

**strut:** An efficient type of *shock absorber.* See also *suspension system.*

**supercharging:** A method of increasing engine power by forcing larger amounts of air into the *cylinders* using an *accessory belt*-driven air compressor (also called a *blower*). Unlike *turbocharging,* which uses air compressed by an exhaust-driven turbine, supercharging decreases fuel economy.

**suspension system:** A system that cushions the passenger compartment of the vehicle from the bumps and shocks caused by the wheels moving over irregular road surfaces. The system includes *springs* or *torsion bars, shock absorbers, steering linkage,* upper and lower *control arms,* and *stabilizers.*

**synchromesh:** A *manual transmission* device that allows two *gears* to mesh more smoothly by causing them to spin at the same rate of speed before coming together.

**system management computers:** Computers that control various systems and features on a vehicle. See also *engine control unit (ECU), electronic sensing device,* and *transmission controller.*

**tachometer:** A device for measuring engine *rpm.* Many vehicles with *manual transmissions* have a dashboard tachometer to aid in changing *gears.* Most cars with *automatic transmissions* also have *tachs* these days because owners seem to expect them.

**tailpipe:** The last link in the *exhaust system.* It conducts *exhaust gases* from the *muffler* to the rear of the vehicle and into the atmosphere.

**telematics:** A word derived from combining "telecommunication" and "informatics," it's the technical term for the wireless systems that enable your vehicle to communicate with the outside world.

**thermostat:** A device that keeps the hot *coolant* confined to the engine cooling passages to help the engine warm up more quickly. After the engine has warmed up, the thermostat allows the coolant to flow to the *radiator,* where it's cooled and recirculated through the engine to prevent overheating. See also *cooling system.*

**throttle:** A device that controls the power produced by a gasoline engine at any given moment by regulating the amount that goes into the *cylinders.* Mechanical throttles consist of a throttle arm located on the outside of the throttle-body on *fuel injection* systems. The throttle arm is connected to the *accelerator* pedal, which activates a throttle valve where it joins the *intake manifold.* Electronic or *throttle-by-wire* systems use a *sensor* on the accelerator pedal to send an electronic signal to the fuel injection system telling it how much fuel to spray into the cylinders based on demand from the accelerator.

**throw-out bearing:** A part of the *clutch,* activated by the clutch pedal, that allows the clutch to disengage. If you allow the car to *idle* in gear with the clutch pedal depressed instead of shifting to Neutral, you can wear out the throw-out bearing. Also called the *clutch release bearing.* See also *pedal free-play.*

**tie rods:** Parts of a rack-and-pinion *steering linkage* that connect the rack to the steering arm.

**timing:** The capability of the *valves, ignition system,* and other engine-driven parts of the vehicle to work together for maximum efficiency. On older cars, timing is checked as part of the basic *tune-up* because if the timing is off, the vehicle can't perform well.

**timing belt:** A *crankshaft*-driven, toothed belt that drives an *overhead cam* or *camshafts* and, in some vehicles, a *water pump.* This belt should be changed at the mileage interval recommended in your *owner's manual.*

**timing chain:** A *crankshaft*-driven chain that drives the *camshaft(s),* which in turn open and close the *intake* and *exhaust valves.* In many modern vehicles, this part has been replaced by a *timing belt.* See also *valve timing.*

**tire valve:** A small valve mounted on the wheel rims of *tires* that allows air to be added to the tire with a properly equipped air hose and allows air to be withdrawn from an over-inflated tire by pressing on the little stem at the end of the valve. Tire valves should have caps to protect against leaks and to keep dirt from fouling the valve.

**tires:** Critical parts of your vehicle that allow braking, accelerating, and cornering on wet or dry roads and contribute significantly to the quality of the ride. All passenger vehicles today use *radial* construction tires. Sidewalls are usually reinforced with polyester, fiberglass, steel, or nylon. Treads are reinforced with a combination of polyester, steel, and sometimes nylon. See also *alignment, ozone checking, retreads,* and *tire valve.*

**toe-in:** An adjustment of front-wheel *alignment* so that the tires are slightly pigeon-toed when the vehicle is standing still. Toe-in is required for proper steering and tire wear.

**toe-out:** A wheel *alignment* angle used to control the way the vehicle tracks on turns. Tires should never be toe-out.

**torque:** Turning or twisting force. See also *torque wrench.*

**torque converter:** A fluid coupling in an *automatic transmission* that transfers power from the engine to the *transmission input shaft*.

**torque wrench:** A special wrench that measures the exact amount of *torque* being applied to tighten a nut or bolt.

**torsion bars:** See *suspension system.*

**traction control system (TCS):** A feature that senses when one wheel is spinning faster than the others and corrects it by automatically applying the brakes, cutting off power to that wheel, and/or reducing acceleration to improve traction and maintain stability. See also *anti-lock braking system (ABS)* and *electronic stability control (ESC).*

**trailer-towing packages:** Optional equipment that usually includes a heavy-duty *suspension,* a larger *radiator,* and a rear bumper with a trailer hitch and wiring for the tow vehicle's lights.

**transaxle:** A single unit combining the *transmission* and the *differential.* The transaxle connects directly to the *driveshafts* on *front-wheel drive* or rear-engine vehicles.

**transfer case:** A unit mounted between the *transmission* and *driveshaft* of *four-wheel drive* vehicles that controls the flow of power to the front and rear drive *axles* when you shift back and forth between two-wheel and four-wheel drive.

**transistor:** A tiny electronic component with at least three connections but no moving parts that functions as a switch or amplifier, by controlling the flow of current.

**transmission:** Typically an assembly of toothed *gears* that mesh in varying arrangements to enable your vehicle to move forward and backward with varying amounts of power to meet a variety of driving situations. *Manual transmissions* are operated by means of a *clutch* and *gearshift. Automatic transmissions* are driven by *hydraulic* pressure. *Continuously variable transmissions (CVT)* are automatic transmissions that use pulleys instead of toothed gears.

**transmission controller:** A computer found on electronic *transmissions* that controls shifting by monitoring engine speed, load, and other factors. See also *system management computers.*

**transmission fluid:** A thin oil that fills the *automatic transmission* so that it can run on *hydraulic* pressure. It's also found in many *power-steering* pumps.

**transmission input shaft:** The turning shaft that carries the power from the engine and *torque converter* or *clutch* into the *transmission.*

**transmission output shaft:** The turning shaft that carries the power out of the *transmission* to the *driveshaft.*

**transverse engine:** An engine that's mounted between the *drive wheels* with its cylinders running parallel to the wheels. Most *front-wheel drive* vehicles have transverse engines.

**trim:** Nonfunctional metal or plastic moldings, frames, and other decorative additions to vehicle bodies and interiors.

**tune-up:** The process of replacing *fuel filters, air filters,* and *spark plugs* to ensure that air, fuel, and spark are available in good condition to obtain maximum engine efficiency.

**turbocharging:** Using an exhaust-driven turbine to compress air and drive it into the *cylinders* in order to increase the power of the engine. See also *supercharging.*

**turn over:** An engine is said to turn over when the *starter* has caused the *crankshaft* to begin to turn, which starts the *pistons* moving so that *combustion* can begin to take place in the *cylinders,* providing power to move the vehicle.

**turning radius:** A measure of how tightly a vehicle can turn when the steering wheel is held all the way in one direction.

**U-joints:** An abbreviation for *universal joints.*

**undercoating:** A protective material applied to the undersides of new vehicles to prevent the formation of rust.

**universal joints:** Couplings located at either end of the *driveshaft* on a *rear-wheel drive* vehicle that allow the shaft to move freely without affecting the more rigid *transmission* shaft and to absorb the movement of the *axle* and wheels. Also called *U-joints.* On cars with *transverse engines,* these are called *constant velocity joints (CV).*

**vacuum modulator:** A device found on some older *automatic transmissions* which controls the pressure in the transmission's *hydraulic* system. If the vacuum modulator malfunctions, it can give the impression of *transmission* failure or can leak *transmission fluid* into the *intake manifold,* producing smoke at the tailpipe.

**valve cover:** A metal lid located on top of the *cylinder head* on vehicles with *overhead valves.* The valve cover is removed when adjustable *valves* need adjusting.

**valves:** Found in the *cylinder head*, valves open and close to allow fuel and air to enter the *combustion chamber* and *exhaust gases* to leave it. They are opened by means of valve lifters, *push rods, rocker arms,* and overhead camshaft lobes, and closed by springs. See also *exhaust valve, intake valve, timing belt,* and *timing chain.*

**vaporize:** To convert a liquid into a mist by breaking it into small particles and mixing it with air. *Fuel injector* nozzles spray tiny amounts of gasoline or other fuel into the ignition chamber, vaporizing it to produce a combustible *fuel/air mixture.*

**VIN (vehicle identification number):** A unique number found on the left-hand corner where the dashboard meets the window as well as on the registration and other paperwork for each vehicle.

**viscosity:** The thickness or pourability of a liquid. *Oil* comes in a variety of thicknesses, or *weights,* as well as in single viscosity (single-weight oil) and in a blend of viscosities (multi-weight oil), which enable it to flow easily in cold weather and reduce thinning in hot weather. The higher the weight, the greater the viscosity of the oil. You can find the weight of the oil on the outside of the bottle.

**voltage regulator:** An electrical device that controls or regulates the electric voltage generated by the *alternator.* On many vehicles this is an integral part of the alternator rather than a separate component, or this function may be performed by the *PCM.*

**V-type engine:** An engine in which the *cylinders* occur in two rows set at an angle to each other, with the *crankshaft* running through the point of the V. V-type engines are identified by number of cylinders as V6, V8, and so on.

**warning lights:** See *malfunction indicator lights (MIL).*

**warranty:** A promise by an automaker or dealership to fix or replace parts on a new vehicle if they malfunction before a specific time or distance has elapsed. See also *guarantee.*

**water jackets:** Channels in the engine through which water and *coolant* (antifreeze) circulate to cool the engine. See also *cooling system.*

**water pump:** A device that circulates the liquid through the *cooling system* by pumping it from the engine *water jackets* to the radiator.

**water separator:** A device found on *diesel* vehicles that removes any water that may have contaminated the *diesel fuel.*

**wheel alignment:** See *alignment.*

**wheel balancing:** A procedure that ensures that the weight of a wheel and tire assembly is distributed evenly so that your vehicle moves smoothly at any speed, with no vibration in the steering wheel or other areas. Usually, the wheel and tire assembly is removed from the vehicle and placed on a balancing machine, which measures imbalance and indicates the points around the rim where small weights must be mounted in order to make the wheel vibration-free, especially at highway speeds.

**wheel bearings:** The inner and outer *bearings* found at each wheel that cushion the contact between the wheel and the *spindle* it sits on. They're packed with grease to prevent wear from the *friction* produced by the turning wheels. See also *bearings.*

**wheel cylinder:** On *drum brake* systems, a small cylinder, located at each wheel brake, that uses *brake fluid* to exert *hydraulic* pressure, which forces the *brake shoes* against the *brake drums* and stops the vehicle. See also *calipers.*

**zero-emission vehicles (ZEV):** Vehicles that produce no emissions when running. Some state laws mandating the production of ZEVs, especially in California, have motivated carmakers to comply, mostly by accelerated research and development of *electric vehicles (EV).* See also *partial zero-emission vehicles (PZEV).*

# Appendix B

# Specifications and Maintenance Records

On the following pages, you'll find a Specifications Record and a Maintenance Record that you can keep and update regularly for your vehicle. Make photocopies of the blank versions before you fill them in, however, so that you have them for several vehicles. Take the Specifications Record to the store with you when you go to buy parts, and take the Maintenance Record to a service facility when you go in for maintenance and repairs to provide technicians with a history of the work done on your vehicle. These records are also valuable when it comes time to offer the vehicle for sale or trade-in.

# Specifications Record

Make _____ Model _____ Year _____

VIN (Vehicle Identification Number) _____

Engine displacement _____ Color _____

Type of vehicle (gasoline, diesel, hybrid, EV, NGV) _____

Engine type and number of cylinders (V-6, and so on) _____

Horsepower _____ Type of fuel injection _____

Air conditioned? Y/N _____ Type of refrigerant _____

Automatic, manual, or CV transmission _____

Type of transmission fluid or grease _____ PCV valve part number _____

Type of power-steering fluid _____ Accessory belt part number _____

Type of ignition (electronic ignition or distributorless?) _____

Spark plug gap and size _____ Cylinder firing order _____

Battery model _____ Date purchased _____ Est. life _____ years

Oil weight (summer/winter) _____ Oil capacity _____ qts. Oil filter number _____

Coolant type _____ Amount required to change _____ qts.

Top radiator hose number _____ Bottom radiator hose number _____

Other hoses (types, inner and outer diameters, and part numbers) _____
_____
_____

Air filter part number _____ Fuel filter part number _____

Tire size _____ Type of spare (full, mini, or run-flat) _____

Min. and max. tire pressure: Front _____ psi Rear _____ psi Spare _____ psi

Disc or drum brakes: Front _____ Rear _____ Brake fluid type _____

Windshield wiper replacement part numbers: Front _____ Rear _____

Additional equipment and parts: _____
_____
_____

# Maintenance Record

Vehicle: _____

From: _____ To: _____

## I. Monthly Under-the-Hood Checklist

**Do once a month or every 1,000 miles**

|  | J | F | M | A | M | J | J | A | S | O | N | D |
|---|---|---|---|---|---|---|---|---|---|---|---|---|
| Checked air filter | ❑ | ❑ | ❑ | ❑ | ❑ | ❑ | ❑ | ❑ | ❑ | ❑ | ❑ | ❑ |
| Replaced air filter (once a year or every 20,000 miles) | ❑ | ❑ | ❑ | ❑ | ❑ | ❑ | ❑ | ❑ | ❑ | ❑ | ❑ | ❑ |
| Checked coolant level | ❑ | ❑ | ❑ | ❑ | ❑ | ❑ | ❑ | ❑ | ❑ | ❑ | ❑ | ❑ |
| Flushed system and changed coolant (once a year) | ❑ | ❑ | ❑ | ❑ | ❑ | ❑ | ❑ | ❑ | ❑ | ❑ | ❑ | ❑ |
| Checked fan belt or serpentine belt | ❑ | ❑ | ❑ | ❑ | ❑ | ❑ | ❑ | ❑ | ❑ | ❑ | ❑ | ❑ |
| Changed fan belt or serpentine belt | ❑ | ❑ | ❑ | ❑ | ❑ | ❑ | ❑ | ❑ | ❑ | ❑ | ❑ | ❑ |
| Checked battery (monthly) | ❑ | ❑ | ❑ | ❑ | ❑ | ❑ | ❑ | ❑ | ❑ | ❑ | ❑ | ❑ |
| Replaced battery (as needed) | ❑ | ❑ | ❑ | ❑ | ❑ | ❑ | ❑ | ❑ | ❑ | ❑ | ❑ | ❑ |
| Checked oil level (monthly) | ❑ | ❑ | ❑ | ❑ | ❑ | ❑ | ❑ | ❑ | ❑ | ❑ | ❑ | ❑ |
| Changed oil (every six months or 5,000 miles) | ❑ | ❑ | ❑ | ❑ | ❑ | ❑ | ❑ | ❑ | ❑ | ❑ | ❑ | ❑ |
| Replaced oil filter (every oil change) | ❑ | ❑ | ❑ | ❑ | ❑ | ❑ | ❑ | ❑ | ❑ | ❑ | ❑ | ❑ |
| Checked automatic transmission fluid level | ❑ | ❑ | ❑ | ❑ | ❑ | ❑ | ❑ | ❑ | ❑ | ❑ | ❑ | ❑ |
| Added automatic transmission fluid | ❑ | ❑ | ❑ | ❑ | ❑ | ❑ | ❑ | ❑ | ❑ | ❑ | ❑ | ❑ |
| Checked brake fluid level | ❑ | ❑ | ❑ | ❑ | ❑ | ❑ | ❑ | ❑ | ❑ | ❑ | ❑ | ❑ |
| Added brake fluid | ❑ | ❑ | ❑ | ❑ | ❑ | ❑ | ❑ | ❑ | ❑ | ❑ | ❑ | ❑ |
| Checked power-steering fluid level | ❑ | ❑ | ❑ | ❑ | ❑ | ❑ | ❑ | ❑ | ❑ | ❑ | ❑ | ❑ |

*(continued)*

## I. MONTHLY UNDER-THE-HOOD CHECKLIST *(continued)*

### Do once a month or every 1,000 miles

| | J | F | M | A | M | J | J | A | S | O | N | D |
|---|---|---|---|---|---|---|---|---|---|---|---|---|
| Added power-steering fluid | ❑ | ❑ | ❑ | ❑ | ❑ | ❑ | ❑ | ❑ | ❑ | ❑ | ❑ | ❑ |
| Checked front and rear windshield washer fluid level | ❑ | ❑ | ❑ | ❑ | ❑ | ❑ | ❑ | ❑ | ❑ | ❑ | ❑ | ❑ |
| Added windshield washer fluid to both | ❑ | ❑ | ❑ | ❑ | ❑ | ❑ | ❑ | ❑ | ❑ | ❑ | ❑ | ❑ |
| Checked front and rear windshield wiper blades | ❑ | ❑ | ❑ | ❑ | ❑ | ❑ | ❑ | ❑ | ❑ | ❑ | ❑ | ❑ |
| Replaced front windshield wiper blades | ❑ | ❑ | ❑ | ❑ | ❑ | ❑ | ❑ | ❑ | ❑ | ❑ | ❑ | ❑ |
| Replaced rear windshield wiper blades | ❑ | ❑ | ❑ | ❑ | ❑ | ❑ | ❑ | ❑ | ❑ | ❑ | ❑ | ❑ |
| Checked tire pressure (don't forget the spare!) | ❑ | ❑ | ❑ | ❑ | ❑ | ❑ | ❑ | ❑ | ❑ | ❑ | ❑ | ❑ |
| Replaced tires (record details in Section IV) | ❑ | ❑ | ❑ | ❑ | ❑ | ❑ | ❑ | ❑ | ❑ | ❑ | ❑ | ❑ |
| Checked wiring | ❑ | ❑ | ❑ | ❑ | ❑ | ❑ | ❑ | ❑ | ❑ | ❑ | ❑ | ❑ |
| Replaced wires (record details in Section IV) | ❑ | ❑ | ❑ | ❑ | ❑ | ❑ | ❑ | ❑ | ❑ | ❑ | ❑ | ❑ |
| Checked hoses | ❑ | ❑ | ❑ | ❑ | ❑ | ❑ | ❑ | ❑ | ❑ | ❑ | ❑ | ❑ |
| Replaced hoses (record details in Section IV) | ❑ | ❑ | ❑ | ❑ | ❑ | ❑ | ❑ | ❑ | ❑ | ❑ | ❑ | ❑ |

## II. Tune-Up Checklist

### Electronic ignitions: Every 18,000 miles or two years
### Non-electronic ignitions: Every 12,000 miles or one year — more often if necessary

| | J | F | M | A | M | J | J | A | S | O | N | D |
|---|---|---|---|---|---|---|---|---|---|---|---|---|
| Checked fuel filter | ❑ | ❑ | ❑ | ❑ | ❑ | ❑ | ❑ | ❑ | ❑ | ❑ | ❑ | ❑ |
| Replaced fuel filter (every tune-up or as manufacturer recommends) | ❑ | ❑ | ❑ | ❑ | ❑ | ❑ | ❑ | ❑ | ❑ | ❑ | ❑ | ❑ |
| Checked PCV valve (if indicator light goes on) | ❑ | ❑ | ❑ | ❑ | ❑ | ❑ | ❑ | ❑ | ❑ | ❑ | ❑ | ❑ |
| Cleaned or replaced PCV valve (every 12,000 miles) | ❑ | ❑ | ❑ | ❑ | ❑ | ❑ | ❑ | ❑ | ❑ | ❑ | ❑ | ❑ |

| Electronic ignitions: Every 18,000 miles or two years |
|---|
| Non-electronic ignitions: Every 12,000 miles or one year — more often if necessary |

|  | J | F | M | A | M | J | J | A | S | O | N | D |
|---|---|---|---|---|---|---|---|---|---|---|---|---|
| Checked spark plugs (if engine performance suffers) | ❑ | ❑ | ❑ | ❑ | ❑ | ❑ | ❑ | ❑ | ❑ | ❑ | ❑ | ❑ |
| Cleaned and re-gapped spark plugs | ❑ | ❑ | ❑ | ❑ | ❑ | ❑ | ❑ | ❑ | ❑ | ❑ | ❑ | ❑ |
| Changed spark plugs (every scheduled tune-up; more often if burnt or worn) | ❑ | ❑ | ❑ | ❑ | ❑ | ❑ | ❑ | ❑ | ❑ | ❑ | ❑ | ❑ |
| Had fuel injectors cleaned (when needed) | ❑ | ❑ | ❑ | ❑ | ❑ | ❑ | ❑ | ❑ | ❑ | ❑ | ❑ | ❑ |

## III. Lubrication and Brake Checklist

|  | J | F | M | A | M | J | J | A | S | O | N | D |
|---|---|---|---|---|---|---|---|---|---|---|---|---|
| Checked grease fittings (every 3,000 miles) | ❑ | ❑ | ❑ | ❑ | ❑ | ❑ | ❑ | ❑ | ❑ | ❑ | ❑ | ❑ |
| Lubricated steering and suspension (every 3,000 miles or as needed) | ❑ | ❑ | ❑ | ❑ | ❑ | ❑ | ❑ | ❑ | ❑ | ❑ | ❑ | ❑ |
| Checked brakes (every 10,000 miles) | ❑ | ❑ | ❑ | ❑ | ❑ | ❑ | ❑ | ❑ | ❑ | ❑ | ❑ | ❑ |
| Had brakes rebuilt (record details in Section IV) | ❑ | ❑ | ❑ | ❑ | ❑ | ❑ | ❑ | ❑ | ❑ | ❑ | ❑ | ❑ |
| Checked wheel bearings (every 10,000 miles) | ❑ | ❑ | ❑ | ❑ | ❑ | ❑ | ❑ | ❑ | ❑ | ❑ | ❑ | ❑ |
| Repacked wheel bearings (every 20,000 miles or as needed) | ❑ | ❑ | ❑ | ❑ | ❑ | ❑ | ❑ | ❑ | ❑ | ❑ | ❑ | ❑ |
| Checked shock absorbers (if ride seems impaired) | ❑ | ❑ | ❑ | ❑ | ❑ | ❑ | ❑ | ❑ | ❑ | ❑ | ❑ | ❑ |
| Replaced shock absorbers (as needed) | ❑ | ❑ | ❑ | ❑ | ❑ | ❑ | ❑ | ❑ | ❑ | ❑ | ❑ | ❑ |
| Had front-end aligned (as needed) | ❑ | ❑ | ❑ | ❑ | ❑ | ❑ | ❑ | ❑ | ❑ | ❑ | ❑ | ❑ |
| Had automatic transmission serviced (every 20,000 to 25,000 miles) | ❑ | ❑ | ❑ | ❑ | ❑ | ❑ | ❑ | ❑ | ❑ | ❑ | ❑ | ❑ |

## IV. Parts Replacement Record

| Part | Date and Details |
|---|---|
| Wiring (ignition wires, spark plug boots, and so on) | _____ |
|  | _____ |
|  | _____ |
|  | _____ |
|  | _____ |
|  | _____ |
|  | _____ |
| Hoses (top or bottom radiator hose, vacuum hoses, fuel lines, and so on) | _____ |
|  | _____ |
|  | _____ |
|  | _____ |
|  | _____ |
|  | _____ |
| Brakes (pads/shoes relined, rotors/drums machined, and so on) | _____ |
|  | _____ |
|  | _____ |
|  | _____ |
|  | _____ |
|  | _____ |

| Part | Date and Details |
|------|------------------|
| Tires (Which one was replaced? Where did the new tire go? What was the mileage on the odometer at tire change?) | _____ |
| | _____ |
| | _____ |
| | _____ |
| | _____ |
| | _____ |
| | _____ |
| Other replacements and repairs | _____ |
| | _____ |
| | _____ |
| | _____ |
| | _____ |
| | _____ |
| | _____ |

# Index

## Numerics

4-cylinder traverse engine, cylinder sequence and firing order in, 94

6-cylinder rear-wheel drive engines, cylinder sequence and firing order in, 94

## A

ABS (anti-lock braking system). *See* anti-lock braking system (ABS)

accelerator, 345

accessory belts

adjusting and replacing, 233–234

checking, 34–35

importance of checking regularly, 31–32

keeping spare set with vehicle, 65

serpentine multiaccessory drive belt, 35

for water pumps, 204–205

acrylic or enamel finishes, cleaning and polishing, 451

adaptive cruise control (ACC), 391

adaptive front lighting systems (AFS). *See also* headlights

future availability of, 101

adjustable devices, for vehicles, 377–378

adjustable vice-grip pliers, for toolbox, 58

adjustable wrenches, 57

for removing oil drain plug, 250

adjusting nut, replacing when reassembling drum brakes, 284–285

ADS (Association of Diesel Specialists), for list of authorized shops, 424

air bag inflator, 372

air bags, 370–376

correct seating position for, 371

how they work, 371–372

ON-OFF switches for, 373

replacing, 373

traveling safely with, 370–371

air cleaner, 33. *See also* air filter

air filter on carbureted vehicles, 34

in fuel system, 73

air conditioners

converting from Freon to R-134a refrigerant, 236

servicing, 104, 236–237

signs of trouble in, 237

air filters

buying and replacing, 152–153

checking, 33–34

checking and cleaning, 151–152

and cold air collector box, 132–133

in fuel systems, 149

inside air cleaner on carbureted vehicles, 34

inside cold air collector box, 150–151

location of under the hood, 32

maintaining, 150–151

air inlet duct, in fuel systems, 150–151

air inlet hose, 150

air intake duct, 133

air pressure, checking for tires, 47

air springs, in suspension systems, 311

air suspension systems, anatomy of, 315

alignment

camber and caster, 337

determining need for, 338

toe-in and toe-out, 338

turning radius, 338

of wheels, 336–338

alloy wheels, potential damage to, 325

all-wheel drive (AWD) vehicles, 349

vs. four-wheel drive vehicles, 349

alternative fuels, how to find, 188

alternatively fueled vehicles, 70, 185–196

alternator

checking accessory belt that drives, 34–35

diagram of, 91

other parts electrical current supplied to by, 101

as part of charging system, 73, 90–92

systems run by, 92

alternator warning light, troubleshooting, 418

aluminum cylinder head, changing spark plugs in, 106

aluminum engines, coolant requirements for, 217

American Petroleum Institute (API), oil classification codes by, 244–245

antifreeze. *See* coolants

anti-lock braking system (ABS), 80, 268–269. *See also* brake systems

checking, 297–298

checking fluid for, 44–45

how they work, 268–269

used by traction control system, 387–388

what they don't do, 268

anti-sway bars, in suspension system, 308

API donut symbol, on oil containers, 262

armature, in electronic ignition systems with distributor, 99

ASA (National Automotive Service Association), Web site address, 424

ASE certification programs, for auto repair technicians, 423–424

auto accidents, recording evidence for, 68

major components of, 139–141

where fuel system and ignition system meet, 139–144

engine control unit (ECU)

electrical system controlled by, 85–86

introduction to, 72

engine displacement, 109

engine fires, causes of, 64

engine flywheel, in drive train, 346

engine lugging, solving with downshifting, 365

engine oil. *See also* motor oil; oil

checking, 40–42

detergents in to dissolve sludge in, 240

engine cooling by, 240

friction reduction by, 241

how it benefits your vehicle, 240–242

reason for checking yourself, 42

EPA Stratospheric Ozone Hotline, contacting, 236

ethanol, methanol, and flex-fuel vehicles, troubleshooting stalling problems, 411

ethanol fuel

fewer emissions produced by, 186–187

usable in flex-fuel vehicles, 186

exhaust manifold, 134

in exhaust system, 79

exhaust pipe, in exhaust system, 79

exhaust stroke, in four-stroke power cycle engine, 143. *See also* four-stroke power cycle

exhaust system

components of, 79, 145–148

controlling noise of escaping gases in, 79

diagram of, 146

muffler heat shield, 79–80

as vehicle waste disposal system, 79

expansion tank. *See* coolant recovery system

external fuel filters, 131–132

**F**

factory representatives, contacting about repair complaints, 436

fan, in cooling system, 78–79, 204

feeler gauge, for gapping spark plugs, 108

Filter Council, Web site address, 255

fire extinguisher

importance of keeping handy, 15

safe use of, 64

storing to keep it handy, 457

firing order. *See also* ignition systems

4-cylinder traverse engine, 94 (AU: The Index term found without locators in input file)

6-cylinder rear-wheel drive engine, 94 (AU: The Index term found without locators in input file)

versus cylinder sequence, 96

and cylinder sequence of engines, 94–96

in four-stroke power cycle engine, 143

first aid kit, in vehicle, 68

five-speed transmissions, 350

fixed-caliper brake systems, 265

flashlights and reflectors, for vehicle safety, 67

*Flat Rate Manual*, service pricing from, 426

flat tires. *See* tires

flex-fuel vehicles (FFVs), 188

E85 fuel for, 186

floor mats, cleaning, 460–461

flywheel, as part of starter system, 89

foreign in-line 4-cylinder engines, cylinder sequence and firing order in, 94

fossil fuels, contribution to global warming, 185

four-stroke power cycle. *See also* compression stroke; exhaust stroke; intake stroke; power stroke

in engines, 141–144

in diesel engines, 172

four-wheel drive vehicles

versus all-wheel drive vehicles, 349

drive train in, 348–349

with transfer case and two differentials, 349

transfer case in, 348–349

freeze plugs. *See* core plugs

Freon. *See* CFC-12 refrigerant

friction bands and plates, in automatic transmissions, 355

frontal air bags, 372–375

front-end alignment. *See* alignment; wheel alignment

front-wheel drive vehicles

crankcase in, 76

cutaway view of, 76

cylinder head in, 76

drive train, 345

dual brake systems on, 261

engine block in, 76

flow of power through transaxle on, 347

fuel tank in, 76

location of transmission in, 75

oil and transmission dipstick locations, 40

oil dipstick in, 76

position of cylinders in, 140

spark plugs in, 76

transaxle fluid dipstick in, 76

transaxle in, 76, 347

transmissions versus rear-wheel drive vehicle transmissions, 75

fuel cell vehicles

components of, 194–195

how they work, 194–195

fuel cells

in fuel cell vehicles, 194

how they work, 194

fuel economy

checking car out ecologically, 489–493

cleaning out junk to lighten load, 492

driving eco-logically for, 489–490

effect of bad PCV valve on, 488

effect of dirty air filter on, 488

effect of improperly tuned ignition system on, 488

effect of loose accessory belts on, 488

how to *(continued)*

jump-start diesel batteries, 181–182

keep electrical system in tune, 103–128

locate the fuel filter, 148–149

locate the PCV valve, 157

loosen lug nuts, 25–26

maintain your air filter, 150–153

measure inside and outside diameter of hoses, 225–226

open car hood, 17–18

read tires for treadwear, 338

reassemble drum brakes after checking, 284–285

remove and repack inner wheel bearings, 289–290

remove and replace gear-type hose clamps, 226

remove and replace screw-type hose clamps, 226

remove and replace the PCV valve, 158

remove and replace wire hose clamps, 226–227

remove pressure cap safely, 210–212

remove wheel covers or hubcaps, 24–25

repack outer wheel bearings, 288–289

repair radiator leaks, 230

replace a battery, 118–121

replace a fuel filter, 153–156

replace an insert in fuel filter, 156

replace and adjust halogen and Xenon headlamps, 124–125

replace and adjust sealed-beam headlights, 124–127

replace directional signals, 128

replace the inner wheel bearing grease seal, 290–291

replace your thermostat, 234–236

rotate your tires, 334–336

safely dispose of empty gas cans, 14

service the PCV valve, 156–157

shop for and use jacks, 62–63

shop for tools, 50

stock your repair toolbox, 65–68

take apart anything and put it back together, 18–20

test for loose accessory belts, 233–234

touch up paint job, 470

troubleshoot catalytic converter, 159–160

troubleshoot headlights, 123–124

use combination wrench, 55

use compression gauge, 60, 162–163

use creepers, 63–64

use gauges, 59

use jack safely, 20–23

use jack stands, 63

use pliers safely, 58

use tire pressure gauges, 60

use wire and taper feeler gauges, 59

hubcap. *See* wheel cover (hubcap)

hybrid vehicles, 71

combination hybrids, 188

parallel hybrids, 188–189

plug-in hybrids, 190–191

regenerative braking systems for, 191–192

troubleshooting stalling problems, 412

two-mode hybrids, 191

types of, 188–192

hydraulic automatic transmission, cutaway view of, 355

hydraulic brakes, 80. *See also* brake systems

hydraulic jack

shopping for, 62

using safely, 22–23

hydrogen and fuel cell vehicles, 194–195

hydrogen gas, in fuel cell vehicles, 194

hydrogen-powered electric vehicles (EV). *See* fuel-cell vehicles

hydrogen-powered fuel cells, how they work, 192–194

hydrogen-powered vehicles, troubleshooting stalling problems, 392

# I

ice and snow equipment, keeping with vehicle, 67

idiot lights. *See* malfunction indicator lights (MIL); warning lights

ignition coil, spark-plug wires running from, 105

ignition control module (ICM)

in distributorless electronic ignition system, 97–98

timing information stored in, 97

ignition switch

in electrical system, 72

in starting system, 87

ignition systems

battery as part of, 35

components of, 92–99

electric current provided by, 77

modern distributorless, 97–99

troubleshooting problems with, 412–413

under-the-hood view, 86

ignitions, override switch for, 28

IIHS list of Ten Safest Vehicles and air bag ratings, Web site address, 370

independent garages, choosing for vehicle service, 422

inflator/sealant, for emergency flat tire repair, 66

injector solenoid, in throttle-body fuel injection systems, 138

in-line engines, 141

finding spark plugs in, 105–106

oil and transmission dipstick locations, 41

intake and exhaust valve, openings in cylinders, 141

intake manifold, 134

checking PCV valve in, 157

fuel pumped into, 74

location of PCV valve in, 155

intake stroke, in four-stroke power cycle engine, 141–144. *See also* four-stroke power cycle

integral parking brakes, anatomy of, 296

internal combustion engine (ICE)

as the heart of most vehicles, 69–70

main parts of, 139, 140

invoices

checking for listing of parts and labor guarantees, 428–430

importance of checking carefully, 428–430

ISOFIX connections, for child safety seats, 382–383

## J

jack stands, 20

importance of for auto repairs, 63

proper positioning of, 22

using safely, 63

jacks

blocking wheels, 20

shopping for, 62–63

types of, 22

using safely, 20–23, 63

jumper cables

for emergency car starting, 66–67

using safely, 435–436

jump-starting engines, 66–67

## K

Kelly Blue Book, Web site address, 231, 466

key code numbers, finding for digital keys, 29

## L

LATCH (Lower Anchors and Tethers for Children) system

for child safety seats, 382

Web site address for information about, 382

leaf springs, in suspension systems, 309

leaks, troubleshooting, 403–405

in engine block core plugs, 231

head gasket, checking for in, 39, 231

locating by pressure testing, 233

LED headlamps, 101. *See also* headlights

lifetime lubrication systems, for steering systems, 303

locked car, getting into when you're locked out, 28

locksmith, calling for locked car assistance, 29

LoJack

Early Warning Recovery System, 393

Stolen Vehicle Recovery System, 393

low-pressure warning systems, types of for tires, 328

lubrication system

components of, 79

for reducing friction on metal engine parts, 241

lug nuts

loosening, 22, 25–26

lug wrench

for changing tires, 24

keeping with vehicle, 66

for removing lug nuts, 66

## M

MacPherson struts, 313

maintenance. *See also* preventive maintenance

finding a reliable diesel mechanic for, 184

finding a reliable service facility, 423–425

importance of monthly, 31–47

location of parts under the hood, 32–33

Maintenance Record, 31

form, 529

importance of keeping, 432

Lubrication and Brake checklist, 531

Monthly Under-the-Hood checklist, 530

Parts Replacement checklist, 532–533

Tune-up checklist, 530–531

malfunction indicator lights (MIL), 208

dealing with, 411

getting report from electronic sensors, 100

showing if alternator isn't working properly, 92

and warning lights, 100

manifolds, intake and exhaust, 134

manual transmissions, 343

components of, 350–352

gear ratio, 352

having fluid level checked for, 42

how they work, 352–354

location of clutch for, 75

shifting actions of, 353

master cylinder

ABS actuator in Japanese cars, 295

activated by the brake booster, 259

bleeding air out of, 294

for brake fluid, 44

in brake system, 80

looking inside of, 277

metal, 260

plastic, 260

removing lid from, 277

types of, 44

mechanic's invoices, sections of, 429–430

metal trim and chrome, polishing, 448

methanol fuel, uses for, 186–187

metric wrenches, 53

mild hybrids. *See* parallel hybrids

monthly under-the-hood check, 31–47, 482

motor oil, used in lubrication system, 79

muffler, in exhaust system, 79, 146

multi-fuel vehicles. *See* flex-fuel vehicles (FFVs)

multigrade oil. *See* multi-viscosity (multi-weight) oil

multi-link suspension systems, anatomy of, 314

multi-port injection (MFI) systems, 136–137

multi-viscosity (multi-weight) oil, 243

Vehicle Safety Hotline, 341
vehicles. *See also* cars
  steps for jacking up, 21–23
  what makes them run, 77–80
vice-grip pliers, for your toolbox, 58
vinyl tops, cleaning and
    repairing, 450
viscosity ratings, for engine oil,
    242–243
volt meter
  checking battery strength with, 38
  gauges showing charging system
    status, 91
voltage regulator, in charging
    system, 92
V-type engines, 141
  finding spark plugs in, 105–106

# W

warning lights and malfunction
    indicator lights (MIL), 100
washing your car, 444–447
  de-bugging safely, 444
  safety tips for using commercial
    products, 444
  waxing or sealing, 447
  windows and mirrors, 447–448
water jackets
  in cooling system, 78–79
  located around combustion
    chambers in cylinders, 204
water pump
  checking accessory belt that drives,
    34–35
  in cooling system, 78–79, 204
  identifying leaks from, 232–233
  rebuilt or remanufactured, 233
water separators, draining on diesel
    vehicles, 180
waxing or sealing
  hard or paste waxes for, 454
  liquid waxes for, 453
  polyglycotes for, 454

polymer preservatives for, 454
  recommended frequency, 453
  soft waxes for, 454
weatherstripping, installing new or
    patching old, 472
Web site address
  AAA or CAA approved repair
    facilities, 423
  ADS (Association of Diesel
    Specialists), 424
  ASA (National Automotive Service
    Association), 424
  Better Business Bureau, 425
  Chilton's subscription service, 71
  Consumer Action Handbook, 437
  Consumer Federation of
    America, 437
  Earth 911 for oil recycling
    information, 219, 255
  Federal Trade Commission
    (FTC), 437
  Filter Council for recycling oil
    filters, 255
  for getting blue book vehicle
    value, 231
  for hazardous materials disposal
    information, 33
  IIHS list of Ten Safest Vehicles and
    air bag ratings, 370
  for list of ASE-certified
    technicians, 424
  Michelin PAX system
    information, 327
  National Automobile Dealers
    Association, 436
  National Ethanol Vehicle
    Coalition, 188
  National Highway Traffic Safety
    Administration (NHTSA), 370
  for tire ratings, 324
  for videos that show deployment
    of air bags, 376
wheel alignment, 336–338. *See also*
    alignment
wheel balancing, 335–336
wheel bearings, 287–288

checking and packing, 287–291
  determining if packable or
    sealed, 287
  on four-wheel drive vehicles, 287
  getting at your brakes, 288
  inspecting and repacking, 287–291
  quick check for wearing of, 291
  replacing when reassembling
    drum brakes, 284
wheel cover (hubcap), removing,
    21–22, 24–25
wheel cylinders
  anatomy of, 263
  checking, 283
  cups inside of that seal, 263
  dust boots on, 263
  function of with drum brakes, 263
windows and mirrors, washing,
    447–448
windshield, dealing with damaged,
    473–474
windshield washer fluid
  checking, 46
  location of under the hood, 32
windshield wipers
  checking and replacing, 46–47
  in electrical system, 101
  keeping spare set with vehicle, 65
wire feeler gauges, for gapping spark
    plugs, 59, 108
wire hose clamps, dealing with, 226
wiring, checking, 46
work lights
  needed for auto repairs, 61–62
  for seeing under vehicles, 251
  tips for selecting, 62
wrenches, types of, 53–57

# X

Xenon headlamps, 101, 124. *See also*
    headlights
  replacing and adjusting, 124–125

# About the Author

**Deanna Sclar** is also the internationally best-selling author of *Buying a Car For Dummies,* a money-saving guide to every aspect of car ownership including buying, selling, financing, auto insurance and claims, and more. A former contributing editor to *Family Circle, Boys' Life, Exploring,* and the *Los Angeles Times,* her articles have appeared in *Redbook, New Woman,* and other national magazines.

As an automotive expert and consumer spokesperson, Deanna has appeared on more than 800 radio and TV shows, including her own segment on *NBC Nightly News with Tom Brokaw; Good Morning America, Today;* the Lifetime, CNN, and National Public Radio networks; and local shows in 30 major cities. Her *Auto Repair For Dummies* video was a National Home Video Awards finalist. She's co-hosted *Outrageous Women,* a weekly TV talk show, and has produced, written, hosted, and edited several documentaries. Her "Auto Repair for Dummies" course at California State University, Northridge, drew the largest crowds ever in their continuing education program.

A life-long environmental activist, Deanna led the group that threw the first Earth Day celebration in New York City and convinced Mayor Lindsay to start the first urban recycling program. The former "Thumbs Sclar" has restored two classic cars, a truck, and three homes. An inveterate gypsy and blue-water sailor, she has crewed her way across the Pacific and Polynesia, sailed and dived Hawaii and the Great Barrier Reef, trekked alone for nine months through southeast Asia and five months through Brazil, and crossed the Atlantic in a small sailboat with a companion and a cat.

"My goal is to prove that we have control over our lives," she says. "Whether you are working on a car or making a lifelong dream come true, it's a do-it-yourself world. Knowing this has turned my life into a great adventure, and I want to pass the good news on to everybody else!"

# Dedication

For my children, Gina and Casey; and my grandchildren, Jesse, Allison, Jacob, and Kylie, who will drive the vehicles of the future.

# Author's Acknowledgments

John O'Dell, for going far beyond all expectations to provide the erudition, insight, and dedication to make sure that this edition is accurate and up-to-date. Thanks so much for always being there for me!

Rosemarie Kitchin, for the support, intelligence, leads, and loving friendship that have been mainstays in my life for over 30 years.

Dave Steventon of the Canadian Automobile Association, for your friendship and guidance through every edition of this book.

Marilyn Levak, for your generosity and skill in organizing more than five years of Internet files and newspaper clippings for this edition.

Joanne Steventon, for researching and obtaining scrap art for this book.

Don Donesley, my first automotive guru, whose classes and advice made the original edition possible. Thanks for introducing me to three of the finest things in life: cars, beer, and the Mojave Desert!

The old Thursday Evening Auto Class at "Uni High," who shared ideas, tools, and elbow grease; served as guinea pigs; and got it all together over beer and pizza afterward.

Lindsay Lefevere, Acquisitions Editor, and Alissa Schwipps, Senior Project Editor, for their heroic efforts and sensitivity from the planning stages right through to publication. Elizabeth Rea, Senior Copy Editor, for her sharp eyes and feel for style. Tracy Barr, Editor, and Bob Freudenberger, Technical Consultant, for shepherding the book through a last-minute review. Janet Wahlfeldt and Thomas Brucker, Technical Illustrator (Precision Graphics), for simple, clear illustrations of complex automotive systems; and the entire Wiley Composition Services crew who worked so long and hard on this edition. May the Fonts be with you!

And, finally, thanks to Tweety Bird, faithful Mustang, who survived all the experiments and mistakes and grew up to be a fine car and a worthy steed; to Honeybun, my dream car come true; and to Esmerelda, my lovely Prius.

## Publisher's Acknowledgments

We're proud of this book; please send us your comments through our Dummies online registration form located at www.dummies.com/register/.

Some of the people who helped bring this book to market include the following:

**Senior Project Editor:** Alissa Schwipps
(*Previous Edition: Pamela Mourouzis*)
**Acquisitions Editor:** Lindsay Lefevere
**Senior Copy Editor:** Elizabeth Rea
(*Previous Edition: Wendy Hatch, Tamara Castleman*)

**Technical Editor:** Karen Greenberg
**Cover Photo:** © JGI/Tom Grill/Blend Images/ Getty Images